SOLVED AND UNSOLVED

SOLVED AND UNSOLVED

CLASSIC TRUE MURDER CASES

Edited and with an introduction by
RICHARD GLYN JONES

Originally published in two separate
volumes as *Solved!* and *Unsolved!*

BONANZA BOOKS
New York

This 1991 edition is published by Bonanza Books, distributed
by Outlet Book Company, Inc., a Random House Company,
225 Park Avenue South, New York, New York 10003, by
arrangement with Peter Bedrick Books, New York.

Printed and bound in the United States of America

Library of Congress Cataloging-in-Publication Data

Solved; and, Unsolved / edited by Richard Glyn Jones.
    p. cm.
    Reprint (1st work). Originally published: New York:
P. Bedrick Books, 1987,
    Reprint (2nd work). Originally published: New York:
P. Bedrick Books, 1987,
    ISBN 0-517-03755-6
    1. Crime – Case studies. 2. Murder – Case studies.
I. Jones, Richard Glyn. II. Title: Solved. III. Title: Unsolved.
HV6251.S65   1990
364.1 – dc20   90-20196
                                   CIP

8 7 6 5 4 3 2 1

SOLVED

Contents

Introduction

The gratifyingly warm welcome afforded to my first collection of true-crime stories[1] prompts another, and this one is designed to complement and extend the first — though it can certainly stand on its own feet. In that first collection I gathered together what I considered to be the finest accounts of some of the world's most notorious unsolved murder cases, and I was delighted to be able to include Colin Wilson on Jack the Ripper, Edmund Pearson on Lizzie Borden, Dorothy L. Sayers on the Wallace Case and other such distinguished pairings. Here, my object is to offer equally distinguished *solutions* to some similarly celebrated cases, but they are the solutions not of detectives or criminologists but of mystery writers. Real criminal puzzles tackled by the creators of fictional ones: it ought to be a stimulating mix, and I think that it is.

—For the relationship between murder in fact and in fiction is fascinating. The methods of Sherlock Holmes, the first fictional detective to attain world-wide popularity, had a considerable influence on real police-work, but when his creator tried to take on the rôle of Holmes he found that real crimes were very much less easy to solve, and — even more annoying — real, flesh-and-blood policemen very much less willing to be made fools of, even if some of them were fools. We'll watch Conan Doyle at work in one of these exploits — not a murder case, in fact, but none the less gripping for that — and discover just how different fact can be from fiction, fantasy from brute reality. If Sherlock Holmes had taken on the case of George Edalji he would have looked over the newspaper reports, made a quick excursion to the scene of the crime later the same day, solved it in a brilliant blend of close observation, shrewd deduction and decisive action, then returned to London to the ringing plaudits of everyone except the villain. The real-life cases of George Edalji occupied Conan Doyle on and off for literally years, and although it did reach a solution it proved an

[1] *Unsolved! Classic True Murder Cases* (1987)

7

extremely vexing business. Reality turned out to be cruel, inconclusive and above all *messy*, and while we applaud Conan Doyle's fine intentions, his courage and his persistence, we can only — I don't want to give too much away — deplore the wretched state of the real world, which has little room for knight-errants.

If Conan Doyle was at heart a romantic, the same can scarcely be said of Damon Runyon. His completely delightful tales of New York's criminal fraternity are, it is true, fairy tales of a sort, but the author of *Guys and Dolls* was also a hardbitten reporter — one of the greatest of his time — who can have had very few illusions about what went on in the real world. He didn't merely report the seamy side of things, but also played quite a lively part in them. His reports on criminal matters are scarcely remembered today, but how good they were! For this book I have chosen his day-by-day reports of the Snyder-Gray trial: a masterpiece of terse, witty writing, and an extremely shrewd ongoing assessment of Ruth Snyder, the so-called 'Granite Woman'. That she and Gray killed her husband was never in much doubt. What was interesting about this trial, apart from the gradual revelation of its horrors, was who was the instigator and who the executor? Would they turn against one another, and would either of them escape? The problem here is not who-done-it? but what the hell was going on inside these people's heads? This is the grim underside of every romantic triangle you've every heard of, miles away from Mindy's but something that Damon Runyon understood perfectly. His analysis of this case is acute, and absolutely right.

To bring that hero of a couple of hundred courtroom dramas, Perry Mason, to life would need, one might think, the creation of a special fantasy court in which he could spring all those last-minute surprises, for surely real courtrooms are like the one at Queen's County where Ruth Snyder and Judd Gray were put through it, and not mere platforms for handsome and heroic lawyers saving innocent and beautiful defendants? In a word, yes. But if Conan Doyle was the romantic and Damon Runyon the realist, Erle Stanley Gardner was practicality personified, and create a court was precisely what he did. He was a man who Got Things Done, working on up to seven novels simultaneously to make himself (without, let's be honest, any tremendous literary talent) one of the best-selling authors of all time. He was also a lawyer, and when *Argosy* magazine ran his series on possible miscarriages of justice it caught the public's imagination, and the Court of Last Resort came into being. It was a means whereby the innocent could indeed be vindicated, and where verdicts could be reversed by the energy of a right-minded group of people. He did it and it worked, though never quite as decisively as any of Perry Mason's triumphs (messy reality again), and not for very long. But the achievement was extraordinary, and Gardner's fascinating account of the setting-up of the Court and its first major case adds the third major aspect to our theme of writers as righters of wrongs.

These three substantial pieces form the tripartite core of this collection and show the writer as detective, reporter and judge, the three major characters in any criminal investigation, and all the more engaging for being an amateur detective, a deeply cynical reporter and an entirely maverick judge. There are other rôles that can be played, however, and the gallery is filled out with some fine examples from some very famous names indeed. The role of Armchair Detective, for instance, is adopted by Ellery Queen in a rare — possibly unique — excursion into these realms, offering a hypothetical solution to the murder of Grace Roberts, the glamorous 'Silk Stocking Girl' once famous throughout America; Freeman Wills Crofts' own novels specialized in the breaking of seemingly watertight alibis, and here he focusses that penetrating mind of the puzzle of the Gorse Hall murder, one of the England's most famous unsolved cases; and F. Tennyson Jesse, the creator of the remarkable Solange Fontaine and a great authority on true-crime cases, makes up her own mind about the guilt or innocence of the fascinating Madeleine Smith.

Julian Symons eschews the armchair and takes matters into his own hands in the most interesting case of 'The Invisible Man'. Robert Graves (not exactly a mystery writer: forgive me) goes back a couple of thousand years to see if he can discover what really happened to the Emperor Claudius, having left the matter rather unclear at the end of *Claudius the God.* And William le Queux provides a personal introduction to the extraordinary Madame Humbert — but then he claimed to know *everyone,* from Rasputin to the Pope.

These shorter pieces are, if you like, embroideries on the main pattern of the collection, and the solutions they offer are sometimes down-to-earth and sometimes fanciful. But in these too we find that the reality of murder seldom resembles its fiction. To make that match we would have to turn to a more documentary kind of writer such as Dashiell Hammett or Hillary Waugh, but the presentation of reality in fiction is not my concern here. Rather, it is the conflict of the novelist's vision with the world as it is, and the problems that inevitably follow when the one meets the other. Does this mean that I am dismissing these fictions as hopelessly implausible? Not at all. That would be to deny art, but we also need our dreams and our fairy-tales, not just to keep reality at bay but also to give us a notion of the world we would like to inhabit. That writers like Conan Doyle and Erle Stanley Gardner were willing to leave their desks and take on the real world is wholly admirable. Certainly, the results make fascinating reading.

— R.G.J.

ELLERY QUEEN

Death in Silk Stockings

Among great beauties a supreme self-confidence is inevitable.

The world, especially the male world, lies at their feet, adoring and grateful for small favors. But it is the love goddess' misfortune if she forgets that not every slave is obedient. And it takes only one rebel to shatter the idol forever.

This is what happened to Maizie Colbert, or 'Grace Roberts,' as she called herself professionally. She thought she could manage Bernard Lewis as safely as she had managed hundreds of other men in her thrall. By the time she discovered her mistake, it was uncorrectable.

In 1916 the body and face of Grace Roberts were as widely known to Americans as, say, those of Woodrow Wilson and John J. Pershing. That hers was held in far more unanimous esteem is no depreciation of those historic gentlemen. They were merely a President and a General; she was 'The Silk Stocking Girl,' whose delectable legs—displayed on magazines, in newspaper ads, on billboards from coast to coast—had no enemies or detractors. By the simple process of posing for lingerie ads she had earned a second title, 'The Girl with the Divine Figure.' With the legs and figure went a face no less heavenly.

This perfect flower had come from a humble garden, endearing her further to the American heart. She had been raised in a grubby little town in north-western Pennsylvania, in a very much lower-middle-class family. In the most romantic tradition of rags-to-riches Maizie Colbert had left home at the age of seventeen to seek fame and fortune in the big city. And in Philadelphia, as a professional model named Grace Roberts, she found both.

Manicure sets, dance halls, beauty parlors, skating rinks came to bear the Grace Roberts label. She was the most sought-after belle of her time. Philadelphia's Main Liners contended for her radiant presence at their posh social functions. The newspapers followed her around as if she were a queen. Among her admirers were financiers, judges, sportsmen, politicos. She was the gracious beneficiary of tens of thousands of dollars' worth of furs, diamonds, antiques. All men are brothers, and in the City of Brotherly Love everyone loved her.

Would success spoil Grace Roberts? Her answer was to lift her family out of their dingy surroundings and deposit them luxuriously in a house in West Philadelphia. The superintendent of the exclusive Wilton Apartments at 15th and Poplar, where she lived in swank, described her tenderly as 'the finest tenant' and 'the best tipper' in the building. To numerous poor Philadelphia families who benefited from her frequent acts of charity, she was Lady Bountiful.

Then, abruptly and beyond recall, during Christmas week of 1916, Grace Roberts' fairy-tale career came tumbling down.

As her family had not heard from her for several days, a sister, Bessie Colbert, paid a visit to the Wilton in the late afternoon of Saturday, December 30th. There was no answer to her rings and knocks on the Roberts door.

The superintendent, a man named Benjamin, had to crawl into the Roberts apartment by way of a fire escape. He scuttled out, ashen. 'Don't go in, Miss Colbert! Something terrible has happened.' Benjamin telephoned the police.

What Police Captain James Tate and his men saw when they set foot in the famous beauty's apartment was not beauty, but death in its ugliest form. Grace Roberts lay on her bed, a twisted thing covered by a red and stiffened sheet. The coat of her lilac silk pajamas had been torn to shreds in some wild, unheard struggle. The face that had launched a thousand advertisements was a pulpy ruin, unrecognizable, it had been worked over with a flatiron that lay bloodily nearby. But death had come through a bedsheet; she had been strangled with it.

Christmas gifts, many still unopened, made a huge pile around the tree in the beautiful living room. The names on the attached cards made the detectives' eyes widen. In an escritoire they found bundles of letters and telegrams from admirers, many of them tycoons and socialites. A photograph album was jammed with the autographed likenesses of young men, middle-aged men, old men, famous men, unknowns.

The apartment was filled with expensive things the killer had not touched—jewels, furs, silver, even a large sum of money. But Captain Tate did not need this evidence to decide that robbery had not been the killer's motive. Frustration and fury had tightened the bedsheet around that lovely throat. Homicidal hate and murderous despair had directed the hand brandishing the flatiron.

Perhaps it is not fair, but beauty desecrated arouses outrage not awakened by ordinary murder. And Grace Roberts had had powerful friends. The police knew that this was one homicide they had to solve.

From the building superintendent they got their first lead. He recalled an incident of the previous day. He had been hauled out of bed very early Friday morning by an irate cabdriver who had complained of depositing a fare at the Wilton in the middle of the night, being told to wait, and having waited three hours before the building with his meter going. The fare had never come out, and it looked as if he was nineteen dollars in the hole. At 9:00 a.m. the angry cabbie had given up and driven away.

It took the police several days to locate Elwood Powell, a veteran of the Philadelphia cabstands. And now they had a description of sorts and a hot lead. The man he had taken to the Wilton Apartments, Powell said, was young—about twenty-five—'rather goodlooking,' and he had worn pince-nez eyeglasses.

Powell had picked up the young man and two girls about 1:00 a.m. that morning at the Bellevue-Stratford Hotel. The girls had called him 'Bernie.' Powell had gathered that 'Bernie' hailed from Pittsburgh.

He had driven the trio to the girls' home in Germantown, and then 'Bernie,' after saying good night to the pair, had had Powell drive him to the Wilton, asking Powell to wait. It was the last the hackman had seen of him.

Grace Roberts' photograph album contained a picture of a nice-looking young man which was signed, 'Love, Bernie.' Powell identified the photo as that of his defaulting fare. And in the murdered beauty's address book was noted one Bernard M. Lewis of Pittsburgh.

The Germantown girls turned out to be sisters—Ethel and Mabel Kyle, both schoolteachers. They had met Bernie Lewis of Pittsburgh by chance at the Philadelphia Auto Show in January, they told police. He had said he was a traveling salesman and a bachelor.

They had dated him several times during 1916, on his visits to Philadelphia. They insisted he was 'always a perfect gentleman.'

He had never mentioned Grace Roberts to them; in fact, it was their impression that they were the only girls he knew in town.

On Friday evening, December 29th, Ethel Kyle said, she had had dinner with Lewis. She had noticed some small, rather odd-looking wounds on three fingers of his left hand. Now that she thought of it, they might have been bites—marks of a woman's teeth.

When Captain Tate's men converged on the Hotel Adelphia, where Lewis had been staying, they found their bird flown. He had decamped without paying his bill.

The alarm went out; Lewis was wanted 'for questioning' in the murder that, as the newspapers were saying, 'had shocked the nation'.

The police stayed close to the Kyle sisters. On Thursday, January 4th, they were rewarded. Lewis phoned. He would not say where he was. On police instructions the girls told him to give himself up. He said he would consult a lawyer and hung up.

But he phoned again. The detectives, listening in, had told one of the girls to say, 'Where did you go after you left us last Friday morning?'

'I'll tell you,' Lewis's voice began. Then it faltered. 'I did wrong. I'll give myself up.'

But he did not.

Other investigators traced his flight from the Adelphia to the

Camden ferry. From Camden he had boarded a train for Atlantic City.

The Lewis family had a summer home, the police knew, in Atlantic City. Quietly they pinpointed Bernard Lewis in a hotel opposite his family's home.

On Friday, January 5, 1917 the knuckles of the law rapped on the door of Lewis's room in the Atlantic City hotel.

They were answered with a shot.

The police broke the door down.

The killer of Grace Roberts had not been shooting at them. In the room they found him sprawled on the floor, clutching a .22 caliber rifle, blood streaming from a wound in his temple, dead.

Why had Bernard Lewis murdered America's favorite lingerie model, the darling of millions?

The question is still officially unanswered. Dead men tell no tales. Dead women are silent too.

But, given the cast of characters, it is possible even after almost fifty years to reconstruct the plot and its bloody climax.

Grace Roberts was a famous sex symbol who had kept her pretty head. Essentially she was what one of her innumerable influential friends, a Philadelphia magistrate, called her—'a fine young lady'.

Bernie Lewis was the prodigal, unpredictable son of a wealthy Pittsburgh coal family. By the time he was twenty-five he had squandered a fortune. He had tried marriage and it had failed—he and his wife were separated.

Lewis met the beautiful young model and, like hundreds of men before him, fell in love with her. Poised, sure of her power over men, Grace undoubtedly thought she could handle him. There is evidence that she went out with him several times.

That was her mistake. What she did not know about this particular man was the black depths of his nature. He was a neurotic, perhaps a psychopathic, personality. His fantasies seized on the beautiful girl as the object of his desires. He must have her. For himself alone.

When he came to her in the middle of that night, pressing his possessive desires upon her, Grace Roberts could only have rejected him. She had had plenty of practice rejecting possessive men. And this one could not even offer marriage.

She must have laughed at him.

That was when Bernie Lewis in a blue-black fury wound the bedsheet around her throat and, when she had stopped struggling, seized a flatiron and with it destroyed every vestige of the beauty she had denied him.

Solving crimes from the armchair is one thing; personal involvement quite another. Arthur Conan Doyle was at the height of his success in 1906 when, after years of struggle as an unsuccessful doctor, his writing had finally supplanted medicine as a career and brought him worldwide fame, especially for his creation of Sherlock Holmes. Yet with the death of his wife and other personal crises his life was in tatters, and when the chance of immersing himself in a new and worthwhile venture appeared he plunged himself into it — the matter of George Edalji.

'It was late in 1906 that I chanced to pick up an obscure paper called The Umpire, *and my eye caught an article which was a statement of his case, made by himself. As I read, the unmistakeable accent of truth forced itself upon my attention and I realized that I was in the presence of an appalling tragedy...' So wrote Conan Doyle afterwards, but in fact it was Edalji himself who had sent* The Umpire *to him ('I knew him only as the author of the Sherlock Holmes detective stories and as the man most likely to be able to unravel the mystery'), when he had been languishing in jail for a series of horrible crimes that might have seemed to be possible only as the work of an out-and-out lunatic. But Edalji was a practicing solicitor, and the mildest of men: what could have happened?*

In true Holmesian style, Conan Doyle made a flying visit to the scene of the outrages, gathered all the evidence he could, and then made his views known publicly in a series of articles in The Daily Telegraph, *which were specified to be free of copyright and which were widely reprinted elsewhere; it is from these articles that the following account of the case is taken.*

SIR ARTHUR CONAN DOYLE

The Case of Mr George Edalji

The first sight which I ever had of Mr George Edalji was enough in itself to convince me both of the extreme improbability of his being guilty of the crime for which he was condemned, and to suggest some at least of the reasons which had led to his being suspected. He had come to my hotel by appointment, but I had been delayed, and he was passing the time by reading the paper. I recognised my man by his dark face, so I stood and observed him. He held the paper close to his eyes and rather sideways, proving not only a high degree of myopia, but marked astigmatism. The idea of such a man scouring fields at night and assaulting cattle while avoiding the watching police was ludicrous to anyone who can imagine what the world looks like to eyes with myopia of eight dioptres—the exact value of Mr Edalji's myopia according to Mr Kenneth Scott of Manchester-Square. But such a condition, so hopelessly bad that no glasses availed in the open air, gave the sufferer a vacant, bulge-eyed, staring appearance, which, when taken with his dark skin, must assuredly have made him seem a very queer man to the eyes of an English village, and therefore to be naturally associated with any queer event. There, in a single physical defect, lay the moral certainty of his innocence, and the reason why he should become the scapegoat.

Before seeing him I had read the considerable literature which had been sent to me about his case. After seeing him I read still more, saw or wrote to everyone who could in any way throw light upon the matter, and finally visited Wyrley and had a useful day's work upon the spot. The upshot of my whole research has been to introduce me to a chain of circumstances which seem so extraordinary that they are far beyond the invention of the writer of fiction. At all times in my inquiries I have kept before my mind the supreme necessity of following truth rather than any preconceived theory, and I was always prepared to examine any point against the accused with as much care as if it made for his innocence, but I have felt at last that it was an insult to my intelligence to hold out any longer against the certainty that there had been an inconceivable miscarriage of justice.

Let me now tell the strange story from the beginning. I hope that the effect of my narrative will be to raise such a wave of feeling in this country as will make some public reconsideration of his case inevitable, for I am convinced that such reconsideration can only end in his complete acquittal and to his restoration to the ranks of that honourable profession from which he has been most unjustly removed.

The story begins as far back as the year 1874, when the Rev S. Edalji, a Church of England clergyman of Parsee origin, was married to Miss C. Stoneham. An uncle of the bride, as I understand it, held the gift of the living of Great Wyrley, which was a parish, half agricultural and half mining, about six miles from Walsall, in Staffordshire. Through this uncle's influence Mr Edalji became vicar of Great Wyrley, a cure which he has now held for thirty-one years, living a blameless life in the sight of all men. Placed in the exceedingly difficult position of a coloured clergyman in an English parish, he seems to have conducted himself with dignity and discretion. The only time that I can ever find that any local feeling was raised against him was during elections, for he was a strong Liberal in politics, and had been known to lend the church school-room for meetings. Some bitterness was aroused among the baser local politicians by this action.

There were three surviving children from this union—George, who was born in 1876, Horace in 1879, and Maud in 1882. Of these Horace received a Government post, and was absent at the time when the long persecution to which the family had been subjected culminated in the tragedy which overwhelmed his brother.

In the year 1888, George Edalji being at that time twelve years of age, a number of threatening anonymous letters were received at the vicarage. The aid of the police was called in, and an arrest was made. This was of the servant-maid at the vicarage, one Elizabeth Foster, who was accused, among other things, of writing up ribald sentences about her employers on outhouses and buildings. She was tried at Cannock in 1889, but her solicitor pleaded that it was all a foolish joke, and she was bound over to keep the peace. An attempt has been made since to contend that she was not guilty, but I take it that no barrister could make such an admission without his client's consent. She and her friends were animated afterwards by bitter feelings of revenge; and there is good reason to believe that in this incident of 1888 is to be found the seed which led to the trouble of 1893–95 and the subsequent trouble of 1903. The 1892–95 letters openly championed Elizabeth Foster; the 1903 ones had no direct allusion to her, but a scurrilous postcard on Aug. 4 contained the words, 'Why not go on with your old game of writing things on walls?' this being the very offence Elizabeth Foster was charged with. The reader must remember that in 1888 George Edalji was a schoolboy of twelve, and that the letters received at that date were in a formed handwriting, which could not possibly have been his.

In 1892 the second singular outbreak of anonymous letters began, some of which were published in the Staffordshire papers at the time by Mr Edalji, in the hope that their style or contents might discover the writer. Many were directed to the vicarage, but many others were sent to different people in the vicinity, so malevolent and so ingenious that it seemed as if a very demon of mischief were endeavouring to set the parish by the ears. They were posted at Walsall, Cannock, and various other towns, but bore internal evidence of a common origin, and were all tainted with the Elizabeth Foster incident. They lasted for three years, and as they were accompanied by a long series of most ingenious and elaborate hoaxes, it is really wonderful that they did not accomplish their proclaimed purpose, which was to drive their victim off his head.

On examination of such of these letters as I have been able to see their prevailing characteristics are:

1   A malignant, diabolical hatred of the whole Edalji family,

Mr. George Edalji without his spectacles.

the 16–17–18-year-old George coming in for his fair share of the gross abuse. This hatred is insane in its intensity, and yet is so coldly resolute that three years of constant persecution caused no mitigation. Here are extracts to illustrate the point: 'I swear by God that I will murder George Edalji soon. The only thing I care about in this world is revenge, revenge, revenge, sweet revenge, I long for, then I shall be happy in hell.' 'Every day, every hour, my hatred is growing against George Edalji.' 'Do you think, you Pharisee, that because you are a parson God will absolve you from your iniquities?' 'May the Lord strike me dead if I don't murder George Edalji.' 'Your damned wife.' 'Your horrid little girl.' 'I will descend into the infernal regions showering curses upon you all.' Such are few of the phrases in which maniacal hatred of the Edalji family is shown.

2   The second characteristic of the letters is a frantic admiration, real or feigned, for the local police. There was a Sergeant Upton on duty in Cannock, who is eulogised in this way: 'Ha, ha, hurrah for Upton! Good old Upton! Blessed Upton. Good old Upton! Upton is blessed! Dear old Upton!

> Stand up, stand up for Upton,
> Ye soldiers of the Cross.
> Lift high your Royal banner,
> It must not suffer loss.'

'The following in this district we love truly—the police of Cannock in general.' Again: 'I love Upton. I love him better than life, because for my sake he lost promotion.'

3   The third characteristic of these letters, besides hatred of Edalji and eulogy of the police, is real or simulated religious mania, taking the form, in some portions of the same letter, that the writer claims to be God, and in others that he is eternally lost in hell. So consistent is this that it is hard to doubt that there was a real streak of madness in the writer.

4   A fourth remarkable characteristic of the letters is the intimacy of the writer with the names and affairs of the people in the district. As many as twenty names will sometimes be given, most of them with opprobious epithets attached. No one can read them and doubt that the writer lived in the immediate neighbourhood, and was intimately acquainted with the people of whom he spoke.

One would imagine that under these circumstances there would be little difficulty in tracing the letters to their source, but, as a matter of fact, the handwriting was never recognised, nor was the culprit discovered. The opinion was strongly held, however, by those who were most concerned, that there was a connection with the former incident, and that the letters were done by some male ally or allies of the discharged maid.

Whilst these letters had been circulating the life of the Edaljis had, as I have already said, been made miserable by a series of most ingenious and daring hoaxes, many of which might have seemed comic had it not been for the tragedy of such a persecution. In all sorts of papers the curious wants of the Rev S. Edalji, of Great Wyrley, broke out by letter and by advertisement. Forgery caused no qualms to the hidden conspirator. Mr Edalji became in these effusions an enterprising matrimonial agent, with a number of ladies, their charms and fortunes most realistically catalogued, whom he was ready to dispose of to any eligible bachelor. His house was advertised to be let for the most extraordinary purposes. His servant-girl was summoned over to Wolverhampton to view the dead body of a non-existent sister supposed to be lying at a public-house. Tradespeople brought cartloads of unordered goods to the vicarage. An unfortunate parson from Norwich flew across to Great Wyrley on the urgent summons of the Rev Shapurji Edalji, only to find himself the victim of a forgery. Finally, to the confusion of anyone who imagines that the youth George Edalji was annoying himself and playing heartless tricks upon his own people, there came a forged apology in the public Press, beginning with the words: 'We, the undersigned, G.E.T. Edalji and Fredk. Brookes, both residing in the parish of Great Wyrley, do hereby declare that we were the sole authors and writers of certain offensive and anonymous letters received by various persons during the last twelve months.' The apology then goes on to express regret for utterances against the favourite protégé of the unknown, Upton, the sergeant of police at Cannock, and also against Elizabeth Foster. This pretended apology was, of course, at once disowned by the Edaljis, and must, I think, convince any reasonable man, if there were already any room for doubt, that the Edaljis were not persecuting themselves in this maddening fashion.

Before leaving this subject of the anonymous letters of 1893, which breathe revenge against the Edalji family, I should like to quote and strongly emphasise two expressions which have a lurid meaning when taken with the actual outcome of the future.

On March 17, 1893, this real or pretended maniac says in a letter to the father: 'Before the end of this year your kid will be either in the graveyard or disgraced for life.' Later, in the same letter, he says: 'Do you think that when we want we cannot copy your kid's writing?' Within ten years of the receipt of that letter the 'kid', or George Edalji, had indeed been disgraced for life, and anonymous letters which imitated his handwriting had played a part in his downfall. It is difficult after this to doubt that the schemer of 1893 was identical with the writer of the letters in 1903.

Among the many hoaxes and annoyances practised during these years was the continual laying of objects within the vicarage grounds and on the window-sills, or under the doors, done with such audacity that the culprit was more than once nearly caught in the act. There was one of these incidents which I must allude to at some length, for though it was trivial in itself, it has considerable importance as forming a link between the outrages of 1893 and of 1903, and also because it shows for the first time the very strong suspicion which Captain the Honourable G.A. Anson, Chief Constable of Staffordshire—influenced no doubt by those reports of his subordinates, which he may or may not have too readily believed—has shown towards George Edalji. Personally I have met with nothing but frankness and courtesy from Captain the Hon G.A. Anson during the course of my investigation, and if in the search after truth I have to criticise any word or action of his, I can assure him that it is with regret and only in pursuit of what seems to me to be a clear duty.

On Dec. 12, 1892, at the very beginning of the series of hoaxes, a large key was discovered lying upon the vicarage doorstep. This key was handed to the police, and was discovered in a few days to be a key which had been taken from Walsall Grammar School. The reason why I say that this

incident has an important bearing upon the connection between the outrages of 1893 and those of 1903 is that the very
first letter in the latter series proclaimed the writer to be a
scholar at Walsall Grammar School. Granting that he could no
longer be a scholar there if he were concerned in the hoaxes of
1893, it is still an argument that the same motive power lay
behind each, since we find Walsall Grammar School obtruding
itself in each case.

The incident of the key was brought before the chief constable of the county, who seems at once to have concluded that
young George Edalji was the culprit. George Edalji was not a
scholar at the Walsall School, having been brought up at
Rugeley, and there does not appear to have been the slightest
reason to suppose that he had procured a key from this six
miles' distant school and laid it on his own doorstep. However,
here is a queer-looking boy, and here are queer doings, and here
is a zealous constable, the very Upton whose praises were later
to be so enthusiastically voiced by the writer of the letters. Some
report was made, and the chief constable believed it. He took
the course of writing in his own hand, over his own name, in an
attempt to bluff the boy into a confession. Under date Jan. 23,
1893, he says to the father, in a letter which now lies before me:
'Will you please ask your son George from whom the key was
obtained which was found on your doorstep on Dec. 12? The
key was stolen, but if it can be shown that the whole thing was
due to some idle freak or practical joke, I should not be inclined
to allow any police proceedings to be taken in regard to it. If,
however, the persons concerned in the removal of the key refuse
to make any explanation of the subject, I must necessarily treat
the matter in all seriousness as a theft. I may say at once that I
shall not pretend to believe any protestations of ignorance
which your son may make about this key. My information on
the subject does not come from the police.'

Considering the diabolical ingenuity of the hoaxer, it would
seem probable that the information came directly or indirectly
from him. In any case, it seems to have been false, or, at least,
incapable of proof, as is shown by the fact that after these
threats from the chief constable no action was taken. But the
point to be noted is that as early as 1893, when Edalji was only

Sir Arthur Conan Doyle at the time of the Edalji case.

seventeen, we have the police force of Staffordshire, through the mouth of their chief, making charges against him, and declaring in advance that they will not believe any protestation of innocence. Two years later, on July 25, 1895, the chief constable goes even further. Still writing to the father he says: 'I did not tell Mr. Perry that I know the name of the offender' (the writer of the letters and author of the hoaxes), 'though I told him that I had my suspicions. I prefer to keep my suspicions to myself until I am able to prove them, and I trust to be able to obtain a dose of penal servitude for the offender; as although great care has apparently been exercised to avoid, as far as possible, anything which would constitute any serious offence in law, the person who writes the letters has overreached himself in two or three instances, in such a manner as to render him liable to the most serious punishment. I have no doubt that the offender will be detected.'

Now, it must be admitted that this is a rather sinister letter. It follows after eighteen months upon the previous one in which he accuses George Edalji by name. The letter was drawn from him by the father's complaint of gossip in the neighbourhood, and the allusion to the skill of the offender in keeping within the law has a special meaning, in view of the fact that young Edalji was already a law student. Without mentioning a name, he assures Edalji's father that the culprit may get a dose of penal servitude. No doubt the chief constable honestly meant every word he said, and thought that he had excellent reasons for his conclusions; but the point is that if the Staffordshire police took this attitude towards young Edalji in 1895, what chance of impartiality had he in 1903, when a culprit was wanted for an entirely new set of crimes? It is evident that their minds were steeped in prejudice against him, and that they were in the mood to view his actions in the darkest light.

At the end of 1895 this persecution ceased. Letters and hoaxes were suddenly switched off. From that date till 1903 peace reigned in Wyrley. But George Edalji was resident at the vicarage all the time. Had he been the culprit there was no reason for change. But in 1903 the troubles broke out in a far more dangerous form than ever.

It was on Feb. 2, 1903, that the first serious outrage occurred at Wyrley. On that date a valuable horse belonging to Mr Joseph Holmes was found to have been ripped up during the night. Two months later, on April 2, a cob belonging to Mr Thomas was treated in a similar fashion; and a month after that a cow of Mrs Bungay's was killed in the same way. Within a fortnight a horse of Mr Badger's was terribly mutilated, and on the same day some sheep were killed. On June 6 two cows suffered the same fate, and three weeks later two valuable horses belonging to the Quinton Colliery Company were also destroyed. Next in order in this monstrous series of barbarities was the killing of a pony at Great Wyrley Colliery, for which George Edalji was arrested and convicted. His disappearance from the scene made no difference at all to the sequence of outrages, for on Sept. 21, betwixt his arrest and his trial, another horse was disembowelled, and, as if expressly to confute the views of those who might say that this outrage was committed by confederates in order to affect the trial, the most diabolical deed of all was committed, after Edalji's conviction upon Nov. 3, when a horse and mare were found mutilated in the same field, an additional touch of horror being added by the discovery of a newly-born foal some little distance from the mare. Three months later, on Feb. 8, 1904, another horse was found to be injured, and finally, on March 24, two sheep and a lamb were found mutilated, and a rough miner named Farrington was convicted, upon entirely circumstantial evidence, and condemned to three years. Now here the results of the police are absolutely illogical and incompatible. Their theory was that of a moon-lighting gang. Edalji is condemned as one member of it, Farrington as another. But no possible connection can be proved or was ever suggested between Edalji and Farrington; the one a rude, illiterate miner, the other the son of the vicar and a rising professional man; the one a loafer at public-houses, the other a total abstainer. It is certainly suggestive, presuming that Farrington did do the deed for which he was convicted, that he was employed at the Wyrley Colliery, and may have had to pass in going to his work that very pony which Edalji was supposed to have injured. It is also, it must be admitted, suggestive that while Edalji's imprisonment had no effect upon the outrages, Farrington's was at once followed by their complete cessation. How monstrous, then, to contend, as the Home Office has done, that no new facts have arisen to justify a revision of Edalji's case. At the same time, I do not mean to imply Farrington's guilt, of which I have grave doubts, but merely that, as compared with Edalji, a strong case could be made out against him.

Now let me, before examining the outrage of Aug. 17, 1903, which proved so fatal to Edalji, give some account of the fresh epidemic of letters which broke out in the district. They were synchronous with the actual outrages, and there were details in them which made it possible, though by no means certain, that they were written by someone who was actually concerned in the crimes.

It cannot be said that there is absolute proof that the letters of 1903 were by the same hand as those of 1895, but there are points about their phrasing, about their audacity and violence of language, finally, about the attentions which they bestow upon the Edalji family, which seem to point to a common origin. Only in this case the Rev Edalji escapes, and it is the son—the same son who had been menaced in the first series with disgrace for life—who receives some of the communications, and is referred to in the others. I may say that this series of letters presents various handwritings, all of which differ from the 1895 letters, but as the original persecutor was fond of boasting that he could change his handwriting, and even that he could imitate that of George Edalji, the variance need not be taken too seriously.

And now for the letters. They were signed by various names, but the more important purported to come from a young schoolboy, named Greatorex. This youth denied all knowledge of them, and was actually away in the Isle of Man when some of them were written, as well as on Aug. 17, the date of the Wyrley outrage. It is a curious fact that this youth, in going up to Walsall every day to school, travelled with a certain number of schoolfellows upon the same errand, and that the names of some of these schoolfellows do find their way into these letters. In the same carriage travelled young Edalji upon some few occasions. 'I have known accused by sight for three or four years,' said Greatorex at the trial, 'he has travelled in the same compartment with me and my schoolmates, going to Walsall. This has not occurred many times during the last twelve months—about a dozen times, in fact.' Now, at first sight, one would think this was a point for the police, as on the presumption that Edalji wrote these anonymous letters it would account for the familiarity with these youths displayed in them. But since Edalji always went to business by the 7.30 train in the morning, and the boys took the same train every day, to find himself in their company twelve times in one year was really rather more seldom than one would expect. He drifted into their compartment as into any other, and he seems to have been in their company but not of it. Yet the anonymous writer knew that group of boys well, and the police, by proving that George Edalji might have known them, seemed to make a distinct point against him.

The 'Greatorex' letters to the police are all to the effect that the writer is a member of the gang for maiming cattle, that George Edalji is another member, and that he (Greatorex) is prepared to give away the gang if certain conditions are complied with. 'I have got a dare-devil face and can run well, and when they formed that gang at Wyrley they got me to join. I knew all about horses and beasts and how to catch them best . . . they said they would do me in if I funked it, so I did, and caught them both lying down at ten minutes to three, and they roused up; and then I caught each under the belly, but they didn't spurt much blood, and one ran away, but the other fell . . . Now I'll tell you who are in the gang, but you can't prove it without me. There is one named —————, from Wyrley, and a porter who they call —————, and he's had to stay away, and there's Edalji, the lawyer . . . Now I have not told you who is at the back of them all, and I shan't unless you promise to do nothing at me. It is not true we always do it when the moon is young, and the one Edalji killed on April 11 was full moon.' (It is worth mentioning here that there was no outrage at all within a week of that date.) 'I've never been locked up yet, and I don't think any of the others have, except the Captain, so I guess they'll get off light.'

I would draw attention in passing to the artistic touch of 'ten minutes to three.' This is realism overdone, as no mutilator on a dark night could readily consult his watch nor care to remember the exact hour to a minute. But it corresponds closely to the remarkable power of imaginative detail—a rather rare gift—shown in the hoaxes of 1893–95.

In the next letter, also to the police, the unknown refers to his previous communication, but is a good deal more truculent and abusive than before. 'There will be merry times at Wyrley in November,' he says, 'when they start on little girls, for they will do twenty wenches like the horses before next March. Don't think you are likely to catch them cutting the beasts; they go too quiet, and lie low for hours, till you men have gone . . . Mr Edalji, him they said was locked up, is going to Brum on Sunday night to see the Captain, near Northfield, about how it's to be carried on with so many detectives about, and I believe they are going to do some cows in the daytime instead of at night . . . I think they are going to kill beasts nearer here soon, and I know Cross Keys Farm and West Cannock Farm are the two first on the list . . . You bloated blackguard, I will shoot you with father's gun through your thick head if you come in my way or go sneaking to any of my pals.'

This letter was addressed, like the last, to:

> The Sergeant,
> Police Station, Hednesford,
> Staffordshire.

bearing a Walsall post mark of July 10, 1903. Edalji is openly accused of the crimes in the letters, and yet the police put forward the theory that he himself wrote them, and founded upon the last sentence of them, which I have quoted, that second charge, which sounded so formidable in his indictment, viz., of threatening to murder Sergeant Robinson.

A few days previously a second police officer, Mr. Rowley, of Bridgtown, had received another letter, evidently from the same hand. Here the detail as to the method of the crime is more realistic than ever, though no accusations against others are made. I quote this letter in extenso:

'Sir—A party whose initials you'll guess will be bringing a new hook home by the train from Walsall on Wednesday night, an he will have it in his special long pocket under his coat, an if you or your pals can get his coat pulled aside a bit you'll get sight of it, as it's an inch and half longer than the one he threw out of sight when he heard someone a slopin it after him this morning. He will come by that after five or six, or if he don't come home tomorrow he is sure on Thursday, an you have made a mistake not keeping all the plain clothes men at hand. You sent them away too soon. Why, just think, he did it close where two of them were hiding only a few days gone by. But, sir, he has got eagle eyes, and his ears is as sharp as a razor, and he is as fleet of foot as a fox, and as noiseless, and he crawls on all fours up to the poor beasts, an fondles them a bit, and then he pulls the hook smart across 'em, and out their entrails fly, before they guess they are hurt. You want 100 detectives to run him in red-handed, because he is so fly, and knows every nook and corner. You know who it is, and I can prove it; but until £100 reward is offered for a conviction, I shan't split no more.'

There is, it must be admitted, striking realism in this account also, but a hook—unless it were a billhook or horticultural hook—could not under any circumstances have inflicted the injuries.

It seems absurd enough that these letters incriminating himself in such violent terms should be attributed to young Edalji, but the climax is reached when a most offensive post-card, handed in at Edalji's own business office, is also sworn to by the expert employed by the police as being in Edalji's own writing. This vile effusion, which cannot be reproduced in full, accuses Edalji of guilty relations with a certain lady, ending up with the words, 'Rather go back to your old game of writing anonymous letters and killing cows and writing on walls.'

Now this postcard was posted at Wolverhampton upon Aug. 4, 1903. As luck would have it, Edalji and his sister had gone upon an excursion to Aberystwyth that day, and were absent from very early morning till late at night. Here is the declaration of the station official upon the point:

'On the night of 4th of August, 1903, and early morning of the 5th I was on duty at Rugely Town Station, and spoke to Mr George Edalji and his sister, who were in the train on their return from Aberystwyth. *William Bullock, Porter-Signalman, Rugeley Town Station.*'

The station-master at Wyrley has made a similar declaration.

It is certain, then, that this postcard could not have been by him, even had the insulting contents not made the supposition absurd. And yet it is included in that list of anonymous letters which the police maintained, and the expert declared, to be in Edalji's own handwriting. If this incident is not enough in itself to break down the whole case, so far as the authorship of the letters goes, then I ask, what in this world would be sufficient to demonstrate its absurdity?

Before leaving this postcard, let me say that it was advanced for the prosecution that if a card were posted at certain country boxes to be found within two and a half miles of Wyrley they would not be cleared till evening, and so would have the Wolverhampton mark of next day. Thus the card might have been posted in one of these out-of-the-way boxes on the 3rd, and yet bear the mark of the 4th. This, however, will not do. The card has the Wolverhampton mark of the evening of the 4th, and was actually delivered in Birmingham on the morning of the 5th. Even granting that one day was Bank Holiday, you cannot stretch the dislocation of the postal service to the point that what was posted on the 3rd took two days to go twenty miles.

Now, during these six months, while Edalji was receiving these scurrilous letters, and while the police were receiving others accusing the young lawyer, you will naturally ask why did he not take some steps himself to prove his innocence and to find out the writer? He did, as a matter of fact, everything in his power. He offered a reward of £25 in the public Press—a reward, according to the police theory, for his own apprehension. He showed the police the letters which he received, and he took a keen interest in the capture of the criminals, making the very sensible suggestion that bloodhounds should be used. It seems hardly conceivable that the prejudice of the police had risen to such a point that both these facts were alleged as suspicious circumstances against him, as though he were endeavouring to worm himself into their confidence, and so find out what measures they were taking for the capture of the offender. I am quite prepared to find that in these dialogues the quick-witted youth showed some impatience at their constant blunders, and that the result was to increase the very great malevolence with which they appear to have regarded him, ever since their chief declared, in 1895, 'I shall not pretend to believe any protestations of ignorance which your son may make.'

And now, having dealt with the letters of 1903, let me, before I proceed to the particular outrage for which Edalji was arrested and convicted, say a few words as to the personality of this unfortunate young man, who was, according to the police theory, an active member, if not the leading spirit, of a gang of village ruffians. Anyone more absurdly constructed to play the rôle could not be imagined. In the first place, he is a total abstainer, which in itself hardly seems to commend him to such a gang. He does not smoke. He is very shy and nervous. He is a most distinguished student, having won the highest legal prizes within his reach, and written, at his early age, a handbook of railway law. Finally, he is as blind as the proverbial bat, but the bat has the advantage of finding its way in the dark, which would be very difficult for him. To find a pony in a dark field, or, indeed, to find the field itself, unless it were easily approached, would be a hard task, while to avoid a lurking watcher would be absolutely impossible. I have myself practised as an oculist, but I can never remember correcting so high a degree of astigmatic myopia as that which afflicts Mr Edalji. 'Like all myopics, Mr Edalji,' says an expert, 'must find it at all times difficult to see clearly any objects more than a few inches off, and in dusk it would be practically impossible for him to find his way about any place with which he was not perfectly familiar.' Fearing lest it might be thought that he was feigning blindness, I asked Mr Kenneth Scott, of Manchester-Square, to paralyse the accommodation by atropine, and then to take the result by means which were independent of the patient. Here is his report:

> Right eye—8.75 Diop Spher.
> —1.75 Diop cylind axis 90°.
> Left eye —8.25 Diop Spher.

'I am prepared to testify as to the accuracy of the above

The Edalji home (top), and one of the thickets that George Edalji would
have had to negotiate on his way to the scene of the crimes (bottom).

under oath,' says Mr Kenneth Scott.

As to what such figures mean, I will bring it home to the uninitiated by saying that a glass made up to that prescription would cause the normal healthy eye to see the world as Edalji's eyes always see it. I am prepared to have such a glass made up, and if any defender of the police will put it on at night, and will make his way over the route the accused is alleged to have taken inside of an hour, I will admit that what seems to me absolutely impossible could be done. I may add that this blindness is a permanent structural condition, the same in 1903 as in 1906.

I appeal to the practising oculists of this country, and I ask whether there is one of them who would not admit that such a condition of the eyes would make such a performance practically impossible, and that the circumstance must add enormously to a defence which is already overwhelmingly strong. And yet this all-important point was never made at the trial.

It is this studious youth who touches neither alcohol nor tobacco, and is so blind that he gropes his way in the dusk, who is the dangerous barbarian who scours the country at night, ripping up horses. Is it not perfectly clear, looking at his strange, swarthy face and bulging eyes, that it is not the village ruffian, but rather the unfortunate village scapegoat, who stands before you?

I have brought the narrative down to the Aug. 17 outrage. At this period twenty constables and detectives had been brought into the district, and several, acting, I presume, upon orders from higher quarters, watched the vicarage at night. On Aug. 17 Edalji, following his own account, returned from his day's work at Birmingham—he had started in practice there as a lawyer—and reached his home about 6.30. He transacted some business, put on a blue serge coat, and then walked down to the bootmaker's in the village, where he arrived about 8.35, according to the independent evidence of John Hands, the tradesman in question. His supper would not be ready before 9.30, and until that hour he took a walk round, being seen by various people. His household depose to his return before supper-time, and their testimony is confirmed by the statement of Walter Whitehouse, who saw the accused enter the vicarage at 9.25. After supper Edalji retired to bed in the same room as his father, the pair having shared an apartment for seventeen years. The old vicar was a light sleeper, his son was within a few feet of him, the whole house was locked up, and the outside was watched by constables, who saw no one leave it. To show how close the inspection was, I may quote the words of Sergeant Robinson, who said, 'I saw four men observing it when I was there . . . I could see the front door and side door. I should say no one could get out on the side I was watching without my seeing.' This was before the night of the outrage, but it is inconceivable that if there was so close a watch then, there was none on the 17th. By the police evidence there were no less than twenty men scattered about waiting for the offender. I may add at this point some surprise has been expressed that the vicar should sleep in the same room as his son with the door locked. They slept thus, and had done for many years, so that the daughter, whose health was precarious, might sleep with the mother, and the service of the house, there being only the one maid, should be minimised. Absurd emphasis has been placed by the police upon the door being locked at night. I can only suppose that the innuendo is that the vicar locked the door to keep his son from roving. Do we not all know that it is the commonest thing for nervous people to lock their doors whether alone or not, and Mr Edalji has been in the habit of doing so all his long life. I have evidence that Mr Edalji always locked his door before he slept with his son, and that he has continued to lock his door after his son left him. If, then—to revert to the evidence—it is possible for a person in this world to establish an alibi, it was successfully established by Edalji that night from 9.30 onwards. Granting the perfectly absurd supposition that the old vicar connived at his son slipping out at night and ripping up cattle, you have still the outside police to deal with. On no possible supposition can George Edalji have gone out after 9.30.

And yet upon that night a pony had been destroyed at the Great Wyrley Colliery. Sergeant Parsons gave evidence that he saw the pony, apparently all right, at eleven o'clock at night. It was very dark, but he was not far off it. It was a wild night, with rain coming in squalls. The rain began about twelve, and cleared about dawn, being very heavy at times. On the 18th, at

6.20, a lad, named Henry Garrett, going to his work at the colliery, observed that the pony was injured. 'It had a cut on the side,' he said. 'The blood was trickling from the wound. It was dropping pretty quickly.' The alarm was at once given. Constables appeared upon the scene. By half-past eight Mr Lewis, a veterinary surgeon, was on the spot. 'The wound,' he deposed, 'was quite fresh, and could not have been done further than six hours from the time he saw it.' The least learned of laymen might be sure that if the pony was standing bleeding freely at six it could not have been so all night, as the drain must have exhausted it. And here, on the top of this obvious consideration, is the opinion of the surgeon, that the injury was inflicted within six hours. Where George Edalji was during those six hours has already been shown beyond all possible question or dispute. So already the whole bottom has dropped out of the case; but, none the less, the indefatigable police went on with their pre-arranged campaign.

That it was pre-arranged is evident, since it was not on account of evidence, but in search of evidence, that the constables raided the vicarage. The young lawyer had already started for his day's work in Birmingham. The startled parents were ordered to produce all the young man's clothing. The mother was asked for his dagger, but could produce nothing more formidable than a botany spud. A hunt was made for weapons, and a set of razors belonging to the vicar were seized. Some were said to be wet—a not uncommon condition for razors in the morning. Dark spots were perceived upon the back of one, but they proved upon chemical examination to be rust stains. Twelve men quartered the small garden, but nothing was found.

The clothes, however, were a more serious matter. One coat was seized by the police and declared to be damp. This is vigorously denied by the vicar, who handled the coat before it was removed. Damp is, of course, a relative term, and all garments may give some feeling of dampness after a rainy night, when the whole atmosphere is humid; but if the condition had been caused by being out in the wild weather which prevailed that night, it is certain that the coat would have been not damp, but sopping wet.

The coat, however, was not one which Edalji used outside, and the evidence of Mr Hands was called to show that he had not worn it the night before. It was an old house-coat, so stained and worn that it is not likely that an ambitious young professional man would, even in the lamplight, walk in the streets and show himself to his neighbours in such a garment. But it was these very stains which naturally attracted the attention of the police. There were some whitish stains—surely these must be the saliva of the unfortunate animal. They were duly tested, and proved to be starch stains, probably from fish sauce or bread and milk. But there was something still more ominous upon this unhappy coat. There were, according to Inspector Campbell, 'dark red or brown stains, right cuff much more stained than the left. There were other stains on each sleeve, further up, reddish brown or white. The coat was damp . . . There are other spots and stains upon it.'

Now the police try to make two points here: that the coat was damp, and that there were stains which might have been the traces of the crime upon it. Each point is good in itself; but, unfortunately, they are incompatible and mutually destructive. If the coat were damp, and if those marks were blood-stains contracted during the night, then those stains were damp also, and the inspector had only to touch them and then to raise his crimson finger in the air to silence all criticism. But since he could not do so it is clear that the stains were not fresh. They fell twelve hours later into the capable hands of the police surgeon, and the sanguinary smears conjured up by the evidence of the constable diminished with absurd swiftness until they became 'two stains in the centre of the right cuff, each about the size of a threepenny bit.' This was declared by Dr Butter to be mammalian blood. He found no more blood at all. How these small stains came there it is difficult to trace—as difficult as to trace a stain which I see now upon the sleeve of my own house-jacket as I look down. A splash from the gravy of underdone meat might well produce it. At any rate, it may most safely be said that the most adept operator who ever lived would not rip up a horse with a razor upon a dark night and have only two threepenny-bit spots of blood to show for it. The idea is beyond argument.

But now, having exhausted the white stains and the dark

stains, we come to the most damning portion of the whole indictment, though a careful consideration may change one's view as to who it is who is damned by it. The police claimed that they discovered horse-hairs upon the coat. 'On the sleeve,' says Inspector Campbell, 'I found brownish hairs, which look like horse-hairs. There are some on now.' Now, let us listen to the very clear statement of the vicar upon the subject. I transcribe it in full:

'On Aug. 18, 1903, they called at the vicarage at about eight o'clock in the morning, and in compliance with their request Mrs Edalji showed them a number of garments belonging to her son, George Edalji. As soon as they saw the old coat they began to examine it, and Inspector Campbell put his finger upon one place and said that there was a hair there. Mrs Edalji told him that it was not a hair, but a thread, and Miss Edalji, who was present then, remarked that it looked like a 'roving.' This was all that Inspector Campbell had said to them about the hair before I came down. When I saw him he told me that he had found horse-hairs upon the coat. The coat was then spread out upon the desk in the study. I asked him to point out the place where the hairs were to be seen. He pointed out a lower part of the coat, and said, "There's a horse-hair there." I examined the place and said, "There is no hair here at all." Some further conversation followed, and then suddenly he put his finger upon another place on the coat nearer to where I was standing, and, drawing two straight lines with his finger, he said, "Look here, Mr Edalji, there's horse-hair here." I looked at the place for a moment, and in order to have more light upon it, I took up the coat with both my hands and drew nearer to the window, and after carefully examining it I said to him, "There is, to be sure, no hair here, it is a clear surface." He then said that he wanted to take the coat with him, and I said, "You can take the coat. I am satisfied there is no horse-hair upon it."

'Now I have said it over and over again, and I say it here once more, that there was absolutely no horse-hair upon the coat. If there had been any I could not have failed to see it, and both Mrs Edalji and Miss Edalji looked at the coat at the same time, and saw no hair of any sort upon it.' Incidentally it may be mentioned in connection with this statement, in which Miss

Edalji entirely concurs, that we have the evidence of Miss Foxley, formerly of Newnham College, and then head mistress of the High School, that Miss Edalji was an exceedingly competent scientific observer. She adds, 'Wilful mis-statement on her part is as impossible in itself as it is inconsistent with her high principles and frank, straightforward character.'

Now, here is a clear conflict of evidence between two groups of interested people—the constables on the one hand, eager to build up their case; the household on the other, eager to confute this terrible accusation. Let us suppose the two statements balance each other. But is it not evident that there was only one course open for the police now to establish their point, and that if they did not avail themselves of it they put themselves out of court? Their obvious course was then and there to send for a referee—the police doctor, or any other doctor—and picking samples of the hair from the coat to have sealed them in an envelope, calling the new-comer to witness when and where they had been obtained. Such a proceeding must silence all doubt. But they did nothing of the kind. What they actually did was to carry off the coat upon which three reputable witnesses have sworn there were no hairs. The coat then disappears from view for twelve hours. In the meantime the pony has been put out of its pain, and a portion of its hide was cut off with the hairs attached, and also secured by the police. The coat had been taken at eight in the morning. It was seen by Dr Butter, the police surgeon, at nine in the evening. At that hour Dr Butter picked twenty-nine undoubted obvious horse-hairs from its surface.

The prosecution have here to break their way through two strong lines of defence, each within the other. On the one hand, if Edalji had done the crime the evening before, it was his blue serge coat, and not his house-coat, that he wore, as is shown by the independent evidence of Mr Hands. In the second line of defence is the oath of the family that there were no hairs in the morning, which is strengthened by the failure of the police to demonstrate there and then a fact which could have been so easily and completely demonstrated. But now we are faced by the undoubted fact that the hairs were there, upon the cuffs and the left breast, by evening. Why was the coat not taken straight to the surgeon? Why was a piece of the animal's hide sent for before the coat was shown to Dr Butter? One need not fly to extreme conclusions. It is to be remembered that the mere carrying of hide and coat together may have caused the transference of hairs, or that the officers may themselves have gathered hairs on their clothes while examining the pony, and so unconsciously transferred them to the coat. But the fact that the hairs were found just on the cuffs and breast will still recur in the mind. It would be sad indeed to commit one injustice while trying to correct another, but when the inevitable inquiry comes this incident must form a salient point of it.

There is one test which occurs to one's mind. Did the hairs all correspond with the type, colour, and texture of the hairs on the sample of hide? If they did, then they were beyond all question conveyed from that sample to the coat. The cut was down the belly, and the portion taken off was from the side of the cut. The under hair of a horse differs greatly from the longer, darker, harsher hair of the sides. A miscreant leaning against a horse would get the side hairs. If all the hairs on the coat were short belly hairs, then there is a suggestive fact for the inquiry. Dr Butter must have compared their appearance.

Since writing the above I have been able to get the words of Dr Butter's evidence. They are quoted: 'Numerous hairs on the jacket, which were similar in colour, length, and structure to those on the piece of skin cut from the horse.' In that case I say, confidently—and all reflection must confirm it—that these hairs could not possibly be from the general body of the pony, but must have been transferred, no doubt unconsciously, from that particular piece of skin. With all desire to be charitable, the incident leaves a most unpleasant impression upon the mind.

If one could for a moment conceive oneself performing this barbarity, one would not expect to find hairs upon one's coat. There is no necessary connection at all. Anxious to avoid the gush of blood, one would imagine that one would hold off the animal with the flat of one hand and attack it with the other. To lean one's coat against its side would be to bring one's trousers and boots in danger of being soaked in blood.

So much for the saliva stains, the blood stains, and the hairs.

There remain the questions of the trousers and the boots. The trousers were said by the police to be damp, and stained with dark mud round the bottom. The boots were very wet. The boots were the same ones which Edalji had admittedly used during his sixty-minutes' walk upon the evening before. It was fine in the evening, but there had been heavy rain during the day, and puddles everywhere. Of course his boots were wet. The trousers were not a pair used the evening before, according to the family. No attempt was made to show blood marks on boots or trousers, though Mr Sewell, a well-known veterinary surgeon, deposed afterwards that in making such an incision a skilled operator would wear an apron to prevent his clothes from being soaked. It is an interesting point, brought out by the evidence of some of the witnesses of the prosecution, that the mud at the place of outrage was yellow-red, a mixture of clay and sand, quite distinct from the road mud, which the police claim to have seen upon the trousers.

And now we come to the farce of the footprints. The outrage had occurred just outside a large colliery, and hundreds of miners going to their work had swarmed along every approach, in order to see the pony. The soft, wet soil was trampled up by them from six o'clock onwards; yet on four o'clock of that afternoon, eight hours after the seizure of the boots, we have Inspector Campbell endeavouring to trace a similarity in tracks. The particular boot was worn at the heel, a fairly common condition, and some tracks among the multitude were down at the heel, and why should not the one be caused by the other? No cast was taken of the tracks. They were not photographed. They were not cut out for purpose of expert comparison. So little were they valued by Inspector Campbell that he did not even mention them to the magistrates on the 19th. But in retrospect they grew more valuable, and they bulked large at the trial.

Now, once again, the police are trying to make a point which in itself would help them, but which is incompatible with their other points. Their original theory was that the crime was done before 9.30. There was heavy rain on and off all night. It is perfectly clear that any well-marked footsteps must have been left after the rain stopped, or when it had nearly stopped. Even granting that the earth was soft enough, as it was, to take footprints before then, this heavy rain would blur them to a point that would make identification by a worn-down heel absurd. What becomes then of all this elaborate business of the footmarks? Every point in this case simply crumbles to pieces as you touch it.

How formidable it all sounds—wet razor, blood on razor, blood and saliva and hair on coat, wet boots, footmark corresponding to boot—and yet how absolutely futile it all is when examined. There is not one single item which will bear serious criticism. Let us pass, however, from these material clues to those more subtle ones which the bearing or remarks of the youth may have furnished. These will bear examination even less than the others. As he waited upon the platform for the 7.30 train an ex-constable, now an innkeeper, named Markhew, came up to him and asked him to stay, as Inspector Campbell wished to see him. At the same moment someone announced that a fresh outrage had been committed, upon which Markhew says that Edalji turned away and smiled. Now, it is perfectly clear that a guilty man would have been much alarmed by the news that the police wished to see him, and that he would have done anything but smile on hearing of the outrage. Edalji's account is that Markhew said, 'Can't you give yourself a holiday for one day?' on which Edalji smiled. Which is the more probable version I leave to the reader. The incident was referred to by the prosecuting counsel as 'the prisoner's extraordinary conduct at the station.'

He went to his office in Birmingham, and there, later in the day, he was arrested by the police.

On the way to the station, after his arrest, this unfortunate youth made another deadly remark: 'I am not surprised at this. I have been expecting it for some time.' It is not a very natural remark for a guilty man to make, if you come to think of it; but it is an extremely probable one from a man who believes that the police have a down on him, and who is aware that he has been accused by name in malignant anonymous letters. What else would he have said? Next day and the following Monday he was before the magistrates, where the police evidence, as already set forth, was given. The magisterial proceedings lasted till Sept. 4, off and on, when a prima facie case was made out, and the prisoner committed to the Staffordshire Quarter Sessions. How far a case of this importance should have been referred to any less tribunal than the assizes I leave to legal opinion. Again the criminal made a remark which rose up in judgment against him. 'I won't have bail,' said he to Police-constable Meredith, 'and when the next horse is killed it will not be by me.' In commenting upon this, Mr Disturnal, the prosecuting counsel, said, 'In refusing bail the prisoner made use of a very significant observation, and it went to suggest that the prisoner knew perfectly well what he was about when he refused bail.' The inference here is that it was pre-arranged that a friend of Edalji's would do a fresh crime, in order to clear him. Was ever a more unfair utterance! It was, 'Heads I win, tails you lose!' If no crimes occur, then it is clear we have the villain under lock and key. If crimes do occur, then it is clear that he is deep in conspiracy with others. As a matter of fact, both Edalji's decision to remain in gaol and his remark were the most proper and natural things in the world. He believed that there was a strong conspiracy against him. In the face of the letters he had every reason to believe so. So long as he was in his cell he was safe, he thought, from this conspiracy. Perhaps another crime would be committed, and in that case, he thought, in the innocence of his heart, that it would clear him. In his wildest dreams he could never have imagined that such a crime would be fitted in as a link in the chain against him.

A crime was committed, and it occurred upon Sept. 21, between Edalji's committal and trial, whilst he lay in Stafford Gaol. The facts are these: Harry Green was the nineteen-year-old son of a farmer who lived somewhere between the vicarage and the scene of the outrage for which Edalji was convicted. He and Edalji knew each other slightly, as neighbours in the country must do, but how slight was their acquaintance may be shown by the fact that when, in the course of my inquiry, I asked Edalji what Green's writing was like, he had to admit that he had never seen it. Consider the utter want of common ground between the two men, the purblind, studious teetotal young lawyer of twenty-seven, and the young Yeomanry trooper of nineteen, one of a set of boisterous young fellows, who made a centre of mirth and also of mischief at each annual training. Edalji entered no public-house, and was at work from early morning to late at night. Where was there room for that blood-brotherhood which would make the one man risk any danger and sacrifice his own horse for the sake of the other?

Green's charger was found disembowelled. It was not a very valuable animal. In one estimate it is placed at five pounds. Whether it was insured or not there is a conflict of evidence. For days there was scare and conjecture. Then, at the end of that time, it was known that Green had signed a confession which admitted that he had himself killed his own horse. That confession undoubtedly exists, but Green, having had a week or two to think things over, and having in the meantime got a ticket to South Africa, suddenly went back on his own confession, and declared, with much circumstantiality of detail, that he had not done it, and that the confession had been bullied out of him by the police. One or other statement of Green's must be a falsehood, and I have sufficient reason myself, in the shape of evidence which has been set before me, to form a very clear opinion what the actual facts of the case were. When a final clearing of the case arrives, and there is a renewed inquiry on the basis that Edalji is innocent, and that the actual perpetrators have never been punished, there are many facts which may be laid before the authority who conducts it. Meanwhile the task which lies immediately before me is not to show who did do the crime—though that, I think, is by no means an insuperable problem—but that Edalji did not and could not have done them. I will leave young Green there, with his two contradictory statements, and I will confine myself to his relation with the case, whichever of the statements is true.

And, first of all, here are the police who claim to hold his written confession. Then why did they not prosecute? It will not do to say that it is not a crime to kill your own horse. It is not a crime to shoot your own horse from humane motives, but it is at all times a crime, as the Society for the Prevention of Cruelty to Animals would very quickly show, to disembowel a horse on a dark night, be it fifty times your own. Here is an outrage of the same sort which has convulsed the countryside for so many months, it is brought home by his own confession to the

offender, and yet the police refuse to prosecute, and connive at
the man's flight from the country. But why? If it was not that
the prosecution of Green would bring out facts which would
interfere with the successful prosecution of Edalji, then, again,
I ask, why? Far be it from me to be unjust to the police, but
again it is their own really extraordinary behaviour which
drives one to seek for hypotheses. The Home Office says that all
inquiry has been made in this case, and that everything has
been investigated and the matter closed. That is the official
answer I received only a fortnight ago. Then can the Home
Office give any good reason why Green was not prosecuted?
The point is a very vital one.

Green was present at Edalji's trial, was not called, and left
afterwards for South Africa. He had been subpœnaed by the
police, and that, no doubt, was what prevented the defence
from calling him. But had they done so, and had he spoken in
public as he has spoken in private, there would have been an
end of all possibility, according to my information, of the great
miscarriage which ensued. It may be noted before leaving this
extraordinary incident that the reason given by Green in his
confession was that the horse had to be killed, having been
injured in the Yeomanry training, but nowhere has he ever said
a word to suggest that he was acting in collusion with George
Edalji.

And now at last we come to the trial. Here, as at every point
of this extraordinary case, there are irregularities which will be
more fitly dealt with by a lawyer. Suffice it that though the case
was of such importance that it is generally thought that it
should not have been at Quarter Sessions at all, it was at the
lesser of the courts which make up that tribunal that it was at
last tried. In Court A a skilled lawyer presided. Sir Reginald
Hardy, who conducted Court B, had no legal training. I have
not a word to say against his desire to be impartial and fair, but
here was a young man, accused of one of a series of crimes for
which the whole county was longing to find someone who might
be made an example of. The jury would naturally have the
same feelings as their fellow-citizens. Hence it was peculiarly
necessary to have a cold legal mind to cool their ardour and
keep them on firm ground of fact, far from prejudice and

emotion. Yet it was in the court of the layman that the case was tried.

The ground over which the prosecution advanced is already familiar to the reader. We have the clothes which have now become 'wet'. They were merely 'damp' in the previous inquiry, and we have the word of the vicar that this dampness was imperceptible to him, coupled with the fact that any bloodstains would then have been liquid. We have the down-at-heel boot, which was fitted into impressions which must have been made after rain, whereas the whole police theory was that the crime was committed before the rain. We have the bloodstains which sank from smears into two threepenny-bit patches, and we have the hairs which made their appearance thirteen hours after the coat had been in the hands of the police, and after it had been associated with the strip of horse's hide. Then came the letters. There was a strong probability that whoever wrote the letters knew something of the crimes. What matter that the letters actually accused Edalji himself and vilified him in all sorts of ways? What matter that one villainous postcard in the same writing as the others was posted at Wolverhampton when he was at Aberystwyth? What matter that in the original series of anonymous letters the writer had said, 'Do you think we cannot imitate your kid's writing?' None of these things weighed as compared with the expression of opinion by an expert that the letters were in George Edalji's own writing. As the unfortunate prisoner listened to such an opinion he must have felt that he was in some nightmare dream. And who was the expert who expressed these views which weighed so heavily with the jury? It was Mr Thomas Gurrin. And what is the record of Mr Thomas Gurrin? His nemesis was soon to come. Within a year he had to present himself before the Beck Committee, and admit the terrible fact that through his evidence an innocent man had suffered prolonged incarceration. Does this fact alone not convince my readers that an entire reconsideration of the Edalji case is a most pressing public duty?

There is absolutely the whole evidence—the coat-boot-razor business, the letter business, the so-called incriminating expressions which I have already analysed, and the one fact, which I admit did really deserve consideration, that a group of schoolboys with whom once a month young Edalji may have travelled were known also to the writer of the letters. That is all. I have shown what each link is worth. And on that evidence a young gentleman, distinguished already in an honourable profession, was torn from his family, suffered all the indignities of a convict, was immured for three of the best years of his life, was struck from the roll on which with such industry and self-denial he had written his name, and had every torture made ten-fold more bitter by the thought of the vicar at home, of his mother and of his sister, so peculiarly sensitive, from their position in the church, to the scoff and the derision of those around them. It is a tale which makes a man hot with indignation as he reads it.

One word as to the evidence of the family, upon which so much depends. It has been asserted that it was given in a peculiar way, which shook the confidence of the jury. I have had some experience of the Edaljis, and I can say with confidence that what seemed peculiar to the jury arose from extreme anxiety to speak the absolute, exact truth. An experienced barrister who knew them well remarked to me that they were the most precisely truthful people he had ever met—'bad witnesses,' he added, 'as they are so conscientious that they lay undue stress upon any point of doubt.'

It must be admitted that the defence was not as strong as it might have been made, which does not seem to have been due to any shortcomings of the counsel so much as to a deficiency in the supply of information. The fact is that the consciousness of innocence was in this case a danger, as it caused some slackness in guarding every point. So far as I can find, the whole story of the early persecutions of 1888 and of 1893–5 was not gone into, nor was their probable connection with that of 1903 pointed out. The blindness of Edalji, a most vital fact, was not supported by an array of evidence; indeed, I think that it was hardly mentioned at all. At all points one finds things which might have been better, but even granting that, one cannot but feel the amazement, which Sir George Lewis has voiced, when the jury brought in 'Guilty,' and Sir Reginald Hardy sentenced the prisoner to seven years.

Now, once again, let me state the double dilemma of the police, before I leave this portion of my statement. Either Edalji did the crime before ten o'clock that night or after ten o'clock that night. The latter case must be laughed out of a common-sense court by the fact that his father, the vicar, spent the night within a few feet of him, that the small vicarage was bolted and barred, no one being heard to leave it, and that the police watchers outside saw no one leave it. If that does not establish an alibi what could? On the other hand, supposing that he did it before ten, or rather before 9.30, the time of his return home. You have to face the supposition that after returning from a long day's work in Birmingham he sallied out in a coat which he was only known to wear in the house, performed a common-place mission at the boot-shop in the village, then, blind as he was, hurried off for three-quarters of a mile, through difficult, tortuous ways, with fences to climb and railway lines to cross (I can answer for it, having myself trod every foot of it), to commit a ghastly and meaningless crime, entirely foreign to his studious and abstinent nature; that he then hurried back another three-quarters of a mile to the vicarage, arrived so composed and tidy as to attract no attention, and sat down quietly to the family supper, the whole expedition from first to last being under an hour. The mere statement of this alternative supposition seems grotesque enough, but on the top of the gross, inherent improbability you are up against the hard facts that the pony was bleeding freely in the morning, and could not have so bled all night, that the veterinary surgeon deposed that the wound could not possibly be more than six hours old, no other veterinary surgeon being called to contradict this statement, and that the footprints on which the police relied were worthless unless left after the rain, which began at twelve. Add to this that the pony was seen standing apparently all right by the police themselves at eleven o'clock, and the case then seems to me to be overpoweringly convincing. Take whichever supposition you like, and I say that it is demonstrably false, and an insult to common-sense, to suppose that George Edalji committed the crime for which, through the action of the Staffordshire police, the error of an expert, and the gross stupidity of a jury, he has been made to suffer so cruelly.

I do not know that there is much to add, save a bare recital of
the events which have occurred since then. After Edalji's
conviction the outrages continued unabated, and the epidemic
of anonymous letters raged as ever. The November outrage
upon Mr Stanley's horses was never traced, but there was some
good local information as to the author of that crime, and a
widespread conviction in the district, which may have been
utterly unjust, that the police were not too anxious to push the
matter, as any conviction would certainly disturb the one
which they had already obtained. This incident, also, will
furnish some evidence for the coming inquiry. Finally, in
March, 1904, a man, named Farrington, was convicted for
injuring some sheep. No attempt has ever been made to trace
any connection between this man and Edalji. In the Green case
not only was there no attempt to prove complicity between
Green and Edalji, but I have evidence to show that the police
had a most positive statement from Green that he had nothing
to do with Edalji, obtained under circumstances which make it
perfectly convincing. And yet, in face of this fact, Mr Disturnal,
the mouthpiece of the police at the trial, was permitted to say,
referring to this outrage: 'The letters which would be read
would show that the writer of them was not acting alone, but in
conjunction with some other people, and he put it to the jury,
what was more likely than that, if there was a gang operating in
the way suggested, one of its members would commit a similar
outrage in order to create evidence for the defence?' Counsel, no
doubt, spoke according to his instructions; but what are we to
think of those from whom such instructions issued, since they
had the clearest proof that there was no connection between
Green and Edalji? Such incidents shake one's confidence in
British justice to the very foundations, for it is clear that the
jury, already prejudiced by the nature of the crimes, were
hoodwinked into giving their conviction.

A few words as to the sequel. The friends of the prisoner,
organised and headed by Mr R.D. Yelverton (late Chief Justice
of the Bahamas), to whose long, ceaseless, and unselfish exertions Edalji will owe so much when the hour of triumph comes,
drew up a memorial to the Home Secretary, setting forth some
of the facts as here recorded. This petition for reconsideration

was signed by ten thousand people, including hundreds of lawyers and many K.C.'s, and was reinforced by the strongest letters testifying to Edalji's character from men who must have known him intimately, including Mr. Denning, his schoolmaster; Mr Ludlow, the solicitor with whom he was for five years articled; the Honorary Secretary and Reader of the Birmingham Law Society, and many others. Now every man of the world will admit that the schoolmaster's testimony is of very great importance, for any traits of cruelty will show themselves most clearly at that age. This is what Mr. Denning says: 'During the five years your son George was here I have never known him commit any acts of cruelty or unkindness. I have always found him a thoroughly upright and well-principled youth, in whom I could place every confidence.' Grier, his school-mate, writes: 'He was several years older than myself, but always treated me with great kindness. I never knew him cruel to any animal, and from what I knew of him then—for I came to know him well—I should say he was quite incapable of any act of cruelty.' How foolish the loose gossip and surmise of Stafford seem in the face of page after page of testimonials such as these.

The memorial had no effect, and some inquiry should certainly be made as to how its fate was determined. It would be indeed a vicious circle if a police prosecution, when doubted, is referred back again to the police for report. I cannot imagine anything more absurd and unjust in an Oriental despotism than this. And yet any superficial independent investigation, or even a careful perusal of the memorial, must have convinced any reasonable human being. The friends of Edalji, headed by Mr Yelverton, naturally demanded to see the dossier at the Home Office, but, as in the Beck case, the seekers after justice were denied access to the very documents which they needed in order to prove their case and confute their opponents.

I have said it was as in the Beck case. I might well have gone to a more classic example, for in all its details this seems to me to form a kind of squalid Dreyfus case. The parallel is extraordinary close. You have a Parsee, instead of a Jew, with a young and promising career blighted, in each case the degradation from a profession and the campaign for redress and restoration, in each case questions of forgery and handwriting arise, with Esterhazy in the one, and the anonymous writer in the other. Finally, I regret to say that in the one case you have a clique of French officials going from excess to excess in order to cover an initial mistake, and that in the other you have the Staffordshire police acting in the way I have described.

And that brings me to what is the most painful part of my statement, and the one which I would be most glad to shirk were it possible for me to do so. No account of the case is complete which does not deal with the attitude taken up by Captain Anson, Chief Constable of Staffordshire, against this unhappy young man. It must, I suppose, have taken its root in those far-off days from 1892 to 1895, when Edalji was little more than a boy, and when Sergeant Upton, for reasons which make a tale by themselves, sent reports against him to his superior at Stafford. It was at that early date that Captain Anson delivered those two memorable dicta: 'You may tell your son at once that I will not believe any profession of ignorance,' and 'I will endeavour to get the offender a dose of penal servitude.'

Now, I have no doubt Captain Anson was quite honest in his dislike, and unconscious of his own prejudice. It would be folly to think otherwise. But men in his position have no right to yield to such feelings. They are too powerful, others are too weak, and the consequences are too terrible. As I trace the course of events this dislike of their chief's filtered down until it came to imbue the whole force, and when they had George Edalji they did not give him the most elementary justice, as is shown by the fact that they did not prosecute Green at a time when his prosecution would have endangered the case against Edalji.

I do not know what subsequent reports prevented justice from being done at the Home Office—(there lies the wickedness of the concealed dossier)—but this I do know, that, instead of leaving the fallen man alone, every possible effort was made after the conviction to blacken his character, and that of his father, so as to frighten off anyone who might be inclined to investigate his case. When Mr Yelverton first took it up, he had a letter over Captain Anson's own signature, saying, under date Nov. 8, 1903: 'It is right to tell you that you will find it a simple waste of time to attempt to prove that George Edalji could not, owing to his position and alleged good character, have been guilty of writing offensive and abominable letters. His father is as well aware as I am of his proclivities in the direction of anonymous writing, and several other people have personal knowledge on the same subject.'

Now, both Edalji and his father declare on oath that the former never wrote an anonymous letter in his life, and on being applied to by Mr Yelverton for the names of the 'several other people' no answer was received. Consider that this letter was written immediately after the conviction, and that it was intended to nip in the bud the movement in the direction of mercy. It is certainly a little like kicking a man when he is down.

Since I took up the case I have myself had a considerable correspondence with Captain Anson. I find myself placed in a difficult position as regards these letters, for while the first was marked 'Confidential,' the others have no reserve. One naturally supposes that when a public official writes upon a public matter to a perfect stranger, the contents are for the public. No doubt one might also add, that when an English gentleman makes most damaging assertions about other people he is prepared to confront these people, and to make good his words. Yet the letters are so courteous to me personally that it makes it exceedingly difficult for me to use them for the purpose of illustrating my thesis—viz., the strong opinion which Captain Anson had formed against the Edalji family. One curious example of this is that during fifteen years that the vicarage has been a centre of debate, the chief constable has never once visited the spot or taken counsel personally with the inmates.

For three years George Edalji endured the privations of Lewes and of Portland. At the end of that time the indefatigable Mr Yelverton woke the case up again, and *Truth* had an excellent series of articles demonstrating the impossibility of the man's guilt. Then the case took a new turn, as irregular and illogical as those which had preceded it. At the end of his third year, out of seven, the young man, though in good health, was suddenly released without a pardon. Evidently the authorities were shaken, and compromised with their consciences in this fashion. But this cannot be final. The man is guilty, or he is not. If he is he deserves every day of his seven years. If he is not, then we must have apology, pardon, and restitution. There can obviously be no middle ground between these extremes.

And what else is needed besides this tardy justice to George Edalji? I should say that several points suggest themselves for the consideration of any small committee. One is the reorganisation of the Staffordshire Constabulary from end to end; a second is an inquiry into any irregularity of procedure at Quarter Sessions; the third and most important is a stringent inquiry as to who is the responsible man at the Home Office, and what is the punishment for his delinquency, when in this case, as in that of Beck, justice has to wait for years upon the threshold, and none will raise the latch. Until each and all of these questions is settled a dark stain will remain upon the administrative annals of this country.

I have every sympathy for those who deprecate public agitations of this kind on the ground that they weaken the power of the forces which make for law and order, by shaking the confidence of the public. No doubt they do so. But every effort has been made in this case to avoid this deplorable necessity. Repeated applications for justice under both Administrations have met with the usual official commonplaces, or have been referred back to those who are obviously interested parties.

Amid the complexity of life and the limitations of intelligence any man may do an injustice, but how is it possible to go on again and again reiterating the same one? If the continuation of the outrages, the continuation of the anonymous letters, the discredit cast upon Gurrin as an expert, the confession of a culprit that he had done a similar outrage, and finally the exposition of Edalji's blindness, do not present new fact to modify a jury's conclusion, what possible new fact would do so? But the door is shut in our faces. Now we turn to the last tribunal of all, a tribunal which never errs when the facts are fairly laid before them, and we ask the public of Great Britain whether this thing is to go on.

Arthur Conan Doyle
Undershaw, Hindhead. January, 1907.

That was the main evidence that Conan Doyle presented as proof of George Edalji's innocence: over-argued in some place and rather dubious in others (Edalji's supposed near-blindness, for instance, must surely have hindered his career as a solicitor and writer if it was as bad as all that), but convincing nonetheless, and further evidence was offered in a detailed analysis of handwriting samples. Edalji was free but not pardoned, and this was what outraged him and his defender: so if George Edalji was not guilty of the crimes, who was? Conan Doyle thought he knew, and sent the following statement to the authorities.

At the time of the outrages, roughly July, 1903, Royden Sharp had a conversation alone with Mrs Greatorex, who is the wife of Mr W.A. Greatorex, Littleworth Farm, Hednesford, who was appointed Trustee at the time of the death of Peter Sharp, the father, in November, 1893. To this gentleman, Mr Greatorex, I owe much assistance in working out the case. In the course of the conversation referred to above, Royden Sharp—after alluding to the outrages—went to a cupboard, and produced a horse lancet of unusual size. He showed this to Mrs Greatorex, saying, 'This is what they kill the cattle with.' Mrs Greatorex was horrified, and told him to put it away, saying, 'You don't want me to think you are the man, do you?' The possession by Sharp of this unusual instrument of so huge a size is to be explained by the fact that he served for ten months of 1902 on board a cattle boat between Liverpool and America. No doubt he took this lancet when he left the boat. I suggest that the instrument is still in the house, and could be secured in case of an arrest.

The fact that this was true, and that this actually was the instrument with which the crimes were committed is corroborated by the following considerations:—

That the wounds in all the earlier outrages up to August 18th were of a peculiar character, which could not have been inflicted by any other weapon. In every case there was a shallow incision which had cut through the skin and muscles, but had not penetrated the gut. Had any knife been plunged in and drawn along it must almost certainly have cut the gut with its point.

The blade in question is like this:

Cutting Edge

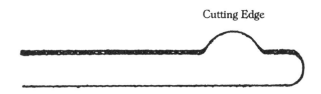

It is very sharp, but could not penetrate further than super-ficially. The witnesses who could testify most clearly as to the nature of the wounds are Mr Sambrook, a butcher, who has now removed from Wyrley to Sheffield, but can, I understand, be easily traced, and Mr Forsyth, a veterinary surgeon, of Cannock. I know that Mr Sambrook was struck by the pecu-liarity of the cuts.

Royden Sharp was in all respects peculiarly fitted to have done these crimes, and there is, apart from this incident, much evidence both before the time of the crimes, during the time and after the time to cause him to be regarded with gravest suspi-cion. I will, for the moment, put on one side the persecution of the Edaljis (in which he was concerned with his elder brother Wallie in 1892–95) and confine the evidence entirely to that which bears upon the outrages and the anonymous letters of 1903. I will first trace his early career.

EVIDENCE OF HIS CHARACTER BEFORE THE CRIMES

Royden Sharp was born in 1879. He very early showed marked criminal tendencies which took a destructive form. When he was 12 years of age he was found to have set a rick on fire at a Cannock Farm (Hatton's Farm at West Cannock) and his father was forced to pay a considerable compensation.

He was sent at the age of eleven to Walsall Grammar School, where his brother Wallie was an elder scholar at the time. His record at the school was as follows: this is an extract which I got from the school books through the courtesy of Mr Mitchell, the present headmaster.

Xmas, 1890.   Lower 1. Order, 23rd out of 23.
                            Very backward and weak. French and Latin not attempted.

Easter, 1891.	Lower 1. Order, 20th out of 20.
	Dull, homework neglected, begins to improve in Drawing.
Midsummer, 1891.	Lower 1. Order, 18th out of 18.
	Beginning to progress, caned for misbehaviour in class, tobacco chewing, prevarication, and nicknaming.
Xmas, 1891.	Lower 1. Order, 16th out of 16.
	Unsatisfactory, often untruthful. Always complaining or being complained of. Detected cheating, and frequently absent without leave. Drawing improved.
Easter, 1892.	Form 1. Order, 8th out of 8.
	Idle and mischievous, caned daily, wrote to father, falsified school-fellows' marks, and lied deliberately about it. Caned 20 times this term.
Midsummer, 1892.	Played truant, forged letters and initials, removed by his father.

It will thus be seen that forgery, which played a part in the anonymous letters of 1903 was familiar to him as a school boy.

Apart from the forgery which the school records show to have been done by him, the disposition to brutal violence was very marked, and so was that of foisting upon others, often with considerable ingenuity, the misdeeds of his own doing. Out of the anonymous letters which are certainly from his hand at this school period 1892–95, I take the two following expressions:

'I will cut your bowels out,'
'I will open your belly,'

showing curiously how his own thoughts were already turning. If he were left in a railway carriage he would turn up the cushion and slit it on the lower side, so as to let out the horse hair. This evidence is given by Mr Wynne, painter, of 'Clovelly,' Cheslyn Hay, who was at school with him. He adds the following anecdote illustrative of his destructiveness, of his bearing false witness, and of his writing vindictive anonymous letters, all of them qualities which came out 10 years later, in 1903.

During the time that the Edalji family had been deluged with anonymous letters from 1892 to 1895 (which letters I have good reason to believe were from the Sharps), another family in the same village, the Brookes, were plagued in the same way, and in the same handwriting, especially the young son, Fred Brookes. I had failed to find any cause, save colour hatred, in the case of the Edaljis, so I hoped I might get something more definite in the case of young Brookes. This is Wynne's story:—

'R.S.,' known as 'Speck,' was a small built youth with sharp features. Generally in a sailor's suit, he was the worst scholar in the school for about three years, and remained at the bottom of the first form. He was very fond of chewing tobacco, and I think it was in the Summer holiday of 1892 that he set a rick on fire near Hednesford . . . One evening we were returning by the usual evening train. F.G. Brookes and myself got in the train when Speck came running into the same compartment straight to the end of the carriage, and put his head through the carriage window smashing it all to bits. We all made our way into another compartment. In a day or two after Brookes and myself were charged by one of the railway officials of breaking the carriage window. We found out that Sharp had told of us, that it was us, not himself. Then we sought the station master, and told him how it happened, and Sharp had to pay for it, and he was also caught cutting the straps of the window, and had to pay, I think, more than once; his father was asked to take him away from the school as they could not do any good with him. He was always into mischief and getting others into trouble. The next I heard was he was sent to sea.

'If my memory serves me right the first letters that I heard of were sent to Mr W.H. Brookes, some time after the railway carriage incident, in a large school handwriting, saying that 'Your kid and Wynn's kid have been spitting in an old woman's face on Walsall station,' and requesting monies to be sent to Walsall Post Office. The second one was threatening to prosecute if the money was not sent.'

Thus the receipt of the anonymous letters by Brookes immediately followed a cause of feud between young Brookes and Royden Sharp.

Having been expelled from school, Royden Sharp was apprenticed to a butcher, thus learning to use a knife upon animals. The butcher's name was Meldon, I think, he still lives at Cannock. In November, 1893, the father died, and W.A. Greatorex, of Littleworth Farm, became Royden's Trustee.

This gentleman is an excellent witness, and ready to help the ends of justice in any way. It was to his wife that the implied confession was made. For two years, 1894 and 1895, this gentleman had much trouble with the lad. Finally he sent him to sea. He went to sea from Liverpool on December 30th in the ship 'General Roberts,' belonging to Lewis Davies & Co., 5, Fenwick Street, Liverpool. He went as apprentice.

From the time he left the letters, hoaxes, &c., which had kept the countryside in a turmoil, ceased completely, and were not renewed until his return in 1903. I may remark in passing that Edalji was at home all this time, and that this fact alone would, one would have thought, have awakened the suspicions of the police and shown them who was the author of the troubles. I am told, but have not verified the fact, that the last anonymous hoax on the Edaljis was an advertisement in a Blackpool paper, about the end of December, 1895—Blackpool being the pleasure resort of Liverpool.

Royden Sharp does not, so far as my enquiries go, appear to have acted badly aboard ship. He finished his apprenticeship in 1900, and afterwards gained a third Mate's certificate. He came home late in 1901, but shortly after got a billet on board a cattle ship to America, where his natural brutality was probably not lessened, and where he, no doubt, got the huge horse lancet which Mrs Greatorex can depose to having seen in his hand.

The Wyrley outrages upon cattle were begun while Royden Sharp was at home, and he was in the district during the whole time of their continuance. Whoever committed the outrages must have been in a position to get into and out of his house at all hours of the night without being observed either by the police or by the other inmates of the house, if they were not conniving at the crimes. Royden Sharp's house was peculiarly well situated for this. He lived alone with his mother and his sister, his brother Wallie coming and going. There was no servant or stranger to check his doings. The back door opened into a garden which led into the fields, so that he could get right away without going down any road or running any risk of being seen. The man who did the outrages must certainly have been a man of cosiderable nerve and activity—able to handle animals, with an almost reckless daring which prompted him to do these outrages under the very nose of the police. As an ex-sailor and an ex-butcher Royden Sharp united all these qualities. Compare him with the purblind and studious young lawyer, Edalji.

The crimes were accompanied by a series of anonymous letters, some of which point straight to the Sharp family. They were so designed as to implicate young Edalji on the one hand, and Wilfred Greatorex on the other. Now Edalji has always been a butt of the Sharp family (Edalji does not know Sharp, so that the origin of this hatred may be mere colour prejudice), and on the other hand the Sharps bore a grudge against their own trustee who had regulated their money matters in a business-like way which was not always to their mind. Therefore, in implicating Edalji and Greatorex, Sharp was bringing down two birds with one stone, and gratifying a double animosity. The second letter of the Greatorex series says, 'I know Holton and Lyndop, Guy, Harvey, Phillips, and many a score.'

Now, these people were as follows:—Holton was the Littleworth doctor, Lyndop the local timekeeper at the Colliery, Guy the local butcher, Harvey an official in the Colliery, Phillips a shopkeeper hard by. They were the people who were not, and could not, be known to young Edalji, living miles away from him; but they belonged to the immediate group who surrounded the Sharp and Greatorex families. They lived two stations down the line from Edalji, whom everyone describes as a very retiring man who made no friends. How could he know these people? But they were put in by Sharp because they were the people whom Greatorex knew, and in putting them in he really proved his own guilt, for he and his family were the only people who could know exactly the same circle. This piece of internal evidence alone must convince any independent and intelligent observer that Edalji could not have written these 'Greatorex' letters, and that if Greatorex did not, which all admit to be true, then all the evidence points to the Sharps, who were accomplished forgers and mystifiers as already shown.

Apart from the letters bearing upon the crimes, other anonymous letters of an obscene description were circulating in the district at this period. I have seen a letter from one who was present dated August 3rd, 1903, saying that a conference was held as to the authorship of these letters that day in the presence of Mr Greatorex, now dead (no relation of the other), who was a local bank manager, and Inspector Campbell, now living at Cannock. The letter wound up, 'I believe that Royden Sharp will be arrested before evening.' From this I infer that the local police had evidence of Sharp's writing anonymous letters at this time. This evidence should be available at the trial, and should show that this was a habit of his. I believe that August 3rd did mark a cessation of letters for some time.

There are many points of internal evidence in the letters (the so-called 'Greatorex' letters) which point to Royden Sharp, apart from the fact that they appeared after his return to the district, and that they deal with a number of people well known to him (and unknown to Edalji). In all the 1892–95 letters there is, so far as I have seen, no mention of the sea. In the very first of the 'Greatorex' letters in 1903 there are two or three allusions to the sea, most natural for anyone who had just left it. He advises in his letter that some boy be sent to sea as an apprentice which was, as I have shown, Royden Sharp's own experience.

The writer uses the curious expression that a hook did the crimes. The instrument which Sharp showed to Mrs Greatorex has a hooky appearance, and could be carried shut in the pocket, as the writer asserts that the 'Hook' actually was. A sharp hook in the ordinary sense of a hook could not be so carried without cutting the cloth.

The writer says that he feels inclined to put his head on the rails where the train runs from Hednesford to Cannock. This is the actual stretch of rail near the Sharp's [sic] house (and is some distance from Wyrley where Edalji lives).

In June, 1903, a letter (still preserved) was received with the Rugeley post mark, signed 'A Lover of Justice,' and addressed to George Edalji. It was asking him to leave the district for a time, so as to be away when the next crime was done, as otherwise he would be in danger of being taken for it. The writer of this letter I identify as being the same as the former anonymous letters of 1895; which I also identify as having been done by Wallie Sharp. There would be no difficulty in getting expert evidence as to the hands being the same. Wallie Sharp was acting as apprentice to an electrical engineer at the time, and was much in the small neighbouring towns of which Rugeley is one. It is to be observed that in the letter in question occurs the phrase 'you are not a right sort.' This phrase occurs also in one of the Greatorex letters. This points to Wallie's complicity in the Greatorex letters, or his brother's phrase may have lingered in his mind. It could hardly be coincidence that the same phrase could occur in both letters. Wallie Sharp died in South Africa in November, 1906.

I now come to what I look upon as a very important piece of evidence, indeed, I think it is conclusive as regards the anonymous letters. Some time after Edalji's arrest there began a series of anonymous letters, signed 'G.H. Darby,' the writer claiming to be Captain of the Wyrley Gang. These letters— many of which I have seen—are all in the same writing and, though very roughly done, contain some of the characteristics of Royden Sharp's writing, especially an r made like x and sometimes so exaggerated as to be almost x which occurs from boyhood in Royden Sharp's writing. About November, 1903, some of these letters arrived from Rotherham, near Sheffield. The police, I think, had some, and others were received by a local paper, the Wolverhampton *Star*. The writer was evidently a Cannock man, and I should think few Cannock men would at any time visit Rotherham. Now, I have found the porter, whose name is A. Beenham, Drayman, near Baptist Chapel, Cannock Road, Chadsmoor, near Cannock, who in November carried Royden Sharp's box to the station, and observed that it was addressed to Rotherham. The Darby letters said that the Captain would return before Xmas, and I believe Sharp actually did so. This seems to me perfectly conclusive, as regards the identity of Royden Sharp with G.H. Darby, and the latter boasted that he was the author of the outrages.

Another significant fact is as follows:—On September 29th, 1903, there was an anonymous notice that 'it was decided to "slice up" ten wenches between November 1st and 20th and 10 after Xmas,' repeating a threat which had already been uttered in the second 'Greatorex' letter. The dates are curious in view of the fact that Royden Sharp would be away as already shown from November to Xmas. The announcement caused much terror in the district, which was increased by the following incident:—A woman and little girl (Mrs Jarius Handley, Great Wyrley, is [the] woman's name) were coming from Wyrley station one evening, soon after, where they had been buying some papers for sale. They met two men in the road. One of them caught the girl by the throat, and held in his hand something that gleamed. They both screamed, on which the man ran away, crying to his comrade who had gone on: 'All right, Jack, I am coming.' I suggest that this man was Royden Sharp, and that his companion was Jack Hart, a dissolute butcher, of the neighbourhood, and a friend of Sharp's. The little girl declared to her mother that she had been stopped once before by the same young man, and proceeded to give a minute description of him. She said that he had a round face, no moustache, about 5ft. 8in. in height, a dark suit, and a shiny peaked cap, which was exactly Royden Sharp's sailor-like costume. I suggest that after Sharp's arrest this girl be allowed an opportunity of identifying him. I am informed that from the time that his description got about Sharp gave up wearing this style of dress.

There was another of the series of anonymous letters which came from London, and was said by the writer to have been written in a Lockhart's coffee-house there. It was dated '————19th' (month can be found by further search) and the writer said he had gone up to London from Birmingham that day. On enquiry Mr Beaumont, of Wolverhampton Road, Cannock,—who has assisted me much—discovered that Royden Sharp had actually left Cannock for Birmingham upon the morning of that same day—19th. Mr Hunt, the local station master, was his informant.

I will now recapitulate in condensed form the statement which has been here set out at length. Royden Sharp can be shown to have been the culprit:

1   Because of his showing the weapon to Mrs Greatorex.

2   Because the wounds could only be produced by such an instrument as he showed.

3   Because only such an instrument fits in with the description in the letters.

4   Because being a butcher and a man from a cattle ship he was able to do such crimes which would be very hard for any ordinary man.

5   Because in many points of the anonymous letters there is internal evidence pointing to Royden Sharp.

6   Because he had a proved record of writing anonymous letters, of forgery, of diabolical mischief, and of bearing false witness, all of which qualities came out here.

7   Because he went to Rotherham at the time when letters bearing on the crimes came from Rotherham.

8   Because he is correctly described by a girl, who saw a man endeavouring to carry out, or pretend to carry out, the threats in the letters.

9   Because the actual handwriting in many of the letters bears a resemblance to Royden Sharp's own old writing. It is impossible now to get any specimen of his actual writing, as he is most guarded in writing anything. Why should he be if he is innocent?

10   I am informed (but have not yet verified the fact) that in one of the anonymous letters occurs the phrase, 'I am as Sharp as Sharp can be.'

This seems to me to be in itself a complete case, and if I—a stranger in the district—have been able to collect it, I cannot doubt that fresh local evidence would come out after his arrest. He appears to have taken very little pains to hide his proceedings, and how there could have been at any time any difficulty in pointing him out as the criminal is to me an extraordinary thing.

If further evidence were needed in order to assure a conviction, there are two men who could certainly supply it. These men are:—

Harry Green, formerly of Wyrley Farm, Wyrley, now in South Africa.

The other is Jack Hart, Butcher, Bridgtown, near Cannock.

Either of these men, if properly handled, would certainly turn King's evidence. They both undoubtedly knew all about

Sharp. Others who know something, but possibly not enough, as they were only on the edge of the affair, are Fred Brookes (formerly of Wyrley, now in Manchester), Thomas and Grinsell, all of the local Yeomanry. It seems to me that Sharp did no more outrages with his own hands after the arrest of Edalji in August. The next outrage was admittedly done by Harry Green, who can be shown, when in doubt as to what he should do, to have sent a note to someone else, which note was answered from London in a letter written on telegram forms, now to be seen in the Home Office. This answer was, I believe from the writing, from Royden Sharp. It is worth noting on the evidence of Mr Arrowsmith, of the Cannock Star Tea Company, who has done most excellent work on this case, that Green accepted all Arrowsmith's remarks good-humouredly, but on the latter saying 'Sharp should be where Edalji now is,' he at once became very angry. The November outrage was done upon Stanley's horses by Jack Hart, the butcher, acting in collusion with Sharp. This makes really a separate case.

If it should be found possible to get Mrs Sharp in the box, she would depose as she has told Mrs Greatorex, that Royden Sharp is strangely affected by the new moon, and that on such occasions she had to closely watch him. At such times he seems to be a maniac, and Mr Greatorex has himself heard him laughing like one. In this connection it is to be observed that the first four outrages occurred on February 2, April 2, May 3, and June 6, which in each case immediately follows the date of the new moon. The point of a connection between the outrages and the moon is referred to in one of the 'Greatorex' letters, so it was present in the mind of the writer.

I cannot end this statement without acknowledging how much I owe to the unselfish exertions of Mr Greatorex, of Littleworth Farm, Mr Arrowsmith, of the Star Tea Company, Cannock, and Mr Beaumont, of Wolverhampton Road, Cannock, without whose help I should have been powerless.

(Signed) *Arthur Conan Doyle.*

Undershaw, Hindhead

AFTERWORD

Did this bring about the immediate arrest of Royden Sharpe, and a trial for these offences, followed by a Free Pardon and compensation for George Edalji, and complete vindication for Conan Doyle? No. And the blank refusal of the authorities to even consider these matters soured Doyle for life. He was never taken into the police's confidence, and became convinced that the case had been mishandled and the resultant mess glossed over: what we would now call a cover-up.

'The mistake that I made, so far as my own interests were concerned,' he wrote later, 'was that having got on the track of the miscreant I let the police and the Home Office know my results before they were absolutely completed.' Whether the case against Sharpe would have stood up in court, founded as it was on hearsay and with little in the way of direct evidence, is a moot point, for likelihood is very different from proof. No writer on the case has disputed George Edalji's innocence, however, and someone committed these crimes, which continued sporadically until 1914.

So messy reality spoiled the neat detective-story ending, though it saved Edalji, and helped Conan Doyle pull his life together again. George Edalji, indeed, was a guest at the reception when Conan Doyle married his second wife, and practised successfully as a solicitor for the rest of his long life.

Now John D. MacDonald tells us just how confusing witnesses can be...

JOHN D. MACDONALD

Coppolino Revisited

Here is a direct quote from the testimony of Doctor Charles J. Umberger, Toxicologist with the office of the Chief Medical Examiner in New York City. He and the late Dr Milton Helpern had gone to Naples, Florida, in April of 1967 to testify for the Prosecution in the trial of Carl Coppolino, anesthesiologist, at which he was convicted of second-degree murder for killing his wife with an injection of succinylcholine chloride, a paralyzing compound used to stop the patient from breathing on his own during major surgery on the lungs or heart.

With the glazed eyes of the jurors upon him, Umberger said, 'Now this case was treated as a general unknown, and when the analysis was started, tissue was set up to cover all categories. For example, one of the first things that was done was to take a piece of kidney. The kidney was ashed and a sample was put on a spectrograph. The purpose of the spectrograph is to determine whether there were any metal compounds. With the spectrographic plate, all but three of the metals can be excluded. Another sample was subjected to what we call a digestion, using an old-fashioned Reinsch Test, plating out the metal on copper. Arsenic, antimony, and mercury, along with silver and bismuth plated out on copper, and from that one can subject the copper plate to an X-ray fluorescent machine and determine whether any of those three metals are there. That is necessary, because in spectrographic analysis there is what is called the volatile metals and these distill out of the crater or the arc and would not produce the spectrum . . .'

As if that wasn't enough, a little further along he got into the procedures by which his lab had isolated and identified the components of the succinylcholine chloride which had killed Carmela Coppolino.

He said, 'The one [test] depends upon the formation of what we call ferric hydroxamic imides. That happens to be what we call a generic test for esters, which is another type of organic structure. Succinic acid is an acid and shouldn't react with this reagent. In working with it, what we discovered is if the succinic acid is sublimed at ordinary atmospheric pressure that as a result of that heating it is turned into the anhydride. In other words the two acid groups kind of lock together and water is lost, and then subsequent to that we found that if we put in a little phosphorous pentoxide in that tube and carried out sublimation we could convert the succinic acid without a lot of manipulation over the anhydride.'

What sort of people were soaking up all this great information?

The jury was composed of twelve men—a retired naval officer, a refrigerator repairman, a construction-crew foreman, two motel owners, a retired clothing salesman, a furniture salesman, a mortgage broker, a maintenance engineer, a fisherman, an air-conditioner serviceman, and a semiretired plumber.

F. Lee Bailey brought on his team of experts to refute the testimony of Helpern and Umberger. I quote from the Naples newspaper the following weekend: 'One of the most fascinating and immediate impressions received by all was the paradox of conclusions reached by these highly qualified scientists in their efforts to determine what happens to the drug after it is injected into a muscle or vein of the human body.'

A Dr Moya, Chairman of the Department of Anesthesiology at the University of Miami, had testified, in just as much stupifying detail as Umberger, that Umberger's experiments were flawed and his conclusions improper. He said that the compounds found in Carmela Coppolino's body were there in normal amounts and had been released for measurement by the embalming fluid.

The newspaper item ends: 'You pays your money and you takes your choice. And a man's life rests on the choice made by the 12 good men and true who listened intently all week from the jury box.'

What do we have then, in this and in other trials where contemporary expert testimony is given by both sides? Not one of those twelve jurors knew diddly about anesthesiology, toxicology, biochemistry, and pharmacology. They could *not* follow and comprehend the expert testimony. The prosecution lawyers and the defense lawyers knew that the jurors could not follow the expert testimony and evaluate it upon its scientific merits. The experts knew this also.

So it is a charade.

Recognizing the fact of charade, one realizes that the jurors will side with that expert who has the best stage presence, who radiates a total confidence in his grasp of the subject at hand, who speaks crisply, with dignity, confidence, and charm, who is neatly and properly dressed and has no distressing mannerisms.

In short, the expert must be precisely the sort of person an advertising agency would select to talk about a new deodorant on national television.

The expert who mumbles, slouches, grimaces, stares into space, and keeps ramming his little finger into his ear and inspecting what he dredges up *might* be a far better scientist than the television commercial chap. But there is no real correlation here. The impressive presence is more likely to be the result of the number of appearances as an expert than the result of academic credentials.

In January of 1977 Melvin M. Belli, sometimes known as the King of Torts, published a syndicated defense of the jury system which appeared op-ed in scores of newspapers.

He wrote:

> After arguing hundreds of cases, both civil and criminal, I do not believe that I have ever seen a jury that did not give the case under submission its honest judgment and deliberation. Contemporary jurors are not swayed by old-fashioned oratory or legal theatrics; thus jury trials have become a precise, orderly business.
>
> Today, jurors take detailed notes during testimony and ask probing questions about the facts and the law. Frequently they will return from their deliberations and ask the judge to have crucial testimony reread or to repeat his instructions on the applicable statutes. Juries do not want to make mistakes—and seldom do.

The question is obvious. How can jurors make honest judgments about a body of knowledge beyond their capacity to
comprehend? Are they going to take notes on the ferric hydroxamic imides, and come back out to ask what a Reinsch Test
might be?

Trial by jury, using expert witnesses to clarify the testimony
of others and add to the body of the case, worked beautifully in
a world which was far simpler in all technologies. In a village
culture a scout could be called in to testify as to the origin of the
arrow which struck the deceased, showing to the jury those
points of difference in fletching and notching which indicated
the tribe where it had been made.

In a world more compartmentalized, knowledge becomes
increasingly impossible to communicate to anyone who has not
had a substantial background in the discipline at hand.

A friend of mine has spent most of his life in pure mathema-
tics, in abstractions as subtle as music. He tells me that up until
perhaps fifteen years ago it was still possible to explain what he
was doing, in rather rough outline, to a bright layman, using
analogy, models, little drawings, and so on. But now he tells me
that he cannot explain to me where he is and where he is going.
He has gone beyond analogy, beyond models and drawings and
comprehensible statements. Think of that. What he is doing is
out of my reach. And yours. Other disciplines are becoming
ever less easy to explain. Computers are playing an ever more
active and forceful role in the designing of computers. IBM had
a computer exhibit in New York City long ago, a big room full
of winking tubes and chuckling sounds. You can hold in one
hand a computer that will do everything that one did, and
faster.

We have all become that Naples fisherman, wondering at the
difference between an ester and an oyster.

Jury trials are becoming ever longer. In notorious trials, the
jurors are sequestered for weeks and months. Deadlocked juries
are more common. Giving expert testimony has become a
profession for scientists who have reason to be disappointed in
the rewards from their career alone.

It is possible that the jury system could be saved from its own
excesses by a revision of the expert-testimony folkdance.

When it appears that medical or scientific testimony will be a key factor in any case, I would suggest that the prosecution select a single expert to present its side, and the defense do the same. These two gentlemen would then select a third man in their field, satisfactory to both of them. After the third man had listened to the scientific evidence and had a chance to read the documentation and do whatever research might be necessary, there would be a meeting between the experts, the judge, and the attorneys for both sides. The selected expert would give his opinion, and it would be binding on both sides. If, for example, in the Coppolino case, the selected expert backed Umberger's procedures and said that he believed that it had been proven that succinylcholine chloride had been injected into the upper outer quadrant of the left buttock in sufficient quantity to cause death, then the defense would be forced to stipulate that this was indeed so, and it would then be up to the defense to change the plea, or try to show that it would not have been done by the defendant.

If such a procedure were to be instituted in civil and criminal trials we would see trials of less duration. Juries would be more prone to reach agreement on the verdicts. Expenses to both the state and the accused would be dramatically reduced in criminal cases, and reduced for the plaintiff and defendant in civil cases.

I would imagine it would make Mr Belli's court appearances of far less duration and hence not quite so burdensome to the insurance companies and to the patients of the doctors who must pass along the high malpractice premiums to their patients in the form of higher charges for office visits.

I have taken my samples of expert-witness jargon from the Coppolino trial only because I happen to have a complete transcript in my files, and not because I have any feeling that Coppolino was done any disservice by this oppressive conflicting testimony. At this writing he has been a prisoner of the state of Florida for over ten years.

By the time the long days of scientific testimony and the direct and cross and redirect examinations of the seven or eight expert witnesses had gone droning on and on, the twelve jurors had already decided that it was of no moment to them whether or not the succinylcholine chloride was detectable or not.

Here is how the state of mind came about. During the prosecution's direct examination of its leading expert, Dr Milton Helpern, there came an opportunity to project onto a large white wall behind and to Judge Lynn Silvertooth's right, some very sharp-focus slides taken by the Medical Examiner's office. The courtroom was darkened. There were a dozen of these slides. The very first one brought a sick gasping sound from the spectators and press. It showed, in about a five-by-eight-foot projection, Carmela Coppolino, clothing removed, face down, full length, after three and a half months in a New Jersey cemetery.

Successive slides moved in closer and closer, focusing on the left buttock, then on the upper outer quadrant of the left buttock to show a tiny crater and, near it and below it, the dark stains of five bruise marks. States Attorney Frank Schaub had asked Dr Helpern, 'Could they be the type consistent with the use of human force, the fingers? Could they be caused by a hand pressing down on the body?' In his quiet clinical voice Helpern testified that they could be consistent, and testified as to how he had proven through micro-examination that the bruises had been inflicted shortly before death.

The final slides showed magnified photographs of the incision Helpern had made adjacent to the crater, showing that it was indeed a puncture wound along with a needle track deep into the subcutaneous fat of the buttock.

Now then, because Helpern had testified that he could find no other cause of death, and because the defense offered no plausible alternative reason for the needle track, and because the jurors could readily believe that Coppolino as a nonpracticing anesthesiologist would have access to the substance in question, and because a reasonably satisfactory motive and a provable opportunity had been established by the State, the jurors did not care whether or not the presence of that suck-something could be proven beyond the shadow of a doubt. They had seen the unforgettable pictures, the fingermark bruises, and the needle track, and nobody had stepped up to show she had died of anything else.

And so they drowsed through a lot of it.

So let us imagine a similar case where there is no needle track, no pitiful and ghastly slides of the slim dead lady, a case where it really *does* hang on the technical evidence presented.

Want to be a defendant? Want to take your chances in a forum where charm rather than fact is the persuader? Want to pay an additional $50,000 to $150,000 for the transportation, housing, fees, and sustenance of your team of experts, plus the additional legal costs of the preparation and the additional days in court?

Or will you choose arbitration?

Final question. *If* it is known that arbitration of conflicting expert testimony *is* available, and the defendant elects to finance a battle of the experts, will it be more difficult to preserve the presumption of innocence?

One solution to the problem posed by the messy nature of evidence is, simply and blandly, to claim inside knowledge. As I remarked earlier, William Le Queux claimed to have known everyone; here is a little story related by Alan Hynd that is perhaps revealing:

'Le Queux had, while prowling a second-hand book store in Stockholm, come upon a rare book, published in 1869, entitled Secrets of the States of Venice. *The volume, printed in Latin and old Italian, both of which Le Queux understood, gave detailed formulas for the slow, lethal and undetectable poisons by which upper-class Venetians abbreviated associations with enemies, friends and chance acquaintances. In one of his novels, Le Queux made casual reference to* Secrets of the States of Venice, *mentioning that the volume detailed the formulas for ancient, and undetectable poisons without dwelling on the formulas themselves.*

'When Dr Crippen, reading Le Queux in his attic retreat, came upon the reference to the rare old book, his professional curiosity was piqued. Having been grounded in the basic poisons during his studies at the Hospital College in Cleveland and at Ophthalmic Hospital in New York, the doctor wondered what the Venetians had had that modern poisoners did not have. Was it possible that the rare book to which Le Queux referred contained the key to some long-lost knowledge that the medical profession could put to advantage — or, more to the point, knowledge that Dr Crippen himself, ever on the qui vive for a stray pound could, monetize?

'Crippen began to spend his spare time in the second-hand book stalls, trying to track down a copy of Secrets of the States of Venice. *Failing to locate the book,*

he wrote to Le Queux, in March of 1908, for an appointment. For some reason or other, perhaps so that his motives wouldn't be misunderstood, Dr Crippen used the name of Dr Adams in writing to the author. Le Queux made an appointment for Dr Adams to have some Scotch and soda with him at the Devonshire Club. Crippen opened the conversation by saying that he liked LeQeux's mysteries even better than those of Conan Doyle — a remark that didn't exactly offend the author — and then got around to the subject of poisons. He wondered if Le Queux might be so kind as to lead him to the whereabouts of that copy of Secrets of the States of Venice *so casually mentioned in one of his books. Le Queux said he would be happy to oblige but the book was in storage in Italy. Crippen seemed deeply disappointed. 'Well', he said, can you tell me anything about those formulas that are in the book — those formulas for poisons that left not the slightest trace?' Le Queux recalled that the volume had mentioned several such poisons, but of course he didn't remember sufficient details to deal them off the cuff now. Anyway, he doubted that many of the so-called undetectable poisons of ancient Venice would be quite so undetectable if subjected to modern toxicological analysis...*

'Crippen decided he might pick up some extra money by contriving a plot for a mystery story and selling it to Le Queux. He immersed himself in volumes on poisons. He read practically everything that was in print on the subject of toxicology; he became an authority on the Manual of Dr Rudolph August Witthaus, the American toxicologist whose conclusions were being generally accepted as standard, particularly at murder trials. Crippen, still calling himself Dr Adams, saw Le Queux several times late in 1908 and early in 1909. At each meeting, the little doctor had a plot for the novelist that turned on a murder by poison. The basic plot was always the same: A man poisoned his wife, secreted her body, and ran off with a mistress. The man in the Crippen plot always got away with murder so that the plot had, from one point of view, a happy ending.

'Le Queux would remonstrate that this was not good, that the reader wanted to have the mystery solved and the guilty man punished. The doctor's answer to that was the chief entertainment to be derived from one of his plots would be to show how easy it was for a man who really knew poisons to get away with murder.'

Convincing? The following story, told by Le Queux himself, is supported by other writers too.

WILLIAM LE QUEUX

The Mysterious Treasure of Mme Humbert

One of the most colossal frauds of modern times was that which was finally exposed on May 9th, 1902, and was known as 'The Humbert Millions.'

Before the great swindle had been disclosed it had been the means of ruining some thousands of people, at least five of whom committed suicide, and there were three other deaths which have never been satisfactorily explained.

As I had some personal knowledge of the perpetrators of this gigantic imposture it may, perhaps, be of interest if I relate the circumstances in which I became acquainted with them.

One day in August 1900, at the invitation of Madame Sarah Bernhardt, I went to a luncheon party at her big white villa close to the lake at Enghien-les-Bains, just outside Paris. Before lunch I, with two other men, took a vivacious, dark-haired girl—whom I had met at a country house near Tours a few months before, and whose name was Marie d'Aurignac—out for a row upon the picturesque lake. We had arrived from Paris a little too early, and as the lawn sloped to the lake we paddled about till lunch was ready.

At the meal I sat next to my old friend Madame Zola. On my right was a stout, rather overdressed, and by no means prepossessing woman to whom I had not been introduced. We began to chat. To me she appeared to be a rather unintelligent and uncultivated woman, for she spoke with a distinctly provincial accent, and her conversation was interlarded with words of Parisian argot.

Presently Madame Zola said:

'I do not think you have been introduced,' and she told the stout, well-preserved woman who I was, adding that I was a friend of her husband, 'dear Emile,' and also a writer.

In a moment her attitude towards me entirely changed. From formal frigidity she became all smiles and geniality. I learnt that she was Madame Thérèse Humbert. But to me it then conveyed no unusual meaning. One meets many people at luncheon parties, and at those given by Sarah Bernhardt celebrities were present by the dozen; and several Parisian operatic stars.

The assembly in that long, old-fashioned dining room, the open French windows of which looked out upon the lake sparkling in the summer sunlight, was a brilliant one, and the chatter was equally vivacious and entertaining. The Divine Sarah was then at the zenith of her popularity, and had just returned from a long tour in the United States and Canada. But the stout woman on my right seemed morose and thoughtful. At last she said:

'What are your movements, Monsieur? I know your name very well. Your father was introduced to me long ago. Sarah told me all about you! You are a friend of Emile Zola, our greatest novelist. And you write too! Ah! I wish you all success. I envy you writers. It is all so clever to publish a book. You know my sister Marie. You took her out on the lake before lunch. So now you know who I am.'

Later, when we walked out upon the lawn and sat beneath the shadow of the trees at the lake-side, I asked Madame Zola about the stout lady who had been my companion at table.

'Oh!' she exclaimed. 'She's a widow—one of the richest women in Paris. She is Madame Humbert. If she invites you to her house in the Avenue de la Grande Armée you must go. All Paris goes there to her dinners and receptions. Frederic Humbert, her husband, was son of the late Minister of Justice, Gustave Humbert; who died five years ago. She is not chic by any means—but she is immensely wealthy.'

'I know her sister, Mademoiselle d'Aurignac, very slightly,' I said. 'But I did know that she was related to Madame Humbert.'

Who in Paris had not heard the fame of the great hostess of

the Avenue de la Grande Armée? Hardly a day passed but one read in the newspapers lists of her guests, which included persons in the most exclusive sets in Parisian society, with diplomats, cabinet ministers, writers, lawyers, dramatists, and the like. If Madame was not in Paris she entertained at her fine old Château de Vellexon, near Vesoul, or at the Villa des Cyclamens, on the road between Beaulieu and Monte Carlo.

Possibly it was through Madame Zola's good offices that a week later I received a card for Madame Humbert's reception.

The great mansion was profusely decorated with choice flowers, and the spacious *salons* were filled with the élite of Paris. I sat in a corner with Emile Zola, Henri Lamorre, Préfet of the Puy de Dôme, and Jules Guyon, the famous painter, and we chatted. Presently, Lamorre, a thin, grey-haired man, mentioned something about a safe.

'What safe?' I asked in my ignorance.

'Why, the safe in the next room,' he replied. 'The safe which contains over four millions sterling! Come and see it,' and he led me to a smaller apartment wherein a few people were seated near the open window, for it was a hot, close night. In a corner against the wall I saw a great fireproof safe about seven feet high and four feet across. There were three keyholes, each being sealed with huge red seals upon broad tapes which had once been white but were now discoloured with age.

I asked my friend what it meant. Whereupon, in an awed voice, he told me of the great fortune therein contained, a mysterious story which, I confess, greatly impressed me as a writer of romance.

As we stood there passed by us the President of the Court of Appeal, chatting with the famous lawyer, Maître Waldeck-Rousseau, and the Italian Ambassador and his wife. Truly Madame Humbert's receptions were the most wonderful in Paris since the downfall of the Empire.

That autumn I was Madame Humbert's guest at the famous old Château de Vellexon, and there again met her sister, Mademoiselle Marie d'Aurignac, and her brother Romain, who was three years her senior. There were some sixteen others of the house-party, and as at that time I was a fair shot—before my eyesight played me false—I enjoyed some good sport in the great woods surrounding the splendid Château.

I

From the first the secret of that great safe with its three big seals laid hold of my imagination. Indeed, that safe, with the mysterious millions it was thought to contain, had captured the imagination of all Paris; as it would naturally attract any novelist.

I am now going to tell the beginning of one of the most impudent frauds ever imposed upon a credulous public. So strange were the whole circumstances that, if written in the form of fiction, they would have been dismissed as being absolutely incredible. But what is here related is actual fact, as was afterwards proved in the Assize Court of the Seine.

It seems that two years after the Prussian invasion there was living at Bauzelles, a village near Toulouse, a young country girl of commonplace appearance. Her father, whose name was Aurignac, was a drunken, incorrigible old peasant, who in his elated moments was fond of declaring himself to be of noble birth. In his cups in the village *estaminet* each night he assumed the self-styled title of Count d'Aurignac. His cronies always addressed him as Monsieur le Comte, and his fame spread far and wide, even into Toulouse itself. At that time there were many scions of noble houses ruined by the Prussian invasion and reduced to beggary, therefore it was not considered very remarkable.

'The Count' lived with his daughters, Thérèse and Marie, and his sons, Romain and Emile. Thérèse did the housework, and the two boys worked in the fields and did odd jobs for anyone who liked to employ them. But the father, obsessed with the idea of his noble ancestry, one day bought for ten francs in the Rue St. Etienne, in Toulouse, an old oak chest studded with brass nails. It was that purchase which was the beginning of the extraordinary sham of the Humbert millions.

The old peasant, who had for years boasted of his noble ancestry, now exhibited to his neighbours the old carved chest, which he had locked and sealed, and which he solemnly declared contained the title-deeds of the great Château d'Aurignac, in Auvergne, and proofs which, upon his death, would entitle his children to a fortune. His friends, ignorant as are most French peasants, were much impressed by his story, but it brought in no money except a few odd francs as loans, so Thérèse was compelled by her father to accept the lowly position of laundry-maid to a family named Humbert, who had befriended the queer old fellow. The family in question consisted of Monsieur Gustave Humbert, Mayor of Toulouse, his wife, and their son Frederic, a slim, impressionable young man with a sloping forehead. Old Madame Humbert took Thérèse into their service out of charity a week after her father died, in January 1874. He did not possess one sou, and when the famous oak box was broken open, only a brick was found in it!

But Thérèse, though not in any way prepossessing, had a sly manner about her, and her eyes were ever open for the main chance. She had been educated to the belief that she was of noble birth, and at length she succeeded in attracting the attention of Frederic, her employer's son, who was then a law student in Toulouse.

All this time the Aurignacs were being laughed at by their neighbours, who knew of the discovery of the sealed-up brick, but so persistent were they all to their claim to nobility that the countryside began to wonder whether, after all, they were not descendants of the great house of d'Aurignac, in Auvergne.

The legend thus born was now to grow, thanks to 'La Grande Thérèse'—as she was later dubbed by the Paris press. She started to carry on the fiction of her absinthe-drinking father and evolved, in her imagination, a great ancestral home, the Château de Marcotte, in the Tarn. In strictest secrecy she disclosed to her lover that the octogenarian Mademoiselle de Marcotte, a very wealthy old lady, who was owner of the château, had bequeathed her entire fortune to her, together with her vast estate. The château, however, never existed, except in Thérèse's imagination, but the story impressed the Humbert family and especially Frederic's father, the Mayor of Toulouse.

Soon afterwards Monsieur and Madame Humbert left Toulouse for Paris, to take up their abode there, where a month later, to their chagrin, they learnt that their son Frederic intended to marry their ex-washerwoman, the girl Thérèse! Frederic had been left in Toulouse to conclude his law studies, and the wily girl had very cleverly entrapped him. So far the facts all read like a sensational novel. But the events which followed and the *dénouement* are far more amazing still.

II

Monsieur Gustave Humbert had, by dint of hard work and considerable shrewdness—some say that his conduct as a lawyer was not altogether above suspicion—come to the fore in politics, and certain of his friends had hinted at his appointment as Minister of Justice. In such circumstances it was but natural that he should be horrified at the suggestion of a laundry-maid becoming his son's wife. He travelled post-haste to Toulouse, and there was a heated scene between father and son. The father threatened to cut off Frederic's allowance, but was only met with defiance. The young man was determined, and so cleverly did Thérèse play her cards that, despite all entreaties, Frederic married her.

There was a queer circumstance on the day of the wedding. Just as she was going to the Hôtel de Ville an official of the Court of Toulouse arrived with a warrant for the arrest of the adventurous Thérèse on account of a debt incurred with a hairdresser. Mademoiselle met the man with perfect sangfroid and told him that she was about to be married, and that in an hour's time if he returned she would obtain the money from her husband and discharge the debt. Thus assured, the warrant was not executed. Indeed, the official could not bring himself to arrest a bride on the eve of her marriage. But on returning at the appointed hour he found that the pair had been registered as man and wife and were already on their way to Paris.

From the first moment of Thérèse's married life her whole career became one of amazing duplicity and adventure. She possessed a subtle cunning, a wheedling manner, a vivid imagination and an utter disregard of honesty or fair dealing. From her reprobate father she seems to have, with her brothers, inherited that same idea of pretence of nobility, an all-absorbing ambition and the gain of money from the credulous. The sealed oak box which was supposed to contain proofs which would secure for his heirs a title and valuable estates and which had only contained a brick—but which had during its existence brought in petty loans from neighbours—had impressed itself upon the mind of 'La Grande Thérèse,' so gradually she evolved from her fertile brain a greater and much more grandiose scheme.

For a time Frederic Humbert and his wife lived in humble circumstances in Paris, occupying a three-roomed flat *au troisième* in the Rue Provence. Her husband, who had now passed his examinations, managed to earn a modest income at his profession, and for several years their existence was quiet and uneventful. From time to time Frederic questioned his wife about the £5000 a year which was coming to her from Mlle de Marcotte, but she was always evasive concerning it, as she well might be. Thérèse had entered the Humbert family and was daughter-in-law of Monsieur Gustave, who had now been appointed Minister of Justice, therefore she had taken a considerable step forward. But, alas! there was no money.

Creditors pressed them in the Rue Provence, so they moved to another flat in the Rue Monge, where her plausible story to the local grocer concerning her expectations from the owner of the mythical Château de Marcotte quickly spread about the neighbourhood, and because of it the pair existed for quite a long time upon credit.

The Marcotte myth proved a very profitable one, but without any tangible proof and no substantiation except the word of the amazing Thérèse it was soon doomed to failure. The local tradesmen began to question the locality in which the Château de Marcotte was situated. The Prefect of the Department was written to, and his reply was that he had no knowledge of any such estate within his jurisdiction. The farm, it may be mentioned, adjoins the Haute Garonne, the capital of which is Toulouse. Sometimes Thérèse had told people that the Château was near Albi, and at others she had mentioned Carmaux and Castres as the nearest towns. The creditors were bewildered, though greatly intrigued. So one of them, who was a native of a village near Castres, went on his summer vacation to his home, and on his return declared that there was no such estate in the Tarn.

Upon that things grew very ugly for the pair. Threats of prosecution for swindling if bills were not paid arrived in a crop, and so serious was the position that Thérèse was compelled to admit to her husband that the whole story was a fabrication. Frederic, greatly alarmed, went to his father, the Minister of Justice, told him the truth, and His Excellency—who could not afford the scandal of his son being arrested for swindling—paid the whole of their debts, much to the relief of 'La Grande Thérèse.'

The latter was sly, unscrupulous and highly ambitious. The sealed oak box with its brick was ever in her mind. For three or four years she slowly evolved plans by which she might, just as her father had done in his own small way to obtain money for drink, impose upon an ever credulous public but on a grander scale.

By this time she had gauged the mind of the French public to a very fine degree. She knew that persons dealing in high finance could not be imposed upon except by some great scheme with enticing profits, and if a little romance were mixed with it then the more certain of success it would be. It was proved in Court that Frederic Humbert had no knowledge that the Marcotte fortune had no foundation until his domineering wife confessed, and that it was he who implored his father to save the family from disgrace.

Yet a few months after the episode, in March 1881, astounding whispers went around Paris—whispers that were not to be repeated. At the salons each evening Paris society discussed the romantic story that M. Gustave Humbert, Minister of Justice, had told his friends vainly that his daughter-in-law had met with a most romantic adventure while travelling on the Ceinture Railway, and that by her brave conduct towards a perfect stranger, an American she had inherited eighty thousand pounds.

His Excellency the Minister had dined at the Elysée, at several of the houses of the great hostesses of Paris, and at one of the Embassies, and had told the story. His son's wife had come into a fortune by reason of her courage and sympathy. The affair at once became the gossip of all Paris. Like all such stories it was not reduced in the telling, so its embroidery increased day by day, just as Thérèse had hoped, until all Paris was gossiping regarding the mysterious fortune of His Excellency's daughter-in-law.

It now became a question, never satisfactorily settled, by the way, whether the Minister of Justice really believed it, or whether in order to increase his own social advancement he readily accepted Thérèse's story, yet believing it to be untrue. He knew the Marcotte myth to have no foundation in fact, therefore it seems incredible that he, a very accomplished lawyer, should have swallowed the strange, romantic tale which the imaginative ex-laundry-maid should have told him.

III

Briefly related, the story, as told by 'La Belle Grande Thérèse,' was as follows: About two years after her marriage she had one hot September afternoon entered a train on the Ceinture Railway in Paris at the Grenelle station to go to Bel-Air. She was in a compartment alone when she heard groans in an adjoining compartment just after they had left Montsouris. She shouted, but there was no response. The cries were of a man in agony. Therefore, at great risk to herself, she got out of the carriage, climbed along the footboard, and in the adjoining compartment found a white-haired old gentleman who had been taken ill. She gave him her smelling-salts, unloosened his collar, and lifting him from the floor dragged him into a corner where, in a sitting position, he soon regained consciousness. He had apparently suffered from a severe heart attack, but it quickly passed. Indeed, before they arrived at Bel-Air the old gentleman thanked her profusely and inquiring her name and address, had written it down upon a scrap of paper.

'We shall meet again one day, Madame, I hope. If not, I wish you to accept my heartfelt thanks for what you have done for me. I happen to have in my pocket a considerable sum of money, and in the hands of unscrupulous folk I might very easily have lost my money—and perhaps even my life!'

They shook hands after the old gentleman had told her that

Madame Humbert and the old gentleman in the train.

he was an American named Robert Henry Crawford, of Chicago, and assured her that he was quite well and able to continue his journey to the next station, which was Avenue de Vincennes. For two years she had forgotten all about the romantic meeting until one day she received a letter from a firm of lawyers in New York enclosing a copy of old Mr Crawford's will, by which she had been left £80,000. That was the original figure which Thérèse stated, but through gossip—no doubt started by His Excellency—the fortune was swiftly increased, first to a million pounds sterling, and then to four millions. This figure the Humbert family never questioned, and for nearly twenty years that followed all Paris believed that Thérèse Humbert was entitled to that sum—after certain divisions.

Whoever prepared the copy of the will, or whoever were the lawyers in New York—these things were never ascertained. It is sure, however, that the documents bore the stamp of authenticity, and were not questioned for the many years the imposture lasted.

The old man from Chicago died suddenly in Nice—the death certificate of a man named Crawford who lived in the Rue de France being produced—and by the conditions of the will his fortune was to be divided between Marie d'Aurignac, Thérèse's sister, who was then a child at school at Neuilly, and two nephews, Robert and Henry Crawford, while out of the fortune the three were to pay Thérèse Humbert fourteen thousand pounds a year.

Madame Humbert at once employed a very reputable firm of Paris lawyers to investigate, and according to their report it was found that the brothers Crawford who lived in America were both millionaires and that the legacy was of but little account to them.

Their American lawyers wrote to Madame's lawyers in Paris, expressing a wish that the money should remain in the Crawford family if possible, that it should remain intact in a safe in Madame Humbert's custody, except for the payment to her of fourteen thousand pounds annually, as the will provided. It was also suggested that as both brothers had seen a photograph of the schoolgirl, Marie d'Aurignac, one or the other of them should marry her when she left school. Then the safe should be opened and the fortune of four millions be divided.

Such was the curious, romancit story that went about Paris and which, coming, as it did, from the lips of the Minister of Justice, nobody dared to doubt. The invention, on the face of it, was ridiculous, though certainly there were letters from lawyers—forged, no doubt—to give it an appearance of fact, which set all Paris agog, and brought Thérèse Humbert fame and credit, so that from her humble home in a side street and her stream of creditors, she assumed the position of a wealthy *grande dame* and the guardian of her young sister's destinies until the marriage of convenience should take place.

Thus it was, in 1881, that the mythical story of the Crawford millions was launched with the connivance of Frederic Humbert and his wife's two brothers, Romain and Emile d'Aurignac—both ne'er-do-wells—and aided and abetted by His Excellency the Minister of Justice. A great white mansion was taken in the Avenue de la Grande Armée and luxuriously furnished as a fitting home for a woman of such great fortune, and in the downstairs room the largest fireproof safe procurable was set up for all to see—the sealed safe containing the four millions sterling, of which Robert Henry Crawford had died possessed.

Because the Minister of Justice himself was a relative and had testified to the truth of the romantic story, not a soul disbelieved it. Madame Humbert became the centre of smart society in Paris, and to be seen at her receptions, or to be a visitor at one or another of her famous country homes was a hall-mark of notoriety. As soon as she was firmly established in that magnificent house in the Avenue de la Grande Armée, the extravagances of the ex-washerwoman became astounding. The most famous people of both sexes in France scrambled for her invitations, and the state she kept up was almost regal. Her dresses and jewels were constantly being described in the Paris Press, for everyone became dazzled by the luxury with which she surrounded herself.

Whence did the money come to keep up that expensive establishment? I will explain.

In 1883, rumours were afloat that Madame had quarrelled with the Crawford brothers, but only after the publication in one of the minor newspapers of an article which threw doubt upon the whole story. An ingenious journalist had summoned courage to question the statement of the most powerful woman in France. As a matter of fact, the journalist in question had been born in Toulouse, had known old Aurignac and his story of nobility, and also of the Marcotte myth.

IV

In this article, Thérèse scented danger lest several people who had lent her money on the security of the safe and its millions should make secret investigations. Therefore she invented the quarrel between old Crawford's nephews and herself. It proved to be a pretty quarrel. The Crawford brothers first began to worry her over small matters of details, one of which was that the money should be removed to the Crédit Lyonnais for safer keeping. To this Madame objected. The matter came to Court, and after much bickering it was at last settled by Madame consenting to have three armed guards placed over the safe from sunset to sunrise each day. It seemed reasonable to suppose that the Crawfords were not imaginary, for non-existent persons do not embark upon expensive law-suits. Indeed, there started an amazing series of actions; some by the Crawfords, and others by Madame Humbert, which were fought out sometimes in the American Courts, and more often in Paris. And so the 'Humbert Millions' became a stock heading in the French newspapers, and the public began to follow the interminable lawsuits which were constantly cropping up.

Huge fees were paid to some of the most famous lawyers in France to defend Madame Humbert's rights, while similar fees were paid to other legal luminaries of equal distinction by the two American millionaires. In her defence, Thérèse was actively aided by her husband's father, the Minister of Justice, and so clever were her poses that everyone believed her to be in the right in resisting the unjust claims of old Crawford's nephews. Indeed, for nearly a generation, these constant law-suits were reappearing, together with occasional affidavits, sworn by either Robert or Henry Crawford, both of whom were in

America, and all sorts of information, evidence taken on commission in Chicago, and squabbles in the French Courts, until such a mass of judgments were obtained and appeals quashed that when the bubble burst nobody could make head or tail of what was the actual commencement of the great litigation upon which lawyers had fattened for years. Indeed, the most ludicrous part of it was that the lawyers themselves very often did not clearly know what they were actually fighting about! But the litigation achieved its purpose, for it seemed to show that the Crawford brothers did actually exist, and that they were endeavouring to obtain possession of the formidable-looking safe.

And all this time Marie d'Aurignac, Thérèse's sister, who had now left school, was the fiancée of Henry Crawford, whom she had, according to her story, met three times while he was on flying visits to Paris to see his French lawyers. During one of the trials in which Maître Waldeck-Rousseau was engaged, he referred to Mademoiselle Marie as 'the eternal fiancée,' a title which stuck to her until the eventual exposure of the swindle.

As was afterwards proved, she had been introduced to an American by her sister, Thérèse, at the Hôtel Continental. The man was represented to be Mr Crawford, and the girl, in her innocence, believed him to be the person whom she was destined to marry. The bogus Crawford was evidently of an engaging character, and good-looking, for Marie seems to have taken a liking to him, and to have met him on other occasions, and had, indeed, sung his praises to her friends. All of this went, of course, to bolster up the great fiction.

Meanwhile 'La Grande Thérèse' had become the most imposing figure in Parisian society. Her expenditure was lavish. Her accounts were investigated after the *débâcle*, and it was discovered that in the year 1897 she spent upon gowns £3780 at Doucet's and £1400 at Worth's, while her hats alone cost her over £850 in the Rue de la Paix. Truly the washerwoman turned adventuress was reckless in her expenditure, and further, such extravagance showed people how very wealthy she really was.

The public never dreamed that from the first moment that great mansion had been rented and furnished, Madame, who gave such expensive and exclusive parties, had existed always upon credit—or rather, upon the credulity of her dupes. That she found level-headed bankers, financiers and business men ready to advance large sums simply upon her assurance that the sealed safe contained four millions sterling in cash and securities was utterly amazing. If the story of Madame's clever duplicity had been written as a novel it would surely have been dismissed as fiction. But in this case we are faced with hard, yet astounding facts. Never in the history of crime had there been such an impudent and colossal fraud, and none so ingeniously conceived. The never-ending series of actions in the Courts between the Crawford brothers and herself established a confidence that the two sons of her late benefactor were alive, yet, as a matter of fact, they had no existence save in the imagination of the public. The whole proceedings, so complex that no lawyer has ever been able to unravel the tangle, was merely 'La Grande Thérèse' fighting herself. And she was paying for it all.

Imagine, then, how cleverly she hoodwinked the lawyers who appeared both for and against her, and how extremely careful she must have been in the preparation of every detail. In this she was assisted by her brothers, Emile and Romain d'Aurignac, who acted as her agents in many of her affairs. But, after all, it was her father's trick of the old oak chest being played again, but this time the harvest was not to be counted in single francs, but millions. Tempted by the promise of high rates of interest, hundreds of people lent Thérèse money in secret, all being assured that when the safe was opened at Marie's marriage they would receive back their loans with profit. The very lawyers who had appeared for her in the Courts became her agents for the borrowing of money, and to anyone who was sceptical, Madame, in great secrecy, would produce a bundle of letters purporting to be from the non-existent Crawfords—a trick which rarely failed to extract money. The time came, of course, when certain creditors desired their money, and became impatient to see the contents of the ponderous safe. But, no! The agreement with the Crawfords was that it was not to be opened until Marie's marriage, and she was not yet out of her teens. So, its creditors became unduly pressing, Madame paid the interest out of further loans from other people. And thus the game proceeded.

V

The first person of importance who seems to have had his
suspicions seriously aroused was a banker from Lyons named
Delatte, who had lent a considerable sum upon the strength of
Madame's story and sight of the sealed safe. To several other
creditors he declared that the whole affair was a fraud, but one
and all disbelieved him. Madame's behaviour, her plausibility,
her proof of the existence of the Crawfords, and her generosity
in the matter of dinners and entertainments disarmed suspicion.

But Monsieur Delatte, pretending that he was reassured and
satisfied, played a waiting game until one day, while guest of
Madame Humbert at the Château de Vellexon, he quite
innocently asked where Henry Crawford was. She declared
that he was living in Boston. He could obtain no further
information except that he had a house in Somerville, a suburb
of Boston, but he acted as nobody else seems to have thought of
acting, for, a week later, without telling anyone of his intentions, he left Havre for New York, and duly arrived in Somerville. Though he made every inquiry he could discover nobody of
the name of Crawford, either in Somerville or in Boston itself.
He engaged a well-known firm of private inquiry agents, but
their search in Chicago also proved futile. To a friend in Paris
he wrote declaring that the Crawford brothers did not exist,
and that he was returning to expose the swindle. His friend
awaited his return, but he never came. A month later, however,
news was received in Lyons that the body of a man who, from
papers found upon him, was identified as M. Delatte, had been
found in the East River between New York and Brooklyn.
Whether the unfortunate man met with an accident, was the
victim of foul play or committed suicide has never been cleared
up. In any case, had he returned to Paris, as was his intention,
he could, no doubt, have made things very uncomfortable for
Madame and her accomplices.

Within two months another of Madame's dupes came to an
untimely end. In this case it was the manager of an important

commercial house in Paris named Henri Vincendon, who, four years before, had lent Thérèse half a million francs. Since then he had been hard pressed for money, and had embezzled one hundred thousand francs belonging to the company which employed him. The books were, he knew, being examined, and soon his defalcations would be discovered, so he rushed to Madame and implored her to at least return him that sum. But he only received the same reply that all creditors' obtained, for Madame, without even expressing regret, told him that the safe could not be opened before the marriage of Marie, 'the eternal fiancée.' He pleaded with her, but although that very day she had obtained a further quarter of a million francs from a fresh victim, she would give him nothing. Therefore in despair the poor fellow went forth, and beneath a tree in the Bois he shot himself. Of almost similar cases there were several, though the actual cause of suicide never leaked out. It was only the ring of creditors themselves who knew.

A German journalist named Haberler, the Paris correspondent of a Berlin newspaper, having met Madame Humbert, considered that she behaved insultingly towards him, so in retaliation began to spread reports to the effect that the Crawford affair was a bogus one. At first nobody took any notice, but Madame's secret agents, her two brothers, came very soon afterwards and declared that the position was perilous, for many people were beginning to believe Haberler's statements. In consequence, Madame very quickly made peace with the journalist by paying him a very large sum, showing him the forged letters of the Crawford brothers, and inviting him to her parties, thus closing his mouth. To those who asked the reason of his change of opinion, the man replied that he had now seen proofs of the existence of the Crawfords, and he deeply regretted that he had defamed the much-criticised holder of the four millions sterling. This was not the only case in which Madame was blackmailed by those who thought they might obtain money by exhibiting animosity, for, of course, to sustain the fiction was vital to her schemes.

Marie d' Aurignac was exhibited everywhere, at Trouville, at Longchamps, at Monte Carlo, Aix, Pau and other places, for in company with her sister she went the usual round of watering-places, where the world gaped at the girl who was affianced to the American multi-millionaire, and at whose marriage the great safe would be opened and the stuffed-in four millions sterling would tumble out upon the floor. This was all a clever ruse on the part of Thérèse, who was nothing if not theatrical in her display. Besides, sight of the fiancée was calculated to attract further moths to the candle. It seems utterly incredible that any woman should carry on such a gigantic swindle against the shrewdest and most competent business men and financiers in France. But the fact was that Madame Humbert's two brothers—who were the forerunners of the modern press-agent—had boomed her to such an extent that, with her father-in-law as Minister of Justice, nobody dared doubt her word.

And so nightly those who were fortunate enough to receive invitations to the great white mansion in the Avenue de la Grande Armée—myself included—stared in awe at the safe containing the huge fortune.

No swindler, however clever he or she can be, can ever carry on the game for all time. A slip of the tongue must come some day, perhaps in a moment of confidence or perhaps after a post-prandial liqueur. Madame Humbert was no exception, despite her marvellous ingenuity and her grasp of complicated legal proceedings. It seems that late one night, while sitting with Jules Bizat in the great conservatory—which led out from the big panelled dining-room which, by the way, I well remember—she was guilty of a very grave indiscretion.

Bizat was a high official of the Banque de France, and though he had not lent Thérèse any money, he was a little inquisitive, because his father-in-law was deeply involved as one of Madame's creditors. Conversation turned upon the contents of the safe, as it so often did, and quite artlessly he asked:

'You, of course, saw what was placed in the safe by Henry Crawford. Of what did the securities mainly consist?'

To this she replied, 'French Rentes.'

That was the first indiscretion which eventually led to her undoing. Hitherto she had always remained silent, declaring complete ignorance. But this admission caused Monsieur Bizat to reflect. If French Rentes were sealed in that safe it would be necessary for her to cash French Rente coupons each year! So pretending ignorance, he at once instituted inquiries at the Banque de France and soon ascertained that no coupons had been cashed. Jules Bizat was a wise man. He held his tongue. But he was the first man to discover the actual fraud.

VI

Thérèse, however, at once discovered her mistake. She had put into the man's hands a weapon against herself. Further, creditors were pressing, and from day to day she did not know when the bubble might burst. For several weeks she existed in hourly anxiety, when once again her fertile brain evolved a further plan by which she might raise money from the public and thus pay the creditors now pressing on every hand for the formal opening of the sealed safe.

To Romain and Emile she disclosed her plans, as result of which another enormous fraud was launched upon the public under the name of the Rente Viagère. Romain d'Aurignac was put up as the figure-head of this new concern, though Thérèse, the ex-washerwoman, had worked out all the details. She had gauged the public of Paris very accurately, and she knew that ultra-luxurious offices would be one of her best assets. So, in the Boulevard des Cappucines, great offices were opened with departments so numerous as to be bewildering, while discreet uniformed attendants wearing white gloves directed clients hither and thither. The place was the biggest 'bluff' ever attempted in modern history.

Now inside those gorgeous offices, which only a genius of make-believe could have ever conceived, a wonderful business was in progress—a business to bolster up the clever manoeuvres of the ex-laundry-maid of His Excellency the Minister of Justice. The Rente Viagère was nothing else than a big bogus insurance company who promised you annuities without any capital to meet its liabilities. Thérèse had started this wonderful insurance company—with the backing of the well-known lawyers who were fighting for her against the inexorable Crawfords—with one object only. It was her master-stroke. She badly wanted money by which to be able to buy French

Rentes, cash the coupons and thus set aside any suspicions which had arisen in the mind of Jules Bizat. If he found that the coupons were cashed, he would surely remain satisfied then!

There is no doubt that when 'La Grande Thérèse' started the Rente Viagère she had no idea of how rapidly the swindle would grow, or of the thousands of people who would invest their small savings in it. The prospectus, drawn up in consultation with her two brothers, was so alluring, and so full of unusual benefits, that thousands of people of the middle classes invested their hard-earned savings, purchased annuities and insured their lives in a concern which was absolutely bogus. The great offices, with their big staff and liveried porters, never had more than a thousand pounds' balance at the bank, though often they took over the counter four or even five thousand pounds a day.

The Rente Viagère was the pet secret scheme of 'La Grande Thérèse.' To those who came each evening to her *salon* she sang its praises as an aid to the poor of France to save and to benefit. But nobody knew of her connection with it. Her brother Romain was full of details as to what they were accomplishing for the benefit of La Belle France, while Gustave Humbert, Minister of Justice, when questioned, expressed the greatest admiration of the scheme.

So the name of Thérèse Humbert became—after the death of her husband Frederic—a name to conjure with. Her critics had been silenced by bribery, or by counter-blackmailing cleverly carried on by her shrewd brothers who were, after all, adventurers after her own heart, and sons of the old peasant who adventured with his battered old box to obtain a few francs from the credulous.

Business went well. Millions of francs poured into the ever-open palm of Thérèse—*alias* the Rent Viagère. Every person who entered the magnificent portals of those fine offices, after being interviewed by suave, black-coated 'directors' who in their gorgeous rooms exuded financial credit—came out the poorer. From every corner of France thrifty working folk invested money in the corporation, bought annuities or insured their lives. With the money thus falling into the lap of 'La Grande Thérèse' she bought French Rentes, the coupons of which she began to cash each quarter-day and thus allayed the suspicion aroused in the mind of M. Bizat. Thus she started a second fraud in order to bolster up the first, and for several years the two big swindles ran side by side. We know that in the first year of the existence of the Rente Viagère Madame paid, in two months, for gloves alone £32, and £220 for hats at shops in the Rue de la Paix, while her florist's bill in the same sixty days amounted to well over £1000.

No doubt the Rente Viagère was much more profitable to Thérèse and her brothers than the sealed safe, the truth of which might at any moment be exposed, even though the Courts had decided that it could not be opened before Marie's marriage. Some say that M. Gustave Humbert, being Minister of Justice and aware of the fraud, had contrived that the Court should make that decree and thus protect his daughter-in-law. There were, however, still people who, unable to get their money back, and seeing no prospect of it, had grown very angry and impatient, and even though the proceeds of the Rente Viagère swindle were being used to stave off such people, they were growing inadequate. Madame Humbert had borrowed three million pounds from unsuspecting people upon no other security than her well-told story of her meeting with old Crawford in the train, and it was becoming clear that the day of reckoning was fast approaching. Yet the creditors were always faced with the decree of the Supreme Court that the safe might not be opened. And at the same time 'the eternal fiancée' was going about Paris happy, smiling, and certainly in ignorance of the part she was playing in the big conspiracy which her sister had engineered so successfully.

In the Courts several persons adjudged bankrupt attributed their insolvency to loans made to Madame Humbert, until at last, early in 1901, a number of her creditors held a meeting, when it was agreed that they had been swindled. One of these pointed out that after Madame had upon borrowed money paid for the defence of those never-ending lawsuits which had gone on for nearly fifteen years, there could not be very much left even if the safe were opened and the money divided. And, after all, the Crawfords would have to have their share. So on the face of it, they argued, Madame had borrowed more than her share of the money, with the result that they, the creditors, would probably obtain nothing.

Unfortunately for Madame Humbert this argument was placed before the great lawyer, M. Waldeck-Rousseau, who had appeared against Madame Humbert many times in Court—though, in his ignorance, paid by 'La Grande Thérèse'—and who had not great liking for her. He had all along been suspicious, being one of the few notable men who would listen to a word said against her genuineness and honesty. In fact, he had for a long time past become convinced that the whole thing was a huge fabrication, and, moreover, he had learnt that in secret the brothers d'Aurignac were the moving spirits in the Rente Viagère, though they were never seen at the offices and their identity was carefully concealed from everyone concerned.

VII

After making a number of secret inquiries, M. Waldeck-Rousseau felt that the time was ripe to prick the bubble. His son-in-law, who had been badly 'bitten' by Madame, had died, leaving his wife in sore straits, and there were other friends of his who had been wickedly imposed upon. Besides, the great game had been in progress for nearly twenty years, and though some people had received interest at times, yet nobody had, in all that period, seen the shadow of the money advanced. Therefore he went to the *Matin* newspaper and placed all the facts he had collected before the Director, who promised to make, in a series of articles, a direct attack upon the myth of the sealed safe.

By some means Madame Humbert heard of this and went boldly to the editor of the *Matin* and threatened an action if he dared to publish anything calling her honesty into question. But the editor coolly replied that he should act as he thought best, and next morning there appeared an article inspired by M. Waldeck-Rousseau, demanding the immediate opening of the safe. For nine days these virulent articles continued, declaring that the story of the Crawford millions had not foundation in fact, until the creditors were practically forced by public opinion to unite and take an action against Madame Humbert for a reversion of the decision against the opening of the safe.

For some months the case was delayed by counsel who defended Madame, and in the meantime the investors in the Rente Viagère suddenly awakened to the fact that they had lost their money, though even at that time there was no suspicion that Madame Humbert had been implicated in the bogus concern.

M. Waldeck-Rousseau was actively assisted in his investigations by M. Emile Zola and an able *juge d'instruction* named Borsant. At length the hearing of the creditors' appeal could no longer be delayed, and the presiding judge who heard the case decided that the only way by which the truth, so long delayed, could be ascertained was to have the seals broken and the safe opened. Notwithstanding a vigorous defence on the part of two famous counsels retained by Madame, May 9th, 1902, was the date fixed for the opening of the mysterious safe, and Madame was ordered to give the key into the custody of the Court.

'La Grande Thérèse,' seeing that the game was up, remained at home until the day before the opening, when, with her two brothers and her young sister Marie, she quietly left the Avenue de la Grande Armée and disappeared.

Next morning four officials of the Court, with M. Waldeck-Rousseau, the editor of the *Matin*, M. Emile Zola, and creditors representing just over three millions sterling, assembled in the room, the seals were broken, the time-stained tapes torn away and the safe was opened!

It was not empty, yet its sole contents consisted of an English halfpenny and a brick—evidently in imitation of the old oak chest trick!

Instantly the news got abroad that the Humbert millions only existed in Madame's imagination. One half of the creditors were furious, the other half hung their heads in shame that they should have been so cleverly imposed upon, while Paris, which always enjoys a good joke, laughed at the unfortunate creditors' plight.

Warrants were issued that day for the arrest of the fugitives. It was known that they had fled to London, but, though three French detectives were sent over, Scotland Yard could discover no trace of them. M. Goron, at that time Chef de la Sureté, has told me of the world search he ordered for Madame and her brothers—her sister not being included in the charges—yet through seven months no trace of them could be found. In the middle of December, however, a cheque upon the Crédit Lyonnais, bearing the name of Romain d'Aurignac, came to Paris, and showed that it had been cashed in Malaga, in Spain. The Spanish police were at once informed, and on December 20th, 1902, 'La Grande Thérèse' and her two brothers were found living in rather poor circumstances in a back street in Madrid.

It seems that the house was surrounded by the police, as the brothers were known to carry firearms, and they first caught sight of Madame's pale, anxious face peering at them from behind a blind. A ring at the door-bell resulted in the appearance of Romain d'Aurignac, who, with a laugh, said: 'I know why you are here! You want me! Here I am!' and he gave himself up, evidently in the hope of allowing his brother and sister to escape. This ruse failed, and all three were promptly arrested, and, after the extradition formalities were concluded, were brought to Paris by six of M. Goron's agents, and eventually tried at the Assize Court of the Seine on February 6th, 1903.

VIII

All three prisoners preserved an amazing calm, while Paris still enjoyed the huge joke, and the creditors were furious. How much Madame Humbert really did borrow on the strength of her unsubstantiated story will never be known, for many creditors of high standing, bankers and others, dared not come forward and confess themselves victims of what was a variation of the old confidence trick. Hence they made no statement or claim. It is, however, estimated that in one way or another five million pounds passed through the ex-washerwoman's hands.

In the trial there were many delays and adjournments, as is usually the case in France, so it dragged on from February until August. To all questions 'La Grande Thérèse' remained mute. She would make no admission. The President of the Court asked her to say where the Château de Marcotte was situated, but she only smiled. And again she smiled when asked for the addresses of the Crawford brothers. Only once did he obtain a direct reply to a question. He asked: 'Who were the Crawfords?' In reply, Madame Humbert, with great dignity, answered: 'Monsieur le Président, I shall tell my secret in due course, when the Public Prosecutor has spoken his last word.'

This attitude amazed all Paris, and the story she told a week later was certainly most astounding. It was decidedly clever, and in telling it she evidently thought she would be believed because of French prejudices against the Germans. She confessed that old Crawford had never existed, but that the person who had bequeathed to her the four millions was none other than Marshal Bazaine, who had surrendered the fortress of Metz to the Germans, the money being the sum paid to him by the enemy as price of his treachery.

'For a long time I was not aware of this, Monsieur le Président,' she went on. 'But as soon as I knew the truth I felt that I could not retain the blood-money. I am a patriotic daughter of France, so I destroyed both the will and the bonds, and burned the many packets of bank-notes which were English, German and French. That, Monsieur, accounts for the emptiness of the safe'.

'Exactly, Madame,' was the judge's retort, 'but it does not account for the brick!'

At which the Court roared with laughter. Of course, not a soul believed her statement, and in the end the jury found her guilty of fraud and she was sentenced to five years' solitary confinement, but, strangely enough, the jury decided that her guilt was in 'extenuating circumstances.' Her brother Romain was also sent to solitary confinement for three years, and Emile for two years, while the celebrated safe was on view for a year or more in a second-hand shop in the Rue Blanche.

Thus ended a most colossal fraud which, engineered by a shrewd and resourceful woman, who must also have possessed great courage and a remarkably clear brain, ran its course for nearly twenty years before final exposure, and which will for ever remain one of the most amazing of all gigantic swindles.

*Julian Symons is one of the most distinguished figures in the
literature of crime, renowned both for his own fiction and for
his critical writings on the genre, especially* Bloody Murder, *his history of crime writing. He has also made several
notable contributions to the field of true-crime writing, and
his book* A Reasonable Doubt *considers a number of cases
where justice might have faltered. In* Unsolved! *I included
one of these pieces, his brilliant analysis of the mystery of Sir
Harry Oakes, and I am delighted to include another Symons
piece here: this time a departure from the desk to carry out his
own investigation...*

JULIAN SYMONS

The Invisible Man

THE PUZZLE

The car was standing at Elishaw Bridge crossroads, on the road from Jedburgh and the Scottish border, as Evelyn Foster drove up. She helped to run her father's taxi service at the village of Otterburn, a mile or two down the road, and was on her way home after taking a party to Rochester.

Now as she drove up, the stranger got out of the car and spoke to her. He said in an accent that she recognized as North Country, although it was not exactly Tyneside, that he wanted to get a bus to Newcastle. The people in the car had brought him this far from Jedburgh, but now they were taking the road south, to Hexham. Could she give him a lift?

He was a pleasantly spoken, dapper little man, neatly dressed in dark blue overcoat, dark tweed suit, and bowler hat. Evelyn Foster considered, told him that her Hudson car was for hire, and said that she would take him into Otterburn, where she wanted to refuel, and then see where he could catch a bus. The occupants of the other car, a man and a woman, did not get out. The stranger thanked them for their hospitality, and the car drove off down the road to Hexham. The stranger got into the Hudson and sat beside her. The time was nearing seven o'clock on a cold, hard January night.

Within a few minutes they were at the Foster garage, in Otterburn's single street. She had told him that the fare to Ponteland, a journey of twenty-odd miles over the North-umbrian moors, would be about £2, and he agreed to this. From Ponteland he could easily get a bus into Newcastle. In the meantime, he said, he would go along to the Percy Arms, just along the road, and have a drink. She could pick him up either there or just beyond, at Otterburn Bridge.

Evelyn left him, and went into the house. There she saw her mother.

'What does he look like?' Mrs Foster asked.

'Oh, very respectable. Gentleman-like—he looks a bit of a knut.'

'Where is the man now?'

'He's gone down to the Percy Arms for a drink.'

Her mother thought that £2 was rather too much to charge, and her father said that the fare should be £1 16s. Her sister Dorothy suggested that it was unwise to travel alone with a stranger over the lonely moor, and said she should take as companion George Phillipson, a joiner in the village with whom Evelyn was friendly.

'I'll call for him,' she agreed.

She borrowed her mother's torch, and she drove away. The time was twenty minutes past seven. She did not see George Phillipson in the village (although in fact he was there), and did not call for him. The stranger hailed her at the Bridge, got into the car, and they began the drive across the moors. While they drove the man in the bowler hat talked to her, and what he said took on some importance in view of what happened afterwards. He did not know much about Newcastle, he told her, but lived in the Midlands. He had a car of his own, he said, and he appeared to know a lot about cars.

So the time passed, pleasantly enough, until they reached Belsay, only six miles from Ponteland. Now he suddenly told her to turn back.

'Why do you want to go back, when we have come so far?'

'That's nothing to do with you,' he said, and now his manner had changed.

She turned the car. He crept along the seat towards her, and took hold of the steering wheel. 'Oh no,' she said. 'I will do the driving.'

He lifted his hand and struck her over the eye, so that she could hardly see out of it. He took the wheel, pushed her over to the side of the car so that she could not move, nipped her arms. Then he drove back most of the way to Otterburn and stopped on the hill at Wolf's Nick, beside the snow-covered Ottercaps.

Now, surprisingly, he offered her a cigarette. She refused it.

'Well, you are an independent young woman,' the stranger said.

Her impressions after this were confused, but terrible. He struck her, kicked her, knocked her into the back of the car. Then he assaulted her, despite her resistance. She became unconscious. Vaguely she was aware that he had taken a bottle or tin from his pocket, that he was pouring something over her, that the something had gone up in a blaze, that she was burning.

There was a bump, as though the car were passing over rough ground. The bump roused her, burning as she was, and she managed to open the car door and push her way out of it. She found herself on the frosty moor. She thought she heard a car draw up, she thought she heard a whistle, but she could not be sure. With agonizing slowness she began to crawl back across the moor towards the road, and help. . . .

At about ten o'clock that night Cecil Johnson, driver of one of Foster's buses, was passing Wolf's Nick, on the journey from Newcastle to Otterburn. He saw something smouldering on the moors and, with the conductor, got out to investigate.

'Why, it's the firm's new Hudson,' Johnson cried as they approached the car. The back of it was almost burned out. The roof was a sheet of glowing embers, fanned by the dry, frosty air. One back tyre was still burning, otherwise there were no flames. There was nobody inside the car. Then they heard groans.

A few yards away they found Evelyn Foster. She was lying face downwards, trying desperately to suck the ice on the moor. The flames had burnt her so that she was practically naked from the waist down.

'It was that awful man,' she said, as they knelt down by her side. 'Oh, that awful man. He has gone in a motor-car.'

Johnson wrapped her in his overcoat, and they took her home. The doctor was summoned and came to Otterburn from Bellingham, nine hilly miles away, but time was of little importance, for there was nothing to be done. Evelyn Foster died early the next morning, but before she died she was able to tell her story to her mother while the Otterburn constable, Andy Ferguson, sat near by taking it down. The account of it that has been written so far is the story that she told to Andy Ferguson in the hours before death. Although in great pain, Evelyn Foster was perfectly lucid while making her statement, and even apologized to the doctor for bringing him out on such a night. What she said about the assault was, in view of what happened afterwards particularly interesting.

'Did he interfere with you?' her mother asked.

'Yes.'

Now Mrs Foster broke down and wept, and Evelyn cried: 'Oh, mother, I couldn't help it. I was fighting for my life.'

Evelyn did not know, as everyone present agreed, that there was no hope for her, but a little while before she died at seven o'clock in the morning, she must have realized it.

'I have been murdered,' she cried. 'I have been murdered.' They were her last words.

It was a horrifying crime, but not, the Northumberland County Police must have thought, one which was likely to resist solution for long. There were a good many clues—the occupants of the car from Jedburgh, who would certainly be able to identify and fully describe the stranger; the barman in the Percy Arms, where he had been going for a drink; possibly the people in the car that had picked him up after the crime. Or if this car did not exist (for she had been vague about the car and the whistle), and the man had tried to escape on foot, he certainly would not get far without being noticed, on the frostbound and lonely moors.

And there were other, material clues, found on the scene of the crime. Near to the car a man's glove was found, and so also was Evelyn's scarf. There was a footprint near by, and a mould of this was taken. Her purse had come out of her pocket and lay on the moor, with the money in it untouched. Altogether, there seemed quite sufficient evidence to discover and identify the murderer, and Captain Fullarton James, the Chief Constable, expressed himself as confident that the case could be handled locally. Neither now, nor at any later time, was Scotland Yard called on for assistance.

But the clues that had seemed so substantial all led nowhere, and to no person. The stranger seemed to have been an invisible man—invisible, at least, to everyone but Evelyn Foster. Several motorists were traced who had been in the vicinity of Jedburgh that Tuesday afternoon and evening, and had taken the road to Hexham, but none had admitted meeting a man like the stranger. The man had told Evelyn that the people in the car had given him tea in Jedburgh, but no hotel or café in the town or near it remembered such a party coming in. Every farmhouse, public house, hotel and café for miles round was visited, and the most dramatic manhunt ever known in Northumberland was carried out on the moors. This search was without result.

There was, of course, the usual crop of false clues. There was a man who had behaved suspiciously and had asked for a lift to Darlington, a local shepherd had seen a stranger on the moors, there was a man in Newcastle who talked like an American and had spoken strangely of the crime, and another man who entered a house in Newcastle and told the occupants that there was a body in the back of his car. All these men were between twenty-five and thirty years of age, all were clean shaven, all wore bowler hats and dark overcoats. They served to confirm the vagueness of a description which applied to hundreds of men in the district.

In Otterburn village, too, the man had been invisible. He had said that he was going to the Percy Arms, but the barman there told the police that no stranger had come in on that Tuesday night. Nor, he added, had Evelyn Foster herself come in to ask for him. This was perhaps the first fact that caused the police to feel doubt about the truth of Evelyn Foster's whole story.

And once doubt was felt, there was plenty of confirmation for it. In one detail at least, Evelyn Foster's story was inaccurate. There were no marks of burning on the heather between the road and the point at which the car stopped. The car was found in gear, and a local motor engineer told the police that it had been driven slowly off the road, and set on fire after it had stopped. The fire had not originated in the front of the car, and there was every indication that petrol from a tin carried in a luggage box at the rear had been used. An empty petrol tin was found on the carrier platform at the back of the car, and the neck and cap were discovered near by.

There was the further point that her story of the man pushing her over in the seat and then driving back from Belsay to Wolf's Nick was very improbable. It is very difficult to drive in such a position, and the handbrake on this Hudson car was on the right. Surely she could have pulled it, or got her foot on to the foot brake, to stop the car?

The evidence which must have finally determined the police view of the case, however, was that of Professor Stuart MacDonald, professor of pathology at Durham University, who examined the body after death. Professor MacDonald found extensive burning, most severe on the middle part of the body and in the front. The distribution and severity of the burns suggested that some portions of her clothing had contained an inflammable substance. The burning had started in front, and was most severe on the upper and inner thighs. Its intensity diminished, both upwards and downwards. The distribution of the burns suggested that the girl had been sitting down during some period of the burning.

But the vital points brought out by Professor MacDonald were two. First, there was no sign whatever that Evelyn Foster had been raped. Second, there was no sign of any blow on the face or head sufficiently violent to have stunned her.

It was four weeks after Evelyn Foster died that the inquest, formally opened within three days of her death, was resumed. It was held in the little War Memorial Hall at Otterburn, next door to the Percy Arms. The Coroner's table was draped with a black cloth, and the jurors sat at the trestle table. They were all local men who had known Evelyn well, the vicar, the sub-postmaster, the proprietor of the Percy Arms, a farmer, mill workers. The hall was lighted by acetylene gas, and the light was needed, for the surrounding moors were now in the grip of winter. Some of the roads to Otterburn were impassable, and

Captain Fullarton James ran into a snowdrift while on the way to the inquest, and had to be dug out.

This jury of local men heard some thirty witnesses out of the two hundred from whom the police had taken statements. There is no doubt that they were expecting to have some account of strangers rumoured to be in the district, and of police investigations into their behaviour. One of the jurymen, indeed, had himself seen a stranger—although not one he could positively identify—near the Post Office at about seven o'clock.

Instead of this, they listened to a step-by-step account designed to show that Evelyn Foster had set fire to the car herself. They heard the engineer, they heard Professor MacDonald. They were warned by the Coroner that Evelyn Foster's statement was not to be taken as evidence of fact.

The Coroner showed clearly enough his own agreement with the police viewpoint, in the questions he asked Professor Mac-Donald:

Coroner: Assuming that the car was standing where you saw it, Professor, and the door was open, and she threw some petrol into the back of the car, and then set fire to it—her left leg probably on the running board, her right on the edge of the step into the back of the car—could flames have come back and blinded her?

MacDonald: I think it is possible.

Coroner: Assuming she herself had upset some petrol over a portion of her clothing and then ignited the car, then that would have been a possible cause?

MacDonald: Yes.

Coroner: If she had taken the petrol tin and poured petrol over herself in that way, is it possible that she might have got two extra splashes on the top above the breast?

MacDonald: It is possible.

Why should Evelyn Foster, a quiet, rather timid, unimpeachably respectable girl of twenty-eight, run her car on to the moors and attempt to burn it? The car had been bought by Evelyn herself out of her savings—she had some £500 in the Post Office when she died—and, to obtain a cheaper rate, had been insured in her father's name. It was suggested by the Coroner that she would have benefitted financially by burning the car—he apparently did not realize that the insurance company would not pay more than the car's current market value.

'On the other hand,' the Coroner added, generously providing another motive, 'you have cases where, for some inexplicable reason, either for notoriety or for the sake of doing something abnormal, a person would do a thing like this.'

The summing up was practically a direction to the jury to say that Evelyn Foster fired the car herself. They were out for just over two hours. When they returned the foreman, McDougal, who was head gardener at Otterburn Towers near by, stood up and read the piece of paper in his hand.

'The jury find a verdict of wilful murder against some person unknown.'

There was silence. Then the Coroner said: 'I suppose you mean that somebody deliberately poured petrol over her and then set her on fire.'

'Yes.'

The Coroner wrote it down. Then he rose. 'That concludes the hearing. Thank you, gentlemen.'

It was not, however, the last comment made on the case. On the day after the verdict Captain Fullarton James made a statement which aroused great indignation in Otterburn. He said:

'We are satisfied that the motor-car in which Miss Foster's supposed murderer is said to have travelled from Jedburgh does not exist.

We are also satisfied that the man she described does not exist.'

INVESTIGATION AND ANALYSIS

Did the man exist? This was the question that I set myself to answer on a visit to Otterburn in a fine week of September 1956, more than twenty years after Evelyn's death. Foster's Garage is still in the main street, but the family's original anger at the attitude of Coroner and police had faded with the years. They could add nothing new to what had appeared in the newspapers, and had no hope of a solution to the crime. I talked, however, to a large number of people in Otterburn, Newcastle and around about, who were more or less directly connected with the case. I also talked to senior officers of the Northumberland County Police at Morpeth.

These gentlemen received me with courtesy and friendliness, but the friendliness was blended with some reserve. There was more reason for this than the rash statement of Captain Fullarton James. At the outset of the case the police had committed a serious blunder. The burnt out car was discovered soon after ten o'clock on Tuesday night, and the police knew of it very shortly afterwards. They put no guard over it, however, until Wednesday morning.

In the meantime (as I learned from a newspaperman in Newcastle) an enterprising journalist had gone out to Wolf's Nick, examined the car thoroughly, lifted the bonnet, found Evelyn Foster's scarf on the ground and put it over the car headlamp, and—it was strongly suggested to me—made the footprint of which the police took a mould. No evidence about this footprint was offered at the inquest. No fingerprint evidence was offered. Nothing was said about the glove found on the scene—was this also perhaps dropped by the reporter?

I should add that this blunder is not officially admitted by the police. A local policeman, now retired, strongly denied that the car had been left unguarded; the police at Morpeth refused to comment on the point. That it is a fact, however, is proved by one small detail of the evidence at the inquest. The police constable who first found Evelyn Foster's scarf, late on Tuesday night, saw it lying on the ground and left it there. When Inspector Russell visited the scene, on Wednesday morning, the scarf was hanging over the car headlamp. If the car was guarded continuously, how had it got there?

This initial error does not, of course, invalidate the theory of arson, but it does suggest that acceptance of this theory would have been welcome to the police. In Otterburn village I found great bitterness about the case, and much criticism of the police. There were roadmenders, I was told, who had seen a car at Elishaw Bridge at the time Evelyn's car drew up; there was a local schoolmistress who had been stopped by a stranger at Otterburn Bridge, a man so unpleasant and strange in his manner that she quickly left him; there was another roadmender who had heard a car turn round outside his house near Belsay (it was suggested by the police that Evelyn Foster had never driven further than Wolf's Nick). None of them was called.

Everybody, police and locals, agreed that the Otterburn police constable, now long retired, was the man who could tell me more about the case and the people involved, than anybody else. When I found Andy Ferguson, living now at Seaton Burn near Newcastle, he refused quite positively to say anything at all. The glove, the scarf, Evelyn Foster's character? His lips were tightly closed.

My own conclusion from those days spent in Otterburn is a firm one: Evelyn Foster was murdered. And there are several points which tell us something positive about her murderer. But before coming to them, let me analyze what may be called the negative side—the case against Evelyn Foster, which was based on her dying statement.

There are four main points to be answered:

1   Her failure to enter the Percy Arms and ask for the stranger.

2   Her unlikely account of the way in which he drove back from Belsay.

3   Her story of being attacked and raped.

4   Her story of the car that approached afterwards, and the whistle.

Let us go through the points in order. She said that the man 'hailed her' at the Bridge, which is no more than a few yards beyond the Percy Arms. If she really meant that he hailed her—called to her—then she might have heard him and not stopped at the hotel. It must also be remembered that her story was told in a low voice and spasmodically, so that the constable taking notes could not always hear what she said.

The second point, like much else in the story, is really in her favour. If she had wished to do so, she could easily have invented so many much more probable incidents which would have involved a change of seats, and his taking the steering wheel.

She said that the man hit her, and this possibility was not denied by Professor MacDonald, who agreed that a light blow in the eye, or even a blow on the head, might well leave no trace. She did not say that the blows stunned her, but that she 'became unconscious,' possibly from shock or fright. The questions put by the Coroner were almost throughout phrased so that her story appeared in the most unfavourable possible light.

The point about the rape is the most interesting of all. When her mother first asked Evelyn what had happened, she replied: 'Oh, it's been that man. He hit me and burned me.' There was nothing here about rape. Later she agreed when her mother asked if the man had 'interfered with her,' but at first Mrs Foster did not necessarily put a sexual interpretation upon this reply. In fact she did so only at the suggestion of the police solicitor.

I should add that the possibility, which was at one time in my own mind, that Evelyn Foster might have been carrying on an affair with a local man, unknown to her family or other Otterburn inhabitants, was decisively disposed of. The police never found anything to support such a theory; and I was assured by more than one person in the village that the community was so closely knit that it would have been absolutely impossible for such a relationship to have existed without being known to people in the district. Professor MacDonald's opinion was that she had died a virgin, although the nature of the burns made it impossible for him to be quite sure.

And finally, a car did stop at Wolf's Nick, at about half past nine. The driver saw smoke and flames from the car on the moor, could see nobody moving out there, and drove on without stopping to investigate. His later movements were checked, and his story authenticated. This could have been the car that Evelyn Foster heard.

There is also what may be called the problem of the missing matches. Evelyn did not smoke, or carry matches. No matches were found in or near the car. She had no lighter. How, then, did she set fire to the car?

And there is another point. If, as was suggested, she meant to set fire to the car and claim that it had been an accident, what would she have said about the missing passenger? Certainly no insurance company would have paid up without verification from him.

Summing up, one may admit that Evelyn Foster's dying statement is not tidy, nor wholly satisfactory. Yet the contradictions involved in denying it are quite staggering. Accept it as a statement basically true (although inaccurate in some details) and we have a picture of the murderer.

He was a man with a criminal record, he probably lived or had lived in the North East, and he was a skillful car driver. It is quite likely that, just before the Otterburn murder, he had committed another crime.

Here is the reasoning behind these conclusions.

His criminal record. Once we accept Evelyn's story, and accept as a fact that there *was* a car at Elishaw Bridge, we must ask: why did not its occupants come forward? There can be only one good reason—that they were afraid of revealing themselves to the police. This would be natural enough if they were criminals, who had recently done a job up in Scotland, and had decided to split up temporarily. It would be interesting to know how far the police pushed this line of enquiry.

He probably lived in the North East. Or at least he knew it very well. The road from Otterburn to Belsay has not greatly changed since 1931, although at Wolf's Nick the embankment has been built up. At that time, however, there was *practically no other spot along this road* where a car could have been driven onto the moor. The bank here was steep, the drop between 4 feet and 4 feet 6 inches, but it was not precipitous. The person who, on this dark night, knew exactly where he should stop to drive the car off the road, obviously had very considerable local knowledge.

He was a skillful driver. To drive the car down the bank was a tricky, and even dangerous, operation. There was no reason why Evelyn Foster should have risked it—or, incidentally, have tried to fire the car from the back rather than from the engine. On the other hand, there was every reason why her murderer should want to get the car off the road and on to the moor. It meant that he ran much less risk of immediate detection by a passing car, and thus helped to facilitate his escape.

There remain two questions. Why did he do it and how did he escape? We are in the region of what is no more than logical conjecture in suggesting that the man had a record not merely of crime, but of violent crime. There can be little doubt that when he first asked for a lift, he genuinely wanted to be driven to Ponteland. Something on the way changed his ·mind. Perhaps Evelyn Foster asked indiscreet questions, perhaps he suddenly felt himself in danger of discovery through her, perhaps his presence alone with her on the moors roused the urge to sadistic violence that is felt by many criminals. We do not know the reasons, only what happened.

Nor do we know how he escaped—whether he had an accomplice who picked him up, whether he managed somehow to get to Newcastle, or made his way to Hexham and there rejoined his companions, or found a hiding place on the moors. He walks out of the story, after killing Evelyn Foster, as abruptly as he had walked into it; but the memory of the invisible man, neat, gentlemanly, bowler-hatted, the man who was seen by nobody but Evelyn Foster but who surely existed, still haunts the people of Otterburn and the moors.

No name this time, alas — but do you get the feeling that perhaps it is only the law of libel that prevents it? Time will tell.

That no such consideration restrained Damon Runyon in the series of pieces that follow is a tribute, in part, to the greater freedom of the press that obtains in America, and there is no doubt at all that US newspapers have had a much greater impact on the cause of justice: witness Watergate, which simply could not have happened in Britain and many other countries, and the recent palaver about the publication of Spycatcher, *still unresolved as this book goes to press.*

The Snyder-Gray case was headline news all over the world as the story broke, and it still ranks as one fo the most celebrated murders of all time. As Damon Runyon says at the end of his reports, 'We have been three-sheeting Henry Judd and Ruth to good purpose.'

Ruth Snyder with her daughter Lorraine.

DAMON RUNYON

The 'Perfect' Crime that was Unspeakably Dumb

Long Island City, New York, April 19, 1927

A chilly looking blonde with frosty eyes and one of those marble, you-bet-you-will chins, and an inert, scare-drunk fellow that you couldn't miss among any hundred men as a dead set-up for a blonde, or the shell game, or maybe a gold brick.

Mrs Ruth Snyder and Henry Judd Gray are on trial in the huge weatherbeaten old court house of Queens County in Long Island City, just across the river from the roar of New York, for what might be called for want of a better name, The Dumbbell Murder. It was so dumb.

They are charged with the slaughter four weeks ago of Albert Snyder, art editor of the magazine, *Motor Boating*, the blonde's husband and father of her nine-year-old daughter, under circumstances that for sheer stupidity and brutality have seldom been equalled in the history of crime.

It was stupid beyond imagination, and so brutal that the thought of it probably makes many a peaceful, home-loving Long Islander of the Albert Snyder type shiver in his pajamas as he prepares for bed.

They killed Snyder as he slumbered, so they both admitted in confessions—Mrs Snyder has since repudiated hers—first whacking him on the head with a sash weight, then giving him a few whiffs of chloroform, and finally tightened a strand of picture wire around his throat so he wouldn't revive.

This matter disposed of, they went into an adjoining room and had a few drinks of whiskey used by some Long Islanders, which is very bad, and talked things over. They thought they had committed 'the perfect crime,' whatever that may be. It was probably the most imperfect crime on record. It was cruel, atrocious and unspeakably dumb.

They were red-hot lovers then, these two, but they are strangers now. They never exchanged a glance yesterday as they sat in the cavernous old court room while the citizenry of Long Island tramped in and out of the jury box, and the attorneys tried to get a jury of twelve men together without success.

Plumbers, clerks, electricians, merchants, bakers, butchers, barbers, painters, salesmen, machinists, delicatessen dealers, garage employers, realtors and gardeners from the cities and the hamlets of the County of Queens were in the procession that marched through the jury box answering questions as to their views on the death penalty, and their sympathies toward women, and other things.

Out of fifty men, old and young, married and single, bald and hairy, not one was found acceptable to both sides. Forty-three were excused, the State challenged one peremptorily, the attorneys for Mrs Snyder five, and the attorneys for Gray one. Each defendant is allowed thirty peremptory challenges, the State thirty against each defendant.

At this rate they may be able to get a jury before the Long Island corn is ripe. The State is asking that Mrs Snyder and her meek looking Lothario be given the well-known 'hot seat' in Sing Sing, more generally known as the electric chair, and a lot of the talesmen interrogated today seemed to have a prejudice against that form of punishment.

Others had opinions as to the guilt or innocence that they said they couldn't possibly change. A few citizens seemed kindly disposed toward jury service, possibly because they haven't anything at hand for the next few weeks, but they got short shrift from the lawyers. The jury box was quite empty at the close of the day's work.

Mrs Snyder, the woman who has been called a Jezebel, a lineal descendant of the Borgia outfit, and a lot of other names, came in for the morning session of court stepping along briskly in her patent-leather pumps, with little short steps.

She is not bad looking. I have seen much worse. She is

thirty-three and looks just about that, though you cannot tell much about blondes. She has a good figure, slim and trim, with narrow shoulders. She is of medium height and I thought she carried her clothes off rather smartly. She wore a black dress and a black silk coat with a collar of black fur. Some of the girl reporters said it was dyed ermine; others pronounced it rabbit.

They made derogatory remarks about her hat. It was a tight-fitting thing called, I believe, a beret. Wisps of her straw-colored hair straggled out from under it. Mrs Snyder wears her hair bobbed, the back of the bobbing rather ragged. She is of the Scandinavian type. Her parents are Norwegian and Swedish.

Her eyes are blue-green, and as chilly looking as an ice cream cone. If all that Henry Judd Gray says of her actions the night of the murder is true, her veins carry ice water. Gray says he dropped the sash weight after slugging the sleeping Snyder with it once and that Mrs Snyder picked it up and finished the job.

Gray's mother and sister, Mrs Margaret Gray, and Mrs Harold Logan, took seats in the court room just behind Mrs Snyder. At the afternoon session, Mrs Gray, a small, determined-looking woman of middle age, hitched her chair over so she was looking right into Mrs Snyder's face.

There was a rather grim expression in Mrs Gray's eyes. She wore a black hat and a black coat with a fur collar, a spray of artificial flowers was pinned to the collar. Her eyelids were red as if she had been weeping.

The sister, Mrs Logan, is plump and pleasant looking. Gray's wife has left him flat, in the midst of his troubles and gone to Norwalk, Conn., with their nine-year-old daughter. She never knew her husband was playing that Don Juan business when she thought he was out peddling corsets. That is she never knew it until the murder.

Gray, a spindly fellow in physical build, entered the court room with quick, jerky little steps behind an officer, and sat down between his attorneys, Samuel L. Miller and William L. Millard. His back was to Mrs Snyder who sat about ten feet distant. Her eyes were on a level with the back of his narrow head.

Gray was neatly dressed in a dark suit, with a white starched collar and subdued tie. He has always been a bit to the dressy side, it is said. He wears big, horn-rimmed spectacles and his eyes have a startled expression. You couldn't find a meeker, milder looking fellow in seven states, this man who is charged with one of the most horrible crimes in history.

He occasionally conferred with his attorneys as the examination of the talesmen was going forward, but not often. He sat in one position almost the entire day, half slumped down in his chair, a melancholy looking figure for a fellow who once thought of 'the perfect crime.'

Mrs Snyder and Gray have been 'hollering copper' on each other lately, as the boys say. That is, they have been telling. Gray's defense goes back to old Mr Adam, that the woman beguiled him, while Mrs Snyder says he is a 'jackal,' and a lot of other things besides that, and claims that he is hiding behind her skirts.

She will claim, it is said, that while she at first entered into the conspiracy to kill her husband, she later tried to dissuade Gray from going through with it, and tried to prevent the crime. The attorneys will undoubtedly try to picture their respective clients as the victims of each other.

Mrs Snyder didn't want to be tried with Gray, but Gray was very anxious to be tried with Mrs Snyder. It is said that no Queens County jury ever sent a woman to death, which is what the State will ask of this jury, if it ever gets one. The relations among the attorneys for the two defendants are evidently not on the theory of 'one for all and all for one.' Probably the attorneys for Gray do not care what happens to Mrs Snyder, and probably the attorneys for Mrs Snyder feel the same way about Gray.

Edgar Hazelton, a close-trimmed dapper looking man, with a jutting chin and with a pince-nez balanced on a hawk beak, who represents Mrs Snyder, did most of the questioning of the talesmen for the defense. His associate, Dana Wallace, is a former district attorney of Queens County, and the pair are said to be among the ablest lawyers on Long Island. It is related that they have defended eleven murder cases without a conviction going against them.

Damon Runyon at the time of the Snyder-Gray trail.

Supreme Court Justice Townsend Scudder is presiding over the court room, which has a towering ceiling with a stained glass skylight, and heavy dark oak furniture with high-backed pews for the spectators. Only no spectators were admitted today because the room was needed for the talesmen.

The court room is so huge it was difficult to hear what was going on at any distance from the bench. I believe it is the largest court room in the country. It was there that the trial scene in the picture *Manslaughter* was filmed.

In the court room on the floor below was held the trial of Mrs Nack in the famous Guldensuppe murder thirty years ago, when the reporters used carrier pigeons to take their copy across the river to Park Row.

Microphones have been posted on the tables, and amplifiers have been rigged up on the walls, probably the first time this was ever done in a murder trial, but the apparatus wasn't working any too well today, and one hundred and twenty newspaper writers scattered around the tables listened with their hands cupped behind their ears.

Here is another record, the number of writers covering the trial. We have novelists, preachers, playwrights, fiction writers, sports writers and journalists at the press benches. Also we have nobility in the persons of the Marquis of Queensbury and Mrs Marquis. The Marquis is a grandson of the gent whose name is attached to the rules governing the manly art of scrambling ears, but the young man wore a pair of fancy-topped shoes yesterday that surprised me. It isn't done you know, really!

The Reverend John Roach Straton was present wearing a Buster Brown necktie that was almost unclerical. A Catholic priest was on hand, but he carried no pad or pencil to deceive us. Some of the writers came attended by their secretaries, which shows you how far we have gone since the days of the carrier pigeons at the Guldensuppe trial.

There were quite a number of philosophers. I have been requested by my Broadway constituency to ascertain if possible what, if anything, philosophy suggests when a hotsy-totsy blonde with whom a guy is enamoured tells him to do thus and so. But then a philosopher probably never gets tangled up with blondes, or he wouldn't be a philosopher.

Mrs Snyder showed signs that might have been either nervousness or just sheer impatience during the day. Her fingers constantly toyed with a string of black beads at her throat. Her entire set-up suggested mourning. She has nice white hands, but they are not so small as Gray's. His hands are quite effeminate.

In fact, the alienists who examined Gray and pronounced him quite sane say he is effeminate in many ways. Gray showed no signs of nervousness or any particular animation whatever. He just sat there. It must be a strain on a man to sit for hours knowing the eyes of a woman who is trying to get him all burned up are beating against the back of his neck and not turn around and give her at least one good hot glare.

April 27, 1927

Some say Mrs Ruth Snyder 'wept silently' in court yesterday. It may be so. I could detect no sparkle of tears against the white marble mask, but it is conceivable that even the very gods were weeping silently as a gruff voice slowly recited the blond woman's own story of the murder of her husband by herself and Henry Judd Gray.

Let no one infer she is altogether without tenderness of heart, for when they were jotting down the confession that was read in the court room in Long Island City, Peter M. Daly, an assistant district attorney, asked her:

'Mrs Snyder, why did you kill your husband?'

He wanted to know.

'Don't put it that way,' she said, according to his testimony yesterday. 'It sounds so cruel.'

'Well, that is what you did, isn't it?' he asked, in some surprise.

'Yes,' he claims she answered, 'but I don't like that term.'

A not astonishing distaste, you must admit.

'Well, why did you kill him?' persisted the curious Daly.

'To get rid of him,' she answered, simply, according to Daly's testimony; and indeed that seems to have been her main idea throughout, if all the evidence the State has so far developed is true.

She afterward repudiated the confession that was presented yesterday, with her attorneys trying to bring out from the State's witnesses that she was sick and confused when she told her bloody yarn five weeks ago.

The woman, in her incongruous widow's weeds sat listening intently to the reading of her original confession to the jury, possibly the most horrible tale that ever fell from human lips, the tale of a crime unutterably brutal and cold-blooded and unspeakably dumb.

Her mouth opened occasionally as if framing words, and once she said no quite distinctly, an unconscious utterance, which may have been a denial of some utterance by the lawyer or perhaps an assurance to her soul that she was not alive and awake.

This is a strange woman, this Mrs Ruth Brown Snyder, a different woman to different men.

To the inert Henry Judd Gray, her partner in crime, sitting at the table just in front of her, as soggy looking as a dummy in his loose hanging clothes, she was a 'woman of great charm,' as he said in his confession which was outlined in court by a police officer yesterday.

To big, hale and hearty George P. McLaughlin, former police commissioner of New York City, who heard her original statement of the butchery, she was a 'woman of great calm,' as he said on the witness stand yesterday.

To the male reporters who have been following the trial she is all that, anyway, though they construe her calm as more the chill of the icy Northland, whence came her parents.

The attorneys for Mrs Snyder, the nimble Dana Wallace and Edgar Hazelton, indicated yesterday clearly that part of their line of defense, in this devil-take-the-hindmost scramble between Ruth and Henry Judd is to be an attempted impeachment of the confession, and Gray's attorneys showed the same thought.

Samuel L. Miller, representing Gray, charged that the confession of the corset salesman was secured while he was under duress and by intimidation and threats.

Gray sat with his chin in his hands, his eyes on the floor, scarcely moving a muscle as Mrs Snyder's confession, damning him in almost every word, was read. I have never seen him show much animation at best, but yesterday he seemed completely sunk. He occasionally conferred in whispers through his fingers with one of his attorneys, but with not the slightest show of interest.

It was Gray who slugged poor Albert Snyder with the five-pound sash weight as the art editor lay asleep in his bed, so Mrs Snyder's confession relates, while Mrs Snyder stood outside in the hall, seeing, by the dim light thrown into the chamber of horror by an arc in the street, the rise and fall of the paper-wrapped weight in Gray's hand.

What a scene that must have been!

Twice she heard her husband groan. Roused from an alcoholic stupor by the first thump on his head, he groaned. Then groaned again. Silence. Out came Henry Judd Gray, saying: 'Well, I guess that's it.'

But the confessions do not jibe here. The outline of Gray's confession, which will be read today, indicates Gray says he dropped the weight after whacking Snyder once, and that Ruth picked it up 'and belabored him.'

'Those were Gray's words—"belabored him,"' ex-Commissioner McLaughlin said yesterday.

District Attorney Newcombe overlooked an opportunity for the dramatic yesterday that old David Belasco, sitting back in the crowd, probably envied, in the reading of Ruth's confession. This was first identified by Peter M. Daly, the assistant mentioned above, after Ruth's attorneys had failed in a hot battle against its admission.

Newcombe stood before the jury with the typewritten sheets in one hand and talked off the words without elocutionary effort, the microphone carrying his voice out over the silent court room. The place was jammed. Women again. At the afternoon session they almost tore the buttons off the uniforms of the coppers on guard at the doors, trying to shove past them. The cops gallantly repulsed the charge.

The first paragraphs of the confession, made to Daly soon after the murder and under circumstances that the defense is attacking, were given over to a recital of Ruth's early life—born on Manhattan Island thirty-three years ago, a schoolgirl, an employee in the same magazine office with Snyder, then an artist when she married him.

The thing has been told so often before that I here go over it sketchily. Soon she was unhappy with her husband, fourteen years older than herself. He constantly belittled her. He threatened to blow out her brains. He was a good provider for herself and their nine-year-old daughter, but wouldn't take her out—so she took to stepping out, as they say. An old, old yarn—Friend Husband a non-stepper, Friend Wife full of go.

She met Henry Judd Gray, the corset salesman, in Henry's restaurant in the once-throbbing Thirties in New York, and the first thing anybody knew she and Henry were thicker than is meet and proper. She told Henry of her matrimonial woes, and Henry, himself a married man, with a young daughter, was duly sympathetic.

But let's get down to the murder.

She wrote Henry and told him how Albert Snyder had threatened her life. She wrote in a code they had rigged up for their own private use, and Henry answered, saying the only thing to do was to get rid of Albert. They had talked of ways and means, and Gray gave her the famous sash weight and went out to Queens Village one night to wipe Albert Snyder out.

They got cold feet that night and Albert lived. Then Snyder again threatened her, the confession said, and told her to get out of his house, so she wrote to Henry once more, and Henry wrote back, saying, 'We will deliver the goods Saturday.' That meant Saturday, March 19. They arranged all the details by correspondence.

Henry arranged his alibi in Syracuse and came to New York the night she and her husband and child were at the Fidgeons' party. She left a door unlocked so Henry could get in the room of her mother, Mrs Josephine Brown, who was away for the night. Ruth saw him there and talked with him a moment when she came back from the party with her husband and child.

Henry had the sash weight which she had left under the pillow in Mrs Brown's room for him. He had chloroform, some cheese-cloth and a blue cotton handkerchief. Also, she had hospitably left a quart of liquor for him of which he drank about half. She put her child to bed, then went into her husband's room and waited until he was asleep, then returned to the waiting Henry.

They talked briefly, and Henry kissed her and went into Albert Snyder's room. She stood in the hallway and saw Gray pummel the sleeping man with the sash weight as related. Then Gray tied Snyder's hands and feet, put the handkerchief, saturated with chloroform, over his face, besides stuffing his mouth and nostrils with the gauze, also soaked with chloroform. Then Henry turned Snyder over so the art editor's face would be buried in a pillow and rejoined Ruth.

Henry Judd wore rubber gloves at his sanguinary task, the confession said, and he went to the bathroom to wash his hands. He found blood on his shirt, so Ruth went into the room where the dead man lay, got one of Albert Snyder's shirts and gave it to Henry Judd. Then they went into the cellar and burned the bloody shirt and put the sash weight into a tool box after rubbing it with ashes.

Now, they returned to the sitting room, this pair, and Henry Judd suddenly thought of some picture wire he had brought alone, presumably to tie Snyder's hands and feet. At least, he had two pieces, Ruth said. One he had lost, so he took the other and went into the death chamber and wrapped the wire around Albert Snyder's throat tightening it with his fingers.

Then he went around and upset the premises generally, to bear out the robbery idea, then sat and gossiped, talking of this and that until daybreak, when Henry Judd tied his sweetheart's hands and feet and left to return to Syracuse. She first went out and got a wallet out of Albert Snyder's pocket and gave it to Henry Judd. She does not know how much it contained.

After Henry's departure, she rolled out of her mother's bed, whereon he had placed her, and aroused her little daughter, telling her to get a neighbor.

Such, in substance and briefly, was the story of that night in Queens Village.

There was a supplemental statement with reference to some letters, including one from Gray, sent from Syracuse after he had departed from New York to join hands with her in the slaughter. Peter M. Daly asked her, at a time when Gray had not yet been definitely hooked with the crime, how she reconciled the postmark with her statement of the murder and she said it was part of Henry's alibi.

Thus Ruth was 'hollering copper' on Henry, even before she knew Henry was 'hollering copper' on her. They didn't stand hitched a minute after the showdown came.

Wallace wanted to know if Mrs Snyder hadn't said she was confused and sick while making the statement, but Daly said no. He admitted Mrs Snyder had a crying spell and that a physician was called in. Wallace mentioned it as a fainting spell, but Daly wouldn't concede it was such. It seemed to be agreed it was some kind of a spell, however.

Daly said she asked if she could see Gray when he got to town. He said she seemed to know that Gray was on his way to New York. The defense devoted more time to Daly than to any other witness so far, Millard of Gray's counsel joining in the cross-examination.

Gray's attorneys had objected to some questions asked by Wallace and now Mrs Snyder's lawyers objected to Millard's questions.

This case has been presented from the beginning in rather a disordered manner, it seems to me, like one of those new-fangled plays that violate all the established rules from the theatre.

For instance, at the morning session, Millard started out cross-examining Lieutenant Dorschell, of the New York Police Department, relative to a drawing made by Gray of the hardware store in Kingston, where he bought the sash weight and the picture wire. This drawing was made at three o'clock in the morning of Gray's arrival in New York after his ride from Syracuse, where he was arrested. Millard inquired into the physical condition of Gray at the time he made the drawing and Dorschell said he seemed to be all right.

Millard then explained to Justice Scudder that he wanted to show under what conditions the drawing was made. He said he desired to present testimony showing that the drawing came after a long examination of Gray by the police, and to that end Justice Scudder gave him permission to call and cross-examine a witness who had not appeared before.

It is certainly somewhat unusual to bring in for cross-examination by the defense a witness who would ordinarily be one of the State's most important witnesses.

The witness was Michael S. McDermott, another lieutenant of New York Police, who brought Gray from Syracuse, and who told with infinite detail of Gray's confession. He said Gray took the thing as a joke at first, maintaining his complete innocence.

McDermott said Gray seemed to find the company he was in 'congenial' most of the journey, a statement that produced a light giggle in the court. He said that Gray at no time seemed to become serious until they told him they had the contents of his wastepaper basket, which included the Pullman stub.

' "Do you know, Judd, we have the Pullman ticket you used from Syracuse to New York?' Then he said, 'Well, gentlemen, I was at the Snyder home that night." '

McDermott said Gray voluntarily launched into a narrative of the bloody night in Queens Village. He told how Gray had subsequently given this same narrative to a stenographer and identified and initialed the various articles used in the commission of the crime.

Now the State proceeded to establish the purchase of the sash weight and picture wire by Gray in Kingston, March 4, last.

Margaret Hamilton, a buyer for a Kingston store, who knows Henry Judd, said she saw him there on that date. She is a stout lady, and wore a startlingly red hat and red scarf.

Arthur R. Bailey, a thin, gray, studious looking man, wearing glasses, a clerk in a Kingston hardware store, didn't seem to remember selling a five-pound sash weight on March 4, although he identified what you might call a bill of sale in his handwriting, taken from the records of the store. He said his store sold any number of sash weights, but he never recalled any transaction involving one sash weight. Mr Bailey obviously didn't care about being mixed up in this trial business, anyway.

John Sanford, a young Negro, testified most briefly to getting this sash weight from the warehouse.

It seemed a lot of bother about a sash weight that has lost some of its importance since the doctors testified that the wallops with it alone did not cause Snyder's death.

Reginald Rose, youthful, black-haired, black-browed and a bit to the sheikish side, a ticket seller for the New York Central, told of selling Gray a railroad ticket to Syracuse and a Pullman seat reservation to Albany on the night of March 19 for the following day, which was the day after the murder. Gray made the return reservation immediately upon his arrival in New York the night he ran down for the killing.

Millard became a bit curious over Rose's clear recollection of this particular sale of a ticket out of the many a ticket seller makes every day and it developed that Rose even remembered how Gray was dressed. He wore a fedora hat and an overcoat.

Rose said he remembered the sale because it wasn't commonplace to sell a railroad ticket to Syracuse and a seat to Albany.

Now came testimony about the party which Mr and Mrs Snyder and their small daughter, Lorraine, attended the night of the murder. It was at the home of Milton C. Fidgeon, and Mr Fidgeon himself took the stand, stout, smooth of face and prosperous-looking.

There had been liquor at the party said Mr Fidgeon. He served one drink, then someone asked if it was not time for another, so he went into the kitchen to produce the second shot.

Mrs Snyder came to him there and said she wasn't drinking, but to give her portion to her husband. The Snyders went home about two o'clock in a pleasant frame of mind, as Mr Fidgeon said on cross-examination by Wallace.

April 28, 1927

Right back to old Father Adam, the original, and perhaps the loudest 'squawker' among mankind against women, went Henry Judd Gray in telling how and why he lent his hand to the butchery of Albert Snyder.

She—she—she—she—she—she—she—she. That was the burden of the bloody song of the little corset salesman as read out in the packed court room in Long Island City yesterday.

She—she—she—she—she—she. 'Twas an echo from across the ages and an old familiar echo, at that. It was the same old 'squawk' of Brother Man whenever and wherever he is in a jam, that was first framed in the words:

'She gave me of the tree, and I did eat.'

It has been put in various forms since then, as Henry Judd Gray, for one notable instance close at hand, put it in the form of eleven long typewritten pages that were read yesterday, but in any form and in any language it remains a 'squawk.'

'She played me pretty hard.' . . . 'She said, "You're going to do it, aren't you?" ' . . . 'She kissed me.' . . . She did this . . . She did that . . . Always she—she—she—she—she ran the confession of Henry Judd.

And 'she'—the woman-accused, how did she take this most gruesome squawk?

Well, on the whole, better than you might expect.

You must remember it was the first time she had ever heard the confession of the man who once called her 'Momsie.' She probably had an inkling of it, but not its exact terms.

For a few minutes her greenish blue eyes roared with such fury that I would not have been surprised to see her leap up, grab the window sash weight that lay among the exhibits on the district attorney's table and perform the same offices on the shrinking Gray that he says she performed on her sleeping husband.

She 'belabored him,' Gray's confession reads, and I half expected her to belabor Gray.

Her thin lips curled to a distinct snarl at some passages in the statement. I thought of a wildcat and a female cat, at that, on a leash. Once or twice she smiled, but it was a smile of insensate rage, not amusement. She once emitted a push of breath in a loud 'phew,' as you have perhaps done yourself over some tall tale.

The marble mask was contorted by her emotions for a time, she often shook her head in silent denial of the astounding charges of Gray, then finally she settled back calmly, watchful, attentive, and with an expression of unutterable contempt as the story of she—she—she—she ran along.

Contempt for Henry Judd, no doubt. True, she herself

squawked on Henry Judd, at about the same time Henry Judd
was squawking on her, but it is a woman's inalienable right to
squawk.

As for Henry Judd, I still doubt he will last it out. He reminds
me of a slowly collapsing lump of tallow. He sat huddled up in
his baggy clothes, his eyes on the floor, his chin in hand, while
the confession was being read. He seems to be folding up inch
by inch every day.

He acts as if he is only semi-conscious. If he was a fighter and
came back to his corner in his present condition, they would
give him smelling salts.

The man is a wreck, a strange contrast to the alert blonde at
the table behind him.

The room was packed with women yesterday, well-dressed,
richly-befurred women from Park Avenue, and Broadway, and
others not so well dressed from Long Island City, and the small
towns farther down the Island. There were giggling young
schoolgirls and staid-looking matrons, and my friends, what do
you think? Their sympathy is for Henry Judd Gray!

I made a point of listening to their opinions as they packed
the hallways and jammed the elevators of the old court house
yesterday and canvassed some of them personally, and they are
all sorry for Gray. Perhaps it is his forlorn looking aspect as he
sits inert, numb, never raising his head, a sad spectacle of a man
who admits he took part in one of the most atrocious murders in
history.

There is no sympathy for Mrs Snyder among the women and
very little among the men. They all say something drastic ought
to be done to her.

How do you account for that—

But while Henry Judd's confession puts most of the blame on
the woman, Mrs Snyder's attorneys, the pugnacious Edgar
Hazelton and the sharp Dana Wallace, who remind me for all
the world of a brace of restless terriers with their brick maneuv-
ers, began making an effort yesterday that shows they intend
trying to make Henry Judd the goat.

When District Attorney Newcombe stood up to read Gray's
confession, a deep silence fell over the room, packed from wall
to wall. Many of the spectators were standing. Mrs Snyder

leaned forward on the table in front of her, but Gray never raised his eyes from the floor, then or thereafter.

You could hear little gasps as of horror or unbelief from some of the women spectators as Newcombe read on in a cold, passionless voice, especially when the confession got down to the actual murder.

It began with the story of their meeting in Henry's restaurant about two years ago. They were introduced by Harry Folsom of New Canaan, Conn., who had picked Mrs Snyder and another up in the restaurant, so ran the confession, rather giving the impression that the blonde was one of those women who can be 'picked up.' Gray said:

'She is a woman of great charm. I probably don't have to tell you that. I did like her very much, and she was good company and apparently a good pal to spend an evening with.'

I looked over at Mrs Snyder as this paragraph was read, and there was a shadow of a smile on the marble mask. The expression altered when the story began to tell an instant later of them starting intimate relations in August. Gray added:

'Prior to that she was just a woman I respected.'

Perhaps I should here explain that most of this confession was made by Gray on the train when he was being brought from Syracuse to New York after the murder and later elaborated in its details by him.

Well, they got very friendly, and soon she was calling him up and writing him. 'She played me pretty hard,' he said. He went out to her house for luncheon, and met her mother, although he did not think the mother knew anything of their relations.

Presently Mrs Snyder got to telling of her unhappiness with Albert. Gray told her, he says, that he himself was married and had a fine wife and was very happy at home, so there could never be anything between him and Mrs Snyder.

She told him of several attempts she had made on Albert Snyder's life, once giving him sleeping powders, and again bichloride of mercury, but Albert kept on living.

Finally, said Gray, 'She started to hound me on this plan to assist her.'

The plan for killing Snyder, presumably. But the little corset salesman added quite naively, 'I have always been a gentleman and I have always been on the level with everybody. I have a good many friends. If I ever have any after this I don't know.'

He said he absolutely refused to listen to the charmer's sanguinary wiles at first, then 'with some veiled threats and intents of love-making, she reached the point where she got me in such a whirl that I didn't know where I was at.'

Clarence A. Stewart, superintendent of the safety deposit vault of the Queens-Bellaire Bank of Queens Village, testified that Mrs Snyder rented two boxes, one under the name of Ruth M. Brown, the other under the name of Ruth M. Snyder. Stewart is a mild-looking man who kept his overcoat on while testifying. He stood up when asked to identify Mrs Snyder and peered at her through his specs.

Edward C. Kern, cashier of the same bank, heavy-set and bland, testified to the contents of these boxes. In the box taken in the name of Ruth M. Brown was $53,000 worth of insurance policies on Albert Snyder and receipts for the payment of the premiums. In the box under the name of Ruth M. Snyder were papers mainly of a family nature relating to the affairs of Ruth and her dead husband, such as fire and burglary insurance policies, receipts and the like.

There seemed to be plenty of fire insurance on the Snyder home. There was some Roxy Theatre stock among other things and papers representing small investments by the dead art editor.

Samuel Willis, a tall, spare, elderly resident of Queens Village, told of seeing Henry Judd Gray waiting for a bus at 5:50 on the morning of March 20, hard by a police booth at Hillside Avenue and Springfield Boulevard, in Queens Village. Police Officer Smith, on duty there, was indulging in a little pistol practice at bottles and Willis said Gray remarked after the officer finished:

'I'd hate to stand in front of him and have him shoot at me.'

The bailiffs had to rap for order. Cross-examined by Samuel L. Miller, the witness said his attention was attracted to Gray 'by that little dimple in his chin.' He said Gray took the bus with him and he saw no more of Henry Judd. This was just after

Gray had left the Snyder home to hurry back to Syracuse, you understand.

April 29, 1927

There was little breathing space left in the yellowish-walled old court room when the morning session opened.

In the jam I observed many ladies and gents with dark circles around their eyes which indicated loss of sleep, or bad livers. I identified them as of the great American stage, playwrights, producers, actors, and even actresses.

They were present, as I gathered, to acquire local color for their current, or future contributions to the thespian art, and the hour was a trifle early for them to be abroad in the land. They sat yesterday writing through the proceedings and perhaps inwardly criticizing the stage setting and thinking how unrealistic the trial is as compared to their own productions.

Among the other spectators comfortably chaired, or standing on tired feet, were ladies running from a couple of inches to three yards wide. They were from all parts of Long Island, and the other boroughs of the large and thriving City of New York, the inmates of which are supposed to be so very blasé but who certainly dearly love their murder cases.

A big crowd waited in the hallways and outside the court house. Tearful females implored the obdurate cops guarding the stairs and the court room doors, to ease them through somehow.

It was a strange gathering. Solid-looking citizens found a morning to waste. They would probably have felt greatly inconvenienced had they been requested to spend the same amount of time on a mission of mercy. Several preachers and some of our best known public 'pests' were scattered around the premises. What a fine commentary, my friends, on what someone has mentioned as our vaunted intelligence.

Peggy Hopkins, Countess Morner and what not, Joyce, the famous grass-widow, came again to dazzle all the beholders with the magnificence of her display. It was Peggy's second visit. Probably she didn't believe her eyes and ears on her first visit that a lady had seemed to have some difficulty in getting rid of her husband. Peggy never did, you can bet on that. She wore a suit of a distressing green and a red fox collar and arrived at the court house in a little old last year's Rolls-Royce.

Paul Mathis, a thin, dark youth, was the first witness. He remembered carting Henry Judd from the Jamaica Station on the subway on Fifty-eighth Street, March 20, the morning of the murder.

The fare was $8.55. Gray gave him a five cent tip. It is not likely Mathis will ever forget Henry Judd if the young man is like the average taxi jockey.

William L. Millard of Gray's counsel, verbally belted away at Mathis rather snappishly, trying to find out if the young man's memory of Henry Judd hadn't been encouraged by the district attorney's office. Millard has a cutting voice when he is cross-examining and is given to sharp asides. The Court has generally admonished him on several occasions.

Justice Scudder does not allow the lawyers to get far out of conversational bounds. My friend, Senator Alexander Simpson, of Hall-Mills fame, would probably feel his style was quite cramped in Justice Scudder's court.

Van Voorhees, a thin, middle-aged man, conductor of the train that carried Gray back to Syracuse from his murder errand, identified Gray. So did George Fullerton, a dusky porter.

'We concede the defendant was on the train,' said Millard, closing that line of testimony.

Now came Haddon Gray, of 207 Clark Street, Syracuse, the insurance man who unwittingly helped Judd Gray with his famous alibi. Haddon and Judd had been friends twenty years, but are not related. Gray is a young man of brisk manner and appearance, of medium height, with black hair parted in the middle and slicked down. He was neatly dressed and displayed a lodge emblem on his watch chain and another on his lapel. He spoke very distinctly.

Haddon Gray said Judd had enlisted his support in Syracuse in the keeping of a date in Albany with a woman Judd referred to as 'Momsie.' Judd had once shown him a photo of 'Momsie.' Haddon Gray said he now knew her as Mrs Snyder.

This obliging Haddon, thinking he was merely assisting an old pal in a little clandestine affair, hung a sign, 'Don't Disturb,' on Judd's door at the Onondaga Hotel, rumpled the bed, called the desk downstairs and left word he was ill and was not to be aroused before a certain hour, and finally mailed some letters that Judd had written. All this after Judd had left Syracuse for New York.

Judd told Haddon he was afraid his firm might check up on him, wherefore the arrangements set forth above. Haddon did not hear from Judd again until Sunday afternoon, March 20, when Judd, just back from his bloody errand to Queens Village, called him on the telephone. Haddon Gray and a friend named Harry Platt went to see Judd at the Onondaga and Judd said he had not kept the 'date' in Albany as a telegram from Momsie had reached him there summoning him on to New York. Then the witness said Judd told him a startling story.

He—Judd—said he had gone to the home of Momsie while she and her husband were out and entered by a side door. He was waiting in a bedroom when he heard Momsie and her husband returning. Then he heard a great commotion and looking out through the door of the room he saw Momsie slugged by a dark man.

Henry Judd told Haddon he hid in a closet, and two men came in and rummaged around in the closet over his head, looking for something. Then they went out and Henry Judd bolstered up his courage and looked about. He went into a bedroom and found Momsie's husband on the floor. He lifted the man onto the bed, and said in doing so he must have gotten blood on his vest and shirt as he bent over the man and listened if his heart was beating.

He showed Haddon Gray the shirt and said it was Snyder's shirt but the witness wasn't clear as to how Judd explained having it. Also Judd had a suitcase containing the suit of clothes he had worn to New York, also the bloody shirt and a briefcase, which Harry Platt took to get rid of at Judd's request. Platt took the suitcase to his office.

After relating this tale Judd went to Haddon's home and spent the evening playing with Haddon's children. Haddon

came to New York after Judd's arrest, saw his old pal in jail and
said:

'Judd, did you do this?'

'Yes, Haddon; I did.'

Henry Judd, inert, head down as usual, never glanced up as
he heard his boyhood friend testify, and Haddon Gray proved
in his testimony that he was about as good a friend as a man
could hope to have.

Harry Platt, an insurance adjuster of Syracuse, very bald,
rather florid, and with glasses, was next. There was a touch of
the old beau to Harry's appearance. He repeated the tale of
slugging told him and Haddon by Judd. He said he gave the
suitcase to his stenographer to be destroyed.

Mrs Anna Boehm, of Syracuse, stenographer for Platt, a
plump lady wearing glasses and obviously a bit nervous, told of
receiving a package from Platt containing a suitcase. In the
suitcase was a suit of clothes and a hat. She gave it to her
husband. The husband, Anthony Boehm, corroborated that
statement. He burned the package in a furnace.

At 12:27, Newcombe stood up and said:

'The People Rest.'

There was a sudden stir and the bailiffs rapped for order. All
the attorneys gathered about Justice Scudder's bench in a
conference with the Court.

When the State rested rather sooner than was generally
expected, the attorneys for the defendants asked for time to
prepare certain motions. They were given until four o'clock in
the afternoon. These motions, all for dismissal on one ground or
another, were probably presented more on the broad premise
that they can't rule you off for trying, rather than the expectation they would be granted. Millard wanted the motions made
in the absence of the jury, but Justice Scudder saw no necessity
for that.

If the jurors didn't understand the motions any better than
most of the laymen collected in the court room, Justice Scudder
was quite right. The language was quite technical.

Now the woman and the crumpled little corset salesman, their once piping-hot passion colder than a dead man's toes, begin trying to save their respective skins from the singeing at Sing Sing, each trying to shove the other into the room with the little green door.

'What did Mrs Snyder say about the confession of Gray's— that squawk?' I asked her attorneys yesterday.

'Well, let's see, she said he—' began Dana Wallace, the buzzing, bustling little man who sits at Mrs Snyder's side in the court room when he isn't on his feet, which is seldom.

'She said—Well, wait now until I recall what she said,' put in Edgar Hazleton, the other attorney for the woman.

They seemed at a loss for words. I suggested: 'Did she say he is a rat?'

'Well I suppose it would amount to that in your language,' replied Wallace. (What did he mean 'my' language?) 'Only she didn't use that term.'

'No, no,' chimed in Hazleton, 'not rat.'

'She said, in substance, 'and to think I once loved that— that—' Well, I think she used a word that means something like coward,' Wallace concluded.

'Do you think she will keep her nerve on the stand?' I asked.

'Yes,' they both answered in unison.

I am inclined to think so, too.

Whatever else she may lack, which seems to be plenty, the woman appears to have nerve. Or maybe she hasn't any nerves. It is about the same thing.

In any event, she has never for a moment cowered like her once little pal of those loving days before the black early morning of March 20. She has been cold, calm, contemptuous, gusty, angry, but never shrinking, save perhaps in that little walk to and from the court between the recesses. She then passes before the hungry eyes of the spectators.

That seems to be her most severe ordeal. She grips her black corded-silk coat in front with both hands, and seems to hasten, her eyes straight ahead. However, we shall see about that nerve now.

April 30, 1927

We were, in a manner of speaking, in the chamber of horrors with Mrs Ruth Brown Snyder yesterday afternoon, mentally tip-toeing along, goggle-eyed and scared, behind her, when the blond woman suddenly gulped, and began weeping.

She had taken us, just before the tears came, step by step to a bedroom in her little home in Queens Village. We were standing there, you might say, all goose-pimply with the awfulness of the situation as we watched, through the medium of the story she told on the witness stand, the butchery of her husband by Henry Judd Gray.

Maybe the ghost of the dead art editor suddenly popped out on her as she got us into that room and was showing us the picture of the little corset salesman at his bloody work while she was trying to stay his murderous hand. Anyway, the tears came, welling up into the frosty eyes of the blonde and trickling down over that marble mask of a face.

Plump Mrs Irele Wolfe, the gray-haired matron of the Queens County jail, hurried to Mrs Snyder's side and put her arms around the weeping woman. A few sips from a glass of water, and Mrs Snyder was again composed sufficiently to go on with the fearful tale of the killing of her husband that she started early in the afternoon and by which she hopes to save herself from the electric chair.

She blamed it all on Gray, even as he will blame it all on her. The baggy little man sitting inertly, as always, in the chair just a few feet from her listened to the woman with only an occasional glance at her.

Yet it would be interesting to know his thoughts. This was his old Momsie. This was the woman he once thought he loved with a great consuming love—this woman who was trying to consign him to the electric juices. He seemed to stagger slightly as he walked out of the court room at the close of the session, whereas before he had tried to put a little snap into his tread.

This woman broke down twice while she was on the witness stand, once when she had us in that death chamber, with Henry Judd Gray pounding the life out of her husband, as she claims, and again when she mentioned the name of her nine-year-old daughter, Lorraine.

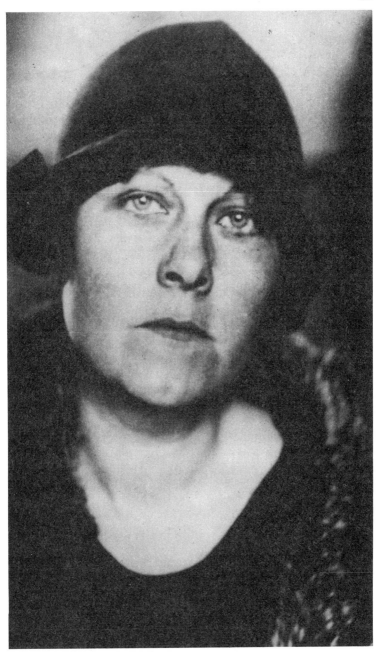

Ruth Snyder in a break during the trial.

But in the main she was as cold and calm sitting there with a thousand people staring at her as if she were at her dinner table discoursing to some guests. She kept her hands folded in her lap. She occasionally glanced at the jury, but mostly kept her eyes on Edgar Hazleton, one of her lawyers who examined her on direct-examination.

This examination was not concluded when Court took a recess at 4:30 until Monday morning. It is the custom of Queens County courts to skip Saturday.

Mrs Snyder wore the same black dress and black coat that has been her attire since the trial started. She made one change in hats since then, discarding a tight-fitting thing that made her chilly chin jut out like an iceberg. Someone probably told her that the hat was most unbecoming, so now she wears one with a brim that takes some of the ice out of the chin.

Her dress and coat are neither fashionable nor well cut, so I am informed by ladies who may be taken as authorities on the subject. Still, they make her look smaller than her weight of around 150 pounds would indicate. She wears black silk stockings and black pumps.

Her face was flushed a bit today, probably from excitement, but she uses no make-up. Slap a little rouge and powder on Mrs Snyder, give her a session with a hairdresser, and put some of Peggy Joyce's clothes on her, and she would be a snappy-looking young matron.

When her name was called by her attorney, Hazelton, soon after court opened this afternoon, she stood up quickly and advanced to the witness chair with a firm step. She had been twisting her hands and biting her nails just before that, however, indicating she felt nervous, which is not surprising, in view of the eyes turned on her.

It seems a great pity that old man Hogarth isn't living to depict the crowd scene in the court room yesterday. Tad* might do it, but Tad has too much sense to risk his life and limbs in any such jams.

Some strange-looking characters almost fought for a chance

---

*Tad was the penname of T.A. Dorgan, satiric artist whose drawings were a popular syndicated newspaper feature in the Twenties.

to leer at the principals in the trial. Apparently respectable men and women showed the court attendants cards, letters, badges, birth certificates and automobile licenses in an effort to impress the guardians of the portals with their importance and the necessity of their getting into the court room.

Dizzy-looking dolls said to represent the social strata of Park Avenue—the upper crust, as I understand—were there, not a little proud of their heroism in getting out so early. Some were escorted by silly-looking 'muggs' wearing canes and spats.

But also there were men who might be business men and women with something better to do, standing chin deep in the bloody scandal of this bloody trial and giving some offense to high heaven, it seems to me, by their very presence.

The aisles were jammed so tightly that even the smallest copy boys, carrying copy of the day as it ran red-hot from the fingers of the scribbling writers of the newspaper delegations, could scarcely wiggle through. The women outnumbered the men about three to one. They stood for hours on their tired feet, their eyes and mouths agape.

Justice Scudder peered over his glasses at a jammed court room and warned the crowd that at the first disturbance he would order the premises cleared.

Then he bowed slightly to the attorneys for the defense and Hazleton arose and stepped up to the table in front of the jury box.

He is a short, serious-looking man, with a hawk nose, and a harsh voice. A pince-nez straddled his beak. He wore a gray suit, and a white starched turned-down collar and a black tie yesterday morning. The collar flew loose from its neck and moorings early in Hazleton's discourse and one end scraped his ear.

He at first stood with his hands behind him, but presently he was gesticulating with his right, waggling a prehensile index-finger most forcibly. He perspired. He stood on his tiptoes. He was so close to Henry Judd that he almost stuck the index-finger in the defendant's eye when he pointed at Judd.

Occasionally a titter ran over the crowded court room at some remark made by Hazleton, who has an idiomatic manner of expression. That's what most of the crowd came for, apparently—to laugh at something, even though it might be human misery! The bailiffs would bawl 'Silence!' and glare around furiously.

The purport of Hazleton's opening was about what had been anticipated. He said he expected to show that Henry Judd Gray was the arch criminal of the whole affair, and he depicted him in the light of a crafty, designing fellow—

'Not the man you see sitting here,' yelled Hazleton, pointing at the cowering Henry Judd, while the eyes of the jurors turned and followed the finger. It was quite possible to believe that the villain described by Hazleton was not the man sitting there. Henry Judd looked anything but villainous.

Hazleton spoke about an hour, then Samuel L. Miller, of Gray's counsel, stepped forward, dark, stout, well-groomed and slick-haired—a New York type of professional young man who is doing all right.

He laid a batch of manuscript on the table in front of the jury and began to read his opening, rather an unusual proceeding. His opening addresses partook more of the nature of closing appeals. Miller had evidently given no little time and thought to his address and had dug up a lot of resounding phrases, but he was comparatively brief.

Harry Hyde, manager of the Jamaica branch of the Prudential Life Insurance Company, was the first witness called for Mrs Snyder. He is a thin man with a Woodrow Wilson face and glasses, and he kept his new spring topcoat on as he sat in the witness chair. His testimony was what you might call vague.

Hazleton tried to show by him that Mrs Snyder had called at his office relative to cancelling the insurance on her late husband's life, but he didn't recognize Mrs Snyder as the woman and didn't remember much of the conversation.

He did faintly recall some woman calling at his office, however, and speaking of the Snyder policies. District Attorney Newcombe moved to strike out the testimony, but the motion was denied.

John Kaiser, Jr., another insurance man of Jamaica, a heavy-set rotund man with a moustache and horn-rimmed specs, testified on the subject of the insurance policies that are said by the State to have been reasons for the murder of Albert Snyder.

He said he recalled Mrs Snyder coming to his offices and discussing the policies, but he couldn't recall the exact nature of the conversation.

Hazleton made a point of a clause in the policy that bore Snyder's signature, reserving the right to change the beneficiary.

Mrs Josephine Brown, mother of Mrs Snyder, was called.

Mrs Brown is a woman who must be around sixty. She speaks with a very slight accent. Mrs Brown is a Scandinavian. Her face is wrinkled and she wears gold-rimmed glasses. She was dressed in black but her black hat had a bright ornament. She gave her answers clearly and quickly.

She said her daughter had been operated on for appendicitis when she was a child and that the wound had to be reopened when she was eighteen. She lived with her daughter and son-in-law for six years and told of the visits to the Snyder home by Gray. On the third visit she told her daughter not to let Gray call again as 'it didn't look right.' Gray came no more.

On the occasions of his visit Mrs Brown said Gray talked mainly about the stock market.

Newcombe examined her closely as to her knowledge of Gray's relations with her daughter. She admitted she called him Judd and had never told Albert Snyder of his visits to the Snyder home. She was away on a professional visit the night Henry Judd hid in her room on murder bent.

So many daffy women and rattle-headed men outside, eager to see whatever they might see, rushed the court house corridors at one o'clock on a rumor that Mrs Snyder was on the stand, that the confusion took on the proportion of a riot. The halls and stairways were packed with struggling females. They pushed and shoved and pulled and hauled, and squealed and squawked. It was a sorry spectacle. The cops on duty at the court house were well nigh helpless against the onrush for a time.

Justice Scudder heard the tumult from his chambers and went out to take a look. Then he ordered the hallways cleared. In the meantime, the court room was jammed, and the spectators piled into the press section, grabbing all unoccupied seats. For half an hour the cops outside the court room would not recognize credentials of any kind until they could stem the human tide to some extent.

I doubt if there has ever been anything quite like it in connection with these trials, and I speak as a survivor of the Hall-Mills trial, and of the Browning trial, which wasn't a murder trial, except with relation to the King's English. The court room is said to be one of the largest in the country, but it could have been three times as large today and there wouldn't have been room for the crush.

A big crowd stood in the street outside all morning and afternoon, though they can see nothing there except the photographers at their sprinting exercises when a witness walks out of the court house.

When Mrs Snyder was sworn as a witness, Justice Scudder told her in a quiet voice that she was not required to testify as the law protected her but that on the stand she is subject to the same cross-examination as any other witness.

She turned in her chair and looked the judge in the face as he talked, and bowed slightly.

Her voice is a soprano, and very clear. It came out through the amplifiers much harsher than its natural tone, of course. The microphone on the desk in front of the witness stand was in the line of vision between Mrs Snyder and Hazleton, and she cocked her head to one side to get a clearer view of the lawyer.

She often emphasized some of her words, for instance, 'We were *not* happy,' when answering Hazleton's question about her married life with Albert Snyder. She never glanced at the staring crowd, though she often looked at the jury. As for the members of that solemn body, most of them watched her closely as she talked for a time, then their attention seemed to wander. Juror No 11 never looked at her at all, but then Juror No 11 never seems to be looking at anyone on the witness stand.

He has a faraway expression. Possibly he is wondering how business is going while he is away listening to all this murder stuff.

Mrs Snyder's first attack of tears came early in the examination, but was very short. The second time court suspended operations for several minutes while she wept. A dead silence reigned. It is well for men to remain silent when women weep, whatever the circumstances.

I asked a lot of men how she impressed them. They said they thought she made a good witness for herself. Then I asked some of the girls, who have been none too strong for Mrs Snyder, just as a general proposition. They, too, thought she had done very well.

You must bear in mind that this woman is talking for her life. If she is the cruel and cunning blond fury that Gray's story would cause you to believe, you would expect her to be calm. But if she is the wronged, home-loving, horror-stricken woman that her own tale would imply, her poise is most surprising.

She always referred to Albert Snyder as 'my husband,' and to her former paramour as 'Mr Gray'—'I tried to stop Mr Gray from hitting my husband and he pushed me to the floor. I fainted and when I came to I pulled the blanket off. . . .'—It was here that she was overcome by tears the second time.

She pictured Gray as the aggressor in the love-making of their early meetings. She wasn't happy at home, and she accepted the advances of the little corset salesman to intimacy. She said Gray was her only love adventure.

He borrowed her money and didn't pay it back, she said. He first suggested the idea of getting rid of her husband, and mentioned poisoning to her. Wherever Gray said 'she' in his confession, Mrs Snyder said 'he' in her testimony today. They have turned on each other with a vengeance, these two once-fervid lovers. There is no doubt they hate each other thoroughly.

It was difficult to tell just what effect Mrs Snyder's tale had on the jury, of course. In fact it would be unfair to make a guess until her tale is finished. It certainly had some elements of plausibility, despite the confession she now says was obtained under duress, and despite the motive of Albert Snyder's life insurance that is advanced by the prosecution.

Mrs Snyder's attorneys attempted to show today that she had tried to have the insurance reduced to cut down the premium, but their evidence on that point did not seem particularly strong. She insisted in her testimony that this had been the purpose.

She smiled just once with any semblance of joy, which was when Justice Scudder admitted, over the objections of the State, the bank books showing that Albert Snyder and Ruth had a joint account. It is by this account that the defense expects to show that Albert Snyder had full cognizance of his wife's payment of the premiums on the policies.

She says Gray always referred to Albert Snyder as 'the governor.' Once she accidentally tripped over a rubber gas tube in the house and pulled it off the jet. She went out and when she came back her husband was out of doors and said he had nearly been asphyxiated. She wrote Gray of the incident, and he wrote back:

'It was too damn bad the hose wasn't long enough to shove in his nose.'

When she testified in just that language there was something in her manner and way of speaking out the word that caused a distinct stiffening among the women in the court room.

'Brazen!' some of them whispered.

This gas jet incident, by the way, was alleged by the State to have been one of the times when Mrs Snyder tried to murder her husband.

She says Gray threatened to kill himself and her if she didn't do what he told her. She was afraid of Gray, she said, although the drooping little man in front of her didn't seem to be anything to be afraid of. She tried to break off with him, she said, and he threatened to expose her.

She said Gray sent her sleeping powers to give 'the governor' on the night of the party at Fidgeons', which was Albert Snyder's last night on earth. Moreover, Gray announced in the letter accompanying the powders, according to her testimony, that he was coming down Saturday to finish 'the governor.'

He came down all right.

'My husband was asleep. I went to my mother's room, where I met Mr Gray. We talked several minutes. He kissed me and I felt the rubber gloves on his hands. He was mad. He said, "If you don't let me go through with this I'll kill us both." He had taken my husband's revolver. I grabbed him by the hand and took him down to the living-room.

'I pleaded with him to stop when we got downstairs, then I

went to the bathroom. I said to Mr Gray, "I'll bring your hat and coat down to you." I heard a terrific thud. I rushed to my husband's room. I found Gray straddling my husband. I pulled the blankets down, grabbing him and then I fainted. I don't remember anything more.'

That's her story and I presume she will stick to it.

May 3, 1927

For five hours and a half yesterday questions went whistling past that marble chin of Mrs Ruth Brown Snyder's, but she kept on sticking it out defiantly from under the little brim of her black hat, like a fighter that can't be hurt.

At a pause just before recess in the old court room with the sickly yellow walls in Long Island City she reached out a steady hand, picked up a glass of water from the table in front of her, took a big swig, and looked at Charles F. Froessel, the assistant district attorney, who had been cross-examining her, as much as to say 'Well, come on.'

But Froessel seemed a bit fagged out, and mopped a steaming brow with a handkerchief as Justice Townsend Scudder granted a motion by one of Mrs Snyder's attorneys for a recess until tomorrow morning.

The dialogue between Froessel and Mrs Snyder toward the close of the day was taking on something of the aspect of a breakfast table argument between a husband and the little woman, who can't exactly explain certain matters that the old boy wants to know.

She is a magnificent liar, if she is lying. You must give her that. She stands out 'mid keen competition these days, if she is lying. And if a liar she is a game liar, one of those 'that's my story and I'll stick to it' liars, which is the mark of the able liar.

And I regret to report that she seems to impress many of her listeners in the light of a wonderful liar rather than as a poor widowed soul falsely accused. The men were rather softening up toward the blond woman at the close yesterday in sheer admiration of her as a possible liar, and even the women who leer at her all day long had stopped hating her. They seemed to be commencing to think that she was reflecting credit to femininity just as a prodigious liar.

Even Henry Judd Gray, the baggy-looking little corset sales-man who was on trial with her for the murder, and who has been sitting inert and completely befogged since the case began, sat up yesterday as if they had suddenly puffed air into him.

He had a fresh haircut and clean linen and looked all sharpened up. He half started when she fairly shrilled 'no' at Froessel when he was asking her about the life insurance on Albert Snyder. Perhaps Gray had heard her say 'no' in that same voice before.

It was about the life insurance for $53,000 on Snyder's life that the assistant district attorney was most curious in his cross-examination, and about which Mrs Ruth Brown Snyder was the least convincing. It was to double in the event of her husband's death by accident, and the State claims that Albert Snyder didn't know his wife had taken it out.

It was a very bad session for her on that particular point. Her answers were at times vague and evasive, but her voice never lost its snap. She said the only motive Gray could have had for killing her husband was to get the life insurance money, and when it was suggested to her that she was the beneficiary, she argued. 'Well, he knew he would get it away from me just as he got money from me before.'

'Isn't it a fact, that you and Gray planned to spend that insurance money together?' she was asked.

'No,' she said quickly.

Most of her answers were sharp yesses, or noes. In fact, Froessel insisted on yes-or-no answers, though sometimes she whipped in a few additional remarks to his great annoyance.

He hectored and badgered the blonde at times until her counsel objected and the Court admonished him. Froessel, a plump-built man of medium height, in the early forties, has a harsh voice and a nagging manner in cross-examination. He wears spectacles and is smooth-shaven and persistent, and there is no doubt that Mrs Snyder at times wished she had a sash weight handy.

She broke down once—that was when she was again leading the way into the room where her husband was butchered, and

Henry Judd Gray: a newspaper photo during the trial.

where she claimed she saw Judd Gray astraddle of Albert Snyder in the bed. She repeated the story she told on her direct-examination.

'I grabbed Judd Gray and he pushed me to the floor and I fainted. When I came to I pulled the blankets off my husband and—'

Then the tears came. There was a microphone on the witness stand, and her sniffles came out through the amplifiers quite audibly. Mrs Irene Wolfe, the plump matron of the county jail, moved to her rescue with water, and presently Mrs Snyder went on.

'Watch her hands,' a woman advised me. 'You can always tell if a lady is nervous by her hands. If she presses them together she is under a strain. If they are relaxed, she isn't nervous.'

So I watched Mrs Snyder's hands as they lay together in her lap. They were limp, inert. Once or twice she raised one to adjust a strand of yellow hair that drifted out under the little black hat, or to apply a small handkerchief to her well-shaped nose.

Under a dim light, backgrounded by the old brown plush hangings behind the judge's bench, and seated on an elevated platform, the black-gowned figure stood out distinctly. Occasionally she fingered the black jet beads at her throat, and she always leaned forward slightly, the white chin pushed out belligerently. Her feet were still. She sometimes shook her head to emphasize a 'no.' Her voice, a little raspy through the 'mike,' has a musical quality.

Her speech is the speech of your average next door neighbor in the matter of grammar. I mean to say she is no better and no worse than millions of the rest of us. She says 'ain't' but I just read a long dissertation by some learned fellow who says 'ain't' will eventually be considered good grammar.

She displayed more boldness than adroitness in her denials when it was patent that she didn't care to go into details.

But she showed no disposition to hide anything about her affair with Henry Judd Gray.

May 4, 1927

That scared-rabbit looking little man, Henry Judd Gray, the corset salesman, is now engaged in what the cops would describe as 'putting the finger' on Mrs Ruth Brown Snyder, only such a short time back his ever-loving, red-hot Momsie.

He seems to be a fairly expert 'finger man,' so far. Perhaps his proficiency goes back to his early youth and much practice pointing the accusatory digit and saying, 'Teacher, he done it.'

He lugged us through many a rendezvous in many a different spot with Mrs Snyder yesterday afternoon, while the lady, who had done a little 'fingering' herself for three days, sat looking daggers at Henry Judd, and probably thinking arsenic, mercury tablets, chloroform, picture wire and sash weights.

This was after she had come out of a spell of weeping when her little daughter, Lorraine, was on the stand. That was a spectacle, my friends—the child in the court room—to make the angels shed tears, and men hide their faces in shame, that such things can be.

Henry Judd had scarcely gotten us out of the hotels which he and Mrs Ruth Brown Snyder infested in the days—ah, yes, and the nights—when their heat for each other was up around 102 Fahrenheit, when a recess was taken until this morning.

Everybody was weary of traipsing up and down hotel corridors and in and out of hotel rooms, but Henry Judd kept making a long story longer under the direct examination of Samuel L. Miller, the stout, sleek-looking young lawyer who is associated with William L. Millard in defending Gray.

Henry Judd hadn't gotten right down to brass tacks, which is after all the story of the butchery of Mrs Snyder's husband, Albert, and which Henry Judd will undoubtedly blame on the blond woman who has made him out the arch-sashweighter of the bloody business.

He had gone over his own early life before he met Mrs Snyder and was a happy little corset salesman, with a wife and child down in New Jersey. He wept when he spoke of that, but composed himself with a stiff jolt of water from the same glass that had but recently been pressed by the lips of his former sweetie.

It was a dull, dry recital, especially those numerous little excursions to hotel rooms. A trip to one hotel room might be made exciting, but when you start going through one of these modern hotels, room by room, the thing lacks zest.

Gray stepped to the stand with a quick tread, and an almost soldierly bearing, which was most surprising in view of the fact he has looked all folded-up like an old accordion since the trial started. He did not commence straightening up until Friday, when he found Mrs Snyder nudging him toward that warm chair at Sing Sing.

He raised his right hand with great gravity as the clerk of the court administered the usual oath. He did not sit down until told to do so by Justice Townsend Scudder, and he listened gravely while Justice Scudder told him he did not have to testify unless he wished. Gray bowed to the Court.

Sitting there was a scholarly-looking young fellow, such a chap as would cause you to remark, 'There's some rising young author,' or maybe a college professor. He wore a dark, double-breasted suit of clothes with a white linen collar and a tie that had an almost indecorous stripe. A white handkerchief peeped out of the breast pocket of the coat.

His dark hair, slightly kinky, made a tall pompadour. His horn-rimmed spectacles have yellowish lenses, which, added to the old jail-house tan he has acquired, gave him a sickly complexion under the stand lamp by the witness stand with its three lights like a pawnbroker's sign.

His hands rested quietly in his lap, but occasionally he raised one to his probably throbbing forehead. His voice is slow and steady, and rather deep-throated. A cleft in the middle of his chin is wide and deep. The psychologists and philosophers have noted it without knowing just what to make of it. He has a strange trick of talking without moving his upper lip. Or maybe there isn't anything strange about it.

He answered Miller's questions without hesitation and with great politeness. You might say with suavity, in fact.

'I did, sir,' he would say. Always the 'sir.' He would impress you as a well-educated, well-bre, WELL-MANNERED YOUNG CHAP. You can't see inside 'em, you know. He has a remarkably bad memory that will probably get him in trouble when the abrupt Froessel, of the district attorney's office, takes hold of him.

'My memory does not serve me well as to conversation,' he remarked on one occasion. He did not seem to be abashed by any of the very personal questions asked him, or rather read by Miller, who has a stack of typewritten notes in front of him. He is obviously frightened, however, which is not surprising when you consider he is facing the electric chair.

He invariably referred to the blond woman, who he says got him in all this mess, as 'Mrs Snyder,' his tale of their introduction in Henry's restaurant by one Harry Folsom not varying from hers. He said he did plenty of drinking when he was with her on those hotel trips, and on jaunts through the night life of New York. She told him of her domestic troubles and he said she talked of leaving her husband and putting their child in a convent. He told her, so he said, that he hated to see a home broken up, which sounded almost ironical coming from a gent with a wife and child himself.

They exchanged Christmas presents, and he bought one for her mother.

Gray's own mother cried bitterly when her son took the stand. Mrs Snyder talked much to him on insurance, Henry Judd said, and once he had induced her to pour out some arsenic which she had in the house to poison rodents, and one thing and another, as she explained to him.

But he hadn't reached sash weights and such matters when Justice Scudder declared the recess. It was a long day in court, with much happening before the defense for Mrs Snyder rested and the defense of Gray began with the immediate production of Henry Judd.

Out of the dark tangles of this bloody morass there stepped for a brief moment a wraith-like little figure all in black— Lorraine Snyder, the nine-year-old daughter of the blond woman and the dead art editor. She was, please God, such a fleeting little shadow that one had scarcely stopped gulping over her appearance before she was gone.

She was asked just three questions by Hazleton as she sat in the big witness chair, a wide-brimmed black hat shading her tiny face, her presence there, it seemed to me, a reproach to civilization.

Justice Scudder called the little girl to his side, and she stood looking bravely into his eyes, the saddest, the most tragic little figure, my friends, ever viewed by gods or men.

'You understand, don't you, that you have to tell the truth?' asked Justice Scudder kindly. I thought he was going to seize the child in his arms.

'Yes,' she said faintly.

'Then sit right down there and listen carefully,' said Justice Scudder. 'If you do not understand the question just say, "I do not understand." Lean back in the chair and be comfortable. The Court rules the child shall not be sworn.'

So she sat down and the jurors gazed at her and everybody in the room felt like bawling. Mrs Snyder gasped and shed tears when her child appeared—tears that probably came from her heart.

She hasn't seen Lorraine since her arrest. I doubt if Lorraine saw her mother across the big room or that the child fully comprehended where she was. Surely she could not know that all these strange-looking men gathered there were trying to kill her mother. It was a relief when Lorraine left the stand. Two minutes more and they would have been short one reporter in the press section.

'Lorraine,' said Hazleton, 'do you remember the morning your mother called you?'

'Yes, sir.'

'Was it daylight or dark?'

'Light.'

'And how long after she called you did you call the Mulhausers?'

'Right away,' piped the child.

'That's all,' said Hazleton.

'Not one question by the district attorney, Your Honor,' said Newcombe.

'No questions,' said Miller of Gray's counsel.

Thereafter while Gray was being examined, Mrs Snyder sat with her elbows on the table, her head bowed, a picture of dejection as great as that presented by Gray for some days. The child seemed to have touched her heart, and the defiant pride with which she has faced her accusers disappeared.

Finally the head came up again and the greenish blue eyes, a bit watery, were leveled on Gray, but it soon drooped once more. The woman seemed a picture of remorse. One-tenth the thoughts she was giving to Lorraine at that moment applied three months ago would have kept her out of that court room.

Mrs Snyder was on the stand three hours and a half yesterday. She quit the witness chair at 2:05 at the afternoon session and walked with slow step back to her seat at her attorneys' table followed by plump Mrs Wolfe, the jail matron.

She was 'all in.' She kept her head down as she passed in review before the leering eyes of the spectators. Her face was a dead, dull white. Her dearest girl friends, as Mrs Snyder calls them, couldn't have called her pretty without being arrested for perjury. She looked very badly indeed. She had no pep left but still I defy any other woman to produce any pep after so many hours of dodging.

The conclusions of some of the more nervous listeners at the close of Mrs Snyder's examination were that hereafter no blonde shall be permitted to purchase a window sash weight without a prescription and that all male suburbanites should cancel their life insurance forthwith and try all the doors before going to bed.

She left not one but two doors open for Henry Judd Gray, so Froessel dug out of her. I think the fact of these unlocked doors will weigh heavily against Mrs Snyder when the jury commences tossing the evidence into the scales of consideration. That, and the insurance that 'the governor' didn't know was loaded on his life. He was carrying plenty of weight along with this mortal coil, was 'the governor.' That was Henry Judd Gray's name for him. Imagine the gall of the little whippet who sneaked into Albert Snyder's home and had a jocular title for him!

Not much jocularity to Henry Judd Gray now as he shrinks in and out of the court room in Long Island City while the ponderous machinery of the law grinds the sausage of circumstance into links of evidence.

It is likely that the case will go to the jury by Friday. It has taken two weeks to try a mother that the citizens of Pueblo County, Colorado, could have settled in two minutes under any cottonwood tree on the banks of the Arkansas, if all the State of New York has developed is true. But the citizens of Pueblo County are forehanded and forthright gents.

Spectators were permitted to remain in the court room during the noon recess and the ladies brought their ham sandwiches and tatting right along with them to while away the hour. They gossiped jovially about the troubles of their sister, Ruth, and a lovely time was apparently had by all. Strange it is, my friends, that morbid impulses move the gals to bite and kick for a place on the premises where a sad, distorted version of life is being aired.

The reader may recall that yesterday I drew attention to the blonde's magnificence as a liar, if she were lying, and today she stepped right out and admitted her qualifications as a prevaricator. She claimed the belt, you might say, when the following tête-à-tête came off between her and Assistant District Attorney Charles F. Froessel when the cross-examination was in progress this morning. 'You lied to the neighbors?' 'Yes.' . . . 'You lied to the policemen?' 'Yes.' . . . 'You lied to the detectives?' 'Yes.' . . . 'You lied to Commissioner McLaughlin?' 'Yes . . . 'You lied to the Assistant District Attorneys?' 'Yes.' . . . 'You lied to your mother?' 'Yes.' . . . 'You lied to your daughter?' 'Yes.' . . . 'You lied to everybody that spoke to you or with you?' 'Yes.'

If that isn't lying it will do until some lying comes along.

Mrs Snyder came in for the morning session looking a bit more marbley than usual. She seemed somewhat listless as Froessel began 'madaming' her again. Her voice was tired. Still, nearly six hours on a witness stand is not calculated to enliven anyone.

Froessel started off in soft accents as if he wished to be a gentleman no matter how painful, possibly in view of the fact that some folks thought he was a little harsh with her Monday. By about the third question, however, he was lifting his voice at the witness. He desired brevity, yes or no, in her answers, since she had a penchant for elucidation. Froessel didn't seem to realize that a blonde loves to talk.

She sat all morning with her hands in her lap; listless, loose hands they were. The familiar black jet beads were missing from the throat in the morning, but she came back with them in the afternoon and toyed with them constantly. Nerves at last!

The greenish blue eyes looked at Froessel so coldly that once he shivered and glanced around to see whence came that draft.

The blond woman wasn't as self-possessed as she had been the day before and she got somewhat tangled up right off the reel as to what she had testified with reference to her knowledge of Gray's murderous intentions against 'the governor.' The poor old 'governor'! There were two strikes on him any time he walked under his own rooftree.

The ice in the blonde cracked up as Froessel kept picking at her, and her voice was petulant as she answered one question with: 'I tell you I don't remember what I did.'

She was sore at Froessel, that was apparent. It takes a bold man to deliberately make a blonde sore, even though she be a prisoner of old John Law. Froessel yelled at her with great violence, especially when she tried to go beyond his questions, and she gave him some very disquieting glares.

'May I explain that?' she asked a couple of times.

'You may not!' he said acidly, and the greenish blue eyes sizzled.

'Just answer questions, madam, and do not attempt to explain matters,' said Justice Scudder from the bench, peering down at her over his glasses.

'Well, yes or no covers so much, Judge, I can't answer,' she replied sulkily.

Froessel escorted the woman back to her home in Queens Village and to that bloody early morning of March 20. He went over her story on that occasion with her, word by word. He got a bit excited at her answers and hammered the table with great violence.

'No buts—no buts!' he yelled.

'I object to the attitude of the district attorney,' interposed Hazleton, and Justice Scudder chided Froessel, but requested Mrs Snyder to be more direct in her answers.

'And when you went into the room of your mother you saw

Henry Judd Gray was there again. . . . And the first thing he did was to kiss you?'

'Yes.'

'And you kissed him?'

'Yes.'

'Knowing, or believing, whatever you want to say, that he was there to kill your husband?'

'Yes.'

Just like that.

Three gentlemen contemplating marriage to blondes hastened to the telephone booths to cancel their troth, shivering in their boots as they went.

She said that the thud she heard while she was in the bathroom was the impact of the sash weight landing on the sleeping Albert Snyder. It must have sounded like Babe Ruth hitting a home run, judging from her description, though the doctors found no fracture of the skull.

Anyway, that was when she rushed to her husband's room to find Gray on the bed astraddle of Albert Snyder, where she grabbed at Gray, when he pushed her away, and when she fainted—as she told it.

Froessel was very curious about her actions after she came out of the faint. He wanted to know if she had tried to do anything for her husband in the way of kindly ministration. Any wifely aid? Any tender care?

'No,' she said, just like that. She hadn't done a thing, merely pulled back the blankets and took a quick look at him. She said she didn't see the wire around his throat or anything like that. She didn't even touch the body to see if it was cold.

Jim Conroy, another assistant district attorney, got out the suitcase that was checked at the Waldorf by Gray and which was recovered by the police after the murder.

'Whose pink pajamas are these?' asked Froessel, as Conroy, a young man, blushingly held up some filmy robes de nuit, as we say at the club.

'Mine,' she said.

'Whose blue pajamas are these?' asked Froessel, and Conroy gingerly exhibited more slumber suitings.

'Gray's,' she answered, grimly. No 'Mr Gray,' not even

'Judd Gray,' today. Just Gray-like.

'Whose toilet articles are in this box?' inquired Froessel.

'Both,' she said, laconically.

Hazelton objected to the district attorney 'parading for the forty-ninth time adultery before this jury—we are not trying that.' The spectators glared at Hazleton for interference with their just due for all the effort it cost to get into the court room.

Froessel picked up a copy of the confession she made immediately after the murder and read it line by line, asking after each line, 'Is that the truth?'

He finally got tired of asking that and requested her to say 'yes' or 'no' at proper intervals and save his breath.

She denied most of the statements attributed to her in the confession, especially with any reference to her part in the actual slaughter of her husband. She had more lingual vigor left at the finish than he did.

May 5, 1927

Bloody apparitions rising out of his memory of that dreadful night in Queens Village probably gibbered at the window of Henry Judd Gray's soul yesterday afternoon.

His voice kept lifting, and hurrying, as he sat on the witness stand, telling his version of the murder, until finally as he reached the climax of the tale, it came pouring out of the amplifiers with a rush, hard driven by a note of terror.

You wouldn't have been much surprised to see the little corset salesman suddenly leap up and go tearing out of the crowded court room with his hair on end. The red fingers of fear were clutching his heart as he said:

'I struck him on the head, as nearly as I could see, one blow. I think I hit him another blow, I think I hit him another blow because with the first blow he raised up in bed and started to holler. I went over on the bed on top of him, and tried to get the bedclothes over his mouth, so as to suppress his cries.' A distinct thud was heard and a commotion stirred the men and women packed like sardines in one part of the court. A couple of court attendants quickly picked up the limp form of Warren

Schneider,* brother of the dead man, and carried him from the court room, beating the air with his hands and crying aloud, 'Albert, Albert.'

Few eyes turned to see. They were all watching the man on the witness stand, up to this moment more like a baggy dummy, popping out, through a mechanical mouth, words thrown in by the ventriloquist's voice.

'He was apparently full of fight. He got me by the necktie. I was getting the worst of it because I was being choked. I hollered, "Momsie, Momsie, for God's sake help me." I had dropped the sash weight. She came over and took the weight and hit him on the head, and throwing the bottle of chloroform and the handkerchief and the wire and everything onto the pillow.'

Necks craned for a look at the woman who has been called 'The Bloody Blonde,' as she sat almost hidden from view among her attorneys and guards, and the spectators crowded in close around her on every side. The blond head, covered with a little black hat was bent low. You could not see the marble white face at that moment. It was between her hands. She was crying. Her mother, Mrs Josephine Brown, was crying. So, too, was the mother of Henry Judd Gray, a small woman in black. She was sitting so close to Mrs Snyder she could have reached out and snatched the black hat off the blond head.

The spectators gasped. For one brief moment, at least, Henry Judd Gray, most of the days of his life a dull, drab sort of a fellow, busied with a corset clientele, attained the proportions of a dramatic figure.

He was gulping as he turned on the high light of his tale, and frequently swigged water from the glass on the table in front of him. His attorney, Samuel L. Miller, stepped to the bench at 4:30, the usual hour of the afternoon recess, and suggested the recess to Justice Scudder.

'Oh, I can go on all night,' Gray spoke up, addressing his remarks to the Court. 'There are some points that I want to clear up.'

Justice Scudder nodded.

---

* Albert Snyder had modified the family name.

The little corset salesman started to backtrack in his story and Justice Scudder said, 'You told us that a moment ago.'

'Well, I'd like to go back if possible, Your Honor, because we went down into the cellar.'

'Very good, but don't repeat.'

'I see,' said Gray, picking up the crimson trend of his story, on down to where he said, his voice now lifting even above any previous note:

'I tied her feet. I tied her hands. I told her it might be two months, it might be a year, and it might be never, before she would see me again—and I left her lying on her mother's bed, and I went out.'

His voice broke. The eyes that show much white, like the eyes of a mean mule, glistened behind the yellowish glasses in the vague light of the old court room. Henry Judd Gray, but a few minutes before the stark figure of a dreadful tale of blood, was close to blubbering.

As the Court announced the recess, a bable of voices broke out in the court room, and men and women stared at one another and argued noisily.

'I say to you that if ever human lips uttered the truth, this was the time!' bawled Willard Mack, the playwright, one fist clutching a wad of paper, the other his hat, as he stared about him wild-eyed and excited. 'They'll never shake that fellow!'

'The man told a good story,' ruminated David Belasco, the famous dramatist and producer, who hasn't missed a day of the trial. 'I thought he would. A good story, indeed—indeed—but,' and he shook his gray head, 'weak in spots, weak in spots.'

Thus the opinions differed among the celebrities, and we had a fresh batch of them, including Olga Petrova, and Irving Berlin, and Ruth Hale, the Lucy Stoner, who would officially be Mrs Heywood Broun if her conscience permitted. Also Frankie Farnum, the hoofer, as well as all our good old standbys like the Marquis of Queensbury.

One thing is certain, Henry Judd Gray made a far stronger impression on the side of veracity than did the lady who is popularly referred to as his paramour. At times I thought Henry Judd was undergoing all the keen pleasure of a small boy telling a swell ghost story to his playmates such was his apparent joy, but along toward the finish my flesh was creeping, like everybody else's.

At first he seemed to have a certain air of bravado, perhaps a remnant of the same curious spirit that may have sent him into the murder in the first place—the desire of a weakling fellow to show off, you might say.

But gradually it became rather apparent it seemed to me, that here was a man who had something on his chest that he greatly desired to unload. He was making public confession, perhaps by way of easement to a sorely harassed conscience.

That is, if he was indeed telling the truth, the whole truth, and nothing but the truth, so help him God. He put all the blame on the woman, to be sure.

He said she egged him on to the murder, steadily, insistently, until he found himself sprawling on top of poor Albert Snyder that night in Queens Village. He said she plied him with liquor at all times. He made himself out pretty much of an 'A-No 1' fathead right from taw, a victim of an insidious blonde, though at no time yesterday did he mention any of his feelings for her, if any.

That will perhaps come today. He babbled all their indiscretions, though it was expected he would tell even more—and worse. In fact, it was rumored during the afternoon that Gray's counsel intended asking the court to bar the ladies from the court room, a canard that had several hundred females prepared to go to law for their rights as listeners.

If anyone retains an impression that Prohibition still prevails in the land, they should read Henry Judd Gray's testimony, although they may get a vicarious snootfull before they have gone very far, if they are susceptible to suggestion.

Henry Judd was quite a rumpot to hear him tell it, especially when he was with Mrs Snyder. He said she cared for gin, while he went in for Scotch. He inhaled all of a small bottle of whiskey left for him by Mrs Snyder and most of a quart that he found himself in the room the night he waited in the Snyder home on murder bent.

In fact, one gathered the murder was conceived in whiskey and executed in whiskey, as is not uncommon with many other forms of crime these days. They were in bed together in the

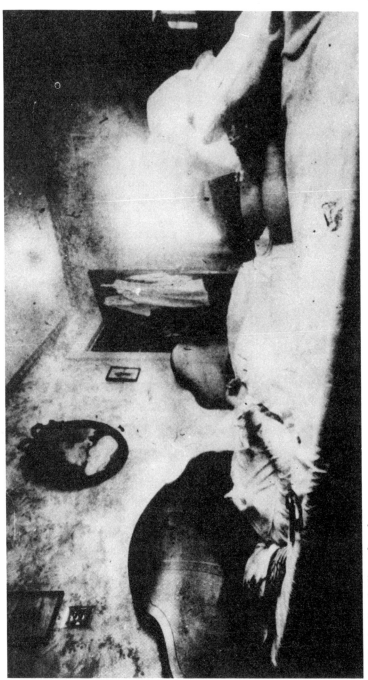

The body of Albert Snyder.

Waldorf, and she had come in 'so plastered up' that he had a lot of trouble getting her into the feathers, when she first suggested the murder to him.

It was born in that bed in the Waldorf, he said, about the third week in February of 1927. 'The plan that was later carried out,' as Henry Judd put it.

One way and another, Henry Judd gave Mrs Ruth Brown Snyder quite a bad reputation with the jurors, who sat listening open-mouthed to his tale, though it must be admitted he didn't spare himself. He pictured himself more as an able two-handed drinker than as a murderer, however. He gave the palm to Mrs Snyder in this respect.

'I had two or three drinks,' or 'I had four or five drinks,' or 'I drank plenty.'

This was the tenor of the early part of his discourse, tending to show no doubt that he was generally well tanked-up when he was with Mrs Snyder. In fact, he said he was usually in a fog. He must have been if he drank all he says, what with the quality of liquor these days.

Mrs Snyder's favorite pastime was trying to knock her husband off, as one gathered from Henry Judd's tale. She told Gray she had tried sleeping powders, gas, auto accidents, and bichloride of mercury, but had no luck. She put it just that way to Gray, he testified—'no luck.'

She gave him four mercury tablets when he had an attack of hiccoughs, so she informed Gray, and the corset salesman says he remarked, 'My God, don't you know that's deadly poison?'

'I thought so, too, but it only made him vomit.'

'It is a wonder it didn't kill him.'

'It is a wonder,' she agreed, 'but it only made him vomit fifteen or sixteen times that night.'

'What were the aftereffects of this?' Gray asked her, he said.

'It apparently cured the hiccoughs,' she replied.

'Well, that's a hell of a way to cure hiccoughs,' Gray said was his comment. There were no titters from the crowded court room. Somehow, the situation in which poor Albert Snyder moved, was commencing to dawn on the spectators. They gazed in wonder and awe at the blond woman who is all the Borgias rolled into one, if what Gray says is true.

She was despondent most of the day. The defiance with which she faced the world at first has faded. Only once or twice she sat up yesterday and glared at Gray. His recital of the ten-day trip that they took through New York State, told without the omission of any of the details, was probably shameful even to this woman who must be shameless, if what the man says is the truth.

He admitted he borrowed money from her, but he claimed he had paid it all back a little at a time, except $25, which he still owes her. Mrs Snyder will probably always have something coming to her. The impression you got from Gray's early recital was of a most despicable little tattle-tale, but you must bear in mind the man is fighting for his life, and men stoop to anything when life is at stake.

Gray's testimony, as drawn from him by Attorney Miller, was really not much different from the story set forth in his original confession made to the police and already read into the records of this case, save in detail, until he came to the murder.

You may remember Mrs Snyder says she was in the bathroom when she heard a thud, and looked into her husband's room to find Gray astride her husband on the bed. She said she tried to pull Gray away, that he pushed her, and that she fainted, and recalls nothing else.

It is for the twelve good men and true to say who is telling the truth. For the first week of the trial, the blond woman appeared to be the stronger character of the two, and with the little corset salesman an inert heap in his chair, she was apt to impress the casual observer.

Now the situation is just reversed. The woman seems to be completely sunk, and while I wouldn't say that Gray stands out as any Gibraltar, he at least shows some signs of life. But where she seemed defiant, he appears repentant in his attitude. He did not hate Albert Snyder—he had never met the man, he testified yesterday, though he may have seen him on one occasion with Mrs Snyder, whereas he claims the woman often expressed to him her dislike of her husband. Gray said:

'She asked me once if I would please help her out by shooting her husband. I said absolutely no. I had never shot a man in my life, and I wasn't going to start in by murder. She asked me if I knew of any other plan, and I said absolutely no, I could not help her out, and she must see the thing through alone.'

But she kept at him, he said. Blondes are persistent, as well as insidious. She kept at him. Drunk, or sober, he was always hearing the suggestion that he step out to Queens Village and slaughter Albert Snyder. You couldn't have seen the average man for heeldust after the first crack from the lady, but Henry Judd held on.

He suggested something of Mrs Snyder's regard for him by testifying she said she would rather have him at home at all times instead of traveling around with those corsets, though he were only a truck driver.

'I told her that was impossible, that I had a family and a home to maintain and that they must be taken care of—that I would not break up my home,' Henry Judd so declared, though it was quite apparent he didn't have any qualms about breaking up Albert Snyder's home.

He often cleared his throat as he talked, probably stalling a bit for time before his answers, though in the main he answered only too readily to suit attorneys for Mrs Snyder. Both Dana Wallace and Edgar Hazleton were on their feet several times objecting to the testimony.

Henry Judd said he didn't know much about life insurance, but testified Mrs Snyder had shown him one of her husband's policies and wanted to know how much she would get from it in case of his death. It would appear Mrs Snyder went to work on that murder thought with Henry Judd soon after they met in the often-mentioned Henry's restaurant.

He at first told her that she was crazy and advised her to have a doctor look at a bump on her blond head. But she kept at him.

She wrote him every day and bought him silk pajamas. She even bought a Christmas present for his little daughter, who is about the same age as Lorraine. This was when there was a general exchange of presents between Henry Judd and Mrs Snyder. She told him she enjoyed spending money on him.

The story of their ten-day trip to Kingston, Albany, Schenectady, Amsterdam, Gloversville, Booneville, Watertown and Syracuse was interesting only in its disclosures of the fact that you can get plenty of liquor in those spots. At least,

Henry Judd did. He took a few drinks about everywhere they stopped, and they both got loaded in Scranton, Pa. when the trip was coming to an end.

It was when they got back from that journey that Henry Judd commenced to be more reasonable when she talked of making a murderer of him. He finally told her he would buy some chloroform for her but wouldn't help her use it. In the end he fell for it.

She had spoken about some heavy instrument, such as a hammer as a good thing to use in tapping Albert Snyder while he slept before the chloroform was applied.

'I think I suggested the window weight,' remarked Gray, quietly. He bought one on a trip to Kingston, a little later, bought the chloroform, the colored handkerchief, and all else.

'I went to Albany and had a lot of drinks, and I got to thinking this thing over, and I thought how terrible it was and I—'

'One moment,' bawled Hazleton, and the Court said never mind what he thought, to Gray.

He said Mrs Snyder wrote him outlining what he should do, just as he related in the original confession, and he obeyed her instructions, he said. He didn't say why. That remains the most interesting thing that he has to tell—Why?

He told of going down to Mrs Snyder's March 7 with the idea of disposing of the murder matter then, but Mrs Snyder met him at the kitchen door and said the time wasn't ripe. He walked around Queens Village quite a bit before he went to the house, Gray said; the mention of his wanderings telling more of his mental trepidations than anything else could have done.

Then came the plans for the second attempt, which proved only too successful.

'My God,' Mrs Snyder said to him at a meeting before the murder, 'you're certainly nervous, aren't you?'

'I certainly am. I hardly know what I am doing.'

Henry Judd shed what we might accept as a sort of sidelight on the Mrs Snyder that was before she bogged down under the strain of the past two weeks, when he testified about the letters she wrote to him when he was on the road, and the murder plot was well afloat.

She asked about his health. About his business. She mentioned little Lorraine. Then she told him to drop down by her home Saturday night and bring the things he carried, which were the murder things. She concluded:

'I hope you aren't as nervous as you were.'

May 6, 1927

Mankind at last has a clue, developed by the Snyder-Gray trial, as to the approximate moment when a blonde becomes very, very dangerous.

Gentlemen, if she asks you to try out a few sleeping powders, that is the instant you are to snatch up the old chapeau and take the air.

Henry Judd Gray gave this valuable tip to his fellow citizens from the witness stand yesterday, when he was under cross-examination.

He said that not until Mrs Ruth Brown Snyder induced him to serve as a sort of guinea pig of experimentation with sleeping powders, which she purposed using on her husband, did he realize he was completely under the spell of her magnetism that caused him to later join hands with her in the slaughter of her husband, Albert Snyder.

It was in May a year ago, that he inhaled the powders for her so she might see how they would work. He had knocked around with her quite a bit up to that time, but it seemed the old spell hadn't got down to business. After that, he said, he knew he would do anything she wanted.

He was in her power. Narrowly did I escape writing it powder. It wasn't fear, he said; no, not fear. She had never threatened him. It was more magnetism than anything else.

'And this magnetic force drew you on even without her presence and was so great it overcame all thoughts of your family—of your wife and child?'

So asked Dana Wallace, one of Mrs Snyder's attorneys, who was cross-examining for her side. There was a note of curiosity in the lawyer's voice.

'Yes,' said Henry Judd Gray, and the spectators turned from

him to peer at Mrs Snyder, the blond magnet. She looked about as magnetical as a potato yesterday. She sat crouched at her attorney's table with her black hat between her hands most of the time, though now and then she lifted her face to glare at Henry Judd.

One side of the marble mask is now red from the pressure of her hand against it as she listens to the man who claims she magnetized him into a murderer. He was surprisingly steady under Wallace's hammering at his story of the crime.

Someone remarked it may be because he is telling the truth. It is always rather difficult to rattle a man who sticks to the truth, a bright and highly original thought for the editorial writers.

Wallace is trying in his cross-examination to make it appear that Henry Judd's was the master mind of the murder, and, while Henry Judd is not dodging a lot of activity in the matter, he is harking back to the original defense of man, the same being woman. I wonder if Eve was a blonde?

Early in cross-examination, Wallace had Henry Judd standing up in the witness chair with the sash weight that figured to such an extent in the butchery held in his hands, showing the pop-eyed jurors just how he slugged the sleeping art editor on the early morning of March 20.

Henry Judd has a sash-weight stance much like the batting form of Waner, of the Pittsburgh Pirates. He first removed his big horn-rimmed glasses at Wallace's request.

'Show us how you struck.'

'I used both hands, like this.'

So explained the corset salesman, lifting the sash weight, which weighs five pounds, and looks like an old-fashioned coupling pin over his right shoulder. He 'cocked it,' as the ball players would say, pretty well back of his right ear. He is a right-hand hitter.

The tags tied to the sash weight to identify it as evidence dangled from the heavy bar below Gray's hands. The jurors and the spectators stared at the weird presentation. Gray did not seem at all abashed or nervous. Wallace asked, 'How hard did you strike?'

'Well, I could not strike very hard.'

He said Mrs Snyder had done a little practicing with the sash weight first—perhaps a bit of fungo hitting—and found that the weight was too heavy for her, and asked him to pinch hit for her when the time came.

'Did you practice with her?' demanded Wallace.

'Well—ultimately,' remarked Gray.

It was a gruesomely humorous reply, though I doubt if Henry Judd intended it that way.

You may recall that he said on direct examination that after he whacked Snyder one or two blows—he is not sure of the number—he dropped the sash weight to pile on top of the struggling art editor, and that Mrs Snyder picked up the weight and beaned her husband.

Wallace picked on Gray on that point no little and in the course of the dialogue the corset salesman uttered one tremendous truism.

'You testified you thought you hit him another blow because at the first blow he raised up in bed and started to holler,' said Wallace. 'Didn't you hear Dr Neail testify here that any of the three blows that struck Snyder would by itself have rendered him unconscious?'

Gray gazed owlishly at the lawyer through his thick yellowish lenses, and said, 'I was there, Mr Wallace, and Dr Neail wasn't.'

One thing Wallace did manage to do was to make it rather clear in his cross-examination that Gray did a lot of able, if murderous thinking, in going about the crime, especially for a man who was as soaked with booze as Gray claims he was. He had already drunk enough in his story to sink the battleship *Mississippi*.

He started out with the inevitable 'I had a few drinks' with which he prefaces most of his answers, and Wallace interrupted.

'Is there any day you know of in connection with this case that you didn't take a lot of drinks?' he demanded.

'Not since I've known Mrs Snyder,' replied Gray with surprising promptness.

When closely pressed, he was almost defiant, and sometimes a trifle stubborn. Wallace kept asking him about the chloroform—whose thought was that?

'Wasn't it your idea?' Wallace asked.

'Well, let it be my idea,' replied Gray.

He admitted he picked up a piece of Italian newspaper on the train en route to New York to kill Snyder and that it was after the murder he had suggested the mention of two foreigners by Mrs Snyder, whereas in the original plan for the crime, a colored man had been in their minds as the fictitious object of suspicion.

It developed, too, from his cross-examination that the murder was finally planned in a chop suey place in Jamaica. He admitted he took the wire from his office with which Snyder's throat was bound. He said she had told him to get rope, but he didn't get the rope because 'his mind was on his work' and he didn't think of it until he was leaving his office.

'Well, was Mrs Snyder's presence or spirit around you in the atmosphere dominating and controlling you when you picked up the wire?' demanded Wallace.

'It might have been,' said Gray.

'Do you believe in such things?' queried Wallace, eyeing the man carefully.

'I might,' answered Gray.

It seems that Henry Judd has some sense of shame left anyway, and probably a lot of remorse. Wallace got to questioning him on his testimony that he and Mrs Snyder occupied Lorraine Snyder's room for their intimacies whenever he went to the Snyder home.

'In spite of the fact that you had a little girl of your own, you did that?' asked Wallace.

'I'm ashamed to say I did,' replied Gray.

'You forgot your own flesh and blood?'

'I'm ashamed to say I did.'

Mrs Snyder raised her head and looked at him. Then she shook her head and dropped her face in her hands again. Gray said that, with only one or two exceptions, they always used the child's room as their trysting place, if that is what you call it.

Wallace referred to the plot for the murder formulated in the chop suey joint as 'the Chinese plan,' and Millard asked, 'Is that facetious, Your Honor?'

'The Court is quite ignorant,' replied Justice Scudder, wearily. 'The Court could not say. Proceed, gentlemen.'

Gray said, rather surprisingly, that he was not thinking of murder when he prepared his Syracuse alibi. He didn't know why he had picked up the waste in the street in Rochester that was used to give Albert Snyder chloroform. At times he didn't remember, too.

Hazleton darted to Wallace's side at intervals and coached his partner on some questions. Gray held himself in such a collected manner that both Miller and Millard, his counsel, were grinning gleefully.

He admitted he had felt the hands of the dead man, Snyder, though later he said it might have been the foot, and 'announced to the widow,' as Wallace casually put it, he thought the art editor was defunct. He said Mrs Snyder was standing at his side at the moment.

But he claimed he never saw the wire around Snyder's neck. He pressed a pistol into Snyder's hand though he couldn't exactly explain why. He denied Wallace's suggestion it was to show Snyder's fingerprints on the gun.

He admitted removing his glasses before entering the bedroom, and said the reason he took them off, he thought, was in case of anything in the way of a fight.

'So your mind was so attuned to the situation, that although you were drinking, you were preparing yourself for a combat?' asked Wallace. 'Not necessarily—no,' replied Gray.

That was where he was weak—on his explanation of his apparently well-planned actions leading up to them.

'And you remember that occasion very well when you struck Snyder, don't you?' asked Wallace.

'I do not remember very well now,' answered Gray.

He claimed he was in a haze from the time of the murder until he had passed Albany on his way back to Syracuse, yet he admitted sweeping up the cellar to hide his footprints and arranging to have the sash weight covered with ashes to make it appear it hadn't been touched. He said he did these things 'automatically.'

'You mean your mind was working to protect yourself?'

'Not necessarily—no.'

'Well, what did you do it for?'

'I don't know.'

Court then recessed until ten o'clock this morning.

Our line-up of celebrities was fairly strong again yesterday taking the field as follows:

Marquis of Queensbury, L.F.

Dave Belasco, R.F.

Olga Petrova, 1 b.

Francine Larrimore, 2 b.

Thurston, 3 b.

Willard Mack, ss.

Clare Briggs, c.f.

Lois Meredith, c.

One-eyed Connolly, p.

Mr Brick Terrett, one of the gentlemanly inmates of the press section, circulated a petition among his brethren that Thurston, the magician, be requested to conjure up a few additional seats from his hat for the newspaper folks.

It was a swell idea.

This remains the best show in town, if I do say so, as I shouldn't. Business couldn't be better. In fact, there is some talk of sending out a No. 2 company and 8,000,000 different blondes are being considered for the leading female role. No one has yet been picked for Henry Judd Gray's part but that will be easy. Almost any citizen will do with a little rehearsal.

May 7, 1927

The Snyder-Gray murder trial—you instinctively put the woman first in this instance–is about over, and the twelve good men and true, who have been stolidly listening to the horrible tale for two weeks will decide soon what shall be done with this precious pair, the cheaters who tried to cheat the laws of God and man and wound up trying to cheat each other.

At about three o'clock yesterday afternoon, all hands rested as they say when they have dug up all the testimony they think will do any good, or any harm, either. If the Sabbath peace and quiet of any neighborhood is offended by loud stentorian voices, that will be the lawyers warming up for a lot of hollering Monday.

Court has taken a recess until then. Dana Wallace will open in defense of Mrs Snyder. William L. Millard will follow Wallace, in an effort to talk Gray out of the chair.

Richard S. Newcombe, the grave district attorney of Queens County, will do most of the arguing for the State of New York.

And what, think you, do the blond woman and the little corset salesman expect from the twelve good men and true?

Gray—nothing. Gray's attorneys say he now has a clean conscience, since relieving it of the details of the butchery of Albert Snyder, and he thinks the jury will believe his story of how the woman wound her insidious blond coils about his life until he couldn't help doing anything she desired.

I gather from the statement that he expects no clemency. Blessed be he who expects nothing, for mayhap he will not be disappointed. I suppose that deep down Gray is hoping for mercy.

And the blonde? You can always look for a blonde to say something unique. Mrs Ruth Brown Snyder says, through her attorneys, Dana Wallace and Edgar Hazleton, that she doesn't see how 'any red-blooded men' can believe Gray's story—that hers was the heavy hand in the hammering and chloroforming and wiring to death of her husband.

He seemed to be red-blooded himself, this Albert Snyder, whose ghostly figure has stalked in the background of this horrible screen presentation of human life and death for two weeks. Much of that red blood is still on a pillow on which his head rested when Gray first beat down upon it with the sash weight, and which was still lying on the district attorney's table along with the other horrible exhibits of the crime after Court took a recess yesterday afternoon.

Two hundred men and women gathered about the table, pushing and struggling with each other for a mere peek at the exhibits. Several hundred others had gone into the street outside to pull and haul for a view of Olga Petrova, as she stood beside her Rolls-Royce, being photographed, and of Leon Errol, the comedian, and other celebrities who honoured us with their presence yesterday.

That scene in the court was one that should give the philosophers and psychologists pause. The women were far more interested in the bloody pillow than they would have been in a baby buggy. It was the last thrill left to them after Gray and Mrs Snyder walked out of the court, the woman passing rows of the leering eyes of her sisters with her head down, but with a dangerous gleam in the greenish blue eyes.

Henry Judd started off the day with a good big jolt of water from the glass on the table in front of the witness stand. He imbibed water while he was on the stand at the same rate at which he used to drink whiskey, if he was the two-handed whiskey-wrestler that his story would indicate.

Wallace touched briefly on Gray's whiskey drinking again as he went into the corset salesman's finances. He wanted to know if Henry Judd always paid for the drinks. Henry said he did, a statement which interested all the bootleggers present. They wondered how he could do so much elbow-bending on his income.

That was about $5500 a year, out of which Gray gave his family $3500 a year. He had around $2000 left for himself. Wallace asked:

'And you visited night clubs and went to parties and did your drinking and clothed yourself on $2000 a year?'

'That is correct.'

And then the philosophers and psychologists really had something to think about. Also the domestic economists then and there present.

Wallace seemed to be trying to connect Gray's purchase of some shares of stock in the corset concern for which he worked with some possible interest in the death of Albert Snyder, for financial reasons.

Q. May I ask you, with your mind in the condition it was under Mrs Snyder's dominance, and being fully aware of your own home conditions and business affairs, what did you expect to gain by aiding and bringing about the death of Albert Snyder? What was your idea, your personal idea, of what you would gain?

A. That is what I would like to know.

Q. What's that?

A. That is what I would like to know.

Q. And without any reason for it that you know of, a man of your intelligence, you struck a man over the head with a sash weight and did the things you say you did?

A. I did.

Q. And you want to tell this jury you do not know why you did it?

A. I am telling.

Q. What did you intend to do after it was all over?

A. I didn't intend to do anything. I was through.

Henry Judd fell into a slightly philosophical strain as he proceeded. He may have been qualifying to cover the next murder case for some newspaper. Also his attitude toward Wallace became gently chiding. He remarked, 'One sometimes does things under the influence of liquor that one does automatically.'

It sounds quite true.

Wallace whipped many a question at Gray and then shouted, 'I withdraw it' before Gray could answer. He could not keep the little corset salesman from going beyond the question at times. Henry Judd was inclined to be verbose while Wallace tried to keep him pinned down to yes and no.

'Are you answering my questions that way because in one form it involves her and in another form it involves you?'

'I am already involved.'

May 9, 1927

If you are asking a medium-boiled reporter of murder trials, I couldn't condemn a woman to death no matter what she had done, and I say this with all due consideration of the future hazards to long-suffering man from sash weights that any lesser verdict than murder in the first degree in the Snyder-Gray case may produce.

It is all very well for the rest of us to say what *ought* to be done to the blond throwback to the jungle cat that they call Mrs Ruth Brown Snyder, but when you get in the jury room and start thinking about going home to tell the neighbors that you have voted to burn a woman—even a blond woman—I imagine the situation has a different aspect. The most astonishing verdict that could be rendered in this case, of course, would be first degree for the woman and something else for the man. I doubt that result. I am inclined to think that the verdict, whatever it may be, will run against both alike—death or life imprisonment.

Henry Judd Gray said he expects to go to the chair, and adds that he is not afraid of death, an enviable frame of mind, indeed. He says that since he told his story to the world from the witness stand he has found tranquility, though his tale may have also condemned his blond partner in blood. But perhaps that's the very reason Henry Judd finds tranquility.

He sat in his cell in the county jail over in Long Island yesterday, and read from one of the epistles of John.

'Marvel not, my brethren, if the world hates you. We know that we have passed from death unto life, because we love the brethren. He that loveth not his brother abideth in death. Whosoever hateth his brother is a murderer: and ye know that no murderer hath eternal life abiding in him.'

A thought for the second Sunday after Pentecost.

In another cell, the blond woman was very mad at everybody because she couldn't get a marcel for her bobbed locks, one hair of which was once stronger with Henry Judd Gray than the Atlantic Cable.

Also she desired a manicure, but the cruel authorities would not permit the selected one to attend the lady.

Thus Mrs Snyder will have to go into court today with hangnails, and just those offices that she can give her bobbed bean herself. I fear that this injustice will prove another argument of sinister persecution when the folks start declaiming against burning the lady, if such should chance to be the verdict of the jury.

However, with all her troubles about her fingernails and the marcel, Mrs Snyder did not forget Mother's Day. She is herself a mother as you may remember, though the fact seemed to skip her mind at times when she was all agog over Henry Judd. Also she has a mother, who spent the Sabbath very quietly in that house of horror in Queens Village with Mrs Snyder's little daughter, Lorraine.

From the old jail Mrs Snyder sent her mother this:

Mother's Day Greeting—I have many blessings and I want you to know how thankful I am for all that you have done for me. Love to you and kiss Lorraine for me. RUTH

Henry Judd Gray, although calm yesterday, declined his breakfast. Moreover, he scarcely touched his lunch. Mrs Snyder, on the other hand, is reported to have breakfasted well and was longing for some of the good Signor Roberto Minotti's spaghetti and roasted chicken at noon.

They both attended divine services at the jail in the afternoon. Mrs Snyder seems quite calm, though at similar services last week she was all broken up. As between the two, the blonde seems to be rallying for the last round better than her former sweet daddy of the days before the murder.

Judge Scudder, the tall, courtly, dignified man, who has impressed all beholders of this proceeding as one of the ablest jurists that ever wrapped a black robe around himself, will charge the jury at some length because he must outline what consists of four different degrees of homicide. He will undoubtedly devote much time to the conspiracy charge in the indictment.

The jurors are men of what you might call average intelligence, I mean to say there are no intellectual giants in the box. They are fellows you might meet in any club or cigar store, or speakeasy. A good jury, I call it. I doubt if they will be influenced by any psychological or philosophical twists that the lawyers may attempt to offer them, if any.

May 10, 1927

Mighty short shrift was made of Mrs Ruth Brown Snyder and Henry Judd Gray by that jury of Long Islanders—the verdict being murder in the first degree for both, the penalty death in the electric chair.

The twelve men went out at 5:20 yesterday afternoon and were back in the box ready to deliver their verdict at 6:57, an hour and thirty-seven minutes. They took off their coats as they entered the jury room, hoisted the windows for a breath of air, and took two ballots.

The first was ten to two for first degree murder, so I

understand, the second was unanimous. Justice moved on the gallop against the murderers once the jury got hold of the case.

Mrs Snyder, standing up to hear the verdict, dropped in her chair and covered her face with her hands. Henry Judd Gray, standing not far from her, held himself stiffly erect for a moment, but more like a man who had been shot and was swaying ever so slightly for a fall. Then he sat down, pulled a prayer book out of his pocket and began reading it.

He kept on reading even while the lawyers were up at Justice Scudder's bench arguing with the Court against immediate sentence. Mrs Snyder sat with her face buried between her hands. Justice Scudder finally fixed the time of sentence for Monday morning at ten o'clock.

Gray finally put the prayer book back in his pocket and sat looking straight ahead of him, as if he had found some comforting passage in the word of the Lord. He said to his guard on his way to his cell, 'I told the truth and my conscience is clear. My mother is glad I told the truth and God Almighty knows I told the truth.'

'Oh, I thought they'd believe me—I thought they'd believe me,' moaned Mrs Snyder to Father Patrick Murphy when she met him in the hallway going back to the jail. But before she left the court room there was a flash of the old defiance that marked her demeanor until the late stages of the trial.

'I haven't lost my nerve. My attorneys know that I have not had a fair trial, and we will fight this verdict with every ounce of strength.'

They have a curious custom in New York State of taking the prisoners before the clerk of the court after a verdict is returned and setting down their 'pedigree'—age, occupation, habits and the like. John Moran, the clerk of the Queens County Court, sits in a little enclosed booth like a bank teller's cage, just in front of the judge's bench, and Mrs Snyder was asked to step up there. Mrs Irene Wolfe, the matron of the county jail, and a guard supported her, the man putting his arm around the blond woman as if he was afraid the black-gowned figure would crumble and fall.

The law is a harsh institution. It would have seemed more merciful to take the woman away at once to some quiet place, where she could allow the tears she was choking back with difficulty to fall as they might.

But they stood her up there and asked her a lot of questions that seemed fatuous in view of what is already known of her, and she answered in a low voice—Ruth Brown Snyder, thirty-two years old, born in New York and all that sort of thing. Married? A widow. The tears began trickling down the marble-white cheeks.

Then they finally took her out of the court room by the same path she had trod so often the last couple of weeks. She was pretty thoroughly licked at that moment, and small wonder, for she had just heard twelve men tell her she must die.

Gray stood up before Moran, still holding himself stiffly, but did not weep. In answer to one of the set questions as to whether he is temperate or otherwise he said temperate, which sounded somewhat ironical in view of Gray's testimony during the trial as to the prodigious amounts of liquor he consumed.

He, too, was finally taken away, still walking as if he had put a ramrod down the back of his coat to hold himself so. Henry Judd Gray had said he expected such a sentence, and he was not disappointed.

The pair probably knew they were gone when they received word to make ready to return to the court room in such a short time after the jury retired. Rumor had tossed the verdict pretty well around Long Island City and the court room when the announcement came that the jury was ready to report, and the verdict was a foregone conclusion.

A few hours' delay might have produced hope for one or the other of the man and woman that fate tossed together with such horrible results. It was still daylight over Long Island City, although the yellowish-walled old court room was vaguely lighted by electric lamps, which shed less illumination than any lights I ever saw.

There was a painful stage wait, and in came Mrs Snyder and Gray, the former between two matrons, Mrs Wolfe and another, and Gray between two guards. Attorney Edgar Hazleton came in with her. He had evidently gone out to steel her for the verdict. He knew what it was, no doubt of that. She walked in with her little quick, short steps, but her face was gray—not white-gray, a dull, sickening gray.

The man walked firmly, too, but you could see by the expression in his eyes he felt what was coming. He seemed to be holding himself together with a strong effort.

Now a stir told of the coming of Justice Scudder, a lean, stooping figure in his black robe, bobbing his head to the right and left with little short bows like an archbishop. The crowd always rises at the entrance of the judge, then sits down again in some confusion, but this time everyone seemed to adjust himself in his seat again noiselessly.

Justice Scudder peered around from under the green-shaded stand lamp on his desk with an inquiring expression, and, as the roll of the jurors was called, they answered in very low voices. Only one said 'here' rather loudly, almost defiantly, it seemed.

The clerk of the court motioned the jurors to stand and then Mrs Snyder and Henry Judd Gray were also told to rise. They stood there, Mrs Snyder just behind Gray, leaning against the table. Gray had no support. They could not see each other.

Ten women fainted in the court room in the course of the day, such was the pulling and hauling and the general excitement of the occasion, but Mrs Ruth Brown Snyder remained as cool as the well-known old cucumber, even when she heard herself termed enough different kinds of animals to populate the zoo.

She was mentioned as a serpent by William L. Millard. Also as a tigress. Still, Millard gave her a back-handed boost, at that, when he called her a sinister, fascinating woman. Perhaps Mrs Snyder would have been just as well pleased if he had left off the sinister.

Cruel, calculating and cunning, he said she was. She kept her eyes closed while Millard was berating her, supporting her head on her right hand, an elbow leaned on the table. Her left hand was across her breast. Once she dabbed her eyes with a little kerchief, as if she might be mopping away a few tears.

But all that Millard said about Mrs Snyder was just a few sweet nothings compared to what Dana Wallace said about Gray. He was 'human filth,' 'diabolical fiend,' 'weak-minded,' 'despicable creature,' 'falsifier,' and finally a 'human anaconda,' which is interesting if true, and ought to get Harry Judd a job in any side show.

The little corset salesman just stared straight ahead while Wallace was blasting him. However, he was upright and alert and heard everything Wallace said, probably figuring it sounded libelous. His mother and his sister sat near by and comforted him.

There was much talk of the Deity on all sides. Both Millard and Wallace appealed to Him, and so, too, did the district attorney, when he came to summing up for the State. Newcombe was brief, and omitted brickbats for the defendants. He did compare Mrs Snyder with a jungle cat, possibly just to make sure that no animals had been left out.

The district attorney was in what you may call a soft spot, anyway, with the defendants at loggerheads, and each trying to push the other into the electric chair. However, from the beginning Newcombe has conducted this case with singular simplicity of method, and without any attempt at red fire.

Millard's argument for Gray was as expected, that Henry Judd was a poor fool, a dupe, and a lot of other things that mean a chump, who was beguiled by the woman.

However, he astonished the populace by advancing the theory that Mrs Snyder slipped Henry Judd a dose of poison the night of the murder, expecting her little playmate in blood would fold up and die also after he had assisted in dispatching Snyder. The poison didn't work, Millard said.

Furthermore, Millard made the first open suggestion of abnormality in Mrs Snyder. I heard hints that Gray's attorneys intended trying to show that the lady wasn't altogether normal, during the trial, but all that junk was kept out—by agreement, as I understand it—and only in his argument yesterday did Millard mention the abnormality.

For Mrs Snyder, the defense was she was the victim of Henry Judd, 'the human anaconda,' and he was but 'hiding behind the woman's skirts.' This caused Lieutenant McDermott, of the Police Department, to suggest mildly to me that it was a great phrase and true, in the old days, but now a woman's skirts are nothing to hide behind if a gent wishes to be really concealed.

Both Millard and Wallace were in favor of their clients being

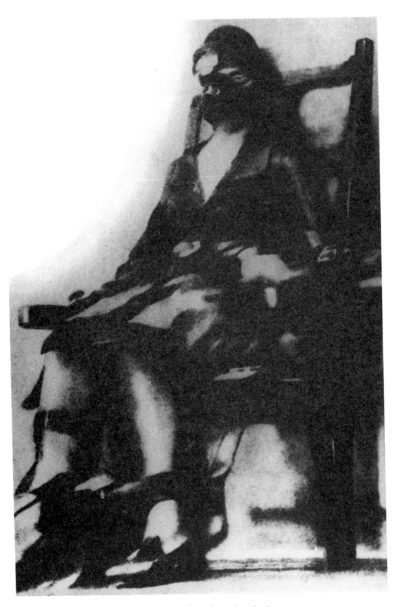

Ruth Snyder's final moment in the electric chair.

acquitted. Millard's was something of an appeal for pity, but Wallace said, in the spirit of Mrs Snyder's defiance throughout this trial, that she was not asking for pity, she was asking for justice.

In some ways it was a disheartening spectacle, if one happened to think how many spectators would have been attracted to Long Island City to hear a few pleas for the Mississippi Flood sufferers. In another, it was something of a tribute to the power of good old publicity. It pays to advertise. We have been three-sheeting Henry Judd and Ruth to good purpose.

F. TENNYSON JESSE

The Trial of Madeleine Smith

The case of Madeleine Smith has a perennial interest for what may be termed mystery fanciers, or, in more modern slang, murder-fans.

And yet, although Madeleine Smith, an old, old woman, died a few years ago in the United States, and one is now, therefore, at liberty to assert the inescapable conviction of all students of the trial that she was guilty, a certain mystery will always hang around this famous trial of 1857. But it is not a mystery of action, but of that strange thing, the human heart.

It was not Madeleine's heart which held mystery. That merely tried to hold its secrets, a very different matter. It is L'Angelier, the victim, who remains an enigma to this day.

I am aware that this statement may bring upon me the wrath of other students of this great trial, but I leave the reader who comes to this article with an open mind to judge for himself.

Madeleine Smith was the eldest daughter of a well-known Glasgow architect. Near her in age came a brother, Jack, and a sister, Bessie. There was a younger boy called James, and a little girl of twelve called Janet.

Only Janet, called by the defence, gave evidence at the trial, although Bessie was with Madeleine when L'Angelier was first introduced to her, and although Jack fetched her back from her father's country house, whither she fled after L'Angelier's death. In fact, the Smith family was protected in every way. Mr and Mrs Smith seemed to have taken to their bed and remained there.

L'Angelier was a penniless young clerk from Jersey, a Frenchman and a foreigner to Scottish eyes. It has always been an interesting question what the result of the trial might have been had Madeleine Smith been the friendless foreigner and the dead man the son of a wealthy and respected local family.

Yet Scottish justice is, as a rule, impartial and as good as can be found in this rough-and-ready world, and I think the answer to the undoubted bias in favour of the accused is to be found not so much in the influence of the Smith family as in the fact that L'Angelier had, after seducing Madeleine, proceeded to blackmail her and make her life a misery.

In fact, the verdict of Not Proven might be summed up as meaning: 'We'll let you off this once, but don't do it again.'

Madeleine Smith was born out of due time. She was beautiful in a handsome, defiant way that was not feminine enough for the period in which she lived. She was a girl of strong physical passion at a time when no woman was supposed to possess such a thing.

She was talented and capable; but arranging the flowers in her parents' home, and, if she were married, being a good housekeeper in her husband's house, was all the mental effort deemed suitable for a woman. In the late war, Madeleine Smith would have driven an ambulance or filled some organising post most admirably.

Pierre Emile L'Angelier, a peculiarly nasty little ladykiller, earning about a pound a week, may have been, and probably was, attracted by Madeleine's bright beauty as she passed about the grey Glasgow streets.

But he also knew that she came of a wealthy family and he pressed a mutual friend, a youth called Robert Baird, to introduce them. Baird asked his mother whether he might bring L'Angelier home one evening when Miss Smith was visiting the house.

But Mrs Baird evidently thought such an acquaintance unsuitable and declined permission, and the introduction took place in the street. A clandestine acquaintance ripened between Madeleine and L'Angelier, but it was discovered by the girl's father, and Madeleine attempted to end the acquaintance in the same month that it had begun.

L'Angelier, however, was not to be shaken off, although Madeleine made another attempt to get free of him in July of 1855. Her heart was not in the business of dismissal, however, and the acquaintance continued, growing more and more intimate.

To Madeleine, L'Angelier's foreign origin, his poverty, his flowing whiskers, and his skilful love-making made of him a figure of romance. L'Angelier's mind was set from the first on marriage with this daughter of a wealthy family, and his seduction of her, if seduction it can be called when her passionate nature was more than ready to submit to him, was merely a step in his campaign.

In June of the following year Madeleine became L'Angelier's mistress. The lovers met sometimes in the woods outside her father's country house, sometimes in the house in Blythswood Square to which she used to admit him after the family were all asleep.

And during all this time a series of passionate love-letters went back and forth. He kept all of hers. She kept but one or two of his. Hers were supposed to show a shocking lack of decency, though nowadays they do not seem strange letters for a woman to have written to her lover whom she thought to marry. His show him as the unpleasing mixture of a sensualist and a preacher that he was.

The raptures of the early months began to fade for Madeleine. Her common sense told her that her father (and Mr Smith seems to have been the very personification of the terrible Jove-like Victorian papa) would never consent to a marriage with L'Angelier.

A Mr Minnoch, a middle-aged man of good standing and a friend of the Smith family, fell in love with her and asked for her hand. The solid comforts of Mr Minnoch's establishment, the charm of being its mistress and a young matron, began to appeal to Madeleine, and her letters to L'Angelier grew perceptibly colder.

He took fright and began to importune her. She definitely tried to break with him, only to find that he refused to let her go, that he even threatened to show her letters—those letters which would damn her for ever in the eyes of her contemporaries—to her father.

Madeleine Smith is not a lovable character, but it is possible to sympathise with the agonies of fear, with the remorse and

Madeleine Smith (top) and Pierre Emile l'Angelier: engravings from
a contemporary report of the trial.

disgust which must have taken hold of her. She had accepted Mr Minnoch's proposal in January, 1857, and she still could not get free of L'Angelier.

In February she told him candidly that she no longer loved him, but she could not pique him into returning her letters. She wrote to him imploringly, but to implore a blackmailer's mercy is a singularly useless proceeding.

She then asked the page boy to go to a chemist to buy her a bottle of prussic acid, saying she wanted it to whiten her hands. The chemist, very sensibly, refused to comply with her request.

She next began to write to Emile in the old strain of affection. While writing these loving epistles, making appointments for him to meet her, she was also employed in buying arsenic. She made three purchases in all, giving the usual well-worn reasons—one, the improvement of her complexion by using the drug as a face wash, and the other the even more hackneyed one of wishing to destroy rats.

Her first purchase, as far as is known, was made on February 21, and there is no doubt that L'Angelier's first bad attack of sickness was in the morning of the 19th. This was a strong argument in favour of her innocence.

But L'Angelier had thrice before been seized with sickness of the same description in the houses of his friends, and it may be that his illness of the 19th was not due to arsenic poisoning. But she was in possession of arsenic on the 21st, and L'Angelier was taken extremely ill on the 22nd. Madeleine bought arsenic again on March 6 and March 18.

Madeleine tried to get him to go away to the Isle of Wight for a holiday, but he refused to go further than Bridge of Allan. Now she began to write to him asking him to come and see her, using the most ardent phrases.

The prosecution maintained that she handed him poisoned cocoa from the window of her basement bedroom where he came there by appointment on the evening of March 22.

But the prosecution was never able to prove this meeting. Had they been able to do so, nothing could have saved Madeleine Smith. L'Angelier, recalled from Bridge of Allan by a letter—from whom the letter came could not be proved—left his lodgings that evening in better health, but at half-past two on Monday morning he was ringing the bell of his lodging-house violently.

His landlady helped him to his room, and there he vomited for about two hours. At five o'clock a doctor was sent for, but refused to come, merely suggesting twenty-five drops of lauda-num and a mustard plaster.

The landlady continued to attend him, and he became so ill that she insisted on the doctor coming at about seven o'clock. The doctor gave him a little morphia and applied a poultice, making the sapient remark that time and quietness were required. By eleven o'clock L'Angelier was quiet enough, for he was dead.

Now the curious thing about L'Angelier's final agonies is this—although he seems to have known that he was dying, he never accused Madeleine Smith, or, indeed, mentioned her name. He did ask his landlady to send for a Miss Perry, a sentimental maiden lady, who had played the part of go-between for him and Madeleine, but by the time Miss Perry arrived he was dead.

Whether he had been going to accuse Madeleine to her we shall never know. According to Miss Perry's evidence at the trial he had said to her after his illness on February 19: 'I can't think why I was so ill after taking that coffee and chocolate from her.' Miss Perry understood her to mean Miss Smith.

He had added: 'It is a perfect fascination, my attachment to that girl. If she were to poison me I should forgive her.'

L'Angelier was an eminently practical person, and there is little doubt that he would not knowingly have taken poison from the hands of Madeleine or anyone else. And so we can be almost certain that in those last hours of agony on the morning of March 23 he realised for the first time that at least one previous attack of sickness may have been due to Madeleine's cocoa, and that the present one must have been caused by her.

If, when dying, he realised what Madeleine had done and yet refrained from naming that girl he had bullied and black-mailed, so much may, at least, be allowed to him for righteous-ness.

But why did this contemptible little lady-killer show such magnanimity? It was suggested, of course, by the defence that he might have taken the poison accidentally, or that some other person, not Madeleine, had murdered him, or that he had committed suicide. The last suggestion is the only one not outside of the region of possibility.

However, if he killed himself by repeated doses of that extremely painful poison, arsenic, he remains unique as a suicide. Also, it is far more in keeping with his character to blackmail Madeleine, or to go to her father and demand from him money for keeping silent.

It is, therefore, not only possible, but perhaps even probable, that a certain remorse entered his heart as he lay dying, for there seems no doubt that he knew that he was dying.

He said to his landlady: 'I'm far worse than the doctor thinks.' His pain and weakness must have been so intense, his knowledge that some lethal substance had been administered to him so certain, that he can have had but little hope, although he murmured: 'Oh, if I could get five minutes' sleep I think I would get better.'

Madeleine's name never passed his lips, nor would he give any hint as to the cause of his illness. This reticence and generosity in a man who had hitherto been completely ruthless is the most mysterious thing in the case.

There is no answer to the riddle, although it may be permitted to hope that the solution is to be found in the theory—which must always remain a theory—that regret touched his scheming little heart in his last hours.

L'Angelier's death seemed so inexplicable that an autopsy was held and more than sufficient arsenic to destroy life was found in the body. L'Angelier's effects were examined and Madeleine's letters were found.

She fled blindly and futilely to her father's country house, but came back unprotestingly with Mr Minnoch and her brother, Jack. All thought of marriage with the respectable Mr Minnoch was, of course, over for good; and, indeed, when that unfortunate man, who seems to have felt the discovery of her previous passion very acutely, had to give evidence against her at her trial, it is said he never looked towards her.

Yet Madeleine was worth looking at, in her full, sweeping, dark silk dress and her bonnet, which, shaped like a halo, showed the front of her sleek, dark head so that her cameo-like profile and beautiful complexion stood out unshadowed.

Rumour has it that one of the judges was peculiarly susceptible to the charms of a pretty foot and ankle, and that Madeleine sat slightly sideways in the dock, her skirt pulled up a little to display this charm, so exciting to the Victorians.

The trial was chiefly noticeable for the magnificent speeches by the Lord Advocate, for the prosecution, and the Dean of Faculty, for the defence. The latter, Lord Inglis, who was to become Lord Justice-General of Scotland, made a closing speech which has remained a model to this day.

The strength, the passion, with which he fought every inch of the ground, the brilliance of his arguments and the closeness of his reasoning, remain untouched by time. And if some of his oratory seems a trifle lush and old-fashioned, the same can be said of that of the late Marshall Hall, and still more so of the sentimental periods of Mr Clarence Darrow, most noted defence counsel in the United States.

Three of the Dean of Faculty's strongest points were:

1 That the prosecution could not show that Madeleine possessed any arsenic before February 21.

2 That there was no proof that L'Angelier had met Madeleine before his attacks of sickness on February 22 and March 22.

3 That it might reasonably be argued that L'Angelier's death placed Madeleine in a very awkward position, as her letters would be bound to be discovered.

There is not, perhaps, much force in the third argument. Madeleine could hardly be in a worse position than if L'Angelier fulfilled his threat of showing her letters to her father, and she may have hoped that if her lover's death passed off without comment the letters would be destroyed. They were, in any case, nearly all signed Mimi, or sometimes even Mimi L'Angelier. But the Dean of Faculty would not have found himself in nearly such a strong position when he argued that there was no meeting between the two on the crucial dates, if a little diary of

L'Angelier's had been allowed to be put into evidence.

The entry for February 19 ran: 'Saw Mimi a few moments. Was very ill during the night.' While that for February 22 read: 'Saw Mimi in drawing-room, promised me French Bible, taken very ill.'

It was ruled, however, that this diary was inadmissible as evidence of a fact against the accused.

The summing up was admirably fair, but certainly it gave the prisoner the benefit of every doubt and it was, probably, a very relieved jury that returned a verdict of Not Proven.

Madeleine Smith, who had remained the calmest and most unmoved person in court throughout the trial, wrote in a letter to the matron of the prison, that she was not at all pleased with the verdict! In the same latter she complained that the feeling of the people towards her round her home was not as kindly as that of 'the good people of Edinburgh' had been.

Apparently she expected to be found Not Guilty and received with acclamation. Even her excellent nervous system, however, found it impossible to bear home life after all the revelations that had been made, and she went to London alone, became a Socialist, and married, the first two steps being rare for a girl of those days, and the third something of an achievement, considering her past.

It is said, with what truth I do not know, that she made an excellent wife, and that her husband was very devoted to her, but that he never allowed her to do any cooking.

There would have been little risk, however, of Madeleine Smith attempting to kill for a second time. She was not a congenital killer, she was merely a woman who knew what she wanted and who, much rarer, knew when she had ceased to want it.

And her resolution was such that she was determined to have her way in both these matters. She was, in short, a woman born at the very worst time in the world's history for such as she; a time when women were not supposed to want much, but were also supposed to want that little long.

'I shall ever remain true to you,' Madeleine had written to L'Angelier. 'I think a woman who can be untrue should be banished from society.'

She had the courage of her change of conviction.

Frederick Seddon.

EDGAR WALLACE

The Trial of the Seddons

Seddon was essentially a business man, shrewd, neat, a little unimaginative. He was the type sometimes met with in the train on the way to the City: a man of dogmatic opinions, a little overbearing, wholly intolerant of other people's opinions. You could imagine Seddon holding rigid political views, and regarding all who did not share them as being outside the pale.

Generally he was accounted, by those who knew him best, as a very excellent manager; a man who gave nothing away, and who was credited with considerable possessions, which his thrift and his gift for driving a hard bargain had accumulated for him.

Seddon lived in a good-sized house at Tollington Park, North London, with his wife and five children. It was a fairly large house and his own property (as he often boasted), and here he carried on his profession of insurance agent, being superintendent of that district and having under his charge a number of collectors, who were kept very busy by their energetic taskmaster. Seddon was certainly a man bound to get on. In the interests of his business he worked day and night; he was indefatigable in his search for new 'lives,' yet found time to indulge in certain social amenities, and was an officer of a very honourable society, where he was considerably respected.

That Seddon was a true Freemason in the real sense of the word can be doubted. Men of his intelligence too often adopt Masonry as a means to an end, believing that fellowship with so many of the best intellects in a district gives them advantages in business. Nevertheless, it was his ambition to rise to the supreme heights of Masonry, and all his spare time was given to the assiduous study of the craft and to fitting himself for higher that which he at present held.

hectoring man, bombastic of speech, loud of voice, that crushed all opposition, his business grew rapidly, but not so fast as he could wish. The dominant passion of Seddon's life was money. Not every miser is a recluse, who hides his bags of gold in inaccessible places and shrinks from the society of his fellow-men. There are some, who are to be met with in every sphere of commercial activity, well-groomed misers who are not to be suspected of their vice, and Seddon was one of these. He worshipped money for money's sake. He never spent a farthing that he could avoid. His household accounts were most minutely examined day by day, and the money he doled out for household expenses was the smallest sum he could in decency offer to his unfortunate wife.

Seddon's dreams had a golden hue. The rich were very wonderful in his eyes, and he would find his recreation in relating to his friends his surprising knowledge of the wealth which was possessed by the great figures of the financial world.

He had saved penny by penny, pound by pound, gradually piling up his assets painfully and slowly. Never once had a large amount come to him in one sum, and one of his bitterest complaints was that he had no rich relations who were likely to die and leave him a fortune. Not the least interesting item of the newspapers was the paragraph which appears every day under the heading 'Latest Wills,' and he would pore over this in the evenings. Sometimes he would learn of a rich man or woman who had died intestate, the money going to the Crown, and this would throw him into a fury.

'All that money wasted! Thrown into the gutter! It is criminal! Why don't people have more common sense?'

I

There was in London, though of her existence Seddon was ignorant for some time, a middle-aged woman who shared Seddon's peculiar passion for money. She, however, had never had to scrape and strive. She had been left a small fortune in the shape of house property—at least it was a small fortune to her—which brought her in £5 or £6 a week. She was as mean as

Seddon, parting with every penny with the greatest reluctance, and worshipping money, even as he did, for money's sake.

It follows that she was a difficult tenant to any landlady who gave her accommodation, and she shifted her lodgings very frequently, taking with her the small boy whom she had adopted, Ernie Grant.

In his restless search for people whom he could persuade to take out insurance policies, Seddon came into contact with this middle-aged spinster, Miss Eliza Barrow, and these two sharp-minded beings recognised in one another kindred souls. Seddon's immediate interest in the woman was a purely business one, but he had ever an eye to the main chance, and it had been his practice to leave no avenue to fortune unexplored.

'Friends should pay dividends,' was one of his mottoes; and there is little doubt, after he had discovered that Miss Barrow was not a likely subject for insurance, that he turned over in his mind a way by which this new acquaintance should 'pay dividends.' Miss Barrow's complaint against landladies was perennial. Her interest in life was confined by the walls of the lodgings she had, and it may be imagined that they had not long met before she was telling him of her various landladies' enormities, the high cost of living, the peculations of lodging-house servants, and the difficulty of finding a home where these causes for distress would be more or less non-existent.

Seddon was a quick thinker. He had a big house in Tollington Park, and several of the upper rooms were unoccupied. This woman could pay dividends in the shape of rent, and in many other ways was a desirable tenant, for he had learnt of her house property and her steady income, and there was no fear that she would come to him on a Monday morning and bring excuses instead of money. So Seddon patted the little boy on the head with easy benevolence, and remembered his empty rooms.

'I think my rooms would suit you very well,' he said. 'We live very quietly; you will be in the house of a successful business man who may be able to help you from time to time in the matter of advice, and I'll arrange it so that you live more cheaply with me than you have been living heretofore.'

The arrangement was most welcome to the woman, who was

in the throes of one of her periodical fits of resentment against her landlady. She had lived in many homes. Once she had stayed with her cousin, Mr Frank Ernest Vonderahe, but that arrangement had not been satisfactory, and she had wandered off with her boy to yet another lodging.

Life at Tollington Park was entirely to Miss Barrow's satisfaction. She had the opportunity of talking business with Seddon; he admitted her to his confidence, allowed her to be present when he was handling the large sums of money which came in from the collectors—a sight very precious to Miss Barrow, who, in spite of her possessions, had probably not seen so much gold before. And the knowledge that he was trusted with such huge sums increased her confidence in him; so that she brought her own financial difficulties to him (the cost of repairs, tenants' demands and the like), and accepted his advice on all matters concerning her estate.

The friendship grew to a stage probably beyond her anticipations. Her confidence came to be a blind trust in his integrity and prescience. It developed, as was subsequently discovered, in her taking the rash step of purchasing an annuity upon his advice.

It is certain that Frederick Henry Seddon saw in Eliza Barrow a greater profit than the meagre sums he obtained by giving her lodging. There was about him the additional flavour of deep religious principles. Seddon had a reputation as a lay preacher and public orator. He was fluent of speech, better educated than most men of his class, and he could be, in his lighter moments, a most entertaining and charming man. He charmed Eliza Barrow to this end, that one day he induced her to sell her Indian stock for £1600, to get rid of her house property and to trust him with the money. She was obviously confident, from his manner to her adopted child, that the boy would lose nothing from being left in Seddon's charge, for she made no provision whatever for his future until a few days before her death.

Seddon had gone to work deliberately, with a set plan, and the first part of his scheme having been brought to a successful issue, nothing remained but to perpetrate the dreadful deed which he may have contemplated from the very moment he had

Eliza Mary Barrow: murdered for a pittance.

obtained Miss Barrow's confidence.

Since no poisoner has ever confessed his method, it is only possible to reconstruct the story of such a murder by an understanding of the murderer's mentality, and by piecing together such scraps of evidence as are available.

Seddon probably purchased a small quantity of arsenic in some part of London in which he was unknown. But he was shrewd enough to prepare, at the same time, a defence for himself. He purchased a number of fly-papers—paper impregnated with arsenic, which, when placed in a wet saucer, destroys any fly who lights upon it—and several of these he placed in Miss Barrow's bedroom.

He knew, for he had made a study of poison trials, that one of the questions which decides the guilt or innocence of any person accused of poisoning, is the accessibility of the poison: in other words, whether it is possible, through accident or design, for poison to be self-administered. The only way that arsenic could be self-administered by a demented or careless woman was to have strong solutions of arsenic in her bedroom. He did not apparently realise that, in ninety-nine cases out of a hundred where a person is found poisoned, the police look for a motive, and find one in a case where a person who had the opportunity of administering the poison directly benefits by the death.

'Seddon always thinks of everything,' said an admiring colleague. 'That is why he has been so successful.'

Undoubtedly Seddon thought of most of the possibilities, but never dreamt that his cunning plan would be exposed.

In many ways Miss Barrow was most favourably placed from his point of view. She had quarrelled with her relations, and those very distant relations. She had no personal friends, and beyond the Vonderahes, who came occasionally to see her, and were received with marked coldness, no interfering individual who would inquire too closely into her sudden demise.

II

The Seddon's family were on very good terms with their lodger. Maggie Seddon and her mother did the cooking for her. Seddon himself was seldom in her room. When she became ill, only on one occasion did Seddon give Miss Barrow her medicine. A doctor was called in, saw nothing suspicious, identified Miss Barrow's symptoms with a natural derangement; and if he was surprised when one day he was summoned to find the unfortunate lady *in extremis*, it was one of those surprises which are the normal experience of every medical practitioner, and he did not hesitate to give a certificate stating that her death was due to natural causes.

Three days before her death, Seddon persuaded Miss Barrow to make a will leaving all that she possessed to Ernest and Hilda Grant, appointing Seddon the sole executor. Again we see the cleverness of the move; for now Seddon had so arranged matters that suspicion would be even more remote from himself. He had no possible interest in her death (unless the secretly-arranged sale of the annuity came to light), and such sums of money and property which had been Miss Barrow's as would be left he might use until the children came of age.

Miss Barrow died on the Thursday, and no sooner was the breath out of her body than Seddon bustled off to interview an undertaker, and arranged for the cheapest possible funeral. Not only did he do this, but he made a gruesome bargain with the man which gives us an interesting insight into his mastering desire to save money at every opportunity. Seddon told the undertaker that an old lady had died in his house, and it would have to be an inexpensive funeral. He had found four pounds ten in the room, he said, and that would not only have to defray the funeral expenses, but find the fees due to the doctor. Thereupon the undertaker bargained to carry out the funeral at an inclusive price of three pounds seven and sixpence and allowed Seddon a small commission on the transaction. Seddon had memorial cards printed, with an appropriate verse of sorrow; he bought a quantity of black-edged envelopes and paper, and wrote a number of letters, which, however, were never delivered or posted.

No man could have taken greater precautions than did Seddon to clear himself of any suspicion that he was implicated in the death of this wretched lady. Miss Barrow died on the Thursday, and on the Saturday was buried in a common grave, although there was a family vault, about which Seddon could not have been ignorant. He was, however, anxious to get the body underground with the least possible delay, for, once buried, he knew that there would be considerable difficulty in getting an exhumation.

Although not on specially good terms, Miss Barrow had been in the habit of calling on the Vonderahes, and the fact that she had not appeared, and that they had seen nothing either of her or the boy, was remarked upon by Mrs Vonderahe.

'I can't understand why we have not seen Miss Barrow for so long,' she said to her husband. 'Why don't you walk round to Tollington Park and see how she is getting on?'

Ernest Vonderahe, who was not particularly interested in his cousin, was nevertheless a dutiful relative, and on the Wednesday evening strolled over to Tollington Park. The door was opened by Seddon's general servant, Mary Chater, who stared at him blankly.

'I've come to see how Miss Barrow is getting on. Is she well?'

The girl gasped.

'Haven't you heard?' she demanded in amazement. 'Miss Barrow is dead and buried—didn't you know?'

Vonderahe could only stare at her.

'Dead and buried?' he said incredulously. 'When did she die?'

'Last Thursday.'

'But this is only Wednesday!'

'She was buried on Saturday,' said the maid.

'Can I see Mr Seddon?'

The girl shook her head.

'He's out, and won't be back for an hour,' she said.

Staggered by this startling news, Vonderahe went back and saw his wife. At his suggestion, she dressed, and they went back again to Tollington Park, arriving about nine o'clock in the evening. This time they saw Maggie Seddon, the daughter, but Seddon was not visible.

'Father has gone to the Finsbury Park Empire and won't be back till very late,' she said, and could give them little or no information about Miss Barrow's illness, nor did they think it worth while to question the child.

The Vonderahes went home and a family council was summoned, consisting of Vonderahe and his brother, with their wives, and they discussed the mysterious suddenness of Miss Barrow's illness until far into the night, arriving at the decision that the two women should interview Seddon the next morning and discover more about the circumstances of the woman's death.

Accordingly, the next morning the two wives went to Tollington Park, and the door was again opened by Maggie Seddon. Apparently they were expected, for they were shown immediately into the dining-room. The visitors were kept for some time before the insurance superintendent and his wife made their appearance. He was his usual self, calm, confident, neatly dressed and in every respect self-possessed. But his wife displayed the greatest nervousness, and, throughout the interview which followed, was on the point of breaking down.

Seddon strode into the apartment, pulled out a watch (which proved to be the property of the late Miss Barrow), looked at it significantly and remarked in a loud tone that he hadn't much time to spare and he hoped that they would be brief. And then, when his wife began to speak, he silenced her firmly but kindly.

'Now,' said Seddon briskly, 'just tell me who you are, and things,' he said, and explained that his wife had been greatly shocked by the death of the lodger and had not yet recovered. 'You sit there and don't upset yourself. I can tell these ladies all they wish to know.'

Mrs Seddon may have had a suspicion that all was not well. The manner of Miss Barrow's death, the haste of the funeral, may have seemed to her suspicious things.

'Now,' said Seddon briskly, 'just tell me who you are, and what relation you are to the deceased Miss Barrow.' And, when he was told, he handed them a copy of a letter written to Vonderahe, which the latter had not received.

The letter was brief and to the effect that Miss Barrow was dead. It invited them to the funeral which had taken place on the previous Saturday. It added that, a few days before her death, Miss Barrow had left a will in which she gave 'what she died possessed of' to Hilda and Ernest Grant, and appointed Seddon as sole executor.

Apparently Seddon had everything prepared: the copy of the will and a large blank envelope into which he put these documents and handed them to one of the ladies present.

So far, in spite of the brusqueness of the man—his callous indifference to the feelings of Miss Barrow's relatives and the scarcely veiled antagonism he showed to these inquirers—there was nothing suspicious beyond his manner; and it is probable that, had Seddon been more conciliatory, expressed a little more sorrow and stage-managed that interview a little more deftly, he might have escaped the consequence of his villainy.

As it was, he again looked at his watch pointedly, and when one of the ladies asked if he would see Mr Ernest Vonderahe he shrugged his shoulders.

'I am a business man, and I think I've wasted quite enough time on this matter,' he said. 'I really can't be bothered answering questions put by inquisitive people.'

These two ladies had gone to Tollington Park with the misguided idea that, because of their relationship, they would be asked to take possession of Miss Barrow's effects. If the will were genuine, and her death had occurred under normal circumstances, they could not, of course, touch a single article without permission from the executor; and legally, Seddon's position was unassailable.

But in their ignorance of the law, they expected to be given certain of Miss Barrow's goods. Their real suspicions began when they found that, justifiably, Seddon meant to retain in his possession all the property the administration of which had been specifically left to him. It was only when they found that they were being sent empty-handed away from Tollington Park that they began to regard Seddon's behaviour as suspicious; and his ignorance of their psychology was responsible for his undoing.

It was not till some weeks later, on October 9th, after many family councils, that Mr Ernest Vonderahe saw Seddon. The insurance agent had gone to Southend for a holiday, feeling, he said, 'a little under the weather.' And that period gave Ernest Vonderahe an opportunity of making closer inquiries into the possessions of Miss Barrow when she died. He discovered something about her investments; she was the landlady of a

Frederick Seddon: tried for the most miserly murder.

public-house called the 'Buck's Head,' and the proprietress of a barber's shop adjoining the public-house; had a considerable sum of money in the bank, and at the time of her death had quite a large sum in ready cash.

Whether the relatives of Miss Barrow were chiefly concerned with the manner of her death, or whether they suffered under an indignant sense of being robbed of that which was rightfully theirs, we need not inquire. All the investigations which went on were in the direction of ascertaining the exact amount of benefit Seddon might have received from the woman's disappearance. It was a very proper and natural line of investigation, to which no exception could be taken. It is perfectly certain that, supposing the will to be genuine—and this was not disputed—whatever might be the result of their inquiries, they themselves could not be benefited by a single penny through the exposure of Seddon as a murderer.

The Vonderahes saw something of one of the 'beneficiaries' under the will. Little Ernie Grant came to see them, but was invariably accompanied by one of Seddon's children, either the girl or the boy, and the suspicions of the Vonderahes were deepened, because they saw, in this chaperonage, an attempt to prevent them questioning the child as to the manner of Miss Barrow's death.

On Seddon's return from Southend, Vonderahe decided to call upon him, and sent him a message to that effect. And the visitor was accompanied by a friend 'as witness.' Seddon had no illusions as to the antagonism of the deceased woman's cousin. He had heard something more than the subterranean rumbling which was to precede the cataclysm, and his line of preparation—to meet the unspoken charges which he knew Vonderahe would have in mind—took the shape of adopting towards his inquisitor a lofty and high-handed manner, which had served him so successfully in dealing with other disagreeable people in his business.

Like all poisoners, Seddon was completely satisfied of his own invincibility. And he could even challenge still greater antagonism by attempting to cow his inquisitive visitors into submission to his point of view. Vonderahe and his friend were in the parlour, cooling their heels, for twenty minutes before

Seddon and his wife came into the room.

III

'Mr Frank Ernest Vonderahe?' asked Seddon, and when the relative had answered in the affirmative, Seddon spoke to the second of the men, under the impression that Vonderahe's companion was his brother.

Seddon was smoking a large cigar, and motioned his visitors to chairs with a lordly air.

'Now what is all this about?' he asked. 'You are under the impression that some money is due to you from the estate of Miss Barrow? The will is perfectly clear, and I don't see why I should give you any further information. If your solicitor cares to see my solicitor, all very well and good.'

In spite of this high-handed proceeding, Ernest Vonderahe began to question the man.

'Who is now the owner of the "Buck's Head"?' he asked, referring to one of the properties which had been Miss Barrow's.

'I am,' said Seddon quickly, 'and the barber's shop next door is also mine. I've bought the property—in fact, I am always open to buy property if it shows any chance of a reasonable return. This house is mine, and I have a number of other properties. That is my private business: I buy and sell whenever a bargain is offered.'

The propriety of Seddon's purchasing properties of which he was the executor for his own benefit did not seem to have occurred to either of the two men, and Ernest Vonderahe shifted his inquiries to a complaint that his relative had been buried in a common grave, when there was a handsome family vault at Highgate available.

Seddon replied that he thought the vault was full up, though this excuse might have been invented on the spur of the moment. The 'Buck's Head' and the barber's shop had, he declared, been bought in the open market. It was his business to dispose of the property, and as his bids were higher than any others, there was nothing remarkable about it being knocked down to him. When they pressed their inquiries, Seddon said (I am quoting the statement of Ernest Vonderahe):

'That is for the proper authorities to find out. I am perfectly willing to meet any solicitor. I am prepared to spend a thousand pounds to prove that all I have done in regard to Miss Barrow is perfectly in order.'

Until this interview, according to the evidence which was subsequently offered at the trial of Seddon, the inquiries and the suspicions had been confined to the narrow circle of the Vonderahes and their intimate friends. But after this point-blank refusal of Seddon to discuss the affairs of the dead woman, and when it seemed that no useful purpose would be served by further interviews, the Vonderahes did what they should have done in the first place—communicated their suspicions to the police.

Such communications are not rare at Scotland Yard, and the police authorities act with the greatest circumspection before they take any drastic action to confirm the suspicions of relatives. There are probably twenty complaints to every exhumation; possibly the number is much larger. But the police, in this case, had something else to work upon than the bald suspicions of the Vonderahes. There was, in the first place, the hasty burial, and, in the second, the fact that, as executor or direct beneficiary, Seddon had obtained a number of effects which were the property of the deceased woman and which were now under his control. The doctor was interviewed by the police and, strengthened by his evidence, the Home Office made an order for the exhumation of the body.

These forces were at work all unknown to Seddon, who went about his daily business, satisfied in his mind that, if he had not allayed the doubts in the mind of Ernest Vonderahe, he had at least so baffled him, by his bold challenge to put the matter into his solicitor's hands, that no further trouble need be anticipated.

Removed to the cemetery mortuary, the body was examined by Drs Wilcox and Spilsbury, now Sir William Wilcox and Sir Bernard Spilsbury, the Home Office pathologists. Certain organs were removed and forwarded for analysis, and the body was reinterred.

It was a grim coincidence that Seddon's business took him to

St Mary's Hospital at the time when Miss Barrow's remains were undergoing chemical examination, and that he was shown over a portion of the laboratory whilst that examination was in progress!

The chemist's report to the Home Office was emphatic: a very large quantity of arsenic had been found in the remains, and on this report the Home Office ordered an inquest.

Seddon was working at his accounts one night when his daughter came to tell him that a policeman wanted to see him.

'A policeman?' said Seddon. 'What does he want? Ask him to come in.'

The officer walked into the room, helmet in hand, and handed him a paper.

'I am the coroner's officer,' he said, 'and this is a summons for you to attend an inquest on the body of Eliza Barrow, which will be held to-morrow.'

Not a muscle of Seddon's face moved. Eliza Barrow! Until that moment he had not known that an exhumation order had been made. This was his first intimation that the net was closing round him.

When the officer had departed, Seddon swept aside the work on which he had been engaged, and sat down, coolly and calmly, to work throughout the night, packing his wife and children off to bed, whilst he prepared answers to such questions as might be put to him.

The grey dawn of a November day found him haggard and drawn, his table littered with papers covered with his clerkly writing. He had prepared for every possible contingency; had an answer for every question which might possibly be put to him; had checked and compared answer with answer, so that his story should be logical and convincing.

The inquest lasted for the greater part of a fortnight. And now suspicion became certainty. Seddon's conduct, tested and probed, did not react, as he had hoped, to his advantage. On December 4th he was arrested on the charge of murdering Eliza Barrow.

For more than a month, while he was under arrest, his wife was allowed her freedom. But as the law officers examined more closely the evidence available, it was obvious that

Seddon's wife was also under suspicion; and, to the amazement and indignation of the murderer, she was arrested on January 15th, 1912.

Seddon plied the detectives with questions as to the nature of the poison, and as to whether it might not have been self-administered. 'It was not carbolic acid, was it?' he asked. 'There was some in her room. Have you found arsenic in the body?'

All Seddon's transactions with the deceased woman now came into the light of day, and, incidentally, the motive for the murder. Miss Barrow had converted a considerable amount of her shares, of which she possessed some £1600 worth, into cash, and purchased from Seddon an annuity of some £155 per annum. Whilst she lived, he had to pay her £3,5s. a week, and it was to save this paltry sum, in the belief that she would live many years, that Seddon had murdered her. The transaction in itself was not unusual. Seddon, as an insurance superintendent, dealt in annuities, but this time the transaction was carried out for his own benefit. The will, therefore, leaving everything she possessed to Ernie and Hilda Grant, was a hollow document which meant nothing, since her only possessions at the time of her death were the cash she had at her bank and her own personal possessions.

The trial, which began at the Old Bailey in March 1912, before Mr Justice Bucknill, excited general interest. The Attorney-General, Sir Rufus Isaacs, now Viceroy of India, appeared for the prosecution; Sir Marshall Hall, then Mr Marshall Hall, defended the man; whilst Mr Rentoul, now Judge Rentoul, defended Mrs Seddon.

Throughout the trial, Seddon kept up that unemotional, detached attitude which he had shown from the very moment of his arrest. Mrs Seddon, on the other hand, was a sad and dejected figure. She could indulge in none of the breezy exchanges which Seddon had with his counsel, nor could she regard with equanimity a visit to the witness-box, which Seddon welcomed rather than otherwise.

Seddon depended upon the fact that no person had seen him administer poison to the deceased woman. And this, as has already been pointed out, is the basis of confidence in the case of every man or woman charged with murder by poison. It was as though he put into words the attitude of such men:

'I am willing to admit that the woman died of poison. I admit that I benefited considerably by her death, but you cannot prove that I gave her the poison. I may have brought food to her, and unless the prosecution can, beyond all possible doubt, prove that poison was in that food, and placed there by me, you must return a verdict of Not Guilty.' Never in the history of criminal jurisprudence has there been a case where a convicted prisoner has been detected in the act of administering poison, either in food or otherwise. The poisoner banks upon suspicion being equally attached to other persons than himself, and thus securing the benefit of the doubt. Seddon's confidence was fated to receive a terrible shock. After an hour's deliberation the jury returned with a verdict of 'Guilty' against Seddon, and 'Not Guilty' against Mrs Seddon. Seddon bent over and kissed his wife; in another minute they were separated, never to see one another again except through the intervening bars.

The Clerk of Arraigns put the usual question: 'What have you to say that the Court should not give you judgment to die according to law?'

And then occurred the most dramatic and, to many people in the court, the most painful incident of the trial. Seddon stood stiffly erect and began a long speech which declared his innocence. He ended by making a Masonic sign which was unmistakable to Mr Justice Bucknill, himself a Freemason: 'I declare before the Great Architect of the Universe that I am not guilty, my lord.' The judge was visibly distressed, but, recovering himself instantly, passed sentence of death, and Seddon paid the penalty for his crime at Pentonville Gaol on April 18th, 1912.

Freeman Wills Crofts was trained as an engineer but suffered, in middle life, a serious illness that required a long and tedious convalescence. He filled the time by writing a detective story, The Cask, *that was subsequently published and later acclaimed as a classic of its kind. He wrote a mystery novel each year afterwards until his death in 1957, many featuring his series detective Inspector French. He wrote very little on true crimes, and so the short piece which follows is — like those by F. Tennyson Jesse and Edgar Wallace — something of a rarity.*

FREEMAN WILLS CROFTS

The Gorse Hall Mystery

At the beginning of November, 1909, Mr George Henry Storrs was murdered at his home, near Stalybridge, under circumstances which have never been cleared up.

Mr Storrs was a wealthy builder and mill-owner, and lived with his wife and his wife's niece, Miss Lindley, in a large house named Gorse Hall. There were three servants—a cook and housemaid resident in the building, and a coachman living with his wife over the stables.

Mr Storrs was a kindly and popular man, a good employer, and had no known enemies. He and his wife were a devoted couple, and both were on affectionate terms with Miss Lindley. The household may, indeed, be called a happy one.

Its peace, however, was destined to be rudely broken. About 9:30 on the night of September 10, 1909, when the family were sitting in the dining-room, a shot was suddenly fired through the window.

Seeing that no one had been hit Mr Storrs rushed to the window and pulled aside the blind. He could just see a dark figure disappearing into the shrubbery. When the ladies asked if he knew the man he replied, after a slight hesitation, that he did not.

Mrs Storrs was more alarmed than her husband, and next day she insisted on the police being informed and asked to keep a special watch on the house. She also had a large alarm bell put on the roof, and it was agreed that if this were sounded the police should instantly hurry over. It was suggested that the man was a homicidal maniac, and she was afraid that he might return.

Nothing unusual happened, however, for some seven weeks,

and then, on the last Saturday of October, Mr Storrs called on the police and asked them to be particularly vigilant in their watch. He said he had no special reason for making the request, but that he 'wanted to be sure.'

That night about midnight the alarm bell sounded and the police hurried to the house. But nothing was wrong. Mr Storrs said apologetically that he had wished to be sure that the alarm was really efficient, and had rung it as a test.

Sunday and Monday passed uneventfully, but on Monday evening tragedy really did visit the house. Some time after dinner the housemaid had to pass the scullery door, when she saw that the gas was alight. She looked in and found that the window had been broken open, but before she could investigate further a man jumped out from behind the door and seized her wrist. He had a revolver in his hand and he swore that if she made a sound he would shoot her.

Instinctively she twisted away from him, running screaming through the house. He did not fire, but followed her till they reached the hall. There Mr Storrs, attracted by the noise, rushed out of the dining-room. As soon as the man saw him he cried: 'I've got you at last!' Again he did not fire, but as Mr Storrs ran forward he closed with him and a terrible fight began.

In the meantime Mrs Storrs and Miss Lindley had also rushed out. For a moment they tried to join in the struggle. Mrs Storrs actually succeeding in tearing away the man's revolver. Then they saw him draw a knife. But Mr Storrs gasped out: 'The bell! Give the alarm!' and Mrs Storrs rushed off to ring it, while Miss Lindley fled down the drive to summon help from the Stalybridge Central Club, which was close by.

When assistance came the murderer had disappeared and Mr Storrs was at the point of death. He had received fifteen terrible knife wounds, and died without making a statement.

While neither the ladies nor the servants were able to give a detailed description of the murderer, declaring that there was nothing distinctive about him, they agreed that he was youngish and poorly dressed, with a slight moustache and long fair hair. The revolver was of a cheap type, and yielded no clue.

A young man called Howard was arrested and charged with

the murder. He was a cousin of Mr Storrs, though he was personally unknown to the ladies. The evidence against him seemed purely circumstantial, but the police had a stronger case than was anticipated. When at the trial Mrs Storrs and Miss Lindley were asked if they could identify the murderer, they pointed dramatically to the prisoner, and swore he was the man.

No possible question of their bona fides arises; at the same time it became evident during the course of the trial that they were mistaken, Howard's innocence being proved beyond question. The verdict of Not Guilty was received with applause, and Howard left the court a popular hero.

Months afterwards a second man named Wilde was charged with the crime, stood his trial at Chester Assizes, and was also acquitted.

Since then the Gorse Hall Tragedy has remained a complete mystery, and no trace of the real murderer has ever been found.

In attempting to reconstruct what may have taken place in this strange tragedy, certain facts at once stand out as significant.

First, the murderer, whom for want of a better name I shall call John, had a definite grievance, real or imaginary, against Mr Storrs. This is proved by the facts that he said: 'I've got you at last,' and that he did not gain materially through his crime.

Second, Mr Storrs knew of this grievance and of his own danger. From his manner on the occasion of the attempt on September 9, it is almost certain that he recognised the man, and when he went to the police on the last Saturday in October, he evidently expected a further attack. Moreover, when he saw his assailant in the hall on the night of his death, he gave no exclamation of surprise, but grappled at once as with a known foe.

Third, Mr Storrs obviously wished to keep the affair secret. If he knew his own danger, as I have suggested he did, the fact that he made no statement on the subject proves this. But it is supported by his other actions. He did not inform the police of the first attack until the assailant had had time to get away. I will suggest presently that a second attack was made on the

Saturday night on which the alarm was sounded, and that on this occasion Mr Storrs suppressed any mention of John's presence for the same reason: to give him time to escape.

Fourth, owing to Mr Storr's upright character and kindly disposition, the secret was nothing with which he could reproach himself.

Fifthly, certain of John's actions seem to indicate an unbalanced mind. He entered the house on the night of the murder by smashing a window, and then committed the folly of turning on the gas. When he was discovered by the housemaid he followed her through the house, though he must have known her screams would attract attention. Again, to strike as many as fifteen times with his knife shows a fury quite abnormal.

With these salient points in mind, can we suggest any circumstances which might meet the facts?

I think we can.

At first sight it might seem as if the crime were committed by some epileptic or homicidal maniac, subject to recurrent fits of illness. But this theory would not account for the facts that Mr Storrs undoubtedly recognised his assailant and yet kept his identity secret. If he had not had some definite and personal reason for silence, he would surely have told the police who the man was.

Let us then try to fit a theory on to the facts we know. Let us begin by assuming that John is like Howard in personal appearance, and of an extremely unbalanced and excitable temperament. Let us further assume that he nurses a bitter hatred against Mr Storrs.

The cause of this hatred—that is, the motive for the crime—we do not know. There is not the slightest indication as to its nature in the evidence. All that we really know is that John had some overwhelming but mistaken sense of grievance against Mr Storrs.

We are probably on firmer ground when we picture John brooding over his fancied wrongs until his desire for revenge grows first into an obsession and then into actual mania.

On going to see Mr Storrs John blurts out his grievance and threatens vengeance. Mr Storrs, however, has no ill-feeling towards his visitor; in fact, he is sorry for him.

His kindly disposition makes him regret the young man's sense of injury, and he is willing to discuss the affair. But John, half insane, will not listen to reason, and Mr Storrs in self-defence is obliged to summon help.

John, seeing his chance gone, hurries away, determined to succeed at the next opportunity. The person who was called does not realise what he has prevented, and Mr Storrs, finding the whole matter painful, does not discuss it.

This reconstruction is still speculative and unsupported by direct evidence. But it is clear that John and Mr Storrs must have had some interview of the kind, in order to account for what follows. This interview, further, was probably not at Gorse Hall, as John was not seen by the inmates.

On September 10, John, who has bought a revolver, goes to Gorse Hall to make his attempt. He reaches the house, creeps up to the only lighted window, finds the blind does not exactly fit and that he can see Mr Storrs, and fires at him through the window. He sees that he has missed, and noticing that there are other people in the room, realises that if he remains for a further attempt he may be identified. So he hurries off.

Mr Storrs realises he is in danger, and asks the police to be specially vigilant. That night John makes his third attempt, but Mr Storrs sees him and rings the alarm. John again finds that if he remains, he will be caught. Mr Storrs, full of pity for the misguided youth, and hoping eventually to bring him to reason, tells the police he was only making a test, in order to give the young fellow time to escape.

It is obvious that there must have been some special circumstances about this attempt which enabled Mr Storrs to ring the alarm before being attacked. Perhaps, for example, he may have discovered John in the act of swarming up a balcony pillar or a waterpipe, or in such other position that the young man could not use his weapon.

On Monday, John again goes to Gorse Hall. Determined this time to make an end of the matter, he breaks in and commits the murder. He escapes from the country and is therefore not found by the police.

The above reconstruction, indicates the lines along which I believe the explanation of this mysterious crime must lie.

In the introduction to this book I have said something about Erle Stanley Gardner and his Court of Last Resort, and in the piece which follows the author tells very entertainingly how it came into being, prompted by a three-part article about him by Alva Johnston. 'A person who hasn't had the actual experience can never visualize what happens when many millions of people see something in print,' he said later. 'All I know for sure is that many, many millions of people read that I was the champion of the underdog. I was therefore literally deluged with underdogs who needed championing.'

For the next decade the Court took up something like eighty percent of Gardner's time, and it was undoubtedly the most important thing in his whole life: a tremendous success, something pioneering and hugely important. It's eventual falling-part was a tragedy, and came about for the most wretched reasons: Argosy magazine had come to depend very heavily on the Court features for its huge circulation, but since it was independent and beyond their ultimate control the Editors felt uncomfortable, which led to tensions that grew and grew, and finally exploded in a welter of resignations, Gardner's included.

It did revive, and Gardner returned to it and Argosy, but the workload proved too much, the articles became thinner and thinner, and eventually the Court died. He continued to be involved in police-work until his death, and wrote other books on real crime, but there was never again anything to rival the Courth of Last Resort, where he could be Perry Mason...

ERLE STANLEY GARDNER

The Court of Last Resort

Man in general doesn't appreciate what he has until he is deprived of it. Then he starts to miss it. He takes good health for granted until sickness comes along. He takes three meals a day for granted until some unusual circumstance makes him go hungry. Liberty is only a term until he is deprived of it, and then he begins to realize what it means to have freedom of motion and freedom of choice.

Strange as it may seem, a diametrically opposite situation led to the origin of the Court of Last Resort.

I learned to value liberty not by having it taken away but by having such a marvelous demonstration of the advantages of freedom that I began to think what it must mean to be deprived of freedom.

In order to understand this somewhat paradoxical situation it is going to be necessary to touch on a most unusual murder case and give a bit of personal history.

The murder case is that of William Marvin Lindley, described in newspapers and magazines as 'The Red-Headed Killer'; the personal history relates to a biographical sketch written by the late Alva Johnston which ran several installments in *The Saturday Evening Post*. This biographical sketch was entitled 'The Case of Erle Stanley Gardner,' and included some of the spectacular and unorthodox methods which I used in connection with the trial of cases when I was a practicing attorney.

I have always claimed that an attorney is not necessarily bound to confine his cross-examination of a hostile witness to questions and answers on the witness stand. If a witness is certain of an identification, he should be absolutely certain of it.

He may testify under oath with all the positive sincerity in the
world that the defendant is the man he saw running away from
the scene of the crime two years ago, but if an attorney can get
him to point to one of the assistant prosecutors by making the
witness feel that the man at whom he is pointing is actually the
defendant in the case, the witness's actions speak louder than
words.

Of course, courts resent attempts to mislead a witness, so an
attorney may well find himself in a position where the procedure, by which he might demonstrate that a witness is mistaken
on a matter of identification, may be frowned upon by the
court.

Therefore the problem of getting a witness to belie his words
by actions, without violating the ethics of the profession or the
rules of court is, at times, a rather tricky business.

During the days when I first engaged in the practice of law,
legal ethics were not as sharply defined nor as rigidly enforced
as they now are, and, with the singular optimism of youth, I
was more confident of my own interpretation of what was
proper.

I mention these matters because the early portion of my legal
career, during which I was trying to build up a law practice in a
city where I was virtually without friends or friendly contacts,
was punctuated with spectacular incidents which made colorful copy for a biographer. As I expressed it at the time in a letter
to my father, 'I have built up a law practice in which I am
dealing with large numbers of clients of all classes—except the
upper and middle class.'

Eventually my courtroom tactics attracted sufficient attention so that my practice became confined exclusively to clients
of the upper and middle class, but Alva Johnston found the
earlier chapters of my legal escapades much more interesting
and therefore emphasized them in considerable detail.

Johnston also emphasized a quixotic streak which has always been part of my nature: to champion the cause of the
underdog, particularly if he is without friends, without money,
and his cause seems to be utterly hopeless.

By the time Johnston had finished stringing colorful incidents into his biographical sketch, his audience might well have

received the impression that I made a habit of entering the lists on behalf of penniless defendants who were in hopeless predicaments, and by legal legerdemain could cause the doors of prison to swing wide open. The result was that just about every hopeless case in the United States was dumped in my lap in a deluge of fan mail.

Among these cases was that of William Marvin Lindley. This case was sent to me by Al Matthews, Jr., a Los Angeles attorney at law who has since become affiliated with the Public Defender's Office, but who, at that time, was a freelance. He had interested himself on behalf of Lindley after Lindley's conviction.

Lindley was at the time in the condemned row at San Quentin awaiting execution. He had been convicted of a brutal sex murder. The evidence against him was so overwhelming that until Al Matthews came along no one had extended the slightest sympathy or had bothered to give the case very much detailed study.

Al Matthews wrote me that he felt absolutely convinced Lindley was innocent, that he had been the victim of a bizarre combination of circumstances, and begged me to study the case.

At the time it seemed to me that every mail was bringing in a dozen similar pleas, but there was something about Al Matthews' letter, a certain sincerity that attracted my attention. I studied the outline Matthews sent down.

The murder had occurred during the aftermath of the great depression, and the characters who were involved in the crime were, for the most part, people who lived in more or less temporary camps along the banks of the Yuba River in California. One gathered the impression that these were persons of limited funds, limited education, and, in some instances, limited intelligence.

Some young girls, around the age of adolescence, had gone in swimming in the Yuba River. As a bathing suit, the victim of the crime wore simply a cotton dress.

William Marvin Lindley, a redhead, was at the time operating a boathouse on the banks of the river.

The victim of the crime had finished her swimming, changed

her clothes, gone into the house where her folks were living, made some remarks to her father, then had gone out again.

Some twenty minutes or half an hour later she was found in a dying condition. She had evidently been attacked after putting up a terrific struggle. She was able to sob out to her father the statement that it was 'that old red-headed liar in the boathouse, the old red-headed liar.' Some time later, and without ever clarifying this statement, she died.

A sheepherder, a young boy whose intelligence was not keen, to say the least, was herding sheep on the other side of the Yuba River, a distance of some two hundred yards. This sheepherder had sat under a tree, watching the girls while they were swimming. They left the water and entered the boathouse. Later on he noticed one of the girls go toward home and another girl went down to the water to wash her feet.

Prior to this time, a man, whom the sheepherder identified as Lindley, had been standing in the willows. He, also, was watching the girls swimming. After the victim had started back toward the levee, the sheepherder stated he had seen her struggling with 'Red,' the man who had been standing in the bushes watching her. They 'went down behind the willows.'

The sheepherder identified the man as 'Red' Lindley, the defendant. He based his identification in part upon the color of clothes that Lindley was wearing that afternoon.

At the time of the trial (and it should be noted that Lindley was not represented at this trial by Al Matthews, who didn't enter the case until after conviction) Lindley tried to produce an alibi. It was a nice alibi except that it broke down for the very period when the crime was being committed.

Apparently none of the persons connected with the case carried a watch, and it was necessary to work out time by depending upon the best estimates of the witnesses, starting from an event which had been pretty well established in the day's schedule.

All in all, Lindley's case seemed hopeless, merely another drab sex crime in which the culprit had become so inflamed at the sight of the adolescent girls bathing in the river that he lost all self-control, and despite the fact that there were witnesses who watched him and who could identify him, proceeded to go completely mad with lust.

Al Matthews had taken over, conducted an investigation and had filed a writ of *habeas corpus* in the State Supreme Court, also an application for a writ of error *Coram Nobis*, and a writ of *Coram Vobis*. Inasmuch as the Supreme Court had already considered the case on appeal and affirmed the conviction and sentence of death, it was necessary for the attorneys to resort to these last named, little used, hardly understood writs in order to have even a leg to stand on.

Enough of a showing had been made so that the Supreme Court had appointed a referee to take testimony, and then peculiar things began to develop. For one thing it turned out that the sheepherder was color-blind; and while he had stated that he had recognized the defendant by the tan-colored khaki clothes he had been wearing, it appeared by the time of the *habeas corpus* hearing that this witness was prone to describe virtually every color as tan. Not only was he color-blind but it developed that he had barely enough intelligence to enable him to testify. At one time he had told the referee that he did not know what it meant to testify under oath. He had identified a brown and white dress, worn by one of the women who was attending the referee's hearing, as black. He had then been asked to identify colored cards at a distance approximately equal to that at which he had seen the murderer, and he had identified a yellow card as being white, a gold one as being brown, an orange one as red, and a gray one as blue. At another time he had said that green was blue, gold was white, light brown was white, and pink was red.

The Supreme Court carefully reviewed the facts in the case as brought out in the hearing before the referee, co-ordinated those facts with the evidence in the case, and decided that Lindley had been properly convicted and must go to the gas chamber.

The date of execution was finally set. (There had been one or two reprieves while the various legal matters were pending, but now the date had been set, and Governor Earl Warren, who had been forced to leave the state temporarily on business, had pointed out to the lieutenant governor who would be in charge during Governor Warren's absence that he wanted no further reprieves in the Lindley case. The execution was to go ahead as scheduled.)

That execution date was but a short distance away. As I remember it, a matter of a week or ten days.

In any event, I telephoned Al Matthews, told him I would study the case, and he sent his wife down to see me, bringing with her the trial transcript and a few facts which would enable me to understand something of the nature of the case.

It was a long and involved transcript, and I labored through it, trying to become familiar with the case from the testimony of the witnesses and the study of the records.

There was one significant thing which Al Matthews had uncovered. There had been *another* red-headed hop picker in the vicinity on the day of the crime. That hop picker had not been working on the day of the murder. He had shown up later with marks on his face which could well have been made by a girl's fingernails. He had reportedly, in a drunken brawl that night, stated that he had been the one who had committed the murder, and he had mysteriously disappeared the next morning without even calling for his pay check. Some of those facts could be verified positively.

That was the case in a nutshell, and William Marvin Lindley was to die.

I carefully studied the evidence submitted by Lindley in support of his defense, and there was no question but what his alibi broke down at the very time the crime was being committed. The attorneys for the prosecution had made the most of that.

So then, having completed a study of the transcript, I decided to tackle the case from another angle.

Strange as it may seem, apparently it had never occurred to anyone to examine Lindley's alibi with reference to the movements of the murderer, whoever that murderer might have been, on the day in question.

I decided to do this and so found it necessary to work out a diagram of the scene of the crime according to distances, and to start co-ordinating the activities of the various people in relation to their contact with other people, forming a species of time schedule that was dependent entirely upon events rather than upon guesswork as to the hour, or the position of clock hands.

Once that was done, a very startling fact became manifest.

At the exact time witnesses had seen the murderer standing in the willows, watching the girls swimming, the defendant, William Marvin Lindley, had been riding in an automobile with the father of the murdered girl.

Again and again I went over this schedule and there simply couldn't be any other possible answer. The evidence given by the father himself, the evidence given by other witnesses, showed that this must be true. There wasn't any escape from it.

At that time there was no opportunity to do anything by strictly legal methods. Lindley's execution was almost a matter of hours. There was no time to make a formal appearance, no time to set in motion any type of legal proceedings even if it had been possible to conceive of any type of legal proceedings which had not been previously tried. The defendant had had the benefit of all the writs that the most adroit and ingenious attorney could possibly have conjured up.

There was only one thing to do.

I sent a letter to each justice of the State Supreme Court; I sent copies of those letters to the State's attorney general; I sent letters to the office of the Governor, pointing out page by page in the transcript the manner in which this synthetic schedule had been built up, making all due allowances for the greatest margin of time-elapse possible. Under this schedule there was no question that at the very moment several witnesses had seen this mysterious man standing in the willows, the man who was positively identified as being the murderer of the victim, the defendant, William Marvin Lindley, had been riding in the automobile with the girl's father some miles from the scene of the crime.

Afterward, and entirely off the record, I learned something of the scene of hectic activity which followed the receipt of these various letters. Still off the record, as I understand it, members of the California Supreme Court unanimously requested Lieutenant Governor Fred Howser, who was in charge at the time, not to permit the execution to take place until there could be a further investigation, and another stay of execution was granted.

The case began to attract quite a bit of attention. The press picked up the fact that I had written a letter in connection with it and set forth some of my contentions.

It will be noted that I am commenting in detail on the Lindley case because of its repercussions. The Lindley case standing by itself, however, is well worth serious study by anyone who is at all interested in the administration of criminal law.

Simply consider the facts of the case at the time Al Matthews, Jr., had taken an interest in it:

The girl had been found in a dying condition. She had made a statement which certainly pointed to the defendant Lindley as the perpetrator of the crime. The police had investigated and found an eyewitness who positively identified Lindley as the man who had been waiting in the bushes, watching the girls swimming, who had subsequently grabbed one of the girls, and, after a terrific struggle, had dropped down out of sight behind the bushes.

Lindley had claimed an alibi, trying to prove that he wasn't there at the time of the commission of the crime. That attempted alibi seemed to have broken down for the exact period that the crime was taking place. Lindley was without funds. An attorney had been appointed by the court to defend him, and the jury, evidently considering Lindley a murderer and a liar, had promptly brought in a verdict finding him guilty of first-degree murder, with no recommendation, thereby automatically making it mandatory that a death sentence be imposed.

I will never know what peculiar hunch attracted Matthews to the case, because a cursory study of the evidence would certainly indicate that the defendant was guilty, but when Matthews began to dig he uncovered new evidence showing that the eyewitness, who had identified Lindley largely because of the color of his clothes, was color-blind; and that another red-headed man, who had been in the vicinity of the crime, had scratch marks on his face, and, in a drunken condition the very night of the crime, had admitted that he was the perpetrator of the offense.

When I interceded on behalf of the defendant the wire services sent out 'copy' which was published in various newspapers throughout the country.

At that time, my friend Raymond Schindler, the famous private detective (with whom I collaborated again on later cases) was an advisory editor of a factual detective magazine, working in connection with Horace Bailey Brown, who was editor in chief. Brown, himself a veteran article writer, with considerable editorial experience, was eagerly looking for new angles on crime stories so that he could get away from the usual hackneyed approach and turn out a magazine that would attract the interests of the reading public.

When Schindler and Brown read the notice in the press stating that I had entered the Lindley case, they wired asking me if I would care to write something about it for the magazine in question.

Nothing could have suited me better.

I was for the moment at an impasse. There was certainly no legal remedy left to the defendant. The lieutenant governor had granted a temporary stay of execution, but Governor Warren's attitude in the matter was quite well known, and now that Governor Warren had returned to the state there was no further authority left in the hands of the lieutenant governor to act in the matter.

So, feeling that nothing remained to be done from a legal standpoint, I decided it would be interesting to see what would happen if the people generally were given some first-hand knowledge of the peculiar situation disclosed by the transcript in the Lindley case.

So I wrote an open letter to Governor Warren, which I sent to the magazine and which was published.

I have been told that the Governor's office received a deluge of mail as a result of this letter. Governor Warren, despite any previous statements he may have made, did the right thing and he did it in a decent manner. He promptly commuted the sentence of the defendant to life imprisonment so that there would be an opportunity for a further investigation.

Lindley—never a robust man emotionally—had been living in the shadow of death for months. He had been figuratively dragged into the death chamber and then hauled out again, only to be once more dragged in and then jerked out. As a result, his mind had become unsettled. The man was, in the opinion of many, hopelessly insane. In fact I understand that some of the members of the Supreme Court had made definite recommendations that because of this insanity alone the execution should not be permitted.

In any event, Lindley was declared insane, and his sentence commuted to life imprisonment. There the case stands to this day.

There is very persuasive evidence that another red-headed man may have committed the crime. An extensive search was made for this mysterious red-headed hop picker who had what may have been fingernail scratches on his face, who had certainly been in a state of extreme nervousness, and who had vanished so mysteriously on the day following the murder of the girl. That search was made far too late. It was made by private parties who did not have the facilities available to the police. The search was fruitless. The man has never been found.

The Lindley case is perhaps as good an example as we can conjure up at the moment of the necessity of making a scientific, careful investigation of all of the facts in a case while those facts are still available.

Because of the identification made by the dying girl (an identification which was, of course, not as definite as should have been the case if Lindley had actually committed the crime), the so-called eyewitness identification by the young sheepherder, the police became convinced that Lindley was the murderer. They diligently searched for any evidence that would enable the prosecutor to build up a good case against Lindley in court, and they brushed aside any evidence which might have pointed to developments that would have been in Lindley's favor.

As a result, this other red-headed suspect, who certainly should have been apprehended and interrogated, was permitted to leave the community without an attempt made to find him or question him. The itinerant witnesses vanished to the four winds, and Lindley was left with a sentence of life imprisonment.

The Lindley case, however, was destined to have far-reaching developments.

Harry Steeger, head of Popular Publications Inc., which publishes *Argosy* Magazine, and for many years a warm personal friend, had been corresponding with me about undertaking an adventure of sorts.

The year before I had taken an expedition down the entire length of the peninsula of Baja California, starting at Tijuana, and, after several weeks of wild adventure over twelve hundred miles of mountain and desert, reaching the very southern tip of the peninsula at Cape San Lucas.

I had written a book about that trip, and since, despite months of careful planning, the whole trip had almost been abandoned because of developments in the Lindley case, I had mentioned briefly the fact that only the commutation of sentence in this case had left us free to make the trip. The point was important in the book because the Lindley matter so materially shortened the time available for preparation that we had no alternative but to throw things into the car helter-skelter, and try to unscramble them on the road.

This book, *The Land of Shorter Shadows,* had fascinated both Harry Steeger and his wife, Shirley, a member of the New York Botanical Gardens, and a tireless and enthusiastic worker.

The upshot of it was that Harry and Shirley Steeger, two of my secretaries, Sam Hicks of Wyoming, and I started once more down the long twelve-hundred-mile route. We had plenty of shorthand notebooks, quantities of film, a veritable battery of cameras, and this time were determined to see that the peninsula was fully covered.

Even with the very best in the line of modern equipment, including jeeps and a 'power wagon' equipped with power winches, four-wheel drive, oversized tires, etc., this trip down the peninsula of Baja California is a long, hard, and at times a dangerous grind. There are days when forty miles is a full day's journey, and several times we went for two days in succession without meeting a single car on the road.

Since this expedition started late in February, the days were short and the nights were long. It was necessary to make camp during the last of the daylight hours, and then after supper, when the dishes were done, the sleeping bags spread on the ground, air mattresses inflated, there would be an hour or two for just sitting around the campfire.

The peninsula of Baja California is distinctly and individually different. The elephant trees are almost exclusively indigenous to that terrain, and, as I understand it, the *cirio* trees are not found in any other spot on earth. The nights were nearly always cool and cloudless. The days were, for the most part, hot with the dry heat of the desert. The air was a tonic and a benediction rolled into one. At night the steady, unwinking stars marched tirelessly across the heavens.

All about us was the immensity of a wild country. The firelight was the only reassuring memento of man's ability to master his environment. It would throw a fitful circle of illumination for some thirty or forty feet and reflect back in a rosy glow from the weird *cardon* trees pushing their cactus-like limbs high into the air. Lower down, on the floor of the desert the flames would illuminate prickly pear, *cholla* cactus, ladyfinger cactus, and, perhaps in the background, a sweet *pitahaya* or organ-pipe cactus.

Beyond the circle of campfire, darkness filled an unknown terrain with a mystery which the human mind instinctively translated into terms of danger. . . . A sudden screaming howl from the encircling darkness caused us to give an involuntary start before we recognized the familiar voice of the coyote, and grinned sheepishly. And just outside of the lighted circle the coyote was probably grinning, too. They are the most daring, saucy, impudent, lovable rascals in the world (unless a man has sheep or chickens, in which event the coyote is a fiend incarnate).

So it was natural that during these long evenings, while we exhausted most of the subjects of conversation, we should find ourselves dwelling on the predicament of men who had been wrongfully imprisoned.

Freedom is, after all, only relative. No man has absolute freedom. We are bound by economic chains, by ties of personal dependency. We have telephones, taxicabs and taxes; work, worry and war. Down there in Baja California life and living became unbelievably simplified. We ate, we slept, and we traveled. We had nothing else to do. There was no schedule, no telephones, no illumination at night save the light of the gasoline lantern which was used sparingly when supper was late.

Against this environment of extreme freedom from care and restraint, the life of a man condemned to live behind barred doors, within gray walls, became a persistent nightmare which colored even our waking hours.

The problem of getting firewood helped determine the length of our sleep at night. We would conscientiously save out enough wood for a breakfast fire, and burn the rest at night. When the evening campfire began to die down to coals we would move closer, until, at length, the last of the flames flickered out. Then we would watch the bed of coals until even the coals began to dull. By that time we would be ready for our sleeping bags.

Many times during those silent watches of the night I lay awake for half or three-quarters of an hour thinking about the problems inherent in the wise administration of justice. And the more I came to revel in my own liberty to go where I wanted to, whenever I wanted to, the more I found myself thinking of innocent men cooped up in cells. It was a nagging worry which I could and sometimes did push into the back of my mind—but not very far back, and it wouldn't stay there.

So one day I mentioned how I felt to Harry Steeger, and I discovered he had been experiencing the same reaction. Every time he wakened at night he found himself speculating on the problem, wondering what he as a publisher could do about it.

On one occasion when we discussed the situation, Harry reached a decision.

'Erle,' he said, 'if you ever find any other case where you think the man has been wrongfully convicted, *Argosy* will donate enough space to see that the case is given ample publicity, and we'll see what the public reaction is.

'You know what I'm trying to do with *Argosy*. When we purchased it from the Munsey Company it was an old-time adventure magazine printed on wood pulp paper. We've turned it into an illustrated magazine for men, and people are beginning to notice it. Of all the magazines we publish I think *Argosy* would be the most available vehicle for this sort of thing.'

In the nights which followed that talk we began to carry this thought to its logical conclusion and to explore possibilities.

Some months previous to this we had discussed the peculiar fact that there was no popular magazine devoted to justice, and yet all of our vaunted American way of life was founded upon our concept of justice.

So, down there in Baja California, we began to speculate on the idea of welding those thoughts together—testing the reaction of the American people to find out if they were really interested in the cause of justice and at the same time using space to correct some specific instance of an injustice.

Night after night, we planned just how a case could be presented to the American people, what their reactions would be and what the effect of those reactions would be upon the governmental agencies who had the final say in the matter.

We realized early in the game that it would never do for a magazine with a national circulation to come out and say in effect, 'This man claims he's innocent. He's been convicted of murder. Erle Stanley Gardner thinks there may be something in the man's contentions, therefore we want the governor to grant a pardon.'

We knew that we'd need facts, and these facts would have to be presented to the reading public in a form that would incite interest. No matter how much space *Argosy* donated to some worthy case, no good would be done unless people read what was printed in that space. And, even then, merely reading about the case wouldn't help unless people became sufficiently aroused to *do* something about it.

Public opinion must be molded, but it must be an enlightened public opinion based on facts, otherwise we would be charged, and justly charged, with the tactics of the rabble rousers.

It is customary in legal circles to refer to the highest tribunal in any jurisdiction as 'the court of last resort.' Out there in the wide open spaces of Baja California, we came to the conclusion that in a country such as ours no officially organized tribunal ever could be the *real* court of last resort. The real court of last resort, we felt, was the people themselves. It was a new and daring concept, yet it was essentially sound. Under our theory of law the people are superior to any department of the government, legislative, executive or judicial. They must, of course, exercise their wishes in accordance with the methods prescribed in the Constitution, but once those methods have been complied with, the will of the people is the supreme law of this land.

That didn't mean that in order to decide whether John Doe had been wrongfully convicted we needed to have the people pass an initiative measure, or, if we decided that John Doe had been wrongfully convicted that we needed to present a Constitutional amendment to get him liberated.

The constitutions of the various states provide that the governors have the power of pardon. The governors, on the other hand, are responsible to the people. Every four years they come up for re-election. They have to stand on their record. If any material thinking segment of a state's population should decide that John Doe had been wrongfully convicted and that the governor's pardoning prerogative was being unjustly withheld, that governor would be faced with a political liability at election time. Governors are not prone to assume political liabilities unless there is a corresponding political credit to be entered on the other side of the ledger.

But how could anyone present a case to the people without following the tactics of the rabble rousers? In the case of John Doe, how could we get the facts, how could we properly marshal those facts, how could we get the public to take a sufficient interest in those facts? How could we persuade a substantial segment of population to take a real interest in John Doe? It was a problem we discussed at length. We felt that we were on the right track if we could once find the proper approach; but the proper approach required that the public should understand the facts, should correlate them, and should then want to take action.

We knew that most magazine readers like detective stories. How about letting the readers study the case of John Doe, fact by fact, until they reached an intelligent opinion?

That would mean investigators in whom the readers would have confidence, and who could unearth those facts. It would mean that reader interest must be kept alive.

Was there any method by which all of this could be accomplished?

Gradually the idea of *Argosy's* board of investigators came into existence.

The basic idea was to get men who were specialists in their line, men who had enough national reputation so readers could have confidence in their judgment, men who would be public-spirited enough to donate their services to the cause of justice (because any question of financial reward would immediately taint the whole proceedings with what might be considered a selfish motivation). We also needed men who had achieved such financial success in their chosen professions that they were in no particular need of personal publicity. Moreover, the aggregate combination must be such that it would be virtually impossible for any prisoner to deceive these men as to the true issues in a case.

It was, of course, a pretty large order.

We thought at once of Dr LeMoyne Snyder.

Dr LeMoyne Snyder is one of the outstanding authorities on homicide investigation in the country. He is not only a doctor of medicine but he is an attorney at law, and he has for some years specialized in the field of legal medicine. His book *Homicide Investigation* is one of the most authoritative technical books on the subject in the country, and is at once a guide for peace officers as well as a treatise for those who are interested in the more highly technical aspects of the subject.

We decided to put the whole idea up to Dr Snyder. Next, we needed some outstanding detective. So we thought of Raymond Schindler.

Raymond Schindler is perhaps the best-known private detective in the country. I had first met him when we were both in the Bahamas. He was then working on the famous case of Alfred de Marigny, who had been accused of murdering his wealthy father-in-law, Sir Harry Oakes. I was covering the case for the New York *Journal-American* and some of its allied newspapers.

Raymond Schindler's career as a private detective dates back to 1906 when he first started work in San Francisco. Later on, it was through the efforts of Raymond Schindler that the

Erle Stanley Gardner: founder of the Court of Last Resort.

corruption which existed in San Francisco under Abe Rueff and 'Big Jim' Gallagher was cleaned up.

Many of Schindler's exploits have found their way from time to time into print, and a year or so ago Rupert Hughes, in a volume entitled *The Complete Detective,* gave a biographical summary of Schindler's life which has, of course, been exceedingly colorful.

So much for the detective end. If Schindler would work with us, we felt he'd be ideal for the job.

It also occurred to us that we'd want to have absolutely accurate information for our own guidance. We had to know whether the men we were talking with were telling the truth. That brought up a consideration of Leonarde Keeler's work with the lie detector. Keeler had not only done a great deal to develop the polygraph but was probably the outstanding polygraph operator in the country. (Before we were able to avail ourselves of Keeler's services to any great extent, he became ill and passed away. His place was taken by Alex Gregory, a man who has an excellent background as an investigator, a careful, conscientious worker, a former member of the Detroit police force, a keen student of psychology.)

There is, of course, some question as to the efficacy of the 'lie detector.'

To my mind the question of, 'How accurate is a lie detector?' is equivalent to asking, 'How good is a camera?'

The answer is, of course, the camera doesn't take the pictures. The photographer takes the pictures. Some photographers using a medium-priced camera can take pictures that win national awards. Some merely take mediocre pictures; others forget to turn the film and so get double exposures, or forget to pull the slide from the plateholder and so get nothing.

I think the same holds true with the polygraph. The polygraph is a scientific instrument. It determines certain specific reactions on the part of the subject. The problem of coordinating the graph of these reactions so as to know whether the subject is or is not telling the truth depends upon numerous factors—the questions which are asked, the manner in which they are asked, the manner in which the subject is prepared for the test, and the skill on the part of the operator.

It is quite possible that Alex Gregory, for instance, won't always be able to tell whether a man is guilty or innocent. But I feel that Alex Gregory would never say that an innocent man was guilty. He might say he didn't know. But if he said a man was definitely guilty, I wouldn't want to run against his judgment. And similarly if Alex Gregory assures us that a man who says he is innocent is telling us the truth, I for one am all in favor of going ahead and launching an investigation which may run into hundreds of hours of time spent.

So much for the polygraph angle.

So far as the legal appraisal was concerned, I promised Steeger I would study the transcripts of testimony in the various cases, and bring to bear such knowledge as I had acquired in twenty-five years of trial work.

Later on this investigating committee was to receive very substantial reinforcements in the persons of Tom Smith and Bob Rhay.

Tom Smith was at the time the warden of the Washington State Penitentiary at Walla Walla. Bob Rhay was working under him, and as presently will be seen, our first case brought us into intimate contact with both of these men. Later on they were destined to become exceedingly interested in the social significance of the program we had undertaken, and when suitable opportunity arose, to affiliate themselves with it.

However, that page in our adventures in justice had not then been written. We were primarily concerned with the problem of getting together a board of investigors who would have enough prestige to influence public opinion, who would have a sufficient love of justice to be willing to donate a large portion of their time, and who had the proper technical qualifications to strip aside all fabrications and arrive at the right answer.

So we worked our way down the peninsula of Baja California, talking around every campfire of plans for our Court of Last Resort, wondering what, if anything, it could accomplish, but each day becoming more and more determined that we would find out by actual experiment just what it could accomplish.

Within a matter of weeks after Steeger and I returned from Baja California I had occasion to consider the case of Clarence

Boggie, prisoner #16587, confined in the Washington State Penitentiary at Walla Walla, serving a life sentence for murder.

Boggie had written a letter enclosing copies of documents compiled by the Reverend Arvid Ohrnell, Protestant chaplain of the Washington State Reformatory at Monroe. This letter had been acknowledged, but was buried in a pile of similar appeals from prisoners sent in from all over the country.

Then I received a communication from the Reverend W.A. Gilbert, a part-time voluntary chaplain at Walla Walla, asking me for an appointment at my ranch.

Gilbert was the rector of St Paul's Episcopal Church at Walla Walla. He also did a great deal of voluntary prison chaplain work purely as an extracurricular activity, donating his time furnishing spiritual guidance to prison inmates.

Bill Gilbert was attending a church convention in Santa Barbara. He drove the two hundred odd miles down to my ranch through Sunday traffic in order to confer with me about the Boggie case and then drove back that afternoon—nearly five hundred miles of Sunday driving in order to try and enlist my aid in the cause of a penniless unfortunate who had then been incarcerated in the Walla Walla prison for some thirteen years, and who was scheduled to remain there the rest of his life.

Bill Gilbert's devotion to a philanthropic cause seemed an unusual sacrifice of time and energy to me then. Now I have seen enough of the work done by prison chaplains to know that it is merely an ordinary incident in their lives.

A book could—and should—be written about the activities of these men. They sacrifice their own time, their own funds, pile up mileage on their automobiles, trying to do what they can to assist in the spiritual and material welfare of prisoners, many of whom shamelessly take advantage of this unselfish devotion to a self-imposed duty.

The best of prison chaplains never worry about what a man has done. They are only interested in trying to see how they can help the man prepare for the future. They know that for the most part they are carving in rotten wood, but they keep carving nevertheless, hoping that when they have stripped away the layers of mental and moral disease they will come to a basic foundation which can take and hold a permanent impression.

In a surprising number of instances they are successful.

At that time I personally had no realization of the extent to which prison inmates are isolated behind a curtain of steel and concrete. I had no realization that their correspondence was limited in many instances as to quantity, and in nearly every instance to a chosen list of approved correspondents.

As a practicing attorney any letters I cared to write to prisoners had been delivered and answered. That, as it turned out, is because an exception is made in the case of attorneys. Prisoners are permitted to correspond freely with attorneys. On the other hand, as a general rule, prisoners are not permitted to correspond at all with representatives of the press, and their personal correspondence is very, very limited.

Since I had left the active practice of law my correspondence with prison inmates had been somewhat limited, and in most of the instances my status as attorney had resolved the doubt in my favor and the correspondence had gone through, but once when I tried to find out something about the facts in a case I had been curtly refused permission to correspond with the inmate.

These instances had served to arouse my ire and I had determined that if we started investigating a case with *Argosy* Magazine behind us, we were going to engage in a verbal slugging match if we weren't premitted to interview the prisoner.

So I explained to Bill Gilbert that I would fly up to Walla Walla to interview Boggie. I told Gilbert to explain this to the warden of the penitentiary and to tell him that I didn't want to have a lot of red tape thrown at me when I arrived.

I remember that I explained to Bill Gilbert that heretofore we had been trying to catch our flies with molasses. I was tired of that, and had decided it might be more effective to catch them with a fly swatter.

Gilbert told me that he felt quite certain I would have no trouble in interviewing Clarence Boggie, but he would sound out the warden in the matter.

Bill Gilbert returned to Walla Walla and wired me that I would have no difficulty.

That was a masterpiece of understatement.

Tom Smith, as has been previously mentioned, was the warden. He was more than ready to meet us halfway.

'Now look,' he said finally, 'you're not going to meet any red-tape opposition up here. If Clarence Boggie is innocent we want to find it out just as much as you do. Bill Gilbert has told me about your organization. I know something about the reputation of these men who are associated with you in the work you're doing. If you're going to make an impartial investigation of the Boggie case, and if it isn't going to cost the State anything, I'll do everything in my power to facilitate the investigation. I also think you'll find the State officials here will have a similar attitude. Anything I can do to help promote such an attitude I'll be glad to do. Now, then, you take over from there.'

In short, I found Tom Smith to be entirely different from the type of warden I had expected to find.

In the intimate association with him which was to come later I learned to know the man's big heart, his almost naïve idealism, and his passionate desire for justice.

At the time, I was surprised to find a warden who had absolutely no resemblance to the type of warden fiction writers are too prone to create. There was nothing of the sadistic disciplinarian about him. He was intensely human, eager to learn everything he could about prison administration, to apply what he had learned, and to see that every man had complete justice.

Later on that day I met the incredible Clarence Boggie.

I refer to him as 'incredible' because everything about the man was completely and utterly incredible. Virtually every time I talked with him I discovered some new facet of the man, some new twist of his background, some episode which seemed to be absolutely incredible, yet which later turned out to be the truth.

For instance, Boggie, a penniless prisoner serving a life sentence, with two previous convictions behind him, maintained stoutly that he had never been guilty of any crime.

That, of course, seemed absurd.

Yet subsequent investigations indicated the man's story might well be true. In each instance of a prior conviction he had received a pardon apparently predicated upon the fact that an investigation showed he had been wrongfully convicted.

The man, of course, had some sort of a prison neurosis. He also had a very strong love for his mother which made him place her on a pedestal. He was emotionally unstable, given to sudden spells of crying, particularly if someone would mention his mother. He had been incarcerated long enough so that he had the mental outlook that is sometimes referred to as being 'stir simple.'

Yet here was this penniless man who would, at a later date, casually mention to us that he was the owner of a copper mine worth several million dollars.

I don't know when he first made that statement. We took it as a complete fairy tale, something that had been conjured up in his dreams during the long period of his confinement.

The story of the copper mine was very interesting. The mine, he explained, had been given to him by a woman whom he had never seen, but she wanted to get rid of her earthly property so she had deeded Boogie the mine. The deed had been lost.

You listen to a story like that from a two-time loser serving a life term in a penitentiary for murder, and it is enough to make you want to forget the whole thing. The guy is not only a crook but a liar. You kick yourself for having traveled twelve or fifteen hundred miles to act the part of a gullible sucker.

Yet essentially this story was true.

It wasn't until we happened to stumble onto certain facts that we learned the background of the story, and I mention it at this time because it is so completely typical of Clarence Boggie.

As mentioned above, Boggie worshiped the ground his mother walked on, and any woman more than twenty years his senior would promptly arouse in him a like feeling of worship.

During the great depression, Boggie, a lumberjack, was out of work, walking the streets of Portland, Oregon, when he saw a frail, white-haired woman, being, as Boggie expressed it, "abused" by the police.

It seemed that a police officer had stopped in front of the woman's house and was pointing out to her that the roots of a tree which was growing at the curb had broken up the cement sidewalk.

The woman apparently either was short of cash or else didn't know how to go about having the repairs made, because she was trying to get an extension of time from the officer, but the officer, according to Clarence Boggie, was "pushing her around."

Boggie said he hung around for a minute or two, listening to the conversation. The woman, he explained, was "a little sweetheart, just a dear little white-haired woman, frail and helpless, but just as sweet as she could be, and the officer was abusive.'

So Boggie, big strapping lumberjack that he was, entered into the argument. As he explained it, he 'chased the officer.'

Apparently what he did was to tell the officer that he, Boggie, would see that the matter was straightened out, to quit annoying the woman and go on about his business. She'd been given a warning and that was all there was to it. The officer had no further business there. The sidewalk would be fixed that afternoon. How did Boggie know? Hell, Boggie was going to fix it himself.

Boggie marched up town, where he went into one of the pool halls, rounded up a squad of lumberjacks who were out of work and weren't doing anything anyway, got some sledge hammers, a crowbar and an ax, and went back to the house of the 'white-haired sweetheart.'

Those lumberjacks put on a job of work that was rarely seen within the city limits. They smashed up the sidewalk, cut the offending roots of the tree, smoothed down the ground, poured cement, erected barriers, kept the cement properly moistened, and within a little more than twenty-four hours had a perfectly brand-new sidewalk, smooth and level.

The 'white-haired sweetheart' was, of course, grateful, but Boggie refused to take a cent. Despite the fact that the lumberjacks were all broke and 'on their uppers,' none of them would take a dime. They wouldn't even let her pay for the cement, which had been procured 'here and there.'

Boggie, of course, was the ringleader and probably the spokesman, but undoubtedly the men all felt very much the same way.

However, the woman did get Boggie's name and address.

It turned out that this woman in turn had a friend in the East who was wealthy and quite elderly. This friend had come to the conclusion that before she died it would be much better for her to strip herself of her property, feeling that worldly wealth and spiritual solace were incompatible.

Looking around for worthy objects of benefaction, she remembered the letter which had been received from her friend in Portland, Oregon. She looked up this letter, and, sure enough, there was the name and address of Clarence Boggie, the man who had made such a chivalrous restoration of the sidewalk.

So the woman promptly made out a deed to Clarence Boggie, giving him title to a piece of ground on which copper had been discovered.

The deed was sent to Boggie at that address. Boggie at that time, however, was in prison. Someone attempted to record the deed and it was lost in transit. Boggie didn't hear about it until some time later. By that time the woman who had made the deed was dead, relatives were in possession of the property, the copper mine had been developed into one of the big copper mines in the country, and Boggie apparently 'didn't have a leg to stand on.' He couldn't even produce the deed, or even testify that he himself had actually seen it.

However, such investigation as we were able to make indicated that he was absolutely truthful in his statement of the facts of the case. The deed actually had been executed and mailed to him, and then, by someone who was trying to record it, had been misaddressed and lost.

Boggie, moreover, told us great stories of his prowess as a logger. These stories made him sound like a reincarnated Paul Bunyan. They were, of course, digested with a tolerant smile. Boggie had been in prison for a long time and doubtless as he thought back over his exploits he kept gilding the lily and painting the rose.

Boggie told us that he could take a crew of men and move more logs in less time, with less expense and greater efficiency, than the average expert.

It is an ironical twist that everyone thought Boggie, because of his emotional instability, his background and his mannerisms, was simply drawing on his imagination in everything that he told us about his background, for a man who is 'stir simple' frequently tries to impress people with tales of his former prowess.

Eventually we learned a lot more about Boggie's abilities, but that is, of course, an entirely different story. What I am trying to convey at this time is a picture of Clarence Boggie as we first saw him, a man with a prison neurosis, a mother fixation, and a well-defined emotional instability.

We found it exceedingly hard to believe his story. However, we had determined to make an investigation of the case, and it was, after all, the case rather than the man that we were primarily interested in.

It was at the time of this first meeting that Boggie turned over to me what, for want of a better name, I have come to refer to as an inmate's 'heartbreak file.'

Just as a girl will keep a hope chest, so does an inmate frequently keep a file which contains the records of his attempts to gain freedom. It is really a heartbreak file.

Here are held the notations on when he is to come before the state parole board, documents setting forth facts in the prisoner's favor, carbon copies of correspondence hopefully sent out. Then the heartbreak. Parole application decision deferred for another year—letters unanswered.

In Boggie's case the heartbreak file was about the most voluminous and the most pathetic I have ever seen.

It is not a simple matter for a prison inmate to write a letter to an official who he thinks may be interested in his case. In the first place there are as a rule only a few typewriters within the walls, and the men who know how to use them are a favored class. A prisoner who wants to have a letter typed must make certain concessions by way of trade.

Money, of course, is contraband within prison. Too many things can be accomplished with money. So the prisoner must make his purchases through the limited credit allowances which can be made by transferring money from his prison account, except, of course, in the case of business transactions which then must have the approval of the warden.

The average prisoner, in order to get a letter written, must turn over his cigarette allowance, or go without some little prison luxury.

For thirteen years Boggie had been forgoing his prison luxuries, getting people to type letters for him. Only by the wildest stretch of imagination could a prisoner have felt that these letters would do any good. They were letters to senators and representatives, even an occasional letter to the President. They had all been neatly typed and had been mailed hopefully whenever Boggie could arrange for the typing and get enough to cover postage. Whenever a new official was elected to office, he could count on receiving a letter from Clarence Boggie.

It was the replies that were heartbreaking. Letters obviously typed by a secretary and signed without reading. Letters that were signed with rubber stamp signatures. Letters that were from secretaries advising Boggie that the matter was being placed in an important file and would be called to Mr Bigboy's attention at the earliest possible moment, that Mr Bigboy, it must be remembered, was swamped with problems incident to his election and a national crisis, but Boggie could rest assured his letter would receive Mr Bigboy's attention just as soon as the matter could be investigated.

In most of the modern penitentiaries a prisoner would not have been permitted to mail the letters that Boggie sent out, but because these were appeals to public officials, to attorneys, and because they were based on Boggie's assertions of complete innocence, the wardens had permitted these letters to be mailed, and the replies to be received.

In one way it was a pathetic heartbreak. In another way it had given Boggie the encouragement necessary to carry on. There was always the hope that one of these days, now that Mr Bigboy had got caught up with the problems incident to assuming his new office, he would remember his promise and turn his attention to the case of Clarence Boggie. . . . So Boggie carried on and waited. Why not? Didn't Boggie have letters over Mr Bigboy's signature assuring that such would be the case?

Then there was Boggie's transcript.

The State of Washington insisted that furnishing a transcript of testimony for use on appeal was a private matter, and as such, entirely up to the defendant.

Without the transcript there could be no appeal. Without

money there could be no transcript.

Boggie had no money. It appeared that the transcript was going to cost some seven hundred and fifty dollars.

Boggie, inside the prison pulled every wire he could think of trying to get money enough to defray the cost of a transcript. His parents were in no position to help. They were elderly and having a hard time to make ends meet. Boggie was penniless— and who was going to help a convicted murderer to the extent of seven hundred and fifty dollars? No one.

Then, after a lapse of some ten years, a peculiar thing happened.

A man who had some few thousand dollars was convicted of crime and sent to the penitentiary. The crime of which this man was convicted is a violation of the moral law and of the statutes. By all man-made standards of conduct this individual is reprehensible.

Yet within the prison this man has done much to help out here and there. Quietly, unostentatiously, he has done the best he could to alleviate the lot of a good many of the inmates. He heard about Clarence Boggie's problem. He heard Clarence Boggie's protestations of innocence. He put up the seven hundred and fifty dollars which enabled Boggie for the first time since his conviction to get a transcript of the testimony taken at the trial. So, when I called on Boggie, he was able to hand me this transcript.

The study of that transcript testimony was a long, uphill job, but reading it, I began to get a picture of the Boggie case.

The case itself was fully as incredible as any of the other things connected with Clarence Boggie.

On June 26, 1933, Moritz Peterson, an elderly recluse seventy-eight years old, was rooming at a private boarding house in Spokane, Washington. He owned a little shack some distance away at the rear of a deep lot on East 20th Avenue in Spokane. There was an occupied dwelling house on the front of this lot, and also one on the adjoining lot.

Peterson was in the habit of leaving his boarding house in the morning, taking a street car to the little shack, and there spending the day puttering around in the garden, taking care of his chickens, pulling weeds, etc. In the evening he'd go back to the place where he boarded. Most of his clothes were kept in the little shack house.

Peterson, in common with most of the world, was in rather straitened circumstances at the time. He had a diamond ring which he believed to be worth five hundred dollars, but he had been trying in vain to sell it for one hundred dollars. (This was at the time when the country was in the depths of a depression and ready money was a very tight commodity.)

The man's financial circumstances are mentioned because it would be almost out of the question to think that anyone who actually knew Moritz Peterson would contemplate trying to rob him. On the other hand there is the distinct possibility that someone who didn't really know him might have thought this eccentric old man, living an ordered life, could well have laid by a little ready cash which he could have kept concealed in his shack or on his person.

Sometime on Saturday night, June 24, 1933, someone broke into Moritz Peterson's shack during the night and made a most thorough job of ransacking the place. Towels having been pinned over the windows so that people in the nearby houses would not notice any light, the intruder proceeded to search every nook and cranny, opening boxes, scattering canceled checks and documents all over the floor.

If one could judge from external appearances the intruder must have been searching for a particular document of some sort. Canceled checks would ordinarily be kept in neat bundles, and it is hardly possible that an intruder would have opened these bundles of checks and strewn the papers over the floor in a search for money, yet that could have been the case. The burglar could well have reasoned that the money might have been secreted in the most unlikely places.

Sunday morning, when Peterson arrived at the shack, he was confronted with the wreckage and complete disorder. He was, of course, very much upset, but he refused to allow the police to be notified. He even went so far as to state that he knew the identity of the intruder and didn't want anything done about it.

Peterson put in Sunday straightening up the place. By afternoon he told the neighbors that the only things which had been taken were a pair of coveralls and a pair of black shoes.

If anyone had wanted to hold up or assault Moritz Peterson the worst day that could possibly have been selected would have been Monday, the conventional washday.

Yet apparently someone was concealed in the Peterson house on Monday, the 26th day of June, 1933, waiting for him to arrive.

The neighbors of course didn't see this person enter, but they did hear the sound of a terrific struggle emanating from the little shack. The time was probably between ten and twenty-five minutes after ten in the morning.

The sounds of that struggle attracted a great deal of attention. Housewives and children ran from their houses. They were in time to see a stocky, heavy-set, bushy-haired individual, who ran with a peculiar 'sideways gait,' running from the house. They chased this individual for some two or three blocks. Then the man disappeared in a wooded area. No one had been able to get a look at his face.

While one of the housewives and some children were chasing the individual who ran away from Moritz Peterson's shack, one of the other women had looked in at his door, found Peterson lying, moaning, with his head virtually beaten in. She dashed to her house and telephoned the police.

What happened after that was what might be called a tragedy of errors.

The little party who were running after the fugitive, trying to keep him in sight, followed him until he entered a thicket of underbrush, whereupon they turned back.

The first officer to arrive on the scene was a motorcycle officer, who came tearing up with siren screaming, and came to a stop before the house at the front of the lot.

The excited audience explained to the motorcycle officer what had happened. The motorcycle officer promptly decided that his duties were along other lines and in other fields. He dashed away from there, fast.

Police officers from the central station tore through the streets with sirens screaming, to come to the Peterson shack.

Apparently it was at this time that the officers found Moritz Peterson lying on the floor, his head so terribly smashed that one of the eye sockets had been completely broken. A homemade weapon was on the floor beside the dying man.

The officers were told by the boys that the assailant had jumped into the brush a couple of blocks up the street, so the officers valiantly permitted themselves to be guided to the spot where the murderer had disappeared, at which time they suddenly discovered they had 'forgotten their guns.' So they returned to their automobile, and, with siren screaming, went tearing back to get their guns.

In the meantime an ambulance had been summoned and the ambulance, also accompanied by the sound of sirens, went to the scene of the crime to pick up Moritz Peterson and transport him to a hospital. The officers, by this time having fully armed themselves, came dashing back to the scene of the crime.

A description of all this confusion and particularly the noise of the sirens is important for reasons which will presently become apparent.

After Peterson had been removed to the hospital, the police made a rather cursory examination of the premises and took into their possession the weapon with which the crime had been committed. It was a homemade bludgeon which had been fashioned with considerable skill and ingenuity, and consisted of a round, water-washed rock wrapped in burlap. This burlap had been tightly twisted and stitched so that the long twisted burlap made a semi-flexible handle. The whole thing was a most potent, deadly weapon, which could strike terrific blows. The assailant had repeatedly struck Moritz Peterson on the head with this weapon.

Strangely enough, however, despite the fact that Peterson had received these fatal injuries, he still remained conscious. The dying man apparently experienced a sensation of great pressure on his brain and thought there was a weight still on his head, but by the time he reached the hospital he was able to talk. He kept complaining of this terrible weight that was crushing his head.

Sometime after reaching the hospital Moritz Peterson's daughter was summoned, and at the bedside of her dying father asked him in the presence of witnesses if he knew who had done this thing to him.

Peterson admitted that he did but didn't want to mention the man's name. The daughter kept insisting, and finally Peterson stated that if she would take the terrific weight off of his head he would tell her; and then, after further questioning, mentioned a name, a name which was heard very distinctly by the daughter.

This name was not the name of Clarence Boggie, nor could that name at any time ever be connected in any way with him. At the time there was nothing to connect Clarence Boggie with Moritz Peterson or with the burglary of the Peterson shack.

The police, in the course of their investigation, were reported to have arrested a suspect who was positively identified by the witnesses who had seen the man running away from the Peterson shack, but after a while the police announced that this man had a perfect alibi and he was released.

This fact, mentioned casually in the local press, was subsequently to assume a very great significance, but at the time it appeared as one of the various diversions, and was snowed under by the conjectures and surmises and press releases given out by the police in order to show that they were diligently working on the case.

Then gradually the case petered out. The police ran down clues, gave the usual optimistic statements to newspaper reporters, and wound up by getting nowhere.

Moritz Peterson died shortly after being admitted to the hospital, and had lost consciousness a very short time after making the statement to his daughter in which he had named his assailant.

At this time, Clarence Boggie was on the streets of Portland, Oregon.

The time, it will be remembered, was during the depression. People who didn't have cash had virtually no way of getting any. People who did have cash didn't know what to do with it. Banks were failing. People were being laid off. Jobs were scarce.

Boggie had no job, and he did have a criminal record.

He had been convicted of a bank robbery in Oregon.

Boggie's story of how he happened to be convicted of that bank robbery is as completely incredible as any of the other Boggie stories. We have never even investigated to find out whether this story was true because apparently the Oregon authorities had made such an investigation and had granted him a pardon—not a parole but a full pardon.

Boggie's story was that he had been camped in the 'jungles' under a bridge across a little creek bed, that a car dashed by at wild speed above the bridge, and someone threw a coat over the bridge. The car went hurtling down the road, and after the car, the sound of screaming sirens indicated pursuing police.

Boggie thought somebody was being pinched for speeding.

He went over and picked up the coat. It was a good fit, and Boggie was badly in need of a coat.

About the time Boggie had nicely adjusted himself to the coat, the creek bed began to swarm with officers. They grabbed Boggie and searched him on suspicion, and in the pockets of the coat they found a lot of currency which had been taken in a bank robbery.

Boggie was convicted. Months passed. Boggie kept protesting his innocence and asking for an investigation. Evidently such an investigation was finally made. He was pardoned, but only after he had spent some years in the Oregon penitentiary.

Now, at about this time, there enters the picture a very interesting character whom we shall refer to as Convict X. This man is, so far as I know, still serving a term in a penitentiary. He is a shrewd, ingenious operator, a clever opportunist, and he may be possessed of a quiet sense of humor. I don't know. I do know that when I was trying to interview him he was completely hostile. He didn't want to talk with me. He didn't want to answer questions.

One of my associates said to him, 'Don't you know who this man is? This is Erle Stanley Gardner. He'll give you a square deal. Haven't you ever read any of his books?'

Convict X twisted his lip in a sneer. 'Bah!' he said. 'Escape fiction.'

This convict came across Boggie on the streets of Oregon at a time when the convict was looking for accomplices. Boggie's story as to why the man wanted them is a story in itself.

In a little town in the state of Idaho the ex-chief of police knew that, because of the instability of the banks, certain relatively affluent citizens were keeping money in large quantities concealed in their houses. Boggie insisted this ex-officer had conceived the idea that if stick-up men should rob one of these houses and should take in a good haul of ready cash, it would be a bad thing for the victim, but it might be turned into a good thing for the ex-chief of police.

The former officer is supposed to have known that a certain individual had thirty thousand dollars concealed in his house. This citizen kept his house carefully locked at all times and had resorted to elaborate safeguards against robbery.

According to Boggie, word went out through the underworld that this ex-chief of police would like to have a sociable talk with some thoroughly competent men who could pull a smooth job. The word trickled through the devious channels of organized crime and reached the ears of Convict X, who promptly got in touch with the former officer. A deal was made.

And this is one place where Boggie's story to us may have been somewhat colored. There is evidence indicating that at the start Boggie may have been the one who passed the story of the ex-chief of police on to Convict X. The history of what happened and what Boggie claimed happened have some variations which are probably significant.

In any event, Convict X and the ex-chief made a deal.

The ex-chief agreed to call on the man who distrusted banks. He would very conveniently leave his car, with its tank filled with gas, on the outside, and the ignition keys would be in the car.

The former official also agreed that when he entered the house he would manage to turn back the spring lock and snap the catch which would hold it back, so that anyone could enter the door by simply turning the knob and pushing.

It was that simple.

Convict X and an accomplice were making the haul, but they wanted someone to sit outside as a watchman. They wanted someone who was so simple that he would follow instructions, so dumb that he could be used as a fall guy in the event anything went wrong.

At this point, stir-simple Clarence Boggie with his mother-complex enters the picture. Boggie was made to order.

According to Boggie's story, the men were to take a trip to Idaho. Boggie was to go along. Some time later he got cold feet. He tried to back out, then he tried to escape. The men wouldn't let him go, but Boggie finally did get away from them.

He started hitchhiking. He was picked up by a man who gave him a ride in return for Boggie's promise to do some of the driving.

So he rode along with this gentleman until it became dark. Then it turned out the man's lights wouldn't work. Boggie decided there was a shorted wire somewhere. He stopped at a sort of service station and general merchandise store and went to work. He had located a short in the wire and was making repairs with tape when another car pulled in and pilloried Boggie in the white lights.

This was the car driven by Convict X; the identical car from which Boggie had made his escape.

There was a short, quiet talk. Convict X quite apparently had associated with Boggie long enough in the Oregon prison to know Boggie's weakness. If Boggie didn't come along and do exactly as they said, Convict X assured him they were going to hunt up 'Mummy' and kill her.

Even after a lapse of some fifteen years, Boggie couldn't tell about this without becoming hysterical. Up to this point he could control himself, but when he reached this phase of the story tears streamed down his cheeks and he completely lost his self-control.

There was never any question in the mind of anyone who talked with Boggie that his fear that these men would have killed his dear 'Mummy' was an actual, tangible force. So far as Boggie was concerned, he accepted it as a basic fact that these men would do exactly what they threatened, and the only way he could save 'Mummy's' life was to go along in absolute docility no matter what happened. From that time on Boggie was their man.

Boggie, Convict X and another accomplice, went to the little town in Idaho which had been picked for the robbery. At the appointed time the ex-chief of police drove up and parked his car. He explained to the owner of the house that he wanted to listen to his radio set for a while.

He was duly admitted and, according to plan, as he stepped inside he turned the spring lock on the door so that anyone could walk right in. Then he carefully closed the door.

Boggie was to be the lookout man. He was to signal the others if anything started to go wrong.

Convict X and his accomplice glided quietly up to the door and tried the knob to make certain that the officer had been able to manipulate the lock. Finding that he had done so, they suddenly pushed the door open and jumped into the room with drawn guns.

It was part of the plan that the former chief, despite the menace of the guns, was to put up a valiant battle.

Convict X told me about all this, a little at a time. For the most part, getting information out of him was pretty much of a job. He was inclined to answer questions in monosyllables or not answer them at all, but when he came to the point where he described the battle with the former chief of police he needed no urging. His eyes lit with enthusiasm. That was one part of the job that he thoroughly enjoyed and he loved to tell about it.

It seemed the two criminals really did a job on the former officer. He had asked to be beaten up, and these boys carried out that part of their assignment with an enthusiastic zeal that gave the man everything he had asked for—and more. He had wanted to be marked up enough so that it would be perfectly apparent he had struggled valiantly against overpowering odds.

'Boy, oh, boy,' Convict X said ecstatically in telling me about it, 'we hung a couple of beautiful shiners on that so-and-so.'

The ex-officer, having been overpowered, was immunized by one of the convicts who held a gun pointed at the man's stomach, while the other intruder went to work on the householder and his wife, trying to find out the place where the thirty thousand dollars were secreted.

Now the story develops a touch of grim humor.

The victim explained to the holdup men that they were acting on a wrong tip, that he didn't have any money in the house. He was supposed to have money concealed but he was too smart for that trap. He preferred to take a chance on a bank despite the fact that there was some chance the bank might fail.

He pulled a checkbook out of his pocket. He showed check stubs to the robbers. And he was so absolutely convincing that he talked them out of it.

Imagine the feelings of the ex-chief of police, standing there with his hands in the air, his face badly banged up, his eyes swelling shut, listening to what was going on, hearing the man who he knew full well had thirty thousand dollars concealed on the premises talking the bandits into believing he had nothing. How he must have wanted to enter the discussion by shouting to the bandits, 'You poor fools. Don't let him talk you out of it. I told you he had thirty thousand dollars here and I wouldn't have told you that unless I'd known. Get busy and find that money, you poor bungling amateurs!'

But the ex-chief, forced to act out the part of a valiant officer, who had been overpowered, beaten up, slugged, and was now facing the gun of a trigger-happy desperado, could only stand there and listen.

The householder, apparently very much frightened, was perfectly willing to surrender 'all the money he had on the premises,' a few hundred dollars. He was so frightened that if he had had any more he would unquestionably have given it up. He put on quite an act. Convict X believed him. So did the other man. They took the money that was available and made a dash out of the front door, piled helter-skelter into the waiting car and took off.

The man who had been held up was nobody's fool. Certain things about the holdup caused him to become suspicious. It had been a little too opportune.

The bandits were apprehended, the whole story came out, and Convict X and Clarence Boggie found themselves facing a long prison term in Idaho.

Boggie made a statement. He wanted to turn State's evidence.

Convict X told him grimly, 'You rat on us and we'll frame something a lot worse than this on you.' (Later on a deputy sheriff, who had overheard this and other remarks, was to make an affidavit that from what he had overheard he had every reason to believe Convict X had framed Boggie for the Peterson murder—and the authorities were to brush that affidavit aside.)

Boggie, Convict X and the accomplice were all sentenced to terms in the Idaho State Penitentiary.

It appeared that on his way north to pull this job Convict X had stopped for a short time in Spokane. Boggie had some people he wanted to see and Convict X wanted to make preparations for a job he was to do.

This was but a short time after Moritz Peterson had been murdered.

Through a fortuitous chain of circumstances Convict X had an absolutely perfect alibi for the Peterson murder. He had been serving a term in a Canadian prison and had been released from that prison on the day *following* the death of Moritz Peterson. Therefore, so far as that crime was concerned, Convict X was in the clear and knew it.

On the other hand, Convict X, who had an adroit, ingenious mind, studied the local newspapers while he was stopping over in Spokane and gave a lot of thought to the Peterson murder, reading about the various clues the police were 'running down.' He noticed the police were going in circles while issuing the usual optimistic reports that they were confident the culprit would be in custody within a short time, etc. So Convict X decided that the Peterson murder might come in very handy in case of necessity.

Just how handy will presently become apparent.

Convict X needed funds and he was a very desperate man. As he explained the matter to me later in a burst of indignation, the Canadian prison had turned him loose with a prison suit of clothes and a Canadian ten-dollar bill in his pocket. 'Why, that wasn't enough,' he charged bitterly, 'for operating capital.'

I asked him what he meant by 'operating capital.'

'Not enough to buy a "rod" with,' he retorted, still angry at this evidence of Canadian lack of hospitality.

So Convict X was in urgent need of 'operating capital.' By the time he reached Spokane he had remedied the defect as far as the 'rod' was concerned, but he was still short of money.

Spokane officers believed he had participated in a robbery and kidnaping while in Spokane, and under the so-called 'Lindbergh Laws' which were being passed by the various states in a wave of indignation over kidnapings, Convict X could have been extradited from Idaho to Washington, and sentenced to death.

The Washington authorities went up to Idaho with the idea of extraditing Convict X to Washington, trying him and demanding the death penalty.

This, it is to be remembered, was after Convict X had been arrested in Idaho but before he had been convicted there. If Idaho was willing to release him to Washington, Washington could prosecute him, and, if convicted, could execute him.

Convict X didn't like that prospect.

At this point it becomes necessary to put two and two together and rely upon a certain amount of surmise and circumstantial evidence. But the indications are quite plain and there is considerable evidence that Convict X said to the officers, 'If you boys will let me stay up here in Idaho and take the rap on this robbery charge without extraditing me back to Washington, I'll do you a favor; I'll solve the Peterson murder for you.'

In any event, and regardless of what actually did happen, the fact remains that the Washington authorities after a talk with Convict X did not extradite him. They let him remain and take the rap in Idaho, and they *did* claim that they now knew the identity of the real murderer of Moritz Peterson. There is reason to believe they returned with a pair of coveralls and a pair of black shoes, which Convict X assured them had been given him by Boggie, and which Boggie had told him were the property of 'the old man.'

Perhaps there was no trade. Perhaps it was all merely coincidental.

The fact remained that the crestfallen officers found that they didn't have a case, because the coveralls did not belong to Moritz Peterson, and the shoes were not the right size.

Rumor has it that on careful investigation the police found a laundry mark in the coveralls, and that this laundry mark established an entirely different chain of ownership.

It is, therefore, apparent that Convict X had formulated some pretty definite plans in his shrewdly ingenious mind. From his viewpoint the Peterson murder case represented an ideal opportunity to buy his way out of any jam in the state of Washington.

The Spokane police were anxious to solve the murder. People

were indignant over the idea of a harmless, inoffensive, well-liked citizen being bludgeoned to death by a murderer who had only a relatively short start on the police and who was never apprehended. Spokane police wanted very much to solve that murder case.

Convict X had an unshakable alibi.

Therefore if Convict X could offer the Spokane police a 'solution' of the Peterson murder, he would be in a marvelous trading position. For a man of Convict X's temperament, personality and occupation, being in a good trading position with the police was well worth the investment in a couple of stage props—a pair of secondhand coveralls and some old shoes.

Of course, Convict X needed just a little more than that. He needed a fall guy, and a man looking for a fall guy couldn't have found anyone more made to order than Clarence Boggie.

So, putting two and two together, it would seem that Clarence Boggie had served several purposes on that fateful trip north from Portland.

And the story that Convict X is known to have told the officers is weird in the extreme. Boggie, he said, had boasted of killing Peterson, had taken Convict X to a place where he had buried the 'loot', had there dug up a small coffee can, had taken off the cover and extracted a worn, empty billfold which he had offered to Convict X and which Convict X had taken.

Thus a pattern of double-crossing chicanery emerged—the dog-eat-dog attitude of factual occurrences in everyday life as opposed to the version that is handed out to the public.

Of course, the Spokane police didn't give up that easily.

They looked up Boggie from all conceivable angles, but all that they had to connect Boggie with the crime was the word of Convict X, and Convict X, of course, with his long criminal record, his extremely personal interest in the matter, would hardly make a witness on whom a district attorney would like to depend.

There must have been a shrewd suspicion in the minds of the officers that they had been taken for a ride by a quick-thinking, fast-talking convict, but if that was the case the officers couldn't do anything about it without publicizing their own gullibility, and Convict X kept assuring them of his complete good faith. Clarence Boggie, he insisted, was the man who committed the crime, even if Boggie had lied about the coveralls and the shoes, and the officers could rest assured that Convict X was giving them the real low-down. If there had been any prevarication about the coveralls and the shoes, it had been Boggie's lie and not that of Convict X, etc.

The Moritz Peterson case went into the unsolved file. The officers busied themselves about other matters; but, always in the back of their minds was the feeling that Clarence Boggie had perhaps outsmarted them in some way and had juggled the evidence. They felt that he was the man who had committed the murder.

Not only did Convict X say that Boggie had confessed to him, but later another Idaho convict claimed Boggie had confessed to him while in the Idaho penitentiary—had, in effect, walked right up to him, and without preliminary conversation said, 'I killed Moritz Peterson,' and then turned and walked away. It was that simple.

In this way, Convict X was able to assure the Washington officers of his entire good faith in the matter. He was never returned to Washington and tried on the kidnap case.

Then, many months later and 'on a tip,' the officers went to a place near a small Oregon town where Boggie had stayed for a while, and there they found an overcoat. There was some evidence that Boggie had worn this overcoat to the house when he arrived. The overcoat had been left there. It had received rather hard usage and was in a dilapidated state.

However, that overcoat was identified by the daughter of Moritz Peterson as having been an overcoat worn by her father during his lifetime.

That did it. The officers came down on Boggie like a thousand ton of bricks.

The murderer of Moritz Peterson had been identified as a person having wild-looking bushy black hair. Clarence Boggie, apparently from the time when he was brought under suspicion, started slicking his hair smoothly down with quantities of hair oil.

This didn't stop the officers. They would bring him in, ruffle his hair up, ask witnesses to identify him, and then take Boggie's picture. Naturally, some of these pictures of Boggie with his thickly greased long hair, pulled up high above his head, resembled the pictures in Frye's geography of a Dyak of Borneo. These pictures were given to the press.

Boggie's story about how he came by the overcoat was incredible.

He had, he said, been in a secondhand clothing store in Portland, Oregon. A man came in with an overcoat, a pretty good-looking overcoat, with a pair of slippers in the pocket. He offered to sell this coat to the proprietor of the store. He wanted a dollar for it. The proprietor hadn't liked the looks of the man and had refused to buy the overcoat.

Boggie spoke up. '*I'll* give you a dollar for it.'

It made the proprietor angry. He didn't think Boggie had any right to interfere in that way. If he had been dickering in the hope the seller would make a lower offer, Boggie's interference would have lost him a good purchase.

The man who was offering the overcoat for sale promptly and eagerly accepted Boggie's dollar. So Boggie bought himself a one-way ticket to a life sentence in the Washington State Penitentiary at Walla Walla.

Little things, which may or may not have been significant so far as the jury were concerned, indicated the background of the Boggie trial. The prosecution, for instance, was permitted to show by witnesses that Boggie had been in a car, with a revolver, and that Boggie's statement explaining the ownership and possession of the revolver was that the authorities had given it to him so he could protect himself.

This, of course, was greeted with the equivalent of hoots of derision.

Later on, the defense tried to prove the actual ownership of the revolver and the reason it was in the car with Boggie by no less person than Fred C. May, the deputy sheriff of Shoshone County, Idaho. The court refused to permit such testimony to go in, on the ground that it was irrelevant.

In vain did counsel protest. The court stated that questions concerning the revolver had been completely irrelevant, and charged the attorneys for the defense that if they permitted irrelevant matter to be brought in by the prosecution they could not thereby make an issue of it. Such are the technicalities of law.

It is to be remembered that the running murderer had a peculiar, 'sideways gait.' Boggie did not have any such gait, but he did have a very slight limp. No one of the witnesses had seen the murderer's face, but witnesses were called upon to identify Boggie as 'looking like' the man who had been seen running away from the scene of the murder two years earlier.

It is to be noted that the witnesses who had seen the murderer running away from the scene of the crime were not given an opportunity to look at Boggie when the police had first had reason to suspect him of the murder. It was not until a lapse of some two years (after the overcoat had been located) that the witnesses were called on to make an identification, and then there was no line-up or anything of that sort. The witnesses were simply brought in to see Boggie and asked if that was the man. There is, in fact, considerable evidence in the record itself that the identification, made in this way, could not have been made if the defendant had been in a line-up.

A junk dealer stated that he had seen Boggie visiting Peterson on the Friday before the murder. Another witness, who had one of the houses in the front of the lot, insisted that she had seen a man whom she thought was Boggie visiting there on a Friday, but on cross-examination, when the witnesses had been separated, it appeared that each was testifying to a different Friday.

It is to be noted that the man who was seen running away from the scene of the murder that twenty-sixth day of June, was not carrying an overcoat, nor, in the heat of a Spokane summer, was he wearing any overcoat. Virtually the entire case against Boggie hinged on the identification of an overcoat, and that identification was made some two years after the crime had been committed.

The murderer, running away from Moritz Peterson's shack that June day, had been followed by one of the housewives who had been doing her washing, and some of the children. The other housewife had been telephoning the police. No one had seen the murderer's face, but one woman had been close enough to see a part of his cheek, the color of his skin, and had observed the running figure closely.

At the time of the trial the prosecution had called her as a witness and the examination had been rather peculiar. For one thing, the prosecution did not ask her to identify Clarence Boggie as the man whom she had seen running away from the house; and when the attorney for the defense cross-examined her, he, probably fearing a trap, was careful not to give her any opportunity to make a positive identification. So this woman was in effect asked a few general questions about hearing the struggle in the shack, seeing the man run away, following him for a couple of blocks, and then she was excused.

One of the other witnesses was much more positive in her identification of Boggie, but there were certain circumstances which tended to weaken the identification. Among other things was the intimation that she had previously identified another person, only to retract that identification when she found out that she must have been mistaken.

There were, of course, other angles to the case. A couple of days after the murder Boggie had been bumming a ride in Pendleton, Oregon. He had spoken in enthusiastic terms of the hunting near a certain place in Oregon, a place where he lived at the time. The driver of the car had expressed a wish to go hunting with Boggie, and Boggie had thoughtfully given him his name and address.

Later on, reading in the newspapers that Boggie was wanted for murder, the driver of the car got in touch with the police.

The prosecution contended that Boggie had made a headlong 'flight' from the scene of the murder. (A strange flight by a man who makes it a point to impress his personality upon the individual with whom he is riding, and gives his name and address.)

However, when Boggie tried to explain away the situation and tell his story, he was asked an impeaching question. Wasn't it true that he had twice been convicted of a felony?

Boggie was forced to admit that such was the case; and that was all there was to it.

Boggie was convicted, and, fortunately for him, escaped the gallows. He was sentenced to life imprisonment. . . .

In summarizing the facts in this case it seems remarkable that even with the urging of the chaplain we would have wasted time investigating the Boggie case. His story was incredible. The case against him, while not particularly sturdy, was, nevertheless, a pretty good case. The penitentiaries are filled with people against whom the prosecution didn't have as good cases as they had against Clarence Boggie. And, on the other hand, there was virtually nothing to establish Boggie's innocence except his word that he wasn't guilty.

The prosecution was able to show that Boggie, with a long criminal record, had the dead man's property in his possession, and had confessed to Convict X, and to another convict in Idaho, that he had killed Moritz Peterson. Witnesses who had seen the murderer running away from the scene of the crime had identified Boggie as being the man.

Despite this positive evidence each link in the chain of evidence had certain weaknesses. Convict X had a definite interest in the matter, or could well have had, if he had made a trade with the Spokane police. The overcoat had not been picked up until two years after the murder. It had been hanging in a barn, and was a fairly worn-out garment by the time it was shown to the daughter of the murdered man for identification. Boggie had not been identified in a line-up, but had simply been exhibited to witnesses who were asked if this was the man they had seen running away from the house at the time of the murder.

Identification evidence is a most tricky subject. The subconscious mind frequently plays tricks upon witnesses who are acting in the greatest good faith, and in the Boggie case witnesses were not called upon to identify him until two years after the date of the crime.

However, as I have said, we can go to any penitentiary in the country and find hundreds of cases where the evidence on which the man was convicted is no more solid than the evidence on which Boggie was convicted.

There was one factor in Boggie's favor. Boggie had made an application for *habeas corpus* and a hearing duly came up in a Federal court. Hon. Lloyd L. Black, the Federal judge before whom that hearing was held, is a patient, a kindly individual who is prone to try to get at the facts of a case and not rush through these numerous *habeas corpus* applications in order to 'clear his calendar.'

He became very much interested in the case when the daughter of Moritz Peterson, the same woman who had been present at the time the dying man had made a statement that he would name the person who had killed him, stated very definitely and positively that she did not believe Clarence Boggie had killed her father or knew anything about the murder, that she simply didn't believe Boggie was known to her father.

Judge Black found no reason to grant the writ of *habeas corpus* but he was very much impressed by the sincerity of the daughter and by her declaration. He at least intimated in open court that he would like to see some further investigation made in the case.

And so those were the facts which confronted me when I arrived in Walla Walla, talked with Tom Smith, met Clarence Boggie, talked with him, went over his heartbreak file and then studied the evidence in the case.

I decided that considerable investigative work was going to be needed and got on the long-distance telephone to Raymond Schindler in New York. I found that he was at the moment in Los Angeles, and was on the point of taking a plane back to New York. I persuaded him he had better fly up to join me, so he took a night plane and arrived in Walla Walla, where I had a chartered plane ready. We flew to Spokane.

Obviously one of the highlights of the case from a legal standpoint was the manner in which the prosecution had interrogated the housewife who had seen the murderer running away from the Peterson shack, yet who wasn't specifically asked to point out Boggie.

My courtroom experience indicated that there must have been a very definite reason for the peculiar type of questions which had been asked this woman on the witness stand. The prosecution had asked all of the usual questions, had got her right up to the point in her testimony where the next logical question would have been to ask her to point out the murderer, and then veered off into a detour from which the attorneys had never returned to the main highway of ordinary procedure.

Frequently those things happen when a prosecutor lays a trap for the defense attorney. Knowing that he has a very positive witness whose testimony would be damning, the prosecutor pretends to fumble around and leaves a beautiful 'opening' for the cross-examiner. The cross-examiner sticks his head through that opening and promptly has it chopped off.

But somehow as Schindler and I read and discussed this woman's testimony, we didn't feel that it had been a trap. We felt that there was something in the background, some reason that the prosecution had pretended to fumble the ball.

Of course, many years had elapsed since the trial, but we felt that if it was still possible to find this woman, we wanted to talk with her.

We found her, and when we did we uncovered a shocking story.

This witness and her young son had seen the murderer emerge from the Peterson shack. They had followed as he ran down the street, not trying to overtake him but trying to keep him in sight. They had never seen his face. (None of the witnesses had ever seen the face of the fleeing man.) But this woman had been in a position to see the side of his cheek and had noticed the color of his skin.

A considerable time after the murder, and apparently at a time when Boggie was under arrest, this woman had seen a man prowling around the vicinity of the Peterson shack. (It is to be noted in passing that long after the time of the murder several other homemade lethal weapons had been found in the bushes nearby, the over-all characteristics being somewhat similar to the murder weapon in the Peterson case.)

This woman felt absolutely certain in her own mind that the man she saw was the same man she had seen running away from the scene of the murder. She went to the telephone and called the police, telling them excitedly that the man who killed Moritz Peterson was outside and to come and pick him up.

The police told her to forget it, that the man who had killed Moritz Peterson was Clarence Boggie, that Boggie had been arrested and was safe in jail awaiting trial.

The woman insisted that this man was the murderer, that in any event he was a prowler who had no business there, and she wanted the police to come out and arrest him.

The police hung up.

After a while the prowler went away.

Nor was this all. The day before Clarence Boggie was to be tried, the deputy prosecutor had gone to the school where this woman's twelve-year-old son was in attendance.

According to this woman the deputy prosecutor painted a very glittering picture. The boy was told he was to be a very important witness. He was to be excused from classes the next day. A big police car with a driver was to come to school and get him. The boy was to go to court. He was to stand up and be sworn as a witness, and for this he would receive witness fees which would be entirely his own money, which he could spend any way he wanted to.

The deputy prosecutor, however, wanted him to be sure and identify Boggie, who would be sitting right there in the courtroom. He wanted the boy to mention that he had seen the face of the murderer who was running away from the Peterson shack, and that this man was Boggie.

But the boy protested he *hadn't* seen the murderer's face.

According to this woman's story the deputy prosecutor had then said, 'But I want you to say that you saw the man's face. You know that I am a public official. I wouldn't ask you to do anything that was wrong. That's the thing I want you to do, to say that you saw the man's face.'

The perplexed, bewildered boy shook his head. He couldn't say he had seen the man's face because he hadn't.

In the end the deputy prosecutor warned the boy against saying anything to his mother about the conversation. So the boy went home from school, a very troubled, worried young man who couldn't eat any supper.

The mother questioned him, trying to find out what was wrong, but, mindful of the warning he had received not to talk to his mother about the conversation, he didn't want to tell her. By this time, very much alarmed and sensing that something was radically wrong, she kept after him until finally he broke down and tearfully told her the story.

This mother was a good, straightforward American woman. She took the boy by the hand and walked up to the prosecutor's office, where lights shining through the windows indicated that last-minute preparations for the courtroom battle the next day were going on.

'What,' she indignantly demanded, 'are you trying to do to my son?'

No wonder the prosecution had handled her with gloves. No wonder they hadn't asked her to identify Clarence Boggie. Had they asked her she would have said that she didn't think Clarence Boggie was the man, that she didn't think he had the same build, that she didn't think he had the same complexion, that she thought the real murderer was the man whom she had seen prowling around the premises at a time when Clarence Boggie was in jail and at a time when the police refused even to come out to investigate.

It is to be remembered that more than fifteen years had passed from the time of the Peterson murder to the date of our investigation. We couldn't talk with the boy because he had grown up to be a young man, had gone to war and had given his life for his country.

On the other hand, the deputy prosecutor had cut one corner too many, had been himself convicted of crime and sent to prison.

So there we had a story on our hands that we couldn't verify. The mother, of course, hadn't heard the conversation with the deputy prosecutor. She only knew what the boy had told her, but the mother had confronted the deputy prosecutor with her boy, and so to that extent was a witness who could testify in any court to that much of the story. . . . And what a sordid story it was. A deputy prosecutor trying to suborn perjury, trying to get a young boy just at the threshold of life to do something that he knew was wrong, trying to send a man to the gallows by assuring a twelve-year-old boy, 'I'm a public official. I wouldn't ask you to do something that was wrong, would I?'

Such was our introduction to the investigation of the Boggie case, the first intimation we had that the Court of Last Resort might be a lot more important than we had at first realized and might find some very tightly closed doors leading into some dark and dingy rooms.

When Steeger and I had discussed the manner in which *Argosy* would donate its space to the activities of the investigating committee for the Court of Last Resort, it was agreed that we wouldn't try to carry the investigation through to completion and then publish what we had found out.

We felt that if we were going to do the job we wanted to do it would be necessary to take the reader right along with us. We wanted to get readers interested in the cause of justice. We wanted to get them interested in a case, and in order to get them interested we wanted them to participate in the investigation.

It was decided we'd make only the most cursory preliminary investigation, that we would then start working on the case, not knowing whether the defendant was guilty or innocent, simply knowing that it was a good case for investigative work, and that the readers of *Argosy* could look over our shoulders while we were making it.

In fact, it is to be continually borne in mind that the Court of Last Resort was not the magazine and was not the investigators, but was the public, the readers of the magazine themselves. The board of investigators was nothing more nor less than an investigative board.

For that reason I carried a portable typewriter along with me when I flew to Washington, and each day I made a summary of what our work had disclosed. Each night we carefully studied the transcript in the Boggie case and made an analysis of the evidence. Since there were several volumes of this transcript the schedule which we set ourselves was a hard one. By day we talked with witnesses. At night we studied transcripts, and put together an analysis and the condensation of the evidence. In the small hours of the morning I would whip out copy to send to the magazine, and when enough copy had been sent in for the first installment of the Boggie case, Schindler flew back to New York and I left for my ranch in California, taking the transcript back with me.

A peculiar situation developed. The authorities in Washington suddenly realized that a case which had taken place in their state was being publicized, and the authorities didn't even know what the case was all about, and didn't have any way of finding out.

The attorney general of Washington called me and wanted to know if I would mail the transcript to his office. I told him I didn't feel I could do that, but that I would be very glad to let anyone whom he might designate study it at my ranch.

So Ed Lehan, a special deputy attorney general, flew down from Washington and spent several days going over the transcript.

At the end of that time Lehan concluded that the evidence had not been such as to warrant a conviction.

Ed Lehan returned to Washington to carry on an investigation for the attorney general.

Raymond Schindler and I flew back to Washington and were joined by Harry Steeger. Here we made a supplemental investigation and learned that the proprietor of the secondhand store, where Boggie claimed he had bought the overcoat, was still in business in Portland, Oregon.

We flew down to Portland, located the man and asked him if he remembered the occasion of the overcoat being purchased while he was contemplating whether or not he would buy it.

The proprietor remembered the occasion perfectly. He was still indignant at the manner in which Boggie had stepped into the picture. According to his understanding, Boggie was a customer. His only excuse for being in the store was to buy something that was on display or to offer to sell something. Aside from that he should keep out of any business transactions.

He remembered the man coming in with the overcoat, with the slippers in his pocket, and he didn't like his looks. The overcoat looked 'hot' to him. He couldn't tell us why he felt that way, but it was simply the reaction of a man who had done business with a lot of people, many of whom were crooks. He thought this man was a crook and didn't want to do business with him. He didn't know whether he would have changed his mind if the price on the overcoat had been lowered or not. But while he was debating the matter with himself, Boggie had stepped in, offered a dollar and taken the coat.

This man had been a witness at the time of Boggie's trial and he felt that a deliberate attempt had been made to intimidate him.

For the most part the proprietor of a secondhand store can't do business unless he has the friendship of the police. It was at least intimated to this man, or he thought it was intimated to him, that it would be exceedingly unwise for him to be a witness on behalf of Boggie. However, he took the stand and told what he knew.

The prosecutor had sought to discredit this testimony by showing that two years after the date of the transaction the witness *couldn't identify the overcoat.*

Of course he couldn't.

If he had, it would have been a most suspicious circumstance.

All that this man remembered was his natural feeling of exasperation when Boggie stepped in to buy the overcoat in question.

Steeger, Schindler and I went back to Washington. We had quite a conference with Smith Troy, the attorney general.

I think Smith Troy is one of the most fair-minded attorneys general I have ever met. He puts his cards face up on the table and he calls the turns as he sees them. As a district attorney he was a remarkably able prosecutor. As an attorney general he is popular, well liked and efficient, and as attorney general he decided that if Clarence Boggie had been improperly convicted it was up to his office to take the responsibility of conducting an investigation, and this was done with vigor and absolute fairness.

When Smith Troy was ready to make a report to Governor Monrad C. Wallgren, Raymond Schindler, Harry Steeger, Tom Smith as warden of the penitentiary, and I went to call on the Governor. He invited us to his executive mansion for cocktails and later on for a supper. We spent the entire evening with him.

Ed Lehan was supposed to join us there earlier, but his plane from Spokane was delayed on account of bad weather, and he didn't arrive until later in the evening. He and Smith Troy gave the Governor the facts in the Boggie case as they understood them and stated they were willing to make a definite recommendation.

Governor Wallgren was very much impressed. He said he certainly didn't want an innocent man in prison, but he did want the report from Ed Lehan and Smith Troy to be in writing.

Ed Lehan agreed to put his report in writing, and Smith Troy agreed to take Lehan's report and supplement it with a report and recommendation from his office as attorney general of the State of Washington.

We felt that the case had been completed, and after shaking hands all around started back to our respective domiciles.

Thereafter, however, things began to drag. There were intimations that someone with considerable political influence in the State of Washington wasn't particularly enthusiastic about having Clarence Boggie pardoned.

And then came a peculiar development.

The Seattle *Times* had in its employ a very alert, able reporter named Don Magnuson. Magnuson had, at one time, talked with Clarence Boggie when he was on a trip to the prison at Walla Walla, and may even have read or glanced through the Boggie transcript.

Nothing had been done about it so far as his paper was concerned.

However, when the articles began to appear in *Argosy* publicizing a case which was, so to speak, in the back yard of the Seattle newspapers, Don Magnuson got busy and proceeded to write a series of articles which very nearly duplicated the legal analysis of the testimony in the case which we had left with the various officials in the state of Washington.

At the time we didn't pay a great deal of attention to these articles. We felt that the Governor had given us his word in the Boggie case; that the attorney general had made an investigation which indicated Boggie had been improperly convicted, and that the Governor was going to grant Boggie a pardon; that if the Seattle *Times* wanted to publish an analysis of the Boggie case based upon work that had been done by *Argosy* investigators they were quite free to do so.

But we couldn't understand the peculiar delay, and it bothered us.

When we had originally set up the Court of Last Resort it had been planned that we would take one case and present it to the readers, letting them look over our shoulders as we made the investigation, and then get their reaction. We had assumed that we could take a case and carry it through in a complete presentation to the reader and have the case closed within two or three installments.

We didn't count on the public reaction, and we didn't count upon the series of interminable delays in the Boggie case. We thought that since we had analyzed the evidence in the case, secured new evidence, made a presentation to the attorney general, secured the Governor's promise that if the attorney general's report was favorable Boggie would be released—that was all there was to it.

But the minute *Argosy* began publishing 'The Court of Last Resort,' letters began coming in, and as they continued coming in we found that readers wanted to know more about the developments in the Boggie case. They wanted to have us bring the case to a satisfactory conclusion one way or the other.

By this time, we began to realize only too well that a magazine of general circulation simply can't 'donate' space to a cause. A magazine is in a highly competitive market. People who pay twenty-five cents for a magazine want to get twenty-five cents' worth of recreation, entertainment, amusement and interesting information. If any substantial part of the magazine is filled with something they don't like, the reading public feels that it has to that extent been deprived of its money's worth and is going to turn to some other magazine.

The letters from readers of 'The Court of Last Resort' made it clear that we would either have to discontinue the feature or put it on a permanent basis. Either course presented very grave problems, particularly in view of the fact that things had come to a standstill in the Boggie case.

So I flew up to Olympia, the state capital of Washington, to find out what was happening.

At first I couldn't seem to get anywhere. Then Smith Troy, the attorney general, asked me if our group would be willing to co-operate with the Seattle *Times*. I told him, sure, we'd be glad to co-operate with anyone, but personally I didn't see why the Governor didn't go ahead and grant Boggie a pardon.

Troy told me that there had been new developments in the case which he wasn't in a position to disclose, but felt that if I talked with Henry MacLeod, the city editor, and Don Magnuson, I might receive some startling information. Smith Troy said he felt that these gentlemen would talk with me if we'd promise to co-operate.

I told Troy I'd be only too·glad to talk with them, and telephoned New York to ask Steeger if he would be willing to co-operate with the Seattle *Times*. Steeger said, 'Certainly,' to go right ahead. We'd co-operate with any newspaper that was trying to get at the facts in any case.

So then MacLeod, Magnuson and I sat down for a talk and I learned that when the first article had appeared in print an individual had telephoned the paper and said in effect, 'Why, I know all about the murder of Moritz Peterson. I know who did it. I told the Spokane police about it at the time. I didn't know that anyone had ever been convicted. I know this man Boggie never did have a thing to do with it. It was another person.'

Naturally the *Times* had rushed Don Magnuson out to see this witness.

The witness had been a businessman in Spokane. A certain peculiar character, whom we will refer to as John Doe, came into the store of this witness on several occasions, and, on one occasion shortly before the murder, had in his possession a weapon which had been made by putting a round, water-worn rock in a piece of burlap, wrapping the burlap around and around, so that the various thicknesses of cloth formed a substantial handle, and stitching the burlap tightly around this handle with the end result of a perfect weapon.

As soon as this witness saw a picture of the weapon that had been used to kill Moritz Peterson he recognized it as being the same weapon which had been in the possession of John Doe a short time earlier. He had promptly notified the Spokane police.

So the police had picked up John Doe. They found that John Doe had been in the neighborhood of the Peterson cabin on the morning that the murder was committed.

But had he been at the scene of the murder *when* it was committed? There was the question.

In investigating this case the police found a witness who had seen John Doe some little distance (as I remember it, it was nearly a mile) from the scene of the murder at '*the time that the sirens went by.*'

What sirens?

The police assumed that the statement of the witness related to the time the sirens had signaled the passing of police cars on their way to answer the frantic telephone calls from Peterson's neighbors.

But had that been the time?

In the first place, the police had no way of knowing exactly what time that was. In the second place, the proceedings had certainly been beautifully mixed up. Just recall the procession of police sirens.

The police knew when the call had been received at the police station. It will be remembered, however, that the first man on the job was the speed cop on his motorcycle. He had listened to the excited story poured in his ears by the witnesses who insisted that the murderer had 'gone thataway,' and had vanished in the wooded lot only a few seconds before.

The officer shook his head. Chasing murderers wasn't part of his duty. He jumped on his motorcycle and tore away.

Then came the police. The police heard the story and the children eagerly escorted the police up to the place where the murderer had gone into the brush. The police, you will recall, had forgotten their guns, and they wouldn't go into the brush without them.

So back they went to the police station to get armed.

Some time along in there, and at a time on which police records are silent, an ambulance came and took Moritz Peterson to the hospital.

All in all, there must have been a whole procession of sirens going back and forth, and the fact that some witness had seen John Doe at a certain place '*when the sirens went by*' was hardly the type of evidence which could be used as an alibi. It hardly seems possible that police could have considered '*the time the sirens went by*' as being any sort of an alibi. It simply didn't prove anything.

What sirens? When?

But the police had turned John Doe loose, and, by the time the Seattle *Times* had dug up this witness, were singularly unenthusiastic about reopening the case.

This was, of course, a very interesting development. Mac-Leod, Magnuson and I talked it over in detail, and it was decided that the first thing to do was to try and locate John Doe.

John Doe had been an itinerant, a man who was, according to the Spokane witness, eccentric to the point of being peculiar. He had vanished and left no trail.

So I moved down to Spokane with Magnuson and an assistant reporter from the Seattle *Times*. Raymond Schindler and Shelby Williams, the manager of his New York office, flew out to Spokane.

Schindler, Williams and the two reporters started running down clues, trying to uncover some lead which would disclose the present whereabouts of John Doe.

The trail was fifteen years old and, of course, as so frequently happens in a case of that kind, ninety-nine per cent of the leads that were investigated turned out to be blind alleys.

They found that John Doe had gone to Arizona, then he had disappeared for a while. They found that he had been in prison, and to add to the long chain of coincidences found that he had actually served a term in the Washington state penitentiary at Walla Walla at the same time Boggie was there serving his life sentence.

Naturally, as a writer, the dramatic possibilities appealed to me. Suppose it should appear that the man who actually murdered Moritz Peterson had rubbed elbows in prison with the man who had been erroneously convicted of that murder. What were his feelings? What would he do? Would he hunt Boggie up and try to form a friendship with him to see how Boggie was taking it, or would he avoid him? Or would he be sufficiently callous to go about the even tenor of his ways, completely ignoring Boggie?

I decided that later on I would make an investigation of this and perhaps confront John Doe with Boggie, but in the meantime, since we were working under cover, we dared not breathe a word of any of this to Boggie or even intimate that we were trying to close in on John Doe.

Finally the investigating team struck pay dirt, and after a long and arduous investigation uncovered a clue which they felt would enable them to put their hands on John Doe within thirty days. In other words, they found where John Doe was going to be thirty days from that date and there was every assurance that he would be there.

So Schindler, Shelby and I went home. The newspapermen stayed on the job, and at the end of thirty days did uncover John Doe and had the Spokane police pick him up for questioning.

They got precisely no place.

At that time Henry MacLeod rang us up and wanted to have Leonarde Keeler come out with a polygraph to give John Doe a lie detector test.

It turned out, however, that this wasn't going to be a simple matter. From telephone descriptions of John Doe's character, Keeler felt that there was a possibility John Doe might not be a 'good subject.' There was also the very strong chance that by the time Keeler got out there John Doe would refuse to take a lie detector test. Nor did Keeler want to fly out on a matter of that importance and make an immediate test. He wanted to take some time to investigate the man with whom he was dealing and familiarize himself with all details of the case.

By that time *Argosy* had spent many thousands of dollars on the Boggie case, and the outlook didn't seem at all promising. The magazine feature, 'The Court of Last Resort,' had proven terribly expensive, and no one knew for certain whether the readers of the magazine cared a hoot if innocent men were imprisoned or freed, or whether they simply wanted an end to a 'story.'

The investigators were all donating their time, but the traveling and incidental expenses had been enormous. We had put in literally months of work. The long-distance and telegraph bills alone were fantastic.

So, while John Doe was being detained, *Argosy* in New York held telephone conversations with Leonarde Keeler in Chicago, and I kept the wires buzzing to Seattle.

Looking back on it, it is incredible to think that we could so have misjudged the American reading public.

Later on it appeared that readers everywhere had been

following the Boggie case; that the reading public cared very much indeed whether innocent men who had been wrongfully convicted were held in prison.

At the time we weren't aware of this. We were feeling our way. The avalanche of public approval that was to dispel all our doubts was just beginning to form. We had no means of knowing what a terrific power it was to become.

In the meantime the Spokane police stated that they wanted to see whether the witness uncovered by the Seattle *Times* could make an identification of the murder weapon which, it is to be remembered, had then been in their hands for sixteen years. The witness had seen that weapon sixteen years earlier and hadn't seen it since.

The Seattle *Times* agreed to have their witness go to Spokane and make an identification of the weapon.

When the witness arrived the Spokane police tossed out a collection of weapons, all as nearly identical as they could make them, and asked the witness to pick out the one he had seen.

It seemed that the Spokane police had been busily engaged in duplicating the murder weapon.

Here again we have another incredible fact in the Boggie case. The witness sat down and carefully examined each of the weapons, and then *picked out the exact weapon which had been used to murder Moritz Peterson sixteen years earlier.*

'This is the one,' he said.

And he was right.

Nor was that identification merely a matter of chance. It happened that this witness was one of those unusually keen observers, who possessed a remarkable ability to recall what he had seen. Moreover, there was one peculiarity about the murder weapon *which had escaped the notice of the Spokane police but which had clung to the memory of the witness.*

I know that it wasn't merely an afterthought or a coincidence because the witness himself had told me about this peculiarity when Don Magnuson had arranged for me to meet him, a meeting which had taken place some weeks before the interview with the police in Spokane.

Then came another development.

Ed Lehan, the deputy attorney general, whom Smith Troy

had delegated to fly down to my ranch and inspect the transcript in the Boggie case, had been very much interested in subsequent developments. He had worked carefully on the case, had made a report to Smith Troy, who, in turn, had made a report to the Governor.

Digging into police records in Spokane, Lehan found that during the time John Doe had first been arrested by the Spokane police, and prior to the time he had been released because he had an alibi for the time that '*the sirens went by,*' every one of the witnesses who had seen the murderer running from the cabin of Moritz Peterson on that fateful Monday morning had positively identified John Doe as being the man they had seen.

The witness who had at the time of Boggie's trial glibly identified him as the man she had seen, had actually, nearly two years before, when the occasion was fresh in her mind, identified John Doe as being the man who had run away from that cabin and had been so positive, according to police records, that she had made the definite statement, 'I'll stake my life on it.'

It will be remembered that when we examined the transcript in the Boggie case there was indication that this witness had previously made an identification of another man, and that there had been a retraction of the identification when it appeared that the other man had a perfect alibi and couldn't possibly have been connected with the crime.

That man was John Doe and the alibi was merely a statement that he had been seen at a certain place some distance from the scene of the crime '*when the sirens went by.*'

As Smith Troy, the attorney general, succinctly stated, 'The State now has a better case against John Doe than it ever had against Clarence Boggie.'

But who was going to prosecute John Doe?

Certainly not the authorities in Spokane.

Clarence Boggie had been convicted by the authorities in Spokane. It would have been a bitter pill to have to swallow, after all these years, to admit a mistake and seek to convict John Doe.

John Doe seemed to sense that if he 'sat tight' he would come out all right.

He sat tight.

After a while John Doe was quietly released.

Those, generally, are the facts of the Boggie case and the murder of Moritz Peterson. There are certain other facts which I could disclose, but I don't think they would do any particular good at this time.

With the Seattle *Times* and *Argosy* Magazine hammering away at the Boggie case, Governor Wallgren finally granted Boggie a conditional pardon in December, 1948.

Don Magnuson received an award for his outstanding reporting, and the Seattle *Times* was showered with congratulations in the press. No one saw fit to mention that *Argosy* Magazine had been investigating the case for months, and even had a virtual commitment from Governor Wallgren long before the Seattle *Times* had even published a word. Bill Gilbert and some of the others who had known of our work started writing indignant letters.

However, I for one am frank to admit that political pressure might well have prevented any action from ever having been taken if it hadn't been for the work of the Seattle *Times* in uncovering the witness, who, apparently, had never read any of the articles in *Argosy*, but who did read that first article in the *Times*.

As I expressed it at one time, I think perhaps *Argosy* was ninety per cent responsible for proving that Boggie had been improperly convicted, whereas the Seattle *Times* was ninety per cent responsible for proving that a case much stronger than the case against Clarence Boggie could have been made against someone else.

Even at this late date the attorney general's office at Washington is looking for further evidence against John Doe in connection with the murder of Moritz Peterson. It has some hope that it may be forthcoming.

I know that I personally welcomed the assistance of the Seattle *Times* at the time we joined forces, and I welcome it now.

Henry MacLeod, Don Magnuson, and Magnuson's assistant, a newspaper reporter who, by the way, took a violent personal dislike to me, were first-class newspapermen. It was a revelation to see the way these men, with their knowledge of local conditions and the power of a local newspaper behind them, dug into the facts of the case. Their work in the Boggie case is one of the best illustrations I know of why we should have a free press, and why readers and advertisers should support powerful local newspapers. An advertiser who buys space in his local newspaper gets value received in terms of a dollars-and-cents return on his investment. In addition to all this he is making a tax-exempt investment in liberty and in freedom of the press. Without our local newspapers citizens would find themselves in a very sorry plight.

The truth of this is so apparent it seems a waste of time to mention it. Yet, strange as it may seem, this is an angle that many local businessmen and newspaper readers overlook.

I know that in my own case I didn't fully realize what a powerful factor a newspaper could be in safeguarding liberties until I saw the way these men from the Seattle *Times* with their knowledge of local conditions could get information that would have been unavailable to us.

From that time on we realized that whenever possible it would pay to have some local newspaper take an interest in our cases.

So far as the Court of Last Resort was concerned, the Boggie case demonstrated certain problems which, incidentally, we have never been able to solve.

In order to secure a committee the personnel of which would command confidence on the part of the public, would carry sufficient prestige to impress state officials, and at the same time be composed of men who were well established financially so that there was no need of personal publicity, it was necessary to get men who had active business interests. If a man is successful he has numerous demands on his time. If he isn't successful people aren't inclined to accept his opinion.

Dr LeMoyne Snyder's services are in constant demand. Leonarde Keeler was tremendously busy during his lifetime, and Alex Gregory at the present time is working on a crowded schedule. Raymond Schindler has the job of co-ordinating the investigation in countless cases. He is constantly flying back and forth from New York to Los Angeles, up to San Francisco, down to Florida, and occasionally over to Europe.

Harry Steeger, in addition to the responsibilities of supervising the destinies of *Argosy* Magazine, has some three dozen magazines in his publishing string. For my part I am always metering minutes, trying to be in two places at once, and do two things at the same time.

The result was that when we would fly to Walla Walla, Olympia or Spokane, and start an investigation, the long-distance telephone would be hammering out a constant succession of calls concerning some 'emergency' which had developed in our various businesses while we were away.

We could only get away a few days at a time; then we would have to go dashing back and face the discouraging prospect of a desk piled high with mail which had accumulated in our absence.

The members of the investigating committee had agreed to donate their time, the magazine had agreed to defray traveling expenses. But when, for instance, a man has to fly from New York to the Pacific Coast to work a few days on a case, then dash back to his office, expenses pile up.

When three or four such individuals get together for a conference, the bill runs into big money.

Those of us who felt that we could afford to do so stopped sending in vouchers and donated all our expenses as well as our time. But some of us simply weren't in a position to do this; contributing the time alone had been a very great sacrifice.

Such factors made the Court of Last Resort terribly costly, and made it debatable as a cold-blooded business proposition. Despite the fact that the reading public was indicating its approval it was, of course, quite clear that if the money spent on the Court of Last Resort should be used to increase promotional allotments and editorial rates, the expenditures would be far more profitable.

But, offsetting this tremendous expense was the knowledge that the work is a badly needed activity in connection with our whole scheme of justice.

Harry Steeger wanted *Argosy* to stand for something. He wanted the magazine not only to entertain, but to be a constructive force, and he overruled his editors when they pointed out how much more desirable it would be to use the money spent on the Court of Last Resort for promotional purposes.

Harry Steeger has a certain bulldog tenacity, and having started the Court of Last Resort he 'stayed put.'

Had we known what we now know about investigating the cases, the investigation of the Boggie case would have been greatly simplified. We learned a lot from that case.

Before finally leaving it, I think it is only fair to mention certain obvious truths which should be given careful consideration.

The police may not have forced the identification of Clarence Boggie in the manner in which a good card magician forces the man from the audience to pick out one particular card from the deck, but there can be no question that the tactics used by the police were such as to greatly influence the witnesses in making an identification.

One of the witnesses who had 'identified' Boggie as 'looking like' the man seen running from the scene of the murder, was asked if she could have made her identification had she been called upon to pick Boggie out of a line-up.

She admitted, at the time the question was first asked, that this would have been most difficult. Later on she said that she hadn't understood the question.

It is also evident that the jurors were out of sympathy with Clarence Boggie, and paid undue attention to his previous record of convictions. A certain amount of persuasive evidence was marshaled against Boggie, but it is difficult to understand how anyone could have felt that this evidence proved him guilty beyond all reasonable doubt.

Identification evidence, even when asserted with vehemence, should always be considered in the light of surrounding circumstances.

Some persons who are inclined to be positive and opinionated will get on a witness stand and swear with every ounce of sincerity at their command that the defendant in the case is the man they saw at such-and-such a time, at such-and-such a place.

Unfortunately the man who should be the most doubtful is, nine times out of ten, the man who is the most positive.

The fair man, whose testimony is apt to be accurate, is more likely to say, 'Well, I can't be absolutely positive, but I *think* that this is the man. Of course, it's been some time ago, but I think this is the man.'

Defense attorneys are inclined to pounce upon such a witness and by showing that he isn't positive and only 'thinks' the defendant is the man, sneeringly subject the witness to ridicule.

In many instances, such tactics are unfair.

Jurors should not readily condone a fair witness being torn to pieces by a jeering, sarcastic defense attorney who is crucifying the witness upon the cross of his own fairness.

On the other hand, juries should not be too much impressed by the testimony of the man who, after seeing some individual for a few seconds during the excitement attending the commission of a crime, swears positively that the man seated in the courtroom is the criminal. Jurors should consider all the facts.

Carefully conducted experiments show that it is rather difficult to make a positive identification, particularly where the individual was seen casually.

I remember at one time when I was attending one of Captain Frances G. Lee's seminars on homicide investigation at the Harvard Medical School, Dr Robert Brittain, a brilliant Scotsman, one of the shrewdest medicolegal brains in the profession (at present Lecturer in Forensic Medicine at Leeds University in England) was lecturing to a class of some fifteen state police officers, men who had been chosen for the course because of aptitude and ability.

Dr Brittain was commenting on description and identification. Abruptly he ceased his lecture, turned to the assembled group and said, 'By the way, how tall am I? Will someone speak up, please?'

Someone said, 'Five foot eight.'

Dr Brittain was like an auctioneer. 'Anyone here who thinks I'm taller than five foot eight?' he asked.

There was something in his voice that made it appear the estimate might have been on the short side, so someone promptly said, 'Five foot eight and a half,' and then someone went to five foot nine.

After a while Dr Brittain said, 'Well, who thinks I'm *shorter* than five foot eight?'

That immediately drew a customer.

Then Dr Brittain went on to the question of his weight and his age. Before he got done he had a series of descriptions which were simply meaningless. Between the extreme estimates there was a margin of difference that represented some fifteen years in age, some twenty pounds in weight and some four inches in height, and it is to be remembered that these descriptions were furnished not by men who were excited because they were being held up, or by men who were getting a fleeting glimpse of an individual in a dim light—they were sitting there looking directly at Dr Brittain, whose figure was only partially obscured by a table, and they were trained observers, men who made it their business to classify and describe.

But what of Clarence Boggie? What of the man himself?

Boggie, it is to be remembered, had been convicted and sent to prison in Idaho for the robbery which had been perpetrated by Convict X.

Boggie had served considerable time in Idaho, always protesting his innocence, and finally, because of various factors in the case, including an affidavit by a sheriff who had overheard conversations which made him believe Boggie might have been forced into the crime, the authorities had launched an investigation.

An investigator had actually found the place where Boggie had been repairing the lights which had short-circuited on the car of the man who had given him a ride. The attendant of that service station remembered that another car had drawn up and Boggie had been forced to get into it. Then the car had driven away.

The Governor of Idaho granted Boggie a pardon, but Boggie never had an opportunity to enjoy even five minutes of liberty under that pardon. The Washington authorities had grabbed him at the moment the pardon was delivered and had whisked him away to try him for the murder of Moritz Peterson, to convict him of that murder and to send him to prison for life.

Boggie at the time of his release found himself in a world that was all but strange to him. He had been in prison for nearly twenty years, and the outside world had made a good many strides during that time.

It was also difficult for him to make an emotional adjustment to freedom.

Moreover Boggie had received quantities of fan mail.

We had relied on publicity to get justice done in his case and the publicity had swelled into a tide which threatened to sweep Boggie off his feet.

Lawyers inspired him with the idea that he could sue the State of Washington for a huge sum of money for false imprisonment. People wrote to Boggie wishing him luck. Some of these fan letters were from women.

Boggie, who had spent some twenty years of his life entirely removed from the company and companionship of women, had placed his mother upon a pedestal and idolized her.

It was no time at all until Boggie was engaged to be married.

The power of the press had brought about Boggie's liberation, and from the moment of Boggie's release he became 'good copy.' Practically everything he did, every floundering mistake made in attempting to adjust himself to his newfound liberty, was publicized in the newspapers.

Then he found himself. He married a childhood sweetheart. He settled down, and finally found someone who had enough confidence in him to put him in charge of a logging crew.

Boggie's previous statements to us that he was one of the best aerial loggers in the country had been taken with a grain of salt and a barrel of pepper. His similar statements to prospective employers had apparently been dismissed as not even worthy of serious consideration.

Now Boggie had a chance to show what he could do.

That was the last unbelievable thing about the unbelievable Boggie. He was just as good as he said he was.

Boggie started breaking all records for handling logs. He tore into the work with a fervor and an efficiency that amazed everyone.

And then just when Boggie had adjusted himself to life on the outside, when he had married and established a home, when he had demonstrated his ability to handle a responsible job of putting out logs, the problem of physical adjustment proved too much for him.

Boggie had one triumphant day in which he broke all previous records for an output of logs.

His heart, which had been weakened by twenty years of confinement within walls, twenty years of routine prison diet, couldn't stand the strain that was thrown on it. Boggie came home. He told his wife that he had broken every previous existing record at the camp for moving logs.

Smiling his tired, twisted smile, Boggie went to the bathroom to wash his hands and fell over dead.

ROBERT GRAVES

New Light on an Old Murder

When, some twenty-five years ago, I wrote a two-volume novel about the Emperor Claudius, my pseudo-autobiographical approach obliged me to break off the story just before he died. However, not to keep my readers guessing, I printed as an epilogue the three main Classical accounts of Claudius's murder, those of Suetonius, Tacitus, and Dio Cassius. For good measure, I added a satire attributed to the Emperor Nero's tutor, the Spanish philosopher and playwright Seneca: 'The *Apocolocyntosis* of Claudius.' *Apocolocyntosis* has always been read as a humorous portmanteau word combining *apotheosis* (deification)—because Claudius was deified immediately after his death—and *colocynthos* (pumpkin)—presumably because Seneca regarded Claudius as a pumpkin-headed fool. The agreed translation therefore is 'Pumpkinfication,' and it never occurred to me that the word could have any other meaning.

Claudius's murder was engineered by his wife Agrippina. He had recently adopted Nero, her seventeen-year-old son by a former marriage, and named him joint-heir to the Empire with twelve-year-old Britannicus, his own son by Messaline. Agrippina decided to oust Britannicus from the succession; Nero's gratitude on becoming sole Emperor ought, she reckoned, to secure her supreme power behind the throne. Meanwhile she did all she could to turn Claudius against Britannicus and kept the two as far apart as possible. At last, fearing that Claudius suspected her of treachery and unfaithfulness, she planned to get rid of him without delay.

In 1949, Dr Valentina Wasson, a New York physician, wrote to enquire whether I had any views on the exact circumstances of the murder, which she and her husband, R. Gordon Wasson, a vice-president of J.P. Morgan and Company, were investigating from the mycological angle. I looked up the sources again, and here they are in what I believe to be the order of their historic trustworthiness:

Most people think that Claudius was poisoned; but when, and by whom, is disputed. Some say that the eunuch Halotus, his official taster, administered the drug while he was dining with the priests of Jupiter in the Citadel; others, that Agrippina did so herself at a family banquet, poisoning a dish of mushrooms, his favourite food. An equal discrepancy exists between the accounts of what happened next. According to many of my informants, he lost his power of speech, suffered frightful pain all night long, and died shortly before dawn. A variant version is that he fell into a coma but vomited up the entire contents of his stomach and was then poisoned a second time, either by a gruel—the excuse being that he needed food to revive him—or by means of an enema, the excuse being that his bowels must be emptied too.

Claudius's death was not revealed until all arrangements had been completed to secure Nero's succession. As a result, people made vows for his safety as though he still lived, and a troop of actors were summoned, under the pretence that he had asked to be diverted by their antics. He died on October 13th, 54 A.D., during the consulship of Asinius Marcellus and Acilius Avola, in his sixty-fourth year, and the fourteenth of his reign. He was given a princely funeral and officially deified, an honour which Nero later neglected and then cancelled; but which Vespasian restored.   Suetonius: *XII Caesars (tr. Robert Graves)*

Agrippina had long decided on murder. Now she saw her opportunity. Her agents were ready. But she wanted advice about poisons. A sudden, drastic effect would give her away. A gradual, wasting recipe might make Claudius, faced with death, love his son again. What was needed was something subtle that would upset the Emperor's faculties but produce a deferred fatal effect. An expert in such matters was selected—a woman called Locusta, recently sentenced for poisoning but with a long career of imperial service ahead of her. By her talents, a preparation was supplied. It was administered by a eunuch who habitually served the Emperor and tasted his food.

Later, the whole story became known. Contemporary writers stated that the poison was sprinkled on a particularly succulent mushroom. But because Claudius was torpid—or drunk—its effect was not at first apparent; and an evacuation of his bowels seemed to have saved him. Agrippina was horrified. But when the ultimate stakes are so alarmingly large, immediate disrepute is brushed aside. She had already secured the complicity of the Emperor's doctor Xenophon; and now she called him in. The story is that, while pretending to help Claudius to vomit, he put a feather dipped in a quick poison down his throat. Xenophon knew that major crimes, though hazardous to undertake, are profitable to achieve.   Tacitus: *Annals (tr. Michael Grant)*

Claudius was angered by Agrippina's actions, of which he was now becoming aware, and sought for his son Britannicus, who had purposely been kept out of his sight by her most of the time (for she was doing everything she could to secure the throne for Nero, inasmuch as he was her own son by her former husband Domitius); and he displayed his affection whenever he met the boy. He would not endure her behaviour, but was preparing to put an end to her power, to cause his son to assume the *toga virilis*, and to declare him heir to the throne. Agrippina, learning of this, became alarmed and made haste to forestall anything of the sort by poisoning Claudius. But since, owing to the great quantity of wine he was forever drinking and his general habits of life, such as all emperors as a rule adopt for their protection, he could not easily be harmed, she sent for a famous dealer in poisons, a woman named Locusta, who had recently been convicted on this very charge; and preparing with her aid a poison whose effect was sure, she put it in one of the vegetables called mushrooms. Then she herself ate of the others, but made her husband eat of the one which contained the poison; for it was the largest and finest of them. And so the victim of the plot was carried from the banquet apparently quite overcome by strong drink, a thing that had happened many times before; but during the night the poison took effect and he passed away, without having been able to say or hear a word. It was the thirteenth of October, and he had lived sixty-three years, two months and thirteen days, having been emperor thirteen years, eight months and twenty days.

Dio Cassius: *Book LXI (tr. E. Cary)*

Mr and Mrs Wasson had gone a long way towards solving their detective problem. The mushrooms, nowhere described as being themselves poisonous, were almost certainly of the wholesome and delicious variety now known, in Claudius's honour, as the *amanita caesarea*. They have round, orange-coloured caps primrose-yellow spores and stalks, and grow plentifully throughout Southern Europe in October, the month of his death. The Wassons believed that Locusta, the professional poisoner employed by Agrippina, made Halotus, the official taster, doctor the mushrooms handed to Claudius with the juice of another mushroom of the same genus—the deadly *amanita phalloides*. The *phalloides* has a yellowish-white slightly pointed cap, white spores and stalk, and grows plentifully near Rome at the same season as the *caesarea*. It seems that Claudius's family and friends were served from a single large dish; and their survival would suggest that he had been unfortunate enough to eat a single poisonous *phalloides* included among the *caesarea* by mistake. Nor was there any chance of

Claudius's detecting the poison—for which no remedy was then, or is now, known—by its taste. All those luckless people who have ever eaten *amanita phalloides* agree (before they die) that it tastes most delicious. They have quite enough time to make this observation, since the ill-effects seldom occur until six hours have elapsed. Sometimes nothing happens for as long as twenty hours. Yet once the poison takes a firm hold, the victim is in no condition to think of anything but his excruciating stomachic pains, which gradually carry him off. One hears vague talk about survivors, but I can find no certain instance of one. Claudius's inability to collect his wits before he died was, Tacitus notes, a condition of the poisoning on which Agrippina insisted.

That Seneca knew the peculiar properties of *amanita phalloides*, the Wassons deduced from a letter he wrote some nine years later to his friend Lucilius the Stoic. While condemning Claudius's gluttony, he exclaims:

> 'Good gods! How many men are employed in the service of a single belly! But can you believe that the tasty poison of those mushrooms does not operate secretly, even if no ill-effect is immediately experienced?'

This seems to me pretty conclusive proof of Seneca's complicity in the murder, and at the same time it explains how Locusta's apparently flawless plot miscarried. Claudius's gross habit, elsewhere attested by Suetonius, of drinking too much and then ridding his stomach of the excess, nearly saved his life. It seems that, soon after being carried from the table dead drunk, he vomited up a part of his meal; which put Agrippina in a most awkward position. (Tacitus's 'an evacuation of the bowels seemed to have saved him' makes no sense and can refer only to the vomiting.) Agrippina had no means of judging how much poison, if any, remained in her husband's stomach; nor, apparently, of preparing the same meal again, even if he could be persuaded to make a second attempt at downing it. Meanwhile, plans had been concluded for Nero's acclamation as the sole Emperor; and, if Claudius were to recover, the news of her attempted coup might well leak out—in which case he would probably appoint Britannicus, who was (according to Suetonius) now officially of age, his co-Emperor, and execute Nero and herself without trial.

The Emperor Claudius: poisoned by a mushroom?

Agrippina and her assistants moved quickly. The best hope of saving their skins lay in reinforcing the action of whatever poison remained in Claudius's system, by administering another drug of the same general effect. A *post-mortem* could then show him to have died by mischance from that single deadly mushroom. So they bribed, or forced, the imperial physician Xenophon to finish his master off. According to Tacitus, Xenophon put a feather smeared with venom down Claudius's throat; but this sounds both difficult and dangerous. The Wassons preferred Suetonius's less melodramatic account, according to which the poison was administered by enema. We were left to discover precisely what drug Xenophon could have chosen and procured at short notice to ensure the desired results.

Then it occurred to me that I had been as stupid as all the long line of Classical scholars who studied these texts before me. The Greek word *colocynthos* does not only mean 'pumpkin'; it also means the wild gourd mentioned in that exciting Biblical passage (II Kings 4: 38–41) about the college of prophets who shredded vegetables into the communal stew and discovered too late that some ignoramus had added a lapful of sliced wild gourd. They cried in agony to their master Elisha: 'O man of God, there is death in the pot!'

Colocynth, though a useful purge in minimal doses, and notorious as the active agent of the powerful No. 9 pill employed by M.O.'s to cure malingerers during the First World War, is a virulent alkaloid poison. Scribonius Largus, the apothecary, in a valuable book of medical prescriptions published around A.D. 45, acknowledges indebtedness for the colocynth recipe to his friend the late Paccius of Antioch. Paccius's No. 9 pill soon became very popular among the Roman aristocracy, most of whom (then as now) ate far too much, slept far too much, and took far too little exercise. But though Xenophon could easily lay his hand on colocynth without exciting suspicion, it tastes exceedingly bitter; and how to make Claudius accept a decisive dose in gruel (as Agrippina seems to have suggested), was a delicate problem. Xenophon's ingenious alternative, that of rectal administration under colour of giving his patient a good turn-out, proved effective.

Hence Seneca's subsequent coinage of the word *Apocolocynto-sis*, the real meaning of which was: 'Deification by means of colocynth.' He celebrated this cruel murder with a light-hearted satire on Claudius's physical and intellectual failings, and it is difficult to forgive the joke about Claudius's miserable last words: '*Vae me, puto me concacavi!*'—'Alas, I think I have messed myself badly!' Seneca writes that Claudius always *did* make a mess of everything. However, to die from colocynth poisoning is at least a swifter and less agonizing fate than to die from *amanita phalloides*.

The farce of pretending, several hours after the end, that Claudius was still alive and being amused by a variety troupe, seems to have been dictated by the change of drugs. Claudius ate his late meal on October 12th, A.D. 54, at about 2:30 P.M. The first gripings from *phalloides* poisoning should have come on between 9 P.M. and midnight; but the 'deferred fatal effect' could not be hoped for until the following evening. Xenophon's colocynth acted far more rapidly. Claudius died before dawn, and Agrippina found herself uncomfortably ahead of schedule. It looks as if the new arrangements for Nero's acclamation as Emperor had been agreed with the Guards Colonel who would begin his turn of duty at noon; because it was not until then that Nero came out from the Palace to receive the soldiers' homage. Agrippina afterwards excused the delay as due to astrological considerations. How much Nero himself already knew about the plot is uncertain; but on a later occasion he laughingly quoted the Greek proverb: 'Mushrooms are the food of the gods,' and added that mushrooms had, in fact, made a god of his predecessor.

Agrippina satisfied herself that Locusta's *amanita phalloides* was a wonderfully effective drug, when (according to Dio Cassius) she killed her enemy Marcus Julius Silanus with a dose of the poison that had been prepared for Claudius. Nor does this seem to have been her last use of it. Tacitus reports that Annaeus Serenus, Commander of Nero's Bodyguard (whom we meet elsewhere as an intimate friend of Seneca's) assisted Nero's secret liaison with a slave-girl named Acte; and that Nero appealed to Seneca for help when Agrippina got wind of the affair. But Tacitus omits to mention Agrippina's revenge of Serenus, and we must turn to Pliny's *Natural History* for the information:

> The safest fungi are those, the flesh of which is red, the colour being more pronounced than that of the mushroom. The next best are the white ones, the stems of which have a head very similar to the cap worn by the Flamens; and a third kind are the *suilli* ('piglets'), very conveniently adapted for poisoning. Indeed, it is but very recently that they have carried off whole families, and all the guests at a banquet; Annaeus Serenus, for instance, the commander of Nero's Guard, together with all the tribunes and centurions. What great pleasure, then, can there be in partaking of a dish of so doubtful a character as this?

Pliny meant, I suppose, that *amanita phalloides* can readily be smuggled into a harmless dish of *amanita caesarea*, with no chance of immediate discovery, and with spectacular success, especially if one does not care how many others, besides the intended victim, die horribly from it.

From the distant past to an even more remote future. Up to here we have concentrated on fairly practical solutions to crimes, but here at the end let's allow the imagination to fly a little. Robert Graves' recreation of Ancient Rome in his two novels about Claudius constitutes an imaginative reconstruction of the first rank; Harlan Ellison's leap into the future is something else again, and not for the squeamish.

Unsolved! opened with perhaps the greatest of all the classic murderers, Jack the Ripper, and to close Solved! the wheel is brought full circle, and posits another kind of solution altogether: the flight of fantasy inspired by real events — a whole genre, and perhaps another collection. Hope to see you there. Meanwhile, here is the inimitable Mr Ellison...

HARLAN ELLISON

The Prowler in the City
At the Edge of the World

First there was the City, never night. Tin and reflective,
walls of antiseptic metal like an immense autoclave. Pure
and dust-free, so silent that even the whirling innards of its
heart and mind were sheathed from notice. The city was
self-contained, and footfalls echoed up and around—flat
slapped notes of an exotic leather-footed instrument. Sounds
that reverberated back to the maker like yodels thrown out
across mountain valleys. Sounds made by humbled inhabitants whose lives were as ordered, as sanitary, as metallic as
the city they had caused to hold them bosom-tight against
the years. The city was a complex artery, the people were
the blood that flowed icily through the artery. They were a
gestalt with one another, forming a unified whole. It was a
city shining in permanence, eternal in concept, flinging itself
up in a formed and molded statement of exaltation; most
modern of all modern structures, conceived as the pluperfect
residence for the perfect people. The final end-result of all
sociological blueprints aimed at Utopia. Living space, it had
been called, and so, doomed to *live* they were, in that
Erewhon of graphed respectability and cleanliness.

Never night.

Never shadowed.

. . . a shadow.

A blot moving against the aluminium cleanliness. The
movement of rags and bits of clinging earth from graves
sealed ages before. A shape.

He touched a gunmetal-gray wall in passing: the imprint
of dusty fingers. A twisted shadow moving through antisep-

tically pure streets, and they become—with his passing—black alleys from another time.

Vaguely, he knew what had happened. Not specifically, not with particulars, but he was strong, and he was able to get away without the eggshell-thin walls of his mind caving in. There was no place in this shining structure to secrete himself, a place to think, but he had to have time. He slowed his walk, seeing no one. Somehow—inexplicably—he felt ... safe? Yes, safe. For the first time in a very long time.

A few minutes before he had been standing in the narrow passageway outside No. 13 Miller's Court. It had been 6:15 in the morning. London had been quiet as he paused in the passageway of M'Carthy's Rents, in that fetid, urine-redolent corridor where the whores of Spitalfields took their clients. A few minutes before, the foetus in its bath of formaldehyde tightly-stoppered in a glass bottle inside his Gladstone bag, he had paused to drink in the thick fog, before taking the circuitous route back to Toynbee Hall. That had been a few minutes before. Then, suddenly, he was in another place and it was no longer 6:15 of a chill November morning in 1888.

He had looked up as light flooded him in that other place. It had been soot silent in Spitalfields, but suddenly, without any sense of having moved or having *been* moved, he was flooded with light. And when he looked up he was in that other place. Paused now, only a few minutes after the transfer, he leaned against the bright wall of the city, and recalled the light. From a thousand mirrors. In the walls, in the ceiling. A bedroom with a girl in it. A lovely girl. Not like Black Mary Kelly or Dark Annie Chapman or Kate Eddowes or any of the other pathetic scum he had been forced to attend ...

A lovely girl. Blonde, wholesome, until she had opened her robe and turned into the same sort of slut he had been compelled to use in his work in Whitechapel ...

A sybarite, a creature of pleasures, a Juliette she had said, before he used the big-bladed knife on her. He had found the knife under the pillow, on the bed to which she had led him—how shameful, unresisting had he been, all confused, clutching his black bag with all the tremors of a child, he who had moved through the London night like oil, moved where he wished, accomplished his ends unchecked eight times, now led toward sin by another, merely another of the tarts, taking advantage of him while he tried to distinguish what had happened to him and where he was, how shameful − and he had used it on her.

That had only been minutes before, though he had worked very efficiently on her.

The knife had been rather unusual. The blade had seemed to be two wafer-thin sheets of metal with a pulsing, glowing *something* between. A kind of sparking, such as might be produced by a Van de Graaff generator. But that was patently ridiculous. It had no wires attached to it, no bus bars, nothing to produce even the crudest electrical discharge. He had thrust the knife into the Gladstone bag, where now it lay beside the scalpels and the spool of catgut and the racked vials in their leather cases, and the foetus in its bottle. Mary Jane Kelly's foetus.

He had worked efficiently, but swiftly, and had laid her out almost exactly in the same fashion as Kate Eddowes: the throat slashed completely through from ear-to-ear, the torso laid open down between the breasts to the vagina, the intestines pulled out and draped over the right shoulder, a piece of the intestines being detached and placed between the left arm and the body. The liver had been punctured with the point of the knife, with a vertical cut slitting the left lobe of the liver. (He had been surprised to find the liver showed none of the signs of cirrhosis so prevalent in these Spitalfields tarts, who drank incessantly to rid themselves of the burden of living the dreary lives they moved through grotesquely. In fact, this one seemed totally unlike the others, even if she had been more brazen in her sexual overtures. And that knife under the bed pillow . . .) He had severed the vena cava leading to the heart. Then he had gone to work on the face.

He had thought of removing the left kidney again, as he had Kate Eddowes's. He smiled to himself as he conjured up the expression that must have been on the face of Mr.

George Lusk, chairman of the Whitechapel Vigilance Committee, when he received the cardboard box in the mail. The box containing Miss Eddowes's kidney, and the letter, impiously misspelled:

> From hell, Mr. Lusk, sir, I send you half the kidne I took from one woman, prasarved it for you, tother piece I fried and ate it; was very nice. I may send you the bloody knif that took it out if you only wate while longer. Catch me when you can, Mr. Lusk.

He had wanted to sign *that* one "Yours Truly, Jack the Ripper" or even Spring-Heeled Jack or maybe Leather Apron, whichever had tickled his fancy, but a sense of style had stopped him. To go too far was to defeat his own purposes. It may even have been too much to suggest to Mr. Lusk that he had eaten the kidney. How hideous. True, he *had* smelled it . . .

This blonde girl, this Juliette with the knife under her pillow. She was the ninth. He leaned against the smooth steel wall without break or seam, and he rubbed his eyes. When would he be able to stop? When would they realize, when would they get his message, a message so clear, written in blood, that only the blindness of their own cupidity forced them to misunderstand! Would he be compelled to decimate the endless regiments of Spitalfields sluts to make them understand? Would he be forced to run the cobbles ankle-deep in black blood before they sensed what he was saying, and were impelled to make reforms?

But as he took his blood-soaked hands from his eyes, he realized what he must have sensed all along: he was no longer in Whitechapel. This was not Miller's Court, nor anywhere in Spitalfields. It might not even be London. But how could *that* be?

Had God taken him?

Had he died, in a senseless instant between the anatomy lesson of Mary Jane Kelly (that filth, she had actually *kissed* him!) and the bedroom disembowelment of this Juliette? Had Heaven finally called him to his reward for the work he had done?

The Reverend Mr. Barnett would love to know about this. But then, he'd have loved to know about it *all*. But "Bloody Jack" wasn't about to tell. Let the reforms come as the Reverend and his wife wished for them, and let them think their pamphleteering had done it, instead of the scalpels of Jack.

If he was dead, would his work be finished? He smiled to himself. If Heaven had taken him, then it must be that the work *was* finished. Successfully. But if *that* was so, then who was this Juliette who now lay spread out moist and cooling in the bedroom of a thousand mirrors? And in that instant he felt fear.

What if even God misinterpreted what he had done?

As the good folk of Queen Victoria's London had misinterpreted. As Sir Charles Warren had misinterpreted. What if God believed the superficial and ignored the *real* reason? But no! Ludicrous. If anyone would understand, it was the good God who had sent him the message that told him to set things a-right.

God loved him, as he loved God, and God would know.

But he felt fear, in that moment.

Because who was the girl he had just carved?

"She was my granddaughter, Juliette," said a voice immediately beside him.

His head refused to move, to turn that few inches to see who spoke. The Gladstone was beside him, resting on the smooth and reflective surface of the street. He could not get to a knife before he was taken. At last they had caught up with Jack. He began to shiver uncontrollably.

"No need to be afraid," the voice said. It was a warm and succoring voice. An older man. He shook as with an ague. But he turned to look. It was a kindly old man with a gentle smile. Who spoke again, without moving his lips. "No one can hurt you. How do you do?"

The man from 1888 sank slowly to his knees. "Forgive me. Dear God, I did not know." The old man's laughter rose inside the head of the man on his knees. It rose like a beam of sunlight moving across a Whitechapel alleyway, from noon to one o'clock, rising and illuminating the gray bricks of soot-coated walls. It rose, and illuminated his mind.

"I'm not God. Marvelous idea, but no, I'm not God. Would you like to meet God? I'm sure we can find one of the artists who would mold one for you. Is it important? No, I can see it isn't. What a strange mind you have. You neither believe nor doubt. How can you contain both concepts at once ... would you like me to straighten some of your brain-patterns? No. I see, you're afraid. Well, let it be for the nonce. We'll do it another time."

He grabbed the kneeling man and drew him erect.

"You're covered with blood. Have to get you cleaned up. There's an ablute near here. Incidentally, I was very impressed with the way you handled Juliette. You're the first, you know. No, how could you know? In any case, you *are* the first to deal her as good as she gave. You would have been amused at what she did to Caspar Hauser. Squeezed part of his brain and then sent him back, let him live out part of his life and then—the little twit—she made me bring him back a second time and used a knife on him. Same knife you took, I believe. Then sent him back to his own time. Marvelous mystery. In all the tapes on unsolved phenomena. But she was much sloppier than you. She had a great verve in her amusements, but very little *éclat*. Except with Judge Crater; there she was—" He paused, and laughed lightly. "I'm an old man and I ramble on like a muskrat. You want to get cleaned up and shown around, I know. And *then* we can talk.

"I just wanted you to know I was satisfied with the way you disposed of her. In a way, I'll miss the little twit. She was such a good fuck."

The old man picked up the Gladstone bag and, holding the man spattered with blood, he moved off down the clean and shimmering street. "You *wanted* her killed?" the man from 1888 asked, unbelieving.

The old man nodded, but his lips never moved. "Of course. Otherwise why bring her Jack the Ripper?"

Oh my dear God, he thought, *I'm in Hell. And I'm entered as Jack.*

"No, my boy, no no no. You're not in Hell at all. You're in the future. For you the future, for me the world of now. You came from 1888 and you're now in—" he stopped, silently speaking for an instant, as though computing apples in terms of dollars, then resumed "—3077. It's a fine world, filled with happy times, and we're glad to have you with us. Come along now, and you'll wash."

In the ablutatorium, the late Juliette's grandfather changed his head.

"I really despise it," he informed the man from 1888, grabbing fingerfuls of his cheeks and stretching the flabby skin like elastic. "But Juliette insisted. I was willing to humor her, if indeed that was what it took to get her to lie down. But what with toys from the past, and changing my head every time I wanted her to fuck me, it was trying; very trying."

He stepped into one of the many identically shaped booths set flush into the walls. The tambour door rolled down and there was a soft *chukk* sound, almost chitinous. The tambour door rolled up and the late Juliette's grandfather, now six years younger than the man from 1888, stepped out, stark naked and wearing a new head. "The body is fine, replaced last year," he said, examining the genitals and a mole on his right shoulder. The man from 1888 looked away. This was Hell and God hated him.

"Well, don't just *stand* there, Jack." Juliette's grandfather smiled. "Hit one of those booths and get your ablutions."

"That isn't my name," said the man from 1888 very softly, as though he had been whipped.

"It'll do, it'll do . . . now go get washed."

Jack approached one of the booths. It was a light green in color, but changed to mauve as he stopped in front of it. "Will it—"

"It will only *clean* you, what are you afraid of?"

"I don't want to be changed."

Juliette's grandfather did not laugh. "That's a mistake," he said cryptically. He made a peremptory motion with his hand and the man from 1888 entered the booth, which promptly revolved in its niche, sank into the floor and made a hearty *zeeeezzzz* sound. When it rose and revolved and opened, Jack stumbled out, looking terribly confused. His long sideburns had been neatly trimmed, his beard stubble had been removed, his hair was three shades lighter and was now parted on the left side, rather than in the middle. He still wore the same long dark coat trimmed with astrakhan, dark suit with white collar and black necktie (in which was fastened a horseshoe stickpin) but now the garments seemed new, unsoiled of course, possibly synthetics built to look like his former garments.

"Now!" Juliette's grandfather said. "Isn't that much better? A good cleansing always sets one's mind to rights." And he stepped into another booth from which he issued in a moment wearing a soft paper jumper that fitted from neck to feet without a break. He moved toward the door.

"Where are we going?" the man from 1888 asked the younger grandfather beside him. "I want you to meet someone," said Juliette's grandfather, and Jack realized that he was moving his lips now. He decided not to comment on it. There had to be a reason.

"I'll walk you there, if you promise not to make gurgling sounds at the city. It's a nice city, but I live here, and frankly, tourism is boring." Jack did not reply. Grandfather took it for acceptance of the terms.

They walked. Jack became overpowered by the sheer *weight* of the city. It was obviously extensive, massive, and terribly clean. It was his dream for Whitechapel come true. He asked about slums, about doss houses. The grandfather shook his head. "Long gone."

So it had come to pass. The reforms for which he had pledged his immortal soul, they had come to pass. He swung the Gladstone and walked jauntily. But after a few minutes his pace sagged once more: there was no one to be seen in the streets.

Just shining clean buildings and streets that ran off in aimless directions and came to unexpected stops as though the builders had decided people might vanish at one point and reappear someplace else, so why bother making a road from one point to the other.

The ground was metal, the sky seemed metallic, the buildings loomed on all sides, featureless explorations of planed space by insensitive metal. The man from 1888 felt terribly alone, as though every act he had performed had led inevitably to his alienation from the very people he had sought to aid.

When he had come to Toynbee Hall, and the Reverend Mr. Barnett had opened his eyes to the slum horrors of Spitalfields, he had vowed to help in any way he could. It had seemed as simple as faith in the Lord, what to do, after a few months in the sinkholes of Whitechapel. The sluts, of what use were they? No more use than the disease germs that had infected these very same whores. So he had set forth as Jack, to perform the will of God and raise the poor dregs who inhabited the East End of London. That Lord Warren, the Metropolitan Police Commissioner, and his Queen, and all the rest thought him a mad doctor, or an amok butcher, or a beast in human form did not distress him. He knew he would remain anonymous through all time, but that the good works he had set in motion would proceed to their wonderful conclusion.

The destruction of the most hideous slum area the country had ever known, and the opening of Victorian eyes. But all the time *had* passed, and now he was here, in a world where slums apparently did not exist, a sterile Utopia that was the personification of the Reverend Mr. Barnett's dreams—but it didn't seem . . . *right.*

This grandfather, with his young head.

Silence in the empty streets.

The girl, Juliette, and her strange hobby.

The lack of concern at her death.

The grandfather's expectation that he, Jack, *would* kill her. And now his friendliness.

Where were they going?

[Around them, the City. As they walked, the grandfather paid no attention, and Jack watched but did not understand. But this was what they saw as they walked:

[Thirteen hundred beams of light, one foot wide and

seven molecules thick, erupted from almost-invisible slits in the metal streets, fanned out and washed the surfaces of the buildings; they altered hue to a vague blue and washed down the surfaces of the buildings; they bent and covered all open surfaces, bent at right angles, then bent again, and again, like origami paper figures; they altered hue a second time, soft gold, and penetrated the surfaces of the buildings, expanding and contracting in solid waves, washing the inner surfaces; they withdrew rapidly into the sidewalks; the entire process had taken twelve seconds.

[Night fell over a sixteen block area of the City. It descended in a solid pillar and was quite sharp-edged, ending at the street corners. From within the area of darkness came the distinct sounds of crickets, marsh frogs belching, night birds, soft breezes in trees, and faint music of unidentifiable instruments.

[Panes of frosted light appeared suspended freely in the air, overhead. A wavery insubstantial quality began to assault the topmost levels of a great structure directly in front of the light-panes. As the panes moved slowly down through the air, the building became indistinct, turned into motes of light, and floated upward. As the panes reached the pavement, the building had been completely dematerialized. The panes shifted color to a deep orange, and began moving upward again. As they moved, a new structure began to form where the previous building had stood, drawing—it seemed—motes of light from the air and forming them into a cohesive whole that became, as the panes ceased their upward movement, a new building. The light-panes winked out of existence.

[The sound of a bumblebee was heard for several seconds. Then it ceased.

[A crowd of people in rubber garments hurried out of a gray pulsing hole in the air, patted the pavement at their feet, then rushed off around a corner, from where emanated the sound of prolonged coughing. Then silence returned.

[A drop of water, thick as quicksilver, plummeted to the pavement, struck, rebounded, rose several inches, then evaporated into a crimson smear in the shape of a whale's tooth, which settled to the pavement and lay still.

[Two blocks of buildings sank into the pavement and the metal covering was smooth and unbroken, save for a metal tree whose trunk was silver and slim, topped by a ball of foliage constructed of golden fibers that radiated brightly in a perfect circle. There was no sound.

[The late Juliette's grandfather and the man from 1888 continued walking.]

"Where are we going?"

"To van Cleef's. We don't usually walk; oh, sometimes; but it isn't as much pleasure as it used to be. I'm doing this primarily for you. Are you enjoying yourself?"

"It's . . . unusual."

"Not much like Spitalfields, is it? But I rather like it back there, at that time. I have the only Traveler, did you know? The only one ever made. Juliette's father constructed it, my son. I had to kill him to get it. He was thoroughly unreasonable about it, really. It was a casual thing for him. He was the last of the tinkerers, and he might just as easily have given it to me. But I suppose he was being cranky. That was why I had you carve up my granddaughter. She would have gotten around to me almost any time now. Bored, just silly bored is what she was—"

The gardenia took shape in the air in front of them, and turned into the face of a woman with long white hair. "Hernon, we can't wait much longer!" She was annoyed.

Juliette's grandfather grew livid. "You scum bitch! I *told* you pace. But no, you just couldn't, could you? Jump jump jump, that's all you ever do. Well, now it'll only be feddels less, that's all. Feddels, damn you! I set it for pace, I was *working* pace, and *you* . . . !"

His hand came up and moss grew instantly toward the face. The face vanished, and a moment later the gardenia reappeared a few feet away. The moss shriveled and Hernon, Juliette's grandfather, dropped his hand, as though weary of the woman's stupidity. A rose, a water lily, a hyacinth, a pair of phlox, a wild celandine, and a bull thistle appeared near the gardenia. As each turned into the face of a different person, Jack stepped back, frightened.

All the faces turned to the one that had been the bull thistle. "Cheat! Rotten bastard!" they screamed at the thin white face that had been the bull thistle. The gardenia-woman's eyes bulged from her face, the deep purple eye-shadow that completely surrounded the eyeball making her look like a deranged animal peering out of a cave. "Turd!" she shrieked at the bull thistle-man. "We all agreed, we all said and agreed; you *had* to formz a thistle, didn't you, scut! Well, now you'll see . . ."

She addressed herself instantly to the others. "Formz now! To hell with waiting, pace fuck! Now!"

"No, dammit!" Hernon shouted. "We were going to *paaaaace!*" But it was too late. Centering in on the bull thistle-man, the air roiled thickly like silt at a river-bottom, and the air blackened as a spiral began with the now terrified face of the bull thistle-man and exploded whirling outward, enveloping Jack and Hernon and all the flower-people and the City and suddenly it was night in Spitalfields and the man from 1888 was *in* 1888, with his Gladstone bag in his hand, and a woman approaching down the street toward him, shrouded in the London fog.

(There were eight additional nodules in Jack's brain.)

The woman was about forty, weary and not too clean. She wore a dark dress of rough material that reached down to her boots. Over the skirt was fastened a white apron that was stained and wrinkled. The bulbed sleeves ended midway up her wrists and the bodice of the dress was buttoned close around her throat. She wore a kerchief tied at the neck, and a hat that looked like a wide-brimmed skimmer with a raised crown. There was a pathetic little flower of unidenti-fiable origin in the band of the hat. She carried a beaded handbag of capacious size, hanging from a wrist-loop.

Her step slowed as she saw him standing there, deep in the shadows. Saw him was hardly accurate: sensed him.

He stepped out and bowed slightly from the waist. "Fair evenin' to ye, Miss. Care for a pint?"

Her features—sunk in misery of a kind known only to women who have taken in numberless shafts of male blood-gorged flesh—rearranged themselves. "Coo, sir, I thought was 'im for true. Old Leather Apron hisself. Gawdamighty, you give me a scare." She tried to smile. It was a rictus. There were bright spots in her cheeks from sickness and too much gin. Her voice was ragged, a broken-edged instrument barely workable.

"Just a solicitor caught out without comp'ny," Jack assured her. "And pleased to buy a handsome lady a pint of stout for a few hours' companionship."

She stepped toward him and linked arms. "Emily Matthewes, sir, an' pleased to go with you. It's a fearsome chill night, and with Slippery Jack abroad not safe for a respectin' woman such's m'self."

They moved off down Thrawl Street, past the doss houses where this drab might flop later, if she could obtain a few coppers from this neat-dressed stranger with the dark eyes.

He turned right onto Commercial Street, and just abreast of a stinking alley almost to Flower & Dean Street, he nudged her sharply sidewise. She went into the alley, and thinking he meant to steal a smooth hand up under her petticoats, she settled back against the wall and opened her legs, starting to lift the skirt around her waist. But Jack had hold of the kerchief and, locking his fingers tightly, he twisted, cutting off her breath. Her cheeks ballooned, and by a vagary of light from a gas standard in the street he could see her eyes go from hazel to a dead-leaf brown in an instant. Her expression was one of terror, naturally, but commingled with it was a deep sadness, at having lost the pint, at having not been able to make her doss for the night, at having had the usual Emily Matthewes bad luck to run afoul this night of the one man who would ill-use her favors. It was a consummate sadness at the inevitability of her fate.

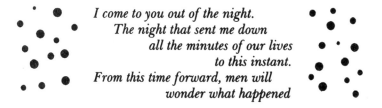

I come to you out of the night.
The night that sent me down
all the minutes of our lives
to this instant.
From this time forward, men will
wonder what happened

*at this instant. They will silently
hunger to go back, to come to my
      instant with you and see my face
      and know my name and perhaps
not even try to stop me, for
      then I would not be who I am,
but only someone who tried
                  and failed. Ah.
For you and me it becomes history
            that will lure men always;
but they will never understand
      why we both suffered, Emily;
      they will never truly understand
why each of us died so terribly.*

A film came over her eyes, and as her breath husked out in wheezing, pleading tremors, his free hand went into the pocket of the greatcoat. He had known he would need it, when they were walking, and he had already invaded the Gladstone bag. Now his hand went into the pocket and came up with the scalpel.

"Emily . . ." softly.

Then he sliced her.

Neatly, angling the point of the scalpel into the soft flesh behind and under her left ear. *Sternocleidomastoideus.* Driving it in to the gentle crunch of cartilage giving way. Then, grasping the instrument tightly, tipping it down and drawing it across the width of the throat, following the line of the firm jaw. *Glandula submandibularis.* The blood poured out over his hands, ran thickly at first and then burst spattering past him, reaching the far wall of the alley. Up his sleeves, soaking his white cuffs. She made a watery rattle and sank limply in his grasp, his fingers still twisted tight in her kerchief; black abrasions where he had scored the flesh. He continued the cut up past the point of the jaw's end, and sliced into the lobe of the ear. He lowered her to the filthy paving. She lay crumpled, and he straightened her. Then he cut away the garments laying her naked belly open to the wan flickering light of the gas standard in the street. Her belly was bloated. He started the primary cut in the hollow of her throat. *Glandula thyreoeidea.* His hand was sure as he drew a thin black line of blood down and down, between the breasts. *Sternum.* Cutting a deep cross in the hole of her navel. Something vaguely yellow oozed up. *Plica umbilicalis medialis.* Down over the rounded hump of the belly, biting more deeply, withdrawing for a neat incision. *Mesenterium dorsale commune.* Down to the matted-with-sweat roundness of her privates. Harder here. *Vesica urinaria.* And finally, to the end, *vagina.*

Filth hole.

Foul-smelling die red lust pit wet hole of sluts.

And in his head, succubi. And in his head, eyes watching. And in his head, minds impinging. And in his head titillation

for a gardenia
   a water lily
   a rose
   a hyacinth
   a pair of phlox
   a wild celandine
and a dark flower with petals of obsidian, a stamen of onyx, pistils of anthracite, and the mind of Hernon, who was the late Juliette's grandfather.

They watched the entire horror of the mad anatomy lesson. They watched him nick the eyelids. They watched him remove the heart. They watched him slice out the fallopian tubes. They watched him squeeze, till it ruptured, the "ginny" kidney. They watched him slice off the sections of breast till they were nothing but shapeless mounds of bloody meat, and arrange them, one mound each on a still-staring, wide-open, nicked-eyelid eye. They watched.

They watched and they drank from the deep troubled pool of his mind. They sucked deeply at the moist quivering core of his id. And they delighted:

Oh God how Delicious look at that It looks like the uneaten rind of a Pizza or look at That It looks like lumaconi *oh god IIIIIwonder what it would be like to Tasteit!*
See how smooth the steel.

He hates them all, every one of them, something about a girl, a venereal disease, fear of his God, Christ, the Reverend Mr. Barnett, he . . . he wants to fuck the reverend's wife!

Social reform can only be brought about by concerted effort of a devoted few. Social reform is a justifiable end, condoning any expedient short of decimation of over fifty percent of the people who will be served by the reforms. The best social reformers are the most audacious. He believes it! How lovely!

You pack of vampires, you filth, you scum, you . . .

He senses us!

Damn him! Damn you, Hernon, you drew off too deeply, he knows we're here, that's disgusting, what's the sense now? I'm withdrawing!

Come back, you'll end the formz . . .

. . . back they plunged in the spiral as it spiraled back in upon itself and the darkness of the night of 1888 withdrew. The spiral drew in and locked at its most infinitesimal point as the charred and blackened face of the man who had been the bull thistle. He was quite dead. His eyeholes had been burned out; charred wreckage lay where intelligence had lived. They had used him as a focus.

The man from 1888 came back to himself instantly, with a full and eidetic memory of what he had just experienced. It had not been a vision, nor a dream, nor a delusion, nor a product of his mind. It had happened. They had sent him back, erased his mind of the transfer into the future, of Juliette, of everything after the moment outside No. 13 Miller's Court. And they had set him to work pleasuring them, while they drained off his feelings, his emotions and his unconscious thoughts; while they battened and gorged themselves with the most private sensations. Most of which, till this moment—in a strange feedback—he had not even known he possessed. As his mind plunged on from one revelation to the next, he felt himself growing ill. At one concept his mind tried to pull back and plunge him into darkness rather than confront it. But the barriers were down, they had opened new patterns and he could read it all, remember it all. *Stinking sex hole, sluts, they have to die.* No, that wasn't the way he thought of women, any women, no matter how low or common. He was a gentleman, and women were to be respected. *She had given him the clap. He remembered.* The shame and the endless fear till he had gone to his physician father and confessed it. The look on the man's face. He remembered it all. The way his father had tended him, the way he would have tended a plague victim. It had never been the same between them again. He had tried for the cloth. *Social reform hahahaha.* All delusion. He had been a mountebank, a clown ... and worse. He had slaughtered for something in which not even he believed. They left his mind wide open, and his thoughts stumbled ... raced further and further toward the thought of

EXPLOSION!IN!HIS!MIND!

He fell face forward on the smooth and polished metal pavement, but he never touched. Something arrested his fall, and he hung suspended, bent over at the waist like a ridiculous Punch divested of strings or manipulation from above. A whiff of something invisible, and he was in full possession of his senses almost before they had left him. His mind was forced to look at it:

He wants to fuck the Reverend Mr. Barnett's wife.

Henrietta, with her pious petition to Queen Victoria— "Madam, we, the women of East London, feel horror at the dreadful sins that have been lately committed in our midst ..."—asking for the capture of himself, of Jack, whom she would never, not *ever* suspect was residing right there with her and the Reverend in Toynbee Hall. The thought was laid as naked as her body in the secret dreams he had never remembered upon awakening. All of it, they had left him with opened doors, with unbounded horizons, and 'he saw himself for what he was.

A psychopath, a butcher, a lecher, a hypocrite, a clown.

"You did this to me! Why did you do this?"

Frenzy cloaked his words. The flower-faces became the solidified hedonists who had taken him back to 1888 on that senseless voyage of slaughter.

van Cleef, the gardenia-woman, sneered. "Why do you think, you ridiculous bumpkin? (Bumpkin, is that the right colloquialism, Hernon? I'm so uncertain in the mid-dialects.) When you'd done in Juliette, Hernon wanted to send you back. But why should he? He owed us at least three formz, and you did passing well for one of them."

Jack shouted at them till the cords stood out in his throat. "Was it necessary, this last one? Was it important to do it, to help my reforms . . . was it?"

Hernon laughed. "Of course not."

Jack sank to his knees. The City let him do it. "Oh God, oh God almighty, I've done what I've done . . . I'm covered with blood . . . and for *nothing*, for *nothing* . . ."

Cashio, who had been one of the phlox, seemed puzzled. "Why is he concerned about *this* one, if the others don't bother him?"

Nosy Verlag, who had been a wild celandine, said sharply, "They do, all of them do. Probe him, you'll see."

Cashio's eyes rolled up in his head an instant, then rolled down and refocused—Jack felt a quicksilver shudder in his mind and it was gone—and he said lackadaisically, "Mm-hmm."

Jack fumbled with the latch of the Gladstone. He opened the bag and pulled out the foetus in the bottle. Mary Jane Kelly's unborn child, from November 9th, 1888. He held it in front of his face a moment, then dashed it to the metal pavement. It never struck. It vanished a fraction of an inch from the clean, sterile surface of the City's street.

"What marvelous loathing!" exulted Rose, who had been a rose.

"Hernon," said van Cleef, "he's centering on you. He begins to blame you for all of this."

Hernon was laughing (without moving his lips) as Jack pulled Juliette's electrical scalpel from the Gladstone, and lunged. Jack's words were incoherent, but what he was saying, as he struck, was: "I'll show you what filth you are! I'll show you you can't do this kind of thing! I'll teach you! You'll die, all of you!" This is what he was saying, but it came out as one long sustained bray of revenge, frustration, hatred and directed frenzy.

Hernon was still laughing as Jack drove the whisper-thin

blade with its shimmering current into his chest. Almost without manipulation on Jack's part, the blade circumscribed a perfect 360° hole that charred and shriveled, exposing Hernon's pulsing heart and wet organs. he had time to shriek with confusion before he received Jack's second thrust, a direct lunge that severed the heart from its attachments. *Vena cava superior. Aorta. Arteria pulmonalis. Bronchus principalis.*

The heart flopped forward and a spreading wedge of blood under tremendous pressure ejaculated, spraying Jack with such force that it knocked his hat from his head and blinded him. His face was now a dripping black-red collage of features and blood.

Hernon followed his heart, and fell forward, into Jack's arms. Then the flower-people screamed as one, vanished, and Hernon's body slipped from Jack's hands to wink out of existence an instant before it struck at Jack's feet. The walls around him were clean, unspotted, sterile, metallic, uncaring.

He stood in the street, holding the bloody knife.

"*Now!*" he screamed, holding the knife aloft. "Now it begins!"

If the city heard, it made no indication, but

[Pressure accelerated in temporal linkages.]

[A section of shining wall on the building eighty miles away changed from silver to rust.]

[In the freezer chambers, two hundred gelatin caps were fed into a ready trough.]

[The weathermaker spoke softly to itself, accepted data and instantly constructed an intangible mnemonic circuit.]

and in the shining eternal city where night only fell when the inhabitants had need of night and called specifically for night . . .

Night fell. With no warning save: "*Now!*"

In the City of sterile loveliness a creature of filth and decaying flesh prowled. In the last City of the world, a City on the edge of the world, where the ones who had devised their own paradise lived, the prowler made his home in shadows. Slipping from darkness to darkness with eyes that saw only movement, he roamed in search of a partner to dance his deadly rigadoon.

He found the first woman as she materialized beside a small waterfall that flowed out of empty air and dropped its shimmering, tinkling moisture into an azure cube of nameless material. He found her and drove the living blade into the back of her neck. Then he sliced out the eyeballs and put them into her open hands.

He found the second woman in one of the towers, making love to a very old man who gasped and wheezed and clutched his heart as the young woman forced him to passion. She was killing him as Jack killed her. He drove the living blade into the lower rounded surface of her belly, piercing her sex organs as she rode astride the old man. She decamped blood and viscous fluids over the prostrate body of the old man, who also died, for Jack's blade had severed the penis within the young woman. She fell forward across the old man and Jack left them that way, joined in the final embrace.

He found a man and throttled him with his bare hands, even as the man tried to dematerialize. Then Jack recognized him as one of the phlox, and made neat incisions in the face, into which he inserted the man's genitals.

He found another woman as she was singing a gentle song about eggs to a group of children. He opened her throat and severed the strings hanging inside. He let the vocal cords drop onto her chest. But he did not touch the children, who watched it all avidly. He liked children.

He prowled through the unending night making a grotesque collection of hearts, which he cut out of one, three, nine people. And when he had a dozen, he took them and laid them as road markers on one of the wide boulevards that never were used by vehicles, for the people of this City had no need of vehicles.

Oddly, the City did not clean up the hearts. Nor were the people vanishing any longer. He was able to move with relative impunity, hiding only when he saw large groups that might be searching for him. But *something* was happening in the City. (Once, he heard the peculiar sound of metal

grating on metal, the *skrikkk* of plastic cutting into plastic—
and he instinctively knew it was the sound of a machine
malfunctioning.)

He found a woman bathing, and tied her up with strips of
his own garments, and cut off her legs at the knees and left
her still sitting up in the swirling crimson bath, screaming as
she bled away her life. The legs he took with him.

When he found a man hurrying to get out of the night,
he pounced on him, cut his throat and sawed off the arms.
He replaced the arms with the bath-woman's legs.

And it went on and on, for a time that had no measure.
He was showing them what evil could produce. He was
showing them their immorality was silly beside his own.

But one thing finally told him he was winning. As he
lurked in an antiseptically pure space between two low
aluminium-cubes, he heard a voice that came from above
him and around him and even from inside him. It was a
public announcement, broadcast by whatever mental communications system the people of the City on the edge of
the World used.

OUR CITY IS PART OF US. WE ARE PART OF
OUR CITY. IT RESPONDS TO OUR MINDS AND
WE CONTROL IT. THE GESTALT THAT WE
HAVE BECOME IS THREATENED. WE HAVE AN
ALIEN FORCE WITHIN THE CITY AND WE ARE
GEARING TO LOCATE IT. BUT THE MIND OF
THIS MAN IS STRONG. IT IS BREAKING DOWN
THE FUNCTIONS OF THE CITY. THIS ENDLESS
NIGHT IS AN EXAMPLE. WE MUST ALL CON-
CENTRATE. WE MUST ALL CONSCIOUSLY
FOCUS OUR THOUGHTS TO MAINTAINING
THE CITY. THIS THREAT IS OF THE FIRST
ORDER. IF OUR CITY DIES, WE DIE.

It was not an announcement in those terms, though that
was how Jack interpreted it. The message was much longer
and much more complex, but that was what it meant, and
he knew he was winning. He was destroying them. Social

reform was laughable, they had said. He would show them.

And so he continued with his lunatic pogrom. He butcher-ed and slaughtered and carved them wherever he found them, and they could not vanish and they could not escape and they could not stop him. The collections of hearts grew to fifty and seventy and then a hundred.

He grew bored with hearts and began cutting out their brains. The collection grew.

For numberless days it went on, and from time to time in the clean, scented autoclaves of the City, he could hear the sounds of screaming. His hands were always sticky.

Then he found van Cleef, and leaped from hiding in the darkness to bring her down. He raised the living blade to drive it into her breast, but she

van   ished

He got to his feet and looked around. van Cleef reappear-ed ten feet from him. He lunged for her and again she was gone. To reappear ten feet away. Finally, when he had struck at her half a dozen times and she had escaped him each time, he stood panting, arms at sides, looking at her.

And she looked back at him with disinterest.

"You no longer amuse us," she said, moving her lips.

Amuse? His mind whirled down into a place far darker than any he had known before, and through the murk of his blood-lust he began to realize. It had all been for their amusement. They had *let* him do it. They had given him the run of the City and he had capered and gibbered for them.

Evil? He had never even suspected the horizons of that word. He went for her, but she disappeared with finality.

He was left standing there as the daylight returned. As the City cleaned up the mess, took the butchered bodies and did with them what it had to do. In the freezer chambers the gelatin caps were returned to their niches, no more inhabitants of the City need be thawed to provide Jack the Ripper with utensils for his amusement of the sybarites. His work was truly finished.

He stood there in the empty street. A street that would *always* be empty to him. The people of the city had all along been able to escape him, and now they would. He was finally and completely the clown they had shown him to be. He was not evil, he was pathetic.

He tried to use the living blade on himself, but it dissolved into motes of light and wafted away on a breeze that had blown up for just that purpose.

Alone, he stood there staring at the victorious cleanliness of this Utopia. With their talents they would keep him alive, possibly alive forever, immortal in the possible expectation of needing him for amusement again someday. He was stripped to raw essentials in a mind that was no longer anything more than jelly matter. To go madder and madder, and never to know peace or end or sleep.

He stood there, a creature of dirt and alleys, in a world as pure as the first breath of a baby.

"My name isn't Jack," he said softly. But they would never know his real name. Nor would they care. *"My name isn't Jack!"* he said loudly. No one heard.

"MY NAME ISN'T JACK, AND I'VE BEEN BAD, VERY BAD, I'M AN EVIL PERSON BUT MY NAME ISN'T JACK!" he screamed, and screamed, and screamed again, walking aimlessly down an empty street, in plain view, no longer forced to prowl. A stranger in the City.

SOURCES AND ACKNOWLEDGEMENTS

'Death in Silk Stockings' by Ellery Queen is from *Deadlier Than The Male* (Corgi, 1967).

The Case of Mr George Edalji' by Sir Arthur Conan Doyle was first published as a series in the *Daily Telegraph* in 1907, subsequently reprinted as a booklet by T. Harrison Roberts, 1907, and later collected in *The Story of Mr George Edalji* (Grey House Books, 1985). The publishers are most grateful to Richard Whittington-Egan, the editor of that collection, for his help with this book, and to Camille Wolff, its publisher.

'Coppolino Revisited' by John D. Macdonald, from *I, Witness* (Times Books, 1978) is reprinted by kind permission of The Mystery Writers of America.

'The Invisible Man' by Julian Symons also from *I, Witness*, is reprinted by kind permission of Curtis Brown Ltd, London.

'The 'Perfect' Crime That Was Unspeakably Dumb' by Damon Runyon, is reprinted by kind permission of King Features, Inc.

'The Trial of Madeleine Smith' by F. Tennyson Jesse and 'The Gorse Hall Mystery' by Freeman Wills Crofts were first published in *Great Unsolved Crimes* (Hutchinson, n.d.).

The Court of Last Resort by Erle Stanley Gardner was first published by William Sloane Associates, 1952; revised edition published by Pocket Books, Inc., 1954.

'New Light on an Old Murder' by Robert Graves was first published in *Food for Centaurs* (Doubleday & Co., Inc., 1960).

'The Prowler In the City At the Edge of the World' originally appeared in DANGEROUS VISIONS; copyright © 1967 by Harlan Ellison. Reprinted by arrangement with, and permission of, the Author and the Author's agent, Richard Curtis Associates, Inc., New York. All rights reserved. This preferred text from THE ESSENTIAL ELLISON (1987).

While every effort has been made to trace authors and copyright holders, in a few cases this has proved impossible; the publishers would be glad to hear from any such parties so that these omissions can be rectified in future editions of the book.

Thanks are due to the following for permission to reproduce the photographs and illustrations of the following pages:

20, courtesy of Richard Whittington-Egan. BBC Hulton Library 25; The Bettmann Archive 119; Topham Picture Library 139, 149, 163; Syndication International 114, 199, 205; William Morrow & Co., Inc 235; Mary Evans Picture Library 291, 294.

UNSOLVED

Contents

Introduction

To fascinate, the mere fact of a murder being unsolved is not enough. After all, hundreds of crimes are committed without even a suspect to show, and thousands of people just vanish never to be seen or heard of again. Nowadays, they do not even make the headlines. No, to fascinate there has to be something more, something to catch the imagination: an unexplained clue, an ambiguity of evidence, a courtroom drama, perhaps with a life hanging in the balance, or simply the sheer thrill of terror.

The cases in this book have all these things in abundance. They are all murders, and every one is a classic of its kind, starting with perhaps the greatest unidentified murderer of them all: Jack the Ripper. Since that appalling series of crimes in 1888, the name of the Ripper has become almost legendary, with a host of books and articles written about him advancing wildly differing theories as to his identity (one of them proposes a Jill the Ripper!), and the case has also inspired movies, novels, plays and even an opera, Alban Berg's *Lulu*. We have been fortunate to be allowed to reprint here for the first time a series of articles by leading Ripperologist Colin Wilson, in which he tells the story of his arrival in London back in 1951 and of his personal quest for the Whitechapel murderer. A worthy opening to our gruesome collection, although Mr Wilson is happy to leave the question of the Ripper's identity as open as ever; which is wise, since however ingenious the theory—and some of them are incredibly complicated—there just isn't the clinching evidence to link the crimes to any one of the suspects proposed so far.

In other unsolved cases there is almost too much evidence.

William Herbert Wallace may or may not have killed his wife on that evening in 1932, but once you have read Dorothy L. Sayers' account of the case you will never forget the telephone box, the defective lock, the roaring fire, the non-existent street—and above all you will not forget the mysterious Qualtrough. This is England's classic 'Did He or Didn't He?', and although the debate still rages there has never been a clearer or more sharply analyzed account of the crime than Miss Sayers'. Raymond Chandler once considered writing an analysis of the Wallace case, which he called 'the nonpareil of all murder mysteries', but in the end he did not because, again in his words, 'it has been done to a turn by Dorothy Sayers'. Her piece offers the additional attraction of seeing a mystery writer playing the part of the detective, and Miss Sayers' powerful mind must have been at full stretch when she tried to disentangle that most complex occurrence.

America offers a case equally rich in clues and equally ambiguous (and even more vicious) in the Borden murders. Did Lizzie take an axe and give her mother forty whacks? Again, there is an abundance of detail, again it is maddeningly incomplete, and again many books and articles have been written using the same evidence to 'prove' Lizzie's innocence or guilt, depending on which side the author takes. Edmund Pearson, perhaps America's finest crime-writer, has been accused of bias in his account of this celebrated case (we shall be talking about that later on), but there is no doubt that his piece is easily the best of its kind: *the* place to open any discussion about the redoubtable Lizzie Borden.

One of the most interesting things about the type of detailed description that we find in Sayers' and Pearson's pieces is the startlingly vivid evocation of previous times; in seeking to understand the crimes we gain a sharply focussed view of life in Fall River in the 1880s, or suburban Liverpool in the 1930s. Social histories and novels can do the same thing in a more generalized way, but murder, by forcing us to concentrate upon the tiny things—the gas jets, the wood-burning stove, the maid's daily routine, the local chess-club—can bring a whole era to life in a uniquely powerful manner. This is particularly so in the next of our 'great' murders, the poisoning of Charles

Bravo in his own bed, for which we move back even further in time. Once again, details are plentiful and almost completely ambiguous in interpretation, but here we have added complications in terms of *motive*. At the heart of this crime is the classic triangle of husband, wife and wife's former lover, made stranger by the advanced age of the lover and the intrusive presence of the sinister Mrs Cox, the wife's companion—in bed as well as about the house. Elizabeth Jenkins' account of the Bravo case is sympathetic, very thorough, and it recreates wonderfully the odd personalities in the Priory, and their even more curious lifestyle. Especially for this book, Miss Jenkins has contributed some fascinating further thoughts to her original view of this problem, which suggests another possible solution to this most tantalizing affair.

The Wallace, Borden and Bravo crimes are perhaps the three most notable unsolved cases in the long history of murder, and accordingly they are examined in some depth in the pages that follow. The shorter accounts included are no less fascinating, but in these there tends to be less detail to consider, less information to speculate upon. In the murder of Joseph Ellwell, for instance, the bizarre circumstances of the killing make for interesting reading (and the story is superbly related by the excellent Alexander Woollcott) but the total absence of anyone who could remotely be considered a suspect leaves nothing much to say beyond a statement of the basic facts. What Woollcott says is really all that there is to be said—and the same sort of considerations apply in the cases of Starr Faithfull, Bela Kiss, and The Minister and the Choir Singer (otherwise known as the Hall-Mills affair), though the last of these benefits enormously from James Thurber's drily humorous re-telling, and Willie Stevens is a character that no-one is subsequently likely to forget. The confusion that surrounds the murder of Sir Harry Oakes in Nassau poses the opposite problem; there is almost too much information here, and the astonishingly inept investigation leaves an enormously wide field for speculation. Distinguished critic and crime-novelist Julian Symons has performed a miracle of clarity and compression in his version of the case.

Beyond the immediate shock of gruesome events and strange

circumstances, what ultimately gives these unsolved crimes their fascination is the human personality itself. In testing our wits against those of William Wallace, Lizzie Borden, Florence Bravo or, indeed, Jack the Ripper himself, we are really looking into the depths of our own psyche. How would *we* have behaved in their position? Could we, by any tortured stretch of our imagination, have done what they are assumed to have done? What we see may not be pleasant but, somewhere in our nature, it is there, and it should not be ignored.

—R.G.J.

SOURCES AND ACKNOWLEDGEMENTS

'My Search for Jack the Ripper' by Colin Wilson (first published as a series in the *Evening Standard*, London, 1960). Reproduced by permission of the author and David Bolt Associates.

'A Sort of Genius' by James Thurber, from *My World and Welcome To It.* (published by Harcourt Brace Jovanovich). Copyright © 1942 James Thurber. Copyright © 1970 Helen W-Thurber and Rosemary A. Thurber.

'The Murder of Julia Wallace' by Dorothy L. Sayers, from *Anatomy of Murder*, (first published by Macmillans, New York, 1937). Reproduced by permission of the publisher and the author.

'The Elwell Case' by Alexander Woollcott, from *Long, Long Ago*, renewed copyright © 1968 by Joseph P. Hennessey. Reprinted by permission of Viking Penguin Inc.

'The Balham Mystery' by Elizabeth Jenkins, from *Six Criminal Woman.* Copyright © 1949 by Elizabeth Jenkins. Reprinted by kind permission of Curtis Brown Ltd on behalf of the author.

'Afterword to the Balham Mystery' by Elizabeth Jenkins. Copyright © 1987 by the author.

'Starr Faithfull, Beautiful Wanton' by Sydney Horler, from *Malefactors' Row* (first published by Robert Hale, London, 1940).

'The Borden Case' by Edmund Pearson, from *Masterpieces in Murder* (first published New York, 1924).

'Death of a Millionaire' by Julian Symons, from *A Reasonable Doubt* (1960). Reproduced by permission of Curtis Brown Ltd, London.

COLIN WILSON

My Search for
Jack the Ripper

COLIN WILSON

My Search for
Jack the Ripper

When I was about eight, someone lent my father a great red volume called *The Fifty Most Amazing Crimes of the Last 100 Years*—I'm not sure why, for I've never yet caught my father reading a book. I was strictly forbidden to read it, in case it gave me nightmares. So I seized on it every time I was left alone in the house, and read it from cover to cover.

I have a copy of it beside me as I write. At the top of every article there is a sketch of the criminal. Landru looks villanous and intellectual; Smith, who drowned his wives in the bath, is an unattractive nondescript. But there is no drawing of Jack the Ripper—only a large black question mark. That question mark started me on my search for Jack the Ripper. It is not logical, of course, but the mind of a child is romantic and not logical. Why should the Ripper be more interesting than Landru, just because he was never caught? No-one has yet discovered how Landru destroyed every trace of his victim's bodies, and, in its way, this mystery is far more interesting than guessing at the identity of Jack the Ripper. And yet it is the Ripper who exercises a fascination beyond that of any other mass murderer.

Most of them are boring little men, like Christie and Haigh— shifty, weak and unimpressive. Many of them have had long criminal records—petty theft, swindling, burglary or confidence trickery—like Heath, Kurten and Dr Marcel Petiot Murder has not yet produced its Caesar, its Napoleon. Murderers are a dull lot.

Perhaps the Ripper was a sneak-thief, with many prison sentences behind him; perhaps it was only Wormwood Scrubs, and not death, that put an end to his amazing career. We shall never be certain. And that is enough to make the Ripper almost unique in the annals of mass murder. We know almost nothing about him.

How many murders did he commit? Even that is the subject of debate. All that we do know is that at least five murders of unparalleled brutality were committed in the latter part of the year 1888. Four of them took place in the Whitechapel district of London, at night; the victims were all prostitutes, although none of them was what we would call 'professionals'. All London panicked. There were meetings in the streets; bands of citizens formed themselves into vigilante groups to patrol Whitechapel at night; thousands of men were questioned, and released; men carrying black bags were attacked by mobs; the Commissioner of Police resigned. And finally, after a lull of more than a month, the Ripper committed yet another crime, this time indoors. The pieces of the victim—a girl in her early twenties—were left spread around the room like bits of a jigsaw puzzle. The panic reached new proportions; there were so many blue uniforms in Whitechapel that the place resembled a police barracks. And then nothing more happened. The murders stopped.

In the following year, 1889, there were two more murders of prostitutes in the Whitechapel area, but without the same appalling mutilations; we shall never know whether the same man was responsible for these.

When I came to London in 1951, Whitechapel exercised a deep and powerful fascination over me, but it was no longer the Whitechapel that Jack the Ripper had wandered around. Whitechapel is still a tough district, but by no means as tough as it had been in 1888. Then, sailors from foreign ships crowded the streets; there were dozens of cheap doss houses where the layabouts could sleep for as little as fourpence a night. And although many 'respectable' married women lived in Whitechapel, a large proportion of the female population was made up of non-professional prostitutes: women without men, women whose men had left them, or simply women whose men had spent their wages on drink.

It was a Whitechapel whose narrow, cobbled alleys were lit by gas lamps that stuck out of the walls; a Whitechapel where human derelicts slept out on the pavements or in entries at night; where murder and robbery were so commonplace that the newspapers didn't even bother to report them. This is the reason why the first two crimes attributed to the Ripper were not mentioned in the newspapers until the inquests.

All this has changed. In 1888, after the Annie Chapman murder, Bernard Shaw wrote a letter to the press in which he suggested that the murderer was a social reformer who wanted to draw attention to social conditions in the East End. He was probably wrong, but German high-explosives have done what Shaw failed to do, and changed the face of Whitechapel. When I first visited the district, bombs had left great empty spaces, and many of the houses were windowless and filled with rubble. After dark, tramps slept on the floors of these ruins. Huge blocks of council flats had sprung up in Hanbury Street, only a hundred yards from the spot where Annie Chapman was murdered, in a yard behind a barber's shop. The council school at the end of Old Montague Street stood black and empty, with political slogans chalked on its walls; now the school has disappeared, with only the black walls of the playground still standing.

The Whitechapel of the Ripper is disappearing day by day. In five years it will be non-existent.

Who was the first victim of the Ripper? It might have been Emma Smith, of George Street, Spitalfield, who was stabbed to death in Osborn Street.

Osborn Street is a sinister little thoroughfare that runs between Old Montague Street and the Whitechapel Road. Emma Smith lived for twenty-four hours after the attack, and stated positively that she had been assaulted and robbed by four men, one of whom had stabbed her with an iron spike in the abdomen. It was a brutal and stupid murder, and its victim was a pathetic, drunken prostitute of forty-five, who had never had more than a few shillings in her purse. She was staggering home drunk at four in the morning when the attack took place. (There were no licensing hours in those days, and many pubs stayed open all night.) An hour later, she was admitted to hospital, her head bruised, her right ear almost torn off. Her death was due to peritonitis.

At the time of the murders, many journalists stated that this was the Ripper's first crime. It seems unlikely, but the murder is worth mentioning for the insight it gives into the Whitechapel of the 1880's. A man or woman might be found like this almost any morning, robbed and battered; it was too commonplace to be reported in the daily press.

Many criminologists believe that the murder of Martha Turner was quite definitely the first Ripper crime. This took place on August Bank Holiday, 1888.

Martha Turner was a prostitute who lived in George Yard Buildings, Commercial Street. In the early hours of the morning, she was found on one of the outside landings of the lodging-house; the post mortem revealed that she had been stabbed thirty-nine times with some weapon like a bayonet, and the coroner stated that the wounds had been inflicted by a left-handed man. Martha Turner had been seen talking to a guardsman on the evening before the murder, and since the injuries resembled bayonet wounds, the police started to look for a left-handed soldier. All the guards in the Tower of London were paraded, but no arrest was made. Within a few weeks, the murder had been forgotten. How could anyone guess that a super-criminal was starting on a series of the most sensational murders of all time?

No-one knows the precise location of George Yard Buildings where Martha Turner, probably the Ripper's first victim, was stabbed to death, but we know the district. If you take a tube to Aldgate East station on a Sunday morning, you will see Whitechapel looking something like the Whitechapel of 1888. Wander up Middlesex Street—known as 'Petticoat Lane'— and you will find it hard to breathe among the crowds jammed around the market stalls. To your right and left there are still cobbled streets that looked exactly the same when Jack the Ripper walked through them in that 'Autumn of Terror'. Turn off to your right, walk fifty yards, and you will find yourself in Commercial Street, the heart and jugular vein of Whitechapel. Late at night, the police still walk two abreast on these pavements. It is a tough district. And yet if you come here at five o'clock on a Sunday afternoon, the quiet will surprise you. The market has closed, and the people of Whitechapel are indoors having their tea, or sleeping off their lunchtime beer.

In 1888, it would have been very different. To begin with, the pubs would still have been open; drunks would have been snoring in the small alleyways off Hanbury Street; but you would have been sensible enough not to explore them, for your chances of being coshed and robbed would have been very high. Probably in no other part of England was so much of the inhabitants' total income spent on beer or spirits—and those were the days when pubs were approximately five times as numerous as they are today. Alcohol was the best chance of forgetfulness, the best way to escape from the dirt and over-crowding and near-starvation.

This may be the reason why Jack the Ripper chose Whitechapel as his hunting-ground. In a sink of human misery, the individual life does not count for much, and the sight of a body prostrate in an alleyway causes no alarm—and, in fact, this is what happened in the case of Mary Anne Nichols, the Ripper's second victim.

In the early hours of the morning of August 31st, 1888, a carter named William Cross was walking along Buck's Row, on his way to work. Buck's Row is another street that has not changed since 1888, although its name is now Durward Street. On one side of the road are small houses, all absolutely uniform, and on the other are blocks of warehouses. Cross noticed something on the other side of the street—a bundle which he took to be a tarpaulin. Then he saw that it was a woman, apparently drunk. She was sprawled in the entrance to an old stable-yard, with her head in the gutter. Another man walked up as he stood there, looking down at her, and the newcomer said: 'Come on, let's get her on her feet.'

They bent down to turn her over, and Cross jumped back, exclaiming: 'Blimey, she's bleeding!'

The other man confirmed this, and commented: 'She's not drunk—she's perishing well dead.'

The two men ran off to find a policeman, and while they were away the body was discovered by another policeman. Within a few minutes, four men were standing around the body. It was about four o'clock in the morning.

Both the policemen were puzzled; they had beats that took them past where the body was now lying, and both of them had been in the street, at either end of Bucks Row, for the past quarter of an hour. Neither had seen anyone. Someone summoned Dr Ralph Llewellyn, who felt the woman's pulse, commented that she had been dead about half an hour, and told the police to take her to the mortuary at the Old Montague Street workhouse. The noise of the discussion attracted several people from the nearby houses. A Mrs Emma Green, whose bedroom was within ten yards of the spot where the body had been found remarked that 'whoever had done it' must have been very quiet, since she had been lying awake for several hours, and had heard no sound.

In the morgue, a young policeman lifted the woman's clothes to gain some idea of the extent of her injuries. What he saw made him vomit. The woman's body had been ripped open from the throat to the stomach. The policeman rushed off to find Dr Llewellyn, who had to give him first aid before he hurried to the morgue.

The first problem was that of identification. This was quickly solved: the woman's name was Mary Anne Nichols, she was forty-two years old, and was known to her friends and acquaintances as Polly. She had been married to a printer's machinist and had born him five children, but they had been separated for seven years; her love of the gin bottle, and the slovenliness that resulted from it, had made him leave her. But as he stood over her body in the mortuary, he was heard to say: 'I forgive you for everything now that I see you like this.'

Since her marriage had broken up, Polly Nichols had sunk steadily lower. She had lived with several men in quick succession and had taken a job as a servant, but she had to steal from her employers to get money for drink, and had then gone to live in Whitechapel. Here she lived as a prostitute, sleeping in nightly doss houses where a bed could be had for fourpence. The main necessity was drink, however, and she would go with a man for the price of a glass of gin—a few pence. A few hours before her death, Polly had arrived at the doss house in Thrawl Street, completely drunk and without money. The lodging-house keeper turned her away. 'Don't

Top: Bucks Row. Bottom: Hanbury Street.

woryy,' she told him, 'I'll soon get the money. Look what a fine hat I've got.'

An hour later, an acquaintance saw her at the corner of Osborn Street, where Emma Smith had met her death a few months earlier. Asked if she was having any luck, Polly replied that she wasn't, but staggered off up Osborn Street, singing cheerfully to herself. She probably then turned right into Old Montague Street and wandered towards Vallance Road at the end. And somewhere along here, she met a man.

It is still not certain how Jack the Ripper killed Polly Nichols with so little sound. A bruise on her face indicates that he clamped his hand over her mouth as he cut her throat, but they were standing on the three-foot-wide pavement of Bucks Row, and people were sleeping within a few yards. A policeman would have been visible at the end of the street, and there were five others within call. Men were climbing out of bed, getting ready to go to work, and others were returning home from Smithfield meat market or from jobs in the docks.

But the luck was with Jack the Ripper; he murdered Polly Nichols without being heard, and walked off into the dawn. Ultimately, this is one of the most amazing features of the whole business—the extraordinary luck that never deserted the Whitechapel sadist. As far as we know.

The nickname 'Jack the Ripper' was not invented until shortly before the notorious double murder of September 30th, but the police were intrigued to hear the phrase 'Leather Apron' used again and again in connection with the killer. Who was he?

No-one seemed to be sure. Some people described him as a short, villanous-looking cobbler who carried his clicking knife in the pocket of his leather apron. Others said that he led a gang that terrorized prostitutes, and demanded a percentage of their earnings. Yet other were of the opinion that he was a maniac who enjoyed frightening women, but who was probably harmless.

The police traced three men whose nickname was Leather Apron. The most likely suspect was a Polish jew named Pizer, who was arrested on suspicion. His alibi proved to be unshakeable, and he was released.

The enquiries came to nothing, but one journalist who visited a doss house in Dorset Street reported an interesting conversation. An old prostitute had wandered in to drink a glass of gin in the early hours of the morning, and the journalist asked her if she was not afraid of meeting Leather Apron. The woman replied: 'I hope I do meet him. I'm sick of this life. I'd rather be dead.'

It throws some light on the mental state of some of these women, and explains why Jack the Ripper never seemed to have had any difficulty finding a victim, even at the height of the terror.

A week after the murder of Mary Anne Nichols the murderer found his third victim, and the pattern of the crime was curiously similar to that in the previous case. Mary Nichols had been turned away from a doss house in Thrawl Street and went off to seek a 'customer'. Annie Chapman was turned out of a doss house in Dorset Street by the keeper, a man named Donovan, and, like Mary Nichols, her life was sacrificed for fourpence, the cost of a bed.

If you walk up Commercial Street from Aldgate, you will pass Dorset Street on your left-hand side. Since 1888, its name had been changed to Duval Street. An extension of Spitalfields market now stands on the site of the lodging-house from which Annie Chapman was turned away in the early hours of Saturday, September 8th. When she left number 35, Dorset Street, she had only a few hundred yards to walk to her death. Halfway down Hanbury Street stands a barber's shop, number 29, which was still a barber's shop when I came to London; I occasionally went there for a haircut. In front of this shop, she met a man who allowed himself to be accosted. As it happened, 29 Hanbury Street was a convenient meeting-place for a prostitute and a prospective client, for a passage runs by the side of the house, with a door at each end. These doors were never kept closed. And at the far end of the passage was a back-yard—a yard that looked exactly as it did 72 years before, when the Ripper entered it with Annie Chapman.

They tiptoed down the passageway, and crept into a corner of the yard by the fence. The man moved closer; she was not even aware of the knife he held in his left hand. A moment later she was dead; the first thrust had severed her windpipe. The man allowed her to slide down the fence. He slipped out of his dark overcoat, and bent over the woman.

The sight of the blood roused in him a kind of frenzy, and for five minutes he remained there, crouched over her. Then he wiped the knife on her skirt, and cleaned some of the blood off his shoes. It was already getting light. He pulled on the overcoat, and crossed to the tap that projected from the fence three feet to the left of the body. From his overcoat he pulled a bundle, which he soaked in water and used to wipe his hands, then he dropped it under the tap. It was a leather apron.

As he pulled it out of his pocket, an envelope dropped out too. The man picked this up, tore off its corner, which was marked with the crest of the Sussex Regiment, and dropped it into Annie Chapman's blood. It would be another false trail for the police to follow. Before leaving the yard, another idea struck him. He searched the pockets of the dead woman's jacket, and removed two brass rings, a few pennies and some farthings, then arranged these carefully by her feet.

A few pennies! Annie Chapman had actually possessed just enough money to stay in the lodging-house! Did she know this? Or could it be that my reconstruction is wrong, and the Ripper took the pennies from his own pocket, as a sort of ironical payment for the pleasure she had given him?

An hour went by, and one of the inhabitants of the house, John Davies, came downstairs and looked into the yard. The body was huddled against a fence. He rushed to Spitalfields Market, where he worked as a porter, and brought two of his fellow-workmen back with him. A few minutes later the police arrived, and the divisional surgeon, Mr Philips, was summoned. His first act was to remove the handkerchief tied around the woman's throat; immediately, the head rolled sideways—it was only just attached to the body. By now, the windows of all the surrounding houses were crowded with sightseers, and some of the local householders even charged a small fee for access to their windows.

Finally, the body was removed to the mortuary, where Mr Philips discovered that the injuries were even more extensive

Contemporary report of the murders in Berners Street and Mitre Square.

than they had been in the case of Mary Nichols. In addition to numerous stab wounds, there were incisions in the woman's back and abdomen. Moreover, a careful examination of the body revealed that certain internal organs had been removed and taken away by the murderer. So too had two of her front teeth—a curious touch that repeated a feature of the murder of Mary Nichols.

At the inquest, Dr Philips expressed the opinion that the murderer must have been a man with some anatomical knowledge and medical skill. And the weapon must have been some kind of long-bladed knife, at least eight inches long, which might have been 'an instrument such as a doctor would use for surgery'.

Of all the Ripper sites, this one is best preserved. When I knocked on the door, it was opened by Mrs Kathleen Manning, who, with her husband and daughter, were the sole occupants of the house; in 1888, sixteen people lived in it! Mrs Manning knew that one of the Ripper murders had been committed there, but she knew no details of the crime. But she told me how, on one occasion, she mentioned casually that Jack the Ripper had committed a murder there. To her surprise, the friend disappeared abruptly into the street, and refused to go back into the house!

Within a hundred yards of this last grim remnant of 1888, blocks of council flats have replaced the insanitary lodging-houses and narrow alleyways through which the Ripper escaped. If the Whitechapel maniac visited his old haunts today, it is doubtful whether he would be able to find his way around!

Children sing and play today on the spot where the Ripper's next victim was killed. It was in the back-yard of the International Working Men's Club at 40, Berners Street, where the Ripper began the most sensational night's work in English criminal history. The yard is now part of the playground of a London council school. No-one I talked to in the area even knew that Jack the Ripper had committed a murder there. But although the club has disappeared, the upper part of Berners Street still looked much as it did when the Ripper walked down it on the night of September 30th, 1888.

The story of that remarkable night begins at 1 a.m., when the steward of the club tried to guide his pony and trap into the back-yard. He had some difficulty, for the pony was obviously unwilling to enter. The cart blocked the gateway, and the man—Louis Delmschutz—dismounted and peered into the darkness, trying to find out what was frightening the pony.

He did not know it, but he was very close to death. A few feet behind him, still holding a knife, was the Whitechapel murderer. But Delmschutz was not aware of this, for he saw the body of a woman lying against the wall, and rushed into the club to raise the alarm.

The man who would soon be known as Jack the Ripper clambered over the wheel of the cart and slipped out into Berners Street. A moment later, he had disappeared into an alleyway.

Delmschutz emerged from the club followed by a crowd of men who babbled in Polish and Russian. Someone struck a light. The body was that of a tall woman, shabbily dressed. Her throat had been cut, and one of her ears was slightly torn. The ripper had been interrupted. The doctor who was called verified that the woman had been killed very recently indeed.

At the moment that the murderer walked out of Berners Street into the Commercial Road, a prostitute named Catherine Eddowes was released from Bishopsgate Police Station, where she had been in charge for drunkenness since 8 o'clock. Five hours in a cell had not sobered her appreciably; she walked down Bishopsgate towards Aldgate, and the man who had just left Berners Street was walking along the commercial road towards his usual haunts. Berners Street was the farthest afield that he had yet ventured; it is on the right as you go down the Commercial Road towards the East India Dock Road—a good half-mile from Commercial Street, the Ripper's usual hunting-ground. Perhaps he was finding the narrow streets of Spitalfields too hot for him; policemen in rubber-soled boots walked through his alleys, and the tradesmen of Whitechapel also prowled around in bands of 'vigilantes' in the hope of catching the murderer. At all events, the Ripper avoided Spitalfields and walked on towards Bishopsgate.

At the corner of Houndsditch he met Catherine Eddowes.

After a brief conversation, the two of them turned off to the right, into Duke Street. Half-way up Duke Street there is a narrow alleyway called St James Passage; in 1888 it had been known as Church Passage. At its far end lies Mitre Square, which looks today almost exactly as it looked in 1888. On its north side stands a warehouse.

The Ripper was standing on the south side of the square, near Church Passage, when PC Watkins walked through the square on his beat; as the policeman walked by, he pressed back into the shadow of a doorway, and, as soon as the steps were out of earshot, he placed a hand over Eddowes' mouth and cut her throat.

Exactly a quarter of an hour later, PC Watkins again walked through Mitre Square, but this time a mutilated body lay in the right-hand corner, near Church Passage. There was no doubt about the identity of the killer, for the body had been stabbed and cut ferociously, and the face had also been mutilated beyond recognition. And two of the woman's internal organs were missing.

The murderer had not given himself much time. The doctor who examined the body agreed that it must have taken at least ten minutes to inflict so many injuries; besides, the removal of the organs revealed some medical skill. And yet the man walked off without fear into Duke Street and right across Whitechapel into Dorset Street, where he found a convenient sink in which to wash his hands. He had torn off a fragment of the woman's apron, and used this to wipe off the blood. Major Smith, of the City Police, actually saw the sink before the bloodstained water had had time to drain away. Possibly some noise frightened the killer there, for he hurried off without finishing the wash, and continued to wipe off the blood as he walked towards Aldgate again. He finally dropped the piece of bloodstained apron in Goulston Street, within a short distance of the scene of the murder.

Although the Ripper did not know it then, Dorset Street was to be the scene of his most horrible murder, six weeks later.

Early the following morning, the Central News Agency received a letter written in red ink, signed 'Jack the Ripper'. It was their second letter bearing this signature. The first had arrived two days before the murder, and promised 'some more work' in the near future. It also promised to clip off the ladies' ears and send them to the police. No-one had taken the first letter seriously—it was assumed to be another practical joke—but this second letter altered the complexion of things. To begin with, it arrived early in the day, before the news of the murders was generally known. Secondly, there *had* been an attempt to cut off the ear of the first victim in Berners Street, and in his second letter the Ripper apologised for not sending it, saying that he had been interrupted!

The murder of Annie Chapman in Hanbury Street had caused a sensation, but it was nothing to the furore that followed the double murder. Hysteria swept the country. Sir Charles Warren, the unpopular Commissioner of Police, was bombarded with furious telegrams demanding his resignation. (He did, in fact, finally resign.) He was also bombarded with letters full of theories about the identity of the murderer and how to catch him.

It is almost impossible to give an adequate idea of the commotion caused by the murders, but the newspapers of the day devoted more space to them than our own journalists give to a royal wedding.

The police arrested about a dozen men a day, but all of them were released after questioning. Sometimes cranks gave themselves up as Jack the Ripper, for after the two letters had been made public the name had caught the popular imagination.

It took the police some time to identify the two women who had been killed that night. The woman who had been killed in Berners Street was finally identified as Elizabeth Stride, a Swedish woman who had taken to drink and prostitution after some emotional tragedy. (One story has it that she saw her children drowned in an accident on a Thames steamer.) The second victim was less easy to trace, because the mutilations to her face made recognition difficult, and there was one stage when she was identified as an Irishwoman named Mary Anne Kelly—an astounding coincidence in view of what was to come. Eventually, the evidence of her clothes established that she was Catherine Eddowes, aged forty-five, and that she had been in

police custody only three-quarters of an hour before she was
murdered.

There are very few streets in London whose names have been
changed because of some evil notoriety associated with the
original name. I know of only one in recent years: Rillington
Place, the site of the Christie murders. There seems no doubt
that Jack the Ripper holds the record for altering street names:
Bucks Row, the scene of the murder of Mary Nichols, is now
Dunward Street; Dorset Street, the scene of his last murder, has
become Duval Street; and I have never been able to discover
what became of George Street, where his first murder took
place.

In 1888, Dorset Street was a narrow and shabby thoroughfare running parallel with Spitalfields market, in Brushfield
Street. On its north side, extending towards the market, was an
entry labelled Millers Court. It was in a house in Millers Court
that the Whitechapel murderer killed and dismembered his last
victim, a twenty-four-year-old prostitute called Mary Jeanette
Kelly.

Five weeks had elapsed since the double murder, and London had begun to hope that the Ripper had left town. The
police and vigilante groups began to relax a little. Then, on the
morning of November 9th, a man knocked on the door of Mary
Kelly to ask for the rent. Getting no reply, he went round to the
window and peered through the half-open curtains. What he
saw was probably the most appalling sight in London's violent
criminal history.

The body that lay on the bed had been taken to pieces like a
jigsaw puzzle, and the pieces had been scattered around the
room, draped over a picture, or piled upon the sideboard. The
heart lay on the pillow, beside the head. The hysteria in
London reached new heights.

At some time after two o'clock on the morning of November
9th, the Ripper had been solicited by Mary Kelly outside her
room in Millers Court. A man named Hutchinson had actually
watched the 'pick-up' and described the man as a 'toff', a short,
thickset man with a curling moustache, and carrying a parcel of
some sort. A short time later, a neighbour heard Mary Kelly

Mary Kelly entering Millers Court with Jack the Ripper.

singing 'Sweet Violets'. At 3.10 the same neighbour heard a cry of 'Murder!' And for the next two hours there was silence, as Jack the Ripper dissected the body. Then the Ripper left, and the great mystery begins.

For how did he walk through London in clothes that must have been soaked in blood? Why did he burn a pile of clothes in the grate of Mary Kelly's room? Above all, what happened to the murderer after November 9th? There is no case in history of a maniacal killer who simply stopped of his own accord. Why did he stop?

These questions have puzzled students of crime ever since. There are theories by the dozen, but no shred of evidence. Is it possible, at this late date, that someone will prove the identity of Jack the Ripper? Are there papers somewhere in police files, or in some mental home, that tell the whole story?

We come, then, to the theories of the case. My own conviction is that the Ripper was a sadist—that is, a mentally sick person who found it impossible to gain sexual satisfaction except by inflicting pain, or producing large quantities of blood. It is just conceivable that he might have stopped killing of his own accord, completely satiated by his final crime.

The best-known theory of the Ripper's identity and motives was propounded by Leonard Matters, who declared—without producing a shred of evidence—that the Ripper was a certain Doctor Stanley, a widower who had been passionately fond of his only son. The son had died of syphilis, contracted from Mary Kelly, and Doctor Stanley had then devoted his life to a search for the woman. He questioned all his victims about her, and murdered them to make sure that they kept silent. Finally, after he found Mary Kelly, he ceased to stalk the East End. Matters alleges that Doctor Stanley died in Buenos Aires, and made a circumstantial deathbed confession.

One of the most popular theories in police circles is that George Chapman was Jack the Ripper. Chapman was actually a Pole whose real name was Severin Klossowski and, at the time of the murders, he was working as a barber in Whitechapel. In 1889, Chapman went to America, returning to London in 1892. During the next ten years, Chapman poisoned three women with whom he cohabited. There was no motive for the murders; he gained nothing by them; it is almost certain that they were purely sadistic. Chapman was executed in 1903, and Chief Inspector Abberline, who had been in charge of the Ripper investigations, stated dogmatically that Chapman was the Ripper.

Certainly, the dates correspond closely enough, and Hargrave Adam, who edited *The Trial of George Chapman*, declared that the 'Ripper murders' took place in Jersey City while Chapman was living there in 1890. But it is hard to believe that the man who dismembered Mary Kelly could have changed his method to antimony poisoning.

One of the most plausible theories of the Ripper's identity was recently put forward by Donald McCormick in his book *The Identity of Jack the Ripper*. McCormick points out that among the papers of Rasputin, the Russian 'monk' who was murdered in 1917, there was a document which claimed that Jack the Ripper was an insane Russian who had been sent to England by the Tsarist police, with the sole aim of embarrassing the English police. McCormick unearthed a great deal of evidence to connect the Ripper murders with Russian immigrants in the East End, and particularly with a barber-surgeon named Pedachenko.

He claims to have seen an issue of a Russian secret police gazette which reports the death of Pedachenko in a Russian mental home, and mentions that he had committed five murders of women in the East End in 1888. If this piece of evidence is still in existence, it is probably the most definite lead we have to the Ripper's identity. According to McCormick's theory, Pedachenko lived in Walworth, and was helped in his murders by two accomplices. His description corresponds closely with that given by the witnesses who claimed to have seen the Ripper: a short, broad-shouldered man, with a large moustache, well-dressed and wearing a gold watch-chain. If it is definitely established that the Ripper was Pedachenko, one of the great mysteries of crime will be at an end.

The East End of Jack theRipper is disappearing fast, but it is still to be found in a few alleyways and narrow entries into old buildings. His murders were a product of these slums and of cheap gin, starving women and fourpence-a-night doss houses. In spite of their 'local colour', it will be as well when they disappear forever.

AFTERWORD

Since Colin Wilson wrote these words in 1960, many of these places have indeed disappeared, although the curious no longer need to hunt for the Ripper murder sites: guided pedestrian tours are regularly held, and they are well attended by Londoners and visitors alike.

But despite much research and many new theories, the identity of the Ripper remains as elusive as ever. In the absence of further evidence, Pedanchenko has fallen from favour as a suspect, but a new candidate was soon afterwards proposed in the person of M.J. Druitt, a young lawyer with a history of mental instability, who may have been in the Whitechapel area at the time of the killings, and who killed himself shortly after the murders ceased. Other potential Rippers include J.K. Stephen, the Duke of Clarence, and—in an extremely complicated theory involving the painter Walter Sickert, freemasonry, more royalty and the Chief of Police—a threefold murderer (for the whole crazy story see Stephen Knight's Jack the Ripper: the Final Solution*).*

The year 1988 is the centenary of Jack the Ripper, and there are rumours of new 'final' solutions to come, including a new book from Colin Wilson himself. There is no doubt that the final word on the Whitechapel murderer will not be written for some considerable time yet.

JAMES THURBER

A Sort of Genius

JAMES THURBER

A Sort of Genius

On the morning of Saturday the 16th of September, 1922, a boy named Raymond Schneider and a girl named Pearl Bahmer, walking down a lonely lane on the outskirts of New Brunswick, New Jersey, came upon something that made them rush to the nearest house in Easton Avenue, around the corner, shouting. In that house an excited woman named Grace Edwards listened to them wide-eyed and then telephoned the police. The police came on the run and examined the young people's discovery: the bodies of a man and a woman. They had been shot to death and the woman's throat was cut. Leaning against one of the man's shoes was his calling card, not as if it had fallen there but as if it had been placed there. It bore the name Rev. Edward W. Hall. He had been the rector of the Protestant Episcopal Church of St John the Evangelist in New Brunswick. The woman was identified as Mrs Eleanor R. Mills, wife of the sexton of that church. Raymond Schneider and Pearl Bahmer had stumbled upon what was to go down finally in the annals of our crime as perhaps the country's most remarkable mystery. Nobody was ever found guilty of the murders. Before the case was officially closed, a hundred and fifty persons had had their day in court and on the front pages of the newspapers. The names of two must already have sprung to your ming: Mrs Jane Gibson, called by the avid press 'the pig woman', and William Carpender Stevens, once known to a hundred million people simply as 'Willie'. The pig woman died eleven years ago, but Willie Stevens is alive. He still lives in the house that he lived in fourteen years ago with Mr and Mrs Hall, at 23 Nichol Avenue, New Brunswick.

It was from that house that the Rev. Mr Hall walked at

35

The four suspects: Henry de la Bruyere Carpender (top left), Henry Stevens (top right), Willie Stevens (bottom left) and Mrs Edward Hall (bottom right).

around 7.30 o'clock on the night of Thursday the 14th of September, 1922, to his peculiar doom. With the activities in that house after Mr Hall's departure the State of New Jersey was to be vitally concerned. No. 23 Nichol Avenue was to share with De Russey's Lane, in which the bodies were found, the morbid interest of a whole nation four years later, when the case was finally brought to trial. What actually happened in De Russey's Lane on the night of September 14th? What actually happened at 23 Nichol Avenue the same night? For the researcher, it is a matter of an involved and voluminous court record, colorful and exciting in places, confused and repetitious in others. Two things, however, stand out as sharply now as they did on the day of their telling: the pig woman's story of the people she saw in De Russey's Lane that night, and Willie Stevens' story of what went on in the house in Nichol Avenue. Willie's story, brought out in cross-examination by a prosecutor whose name you may have forgotten (it was Alexander Simpson), lacked all the gaudy melodrama of the pig woman's tale, but in it, and in the way he told it on the stand, was the real drama of the Hall-Mills trial. When the State failed miserably in its confident purpose of breaking Willie Stevens down, the verdict was already written on the wall. The rest of the trial was anticlimax. The jury that acquitted Willie, and his sister, Mrs Frances Stevens Hall, and his brother, Henry Stevens, was out only five hours.

A detailed recital of all the fantastic events and circumstances of the Hall-Mills case would fill a large volume. If the story is vague in your mind, it is partly because its edges, even under the harsh glare of investigation, remained curiously obscure and fuzzy. Everyone remembers, of course, that the minister was deeply involved with Mrs Mills, who sang in his choir; their affair had been for some time the gossip of their circle. He was forty-one, she was in her early thirties; Mrs Hall was past fifty. On the 14th of September, Mr Hall had dinner at home with his wife, Willie Stevens, and a little niece of Mrs Hall's. After dinner, he said, according to his wife and his brother-in-law, that he was going to call on Mrs Mills. There was something about a payment on a doctor's bill. Mrs Mills had had an operation and the Halls had paid for it (Mrs Hall had inherited considerable wealth from her parents). He left the house at about the same time, it came out later, that Mrs Mills left her house, and the two were found murdered, under a crab apple tree in De Russey's Lane, on the edge of town, some forty hours later. Around the bodies were scattered love letters which the choir singer had written to the minister. No weapons were found, but there were several cartridge shells from an automatic pistol.

The investigation that followed—marked, said one New Jersey lawyer, by 'bungling stupidity'—resulted in the failure of the Grand Jury to indict anyone. Willie Stevens was questioned for hours, and so was Mrs Hall. The pig woman told her extraordinary story of what she saw and heard in the lane that night, but she failed to impress the Grand Jurors. Four years went by, and the Hall-Mills case was almost forgotten by people outside of New Brunswick when, in a New Jersey court, one Arthur Riehl brought suit against his wife, the former Louise Geist, for annulment of their marriage. Louise Geist had been, at the time of the murders, a maid in the Hall household. Riehl said in the course of his testimony that his wife had told him 'she knew all about the case but had been given $5,000 to hold her tongue.' This was all that Mr Philip Payne, managing editor of the *Daily Mirror*, nosing around for a big scandal of some sort, needed. His newspaper 'played up' the story until finally, under its goading, Governor Moore of New Jersey appointed Alexander Simpson special prosecutor with orders to reopen the case. Mrs Hall and Willie Stevens were arrested and so was their brother, Henry Stevens, and a cousin, Henry de la Bruyere Carpender.

At a preliminary hearing in Somerville the pig woman, with eager stridency, told her story again. About 9 o'clock on the night of September 14th, she heard a wagon going along Hamilton Road near the farm on which she raised her pigs. Thieves had been stealing her corn and she thought maybe they were at it again. So she saddled her mule, Jenny (soon to become the most famous quadruped in the country), and set off in grotesque pursuit. In the glare of an automobile's headlights in De Russey's Lane, she saw a woman with white hair who was wearing a tan coat, and a man with a heavy mustache, who

looked like a colored man. These figures she identified as Mrs
Hall and Willie Stevens. Tying her mule to a cedar tree, she
started toward the scene on foot and heard voices raised in
quarrel: 'Somebody said something about letters.' She now saw
three persons (later on she increased this to four), and a
flashlight held by one of them illumined the face of a man she
identified first as Henry Carpender, later as Henry Stevens,
and it 'glittered on something' in the man's hand. Suddenly
there was a shot, and as she turned and ran for her mule, there
were three more shots; a woman's voice screamed, 'Oh, my!
Oh, my! Oh, my!' and the voice of another woman moaned,
'Oh, Henry!' The pig woman rode wildly home on her mule,
without investigating further. But she had lost one of her
moccasins in her flight, and some three hours later, at 1 o'clock,
she rode her mule back again to see if she could find it. This
time, by the light of the moon, she saw Mrs Hall, she said,
kneeling in the lane, weeping. There was no one else there. The
pig woman did not see any bodies.

Mrs Jane Gibson became, because of her remarkable story,
the chief witness for the State, as Willie Stevens was to become
the chief witness for the defense. If he and his sister were not in
De Russey's Lane, as the pig woman had shrilly insisted, it
remained for them to tell the detailed story of their whereabouts
and their actions that night after Mr Hall left the house. The
Grand Jury this time indicted all four persons implicated by the
pig woman, and the trial began on November 3rd, 1926.

The first persons Alexander Simpson called to the stand were
'surprise witnesses'. They were a Mr and Mrs John S. Dixon,
who lived in North Plainfield, New Jersey, about twelve miles
from New Brunswick. It soon became apparent that they were
to form part of a net that Simpson was preparing to draw
around Willie Stevens. They testified that at about 8.30 on the
night of the murders Willie had appeared at their house,
wearing a loose-fitting suit, a derby, a wing collar with bow tie,
and across his vest, a heavy gold chain to which was attached a
gold watch. He had said that his sister had let him out there
from her automobile and that he was trying to find the Parker
Home for the Aged, which was at Bound Brook. He stuttered
and he told them that he was an epileptic. They directed him to

a trolley car and he went stumbling away. When Mrs Dixon identified Willie as her visitor, she walked over to him and took his right hand and shook it vigorously, as if to wring recognition out of him. Willie stared at her, said nothing. When she returned to the stand, he grinned widely. That was one of many bizarre incidents which marked the progress of the famous murder trial. It deepened the mystery that hung about the strange figure of Willie Stevens. People could hardly wait for him to take the stand.

William Carpender Stevens had sat in court for sixteen days before he was called to the witness chair, on the 23rd of November, 1926. On that day the trial of Albert B. Fall and Edward L. Doheny, defendants in the notorious Teapot Dome scandal, opened in Washington, but the nation had eyes only for a small, crowded courtroom in Somerville, New Jersey. Willie Stevens, after all these weeks, after all these years, was to speak out in public for the first time. As the New York *Times* said, 'He had been pictured as "Crazy Willie", as a town character, as an oddity, as a butt for all manner of jokes. He had been compared inferentially to an animal, and the hint of an alien racial strain in his parentage had been thrown at him.' Moreover, it had been prophesied that Willie would 'blow up' on the stand, that he would be trapped into contradictions by the 'wily' and 'crafty' Alexander Simpson, that he would be tricked finally into blurting out his guilt. No wonder there was no sound in the courtroom except the heavy tread of Willie Stevens' feet as he walked briskly to the witness stand.

Willie Stevens was an ungainly, rather lumpish man, about five feet ten inches tall. Although he looked flabby, this was only because of his loose-fitting colthes and the way he wore them; despite his fifty-four years, he was a man of great physical strength. He had a large head and a face that would be hard to forget. His head was covered with a thatch of thick, bushy hair, and his heavy black eyebrows seemed always to be arched, giving him an expression of perpetual surprise. This expression was strikingly accentuated by large, prominent eyes which, seen through the thick lenses of the spectacles he always wore, seemed to bulge unnaturally. He had a heavy, drooping, walrus mustache, and his complexion was dark. His glare was sudden and fierce; his smile, which came just as quickly, lighted up his whole face and gave him a wide, beaming look of an enormously pleased child. Born in Aiken, South Carolina, Willie Stevens had been brought to New Brunswick when he was two years old. When his wealthy parents died, a comfortable trust fund was left to Willie. The other children, Frances and Henry, had inherited their money directly. Once, when Mrs Hall was asked if it was not true that Willie was 'regarded as essential to be taken care of in certain things,' she replied, 'In certain aspects.' The quality of Willie's mentality, the extent of his eccentricity, were matters the prosecution strove to establish on several occasions. Dr Laurence Runyon, called by the defense to testify that Willie was not an epileptic and had never stuttered, was cross-examined by Simpson. Said the Doctor, 'He may not be absolutely normal mentally, but he is able to take care of himself perfectly well. He is brighter than the average person, although he has never advanced as far in school learning as some others. He reads books that are above the average and makes a good many people look like fools.' 'A sort of genius, in a way, I suppose?' said Simpson. To which the Doctor quietly replied, 'Yes, that is just what I mean.'

There were all sorts of stories about Willie. One of them was that he had once started a fire in his back yard and then, putting on a fireman's helmet, had doused it gleefully with a pail of water. It was known that for years he had spent most of every day at the firehouse of Engine Company No. 3 in Dennis Street, New Brunswick. He played cards with the firemen, ran errands for them, argued and joked with them, and was a general favorite. Sometimes he went out and bought a steak, or a chicken, and it was prepared and eaten in the firehouse by the firemen and Willie. In the days when the engine company had been a volunteer organization, Willie was an honorary member and always carried, in the firemen's parades, a flag he had bought and presented to the firehouse, an elaborate banner costing sixty or seventy dollars. He had also bought the black-and-white bunting with which the front of the firehouse was draped whenever a member of the company died.

After his arrest, he had whiled away the time in his c
reading books on metallurgy. There was a story that w

sister-in-law, Mrs Henry Stevens, once twitted him on his heavy reading, he said, 'Oh, that is merely the bread and butter of my literary repast.' The night before the trial opened, Willie's chief concern was about a new blue suit that had been ordered for him and that did not fit him to his satisfaction. He had also lost a collar button, and that worried him; Mrs Henry Stevens hurried to the jail before the court convened and brought him another one, and he was happy. At the preliminary hearing weeks before, Simpson had declared with brutal directness that Willie Stevens did indeed look like a colored man, as the pig woman had said. At this Willie had half risen from his chair and bared his teeth, as if about to leap on the prosecutor. But he had quickly subsided. All through the trial he had sat quietly, staring. He had been enormously interested when the pig woman, attended by a doctor and a nurse, was brought in on a stretcher to give her testimony. This was the man who now, on trial for his life, climbed into the witness chair in the courtroom at Somerville.

There was an immense stir. Justice Charles W. Parker rapped with his gavel. Mrs Hall's face was strained and white; this was an ordeal she and her family had been dreading for weeks. Willie's left hand gripped his chair tightly, his right hand held a yellow pencil with which he had fiddled all during the trial. He faced the roomful of eyes tensely. His own lawyer, Senator Clarence E. Case, took the witness first. Willie started badly by understating his age ten years. He said he was forty-four. 'Isn't it fifty-four?' asked Case. Willie gave the room his great, beaming smile. 'Yes,' he chortled, boyishly, as if amused by his slip. The spectators smiled. It didn't take Willie long to dispose of the Dixons, the couple who had sworn he stumbled into their house the night of the murder. He answered half a d̶ ̶n questions on this point with strong emphasis, s̶ ̶vly and clearly: he had never worn a derby, he had ld watch and chain. Mr Case held up Willie's old d chain for the jury to see. When he handed e, with fine nonchalance, compared his watch the courtroom wall, gave his sister a large, nd turned to his questioner with respectful ibed, with technical accuracy, an old revolver of his (the murders had been done with an automatic pistol, not a revolver, but a weapon of the same caliber as Willie's). He said he used to fire off the gun on the Fourth of July; remembering these old holidays, his eyes lighted up with childish glee. From this mood he veered suddenly into indignation and anger. 'When was the last time you saw the revolver?' was what set him off. 'The last time I saw it was in the courthouse!' Willie almost shouted. 'I think it was in October, 1922, when I was taken and put through a very severe grilling by—I cannot mention every person's name, but I remember Mr Toolan, Mr Lamb, and Detective David, and they did everything but strike me. They cursed me frightfully.' The officers had got him into an automobile 'by a subterfuge', he charged. 'Mr David said he simply wanted me to go out in the country, to ask me a very few questions, that I would not be very long.' It transpired later that on this trip Willie himself had had a question to ask Detective David: would the detective, if they passed De Russey's Lane, be kind enough to point it out to him? Willie had never seen the place, he told the detective, in his life. He said that Mr David showed him where it was.

When Willie got to the night of September 14th, 1922, in his testimony his anger and indignation were gone; he was placid, attentive, and courteous. He explained quietly that he had come home for supper that night, had gone to his room afterward, and 'remained in the house, leaving it at 2.30 in the morning with my sister.' Before he went to bed, he said, he had closed his door to confine to his own room the odor of tobacco smoke from his pipe. 'Who objected to that?' asked Mr Case. Willie gave his sudden, beaming grin. 'Everybody,' he said, and won the first of several general laughs from the courtroom. Then he told the story of what happened at 2.30 in the morning. It is necessary, for a well-rounded picture of Willie Stevens, to give it here at some length. 'I was awakened by my sister knocking at my door,' said Willie, 'and I immediately rose and went to the door and she said, "I want you to come down to the church, as Edward has not come home; I am very much worried"—or words to that effect. I immediately got dressed and accompanied her down to the church. I went through the front door, followed a small path that led directly to the back of the house past the cellar door. We went directly down Redmond Street to Jones Avenue, from Jones Avenue we went to George Street; turning into George Street we went directly down to Commercial Avenue. There our movements were blocked by an immense big freight automobile. We had to wait there maybe half a minute until it went by, going toward New York.

'I am not at all sure whether we crossed right there at Commercial Avenue or went a little further down George Street and went diagonally across to the church. Then we stopped there and looked at the church to see whether there were any lights. There were no lights burning. Then Mrs Hall said, "We might as well go down and see if it could not be possible that he was at the Mills' house." We went down there, down George Street until we came to Carman Street, turned down Carman Street, and got in front of the Mills' house and stood there two or three minutes to see if there were any lights in the Mills' apartment. There were none.' Willie then described, street by street, the return home, and ended with 'I opened the front door with my latchkey. If you wish me, I will show it to you. My sister said, "You might as well go to bed. You can do no more good." With that I went upstairs to bed.' This was the story that Alexander Simpson had to shake. But before Willie was turned over to him, the witness told how he heard that his brother-in-law had been killed. 'I remember I was in the parlor,' said Willie, 'reading a copy of the New York *Times*. I heard someone coming up the steps and I glanced up and I heard my aunt, Mrs Charles J. Carpender, say, "Well, you might as well know it—Edward has been shot." ' Willie's voice was thick with emotion. He was asked what happened then. 'Well,' he said, 'I simply let the paper go—that way' (he let his left hand fall slowly and limply to his side) 'and I put my head down, and I cried.' Mr Case asked him if he was present at, or had anything to do with, the murder of Mr Hall and Mrs Mills. 'Absolutely nothing at all!' boomed Willie, coming out of his posture of sorrow, belligerently erect. The attorney for the defense turned, with a confident little bow, to Alexander Simpson. The special prosecutor sauntered over and stood in front of the witness. Willie took in his breath sharply.

Alexander Simpson, a lawyer, a state senator, slight, perky, capable of harsh tongue-lashings, given to sarcasm and innuendo, had intimated that he would 'tie Willie Stevens into knots'. Word had gone around that he intended to 'flay' the eccentric fellow. Hence his manner now came as a surprise. He spoke in a gentle, almost inaudible voice, and his attitude was one of solicitous friendliness. Willie, quite unexpectedly, drew first blood. Simpson asked him if he had ever earned his livelihood. 'For about four or five years,' said Willie, 'I was employed by Mr Siebold, a contractor.' Not having anticipated an affirmative reply, Simpson paused. Willie leaned forward and said, politely, 'Do you wish his address?' He did this in good faith, but the spectators took it for what the *Times* called a 'sally', because Simpson had been in the habit of letting loose a swarm of investigators on anyone whose name was brought into the case. 'No, thank you,' muttered Simpson, above a roar of laughter. The prosecutor now set about picking at Willie's story of the night of September 14th: he tried to find out why the witness and his sister had not knocked on the Mills' door to see if Mr Hall were there. Unfortunately for the steady drumming of questions, Willie soon broke the prosecutor up with another laugh. Simpson had occasion to mention a New Brunswick boarding house called The Bayard, and he pronounced 'Bay' as it is spelled. With easy politeness, Willie corrected him. '*Bi*yard', said Willie. 'Biyard?' repeated Simpson. Willie smiled, as at an apt pupil. Simpson bowed slightly. The spectators laughed again.

Presently the witness made a slip, and Simpson pounced on it like a swooping falcon. Asked if he had not, at the scene of the murder, stood 'in the light of an automobile while a woman on a mule went by', Willie replied, 'I never remember that occurrence.' Let us take up the court record from there. 'Q.—You would remember if it occurred, wouldn't you? A.—I certainly would, but I don't remember of ever being in an automobile and the light from the automobile shone on a woman on a mule. Q.—Do you say you were not there, or you don't remember? A.—I say positively I was not there. Q.—Why did you say you don't *remember*? A.—Does not that cover the same thing? Q.— No, it don't, because you might be there and not remember it.

A.—Well, I will withdraw that, if I may, and say I was not there positively.' Willie assumed an air of judicial authority as he 'withdrew' his previous answer, and he spoke his positive denial with sharp decision. Mr Simpson abruptly tried a new tack. 'You have had a great deal of experience in life, Mr Stevens,' he said, 'and have read a great deal, they say, and know a lot about human affairs. Don't you think it sounds rather fishy when you say you got up in the middle of the night to go and look for Dr Hall and went to the house and never even knocked on the door—with your experience of human affairs and people that you met and all that sort of thing—don't that seem rather fishy to you?' There was a loud bickering of attorneys before Willie could say anything to this. Finally Judge Parker turned to the witness and said, 'Can you answer that, Mr Stevens?' 'The only way I can answer it, Your Honor,' said Willie, scornfully, 'is that I don't see that it is at all "fishy".' The prosecutor jumped to something else: 'Dr Hall's church was not your church, was it?' hs asked. 'He was not a *Doctor*, sir,' said Willie, once more the instructor. 'He was the Reverend *Mister* Hall.' Simpson paused, nettled. 'I am glad you corrected me on that,' he said. The courtroom laughed again.

The prosecutor now demanded that Willie repeat his story of what happened at 2.30 a.m. He hoped to establish, he intimated, that the witness had learned it 'by rote'. Willie calmly went over the whole thing again, in complete detail, but no one of his sentences was the same as it had been. The prosecutor asked him to tell it a third time. The defense objected vehemently. Simpson vehemently objected to the defense's objection. The Court: 'We will let him tell it once more.' At this point Willie said, 'May I say a word?' 'Certainly,' said Simpson. 'Say all you want.' Weighing his words carefully, speaking with slow emphasis, Willie said, 'All I have to say is I was never taught, as you insinuate, by any person whatsoever. That is my best recollection from the time I started out with my sister to this present minute.' Simpson did not insist further on a third recital. He wanted to know now how Willie could establish the truth of his statement that he was in his room from 8 or 9 o'clock until his sister knocked on the door at 2.30 a.m. 'Why,' said Willie, 'if a person sees me go upstairs and does not see me come downstairs, isn't that a conclusion that I was in my room?' The court record shows that Mr Simpson replied, 'Absolutely.' 'Well,' said Willie expansively, 'that is all there was to it.' Nobody but the pig woman had testified to seeing Willie after he went up to his room that night. Barbara Tough, a servant who had been off during the day, testified that she got back to the Hall home about 10 o'clock and noticed that Willie's door was closed (Willie had testified that it wouldn't stay closed unless he locked it). Louise Geist, of the annulment suit, had testified that she had not seen Willie that night after dinner. It was Willie's story against the pig woman's. That day in court he overshadowed her. When he stepped down from the witness chair, his shoulders were back and he was smiling broadly. Headlines in the *Times* the next day said, 'Willie Stevens Remains Calm Under Cross-Examination. Witness a Great Surprise.' There was a touch of admiration, almost of partisanship, in most of the reporters' stories. The final verdict could be read between the lines. The trial dragged on for another ten days, but on the 3rd of December, Willie Stevens was a free man.

He was glad to get home. He stood on the porch of 23 Nichol Avenue, beaming at the house. Reporters had followed him there. He turned to them and said solemnly, 'It is one hundred and four days since I've been here. And I want to get in.' They let him go. But two days later, on a Sunday, they came back and Mrs Hall received them in the drawing room. They could hear Willie in an adjoining room, talking spiritedly. He was, it came out, discussing metallurgy with the Rev. J. Mervin Pettit, who had succeeded Mr Hall as rector of the Church of St John the Evangelist.

Willie Stevens, going on seventy, no longer visits the firehouse of No. 3 Engine Company. His old friends have caught only glimpses of him in the past few years, for he has been in feeble health, and spends most of his time in his room, going for a short ride now and then in his chauffeur-driven car. The passerby, glancing casually into the car, would not recognize the famous figure of the middle 1920's. Willie has lost a great deal of weight, and the familiar beaming light no longer comes easily to his eyes.

After Willie had been acquitted and sent home, he tried to pick up the old routine of life where he had left it, but people turned to stare after him in the street, and boys were forever at his heels, shouting, 'Look out, Willie, Simpson is after you!' The younger children were fond of him and did not tease him, and once in a while Willie could be seen playing with them, as boisterously and whimsically as ever. The firemen say that if he encountered a ragged child he would find out where it lived, and then give one of his friends the money to buy new clothes for it. But Willie's adventures in the streets of the town became fewer and farther apart. Sometimes months would elapse between his visits to the firehouse. When he did show up in his old haunts, he complained of headaches, and while he was still in his fifties, he spent a month in bed with a heart ailment. After that, he stayed close to home, and the firemen rarely saw him. If you should drop by the firehouse, and your interest in Willie seems friendly, they will tell you some fond stories about him.

One winter Willie took a Cook's tour to Hawaii. When he came back, he told the firemen he had joined an organization which, for five dollars, gave its subscribers a closer view of the volcanoes than the ordinary tourist could get. Willie was crazy about the volcanoes. His trip, however, was spoiled, it came out, because someone recognized and pointed him out as the famous Willie Stevens of the Hall-Mills case. He had the Cook's agent cancel a month's reservation at a hotel and rearrange his schedule so that he could leave on the next ship. He is infuriated by any reference to the murders or to the trial. Some years ago a newspaper printed a paragraph about a man out West who was 'a perfect double for Willie Stevens'. Someone in the firehouse showed it to Willie and he tore the paper to shreds in a rage.

Willie still spends a great deal of time reading 'heavy books'—on engineering, on entomology, on botany. Those who have seen his famous room at 23 Nichol Avenue—he has a friend in to visit him once in a while—say that it is filled with books. He has no use for detective stories or the Western and adventure magazines his friends the firemen read. When he is not reading scientific tomes, he dips into the classics or what he calls the 'worth-while poets'. He used to astound the firemen with his wide range of knowledge. There was a day a salesman of shaving materials dropped in at the enginehouse. Finding that Willie had visited St Augustine, Florida, he mentioned an old Spanish chapel there. Willie described it and gave its history, replete with dates, and greatly impressed the caller. Another time someone mentioned a certain kind of insect which he said was found in this country. 'You mean they used to be,' said Willie. 'That type of insect has been extinct in this country for forty years.' It turned out that it had been, too. On still another occasion Willie fell to discussing flowers with some visitor at the firehouse and reeled off a Latin designation— *crassinae carduaceae*, or something of the sort. Then he turned, grinning, to the listening firemen. 'Zinnias to you,' he said.

Willie Stevens' income from the trust fund established for him is said to be around forty dollars a week. His expenditures are few, now that he is no longer able to go on long trips. The firemen like especially to tell about the time that Willie went to Wyoming, and attended a rodeo. He told the ticket-seller he wanted to sit in a box and the man gave him a single ticket. Willie explained that he wanted the whole box to himself, and he planked down a ten-dollar bill for it. Then he went in and sat in the box all alone. 'I had a hell of a time!' he told the firemen gleefully when he came back home.

De Russey's Lane, which Detective David once pointed out to Willie Stevens, is now, you may have heard, entirely changed. Several years ago it was renamed Franklin Boulevard, and where the Rev. Mr Edward W. Hall and Mrs Eleanor Mills lay murdered there is now a row of neat brick and stucco houses. The famous crab apple tree under which the bodies were found disappeared the first weekend after the murders. It was hacked to pieces, roots and all, by souvenir-hunters.

AFTERWORD

One of the theories about the Hall-Mills case not mentioned by Thurber— perhaps he considered it too ridiculous, although others have taken it seriously enough—is that the murders were committed by the Klu Klux Klan. Apparently the Klan was active and powerful in rural New Jersey at that time, and had a reputation for punishing what it considered to be 'sins against morality' by its own violent actions. Certainly, the affair between the Reverend Edward Hall and Eleanor Mills was no great secret in the neighbourhood, and it is possible that it might have attracted the Klan's attention.

On balance, however, it seems that personal jealousy would have provided a much stronger motive, though whether Mrs Hall's family took matters into its own hands or hired others to take action on their behalf (they could have afforded it) will probably now never be known. All the participants in the case, including Willie Stevens, are now dead, of course, and they died without shedding any further light on the matter.

If the Hall-Mills murders seem destined to be forever labelled 'unsolved', that is certainly not the case in our next murder: that of Julia Wallace in Liverpool in 1931. We have already quoted Raymond Chandler's admiring comments on Dorothy L. Sayers' handling of it; now we skip back across the Atlantic Ocean and settle down to let Miss Sayers guide us through the intricacies of this most fascinating of crimes. To quote another remark of Chandler's: 'The Wallace case is unbeatable; it will always be unbeatable.'

DOROTHY L. SAYERS

The Murder of Julia Wallace

DOROTHY L. SAYERS

The Murder of Julia Wallace

The question is not: Who did this crime? The question is: Did the prisoner do it?—or rather, to put it more accurately: Is it proved to your reasonable satisfaction and beyond all reasonable doubt that the prisoner did it? It is a fallacy to say: 'If the prisoner did not do it, who did?' It is a fallacy to look at it and say: 'It is very difficult to think the prisoner did not do it'; and it may be equally difficult to think the prisoner did do it. . . . Can you say, taking all this evidence as a whole . . . that you are satisfied beyond reasonable doubt that it was the hand of the prisoner, and no other hand that murdered this woman? If you are not so satisfied . . . if it is not established to your reasonable satisfaction as a matter of evidence, as a matter of fact, of legal evidence and legal proof, then it is your duty to find the prisoner not guilty.— *Mr Justice Wright's summing-up in the trial of William Herbert Wallace.*

When a crime has been committed, the facts may be examined from three different points of view, very carefully distinguished by the learned Judge whose words I have just quoted. The people ask at once: 'Who did it?' The law never has to ask this question; it waits until the people, through their representatives, the police, have produced a tentative answer by accusing a suspect, and it then asks one question only: 'Did the prisoner do it?'—which is not at all the same thing. The detective novelist, a special sort of person among the people, also asks: 'Who did it?' And his professional bias also prompts him to add, and to press with peculiar interest, that further question of which the law can take no cognisance: 'If the prisoner did not do it, who did?'

The people, guided by instinct and communal experience, are naturally inclined to favour the most simple and obvious explanation of the facts; also it is a relief to their minds if they can believe that the right person has been accused, convicted and put out of the way; they prefer, therefore, on the whole, that the accused person should be convicted. The detective novelist, as a class, hankers after complication and ingenuity, and is disposed to reject the obvious and acquit the accused, if possible; and having done this, the law makes an end of the matter. But the detective novelist is uneasy until he has gone further and found some new and satisfying explanation of the problem.

The case of the Wallace murder shows law and people strangely and interestingly at odds, and provides for the detective novelist an unrivalled field of speculation. William Herbert Wallace was convicted by the people and acquitted by the law; and whether he was guilty or innocent the story is of a sort that (one would think) could only have been put together by the perverted ingenuity of a detective novelist. For if he was guilty, then he was the classic contriver and alibi-monger that adorns the pages of a thousand mystery novels; and if he was innocent, then the real murderer was still more typically the classic villain of fiction. And, since law and people pronounced opposing judgments, any explanation that the novelist can suggest will have the professional merit of flouting opinion and avoiding the obvious.

As in every criminal case that comes to trial, the available facts are only such as were openly produced in court. This restricted material is that upon which people, law and novelist alike have to work. The police, indeed, and the solicitors for the defence, may have had other material at their disposal; but since they did not produce it we may suppose that it was not helpful to them; and the law had to base its decision upon the evidence given at the trial. For the purpose of this article I propose, therefore, to use only the published evidence, so as to place law, people and novelist all in the same position. This is the more easy and suitable since there was, throughout the trial, remarkably little conflict of evidence. With a few trifling exceptions the facts were admitted by both sides; the only difficulty was how to interpret them. It will be seen that there is, from first to last, no single incident which is not susceptible of at least two interpretations, according to whether one considers that the prisoner was, in fact, an innocent man caught in a trap or a guilty man pretending to have been caught in a trap. Nowhere shall we find that 'master-clue' beloved of the detective novelist, which can only lead in one direction. The problem of the Wallace murder had no key-move and ended, in fact, in stalemate.

Nothing could be more respectable, more harmless, more remote from savage violence, than the antecedents of the man who in 1931 was accused of brutally beating out his wife's brains with a poker. Born in 1878, in the Lake District, William Herbert Wallace was apprenticed to the drapery trade. At the age of twenty-three (driven, according to his own statement, by a romantic *Wanderlust*) he sailed for India to take up a post as salesman in Calcutta. Here he fell seriously ill, and, after a period of employment as advertising manager in the less trying climate of Shanghai, was forced for his health's sake to return to England. He obtained a situation in Manchester, where he interested himself in politics and was appointed Liberal Agent for the Ripon Division of the West Riding. While visiting Harrogate, in 1911, he made the acquaintance of his future wife, and on March 24, 1913, he married her. When the war put an end to his political work, he obtained employment as a district agent for the Prudential Assurance Company, and moved with his wife to Liverpool. Here they rented a small, two-storeyed house, No. 29 Wolverton Street, in the suburb of Anfield, and here they lived for sixteen uneventful years, in what seemed to be, in the words of a witness, 'the best relations possible'.

It is, of course, always difficult to be certain how far an appearance of married harmony may not conceal elements of disruption. Unless the parties attract the notice of neighbours or servants by the throwing of crockery, by loud and abusive language, by open infidelities or by open complaints, a great deal of quiet mutual irritation may go on without anybody's being much the wiser. The Wallaces had no children, kept no servant but a charwoman who came in once a week, and saw but few friends; so that, if indeed they had any disagreements, they were better placed than many people for keeping their troubles to themselves. A caustic judge once expressed the opinion that, in the case of a married couple, there was no need

William Herbert Wallace.

to look for the motive for murder, since marriage was a motive in itself; while a cynic once argued upon the same lines to the present writer that, who but the husband *could* want to get rid of the wife? Since nobody else could be shown to have any motive for murdering Mrs Wallace, the murderer *must* be the husband, since after all he *was* her husband, and so had his motive ready made. After his release, Wallace wrote:

> Our days and months and years were filled with complete enjoyment, placid, perhaps, but with all the happiness of quietude and mutual interest and affection. Neither of us cared very much for entertaining other people or for being entertained; we were sufficient in ourselves.

It is in that very self-sufficiency, that intimate companionship extended over days and months and years, that some writers have discovered the hidden motive for the crime: they were too close to one another, the monotony was unendurable, the husband's nerves gave way under the silent strain and he killed his wife because he was bored with her. If there had been open quarrels, that fact would have told against the husband; equally, the fact that there were no such quarrels may be held to tell against him also. Where human nature is concerned, there can never be any certainty; it all depends on the way you look at these things.

And yet it is exceedingly rare, when a husband and wife are at odds, that nobody at all should have any knowledge of their difficulties. One might think that, at some time or other during those sixteen years, the self-control of a hopelessly irritated husband would have given way. It is quite certain that, had there been any evidence at all of domestic trouble, the prosecution would have produced it, for the sheer absence of any comprehensible motive was the weakest point in their case against Wallace. There was, at any rate, no 'eternal triangle'— no other woman and no other man; if there had been any such persons it is almost inconceivable that the researches of the police could have failed to unearth them. Nor could Wallace have had any financial motive for murdering his wife, since, though she was insured for a small sum, his accounts were in perfect order and he had a sufficient balance in the bank. We may weave what fancies we like about the situation; the *fact* remains that no evidence of motive was ever put forward for the murder of Julia Wallace by her husband or anybody else.

What evidence can we, *in fact*, produce about the relations between the Wallaces?

There is, first of all, the undisputed fact that they lived together for nearly eighteen years and had no children. What conclusion we ought to draw from this circumstance we do not know, for nothing was ever said about it. Had their married relations always been normal? We do not know; at any rate, no evidence was brought to the contrary. Did Wallace, perhaps, blame his wife for their childlessness and determine to put her out of the way so that he might marry someone else before it was too late? It is a possibility; he was in no position to get a divorce, and the scandal of an irregular relation with another partner would no doubt have prejudiced him in his employment. We can only say that the prosecution made no suggestion of any such motive. Or did Mrs Wallace perhaps lay the blame on her husband and drive him to murderous fury by taunts and insults? There was a case in the last century—closely parallel in some respects to the Wallace case—in which that situation does seem to have occurred; but here, there is again no evidence. Neither William nor Julia Wallace was of strong physique, and their means, though sufficient, were not ample; they may have been incapable of having children, or they may, for reasons of health or finance, have agreed to remain childless; we do not know—all is conjecture.

In the absence of a family, what were their common interests? Here we can draw upon the evidence of the witnesses, on the evidence of Wallace himself at the time of the trial and after, and on the evidence of Wallace's diaries—of which those portions at any rate which were written before the murder may be supposed to be fairly reliable.

In Wallace, then, we have one of those mild dabblers in science and philosophy common among self-educated men of a speculative turn of mind. A witness for the prosecution described him, aptly enough, as ' a man who is intellectual, and varied in his habit of study, and that sort of thing'. It was, indeed, exactly that sort of thing. He 'looked at all things with the eyes of a naturalist'; he read and noted in his journal the newest theories about atomic physics; he made amateur chemical experiments in a back bedroom, which he had fitted up as a laboratory; he strove to model his behaviour upon the stoic precepts of Marcus Aurelius; he was interested in music, and at the age of fifty 'took up' the violin (in half a dozen lessons from a friend); and he was a keen and skilful chess-player. Witnesses spoke of him as 'a placid man', 'scrupulously honest', 'an absolute gentleman in every respect'; one feels that he was perhaps a little fussy, a little pedantic, a little too fond of improving himself and other people, and something perhaps of an old maid married.

His wife Julia was, in his own words, 'an excellent pianist, no mean artist in water-colour, a fluent French scholar, and of a cultured literary taste'. She was dark and small, not very robust, but apparently capable of doing the greater part of the work of their little six-roomed house. One gathers that they enjoyed country rambles and excursions together (he, the naturalist, and she, the artist); that in the evenings they sometimes went out together to a play or cinema, or enjoyed a musical evening at home (she, the pianist and he, the fiddler) in the front sitting-room that was otherwise only used for 'company'. True, Julia failed to appreciate the 'inner significance and real meaning' of *The Master Builder*, and her husband thought this strange; but she evidently did her best to share his interests.

> When she was with me [he wrote after the trial] her passion for novelty and discovery gave me countless hours of joy in explaining, as far as I could, the great riddles of the universe. . . . As I passed from practical to theoretical science my wife tried hard to keep pace with me in the newer problems of physics. . . . The hours and hours we spent together examining specimens under the microscope.

The perfect wife, surely, and model womanly woman! Only one phrase in the diary may perhaps reveal the more trying side of womanliness:

> Nothing can ever bring her back, and however much I want her, or however much I miss her loving smiles and aimless chatter . . .

Was that aimless chatter perhaps less lovable in reality than in retrospect? But probably the plainest expression of the feeling between them is to be found in Wallace's sober entry for March 25, 1929, nearly two years before the murder:

> Julia reminds me to-day it was fifteen years ago yesterday since we were married. Well, I don't think either of us regrets the step. We seem to have pulled well together, and I think we both get as much pleasure and contentment out of life as most people . . .

One feels, perhaps, that here the pupil of the stoics is controlling the pen more firmly than on some other occasions; but it is scarcely the expression of a man driven to madness by disillusionment and exasperation.

And now, having made ourselves acquainted with the principal characters, we come to the strange plot of the melodrama.

> The only time I left my wife alone in our little home [wrote Wallace in a published article] was to visit the Chess Club at the City Café, to deliver my lectures [on chemistry] at the Technical College, or to attend to my insurance business. On all other occasions my wife was my inseparable companion.

Monday was one of the days on which the Liverpool Central Chess Club held its regular meetings, and accordingly, on the night of Monday, January 19, 1931, Wallace left his inseparable companion at about a quarter-past seven, in order to attend the meeting and take part in a championship competition in which his name was down to play that evening. At about 7.20 the telephone rang in the café and was answered by the waitress, who then called Mr Beattie, the captain of the Chess Club, to come and take the message. The caller, who spoke in 'a strong rather gruff voice', asked whether Mr Wallace was in the club. Mr Beattie said no, he was not, but would be there presently; would the caller ring up again. The caller said, 'No, I am too busy; I have got my girl's twenty-first birthday on, and I want to see Mr Wallace on a matter of business; it is something in the nature of his business.' Mr Beattie then offered to take a message, and the caller said he wanted Wallace to come and see him the following evening at 7.30, giving his name as 'R.M. Qualtrough', and his address as 25 Menlove Gardens East, Mossley Hill'.

Half an hour or so later, that is, at about a quarter to eight, Mr Beattie saw that Wallace had come into the café and started a game of chess with a man called McCartney. 'Oh, Wallace,' said Mr Beattie, 'I have a message for you.' 'Oh, who from?' said Wallace. 'From a man named Qualtrough,' replied Mr

Beattie. 'Qualtrough, Qualtrough,' repeated Wallace. 'Who is Qualtrough?' Mr Beattie said, 'Well, if you don't know, I don't,' and gave the message. Wallace again said, 'I don't know the chap. Where is Menlove Gardens East?' Mr Beattie did not know, nor did another member of the club whom they consulted, but they all agreed that it was probably to be found in the same district as Menlove Avenue. Having noted down the name and address in his diary, Wallace went on to finish and win his game of chess. Nothing further seems to have been said about the mysterious message until Wallace was going home, accompanied by two other members of the club. He then asked, 'Qualtrough? Have you heard of that name before?' His friend said he had only heard of one person of that name, and they then discussed the best way of getting to Menlove Gardens. Wallace said he was not sure whether he would go at all, but if he did, he would take the tram to Menlove Avenue. So ended the first act of the tragedy.

Now, whatever else is uncertain about the Wallace case, one thing is abundantly clear: that, whoever sent the telephone message from 'Qualtrough', it was not a genuine message but the first deliberate step towards the commission of a crime. At the trial, Wallace was accused of having sent the message himself, by way of establishing an alibi for the Tuesday evening; he himself maintained that it was sent by an enemy, so as to lure him away from home. Any argument directed to prove or disprove the genuiness of the message is beside the point: there never was an R. M. Qualtrough; there never was a Menlove Gardens East; there never was any genuine insurance business to be transacted. Whoever sent the message was the murderer; all we have to inqure is, was 'Qualtrough' Wallace, or was he somebody else?

The first interesting fact is that the message was sent from a telephone kiosk about four hundred yards from Wallace's own house, and sent at exactly the time that Wallace was due to pass that kiosk on his way to the Central Café. Counsel for the prosecution made great play with this fact.

Assuming he [Wallace] left the house on his three minutes journey at 7.15, he could easily have been in the box by 7.18; but by a singular coincidence the man who wanted him, Qualtrough, was in that telephone box at the identical time at which Mr Wallace might have been there, and, by another singular coincidence, was trying to ring up Mr Wallace. . . . It was a box that he [Wallace] has used. . . . The man in the box telephoned through to the Central Café. Nobody but Wallace knew that Wallace was going to be at the café; no one. . . . The man rings up, and . . . assuming that it was the prisoner . . . no doubt disguising his voice. . . . He is asked if he will ring up later. . . . He says 'No.' . . . If it was Wallace, obviously he would say he could not ring up later, because he would not be there. If the man had important business, and he wanted to speak to a man he did not know, do you not think he would then want to ring up later? And remember, when he was ringing up he was four hundred yards only from the house of Mr Wallace, and it is perfectly clear that he did not call there, and he did not leave any note there. What he did do, was to telephone up to a place where he could not know he [Wallace] was going to be—it is common ground that the man who rang up . . . was planning the murder. . . . You would have thought he would be certain to see that his message . . . would get home. . . . He does nothing of the sort. . . . He never inquires afterwards whether Wallace came there and got his message, but he leaves the whole thing in the air.

Now this argument is curiously contradictory. At one point, counsel asks, 'If the man had important business, would he not have done so-and-so?' But in the next breath he admits that the man had no important business, except crime; therefore it is clear that whatever his actions might be, they could not be such as one would expect of an innocent man making a business appointment. The question that counsel was really trying to ask was not: 'Can we now believe the message genuine?' but: 'Could Wallace at that time have innocently believed the message genuine?' But let us examine the whole business of the telephone call carefully, point by point; for it is the very centre of the problem.

First of all: Is it true that nobody but Wallace could possibly have known that he was going to the City Café on January 19th? It is not true. Wallace was scheduled to play a championship game that night, and the list of fixtures was openly displayed in the café where anybody might see it. The meetings of the chess club always began at about the same time—roughly 7.45. Wallace was a fairly regular attendant, and we know that he was definitely expected on the Monday, because Mr Beattie said as much to 'Qualtrough'. Therefore, any frequenter of the café might reasonably have looked to find him there.

Secondly: Where was the famous telephone kiosk, and what was it like? The Wallaces' house was one of a row, all having their front doors upon Wolverton Street and their back doors upon a lane running roughly parallel to the street. At a point some four hundred yards from No. 29 street and lane converged, and at this strategic point stood the kiosk—a dim little erection, lit only by the reflected rays of a street-lamp. Whether Wallace left his house by the front or the back door, he was bound to pass the kiosk on the way to the Central Café. Equally, anybody who wanted to know whether he was going to the Central Café that night had only to stand at the corner of the two streets and see whether he passed the kiosk. Thus counsel's 'coincidence' turns out to be no coincidence at all, for if 'Qualtrough' was not Wallace, then he must have been watching in or near the kiosk to make sure that Wallace went to the café, and, having made sure, he telephoned.

Is there anything that might indicate whether 'Qualtrough' was Wallace or somebody else? There is the curious evidence of the girl at the telephone exchange. She was spoken to by the caller, who said: 'Operator, I have pressed button A, but have not had my correspondent yet.' She then connected him and thought no more about it. Now, counsel drew attention to the fact that Wallace often spoke from that call-box; he should, therefore, have known how to use it. But the whole point of button A's existence is that you should *not* press button A *until* you have heard your 'correspondent' speak. Either, then, 'Qualtrough' was unfamiliar with a public call-box, or he was too much agitated to remember the procedure. Whoever he was, he may well have been agitated: but the more usual mistake with button A is to forget to press it at all. The point is a trifling one; but, such as it is, it tells, perhaps, slightly in Wallace's favour.

Now comes the question why 'Qualtrough' rang up when he did. If he was Wallace, then 7.18 was obviously the only time at which he could ring up. If not, then why did he not wait till Wallace had reached the café, or deliver a note or message at the house? There can be only one answer to this: that his face, voice and handwriting were known to the Wallaces and that he did not dare to risk recognition. Still less could he ring again

later in the evening. The voice might have been disguised; Mr
Beattie said that at the time it did not seem to him to be
anything but a natural one, and that it 'would be a great stretch
of imagination' to say that it was anything like Wallace's. But
supposing it was not Wallace, how could 'Qualtrough' venture,
in his own voice or a disguised one, on a prolonged conversation
with Wallace? He would have had to answer every kind of
inconvenient question: details about himself, details about
'Menlove Gardens East', details about the mysterious 'business', and he would have had to be an uncommonly skilful liar
to get through without letting Wallace smell a rat. The tale of
the birthday party was a little fishy; but the vague message sent
through Mr Beattie had its merits, for it held out a bait of
indeterminate size and splendour.

> Seeing the name and the daughter coming of age had been suggested
> [said Wallace in court] I considered it might result in a policy of
> something like £100 endowment, or something of that nature. I did not
> expect it would be less than that.

To a man in Wallace's position, that would have been
business worth getting. Besides, if the name was not to be found
in the directory, or the address was discovered to be non-
existent, how easy to suppose that Mr Beattie had heard
wrongly or noted the details carelessly.

All through this case one has to remember that Wallace lived
in a small way and worked for very small profits. Nobody is
more pertinacious than your small insurance agent. He will go
miles to secure a few shillings. He would not be disconcerted by
failing to find 'R. M. Qualtrough' in a list of householders; the
man might be a lodger, a domestic servant, a newcomer to the
district. Wallace said afterwards that he had not thought to
look up the address in the directory; but in any case, new streets
and houses were being run up all over the place at a great rate,
and it might have been one of those. It was nearly as certain as
death and taxation that Wallace would never rest content till he
had investigated the whole matter personally and on the spot.

And finally, did 'Qualtrough' take no steps to ascertain that
his message had 'gone home'? We cannot say that. He had only
to follow Wallace to the café. Whoever he was, he must have
been a habitué of the place to have known of Wallace's engage-

ment to play there that night. It is possible that he actually arrived in time to hear the message delivered. Once we admit that he must have known Wallace and the café, all the rest follows. Any explanation that fits Wallace as the murderer also fits any murderer we may like to postulate.

The stage being now set, the curtain goes up on Act II. It is preceded by a curious little interlude. At 3.30 on the following afternoon, James Edward Rothwell, a police constable, was bicycling along a street called Maiden Lane, and saw Wallace walking on the pavement.

> He was dressed in a tweed suit and a light fawn raincoat. His face was haggard and drawn, and he seemed very distressed. He was dabbing his eye with his coat-sleeve, and he appeared to me as if he had been crying.

It was suggested to P.C. Rothwell that Wallace's eyes might have been merely watering from the cold, but the constable stuck to his opinion. On the other hand, we have the evidence of three women upon whom Wallace called between 3.30 and 5.45 to collect their insurance, that he seemed 'calm' and 'just as usual', that he cracked jokes with one and enjoyed a cup of tea with another. Whether the constable or the ladies were the better qualified to detect signs of emotion in an insurance agent is a question. Women are said to be observant by nature, and policemen should be observant by profession. The one certain fact is that, on that morning and afternoon of Tuesday, January 29th, Wallace transacted all his business in his ordinary accurate manner.

He stopped collecting, by his own account, at a few minutes to six and then went home for his tea. And it is now that we come to the one serious conflict of evidence in the whole case. Some time between 6.30 and 6.45 the milk-boy called with the milk; Mrs Wallace took it in, and that is the last occasion on which she was seen alive by any disinterested person. The milk-boy, Alan Croxton Close, was 14 years old, and in his evidence he said he knew he delivered the milk at 6.30, because when he passed Holy Trinity Church it was 6.25, and it took him five minutes to get from there to 29 Wolverton Street.

On the other hand, Allison Wildman, aged 16, who was delivering a newspaper at No. 27, next door, said she got there at 6.43, and that when she had delivered her paper and gone,

Close was still standing at the door of No. 29. She, too, relied on Holy Trinity Church clock. Moreover, she was seen by some boys leaving Wolverton Street some minutes after 6.40. Further doubt was thrown on Close's evidence by a number of other little boys who maintained that on the day after the murder he had told them, 'I saw Mrs Wallace at a quarter to seven'; and it was rather suggested that young Close had altered his opinion to fit the police case against Wallace. It is a close thing—a matter of five or eight minutes—the kind of point on which nobody but the characters in a detective novel can reasonably be expected to be accurate; its importance (just as in a detective story) lies in the fact that, if Mrs Wallace was alive at 6.45 it was almost impossible that Wallace could have murdered her; for at 7.10 at the very latest he was changing trams at the junction of Smithdown Road and Lodge Lane, a good twenty minutes' ride from his home. To commit the murder between 6.30 and 6.50 would have been pretty quick work; to commit it between 6.45 and 6.50 would have been something like a conjuring trick.

Wallace stated that he left the house that evening by the back door. This, he explained, was his usual custom in the early part of the evening.

> If I was going out after six, and I knew I was going to be out an hour or two, I might go out by the back door and ask my wife to come down and bolt it after me, and on my return come in by the front door, because I would have my key.

This seems reasonable; we get the picture of the front door with its patent lock and the backyard door with its builder's lock and iron bolts, which (and this must be borne in mind) the householder would *expect* to find bolted against him on his return. Mrs Wallace, on this occasion, accompanied her husband—or so he said—by way of the back as far as the backyard gate and there he left her, with instructions to bolt the door after him.

Now, if 'Qualtrough' was lurking about the telephone kiosk at ten minutes to seven on that dark January night, what might he have seen? In the light of the adjacent street-lamp he would have seen Wallace's slight figure, dressed, not in the fawn raincoat (for the weather had cleared), but in an overcoat, come briskly up from the back lane towards the tramway stop.

That would have been his cue that the coast was clear at No. 29, and that his dupe was out of the way for a good hour at least. Now would be his moment for going to the house. If, by any chance, Mrs Wallace had somebody with her, he could still make some excuse and withdraw; but if she was alone, the path to crime lay open.

Nobody (except the not impossible 'Qualtrough') seems to have seen Wallace at this stage of his journey. He is next heard of some time between 7.6 and 7.10, at the tram-junction at Smithdown Road, asking the conductor, one Thomas Charles Phillips, whether the tram went from there to Menlove Gardens East. Phillips replied, 'No, you can get on No. 5, 5A, 5W or a No. 7 car.' There was nothing in this to suggest to Wallace that Menlove Gardens East might not exist, so he got on, observing that he was a stranger in the district and had important business at Menlove Gardens East. Later, while paying his fare, he reminded the conductor that he wanted to be put off at Menlove Gardens East, and a little later mentioned his destination for the third time and was told to change at Penny Lane. When they got there, Phillips shouted 'Menlove Gardens, change here,' and saw his fussy passenger sprinting to catch the No. 7 car, which went to Calderstone. The time was then 7.15.

On the Calderstone car, Wallace again anxiously asked the conductor to put him off at Menlove Gardens East. Accordingly, he was put off at Menlove Gardens West, the conductor saying to him, 'You will probably find Menlove Gardens East in that direction.' Wallace replied, 'Thank you; I am a complete stranger round here.'

Now, it was said afterwards that these persistent inquiries and repeated asserverations that he was a stranger in the district and had important business there, were unnatural, and showed that Wallace was eager to impress his personality upon the tram-conductors in order to establish his alibi. This may be so—though, if fussy inquiries and irrelevant personal confidences are a proof of criminal intent, then the proportion of criminals engaged daily in establishing alibis on public vehicles must be a shockingly high one.

It is interesting that he did not succeed in impressing himself

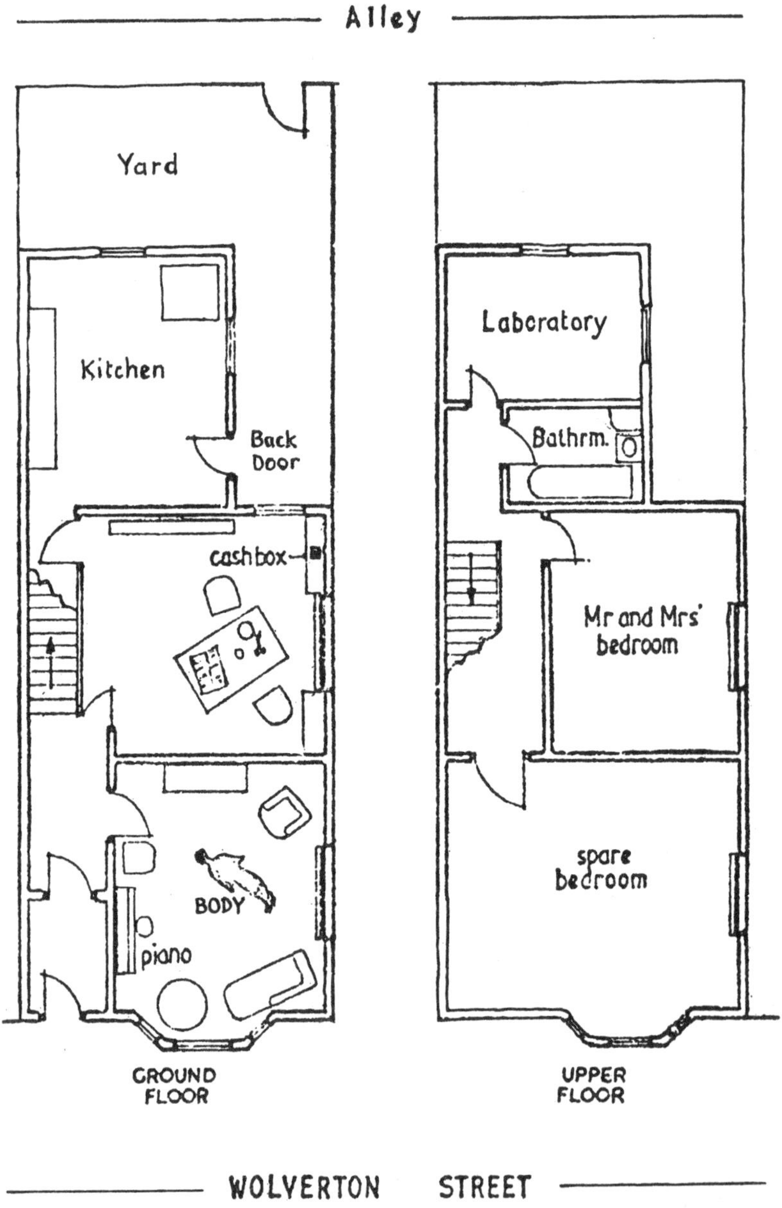

Alley

Yard

Kitchen

Back Door

cashbox

Laboratory

Bathrm.

Mr and Mrs' bedroom

BODY

piano

spare bedroom

GROUND FLOOR

UPPER FLOOR

WOLVERTON STREET

Plan of the Wallace house.

upon the conductor of the first tram—the one nearest home. The early part of the alibi is obviously the most important; did he, being guilty, think it dangerous to attract attention to himself at that stage in the proceedings? Or did he, being innocent, make no inquiry, merely because he knew the way as far as Smithdown Road? We may note at this point that Wallace appears never to have tried to establish an alibi in the strict sense of the word. He never suggested, for instance, that he was already out of the house by the time the milk-boy came. A villain in a book would, one feels, not have neglected this important point; but the argument cuts both ways, since a definite statement about times may be challenged; a mere vagueness leaves the onus of proof upon the prosecution.

Next comes the evidence of Sydney Herbert Green, a clerk, who found Wallace wandering about Menlove Gardens West and looking in vain for Menlove Gardens East. Green informed him that there was no such place. Wallace then said he would try 25 Menlove Gardens West. This he did, asking the wife of the occupier whether anybody called 'Qualtrough' lived there. She said no, and he went away.

Then came a complication which was very damaging for Wallace, for whem he had inspected Menlove Gardens North and South he roamed along Menlove Avenue and then found himself (by his own account unexpectedly) in a road which he did know. Between Menlove Avenue and Allerton Road runs Green Lane, and in Green Lane lived a Mr Crew, who was a superintendent of the Prudential Assurance Company and whom Wallace had visited on five occasions to take violin lessons. This, said the prosecution, proved that Wallace was lying when he said he did not know the district. Mr Crewe said in cross-examination that the violin lessons had been given two years ago and always on winter evenings after dark. There are, of course, some people who, after passing half a dozen times along a tram-route by night are familiar with every crossing and turning to left and right of the route, and who never visit a house without making themselves acquainted with all the surrounding streets. Others (of whom the present writer is one) allow themselves to be carted incuriously from point to point, remaining in the end as ignorant of the general topography of

the district as when they started. Wallace, if one may trust to
his evidence, was of the latter sort. 'How used you to go to
Woolton Woods with your wife?'—'I probably inquired of
some driver of a car, which car would take us there and got on
that car.' A statement which, if untrue, was well invented to
square with his known behaviour on the night of the crime. As
for knowing the lay-out of Menlove Gardens, Mr Crewe, who
had lived just round the corner for three and a half years, said
definitely in evidence that, previously to the trial, he himself
had not had any idea whether there was a Menlove Gardens
East or not.

At any rate, suggested counsel, when Wallace found himself
in Green Lane, why did he not call at Mr Crewe's house and ask
his assistance in finding 'Qualtrough's' address? Wallace replied that he did; he knocked at the door but could get no
answer. Mr Crew was, in fact, out that night; so that the
statement was not capable of disproof.

Having failed here, Wallace met a policeman and again
inquired for Menlove Gardens East. The constable said, cate-
gorically, that there was no such place: there was Menlove
Gardens, North, South and West, and Menlove Avenue, but no
Menlove Gardens East. He suggested that Wallace should try
25 Menlove Avenue (which he pointed out); Wallace thanked
him and then asked where he could find a directory. The
constable said he could see one at the newsagent's in Allerton
Road, or at the police station or post office. Wallace then
explained, 'I am an insurance agent looking for a Mr Qualtrough who rang up the club and left a message for me with my
colleague to ring up [? visit] Mr Qualtrough at 25 Menlove
Gardens East.' Whether this outburst of confidence was a
necessary part of alibi-faking, or was merely the ordinary
citizen's apologetic anxiety to justify his existence in the eyes of
the police, is again a matter of interpretation. Wallace then
said, 'It is not 8 o'clock yet?' and the constable agreed that it
was only a quarter to. The alibi again? or only a reasonable
desire to know whether the newspaper shop would still be
open? However that may be, it is in the shop that we next find
Wallace at 8.10, searching the directory for Menlove Gardens
East. In the meantime, he had apparently been looking for the

post office, but could not find it. He hunted the directory for some time, and then said, 'Do you know what I am looking for?' The manageress said (not unnaturally) that she did not, he then told her that he was looking for 25 Menlove Gardens East. She then assured him that there was no such place. Curiously enough, he does not seem to have mentioned the name of Qualtrough in the shop; he said that he looked for the name in the book and could not find it; and by this time he was probably convinced that, whoever Qualtrough was, he was not a householder.

It was now about 8.20, and according to Wallace himself, he was beginning to get a little alarmed. If he was innocent, this was perhaps not unnatural. There did seem to be something rather queer about 'Qualtrough', and he could not but remember that there had been one or two recent burglaries in the neighbourhood of Wolverton Street, and that it was a well-known trick of burglars to lure away householders with bogus telephone messages. Further, this was a Tuesday night—the night when, as a rule, he had a good deal of the insurance money in the house. So, giving up the vain search for Qualtrough, he walked to the nearest tram-stop to begin the journey home.

In the meantime, Mr John Sharpe Johnston, an engineer, who lived next door to the Wallaces at 31 Wolverton Street, was getting ready to go out with his wife for the evening. The two families had been neighbours for the last ten years, and knew one another, in Mrs Johnston's own words, 'as neighbours'. There seems to have been no very great intimacy. In all those years Mrs Johnston had been into No. 29 'about three times', and then only into the front sitting-room. On all three occasions Wallace had been absent, so that Mrs Johnston had never seen the Wallaces together in their own home; nor, evidently, had the two women been accustomed to run in and out of each other's back kitchens in the informal way that neighbours sometimes fall into. Mr Johnston had, indeed, seen the Wallaces together from time to time, and thought them 'a very loving couple, very affectionate'; but he cannot have known them very well, for he had never heard Mrs Wallace's Christian name—or, if he had, not often enough to remember what it was. Of one thing, however, the Johnstons were quite certain: they had never heard any quarrelling going on next door, though, since the houses shared a party-wall, they would have been likely to hear anything exciting that there was to be heard.

A little before 8.45 on the Tuesday evening, the Johnstons heard somebody knocking, as it might be with a fist or palm of the hand, at the Wallaces' back door. This was nothing unusual, so they paid no particular attention to it. On going out, by way of the back door, into the entry that runs parallel to Wolverton Street, they met Wallace, just coming down at an ordinary walking pace from the Breck Road end of the entry towards his own back door. To Mrs Johnston's polite 'Good evening, Mr Wallace,' he replied only with the question. 'Have you heard anything unusual tonight?' Mrs Johnston said, in some surprise, 'No—why? What has happened?' To which Wallace replied: 'I have been round to the front door and also to the back, and they are both fastened against me.'

It is at this point that the detective-story writer becomes exasperated with the published accounts of the case. To him the exact mechanism of locks and bolts is meat and drink, and in writing his books he makes his witnesses offer precise information on the subject, illustrating his points, if necessary, with neat diagrams. Now, in the Wallace case, we are concerned with no less than three doors and their fastenings, all of which are of the utmost importance; yet, of these, one lock only seems to have been brought into court, and of that there is no published description, while the witnesses are maddening vague in their evidence, so that it is often difficult to say whether by 'lock' they mean a mortice-lock or a safety-lock, or even the mechanism of the door *handle*; whether by 'bolt' they mean an iron bolt, or the catch of a safety-lock; and even whether by 'back door' they mean the kitchen door or the yard door leading to the entry. By careful piecing together of the various statements, we may, however, come to the following conclusions.

1. The front door was the one by which Wallace was accustomed to let himself in with his own key on returning home at night. From the data furnished in evidence, it seems likely that

the lock was an automatic lock, though not of the 'Yale' type; but it is clear that no key can have been left in it on the inside, as this would prevent its being opened by another key from without. It may even have been a small mortice-lock, which Wallace would lock after him, removing and carrying away the key. This door also had a bolt, which is not described. It may have been a safety-catch or a small and easily sliding bolt immediately beneath the lock-plate. If it was a stiff, heavy or double bolt, then one suggestion that was made becomes quite incredible, as will be seen. It is really extraordinary that so few details should have been reported about this bolt.

2. The back *kitchen* door seems to have had a handle, a bolt or bolts, and possibly also a lock. The mechanism of the handle seems to have been stiff and faulty.

3. The back *yard* door had apparently a latch and a bolt. It is not perfectly clear from the evidence whether it was this door or the back kitchen door which Wallace expected his wife to have bolted after him when he left; he apparently contradicted himself a little about this, but no energetic effort seems to have been made to clear the matter up.

In any case, when Wallace told the Johnstons that both doors were fastened against him, they were 'all standing in the entry before the door into the entry had been opened'. As to what followed, let us look first at Mr Johnston's evidence as given at the trial:

> What did you say to him then?—I suggested that he tried the door again, as if it was the back door, and if he could not open it, I would get the key of my back door and try.

[By a process of deduction, we may see what Mr Johnston had in his mind. Here was no question of a Yale lock, for which another person's key would be useless; and it would be equally useless to try to open an ordinary lock from outside if the key had been left in the lock *inside*. Therefore, he must have thought that Mrs Wallace had gone out by the back and taken the key with her.]

> When you said, 'Try again' and you would see, what did he do?—He went up to the door.

[Apparently the back door of the house; see later.]

> Did Mr Wallace say anything when he went in, or when he went up the
> yard?—When he got to the door, he called out, 'It opens now.'

[Mrs Johnston's evidence here interestingly supplements her husband's. She remembered that Wallace, as he crossed the yard, looked back over his shoulder and said: 'She (meaning his wife) will not have gone out; she has such a bad cold.' Here we have then, Wallace answering, and rebutting, Mr Johnston's unspoken assumption in the matter of the key.]

> Were you able to hear, from where you were, whether he tried with his
> key or anything?—No, he did not seem to try the key; he seemed to turn the
> knob in the usual way.—And said, 'It opens now?'—Yes.
> Mr Justice Wright: Could you see?—Yes; I could see him at the door,
> my lord.

To supplement this, we have Wallace's own statement made at the police station.

> I . . . then pulled out my key and went to open the front door and found
> it secure and could not open it with my key. I then went round to the back.
> The door leading from the entry to the back yard was closed, but not
> bolted. I went to the back door of the house and I was unable to get in. I do
> not know if the door was bolted or not; it sticks sometimes, but I think the
> door was bolted, though I am not sure. . . . I tried my key in the front door
> again and found the lock did not work properly.

Putting these two statements together, it is clear that Wallace meant it to be understood that he had tried first the front door, then the back door *of the house*, and then the front door again, and that he was coming round to the back for the second time when he met the Johnstons in the entry. It is perhaps a little surprising to find Mr Johnston asserting that their conversation took place 'before the door into the entry had been opened'. Did Wallace, then, carefully shut it behind him after his first fruitless attempt on the back door of the house? Unless the door had a spring, and shut to of itself, he must have done; and this does not look very much like agitation of mind. A similar unnecessary carefulness proved the downfall, under cross-examination, of Fox the matricide. Curiously enough, nothing seems to have been made of this point by the prosecution.

Now, with regard to the back door of the house: nobody, except Mr Johnston when he offered the help of his own key, seems to have suggested that it was locked at any time. Wallace said he thought at first that it was bolted, and subsequently came to the conclusion that the handle was merely stiff. At any rate, he eventually got in without using any key. And at this point we may take the evidence given subsequently by a locksmith.

> Witness produced another lock which he said was from the back kitchen door and found to be rusty. When the knob was turned, with difficulty, the spring bolt remained inside the lock and the knob returned to its former position.

The mention of the 'knob' seems to show definitely that the reference is not to the lock, but to the latching mechanism operated by the door handle. This evidence gives support to the theory that Wallace, when he first tried the door, was misled by its stiffness into supposing it to be bolted when, as a matter of fact, the latch had merely stuck.

We shall have to come back later to this question about the locks. We will take up the story at the point where Wallace opened the door, as described by Mr Johnston, and went in, leaving his neighbours in the yard. They do not seem to have noticed any light in the back kitchen (Wallace said that there was a gas-jet, reduced to a very feeble glimmer, over the sink); upstairs, however, the windows of the 'middle bedroom' where the Wallaces slept, and of the 'back room' which Wallace used as a workshop, were dimly lit, as though the gas had been left on, but turned down low.

After Wallace entered the house the Johnstons heard him call out twice, and shortly afterwards they saw first the light in the middle bedroom turned up full and then a match struck in 'the small room at the top of the stairs'. In 'about a minute and a half' Wallace came hurrying out, saying to them: 'Come and see; she has been killed.' His manner, observed Mr Johnston, who was a witness commendably free from any tendency to exaggerate language, 'seemed a bit excited'. Mrs Johnston said he spoke 'in a distressed tone, his words were very hurried you know'—by which, as she explained, she meant 'agitated'.

At this news they all went into the house. Wallace led them through the back kitchen and the main kitchen, where he had already lit the gas, and into the front sitting-room, where a dreadful sight awaited them. The body of Mrs Wallace lay stretched upon the hearth-rug, her feet near the gas-fire and her head towards the door. Her skull had been brutally battered in with such force as to scatter her brains about the floor, and her blood was splashed all around—on the carpet, on the arm-chair by the fireplace, on the violin-case lying on the seat of the chair, and on the wall behind. Mrs Johnston cried out, 'Oh, you poor darling!' and felt the dead woman's hand. It is not recorded what either of the two men said; but Mr Johnston reported that Wallace appeared, all the time, 'as though he was suffering from a shock. He was quiet, walking round; he did not shout, or anything like that.'

There was plenty of light to see the grisly state of things, because, when Wallace had first gone into the house he had lit the gas in the sitting-room. He was cross-examined over and over again about his movements, and nothing could be clearer, or one might think, more natural, than the account he gave. He said that, after passing through the back kitchen, he opened the door into the main kitchen, which was where he would have expected to find his wife, if she was still sitting up. It was dark, and he lit the gas (which was sensible of him if he wanted to see where he was going), and then, matchbox in hand, he went straight upstairs to see if his wife was in the bedroom, calling to her as he went. Here he turned up the light, and, finding the room empty, searched the other rooms on that floor with the aid of his matches, and then came down again to try the front sitting-room—the last place where she might be expected to be, but the only other room in the house.

> The door was closed to, and I pushed it a little open, and then I struck a match in quite the ordinary way, that I probably did every night I went into the room in the dark. I held it up, and as I held it up I could see my wife was lying there on the floor.
>
> You told the officer that you thought she was in a fit?—That was my first impression, but it only lasted possibly a fraction of a second, because I stooped down, with the same match, and I could see there was evidence of signs of a disturbance and blood, and I saw that she had been hit.
>
> Did you light the light?—Yes, I did.
>
> Which light?—The one on the right-hand side near the window.
>
> Why did you light that one?—It is the one we always use.

Now, the questions asked by the prosecution about this were directed to two points. First: Why, unless he knew beforehand that he was going to find a body on the floor, did he strike a match on the sitting-room threshold at all? He could have seen his way into the room quite well by reflected light from the kitchen. And secondly: Why did he walk round the body to light the farther of the two gas-jets, instead of the one nearest to him?

Now these, one would say, were the sort of questions that could only occur to a man who had never in his life had anything to do with gas. It is absolutely automatic with anyone who lives in a house with gas-lighting, to strike the match *at the threshold*, if he thinks he may have occasion to light the gas; so much so, that the present writer, for some time after making the changeover from gas to electricity, could seldom enter a room at night without first striking a match in the doorway or, at least, making a tentative gesture towards the pocket that held the matchbox. Equally automatic would be the action of lighting the accustomed gas-jet; since a jet that is seldom used may easily turn out to have a clogged burner or a broken mantle, and the realization of this, though quite subconscious, is enough to inhibit entirely any recourse to that jet in an emergency.

Having lit the gas, felt his wife's hand and looked at her injuries, Wallace, as he said, saw that she was quite dead, and at once rushed out and called his friends. It is difficult to see what else he could have done; and all this part of the story seems perfectly consistent with his innocence.

Seeing that poor Mrs Wallace was past all help, they all three went back into the kitchen, and there Wallace drew their attention to the lid of a cabinet, which appeared to have been wrenched off and was lying on the floor. Then he reached up to a shelf and took down a cash-box. Mr Johnston asked whether anything was missing. Wallace said he thought about £4 had gone, though he could not be certain until he looked through his books.

This business of the cash-box is rather mysterious. It was presumably examined for finger-prints, but no evidence about this seems to have been given.[1] Wallace's prints would have

[1] The point was put to Detective-Sergeant Bailey in cross-examination, but he replied vaguely, and the matter was apparently never cleared up.

Julia Wallace.

been on it in any case, since he handled it to take it down; if there were others, we hear nothing of them. It was said, 'Why, if an outside murderer had stolen the money, should he have so carefully replaced the box on the shelf?' It might, with equal force, have been asked why, if Wallace wanted to pretend that the murderer had been there, did *he* put it back? Common sense would have suggested that he should produce the appearance of as much disorder as possible. Like almost everything else in this extraordinary case the question cuts two ways. Then, how did it happen that there had been so little money in the box? Wallace's accounts were gone into very carefully at the trial, and everything he then said was found to be correct. On an ordinary Tuesday he would have had about £30 or £40 of the company's in his possession, ready for paying in on the Wednesday, which was the regular accounting day; on one Tuesday in each month he might have as much as £80 or £100, or even more. On this particular Tuesday, however, he had less than usual, first, because he had been laid up with influenza on the Saturday and had not made his round; secondly, because out of the £14 or so he had collected on the Monday and Tuesday (his other regular collecting-days) he had paid away about £10 10s. 0d., in sick benefit; thus leaving about £4. Let us see which way this evidence tells.

1. Supposing that there was an outside murderer, why did he not come on the Monday night, when he knew that Wallace was safely occupied with his chess-match?—Answer: Because his intention was to steal the insurance money, and what he wanted was to get Wallace out of the way on the *Tuesday* night, when a bigger sum would have been collected.

2. If the intention was to steal, why did not the thief select some night when both Wallace and his wife were out of the house?—Answer: Because (as Wallace said in evidence) when they were both out of the house they always took any of the company's money with them for greater safety.

3. But how could an outside murderer have known this?—Answer: If there was an outside murderer, he was obviously somebody well acquainted with Wallace and his habits, as is clear from other considerations mentioned earlier.

4. If Wallace himself was the murderer, would he not also

select the Tuesday night, in order to suggest that the murderer was a thief in search of the insurance money?—Certainly he would.

5. In that case, since he *did* know and was probably the only person who *could* know that there would be less money that week than usual, why did he not postpone the crime a day when he could stage a really impressive robbery?—This question is difficult to answer; unless, of course, Wallace had some idea that he might be called upon to make good the loss; in which case his failure to collect on the Saturday might all be part of the plan.

It should be said at once that there was never any suggestion that Wallace himself committed the crime for money: his accounts were all in order; there was only the £4 of insurance money; no private liabilities were disclosed; his wife was insured for the trifling sum of £20, and, though she had £90 in the savings-bank, Wallace's own bank balance was £152—ample for any emergency.

After looking at the cash-box Mr Johnston suggested that Wallace should go and see if anything had been taken from upstairs. Wallace went up and came down almost at once, saying: 'There is £5 in a jar they have not taken.'

Mr Johnston then went out for the police, and Mrs Johnston went back with Wallace into the blood-bespattered sitting-room. Here, he stooped over his wife, and said, 'They have finished her; look at the brains.' Mrs Johnston, not unnaturally, seems to have preferred not to look at any such thing; instead, she gazed round the room and said, 'What ever have they used?'

Wallace made no suggestion about this; he got up and came round to the other side of the body and then said, 'Why, what ever was she doing with her mackintosh, and my mackintosh?'

Mrs Johnston then saw that there was a mackintosh lying, as she expressed it, 'roughed up' and almost hidden under the body. (Later, a policeman with a gift for description said it was 'as though it had been put in this position round the shoulder, and tucked in by the side, as though the body was a living person and you were trying to make it comfortable.') Mrs Johnston was not quite sure whether Wallace had said 'her' or

'a' mackintosh; she was, however, quite positive that he ended
his sentence by identifying the mackintosh as his own. Aban-
doning the problem of how the garment came there, the two of
them then went into the kitchen. The fire was nearly out—'just
a few live embers'—and Mrs Johnston, 'feeling that she must
do something', relit it, with Wallace's assistance. Then, while
they waited together in the kitchen, Wallace, who till then had
been 'quite collected', twice broke down and sobbed for a
moment, with his head in his hands.

Now Mrs Johnston offers us a little more evidence about the
front door:

> A little later there was a knock at the door, I understand?—Yes.
>
> Did you try to open the door?—Yes.
>
> Were you able to?—No; it is a different lock to mine, and I think I was
> agitated, and I drew back and let Mr Wallace open it.
>
> Do you know whether or not the door was bolted?—I do not.
>
> If he [Wallace] says he undid the bolt, you would not contradict him,
> would you?—I do not know whether he did, but I cannot remember that.

Nothing here is said about the necessity of a key to open the
door from the inside: Mrs Johnston merely attributes her
failure to agitation and the fact that the lock was of another
pattern from her own. Nor does it seem likely that she could
have failed to notice the drawing of a heavy bolt or of the double
bolt. The door, at any rate, was opened to admit a policeman;
and he said that he did not hear any bolt withdrawn.

To this policeman, by name Frederick Robert Williams,
Wallace said: 'Something terrible has happened, officer.' The
policeman came in, examined the body, and then heard Wallace's account of his efforts to enter the house, at the front, at the
back, at the front again—'this time I found the door was
bolted'—again at the back—'this time I found it would open.'
Both then, and later, at the trial, Wallace asserted quite
definitely and positively that the front door was actually bolted
when he let P.C. Williams in, and this is one of the most
extraordinary points about the case. If Wallace was innocent,
then it is difficult to see why the real murderer or anybody else
should have bolted the door; if he was guilty, then, by sticking
to the tale of the bolted door (which rested on no evidence but
his own), he probably did more damage to his own case than by
any other thing he said.

Leaving the matter of the bolts for a moment, let us accompany P.C. Williams on his tour of the house. Omitting the questions of examining counsel, his story ran more or less like this:

> In the middle bedroom the gas-jet was lit; accused said he changed in this room before going out and left the light burning. On the mantelpiece I noticed an ornament from which five or six £1 notes were protruding. Accused partly extracted the notes, and said, 'Here is some money which has not been touched.' I requested him to put the ornament and notes back, which he did.

P.C. Williams should have spoken sooner; a smear of blood was subsequently found on one of the notes, but by that time it was impossible to say that it had not got there from Wallace's hands after his examination of the corpse.

> I approached a curtained recess to the right of the fireplace. Accused said, 'My wife's clothes are there, they have not been touched.' I looked in, and apparently they were undisturbed. In the back room which has been converted into a laboratory, accused said, 'Everything seems all right here'. In the bathroom there was a small light; accused said, 'We usually have a light here.'

So far, everything seemed to square with Wallace's story. Next comes a very curious little circumstance, which squares with no imaginable theory of the crime.

> We went into the front bedroom. It was in a state of disorder; the bed-clothes were half on the bed and half on the floor; there were a couple of pillows lying near the fireplace; there was a dressing-table in the room, containing drawers and a mirror, and also a wardrobe; the drawers of the dressing-table were shut and the drawers of the wardrobe were shut.

On the subject of the front bedroom, the published evidence is more vague and unsatisfactory even than it is about the locks. Counsel for the defence seems to have asked the prisoner:

> It is said that the bed in the front bedroom was somehow disarranged, and there were some of your wife's hats on it?—Yes.

[This is all we ever hear about the hats.]

> Do you know anything about that?—I do not think I had been in that room for probably a fortnight before the 20th or the 19th January.

Here the detective-story writer (and, one would think, everybody else) would ask instantly: Did your wife often go into the room? Were there sheets on the bed? If so, were you, or was your wife proposing to sleep there on the night of the 20th? Why? Did you always occupy the same room as your wife, and if not, why not? According to Wallace, his wife's bedroom 'would look down on the yard' (i.e. she slept in the 'middle bedroom'), and, since he himself changed his clothes in that room, the presumption is that he occupied it with her; but the position is never made clear. If the room was merely a spare room, then, one asks: What is the meaning of the disorder? Would an outside thief and murderer overlook the occupied bedroom with its five £1 notes on the mantelpiece, and make straight for the spare room? And why should he there confine himself to ransacking the bed, either omitting to open any drawers and cupboards, or else carefully shutting them all up after him? And if the murderer was Wallace, trying to present a convincing picture of a search for valuables, then why did he stage it, so absurdly, in this room rather than in the other?

It seems highly probable that the disorder in the front room had nothing to do with the murder; there is, however, a curious and interesting parallel in the case of the Gilchrist murder (Edinburgh, 1909). Here, the murderer, after battering his victim to death, made straight, not for the old lady's own bedroom where she kept her jewels in the wardrobe, but for the spare bedroom, where, disregarding various articles of value upon the dressing-table, he broke open a box containing papers. In this case, however, the murderer is known to have been interrupted in the middle of his activities, and it has been suggested that some paper, and no ordinary valuable, was the real object of his search. Our detective novelist might play with two theories in this connection: (1) The rather melodramatic one that the murderer of Julia Wallace was in search of something that he had cause to believe might be found secreted under the spare room mattress; or (2), the idea that Wallace, in staging his murder, deliberately modelled his effects upon the Gilchrist case; this might explain his curious insistence in the matter of the bolted front door, and his subsequent statement that he at first believed the murderer to be still in the house.

Having searched the bedrooms, they went downstairs again. In the kitchen Wallace showed P.C. Williams the cabinet and the cash-box, and also picked up a lady's handbag from a chair, saying that it belonged to his wife. It contained a £1 note and some small change. They were then joined in the sitting-room by Police Sergeant Breslin, in whose presence Williams observed: 'That looks like a mackintosh.' Wallace, who was standing in the doorway, said, 'Yes, it is an old one of mine,' and, glancing out into the hall, added, 'it usually hangs here.' It was not until past 10 o'clock that the mackintosh was closely examined. By that time Superintendent Moore had arrived, and he, after hearing Wallace's story and examining the rooms and doors of the house, again asked Wallace whose the mackintosh was. This time Wallace seemed to hesitate in his answer, and the Superintendent pulled the mackintosh out, saying, 'Take it up and let's have a look at it. It's a gent's mackintosh.' Wallace said, 'If there are two patches on the inside it is mine,' and, finding the patches, continued in the same breath, 'It is mine.' A great deal was made, later, of this brief hesitation; it appears, however, quite natural that, seeing the importance the police were inclined to attach to the mackintosh, Wallace should have thought it well to verify, by proof, his first general impression that the garment was his.

When the mackintosh was pulled out it was found to be heavily spattered with blood on the right side, both inside and out. Also—which was more remarkable—it was very much burnt, and part of Mrs Wallace's skirt was burnt also. Yet the gas-fire before which she lay was not alight when the body was found. Two theories were advanced to account for the burning. One was that the murderer (in that case Wallace) had tried to destroy the mackintosh by burning it at the gas-fire and had accidentally burnt Mrs Wallace's skirt in the process; the other, that the fire had been alight when the murder was committed, that Mrs Wallace had fallen against it and set her skirt alight, and that either she was wearing the mackintosh at the time, or that the murderer had been wearing it and had burnt it in stooping to turn out the gas.

In the same way, two theories were advanced to account for the blood. Mrs Wallace (who had a cold) might have slipped the mackintosh loosely about her shoulders for warmth, let the murderer in at the door, stooped down to light the gas fire and been struck down with the mackintosh still about her; or else, the murderer might himself have put on the mackintosh to protect himself from bloodstains.

One thing seemed fairly clear: unless the murderer had had some sort of protection he must have been heavily spattered and stained with blood. Now, throughout the house, there were no signs of bloodstains (except, of course, in the sitting-room), other than the smear on the £1 note in the bedroom and a small clot on the lavatory pan in the bathroom, which, it was admitted, might have been dropped there by one of the numerous policemen[1] who were roaming about the place all night. There were no damp towels in the bathroom and no appearance that anybody had recently taken a bath. Nor was any blood found on Wallace, nor on any clothes belonging to him.

Next comes the question of the weapon. The charwoman, Sarah Jane Draper, gave evidence that since her last visit on January 7th two objects had disappeared from the house: the kitchen poker and an iron bar that was usually kept in the sitting-room for cleaning under the gas fire. Search was made for these all about the house and yard and in every conceivable place, including the drains, along the tram route between Wolverton Street and Menlove Gardens where they or one of them might have been thrown away; but neither of them was ever found. Nor was any suggestion ever put forward why two weapons should have been used or why either of them should have been removed (unless, indeed, on the general principle of 'making it more difficult'). For consider: whoever did the murder, it was to his advantage to leave the weapon in the house. There are only three reasons for getting rid of a weapon: (1) To conceal the fact that a murder has been committed at all; in this case no attempt was made to pretend that the death was suicide or accident. (2) To prevent identification by finger-prints; in this case finger-prints could easily have been wiped off. (3) To destroy a ready means of identification, as, for instance, where the murderer uses his own pistol or walking-

---

[1] These included a constable, a police-sergeant, a detective-sergeant, a detective-inspector and a detective-superintendent. Novelists who restrict their commission of inquiry to a 'man from the Yard' and a gifted amateur are letting themselves off too easily. But it is hard work inventing names and characteristics for so many different policemen.

stick; in this case the weapon was identified only with the house itself, and if the murderer came from outside, the use of a weapon identified with the house would assist him in throwing the blame on Wallace, whereas, if Wallace himself was the murderer, by far the readiest way of fixing suspicion upon himself was to use a weapon belonging to the house *and remove it*, since its removal created a strong presumption that no weapon had been brought from outside. Whichever way one looks at it, the carrying away of the weapon (still more, two weapons) was an idiotic and entirely unnecessary error, involving the risk of discovery. Still, somebody made that error and took that risk, and since it could benefit nobody it gives us no help in solving the mystery. It seems likely that the weapon actually used was the iron bar; the poker, if it was not used to break open the cabinet, may have been lost on some other occasion, or Mrs Draper have merely imagined the loss of a poker.

The body itself was examined by various medical witnesses, who, as usual, differed a good deal about the probable time of death. Professor MacFall, called by the prosecution, judged, from the fact that *rigor mortis* was present in the neck and upper part of the right arm when he saw the corpse at ten o'clock, that death had taken place 'four hours or more' before his arrival. Since Mrs Wallace had been seen alive by the milk-boy certainly not *earlier* than 6.30, this witness *must* have been at least half an hour out in his calculations. Dr Pierce, also a witness for the prosecution, agreed with him in giving 'about six o'clock' as the probable time of death. Prosecuting counsel at this point supplied the world with an admirable example of the folly of not letting well alone:

> You say about six o'clock. What limit on either side would you give?—I would give two hours' limit on either side.
> Mr Justice Wright (*pouncing on this admission of human fallibility*): It might have been between four and eight?—Yes, my lord.
> Counsel (*making the best of it*): Would you say that death could not possibly have occured after eight o'clock?—I would say definitely it could not have occurred after eight o'clock.
> Cross-examining Counsel (*consolidating his advantage, after ascertaining that witness had omitted to apply all the tests he might have applied*): When you say you think it was six o'clock, it might have been four o'clock in the afternoon or might have been eight o'clock?—And there were other factors as well.
> So it follows she might have met her death at any hour within this time that night?—Yes.

From all this the detective novelist may well conclude that he ought not to allow his medical men to be too dogmatic in deducing the exact time of death from the appearance of the body. In fact, in the words of Professor Dibble, F.R.C.S., who was called for the defence, 'it is an enormously difficult subject, full of pitfalls'. Nothing, in fact, emerged at the trial except that it was probable, on the whole, that Mrs Wallace was murdered round about the time that Wallace left the house. This is exactly what one would expect. If Wallace did it, the only possible time was between about 6.30 and about 6.50; if anybody else did it, he would no doubt have entered the house as early as possible after Wallace's departure, so as to give himself an ample margin for retreat.

To go back to the night of the murder: Superintendent Moore, who came on the scene at 10.5, carefully examined all the doors and windows of the house, and found no signs that anyone had broken in. Having borrowed Wallace's latchkey and tried it in the front door, he found that, though it would open the door with a little trouble, the lock was defective. Wallace, when told, said, 'It was not like that this morning'— though, actually, it turned out that the lock must have been out of order for some time. Wallace's first account was that the first time he tried the front door lock the key would not turn and that the second time he became convinced that the door was bolted. Superintendent Moore's account was that the key had a tendency to slip round in the lock, and 'that if the key was turned beyond a certain point it would re-lock the door'. At one point Wallace adopted Superintendent Moore's explanation, and was much criticized because this did not agree with his earlier account of the matter.

It seems quite possible that both Wallace's accounts were perfectly honest. When he first arrived at the house the key may have stuck in the defective lock as he said. The second time it may have turned too far, as it did with Superintendent Moore, and re-locked the door. Wallace, in the flustered state of his mind, finding that, though the key turned, the door would not open, may have jumped to the conclusion that the bolt had been shot between his two attempts. As to his saying, 'it was not like that this morning', that may amount to no more than any

man's natural reluctance to admit that he can have made a
conspicuous ass of himself. It is curious that he did not,
apparently, on that night, inform Superintendent Moore that
the door had been actually bolted when he opened it to admit
P.C. Williams.

Apparently, however, he had told P.C. Williams and he may
well have thought this enough. At the trial he said, wearily, that
he really could not remember what he *had* said to the Superintendent. After all, when one has had to tell the same story half a
dozen times in one night, and innumerable times since then, it
may be difficult to remember exactly to which policeman one
told what details of it.

We may bring down the curtain upon the third act of the
tragedy by quoting two little word-pictures of Wallace's de-
meanour on that memorable night. Professor MacFall said:

> I was very struck with it, it was abnormal. He was too quiet, too
> collected, for a person whose wife had been killed in that way that he
> described. He was not nearly so affected as I was myself. . . . I think he was
> smoking cigarettes most of the time. Whilst I was in the room, examining
> the body and the blood, he came in smoking a cigarette, and he leaned over
> in front of the sideboard and flicked the ash into a bowl upon the
> sideboard. It struck me at the time as being unnatural.

Detective Inspector Herbert Gold, who arrived on the scene
at 10.30, agreed that Wallace was 'cool and calm'.

> When I first went into the house on the night of the murder, he was
> sitting in the kitchen. In fact, he had the cat on his knee and was stroking
> the cat, and he did not look to me like a man who had just battered his wife
> to death.

Wallace's own comment, in an article written after the trial,
was:

> For forty years I had drilled myself in iron control and prided myself on
> never displaying an emotion outwardly in public. I trained myself to be a
> stoic. My griefs and joys can be as intense as those of any man, but the rule
> of my life has always been to give them expression only in privacy.
> Stoicism is so little practised today that when seen it is called callousness.

The Emperor Marcus Aurelius is, it would seem, not the
wisest counsellor for those who may have to make their appearance before a British jury.

At about four or five o'clock on the Wednesday morning,

Wallace was allowed to leave the house to sleep—supposing he could sleep—at his sister-in-law's. During twelve hours of the next day he was detained at the police station, making a statement and answering questions about his movements on the Monday and Tuesday evenings. In particular, he was told that the fateful telephone call had been put in from a call-box in the Anfield district near his own home.

The consequence of this was that on January 22nd, happening to meet Mr Beattie, Wallace questioned him very closely about the exact time of the call, adding, most unfortunately for himself: 'I have just left the police; they have cleared me.'

This conversation was reported back to the police, who, of course, pounced on it like tigers. Why should Wallace be so much interested in the time? Why should he announce that he was 'cleared' when nobody, so far, had suggested that he was suspected? As to the first, Wallace replied: 'I had an idea; we all have ideas; it was indiscreet of me.'

Asked at the trial to amplify this cryptic remark, he explained that by this time he had realized he might be suspected and thought that, if he could ascertain from Mr Beattie that the call had been put through at seven, whereas he himself did not leave his house till 7.15, it would be a complete proof of his innocence. Thinking it over, he saw that for him, a suspected person, to be seen talking to a witness in the case, was an indiscretion. Yes; but *why* should he imagine himself suspected? To which Wallace replied that if his conversation with Mr Beattie had been reported he must have been followed and watched, and that this showed clearly that he *was* suspected, a fact which he realized at the time. Looking at it from the purely common-sense point of view, one must confess that Wallace would have been a fool indeed *not* to realize that, in a case where a married woman is murdered, the husband is always the first person to be suspected. It was in fact admitted by the police witnesses at the trial that, between the time of the murder and of the arrest, Wallace had to be given police protection while he was collecting his insurance money because the people in the district were hostile to him. Some further light may be thrown on his statement, 'I had ideas; we all have ideas,' by the fact that on that same January 22nd he mentioned the name of a

certain man, known to him and his wife and connected with the
Prudential, who was the object of his own suspicions. This
person turned out to have an alibi, and nothing, of course, was
said about him at the trial; but it is quite likely that he may have
had something to do with Wallace's indiscreet 'ideas'. On the
same occasion, Wallace mentioned the name of another possible suspect, and, after his death in 1933, papers were found
among his belongings in which he named the murderer. Nothing, however, was discovered that definitely pointed to the
guilt of anyone else, so on February 2nd Wallace was arrested
and charged, and on March 4th, at the conclusion of the police
court inquiry, was sent up for trial at Liverpool Assizes.

It is not necessary to go through the trial[1] itself, since most of
the important points in the evidence have already been discussed. We may, however, spend a little time in examining the
theory of the prosecution as it eventually took shape in court.

The theory was that Wallace, having prepared his alibi the
evening before, suggested to his wife after tea that they should
have one of their customary violin practices in the front room.
While she went to light the gas fire and get the music ready
Wallace went upstairs and stripped himself naked, so that his
clothes should not be stained with blood. He then slipped on
the mackintosh, came down, and, catching his wife just as she
was stooping to light the fire, struck her dead with repeated
blows from the iron bar, with which he had already armed
himself. Then, wiping his bare feet on the hearth rug, and
perhaps making a hasty attempt to burn the incriminating
mackintosh at the gas fire, he went upstairs, dressed, dis-
arranged the front room and broke open the cabinet in the
kitchen and then hurried out to catch his tram and establish his
alibi, taking (for some reason or other) the bloodstained
weapon with him.

As regards this part of the theory, several criticisms may
occur to us. To commit a murder naked is no new idea; the
thing was done by Courvoisier, who murdered Lord William

---

[1] April 22, 1931, before Mr Justice Wright; for the Crown, Mr E. G. Hemmerde, K.C.,
Recorder of Liverpool, and Mr Leslie Walsh; for the defence, Mr Roland Oliver, K.C.,
and Mr S. Scholefield Allen.

Russell in 1840, and it was suspected in the case of Lizzie Borden, tried for murdering her father and stepmother in Fall River, Massachusetts, in 1892. But the mackintosh complicates the matter. It can scarcely be supposed to have been slipped on in order to take Mrs Wallace more effectively by surprise; even if the poor woman had been given a preliminary warning by the startling apparition of a naked husband on the threshold, the smallness of the room would have enabled him to spring upon her before she could escape or call for assistance. The only conceivable justification for the mackintosh would be a curious prudery. That is not impossible. In the lower middle class there is no doubt many a man who would not—literally to save his life—appear mother-naked before his wife, even if he knew for certain that that astonishing sight was the last sight she was doomed ever to see in the world. Yet it seems strange that a murderer who had shown so much foresight in preparing the alibi should have allowed such a consideration to influence him. As for the suggested attempt to burn the mackintosh, a moment's thought would suggest that the proper place for that was not the gas-fire in the sitting-room, but the coal fire in the kitchen, which, at 6.30, when they had just finished tea, must have been burning cheerfully. It was stated in evidence that the mackintosh was of a material that would burn easily; an hour in the kitchen grate would probably have destroyed all but the buckle and buttons, which might easily have escaped search or identification. It is most unlikely that the burning of the mackintosh was anything but accidental, whoever committed the murder.

The second point is, of course, the witlessness of the disturbance created in the front room and elsewhere. Anybody wishing to suggest that a thief had gone upstairs would have removed the £1 notes from the middle bedroom and flung open the drawers and wardrobe as though in search for money.

The third unsatisfactory point is the time factor. It is astonishing what can be done in twenty minutes, which was the longest time possible that Wallace can have had at his disposal. Still, he must, at any rate, have washed his face, hands and feet, and that so carefully as to leave no smear of blood anywhere in the bathroom, dressed from top to toe, broken open the cabinet

and rifled the cash-box and administered (again without leaving a trace) as much rough cleaning to the iron bar as would
enable him to carry it away without staining anything it
touched. The thorough removal of bloodstains is no very quick
or easy matter, as anybody knows well who has tried to clean up
the mess produced by a cut finger.

The other part of the theory brings us back to the vexed
question of the locked doors. The theory was that Wallace, in
order to get witnesses to his discovery of the body, pretended
that he could not get in, when, in fact, he could have done so.
We may, I think, dismiss any suggestion that he had in fact
entered the house before encountering the Johnstons. What
they heard and saw agreed very well with the estimated time of
his arrival home and his account of his own actions. They heard
him knocking, as he said, at the back door and, a few minutes
later, met him coming down from the end of the entry as
though, in the interval, he had been round to the front. If he was
the murderer he would probably not risk making an actual
entry, which might be observed by someone living in the street,
if he was going to deny it afterwards.

Let us assume that Wallace is guity and is endeavouring to
present a picture of a murder committed by a third party. It is
going to be a ticklish business—more ticklish than it appears at
first sight. The proper handling of bolts and locks has in all
likelihood planted more grey hairs in the heads of detective
novelists and other planners of perfect murders than any other
branch of this amiable study. Let us see how it must have
presented itself to him—remembering that his meeting with the
Johnstons was entirely fortuitous, and could not have entered
into his calculations one way or the other.

First, then, the simplest way to suggest an intruder from
without is, obviously, to follow the excellent example set by the
wicked Elders who accused Susannah. They, it will be remembered, 'opened the garden doors' and subsequently testified
that an apocryphal young man had been in the garden 'and
opened the doors and leaped out'. So, the apocryphal murderer
must be supposed to have left the house by some means or
other, and the most natural thing would be to make it appear
that he escaped either by the front, leaving the door on the

automatic lock, or by the back, leaving the door latched, or—more picturesquely—wide open as though in rapid flight. But alas! Where a murderer could get out Wallace could get in, and this would mean 'discovering' the body without any witness to support him. He must, therefore, find 'both doors locked against him'. But he cannot *really* find them so, for two reasons: (1) because he is not skilled as the murderers of fiction in shooting inside bolts from the outside by means of strings and other gadgets, and (2) because, if he did, then by hypothesis the murderer would be still inside the house when Wallace arrived with his witnesses, and it would be exceedingly difficult to fake the hasty departure of a non-existent murderer after the door was opened. He must, then, only *pretend* to be unable to get in, and *pretend* to suppose that the murderer might be still in the house. As a matter of fact, he did say all along that his first thought was that the murderer was still there, but that he abandoned that theory when they got in and found the house empty. Now, it is at this point that the emergence of the Johnstons from their back door must have upset the plans of a guilty Wallace most horribly. But for them he might have pretended that his knocking at the back door had disturbed the murderer, who must have then opened the kitchen door and fled while Wallace was trying the front for the second time. With the Johnstons there to see and hear anybody escaping, he could not very well put up that story.

Supposing the Johnstons had not come out, could the story have held water? The detective of fiction would say no; and for this reason: A cautious medical witness, inspecting a corpse at 9 o'clock, may find it difficult to say precisely whether the person was killed within two hours either way of 6 o'clock. But he will have no hesitation in saying whether or not death took place within the last quarter of an hour or so. 'I would say definitely,' said Mr Pierce, 'it could not have occurred after 8 o'clock.' That being so, how could the murderer be supposed to have been occupying the time between the murder and Wallace's return? To explain such unaccountable lingering on the scene of the crime, one would have to present the picture of a thorough ransacking of the house from top to bottom; and this, as we know, was not done. But a consideration of this kind would probably not have occurred to Wallace beforehand, or perhaps to anybody except a detective novelist.

But, as things turned out, there the Johnstons were: and now what was Wallace to do about the front door? Was he still to insist that it had been bolted, put it on the bolt (if this had not been already done), and draw the Johnstons' attention to the bolt? This he certainly did not do, and it is odd that it does not seem to have occurred, either to him or to Mrs Johnston, to verify that matter of the front door bolt while they were waiting for the police. If, on the other hand, Wallace, thinking his story over, had decided to leave the question of the bolt in a decent obscurity, it is odd that he should have persisted at the trial in asserting that it *was* bolted, when, in the meantime, the police themselves had offered him a perfectly good explanation for his inability to make the door open. Perhaps he felt that, having once told P.C. Williams the door was bolted, he had better stick to his story. Perhaps, when all is said and done, it really was bolted and he was telling the truth. The more we examine the question the more complicated it becomes, espeically when we are left in such doubt as to the exact machinery of the lock.

Then again, if Wallace, having come back in the ordinary way and been unable to get in at the front, had gone round to the back and found the door locked, this ought not to have surprised or alarmed him. In the ordinary way it would be locked, since Mrs Wallace would expect him to enter by the front. His story was that he was both surprised and alarmed. Why? Because of the queerness of the telephone call and the fact that he could see no light in the front kitchen. But if the curtains of the front kitchen window were drawn he could not have seen a light in any case, so why the alarm? To this he replied that by looking sideways at the back kitchen window one could have seen the light shining through from the front kitchen. Not if the door between the two kitchens was shut? Well, no. This did not seem satisfactory. If he thought his wife was upstairs, why did he not shout to her instead of knocking gently? Wallace replied simply that he did not think of it. If he had been trying to give the impression that the noise he made had scared the murderer away, one would rather expect him to make as much hullabaloo as possible. On the other hand, too much hullabaloo might have brought out the neighbours. The neighbours did, in point of fact, come out for another reason.

That Wallace's mind was confused, both at the time and after, about the locked doors is evident. He said, for instance, that when he could get in by neither door, he at first thought his wife might have slipped out to the post. This is inconsistent with the statement that he thought a man was in the house, but is not in itself unreasonable, and is supported by his remark to the Johnstons as he crossed the yard. He might, in that case, having tried and failed at the front door and got no answer at the back, have thought that Mrs Wallace had 'slipped out' the back way, locking the back door after her and taking the key. If so, it would naturally be useless to shout at her bedroom window, and he would go round and make another attempt on the front door while waiting for her return. And it was possibly then that he first became really disturbed in his mind. It is not easy to remember the exact sequence of one's actions or thoughts in a moment of agitation. His own phrase, used in the course of cross-examination, probably corresponds with the feelings of the normal person in such a situation: 'I was both uneasy and not uneasy, if you follow me.' One has often felt like that: vaguely worried yet able to present one's self with a number of possible explanations, inconsistent with one another, but all quite credible separately.

And, of course, the fact remains that both those locks *were* defective, and had been so for a long time. Whether Wallace, knowing this, used the circumstance deliberately to throw an atmosphere of confusion about the whole case, or whether he was genuinely mistaken in supposing both or either of the doors to be fastened, it seems not impossible to say. It is pretty certain that he did not himself deliberately damage either of the locks in advance in order to support his story.

Now let us take the other side of the question. Suppose Wallace was innocent, how did the murderer get in? The answer was suggested by the defence. He presented himself at the front door and was let in by Mrs Wallace, saying that he wanted to leave a note for Wallace or wait for his return. She had thrown Wallace's mackintosh over her shoulders before opening the front door (we know she had a slight cold at the time). She took the murderer into the front parlour (the usual place for receiving guests and strangers) and was there struck down. Her skirt caught fire. The murderer extinguished the flames with the bloodstained mackintosh, turned out fire and gas-light, bolted both doors in order to have notice of Wallace's return (?), washed his hands in the back kitchen (?), refled the cash-box and cabinet, and departed, leaving the back door latched (and the front door still bolted?) and carrying the iron bar with him (!)

There are, of course, difficulties about this too. We know that there were several people, including the two men suspected by Wallace, whom Mrs Wallace would readily have let in if they had called. She would also, if Wallace had told her (as he said he did) about the message from 'Qualtrough', have let in anyone giving that name. Whoever the caller was, he was probably known to Mrs Wallace, so that she had to be murdered lest she should identify him later. Would not the intending murderer in that case have brought his own weapon with him? We do not know that he did not. We have no evidence that the iron bar was the weapon used. We know only that it disappeared. An outside murderer might, seeing it handy, have used it in preference to his own or, more subtly, having used his own, he might have removed the iron bar for the express purpose of incriminating Wallace. In fact, the only thoroughly satisfactory reason anybody could possibly have for taking it away would be that it was clean and, therefore, if left behind, could *not* incriminate Wallace. But one cannot expect (outside a detective novel) a thoroughly satisfactory reason for any person's actions.

An explanation of the iron bar's disappearance is offered by Miss Winifred Duke in her novel, *Skin for Skin*, which presents a reconstruction of the crime on the hypothesis that Wallace was the murderer. She makes him conceal the bar in his umbrella and drop it down a drain at the far end of his tram journey, in the neighbourhood of Menlove Gardens. The only reply that can be made to this is that the police said they had searched 'everywhere', and they can scarcely have omitted to search the Menlove Gardens district. Wallace could scarcely have carried it very far afield, for his time-table leaves no room for such an excursion. If the bar had been found in the neighbourhood, it would have certainly incriminated Wallace. Since it was never found it incriminates nobody, and such witness as it bears is slightly in Wallace's favour. Its chief function is to darken counsel. Indeed, the iron bar has bothered everybody who has attempted to deal critically with the case.

Our alternative theory does indeed leave us with the blood-stained murderer obliged to clean himself and escape. But whereas Wallace had twenty minutes only in which to do everything and then travel by tram, the 'other man' had getting on for two hours and might then remove himself inconspicuously on foot (possibly to a bicycle, or a car parked somewhere handy). He had more time for cleaning, and he need not appear so scrupulously clean.

Further, we are not obliged to suppose that the outside murderer went upstairs at all. The £1 notes would then be left unappropriated because he never went near them, and the bathroom clean and dry because he did not wash himself there. As for the front bedroom, the likeliest explanation of all is that the murderer never went there and had nothing to do with it. His ring at the door may have disturbed Mrs Wallace when she was engaged in turning over the bedding for some domestic purpose of her own. Perhaps she had piled the bed-clothes and pillows on the foot of the bed, and they fell off, as they usually do in such circumstances. The appearance of the room, as described, is more suggestive of some such household accident than of a search by a thief.

The trial itself occupied four days. Wallace himself made a very good witness—too good, perhaps, for a jury. He was, as ever, 'cool and collected', and there is no kind of prisoner a jury dislikes so much, except, indeed, a hot and agitated one. But he impressed the judge. 'When reference is made to discrepancies in his statement,' said Mr Justice Wright summing up, 'I cannot help thinking it is wonderful how his statements are as lucid and consistent as they have been.' Counsel for the prosecution, though as usual conspicuously fair in the general treatment of the case, perhaps helped a little to confuse the issues by arguing, from time to time, as though the defence was that 'Qualtrough's' call was a genuine business inquiry, which

it could not on any hypothesis have been; while Mr Roland
Oliver, in endeavouring to cast contempt upon the theory of the
prosecution, asked the prisoner, absurdly enough, 'Were you
accustomed to play the violin naked in a mackintosh?' which
again confused the issue. The defence also attacked the police
vigorously for not having called the newspaper girl and the
little boys who supported her testimony, going so far as to
accuse them of deliberately suppressing evidence in order to
give colour to their case. This may have prejudiced the jury,
who commonly do not care to hear the police attacked, though
the judge, while deprecating the attack, said he thought the
police had committed an error of judgment. There was probably also a certain amount of prejudice arising from the evidence that had already come out in the magistrate's court, and
from the general tendency to suspect married persons of
murdering one another. But the chief difficulty in the way of the
defence was the difficulty with which we started out: that the
common man, however well he knows that his duty is to ask,
'Did this man do it?' will insist on asking instead, 'Who could
have done it, if not this man?' It is perfectly evident, in the
judge's summing-up, that he was aware of this difficulty. He
summed up dead in the prisoner's favour, and again and again
repeated his caution that the verdict must be given according to
the evidence.

> Members of the jury, you, I believe, are living more or less in this
> neighbourhood: I come here as a stranger . . . you must approach this
> matter without any preconceived notions at all. Your business here is to
> listen to the evidence, and to consider the evidence and nothing else. A
> man cannot be convicted of any crime, least of all murder, merely on
> probabilities . . . if you have other possibilities, a jury would not, and I
> believe ought not to, come to the conclusion that the charge is estab-
> lished. . . . The question is not: Who did this crime? The question is: Did
> the prisoner do it? . . . It is not a question of determining who or what sort
> of person other than the prisoner did the crime or could have done the
> crime; it is a question whether it is brought home to the prisoner, and
> whether it is brought home by the evidence. If every matter relied on as
> circumstantial is equally or substantially consistent both with the guilt or
> innocence of the prisoner, the multiplication of those instances may not
> take you any further in coming to a conclusion of guilt. . . . In conclusion I
> will only remind you what the question you have to determine is. The
> question is: Can you have any doubt that the prisoner did it? You may
> think: 'Well, some one did it.' . . . Can you say it was absolutely impossible

Menlove Gardens North – an important part of Wallace's alibi.

that there was no such person [as an unknown murderer]? . . . Can you say . . . that you are satisfied beyond reasonable doubt that it was the hand of the prisoner, and no other hand, that murdered this woman? If you are not so satisfied, if it is not proved, whatever your feelings may be . . . then it is your duty to find the prisoner not guilty.

The jury, after an hour's retirement, found the prisoner guilty.

The prisoner, being asked if he had anything to say, briefly replied: 'I am not guilty. I don't want to say anything else.'

In passing sentence, the judge, whose summing-up had been a most brilliant exposition of the inconclusive nature of the evidence, pointedly omitted the customary expression of agreement with the verdict.

It is said that, when the verdict was announced, a gasp of surprise went round the court. On the general public, if not on the jury, the summing-up had produced a deep impression.

Nor, whatever rumours may have been going about beforehand in the neighbourhood of Wolverton Street, was the main body of Liverpudlians at all happy about the conviction. Their extreme uneasiness led to one result which was logical enough, no doubt, but highly unusual in this Christian country: a special Service of Intercession was held in Liverpool Cathedral that God might guide the Court of Criminal Appeal to a right decision when the case of Wallace came before it.

The answer to prayer might be considered spectacular. On May 19th, the Lords of Appeal, after a two days' hearing quashed the conviction on the ground that the evidence was insufficient to support the verdict; this being the first time in English legal history that a conviction for murder had been set aside on those grounds. The phrasing of the judgment is exceedingly cautious, but, in the words of the learned barrister to whom we owe the best and fullest study of this extraordinary case:

> The fact that the Court of Criminal Appeal decided to quash the conviction shows how strong must have been the views of the judges that the verdict was not merely against the weight of evidence, but that it was unreasonable.

Judges in this country are, indeed, exceedingly jealous of any interference with the powers and privileges of a jury, and will in general always uphold its verdict unless they see very strong reason to the contrary.

The judgments of God, unlike those of earthly judges, are, however, inscrutable. Any writer of fiction rash enough to embellish his *dénouement* with an incident so unlikely as a public appeal to Divine Justice must interpret the answer according to his own theological fancy. If he believes that the All-Just and All-Merciful declared for the innocent through the mouths of the Lords of Appeal, the facts will support that theory; but if he believes that the world is ruled by an ingenious sadist, eager to wring the last ounce of suffering out of an offending creature, he may point out that Wallace was preserved only to suffer two years of complicated mental torture and to die at length by a far crueller death than the hangman's rope. Like every other piece of testimony in the Wallace case, the evidence may be interpreted both ways.

The Prudential Assurance Company, who had behaved throughout in a very friendly way to Wallace, expressed their full belief in his innocence by at once taking him back and giving him a new job in their employment. It was, however, impossible for him to continue with his work as a collector on account of the suspicion which still clung about him. He was, in fact, obliged to leave Liverpool and retire to a cottage in Cheshire. The diary which he kept for a year after his release contains many references to the rebuffs he received from his former acquaintances, together with expressions of his love for his wife which have every appearance of being genuine. He seems to have spent his spare time pottering about his garden and equipping his home with little ingenious household gadgets, and trying every means to fight off the appalling loneliness of spirit which threatened to overcome him. 'What I fear most is the long nights.' 'I seem to miss her more and more, and cannot drive the thought of her cruel end out of my mind.' 'There are now several daffodils in bloom, and lots of tulips coming along. How delighted dear Julia would have been, and I can only too sadly picture how lovingly she would have tended the garden.'

On September 14, 1931, occurs a remarkable passage:

Just as I was going to dinner —— stopped me, and said he wanted to talk to me for a few minutes. It was a desperately awkward position. Eventually I decided not to hear what he had to say. I told him I would talk to him some day and give him something to think about. He must realize that I suspect him of the terrible crime. I fear I let him see clearly what I thought, and it may unfortunately put him on his guard. I wonder if it is any good putting a private detective on to his track in the hope of something coming to light. I am more than half persuaded to try it.

Other allusions to the same person are made from time to time. Are we to believe them sincere? Or must we suppose that all this was part of some strange elaborate scheme for bamboozling the world through the medium of a private diary, which there was no reason to suppose that anyone was likely to see but Wallace himself? That he should have made this kind of accusation (as he did) in newspaper articles proves nothing; but the diary (which is far more restrained and convincing in style than the statements published over his signature) is another matter. One can only say that, if he was a guilty man, he kept up the pretence of innocence to himself with an extraordinary assiduity and appearance of sincerity.

On February 26, 1933, Wallace died of cancer of the kidneys. It is, of course, well known that disease affecting those organs produces very remarkable and deleterious changes in a person's character; but whether the trouble had already begun in 1931, and if so, whether it could have resulted in so strange a madness, with such a combination of cunning and bestial ferocity as the murderer of Julia Wallace displayed, is a matter for physicians to judge. So far as can be seen, Wallace showed no signs of mental or spiritual deterioration either before or after the crume.

It is interesting to compare the case of Wallace with that of the unfortunate clergyman, the Rev. J. S. Watson, who in 1869 murdered his wife under rather similar circumstances. Here, again, it was the case of a childless couple who had married for love and lived peaceably together for many years. The husband, a man of mild behaviour and considerable literary ability, suddenly seized the opportunity one afternoon, when the servant was out of the house, to batter his wife to death with exactly the same uncontrolled brutality as was used on Mrs Wallace. But here the resemblance ends. Poor Mr Watson had for some time shown symptoms of melancholia and disturbance of mind; the wife was known to drink; there had been quarrels; and the husband, though at first he denied his guilt, soon after made an attempt at suicide and confessed the crime; nor, though he at first made some blundering efforts to cover up his tracks, did Watson contrive anything remotely approaching the elaborate ingenuity of the 'Qualtrough' alibi. The superficial resemblances only serve to emphasize the fundamental disparity between the two cases.

Though a man apparently well-balanced may give way to a sudden murderous frenzy, and may even combine that frenzy with a surprising amount of coolness and cunning, it is rare for him to show *no* premonitory or subsequent symptoms of mental disturbance. This was one of the psychological difficulties in the way of the prosecution against Wallace. Dr MacFall gave it as his opinion that the brutality of the murder was a sign of frenzy. He was asked:

> So, if this is the work of a maniac, and Wallace is a sane man, he did not do it?—He may be sane now.
>
> If he has been sane all his life, and is sane now, it would be some momentary frenzy?—The mind is very peculiar.
>
> The fact that a man has been sane fifty-two years, and has been sane while in custody for the last three months, would rather tend to prove that he has always been sane?—Not necessarily. . . . We know very little about the private lives of persons or their thoughts.

The mind is indeed peculiar and the thoughts of the heart hidden. It is hopeless to explain the murder of Julia Wallace as the result of a momentary frenzy, whether Wallace was the criminal or another. The crime was carefully prepared in cold blood; the extraordinary ferocity of the actual assault was probably due less to frenzied savagery than to sudden alarm at the actual moment of the murder. It has, over and over again, come as a shocking surprise to murderers that their victims took so long to die and make such a mess about it; they have struck repeated blows, to make sure, confessing afterwards, 'I thought she would never die'; 'Who could have thought that the old man had so much blood in him?'

Before leaving the case for the consideration of those who may like to make of it a 'tale for a chimney-corner', two small points ought perhaps to be mentioned. One is the statement

made by a young woman at the trial that on the night of the
murder she saw Wallace at about 8.40 at night 'talking to a
man' at the bottom of the entry to Richmond Park, near Breck
Road. She did not know Wallace at all well, and he himself
denied the whole episode. In all probability she was quite
mistaken, nor could anything very much be made out of the
story either by the prosecution or the defence; it is mentioned
here only for completeness and for the sake of any suggestion it
may offer for the novelist's ingenuity to work upon. The only
practical step that was taken about it seems to have been that
the police made an especially careful search of the waste ground
in and about Richmond Park in the hope of finding the iron bar;
but without success.

The second point concerns the choice of the name 'Qualtrough'. This name is extremely common in the Isle of Man,
and should also, therefore, be pretty familiar to Liverpudlians.
It might therefore seem a suspicious circumstance that Wallace
should have professed never to have heard it before, but that it
was apparently unknown also to Mr Beattie, and that among
Wallace's other acquaintances at the chess club only one said
he had 'heard it once before'. Now, if one is preparing to give a
false name, one will, as a rule, give a name that is exceedingly
common, such as Brown or Smith, or one that is subconsciously
already in one's mind for some reason or another. Since, to
Manxmen, the name 'Qualtrough' is apparently as familiar as
'Smith' to an Englishman, it might seem reasonable to look for
a murderer who either came from Man, or frequently went
there for reasons of business or pleasure. On the other hand, if it
could be shown that Wallace (either through the books of the
Prudential or in some other connexion) had recently had the
name brought to his notice, then that fact would strengthen
suspicion against him, particularly in view of his categorical
statement that he had never heard it before. It is a little curious
that if the name was exceedingly well known in that part of
Liverpool, no one should have drawn attention to the fact in
evidence. The detective writer ought not, I think, to neglect
that line of investigation.

There, then, the story remains, a mystery as insoluble as
when the Court of Appeal decided that there was no evidence

upon which to come to a conclusion. 'We are not,' said the Lord Chief Justice, 'concerned here with suspicion, however gravε, or with theories, however ingenious.' But the detective novelist does, and must, concern himself with ingenious theories, and here is a case ready made for him, in which scarcely any 'theory, however ingenious' could very well come amiss. It is interesting that the story should already have been handled twice by writers of fiction, and both times from the point of view that Wallace may have been guilty. Mr George Goodchild and Mr C. E. Bechhofer Roberts in *The Jury Disagree* have used the case only as a basis on which to erect a story which includes fresh incidents and complications not forming part of the actual evidence, and have given it a 'key-incident' solution in the recognized 'detective' manner. Miss Winifred Duke, in *Skin for Skin*, has followed the facts with scrupulous exactness, concerning herself almost exclusively with the psychological problem of how Wallace might have come to do it (if he did do it) and what effect it had upon him.

With both novels, the criminal's motive may be summed-up in the cynical words of *Marriage à la Mode*:

> Palamede: O, now I have found it! you dislike her for no other reason but that she's your wife.
> Rhodophil: And is not that enough?

It remains for some other writer, who does not find it 'enough', or who is convinced by his study of the case that Wallace was telling the truth, or who merely prefers the more out-of-the-way solution to the more obvious one, to tell the story again, identifying 'Qualtrough' with that to us unknown man whom Wallace himself named as the murderer.

AFTERWORD

A personal note: when I was twelve, my family moved to the Merseyside village of Bromborough. I had just built myself a canoe, and the couple living in the bungalow opposite our house kindly offered to let me keep it in their loft. I was astonished and not a little thrilled when the local boys told me not to set foot in the bungalow because a murderer *had once lived there. The older villagers remembered him well. They at least had no doubt that he had 'done away with' his wife and, I gathered, had taken every opportunity to make their views clear to him.*

More than twenty years after Wallace's death, in the village to which he had retired he was still a sort of bogeyman.

For someone who was acquitted it seems a harsh fate, and most modern criminologists would uphold that final verdict—indeed, they have gone to great pains to try and establish once and for all Wallace's innocence. Not long ago there was an unofficial re-trial in Liverpool, where the evidence was reconsidered and, I gather, the 'real' murderer was identified: a man known to both Wallace and his wife, but still alive and who therefore could not be named publicly. For obvious reasons, this cannot be explored further at this moment, but it is highly probable that some day soon the Wallace case will be—well, perhaps not solved, but certainly re-opened.

Sightseers often visit the Menlove complex of streets in Liverpool, but not to try and find Menlove Gardens East or anything else to do with William Herbert Wallace. They are looking for Penny Lane, which is just around the corner, or Strawberry Fields, or Menlove Avenue, where Auntie Mimi looked after the young John Lennon, another victim.

ALEXANDER WOOLLCOTT

The Elwell Case

ALEXANDER WOOLLCOTT

The Elwell Case

In a sense which would have delighted Sherlock Holmes, the Elwell murder was marked by a set of extremely prominent teeth. You may remember the mystery in which Holmes called the attention of the Scotland Yard inspector to the curious incident of the dog in the nighttime.

'But,' said the obliging inspector, 'the dog did nothing in the nighttime.'

'That,' said Holmes, 'was the curious incident.'

In the murder of Joseph B. Elwell, his false teeth provided a similarly curious incident. In fact they were so conspicuous by their absence that they became important evidence in the case.

When Elwell's housekeeper, arriving for work as usual on the morning of June 11, 1920, found her kind employer dying in the reception room with a bullet wound in his forehead, the gleaming teeth which had illumined many a seductive smile in his career as a philanderer, were not where she had always seen them. They were upstairs in the glass of water beside his bed.

Upstairs also was the entire collection of toupees which had long helped to maintain the illusion that he was still a dashing young blade. Forty wigs there were in that hidden collection, yet not one of them was on his head when his fate came roaring at him out of the muzzle of a .45 automatic on that June morning twenty-three years ago.

Before that day's sun was high in the heavens, detectives and reporters were delightedly swarming over the Elwell house, which, since his housekeeper, valet and chauffeur all slept out, was exceptionally convenient for hanky-panky.

In particular the reporters relished the boudoir delicately furnished for a guest, the monogrammed pajamas left behind

Joseph Elwell on one of his racehorses.

there by one greatly embarrassed visitor, and the long telephone directory—obviously compiled with loving care—of fair ladies, each of whom was promptly called upon for an alibi.

But if one thing is certain about Joseph Elwell's death, it is that he would have shot himself rather than let one of these ladies see him as the bald and toothless old sport he really was.

The press yearned to assume that that bullet was fired by a woman scorned, but although there is no doubt that Elwell was a ladies' man, the one who killed him was certainly no lady.

This case caused the greater stir at the time because not since a Pittsburgh defective named Harry Thaw shot and killed the great Stanford White had the victim of a murder been a man already so widely known. For this Joseph B. Elwell was the Ely Culbertson of the bridge world shortly after the turn of the century.

In the days when contract was undreamed of and the courtesy of the time said that one might not even lead at all until one's partner had replied, 'Pray do,' to the question, 'Partner, may I play?' all earnest addicts studied *Elwell on Bridge*.

Elwell left the writing of these textbooks to his wife, and he also left his wife.

After their separation, he moved on up in the sporting world, with houses of his own at Palm Beach, Saratoga Springs, and Long Beach and, for a final touch of magnificence, a racing stable in Kentucky.

It was, however, in his New York house at 244 West 70th Street that he was killed, and only the night before he had been dining at the Ritz and attending the Midnight Frolic of the Ziegfeld Roof in company with men and women whose names and faces were already familiar in what later was to be known as Café Society.

All the evidence tends to suggest that he went home alone and remained alone at least until after the first visit of the postman next morning, for he had come downstairs barefoot and in his wrinkled pajamas, and was reading a letter out of the morning mail when he was shot.

Now the postman dropped that mail at 7.10 and the murderer had departed before the arrival of the housekeeper one hour later. It is difficult to escape the conclusion that the murderer was someone Elwell himself admitted, maybe someone he had sent for and was expecting, perhaps someone bringing a report from the early morning workout at a racing stable, certainly someone in whose presence he would not mind sitting with his wig off and his teeth out, reading a letter.

But why not a burglar trapped in the house and shooting his way out? Or why not an enemy—Elwell had more than one man's share of enemies—who, having gained access the day before, had been biding his time ever since? To each of these questions there are many answers, but one conclusive answer fits them both. It is difficult to imagine why an unexpected person would (or how any unexpected person could) have come around the calmly seated Elwell (whose chair, with its back to the wall, faced the fireplace), stood squarely in front of him and shot him between the eyes.

No, Elwell must have known Mr X was there. He merely did not know that Mr X was going to kill him.

One other point. The upward course of the bullet led the police to suspect that Mr X shot from the pocket or from the hip. Of course there is always the possibility that he may have been a midget, a belated suggestion which will either amuse or annoy him if he happens to read this memoir of his successful but anonymous achievement. Whoever he was, or wherever he is, he also has it on his conscience that he brought into this world one of the most irritating detectives in the whole library of criminous fiction.

It was the nice police problem presented by the Elwell murder which prompted a previously obscure pundit named Willard Huntington Wright to try his hand at his first of many detective stories. Under the pen name of S. S. Van Dine he turned Elwell's obituary into *The Benson Murder Case*, introducing for the first time that laboriously nonchalant, cultured, and tedious detective, Philo Vance.

ELIZABETH JENKINS

The Balham
Mystery

ELIZABETH JENKINS

The Balham Mystery

Some lives suggest irresistibly the theory of reincarnation; actions which their possessors commit appear to us no worse or more momentous than the identical actions committed by scores of others with complete impunity, yet in these lives their consequences are so profound, so ruinous, it seems impossible to believe that the cruel punishment was earned by the single act. We feel that some awful pattern of cause and effect is being woven on a plane that is beyond our immediate vision; that the retribution has been set in motion by the single act, but that it was earned elsewhere and at another time; that what we see in front of us is a short length of a chain whose beginning and end are hidden from us in this existence.

Such feelings are hard to withstand when one thinks about the Balham Mystery, with its victim, its criminal who was never named and the broken lives left in its wake.

The Campbells were a wealthy merchant family, with a country house, Buscot Park, in Berkshire, and a town house in Lowndes Square. They had several children, of whom the most interesting was their daughter Florence. This was an unusually attractive girl, radiant and gentle, but with a somewhat erratic strain of self-will. She was of a small, pretty, rounded figure, with large and widely set blue eyes, and a mass of hair that is variously described as red-gold and bright chestnut. There was no difficulty in marrying off such a charming creature, and in 1864, when she was nineteen, she was married to Captain Ricardo, a wealthy young guards officer of twenty-three.

Captain Ricardo undoubtedly had a great deal of money, but there his eligibility as a husband might be said to have begun and ended. The fact that he had married a beautiful girl of nineteen did not deter him from keeping a mistress, and the amount he drank seemed deplorable even to a hard-drinking age. Nor was he a man who could be left to drink himself under the table while a wife quietly pursued an independent existence; the unhappy bride was subjected to all the harassing torments of reconciliations, promises, relapses and promises again. Such an introduction to married life would have broken down most girls, and Florence was particularly unfitted to bear it. Her vitality was high—her glowing appearance and her strong natural faculty for enjoyment proclaimed it—but it was a purely physical characteristic. When she was subjected to any emotional strain she went to pieces, and the experiences of five years as Captain Ricardo's wife had all but reduced her to a nervous wreck. If she had been a plain woman, who had learned to adapt herself to slights and to make the best of what was going, she would have managed better; but she had come from an affectionate home, in all the natural self-confidence of a lovely girl. The shock and bewilderment, the undreamed-of humiliations of her position, had undermined her completely. There was only one consolation which she had found in her married life. It was drink, She had found out that the best way to endure Captain Ricardo's weakness was to share it.

By the time she was twenty-four she had sunk into absolute ill-health. Her mother persuaded her to come away to Malvern to try the hydropathic cure, and Captain Ricardo in one of his fits of reconciliation and promised amendment was to join her there. It was hoped, with singular optimism, that he, too, might find benefit from the water treatment.

Malvern had long been a spa, but it had developed with great rapidity as the Metropolis of the Water Cure, since 1842, when Dr Wilson and Dr Gully had settled there and introduced their system which had become nationally famous. Though Wilson had introduced the idea of hydrotherapy, which he had picked up abroad from a Bavarian peasant named Preissnitz, Gully was so much the abler man of the two that he soon became the leading figure, and in a few years had made Malver famous all over the British Isles. His system consisted in the application of water in every form: packing in wet sheets, sitz baths, douches, compresses, showers whether lateral or horizontal, spinal washings, foot baths, plunge baths and friction with dripping towels. His patients included Tennyson, Carlyle, Charles Reade, Bulwer Lytton, Bishop Wilberforce and 'a host of the favourites of society'. Though his success was sensational, there was no suspicion of quackery about him. He was a thoroughly trained medical man; and though his success was no doubt assisted by his great personal magnetism, the influence this gave him over his patients was a legitimate attribute of the eminent doctor. He was now sixty-two, not tall, but dignified and erect, with handsome, clear-cut features and an expression of warmth and candour.

Florence Ricardo had once been taken to Dr Gully when she was a child of twelve, so that her present visit to Malvern was in a sense the renewal of an old acquaintance. That she succumbed at once to the influence of Dr Gully's personality needs no explanation and hardly an excuse. She was ill because she was miserable and miserable because she was ill. Dr Gully treated her with the profound sympathy and scientific understanding, the warm, impersonal kindness, which only a doctor can bestow. She had never known anything like it. Her experience of men had begun at nineteen when she found herself married to a husband who left the house to go to a mistress and drank himself silly when he stopped at home. Though she was headstrong she was not self-reliant; she would have leaned on a husband if she could. As it was, her husband was weaker than she, and his scandalous ill-treatment of her alternated with fits of grovelling repentance and self-abasement. Dr Gully, who was authoritative, calm and kind, provided exactly the support that her unhappy state cried aloud for; above all, he was an exceptionally able physician, under whose care she got well again. It was no wonder that when her whole nature turned towards him with gratitude and admiration, her emotion overpassed the prescribed boundary and turned into romantic love. The fact that Dr Gully was old enough to be her father was no hindrance to this. Her devastating experience of a young husband made her yearn for the lover who would be also a father.

Matters were in this somewhat equivocal state when fresh outbursts on Captain Ricardo's part decided the Campbells that their daughter should not be asked to continue this existence; the outcome of their decision was that Captain Ricardo consented to a deed of separation by which Florence was to live apart from him and to receive an allowance of one thousand two hundred pounds a year. This took place in 1870. The following year, Captain Ricardo, who had retired to Cologne with a mistress, died there suddenly, before he had revoked the will made on his marriage. Thus at twenty-five Florence was left a widow, with four thousand pounds a year in her own right.

Her family regarded the event as a release, and yet the position was far from reassuring. Up till now Florence had been first under her parents' control, and then under the nominal control of a husband. She had not caused anybody anxiety, except by her unhappiness and ill-health, but if she had, her father or her husband could have exerted considerable pressure on her by the mere fact that she had no means of support except what either of them chose to give her. Now it was very different. As a widow, she was completely her own mistress, with a large income entirely at her own disposal. There she was, in Malvern, and there was Dr Gully.

Released from the monstrous bondage in which the first years of her adult life had been passed, her wilful, luxurious nature now asserted itself. To look at the likeness of her face, with its large, emotional eyes, its expression of mingled softness and intensity, is to feel that it is no unkind or unreasonable judgment that the motive force which brought together her and Dr Gully came from her. Dr Gully was a very busy man, in a large and exacting practice; not only had he been grounded in the high traditions of his profession, but if he had not been a man whose emotions were under his own control he would never have achieved his remarkable success. On the other hand, if a determined siege were to be laid to him, this of all others was the time of his life when it might be expected to succeed. He was nearing the end of his professional life. Though left to himself he would no doubt have continued in practice for some time longer, he was within sight of the time when he would have relinquished it in any case. He was extremely well-to-do (the income from his practice was estimated at ten thousand pounds), and though he was in fact a married man, his son was grown up and his wife, who was in an asylum, had been separated from him for thirty years. If anyone could be excused for regarding himself as a free agent when in actual fact he was not it was surely a man in the position of Dr Gully. On the other side Florence was very young, but she was not inexperienced. However impetuous her approaches had been, he would have been very unlikely to admit them had she been an unmarried girl, but her misfortunes had made her a woman of the world, and she was responsible to nobody but herself. At the same time, she was not only fascinating but she had the charm of youth, and to Dr Gully as a man of over sixty her devotion was not only enchanting, it was flattering to an unusual degree. It was difficult to prove at what date they became lovers, but it was afterwards considered certain that it was while Dr Gully was still in practice at Malvern. A great deal depended on this point, and when it was regarded as having been proved the decision was fatally unfortunate for him.

Florence very early in her widowhood became at variance with her family, who strongly disapproved of her infatuation for Dr Gully, and before long her parents told her that they would have no communication with her until she gave it up. So strong was the convention of the time that Mr and Mrs Campbell took this drastic step of refusing all intercourse with their daughter, although they imagined her infatuation to be indiscreet rather than actually immoral. It was a strange characteristic in a charming young woman that she was almost friendless. Perhaps her capacity to absorb herself in an emotional adventure argued a certain self-centredness that would repel a friend as it would attract a lover. At all events, her separation from her family left her without a social circle, and she accepted the offer of accommodation from her solicitor, Mr Brooks, in his house on Tooting Common. Mr Brooks had three daughters, for whom he employed a daily governess, an unremarkable woman of middle age, a widow named Jane Cannon Cox. The most noticeable feature of Mrs Cox's appearance was her spectacles, which apparently had the effect of quite obscuring the expression of her face. Drawings of her emphasize this so much that it seems likely the glasses were tinted. Her dark hair, in one of the less prepossessing fashions of the time, was scraped back from her temples and so arranged that the top of her head looked pointed like a bee-hive. The dress of the 'seventies, which concentrated all the fullness of the drapery at the back, left the front of the figure, rigidly corseted, tightly outlined from the shoulder to the knee. The effect on Mrs Cox's somewhat low and meagre frame was to give her the outline of a black beetle.

Mrs Cox had the efficiency and self-possession of a woman who has had to make her way against odds. Her husband had been an engineer in Jamaica, but he had died and left her to provide for three young sons. She had been assisted by a wealthy friend, a Mr Joseph Bravo. By his advice she had invested her small amount of money in a furnished house in Lancaster Road, Notting Hill, which she let, while she herself went out as a governess to Mr Brooks's family. Her three boys were placed at a school in Streatham for the sons of distressed gentlefolk. Quietness, respectability, usefulness and pleasantness to an employer were not, in Mrs Cox's case, mere unselfconscious traits of character; they would more properly be described as weapons, held in an unfaltering grasp, with which she waged the battle with the world that was to win the livelihood of her children and herself. She was not in any sense attractive, but her powers of mind were considerable, and since these were all directed towards making herself agreeable to people more fortunately placed than herself it was not surprising that she was successful. She soon made herself pleasant to the rich, voluptuous young widow, then useful and at last indispensible. Dr Gulley meanwhile, in 1872, sold his practice and retired from Malvern. His retirement was a civic event; demonstrations of respect and gratitude were made by every clas of society and the town acknowledged that it was his working there for thirty years which had brought prosperity to it. He did not immediately settle upon a house. He took lodgings opposite to Mr Brooks's house on Tooting Common.

That Florence had no friends of her own did not mean that she felt able to do without them. Her infatuation for Dr Gully was the most important thing in her life, but their liaison could not supply the want of a social circle. The usage of the time obliged the lovers to behave with the utmost secrecy and discretion. They could enjoy very little of each other's society in an open manner. Florence still needed a friend for daily wear, and as a rich and somewhat self-indulgent young woman she also wanted somebody to take the troubles of her establishment off her hands. It was not long before the idea of Mrs Cox presented itself to her, irresistibly. Mrs Cox seemed to have every qualification that Florence could imagine as desirable. She was excellent in household management, and she knew how to order an establishment for rich people, how to control a large staff of servants and to see that a high standard of comfort and elegance was maintained. Nothing was irksome to her, no trouble was too great; in a quiet and unobstrusive way she whole-heartedly identified herself with the owner of the establishment. Then, too, she was a gentlewoman; and though personally unattractive and in narrow circumstances, she was presentable as a companion, and in her tact, sympathy, affection and common sense she was quite invaluable. Mrs Cox, on her part, was exceedingly happy to exchange the drudgery and poor pay of a governess for the luxury and freedom, the authority, of friend and companion to such an employer as Florence Ricardo. The opportunity was indeed exceptionally fortunate. The generosity of Florence's nature had had few outlets, and she thoroughly enjoyed being good to Mrs Cox. Their footing was one of complete social equality; they called each other Florence and Janie. And Florence not only did everything possible to make her companion happy under her roof—Mrs Cox received a salary of one hundred pounds a year, but her incidental expenses, which were all paid for her, including many items of her dress, came to three times this amount—but her employer took a warm interest in Mrs Cox's three boys. Their school holidays were spent with their mother in Mrs Ricardo's house.

When Florence left Mr Brooks's house, taking Mrs Cox with her, she settled herself for the time being in a house in Leigham Court Road, Streatham Hill. The house she had occupied in Malvern, where the great bliss of her life had come to her, had been called Stokefield, and she named this house Stokefield also. At her suggestion Dr Gully bought a house which was available on the opposite side of the road. That a woman so astute as Mrs Cox should not have realized on what terms her employer and Dr Gully were anyone may believe who likes; but at least the polite fiction was kept up that the relationship was merely one of devoted friendship. Dr Gully often came to meals. He called his hostess by her Christian name, and they kissed each other. In Mrs Cox's opinion, he was 'a very fascinating man, likely to be of great interest to women'. She went so far as to say that, though she believed the friendship to be quite innocent, had Dr Gully been unmarried it would no doubt 'have been a match.'

In this year, 1872, Dr Gully and Mrs Ricardo went for a holiday to the baths at Kissingen. They attempted no deceit; they travelled under their own names and occupied separate rooms in their hotels, but as a result of their time abroad Florence had a miscarriage when she came home. Dr Gully attended her, but she was nursed by Mrs Cox. She said that she had at the time entirely concealed from Mrs Cox the cause of the illness, and made out, what she had in fact at first thought to be the case, that it was the result of a severe internal derangement brought on by the baths at Kissingen. Mrs Cox's untiring devotion to her during weeks of illness and prostration established the companion's claim on her more firmly than ever.

In 1874 Florence decided upon a permanent house. This was an estate of ten acres known as the Priory at Balham. The house had been built in the early 1800s and was a charming example of the Walpole Gothic, simple, airy, graceful, that was later to be submerged in the hideous Municipal Gothic of the Victorian age. The Priory, with its pale tint, its crenellated roof, its arched doorway, and windows with pointed upper panes, belonged to the last era in English social life that produced charming architecture. On the front lawn stood a giant oak tree, said to be a hundred and fifty years old. Behind was the sunny 'garden front', laid out in turf, gravelled paths and numerous flower-beds. There were a greenhouse, a grapehouse, a melon pit, large strawberry beds and a vegetable garden. Florence filled the house with luxury, gaiety and comfort. Her morning-room housed a sparkling collection of Venetian glass and opened into

The Priory, Balham.

a small conservatory. She liked this effect so much that she repeated it in the drawing-room, where she threw out one of the windows to make a fernery. Here she assembled a grove of exquisite ferns, for some of which she had paid twenty guineas each. Horticulture was one of her keenest enjoyments and she kept the garden in a high state of perfection, filling the beds with flowers and planting standard rose trees everywhere. The Victorian age was one of hot summers, and the windows of the Priory were shaded with striped awnings, which added their inimitable touch of festivity to the scene of a well-kept English garden on a hot summer day. Another of Florence's pleasures was driving. She kept one carriage horse for her landau—this was driven by her coachman; but she drove herself in a phaeton with two 'handsome actioned' cobs, called Victor and Cremorne. The pamphlet, *The Balham Mystery*, issued in seven numbers in 1876, contains instead of press photographs a series of pen-and-ink drawings of remarkable vividness. The press photographer has superseded the press artist, and it comes as a surprise to our generation to see how excellent the latter was. One of the illustrations shows Florence driving her cobs. The tiger sits behind with folded arms while she bowls along at a smart pace. The drawing shows a woman who drove very well. She wears a close-fitting jacket with a bow under her chin, and a wide-brimmed hat shaded by a feather, under which her hair streams away behind her ears. By her side, upright, collected and demure, sits Mrs Cox.

Within a few months of Florence's having bought the Priory Dr Gully bought a house in Bedford Hill Road, a few minutes away from the Priory lodge. The long slope of grass and trees terminating in the level ground of the Priory was unbuilt on, except for six houses, all of the same design, halfway up on the left-hand side. Dr Gully took the first, which was called Orwell Lodge. He, like Florence, seemed to regard his new establishments as a permanent one. He furnished it from top to bottom and installed his own servants, of whom the chief was his butler Pritchard, who was devoted to him and had been with him for twenty years. The neighbourhood in 1875 was still extremely retired. Bedford Hill Road was so quiet that when Florence built a second lodge to open the estate on that side, though the new lodge stood directly upon the road without the protection even of a paling, the climbing roses she trained all over its front hung undisturbed. There were no censorious neighbours to overlook their private lives. Dr Gully had a key to one of the doors of the Priory. The parlour-maid said: 'I never opened the door to him, but I have found him in the house.' He came frequently to lunch and stayed to dine. Once or twice when Mrs Cox was away he stayed the night. The Priory coachman, Griffiths, had previously been in Dr Gully's service. Now that Dr Gully had left off practice, he did not keep a carriage and Florence had taken Griffiths on. He and his wife lived in the new lodge. Three or four times a week Griffiths drove the doctor and Mrs Ricardo out in the landau. He would take up Dr Gully in one of the quiet roads near his house, and set him down again before he reached the gate of Orwell Lodge. Sometimes they drove in to London, but more often their drives were through the undisturbed country about Tooting Common. On frequent occasions Florence, accompanied by her chaperone, would come to meals at the doctor's house. When this happened, the butler Pritchard could see that, though his master and Mrs Ricardo were still very much attached to each other, the affair had become worn down to the level of ordinary existence. 'They often quarrelled,' he said.

The Bravos who had befriended Mrs Cox lived in a large house on Palace Green, Kensington. The family of three were Mr and Mrs Bravo and the latter's son by a previous marriage. Charles Bravo, who had taken his stepfather's name, was the idol, not only of his mother, but of his stepfather also. He was a good-looking young man, with dark hair, rounded features and an expression at once pugnacious and egotistical. Mr Joseph Bravo had brought him up from a child, educated him and seen him established at the bar. He doted on what he took to be the young man's great cleverness, and he loved him as fondly as if Charles had been in fact his son. Charles Bravo would not appear to have been strikingly gifted in the profession had had chosen. He was nearly thirty and his gains as a barrister were still almost nominal; but despite the fact that his stepfather gave him as much money as he could want, and that he had therefore no financial incentive to work very hard at an unrewarding profession, he did not the less devote himself to it. He went to his chambers every day and followed his profession as if his bread had depended on it. He had kept a mistress for the past four years, but the intense possessiveness of his mother and the indulgent kindness of his stepfather had so far prevented him from any inclination to be married.

One day Florence Ricardo went in the carriage to London to do a day's shopping and arranged to drop Mrs Cox at Palace Green to call upon her friends, and to pick her up again on the way home. When, later in the day, Mrs Ricardo's carriage was announced at the Bravos' door, Mrs Bravo courteously sent out a request that Mrs Ricardo would come in for a few minutes. It so happened that Charles Bravo was in his mother's drawing-room when the lady with bright auburn hair was shown in, but neither he nor she seemed at that time to take much notice of each other. The visit was short and, though extremely civil, was purely formal one.

In 1875 Dr Gully went abroad with some of his own relations. Though she might quarrel with him, Florence found her house dull and wearisome when he was not at hand, and to relieve the tedium of her lover's absence she took Mrs Cox on a visit to Brighton. It was autumn, and Brighton was not gay. The beauty of the Regency squares and terraces was not appreciated by the taste of the 1870s, and the half-empty streets and the sea under autumnal mists and gales did not restore Florence's spirits. They had themselves photographed, but there was really very little to do.

Brighton, however, is within very easy distance of London and its advantage as a resort is that so many people run down from London for the day. By a really remarkable coincidence, in one of their walks they met Charles Bravo. The first meeting between him and Florence had passed off apparently in complete indifference on both sides, but on the second one it seemed as if a seed, long germinating, had suddenly burst into flower. Mrs Cox was of course polite and cordial. It was not open to her to be anything else. Her paramount duty to herself and her children was to be pleasant to her employer, and whatever her opinion of the rapidly-forming intimacy might have been it would have had no weight with Florence. The latter might be dependent on her friend up to a certain point, but in anything which concerned her pleasures she was entirely her own mistress and intended to remain so.

Florence had not an admirable character, but one of her strongest charms was naturalness, and though her actions might be unwise or even discreditable they were always understandable and such as would arouse sympathy. Her passion for Dr Gully was almost inevitable and the same might be said of its termination. She needed the love and protection of an elderly man to restore her after the shattering experiences of her first marriage, but when this influence had done its work and her being had recovered its normal balance she was ready to fall in love again with a man of her own age. Charles Bravo and she were both nearly thirty. She was independent by legal settlements and he was virtually so through the affection of his stepfather. If they chose to marry there would be no need of a long engagement. Charles Bravo was undoubtedly much attracted by Florence, but it is equally certain that what induced him to think of marrying her was her income. They were, however, well suited personally: young, vigorous, pleasure-loving, a virile man and an extremely feminine woman. The growth of mutual attraction went on fast and it was obvious that Charles Bravo's proposal would soon be made.

In October Dr Gully returned to England and he came down to see Florence at Brighton. She now acted with great duplicity. She told Dr Gully that the estrangement from her family, which could never be ended as long as her liaison with him lasted, had made her very unhappy for some time, and as her mother was now ill she wished earnestly to be reunited to her parents. She had decided therefore that the time had come for them to part. Dr Gully behaved with the unselfish kindness of real affection, in spite of having received a very disagreeable shock. He had had no preparation for this event. He said afterwards: 'I was very much attached to her at the time, and I had thought that she was fondly attached to me.' But he said that she must do whatever she felt was necessary to her own happiness and well-being. In November Charles Bravo proposed to her and she accepted him. When Dr Gully heard of this, he was at first thoroughly angry. After giving up his practice and his public position as one of the most eminent doctors of the day, and being at her beck and call for five years, he now found himself cavalierly thrown over for another man and shamelessly deceived as well. He wrote her one angry letter, but after that his anger subsided. He was sixty-six; and though the love affair had been an enchanting embellishment to his existence, what he really wanted now was peace and quiet, and a connection with a spoilt and exacting young woman, particularly one who was inclined to drink too much, was probably, as Sir John Hall suggests, something that on calmer reflection he was quite prepared to give up.

In the rest of Florence's small circle feeling was much mixed. Her own parents were delighted, first that she should have put an end to the liaison for which they had felt obliged to disown her, and secondly that she was going to marry a man of suitable age, steady character and the prospect of great wealth. Their reconciliation with their daughter was complete. On the other side, however, the idea was received with open animosity Mr Bravo's feelings were not disclosed, but Mrs Bravo, who would have been unwilling to see her son marry anybody, was horrified that he should marry Florence, whose independence, worldliness and sensual attractions filled her with hostile dismay. She would have stopped the marriage if she could, and once it was an accomplished fact she did the little that was in her power to upset its smoothness.

Mrs Bravo's enmity to the match was open enough, but there was some elsewhere that expressed itself in a more subtle and tortuous manner. Florence had not been candid with Dr Gully, but it was to the credit of her good feeling and also her common sense that she was perfectly open with Charles Bravo about her past. She told him the whole story of her affair with Dr Gully and he in return told her of his having had a mistress for the past four years, and each agreed that now all had been admitted they would never speak of the past again. Charles Bravo even discussed the matter with his future wife's companion. He said he should imagine that a woman who had once gone wrong would be even more likely to go straight in the future than one who had never strayed. What, he asked, was Mrs Cox's opinion? Mrs Cox had no doubt that he was quite right; but she did not stop there. She so much approved of the frankness the parties had shown to each other, that she wanted to see it carried even further. She suggested that the whole story of Dr Gully's relation with her future daughter-in-law should be explained to Mrs Bravo. Charles flatly refused to consider any such idea. His mother was so much against the marriage already that to tell her such a thing as that was absolutely out of the question. It was, in any case, a private matter between his wife and himself and no concern of anybody else, even of his mother's. Still Mrs Cox was urging her opinion to the contrary. It would be so much better, she thought, to have everything open and above-board. She was obliged, however, to give up the point. Charles Bravo, brusque, determined and short-tempered, was not amenable to unwelcome suggestions, especially from a paid companion.

The wedding was fixed for December 7, and meantime the settlements were being prepared. The Married Woman's Property Acts were not yet in operation and therefore everything in Florence's possession would become her husband's unless it were previously secured to her by settlement. Charles Bravo made a disagreeable impression on her solicitors because when he came to discuss the settlements and one of the firm offered him congratulations on the approaching marriage, he exclaimed: 'Damn your congratulations! I have come about the money.' His overbearing nature showed itself again on the question of the settlement itself. Florence's solicitor had wanted to secure to her, besides the income from her first husband's fortune, the Priory and all its furniture and movables. Charles Bravo acquiesced in her keeping the four thousand pounds a year in her own hands, but he demanded that the house and furniture should be taken out of the settlement and therefore become his. Florence took a keen delight in her charming estate and all her pretty furniture, her horses and carriage, and her jewellery, and in love though she was, a streak of her wilfulness showed itself. She refused to have these things removed from the settlement. The violence of Charles Bravo's temper now showed itself. He swore that rather than submit to sitting on a dining-room chair that was not 'his own' he would break off the marriage, and she might take it or leave it.

Florence was in a quandary, and she did what she had done for the last five years, what was now second nature to her. She consulted Dr Gully. They met in the Griffiths' lodge, and she told him her perplexity and asked his advice. She had already written to say that they must never see each other's face again, and Dr Gully had accepted this decision as perfectly proper in the circumstances; but now that he had been sent for, he did not refuse to come. He behaved with the utmost kindness and sense. He said it was natural that Bravo should feel as he did, and the matter was not worth upsetting the marriage over. He advised her to give way. Then he wished her every happiness, kissed her hand and said good-bye.

Though it was Florence herself who had stated dramatically that they must never meet again, she did not seem entirely prepared to carry out her own edict. Dr Gully, however, was prepared to do it for her. He saw that no other course was possible to a gentleman and a man of sense. He sent back the key he had made use of by Griffiths to Mrs Cox, and he told Pritchard that in no circumstances were Mrs Bravo or Mrs Cox ever to be admitted to Orwell Lodge. Pritchard was pleased enough to receive such orders; he said, 'I had had quite enough trouble before when we had to do with them. I did not want my master bothered any more with them.'

Florence was married on December 7, 1875, from her parents' house in Lowndes Square. It was a pleasant occasion, a marriage of affection between a good-looking young pair, with family approval and excellent prospects. The bridegroom's mother, however, had not brought herself to be present at the ceremony. She would only say that she hoped she might, in time, be able to feel more charitably towards her daughter-in-law.

Notwithstanding this piece of bad behaviour from old Mrs Bravo, life at the Priory appeared to begin very happily; but there were indications, even in a month's time, that causes of disquiet existed, and that they showed themselves unusually soon. There was no doubt that husband and wife were strongly attracted to each other, but their happiness was made by their mutual passion, and it was sometimes threatened by the conditions of their daily existence. Charles Bravo had the power of arousing strong affection, but he was violent, and egotistical to the point of arrogance. On his marriage, twenty thousand pounds had been settled on him by his stepfather, and Mr Bravo had afterwards given him another present of one thousand two hundred pounds; but apart from the stable expenses of the Priory, which he paid himself, all the expenses of the establishment, of any kind whatever, were paid out of his wife's income, while he had seen to it that all the property of the house was his. Florence spent freely, but she had always lived within her means; now, however, her husband began to domineer over her expenditure. Charles Bravo had certainly not been demoralized by the prospect of inherited wealth; not only did he work hard, but he was what his friends called careful, and those who disliked him mean. To a man of this temper a wife who would spend twenty guineas on a fern was a subject of considerable disquiet. Using his legal powers as a husband and his influence as a newly married bridegroom, he began to consider where retrenchments might be made. As he visited his mother in Palace Green almost daily, he had plenty of opportunity to discuss his ménage with her, and old Mrs Bravo was at no loss to suggest ways in which her daughter-in-law's pleasures might be curtailed. Florence had always kept a personal maid, but Charles, primed by his mother, persuaded her that she could do without one and manage with the help of the head housemaid. The fact that this housemaid, Mary Ann Keeber, was an exceptionally nice and sensible girl, perhaps made Florence acquiesce in the arrangement more easily than she might otherwise have done. The Priory gardens required the services of three gardeners; this, old Mrs Bravo thought, and Charles agreed, was excessive, and he discussed with Florence a scheme for letting some of the beds go under grass. She was reluctant to give up one of her favourite pastimes, but to please her husband she was willing to entertain the idea. On her marriage the landau had been replaced by a carriage, for which two horses were jobbed. With Victor and Cremorne, this meant a stable of four. 'What does one couple want with four horses?' exclaimed Charles. His mother agreed with him; Florence's cobs, she thought, were a quite unwarrantable expense. Florence was much annoyed at this final piece of interference, the more so because she knew who was behind it. She would not agree to parting with the cobs, and Charles Bravo relinquished the idea for the time being. His mind, however, was still earnestly bent upon saving his wife's money, and it occurred to him that with a husband, a butler, a footman, six women servants, three gardeners, a coachman and a groom, she really did not need the services of a companion. He began to look into the financial aspect of Mrs Cox's employment. One day at his chambers, as he sat with his pen in his hand, calculating, he said to the barrister beside him that with salary, board and incidental expenses Mrs Cox was costing them four hundred pounds a year. 'Why,' exclaimed his friend, 'you could keep another pair of horses for that!'

Charles Bravo had no personal objection to Mrs Cox. She lived as a member of his family and called him by his Christian name, and he spoke highly to his stepfather of her usefulness and her devotion to Florence; but the matter of four hundred pounds a year weighed on his mind considerably. Old Mr Bravo knew that Mrs Cox had an aunt in Jamaica from whom she had some modest expectations, and he advised her to go back to Jamaica with her boys. Mrs Cox did not enlarge upon the topic; she merely said that she was not going.

She could of course decide whether or not she would go to Jamaica, but it would not be open to her to remain at the Priory once Charles Bravo had made up his mind to get rid of her. Florence was wilful and self-centred, but beneath her bright, petulant manner there was a pronounced weakness and dependence; she could be overpersuaded by affection and though emotional she had very little stamina. It would be only a matter of time before the cobs were laid down, and any other retrenchment Charles had in view would inevitably come about sooner or later. He had a passion for his wife and considerable affection for her when everything was going as he liked, but his method of achieving domestic tranquillity was by crushing all opposition.

Yet the recipe for a happy marriage cannot be defined like the recipe for a good pudding. Though Charles Bravo sounds as if he were in some ways almost as odious as Captain Ricardo, he and Florence were happy. Their domestic servants who saw them at all hours, and especially Mary Ann Keeber, who was often in their bedroom, all said that the pair were on the most affectionate and happy terms. His wife was not even disturbed by his occasional violence. Once he struck her, but the next moment his passion had subsided. 'It was like a child's anger,' she said.

Unknown to the servants, however, unknown to anybody except themselves and Mrs Cox, there was, it is believed, one cause of very serious discord between husband and wife. That it existed is almost certain, but how acute it had become or what degree of importance was attached to it was never found out, and for more than seventy years the matter has aroused speculation and bewilderment. Florence Bravo asserted, and her statement was supported and amplified by Mrs Cox, that after the marriage Charles Bravo developed a violent, re-trospective jealousy of Dr Gully. Though Mrs Cox's statements are highly suspect, the wife's story, even though supported by no more trustworthy witness than Mrs Cox, deserves at least a hearing. In their mutual confessions before the marriage she and Charles Bravo had agreed to overlook the other's past. It was common enough for a man to have had pre-marital entanglements, but in overlooking one on the part of his future wife Charles Bravo did what few men of the time would have been prepared to do. But just as he was not a sensitive man, so, too, he was not imaginative, and it was not until he himself was in possession of the woman he loved that the full realization of her having been Dr Gully's mistress was brought home to him. The torment of sexual jealousy grew side by side with the delight of sexual love. Florence said that in spite of his promise he frequently upbraided her with her past love, that he cursed Dr Gully as 'a wretch' and said he would like to annihilate him. Meantime, so strictly did Dr Gully keep to his seclusion that Charles Bravo had never once set eyes on him.

In spite of her brilliant colouring. Florence was not robust. In January, the month after the wedding, she had a miscar-riage, and in February 1876 she went to Brighton to recover. While she was there her husband wrote to her every day; the letters were afterwards read at a legal inquiry, and they were put in as showing nothing but the feeling of an anxious, devoted young husband who missed his wife. But one of them, Florence maintained, referred to their cause of distress. It was dated February 15 and written from Palace Green. It said: 'I hold you to be the best of wives. We have had bitter troubles, but I trust every day to come the sweet peace of our lives will not so much as be disturbed by memories like those. . . . I wish I could sleep away my life till you return.' It was suggested that the bitter troubles and the memories of them were those of the miscarriage. Florence declared that they were the raking up of burning grievance over Dr Gully.

Neither Charles nor Florence Bravo had seen a sign of Dr Gully since November of the previous year, but Mrs Cox had seen him more than once. She fairly frequently made the short journey to town, on business about her house in Lancaster Road or to see her boys at St Ann's School. On one occasion she met Dr Gully in Victoria Street outside the Army and Navy Stores and he spoke civilly, and asked her to send him a book of press cuttings which he had once lent Florence and which had never been returned. Another time she met him on Balham Station. Dr Gully had a cure for what was known as Jamaica fever, and Mrs Cox asked him to let her have the prescription. He promised to do so, and a few days later it came to her by post addressed to the Priory. It was Charles Bravo's habit to meet the postman, take his wife's letters and open them before he gave them to her. On this occasion, Mrs Cox declared, he met her with the letter in his hand and asked her if he might open it as it was addressed in Dr Gully's hand. Mrs Cox providently added that she had no idea how he had been able to recognize Dr Gully's writing. She resented the request, she said, but she opened the envelope before his eyes and showed him that it contained nothing but the prescription. In the extraordinary maze to which the clue has never been found, incidents like this, with their double-edged aspect, add to the confusion like mirrors which are placed so to reflect turnings that the eye is lost between the reflection and the reality. Was this statement true? Grave doubts are cast upon it by the fact (of which Mrs Cox's parenthesis looks like a clumsy attempt at covering-up) that it was scarcely possible that Charles Bravo should have been able to recognize Dr Gully's handwriting. If it were not true, then it was obviously designed as an alibi for another incident, and if the second incident were not accounted for by the first's being true, then a new vista of murky possibilities is opened.

Florence returned from Brighton in recovered health, but shortly afterwards, on April 6, she miscarried again. The second miscarriage was more serious. She suffered much pain, weakness and sleeplessness. She stayed in bed for ten days, and her husband moved out of their bedroom and went to a spare room on the same landing, on the other side of an adjoining dressing-room. Mrs Cox, whose own bedroom was on the floor above, came down and shared Florence's bed. During these ten days she met Dr Gully again, on his way to Bayswater to stay with his son and daughter-in-law. Mrs Cox told him how ill Florence was, of her pain, her backache and her sleeplessness and asked him what he would advise. The discreet reply on Dr Gully's part would no doubt have been that Mrs Cox should consult another doctor, but it was scarcely to be expected that Dr Gully would make it. He recommended spinal washings and cold sitz baths, and knowing from his experience of her that Florence was 'driven frantic by ordinary opiates' he said he would try to think of some sedative that might suit her and would sent it to the Priory. Mrs Cox hurriedly interposed, and giving as her reason the vigilance which Charles Bravo exercised over the post, asked Dr Gully to send his prescription instead to her own house in Lancaster Road, where she would call for it. Dr Gully did so. He left a half ounce green bottle, with a stopper covered in white kid, to be called for by Mrs Cox. It contained laurel water. He had chosen it as something mild and incapable of producing disagreeable results.

Good Friday that year came on April 14. The weather was lovely, and Florence was getting up in the middle of the day. Over the holiday, Charles Bravo did not go up to his chambers; he stayed in the Priory, and Florence wrote a letter to his mother — so binding was the family etiquette of the time — in pleasant, domestic vein, saying, 'Charlie is walking about the garden with a book under his arm, as happy as a king.' He was in good spirits at the holiday, the fine weather and at his wife's recovering. Yet there was a slight upset after lunch. Florence

had gone to her room to lie down, and her husband followed
her, wanting to talk and be amused. She was weak and irritable
and wanted him to go away and leave her to her rest. At last she
absolutely ordered him out of the room. He was angry, and Mrs
Cox followed, attempting to soothe him. It was her own version
of the affair that he shouted: 'She's a selfish pig,' and then said:
'Let her go back to Gully.' According to her, he was still angry
that evening, and threatened to leave the house. By her own
account, she went to his bedroom door and spoke to him in a
placating manner. He replied, she said, by saying that he had
no quarrel with *her*. 'You are a good little woman,' he said, and
kissed her cheek.

As the weather was very fine, the Easter moon at its full must
have filled the sky with light. In the tranquillity and silence of
that quiet scene no sound from the outside world disturbed the
sleeping Priory. On the garden side gravel paths glistened and
conservatory panes glittered. In front, against the pale stuc-
coed façade, the giant oak tree stretched its arms, its black
shadow thrown across the grass. The servants were all sleep in
their quarters, the master was shut away in his single room. In
the large bedroom at the head of the stairs Florence was in her
bed, and beside her was Mrs Cox. In the moonlight and the
silence, what was said? It is as if the box containing the secret
were in full view but the key is irretrievable.

On Easter Saturday the weather continued brilliantly fine
and Florence and Mrs Cox drove in the carriage to Streatham,
meaning to bring the three boys to the Priory for the weekend,
but the headmaster would only allow them out for Easter
Monday. Florence arranged to send for them early on Monday
morning and they drove back to Balham. Charles Bravo had
had a tennis court laid out and was superintending the putting
up of the net. He had a vigorous game with the butler, and
when the boys arrived on Monday morning he at once started
to play with them. He wrote a letter to his father (those daily
letters which telephone conversations now replace) saying that
he had 'loafed vigorously' and thoroughly enjoyed the
weekend.

To help Florence's recovery, they had decided to go to
Worthing, and to take a house there as more comfortable than

lodgings. On Tuesday, April 18, Mrs Cox set off to Worthing to find a suitable house. Good living was the rule of the Priory and Mrs Cox took a flask of sherry with her to recruit her in her exertions. Meanwhile Florence ordered the carriage to drive in to town and her husband was to accompany her. The carriage turned out of the gates into Bedford Hill Road and when a few minutes later it passed Orwell Lodge Florence turned her head away in the gesture that had become instinctive. Charles Bravo noticed it and said savagely: 'Do you see anybody?' 'No,' she said. He then muttered some abuse of Dr Gully, and she exclaimed that he was very unkind to be always bringing up that name after the solemn promise he had made never to refer to the past. He would not like it, she said, if she were to be always taunting him about that woman! Her husband was touched by this, and asked her to forgive him. Then he said pleadingly: 'Kiss me!' She was too much ruffled, and refused; whereupon, she afterwards declared, he exclaimed: 'Then you shall see what I will do when we get home!' This frightened her, she said, and she did kiss him.

The carriage put him down at the Turkish Baths in Jermyn Street, and then took her to the Haymarket Stores, where she did some shopping. She drove back to the Priory for lunch. Charles Bravo lunched with a friend at St James's Hall, and came back to Balham in the afternoon. Florence gave him some tobacco she had bought him at the Stores, and he was very much pleased by the little gift, which was indeed a gesture of reconciliation, since in the 'seventies the mistress of the house, so far from encouraging smoking, was understood barely to tolerate it. Charles Bravo said he would now go and smoke in his room, for it was out of the question that he should do it in his wife's drawing-room or morning-room. Florence thought that he would spend the time up there till dinner, but, to her surprise, in the late afternoon he came down dressed for riding and said he was going out on Cremorne. His horsemanship was characteristic of him; he rode badly but with pertinacity and courage. This was the first evening that Florence had stayed up to dinner since her illness, but the meal, which should have been a little domestic celebration, did not go off well. First, Charles Bravo arrived home much shaken, saying the cob had run away with him. The groom told him it was his own fault for riding it on a snaffle instead of a curb. Charles admitted this and said he would not do so next time. When he came in he looked pale and complained of stiffness. Florence said he must have a mustard bath and sent the butler upstairs to get it ready. She then went upstairs herself to dress. Meanwhile the butler, having prepared his master's bath, came down to the dining-room to finish laying the table. A bottle of burgundy was decanted and placed in the middle of the table. Dinner had to be kept back because Mrs Cox had not returned, but she arrived a little after half-past seven. She went upstairs, but did not stay to dress as it was too late. When she came down a few minutes afterwards they all went into the dining-room.

The meal was a simple one: whiting, roast lamb and a dish of eggs and anchovies. Charles Bravo seemed unwell and was certainly ill-humoured. Mrs Cox produced a photograph of the house she had chosen, but he brushed it aside, and said the whole project of going there was an unnecessary expense. Then he was annoyed because a letter from a stockbroker addressed to himself had been sent by mistake to his stepfather. The letter gave an account of some very mild flutters in which Charles had engaged and showed that he had lost twenty pounds. The elder Mr Bravo disapproved of gambling on the Stock Exchange even to such a trivial extent as this, and he forwarded the letter with a few grave observations of his own. Charles Bravo was the more irritated because his stepfather had had no business to see the letter, anyway. He said he should 'write the governor a shirty letter about it.' The butler noticed that his master was pale and quite unlike himself, and put it down to the shock of being bolted with; but though he did not complain of it that evening, Charles had been suffering a good deal from toothache and this trouble may have accounted for some of his pallor and moroseness. He drank three glasses of burgundy, about his usual measure. The ladies, it is somewhat startling to learn, drank nearly two bottles of sherry between them.

At a little after half-past eight Charles told his wife she had sat up long enough for a first evening. She agreed and went upstairs, followed by Mrs Cox, but half-way up the staircase she asked Mrs Cox to bring her up another glass of sherry. Mrs

Cox at once returned for it to the dining-room and carried it upstairs. She helped Florence to undress, because Mary Ann Keeber, who would ordinarily have done so, was now at her supper. It therefore happened that the two women were quite alone on the first floor, from just after half-past eight until Charles Bravo came upstairs at about half-past nine.

Mary Ann was going upstairs to Mrs Bravo's bedroom at the same time, and she stood back to let her master go up first. She particularly noted his distraught appearance. He was extremely pleasant and friendly with servants, and it was unlike him to walk upstairs with one of them without speaking. As it was, he looked round at her twice, and she thought he seemed angry. It must be admitted, however, that this would describe the appearance of a man gnawed by toothache. He went to his bedroom and she went to Mrs Bravo's. Florence asked the girl to bring her a glass of Marsala from the dining-room. Mary Ann went downstairs and returned with half a tumbler full. The master followed her into the bedroom and began to reproach his wife with taking too much wine. As she always took a glass of sherry while she was dressing, she had now swallowed more than a bottleful and half a tumbler of Marsala in the course of the evening. Mary Ann had discreetly gone away into the dressing-room, where she was busy in tidying away Florence's clothes. When she had finished, she went back to Florence's bedroom. Florence was lying in bed, and Mrs Cox was sitting at the bedside. Mary Ann was accustomed to seeing her sitting there. The maid asked if anything more were wanted and Mrs Cox said softly, 'No,' and asked her to take the dogs downstairs. Mary Ann collected the two small dogs who were in the bedroom and was half-way down the stairs with them when Charles Bravo appeared at the door of his room in desperate plight, calling loudly: 'Florence! Florence! Hot water!'

The startled maid turned back and ran to the big bedroom. Strange as it might appear, Mrs Cox had not heard these frantic cries which were uttered a few feet away from her. She still sat dreamily in her post by the bed. In the bed, Florence, overcome by the fumes of alcohol, was already fast asleep.

Roused by Mary Ann, Mrs Cox bustled off to Charles

UNSOLVED!

PRICE THREEPENCE.

PICTORIAL WORLD

AN ILLUSTRATED WEEKLY NEWSPAPER

No. 128. Vol. V. {Registered at the General Post Office as a Newspaper.}   *SATURDAY, AUGUST 12th, 1876.*   THREEPENCE. Per Post, 3½d.

THE "BALHAM MYSTERY"; PORTRAITS OF THE LATE MR. BRAVO, MRS. C. BRAVO, MRS. COX, AND DR. GULLY

The victim and suspects in the Bravo case.

Bravo's room, and as she and the maid came in they saw him standing at the window, vomiting. Mrs Cox at once sent Mary Ann down to the kitchen for a can of hot water. When the girl came back with it Bravo was lying on the floor and Mrs Cox was rubbing his chest. She now told Mary Ann to go for mustard, for an emetic, and in the course of her errand Mary Ann, thinking it strange the wife should not have been called to a husband in such an alarming crisis, went into Mrs Bravo's bedroom and succeeded in rousing her from her stupor. As soon as Florence could be made to understand what had happened, she hurried on her dressing-gown and rushed to the spare room. From that moment everyone who saw her agreed that her behaviour was that of a completely innocent woman, distracted with anxiety at her husband's state. Mrs Cox had sent one of the servants for Dr Harrison of Streatham, but Mrs Bravo now insisted on Dr Moore's being sent for, since he was much the nearer, as he lived in Balham itself.

When Dr Harrison arrived, Mrs Cox met him in the hall and told him she was sure Charlie had taken chloroform. She said afterwards that she had not mentioned this to Dr Moore because the latter was a local man and Charlie would not wish anyone in the neighbourhood to know what he had done. Harrison at once went up to join his colleague and they both tried to detect any odour of chloroform on the patient's breath, but there was none.

In her recent illness Florence had been attended by Mr Royes Bell of Harley Street, who was a connection of her husband's and an intimate friend of the Bravo family. She now suggested that he should be sent for. Dr Harrison wrote a note asking Mr Royes Bell to come at once and to bring someone with him. This note was given to the coachman, who drove with it to Harley Street, and at the end of the two hours necessary to go and come, returned bringing Mr Royes Bell and Dr Johnson.

Meantime Florence, with every sign of passionate distress, threw himself on the bed beside her husband; but, weak from illness, overpowered by grief and having had far too much to drink, she soon fell asleep. Dr Harrison roused her and got her off the bed; he was afraid she would interfere with the sick man's breathing. Presently Charles Bravo came to again; he began to vomit, and the doctors could now be sure that he had taken a strong dose of irritant poison. When Mr Royes Bell and Dr Johnson were brought up to the bedroom and had made their examinations, Mr Royes Bell took advantage of the patient's returning consciousness to ask him what he had taken. 'I took some laudanum for toothache,' he said. 'Laudanum will not account for your symptoms,' said Dr Johnson.

Mrs Cox now glided up to Mr Royes Bell and, drawing him aside, she made the extraordinary statement that when she had answered Charles Bravo's cries for help he had said: 'I have taken poison. Don't tell Florence.' Royes Bell was astonished that she had not said so at once. 'It's no good sending for a doctor if you don't tell him what's the matter,' he said, and hurriedly returned to his colleagues with the news. Dr Harrison was extremely annoyed that Mrs Cox had not made the disclosure to him. Mrs Cox, blandly obstinate, replied that she had done so. 'I told you when you arrived,' she said. 'You did nothing of the sort,' replied Dr Harrison heatedly; 'you said he had taken chloroform.' The night passed with no improvement and at five o'clock in the morning Dr Harrison, Dr Moore and Dr Johnson went home, the latter taking with him a specimen of the vomit for analysis. Mr Royes Bell, who was now in charge of the case, remained at the Priory.

The day was Wednesday, April 19. It wore on slowly, the patient suffering agonies of pain succeeded by periods of profound exhaustion. During one of his calmer moments he saw his wife bending over him. A memory seemed to cross him of their miserable altercation in the carriage. 'Kiss me!' he pleaded. She did so. Many times during the day he asked her to kiss him. At noon he had a short will made in which he left her everything, and he told Royes Bell that if his mother arrived too late to see him alive she must be given a message from him. It was: 'Be kind to Florence.'

At three o'clock that afternoon the three doctors, once more gathered at his bed, tried again to make him say whether he had taken anything. The butler heard his master exclaim in weak but irritable accents: 'Why the devil should I have sent for you if I knew what was the matter with me?'

That same afternoon old Mr and Mrs Bravo, who had been

telegraphed for, arrived from St Leonards. They brought with them Mr Bravo's brother-in-law, Dr Henry Smith, Miss Bell, the surgeon's sister, and their maid Amelia Bushell, who had known Charles from a small child. Mrs Cox met them at the station with the appalling news that Charles had poisoned himself. The whole party disbelieved it, and Mr Bravo stoutly denied that such a thing was possible.

When they arrived at the Priory, Mrs Bravo told Florence that she had always nursed Charles in all his ailments and begged that she might take charge of the sickroom now. Florence, distracted and incapable, agreed willingly. She gave up the double bedroom to the Bravos and went upstairs to share Mrs Cox's.

Next morning, Thursday, the twentieth, there was no alteration and very little hope, and Florence, acting on a natural impulse, sent Mrs Cox round to Orwell Lodge. She afterwards said pathetically that she had always thought Dr Gully 'the cleverest doctor in the world'. When everyone else had failed, she instinctively turned for help to him. There was no room for embarrassment. Mrs Cox presented herself boldly, and Pritchard, putting her in the drawing-room, went to announce her to his master. 'You shouldn't have let her in, Pritchard,' said Dr Gully, but he went to see what was the matter. When he heard the trouble, he suggested mustard plaster, and small doses of arsenicum. Within five minutes of her arrival Mrs Cox was walking down the drive again.

Meanwhile Florence, in her desperate search for succour, had bethought her of a friend of her father's, the famous Sir William Gull. This doctor, who was short-tempered and domineering, and bore a curious resemblance to Napoleon, was the most eminent physician of the day and was considered to be unrivalled in diagnosis. Though, as Mr Royes Bell was in charge of the case, she ought not to have summoned another doctor without consulting him, the distraught wife sent Sir William Gull a note saying her husband was desperately ill and could he come at once? This note made no mention of poison.

Sir William Gull and Mr Royes Bell agreed to ignore this breach of etiquette and they drove out to Balham together, arriving at the Priory at six o'clock that evening. When Sir

William Gull entered the bedroom he told everybody to leave it except the five other doctors there already. Then he made his examination. Bending over Charles Bravo, he said: 'This is not disease. You have been poisoned. Pray tell us how you came by it.' In weak but unfaltering tones the dying man swore solemnly that he had taken nothing except laudanum for his toothache. 'You have taken a great deal more than that,' said Sir William Gull. Dr Johnson from his post at the foot of the bed said that if the patient could tell them no more, someone might be accused of poisoning him. 'I cannot help that,' said Charles Bravo; 'I have taken nothing else.'

Mrs Cox had already made two statements, to Dr Harrison and Mr Royes Bell, each one more important than the last. She now capped them with a third to Sir William Gull. She explained that what Charles Bravo had really said to her was: 'I have taken poison for Gully. Don't tell Florence.' How Sir William Gull received this is not known, but he, alone of the seven doctors, inclined to the theory of suicide. Dr Johnson's analysis of the vomit proved useless, for it had been tested for arsenic only, of which it contained no trace. It appeared at first as if no other specimen were obtainable, for when Mary Ann had attended Charles Bravo in his first seizure Mrs Cox had ordered her to wash the basin and throw away the contents. However, Sir William Gull stood at the window from which he had been told that Charles Bravo had vomited, and he saw traces of the rejected matter on the leads beneath. He ordered some to be collected and took it back with him to London. He had left the sickroom for a few moments only when he was hastily called back; but the patient only wanted to repeat his solemn assurance that he had not poisoned himself and to ask if there were any hope? Sir William Gull would not deceive him. He told him that he was half dead already. To the parents he said he doubted if their son would last the night. He then left the Priory and his prognostication was soon fulfilled.

At four o'clock on the morning of April 21 Charles Bravo died, within five months of his wedding day.

In the shock of grief, terror and dismay that swept the household, the only person to remain calm, useful, practical and thoughtful for others was Mrs Cox. There could be no question of granting a death certificate, and it was realized that a coroner's inquest must be prepared for. The coroner for East Surrey was Mr Carter, and Mrs Cox at once got into touch with him. She gave him to understand that this was a case of suicide and that it was an object to spare the family's feelings as far as possible. She suggested that the inquest should be held in the Priory itself, to avoid distressing publicity, and added, with her usual attention to detail, that refreshments would be provided for the jurors. Mr Carter fell in with these arrangements in the most obliging way. No notice of the inquest was sent to any of the papers, and no reporters were present. The ceremony, conducted in the pleasant seclusion of the Priory dining-room, was almost a family affair, except that a few of the late Charles Bravo's barrister friends had wormed themselves in. However, no one paid them any attention.

The proceedings opened on April 28, and the coroner had clearly taken it for granted that the case was one of suicide about which it would be well to say as little as might be. Meanwhile, however, the pathologist to whom Sir William Gull had submitted the specimen for analysis had revealed the fact that Charles Bravo had died from a large dose of antimony, taken in the form of tartar emetic. On the advice of Dr Smith, Mr Bravo took this report to Scotland Yard, who sent 'down Inspector Clarke to see if he could trace tartar emetic in the possession of anyone in the Priory. This he entirely failed to do. The rooms both of Mrs Bravo and Mrs Cox were full of patent medicines, but all of a quite harmless character. Meanwhile, evidence was given at the inquest that was difficult to reconcile with the idea of suicide, for Mary Ann Keeber showed that the couple were on terms of devoted affection, and Mr Royes Bell repeated the impressive denials of the victim that he had taken anything to poison himself. Nevertheless, Mr Carter appeared anxious to hurry through a verdict in accordance with his own view. He refused to hear the testimony of Dr Moore and Dr Johnson, both of whom wanted to speak, and he refused to allow Florence to be called, as he understood that she was prostrated by shock. The jury, however, were far from satisfied. They returned a verdict to the effect that Charles Bravo had died from a dose of tartar emetic but that there was no proof as to how he had come by it.

The next day, April 29, the funeral took place at Norwood

cemetery, and on the thirtieth, Florence retired with Mrs Cox to Brighton, where Mrs Cox had found them apartments at 38 Brunswick Terrace. Mr Joseph Bravo remained at the Priory, and he had all his son's drawers sealed up. Florence heard of this in her retreat, and she at once wrote to her father-in-law about it. She said that all her husband's possessions belonged now to her, and no one else had the right to touch 'one single thing'. At the same time she took the opportunity of suggesting to Mr Bravo that any money he had been in the habit of giving his son should now be considered as due to her. 'What he died possessed of I must leave to you; he told me that he had two hundred pounds a year from investments, and of course his books and pictures and private papers at Palace Green are now mine. . . . P.S. Poor Charlie told me that you promised to allow him eight hundred pounds a year.'

Such a letter, at such a time, does not put her in an amiable light; but a childish greed and selfishness was the reverse side of her emotional nature. Charles Bravo had insisted, with brutal and insulting harshness, that all her possessions should be his; he had said if he were not to have everything for his own then he would not marry her at all. She had acquiesced at the time, but now she was particularly alive to the idea that she ought to reap her side of the bargain. She wrote a little later apologizing to Mr Bravo for the disagreeable tone of her last letter; she had quite misunderstood his intentions, she said; she added that a letter from Mr Royes Bell had convinced her that poor Charlie had committed suicide, and she believed it had been because 'that dreadful woman' had been pressing him for money; this, too, was why he had been so anxious to cut down their expenses. This was the letter of a woman who was either genuinely stupid or a very incompetent deceiver. There had been no trouble from Charles Bravo's mistress, who had made no claim on him at all; she would not have got very far with such a man if she had; whereas the cutting down of expenses required no explanation beyond the fact that Charles Bravo was exceedingly careful about money and was supported by a woman who disliked and disapproved of her daughter-in-law.

Dissatisfaction with the conduct of the inquest was growing. It showed itself in a flood of anonymous letters which reached

Florence in her rooms at Brunswick Terrace, but it was also making its way among the reputable part of society. One of Charles Bravo's friends who had been present at the inquest, a Mr Willoughby, went and explained his uneasiness at Scotland Yard; while several newspapers, notably the *Telegraph*, began an agitation to have the proceedings reopened. Florence felt herself to be in a position of odious notoriety, which threatened to become something worse. On her father's advice she published the offer of a reward of five hundred pounds to anyone who could prove the sale of tartar emetic in the neighbourhood of the Priory.

The result of the pressure that was brought to bear was that an enquiry was held at the Treasury, at which Mrs Bravo and Mrs Cox each made a voluntary statement. The latter's was so startling that a second inquest was ordered to take place on July 11.

This time it was entirely out of private hands. Far from the pleasant seclusion of the Priory dining-room, the jurors met in the billiard-room of the Bedford Hotel, outside Balham Station. It was very hot, and the billiard-room windows were open, with the Venetian blinds half down. Public interest was enormous. Every available inch of space not occupied by the performers of the inquest was filled with a mob of intensely curious spectators. The possible issues were of the utmost seriousness, and the persons chiefly concerned were all able to pay for the best legal assistance, and consequently a most impressive collection of counsel was assembled in these incongruous surroundings. The Crown counsel were Sir John Holker, Mr Gorst, Q.C., and Mr, afterwards Sir, Harry Poland. For Mrs Charles Bravo there appeared Sir Henry James, Q.C., and Mr Biron; and Florence had also retained Mr Murphy, Q.C., to act for Mrs Cox. Mr Joseph Bravo was represented by Mr Lewis, a partner of Messrs Lewis & Lewis, the famous firm of solicitors. Half-way through, the proceedings took such an ominous turn that Mr Sergeant Parry and Mr Archibald Smith presented themselves, saying they had been instructed to watch the case for Dr Gully.

The legal gentlemen were indeed eminent, so eminent that they defied all control. In a court of law a judge would have managed them, but in the billiard-room of the Bedford Hotel there was nobody but Mr Carter. His unhappy position was rather that of Phaeton, who attempted to drive the coursers of the sun and was tumbled ignominiously into the ocean.

Before the inquest opened a macabre ceremony was performed. It was necessary for the jurors to view the body, and the coffin was therefore taken up out of its brick vault in Norwood cemetery and placed on wooden blocks under a canvas shelter. That the formality of viewing might be accomplished, the undertakers had cut away a square of the lead casing and left the dead man's face in sight under a pane of glass. The face was as dark as a mummy's, the teeth, exposed by rigor, were entirely black. The jurors filed past the coffin, raising their tall hats as they did so. A heavy, overpowering smell of disinfectants added to the oppressiveness of the sultry day.

The inquest was considered afterwards to have been conducted in a most undisciplined manner. Not only was Mr Carter unable to control the loud-voiced comments of the crowd or to prevent the jury from making unsuitable demonstrations; he could not prevent the lawyers from extorting by relentless cross-examination, much material that would probably have been ruled as inadmissible in a proper court. A domestic picture of the most graphic detail was built up by the statements of a wide variety of witnesses, but the three most important were Mrs Bravo, Dr Gully and Mrs Cox.

In Mrs Cox's examination, which was the longest, she quietly and persistently maintained that Charles Bravo had committed suicide and that he had done so out of retrospective jealousy of Dr Gully. Her story which had grown in circumstantial detail from the time she made her first communication to Dr Harrison now received its crowning touch. She said that at one of the moments when she was alone with Charles he had said: 'Why did you tell them?' and she had answered: 'I had to tell them. I could not let you die.' The only creature who could have contradicted her was now a blackened corpse. When she was asked why she had not at once reported that Charles Bravo had said he had taken poison 'for Dr Gully', she replied that it had been with a view of shielding Mrs Bravo's character.

As she and Florence both adhered to this story of the death, the story of the liaison with Dr Gully was pushed forward into a position of the utmost importance. It acquired in fact an importance in the minds of the lawyers which Mrs Cox had perhaps not foreseen, for if the liaison could account for the suicide, if still existing, it might equally be held to account for a murder. This perhaps accounts for the remarkable lengths to which the Crown counsel and Mr Lewis went in attempting to find out when the relationship had begun — a matter, after all, of some four years before Charles Bravo and Florence had ever set eyes on each other. When Mrs Cox was asked twice over whether she was not aware of the fact that her employer and Dr Gully were lovers, she looked down and gently brushed the tablecloth with her gloved hand. She admitted at last that she had suspected it. She was now called upon sharply to speak up, and this request was received with clamorous delight by the onlookers. Mr Sergeant Parry was appalled by these proceedings. 'Applause in a court of justice!' he exclaimed. 'It is terrible! It is fearful!' But Mr Carter was helpless.

When Florence Bravo was called her appearance created a sensation. In her widow's dress of black crêpe, her bright hair strained back under a bonnet with a crêpe veil, her large blue eyes sunken in her pale face, she appeared on the verge of breaking down, but she spoke with unexpected firmness, until Mr Lewis, after a long cross-examination on her relations with Dr Gully, began with savage persistence to demand at what point they had begun. She denied that this had been while she was at Malvern, but Mr Lewis produced a letter she had written six years ago to a maid called Laundon, in which she promised to recommend her to another place and said, 'I hope you will never mention what passed at Malvern.' 'What did that mean, Mrs Bravo?' asked Mr Lewis and he repeated the question until her merciless reiteration broke her self-control. Sobbing wildly, she implored the coroner for protection, which he was powerless to extend. He could not control the counsel any more than she could.

Dr Gully's examination aroused a great deal of unfavourable comment, both in the press and at the actual scene of the inquest, where several jurors showed disapproval because the coroner allowed him to sit down during his lengthy ordeal.

There was by the end of the proceedings no shred of evidence, no shade of implication, to connect him with the crime, but public opinion was weighted against him almost as if he had been proved a murderer. It was of course right that so serious a breach of professional etiquette, particularly on the part of such an eminent man, should be strongly condemned, but the tragedy of Dr Gully's fall after a long and distinguished career seems to have passed unregarded. This was no doubt partly or even largely due to the fact that a fellow human being always arouses hostility and resentment if he or she is felt to have enjoyed a sexual success out of proportion to any physical or social advantages. That Dr Gully, a man well over sixty, should have had a pretty young woman as his adoring mistress, unloosed a flood of vindictive taunts and scathing vituperation.

Once the discreditable fact had been admitted in its full culpability the rest of Dr Gully's evidence was that of an upright, distinguished man with every instinct of a gentleman. He spoke honestly, simply, and with a keen sense of regret for his backsliding. 'Too true, sir, too true,' he said, when the Crown counsel flung his past indiscretion in his face. At one point of the proceedings the horrible implication was made that he had prescribed medicines for Mrs Ricardo to bring on a miscarriage. His prescriptions had been traced to the chemists who dispensed them. Dr Gully replied with effective simplicity that to any medical man the prescriptions would speak for themselves; they were not such as would be used to procure abortion. All his evidence went to show, just as Florence Bravo's had shown, that after she had dismissed him in October of 1875 he had never attempted to have any further communication with her. He had seen her once at her own request, when he advised her to give way about the marriage settlement. After that, he had never even laid eyes on her. Nor, apart from the one interview in the coachman's lodge, had she ever attempted to get into touch with him till she sent Mrs Cox to ask his advice for her dying husband. He had prescribed for her pains, and he had sent her a bottle of laurel water: both these acts had been brought about by the agency of Mrs Cox.

The dead man, according to the pathologist, had taken the enormous quantity of some forty grains of antimony, and a thorough search of the Priory, including the medicine chests of Mrs Bravo and Mrs Cox and the numerous bottles that were littered about in both ladies' rooms, had revealed no trace of anything likely to contain antimony in any form. The reward of five hundred pounds offered by Florence to anyone who could prove a sale of tartar emetic in the neighbourhood had produced no response. But now it came to light that a large amount of tartar emetic had been on the premises no later than the preceding January, three months before Charles Bravo's death. The then coachman at the Priory, Griffiths, had bought tartar emetic to doctor Florence's horses, and he had also used it in Dr Gully's stables at Malvern. Dr Gully had not known of this; he had forbidden Griffiths to physic the horses, as he himself treated them by hydropathy, 'with marvellous results'. In the Priory stables, however, Griffiths had it all his own way, and he made a profuse purchase of tartar emetic, regardless of the fact that he had only four horses under his charge. He was asked why he had bought physic enough for at least a hundred, and he explained that he liked to have things by him. On the day of the Lord Mayor's Show, 1875, he was driving his mistress, accompanied of course by Mrs Cox, in the London streets, and the carriage was involved in a serious collision. Griffiths denied that he was to blame, but Charles Bravo, harsh, impetuous and alarmed for Florence's safety, insisted on his being dismissed. He left the Priory in January. Griffiths bore Charles Bravo a bitter grudge in consequence, though he went at once into the service of Lady Prescott. He said that while the tartar emetic was in his possession he had kept it locked in a cupboard in the harness room, and that before he left he had poured it down a drain in the stable yard. Unfortunately, though there was no reason to suppose Griffiths a deliberate liar, he was excitable and loquacious and his evidence was full of contradictions and inconsistencies. That he said he had kept the poison locked up and thrown away the remainder before he left was nothing like so significant as the fact that a large quantity of tartar emetic had actually been on the premises.

It was an accepted fact that Charles Bravo must have taken the poison in some form of drink after the dinner hour of seven-thirty. As Florence had gone upstairs immediately after dinner, no coffee had been served that evening. Therefore the two mediums in which he could have taken the poison were the Burgundy he drank at dinner or the water in the bottle on his bedroom washstand from which he always drank a glassful before going to bed. The medical evidence inclined to its having been taken in the water, and this view was supported by the fact that the butler had been near at hand, in dining-room or hall, ever since the wine was decanted some half an hour before dinner. Though it would not have been impossible, it would have been exceedingly difficult for anyone to enter the dining-room and doctor the Burgundy unobserved. But with regard to the water in the bedroom: Florence and Mrs Cox had the first floor entirely to themselves between the time of their going upstairs at eight-thirty and Charles Bravo and Mary Ann's appearance at about half-past nine. The matter could have been decided by the examination of what remained of wine and water; but by the same perverse good fortune which had supported the criminal in every aspect of the crime the remains of wine and water could, neither of them, be accounted for. The butler had opened a fresh bottle of Burgundy for Dr Harrison and Dr Moore; he could not say what had happened to the remains of the other; the house had been in confusion and he could not remember if anyone had drunk it or not. (Similarly he would not, of course, have known if anyone had poured it away.) The remains of the water bottle had not been noticed either. The doctors had noticed the bottle in the room, but at that time they had naturally attached no importance to it. They were not continuously present with the patient, and any care-ful, attentive soul refilling the bottle with fresh water would scarcely attract attention.

The verdict which was finally pronounced after the sittings had lasted three weeks was that Charles Bravo had not died by misadventure and not committed suicide, but that he had been poisoned, though there was not sufficient evidence to say by whom. This statement came as a stunning blow, because it at once branded Mrs Cox as a liar, and therefore it was next door to an indictment of murder of either herself or Florence or both, with the possibility of suspicion resting upon Dr Gully. The pamphlet, *The Balham Mystery*, is exceptionally interesting, as it not only supplies an exhaustive account of the proceedings at the inquest and drawings of the scenes and people involved, but it conveys the public feeling of the time in three fanciful drawings, crude and morbid and of astonishing effectiveness. One is of the devil dressed as a showman at a fair, with three thimbles standing on a board. The drawing is headed: 'Rather a Poser. Under which thimble is the P——?' Does P stand for prisoner? At all events there is no doubt as to whom the three thimbles represent. The second of these full-page drawings is in vivid chiaroscuro. It shows the setting sun from which a stony road leads up to the foreground. Here in deep shadow a gallows stands, and beneath it, sitting at the edge of an open pit strewed with bones, is a figure of such terror as is seldom seen outside nightmare. The hooded cloak reveals one hoof, and a head that would be a skull except that the features are still there. The expression of intense personal misery such as the devil might be supposed to bear is combined with an indrawn, waiting look and a hideous smile. On the lap a skeleton hand holds a whip. The picture is called: 'Waiting for the culprit.' But even more interesting is a small illustration at the end. This is a murky-looking corner where several phials and a glass jar containing what looks like an anatomical specimen are standing on a shelf. A single beam of light illuminates a woman's hand which stretches out towards one of the small bottles. A careful examination of the drawings of Mrs Bravo and Mrs Cox shows that the sleeve, banded with dark ribbon and finished with a deep fall of lace, is not identifiable with any dress which either of them is shown as wearing; but it is an elegant hand, with a massive bracelet on the wrist; this, and the richness of the sleeve, suggests inescapably that it is meant for Florence Bravo, while the anatomical specimen carries an equally inescapable suggestion of Dr Gully.

There are two authoritative pronouncements on this crime which after seventy years still holds its secret. In his memoir of Sir Harry Poland, *Seventy-two Years at the Bar*, Mr Ernest Rowlands says that Sir Harry Poland told him that he had his theory, though it was not for publication, and there was not enough evidence for a prosecution. It is tantalizing to read such words, because this theory, formed by a man who was one of the counsel, would be as near to the actual truth as the rest of us could hope ever to come. But Sir Harry Poland's other observations are extremely interesting. He entirely exonerates Dr Gully, and he mentions a possible motive for each of the women: that Mrs Cox was threatened by Charles Bravo with the loss of her pleasant life at the Priory to which the alternative was drudgery and insecurity and the anxiety for her sons' future, and that Mrs Bravo murdered her husband to avoid losing her companion, but he says that the first motive was scarcely sufficient and the second was not credible. Nevertheless the effect of that paragraph is that he thought it was the motive rather than the identity of the culprit which remained obscure.

Sir John Hall in *The Bravo Mystery and other Cases* also clears Dr Gully from all suspicion of complicity in the murder and says that there is no evidence of Florence Bravo's having wanted to renew her liaison, of her having procured poison, or behaved in any way but one natural to an affectionate and single-hearted wife; but he also says that what lays her open to grave suspicion is the way in which she supported every statement of Mrs Cox, and the extraordinary intimacy in which she lived with her; not only were they the closest friends, but for the last fortnight they had been sleeping in the same bed. Sir John Hall says: 'If one be guilty the other cannot be innocent.'

It would be presumptuous to hazard any theory which was not closely conformable with what has been said by these two writers, but it is, one hopes, not going beyond the lines thus laid down to say that the murder was certainly done and almost certainly planned by Mrs Cox, and that all that is doubtful is her motive for it. The Marxist trend of present-day thought perhaps inclines our generation to attach more importance to economic motive than the men of Sir Harry Poland's day were prepared to allow. To us it does not seem incredible that a woman of such calibre as Mrs Cox should be prepared to commit murder in order to maintain her own security and that of her children. On the other hand, it seems likely that though Florence Bravo did not know that the crime was to be committed at that time, or, perhaps, that it was ever actually to be committed at all she knew afterwards how and by whom it had been done. Though very little is known of her subsequent story, that little is of extreme significance: it is simply that she died within fourteen months of the second inquest. It is not generally known whether her support of Mrs Cox continued during the short remainder of her own life. A theory (in default of any evidence) is sometimes suggested, more or less facetiously, that her death may have been a second murder, but by far the most probable explanation is that after the second inquest the truth about her husband's death became known to her, and that the strain of enduring this knowledge was more than she could bear. What is dreadfully clear is the influence of the controlled, secretive, ruthless character over the sensuous, impulsive, helpless one. Had Florence Bravo been another sort of woman she might be thought the victim of some morbid attachment to Mrs Cox, but the history of her love affair and her marriage puts this out of court. Mrs Cox dominated her because she ran her house, attended to her wants, promoted her comforts and pleasures and enabled her to lead her life as she wanted to lead it. Mrs Cox was the evil spirit whose power over us is the power we ourselves have given it. Florence's character, self-indulgent, greedy, impetuous, pleasure-loving, had its exact complement in the character that was vigilant, cautious, hard-working, self-reliant, capable of any self-denial to achieve a particular end, just as her appearance with its Rubens-like colouring, its feminine softness and grace, was the opposite of the plain, dark, unobtrusive figure, which had developed a self-protective obscurity.

In the infinite complexities of the mind it is possible to know without realizing the knowledge, until circumstances force the mind to admit it. In their extreme intimacy before the death of Charles Bravo, when Mrs Cox nursed her, waited on her and slept in her bed, Florence must have confided to her friend whatever causes of resentment and dislike she may have had against her husband, and she must have felt assured that her own feelings were met by a profound agreement. Yet nothing would be more natural than that she should accept, at first, Mrs Cox's version of the tragedy which had overtaken the household when she herself was weak from illness and bemused by a drunken sleep, and that at the actual moment of calamity all her other feelings should be submerged in dismay and terror at the sight of her husband's agonies.

It is of course impossible to say what may have been the extent of her complicity, whether she were an accessory before or after the event, whether her silence were willing or unwilling, but her early death seems to speak volumes on her sufferings. Hers was an organism that collapses in physical ill health whenever it is placed under a nervous strain, and if she ceased to want to live there would be no recovery. The force that killed her husband killed her also.

Mrs Cox was heard of many years after, visiting an elderly invalid with fruit and flowers. 'She was quiet and so *very* kind,' said those who remembered her visits.

Dr Gully died seven years later, and for those remaining years his penance was heavy. During a long life he had built up for himself a position of public respect and admiration such as very few men enjoy. As a result of the disclosures at the Balham inquest this was blasted overnight. Not only was his name trampled on by the public, but he had to bear the ruin of his professional reputation. His name was removed from all the societies to which he belonged and from all the journals and papers to which he had been one of the most distinguished contributors. That he bitterly regretted the love affair that had proved fatal to him, he had said himself; but however much his feelings might have altered towards her, the anguish and death of the woman he had loved must have caused him deep grief. He was a man of unusual gifts of personality and intellect, but, with all his good qualities, he had neglected the Wisdom of Solomon:

'Discretion shall preserve thee, understanding shall keep thee.

'To deliver thee from the strange woman, even from the stranger which flattereth with her tongue.

'Which forsaketh the guide of her youth and forgetteth the convenant of her God.

'For her house inclineth unto death, and her paths unto the dead.'

AFTERWORD by Elizabeth Jenkins

*Since I wrote this account of the Balham Mystery in 1949, I have read a great · deal more about the matter and I do not now altogether hold the view of it I presented then. I assumed that the murder had been committed by Mrs Cox, as this was the opinion of the distinguished authority Sir John Hall (*The Bravo

Mystery and other cases*); also, it would appear, of Sir Harry Poland, one of the Crown counsel at the second inquest, and of Sir George Lewis, the solicitor who represented the Bravo family. This is a formidable body of opinion, but in this century a more modern alternative suggests itself. Florence Bravo had had a miscarriage on December 7, 1875, seven weeks after her marriage; she suffered another one on April 7, 1876. (Had she been brought to trial this would, today, almost certainly have entitled her to plead diminished responsibility.) In the 19th century, contraception, though known, was not widely practised, and a device sometimes resorted to by women anxious to postpone another pregnancy was to administer an emetic to make the husband sick. Charles Bravo had shown signs of wanting to return to his wife's bed, and I, for one, subscribe to the theory that with Mrs Cox's connivance, she doctored the water-bottle on his wash-stand with a dose that she meant to incapacitate him for the time being; as she was half-tipsy, she put into the water a quantity of tartar emetic that was lethal. It was only when Mrs Cox, summoned to his bedroom, found him passing out on the floor, that the dreadful consequences were brought home to them. Florence, who, innocent of attempted murder, had none the less brought about her husband's death, was too much frightened to admit what she had done; this theory would account for Mrs Cox's self-contradictions in her first statements made to the doctors impromptu, and for Florence's desperate anxiety to save her husband, by calling in six doctors one after another. In their frantic attempts to protect themselves from a capital charge, she and Mrs Cox claimed that Charles Bravo had committed suicide out of retrospective jealousy of Dr Gully, and to build up this statement, Mrs Cox, in her cross-examination at the inquest, remorselessly exposed the love affair between himself and Florence which had existed before her marriage to Charles Bravo.

I was wrong in accepting, on the authority of the article on Dr Gully in the Dictionary of National Biography, the statement that after the inquest his name was removed from the medical societies to which he belonged. I have learned from the Library of the Wellcome Institute of the History of Medicine that this was not so; it should be added that the Garrick Club, of which he was a member, did not ask for his resignation. The attendance at his funeral and his obituary notices proved that though his reputation had ben injured much of it was left to him.

SYDNEY HORLER

Starr Faithfull, Beautiful Wanton

SYDNEY HORLER

Starr Faithfull, Beautiful Wanton

Perhaps the most famous of all unsolved crimes is that of the murder of a beautiful American girl named Starr Faithfull, whose body, clothed only in a dress—the shoes, stockings and underclothing were all absent—was found floating very near the edge of the waves at Long Beach, Long Island, at nine o'clock on Monday morning, June 8th, 1931.

The discovery was made by a man named Daniel Moriarity, who was strolling idly along the shore near the water's edge.

After taking one horrified glance at the corpse, he ran to find the nearest policeman, and in a few minutes Officer Patrick O'Connor arrived and superintended the carrying of the body up on the beach.

Long Beach, Long Island, is a fashionable summer resort, and soon many residents from the neighbouring cottages flocked to see what had happened.

Even in death the features of the unfortunate girl showed refinement and outstanding beauty; everyone who was present remarked on this fact. Naturally enough, the newspaper reports made the most of these attributes, and before many hours had passed, the affair had become an outstanding newspaper sensation.

The Police early came to the conclusion that the girl had been murdered, but there was no jewellery on the body and very few characteristics from which any attempt at identification could be made. The corpse was taken to the nearest Morgue, where Dr Otto Schultz made a post mortem. He declared that death had been caused by drowning, and that before her end the girl had been the victim of a criminal attack. As evidence of this, he pointed out that both arms and eyes were

Starr Faithfull.

covered with many marks and bruises which must have been made before death, and which from their positions on the body bore out the other indications that the girl had been violated.

It was not long, in spite of the lack of clues, before the Police were able to identify the body. The Long Beach authorities had only to glance through their file of persons reported missing to find that they had the exact description of a girl calling herself Starr Faithfull—here was a melodramatic nomenclature, if you like!—which tallied exactly with that of the corpse found on the beach.

The bereaved parents were quickly found, and Mr Faithfull, upon being notified, identified the corpse in the Nassau County Morgue as that of his daughter, Starr.

It was a shocking revelation to this man, a retired chemical manufacturer, who was not only wealthy but well respected.

Mr Faithfull informed the Police that his daughter had been missing since the previous Friday—that was since June 5th. On the next day, he had made a confidential report to the Charles Street Police Station saying that his daughter was missing. He described her as being twenty-five years of age, five feet three inches in height, and weighing 110 lbs. He added that his daughter was a graduate of two New England finishing schools, and had travelled extensively, having only returned recently from Europe.

Soon everyone in America was asking this question: *How did Starr Faithfull meet her end?* Not only was the mystery discussed in the newspapers, but it became a subject of universal conversation.

The situation was complicated by the fact that Dr Schultz, as a result of his autopsy, had announced that sand had been found in the dead girl's lungs. This indicated, of course, that she had been drowned in shallow water. But Starr Faithfull was known by all her intimates to be not only a strong but an expert swimmer. How was it possible then that such a girl could be drowned under those conditions? Could the explanation be found in the fact that someone had forcibly held her down under water until she died?

Such a case was naturally enough the cause of heated

controversy: experts were equally divided: some said that it was an open and shut murder case; others declared that Starr Faithfull had committed suicide.

The adherents to this latter theory pointed out that the bruises on the body could have been caused after death through contact with heavy objects—rocks, piers, etc.,—as the corpse floated in the water. Dr Schultz, when pressed on the point, admitted that such a possibility certainly existed, but that, in his opinion, it was a remote one. He still clung to the theory that the girl had been murdered.

It was whilst the controversy was raging at its height that another medical man, a Dr Alexander G. Goettler, and an eminent toxicologist, caused a fresh sensation by stating that death was undoubtedly due to submersion, as he had found traces of salt water in the left ventricle of the heart.

Dr Goettler went further; he was able to provide sensation in a large way. After making this first announcement, he stated that he had also found a large quantity of veronal in the girl's kidneys. Veronal is an opiate which may be bought in any chemist's shop and is taken by many people to induce sleep. It has its dangers, however, for it is habit-forming, and there have been many cases on record in which an overdose taken to induce sleep has ended in death.

But in this case the quantity of veronal found in the girl's system was proved not to be sufficient to have made her even unconscious; nevertheless, Dr Goettler persisted that Starr Faithfull must have been a veronal-addict. He said further that he had definitely come to the opinion that the girl had not been drinking at the time she died, and that in all probability she had been in full possession of her faculties.

Well, here was mystery indeed! Whilst the adherents of the suicide theory maintained that they alone were right, the opposite camp were more than ever convinced that this lovely girl of twenty-five had been done to death by a criminal lunatic.

A fresh development was soon forthcoming; as a result of an immediate investigation into Starr Faithfull's movements on the day she disappeared, it was discovered that the dead girl had been in love with a Dr James Carr, who acted as ship's surgeon on the *Franconia*. It was also disclosed that on May 29th she had gone down to the 14th Street Dock, New York, to see the ship off. There had been a cocktail party on board, and Starr had over-indulged with the result that when the gangway was taken off, the girl was still on the ship and had to be taken ashore in a tender. The famous *Mauretania* had sailed for a southern trip on the Friday on which the girl had disappeared, and as Starr Faithfull had a large acquaintance among the officers on board, it was presumed that she might have gone to say farewell to some of these friends and had remained on board in similar circumstances to what had happened to her in the case of the *Franconia*.

Spurred on by the previous melodramatic features of the case, several amateur investigators thought it was quite likely that once on board the *Mauretania*, the girl had been attacked and thrown overboard. Completely exhausted after her long swim, she might have been drowned in shallow water. There was certainly some point to this, considering that the course of the *Mauretania* had lain close to Long Beach.

One disclosure led to another. The investigators soon learned that Stanley Faithfull was not Starr Faithfull's father! The girl's real father was declared to be a Stanley Wyman. The latter had secured a divorce from Starr's mother in 1924, and in 1925 Faithfull had married the divorcée and Starr had taken his name.

Arrangements were quickly made for the body of the unfortunate girl to be cremated in the Fresh Pond Crematorium, but when the private cremation ceremonies were about to begin, the Police entered and stopped the proceedings. They explained that they wanted several taxi-drivers, steamship company agents and other people to view the body.

One cab-driver testified that the remains were undoubtedly those of a girl whom he had driven to the Cunard Line dock on the very day that Starr Faithfull was reported to have disappeared. The Faithfull family had all along been of the opinion that Starr had been murdered, and on hearing this evidence, they declared themselves willing to postpone cremation, so that more witnesses, if the latter could be found, might also give evidence.

Ever since the finding of the body, the New York Police had

been delving industriously into the past of the dead girl. It was not long before they were able to learn that in the previous March the girl had been brutally beaten by a man in an hotel room. Both Starr and this man had been taken to the psychopathic ward of the famous Bellevue Hospital. They were both stated to be suffering from acute alcoholism.

A page boy, in telling the Police of this occurrence, said that other guests in the hotel had reported a 'row' in a room occupied by a 'Mr and Mrs Collins.' The witness had entered the room with a pass key and had found there a young woman—later identified by him as Starr Faithfull—lying completely nude on the bed, while the man in his underwear was sitting on the edge of the bed. The girl showed signs of having just received a terrific beating. A policeman was called, and the pair, who were both still very drunk, were removed to hospital.

The detectives employed on the case also discovered that Starr Faithfull had been under observation at the Channing Sanatorium for a short period during 1925—that was six years before. She had been discharged nine days after entering the institution, and her card marked 'improved'.

It was also discovered by the detectives that in the previous autumn, Starr Faithfull had visited Europe with her mother and sister, and that whilst there she had spent a good deal of time buying clothes and frequenting nightclubs. A reluctant witness, who had known Starr in London, told the detectives that one night the girl had danced in the nude in a certain night-club upon being challenged to do so. One of the group of people who had accompanied her to the club tried to hide her nakedness with his overcoat, whereupon Starr's escort had taken a revolver from his overcoat pocket and fired at the Puritanic interrupter. The incident, it was stated, had caused a 'good deal of comment in the English Press'. And small wonder!

A scenic artist by the name of Rudolph Haybrook, now came on the scene. He told the Police that he was absolutely certain that Starr had been murdered, the reason being the result of a 25,000 dollar settlement case in which she was the principal witness. It was in order to stop these fresh sensational rumours, that Stanley Faithfull issued a statement to the Press declaring that his adopted daughter had never been involved in any such type of litigation.

Meanwhile, fresh inquiries were being prosecuted in England, and these disclosed the fact that Starr Faithfull had attempted suicide whilst a guest in a certain London hotel; she had only been thwarted by a chambermaid coming in at a critical moment.

It can easily be imagined that all this sensational rumour and counter-rumour was greedily printed by the New York Press—indeed, by a Press of the whole world. The Faithfull case was a 'natural' as a news story. But the vital questions, (1) How Starr Faithfull had died? and (2) Who was her murderer? still remained unsolved.

It was while the investigations were in this unsatisfactory state that District Attorney Edwards came into prominence. Placed in charge of the case, he declared that he was convinced that the dead girl's family was not telling the whole truth about her, but was trying to hide many vital facts. He went to the Faithfull home and asked to examine the dead girl's room. Here, behind a volume of Tennyson's poems in the bookcase, he found a small book marked 'My Diary'.

It did not take Edwards long to be convinced that the contents of this small volume was bound to add more sensation to the case, and increase the fury of the 'murder v. suicide' controversy.

For the diary made frequent references to a man whose initials were 'A.J.P.' Excitement followed upon excitement, for these initials were those of a former mayor of Boston, by the name of Andrew J. Peters! It was not determined, however, whether or not the notations in the diary referred to Mr Peters; the former Mayor, when questioned, admitted readily that he had known Starr but that he could give no information which was not already in possession of the Police.

But the diary certainly revealed that the dead girl had had a peculiarly warped and morbid mind. For instance, there were several references to suicide and the general futility of modern existence; and—an even more sensational feature—there were frank confessions of sexual perversion and promiscuity.

Faced by these disclosures, the Faithfull family were forced

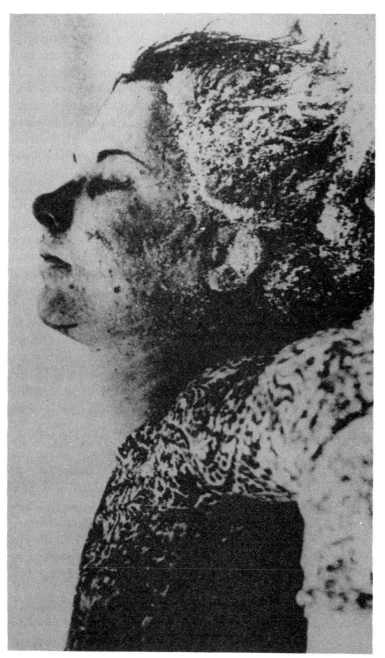

Starr Faithfull – the body on the beach.

to admit that the girl's conduct had been a constant worry and problem to them. Mr Faithfull even went to the extent of revealing that when Starr was only eleven years old, she had allowed herself to be seduced by a man four times her age. It was this man who had taken her on various trips to Europe and had entirely warped her personality as well as her outlook on life. In her diary, Starr had told with the utmost frankness of her relations with this man—and even the Press of America could not print the full details, because of their revolting nature.

It was as a result of these sexual relations that the girl had had to be confined in a sanatorium, where she remained under the care of doctors for some time. A relative of the family, a lawyer by profession, had advised Mr Faithfull to sue Starr's 'lover' for the medical expenses. The result of the suit was that the man had settled out of Court, giving Starr 22,000 dollars in cash.

Ten days after the discovery of the body, Dr Carr of the *Franconia*, with whom it had been stated the girl had been in love, returned to New York and submitted to questioning by detectives. He showed the police officials a letter which Starr had written to him a few days before her disappearance. In this letter, the girl had said that she intended, at some time in the future, to take her own life, as she was 'fed up'.

Naturally enough, this statement was seized upon by the adherents of the suicide theory who claimed that the letter clinched their case, and that there could no longer be any possible doubt that Starr killed herself in a fit of morbid despondency.

But those on the other side were still not satisfied. They pointed out that there were yet many questions about the case that remained mysterious. Why, they put forward, had the girl been criminally violated before she committed her last dread act? Undoubtedly, they went on, she had been murdered. The assault would be ample motive for the killer.

Then again, if Starr had committed suicide (by jumping off a pier), why were her undergarments, coat, hat, shoes and stockings not found at the spot where she had entered the water?

These burning questions have been unanswered to this day. The Starr Faithfull case is still unsolved. But one point of interest in the affair has developed quite recently: a taxi-driver has come forward to state that on the afternoon of Starr Faithfull's disappearance, he carried a man and woman in his cab away from the Manhattan dock. They were both quite drunk. After riding for a few blocks, the man got out of the cab and the girl returned to the docks from whence she had come.

When asked why he had kept this story for so long, the taxi-driver explained that he was forced to keep silent for 'personal reasons'.

Will the truth ever be known? After this long period it seems doubtful, but even to this day the Starr Faithfull case is numbered amongst the most notorious murder-mysteries of modern America.

AFTERWORD

The passage of time has, alas, added absolutely nothing to our knowledge of how Starr Faithfull met her end. The case continues to fascinate, however, and regularly pops up in newspapers, magazines and books. For anyone wanting to pursue the problem, an entertaining solution is to be found in Sandra Scoppettone's 1977 novel, Some Unknown Person.

WILLIAM LE QUEUX

Bela Kiss, the Mystery Man of Europe

WILLIAM LE QUEUX

Bela Kiss, the Mystery Man of Europe

In the early spring of 1912 a tall, rather elegant man of exquisite manner, thin-faced, black-haired, with high cheek-bones and a countenance of almost Tartar type, arrived with his young and pretty wife from Budapest at the charming little summer resort of Czinkota, a few miles from the Hungarian capital. The place is much frequented by holiday folk on Sundays, it being a centre for excursions to Visegrad, Nagy-Moros and Budafok. The stranger, who was about forty years of age, was named Bela Kiss, his wife being about fifteen years younger. After searching the district for a house he eventually took a rather spacious one standing back in a large garden on the Matyasfold road, in a somewhat isolated position, and for a few months lived happily there, going into Budapest alone about once or twice a week. It afterwards transpired that he had been a tinsmith in a large way of business, but had retired.

The pair formed few friendships, for Kiss seemed a somewhat mystical person, and had often been heard to discuss psychic subjects with his wife. He was also something of an amateur astrologer and possessed many books upon the subject, while his wife had a small crystal globe into which she was fond of gazing. The pair seemed a most devoted couple, and went about together in the small and rather dilapidated car which the husband possessed, and in which he often went into Budapest.

The wife was extremely good-looking, and Kiss was apparently extremely jealous of her. Indeed, he forbade her to make any male acquaintances. She was a native of Zimony, on the Danube, in the extreme south of Hungary, a place long noted for its handsome female inhabitants. According to village

gossip, however, little Madame Kiss had a friend in a certain
Paul Bihari, an artist of Budapest, who sometimes spent the
day with her wandering in the acacia woods and picnicking
together during her husband's absence. The handsome young
fellow was well known in the capital and especially at the
Otthon Club, where Hungarian authors, artists and journalists
assemble nightly.

I

Matters proceeded in this manner for nearly six months, Paul
being a frequent visitor to the house, and the pair making many
excursions to the beauty spots in the vicinity. One evening,
however, Bela Kiss on his return from Budapest found the
house locked up. After waiting till near nightfall he broke open
the door, and found, lying upon the dining-table, a note from
his wife saying that she had fled with her lover, and asking
forgiveness. In a frenzy of anger he burnt the note, and then
rushing to a neighbour named Littman, who lived in the
vicinity and who was one of the few persons with whom he had
formed a friendship, told him of the staggering blow he had
received.

Next day all Czinkota was agog, knowing what had occurred. But it was only what they had long expected.

Crushed by his disillusionment, the heart-broken husband
shut himself up and became almost a recluse. He drove sometimes to Budapest, but he had no servant and did his own
cooking and looked after his few daily wants himself. In fact, he
became a woman-hater and devoted his time to the study of
psychometry and mysticism. His eccentricity now became the
more marked, but as months wore on his health appeared to be
failing, until it was noticed that he had not been seen out for
over a week, while the house appeared to be closed. Yet each
night there appeared a light in his bedroom.

The neighbour in whom he had confided how his wife had
deserted him began to wonder, so one day he called. The knock
on the door's brought Bela, pale, half-clad and very feeble. He
told his friend that he had been ill in bed for some days. The
friend at once suggested that he should have somebody to nurse
him, and that the village doctor should be called. At first Kiss

demurred, saying: 'After all, if I die what matters? I have nothing to live for, now that my dear one has left me!'

The neighbour uttered comforting words, and eventually the doctor visited him—much against his will—and an old woman from the village, named Kalman, was left in charge.

His eccentricity had, it seems, increased to a marked degree. In one room there were laid out carefully upon the table the clothes and shoes that his wife had left behind, and into that room the invalid forbade the old woman to enter. For nearly three weeks the village woman was most assiduous, and carefully nursed him back to health, until at last he became quite well again. So he paid her and she left, leaving him to the dull, isolated life which he had lived ever since his young wife had gone.

II

Soon he resumed his business visits to Budapest, usually leaving the house in the afternoon and often not returning until midnight and after. Very naturally the woman Kalman was questioned by her friends as to the condition of the house of the poor grief-stricken man. It was also but natural that she should describe to her neighbours what she had seen—how, though forbidden to enter the room where the erring wife's clothes were displayed, she had entered it in secret while her patient was asleep, and passing through it had peered through the keyhole of the room beyond, where she saw five large tin drums ranged along by the wall.

The old woman's curiosity had been aroused by sight of these, and soon her friends, to whom she described what she had seen, suspected the eccentric, grief-stricken man to be in league with some illicit distillers who had their secret factory somewhere in the neighbourhood. The gossips were naturally sorely puzzled to account for those big receptacles for fluid. Some laughed and said that he had a big store of wine bought at the previous year's vintage. Littman, his neighbour and confidant, hearing about it, one day mentioned to him what the old woman Kalman had seen, whereupon Kiss laughed heartily and replied:

'Well, that is really amusing! They think I am one of those

who distil alcohol against the law and sell it in secret to the night cafés in Budapest—eh? Well, let them think so! I would be afraid to engage in such a dangerous trade, lucrative as it is. No. The fact is that I have my store of petrol there. I bought it cheaply from a man who was about to be made bankrupt.'

Quickly the truth went round the village, and suspicion was at once allayed. Indeed, a man of such exemplary conduct as Bela Kiss surely could never be engaged in any illicit transactions.

Once Littman expressed surprise that he had not followed the runaway pair and divorced his wife. To this, Kiss replied: 'If they are happy in Vienna, as I hear they are, why should I wreck her life? I loved her more than anything on earth. So that is enough. I was a fool! That's all!' And he refused to discuss the matter further.

From that moment, however, suspicions regarding Kiss became increased. His many journeys to Budapest were regarded as mysterious, and an evil-tongued woman who distrusted him declared that he practised black magic. He had drawn the horoscope of a woman of her acquaintance who believed in astrology, and thus a fresh theory was set up to account for his aloofness and eccentricity.

Whenever he motored to Budapest, as he did twice a week, it was noted that he never returned until the early hours of the morning, when the whole village was asleep. The villagers heard his noisy, ramshackle car speeding through the streets homeward bound. Of money this retired tinsmith had plenty. The village policeman, who, by the way, had also had his curiosity aroused by the malicious gossip, struck up an acquaintance with him, and soon discovered him to be a real good fellow, kind, generous and hospitable. They often spent evenings together, for the representative of the law was, in addition to Littman, the only person he ever invited to cross his threshold since his wife's flight. The constable naturally reported the result of his inquiries to his chief, and all suspicions were set at rest.

III

One wintry morning in January 1914, the exquisitely dressed Bela Kiss was seen walking with a pretty young woman, also handsomely attired in furs, about half a mile from the village, and this fact, which soon got about, gave rise to the theory that the disillusioned husband had fallen in love again. The gossips kept watch, but only on that one occasion was the lady seen. It, was, no doubt, an illicit meeting, for the well-dressed lady had, it was known, come from Budapest and had spent the day with her admirer.

About a month later a farmer driving from Czinkota to Rakosfalva noticed a man and a woman walking in the afternoon along a secluded footpath on the edge of a wood, and on approaching recognised Kiss arm in arm with a well-dressed young girl, to whom he was earnestly talking. The spot was nearly four miles from the village, and near by stood Kiss's old motor-car, muddy and unwashed.

Just about that time a strange story was told to the police of the Josefvaros quarter in Budapest by a young girl named Luisa Ruszt, daughter of a well-known draper in the Karoly Korut, one of the principal shopping thoroughfares.

She said that one evening she had met a man in the Somossy variety theatre, and he had taken her next day for a long motor drive. On their way back to Budapest, they had stopped at his country house and there had some refreshment. Afterwards they returned to the city, when he invited her to his flat somewhere near the Margaret Bridge. They had had dinner at a restaurant, when he told her that if she cared to go back to his flat he would tell her fortune. Like most girls she was eager to know her future, therefore she consented and went.

On arrival he offered her some pale yellow liqueur which seemed very strong, and then setting her at a table he told her to gaze intently into a small crystal globe. In fun he promised that she would see her future husband.

She did as he instructed, and had been gazing intently for some time when she began to experience a strange dizziness, probably due to the liqueur. Suddenly, on looking up from the crystal she saw in a mirror at her side the man standing behind her with a piece of green silk cord in his hand. It had a noose and a slip-knot, and he was about to place it over her head!

Sight of the changed face of her friend—a pale, evil countenance, with glaring dark eyes which had in them the spirit of murder—held her breathless. She fainted, and knew no more until she found herself lying beneath the trees in the Erszebet Park at dawn with all her jewellery and money gone.

She described to the police, as well as she could, the man with his house in the country and his flat in the town, but, though some inquiries were made, neither flat nor house could be identified, and they apparently dismissed the story as the imaginings of a romantic girl.

Curiously enough, however, about three weeks later a very similar story was told by a young married woman of good family, and whose husband was a wealthy merchant, to the police of the Belvaros quarter of Budapest. The lady, who lived on the handsome Franz Josef's Quai, facing the Danube, had met a smartly dressed man one Sunday morning as she came out alone after service in the Terezvaros Church, which is highly fashionable during the Budapest season. She was nearly run down by a passing taxi when he had grabbed her arm and pulled her back. Thus they became acquainted. They walked together for some distance, when he told her that his name was Franz Hofmann, a jeweller's traveller, and that he was greatly interested in spiritualism. She happened to be also interested in spiritualism, hence a friendship was formed. Her husband was away in Paris, therefore she invited him to dine at her house a few days later, and at the dinner she appeared wearing some valuable jewellery, while he, as a jeweller, admired it greatly.

Later that evening Hofmann invited her to go to one of the most select night cafés for which Budapest is famous, and she accepted. Afterwards, at two o'clock in the morning, he persuaded her to accompany him to his flat, where he would tell her fortune by the crystal. She went, and almost the same thing happened. She drank the liqueur, and he tried to strangle her. She fought with him, was overpowered, and when she came to her senses found herself in the hands of the police devoid of her jewellery. She had been found lying in a doorway unconscious.

This second story aroused the interest of the Budapest police, and inquiries were made, but neither woman could say where the flat in question was situated. They had been taken there, they said, by a roundabout route. The taxi had been dismissed in what seemed to be a cul-de-sac, and they had walked the remainder of the distance. They both described the interior in identical terms, and their description of the man left no doubt that it was the same individual in each case.

Then, when a third girl told a similar story a fortnight later, and when a dealer in second-hand jewellery had shown the police a ring the description of which had been circulated, a real hue and cry was raised. But just at that moment war broke out, and the country was thrown into disorder. The police system quickly broke down, and every available man was called up to fight against the Allies on the side of the Germans.

Bela Kiss was among those called up. He had been living a quiet, lonely, uneventful life, and as soon as the call to arms came he ordered from a blacksmith a number of iron bars, which he fixed inside the windows of his house to keep out thieves during his absence. Then, a week later, he left Czinkota and joined the colours.

IV

Eighteen months passed. He fought in Serbia, and once wrote to his friend Littman from Semendria, on the Serbian shore of the Danube, after a great battle had been fought. Littman, who was over military age, replied, but the letter was returned some four months later with an official intimation that Kiss had died of wounds in a military hospital near Belgrade. Then the village gossips of Czinkota knew that the poor deserted husband, who had led such a lonely life, had given his life for his country, and his name was later on engraved upon the local war memorial.

In the meantime, however, a sensational discovery had been made, quite by accident, of the body of a young woman in an advanced state of decomposition buried under about six inches of earth in the same wood of acacias wherein the farmer had seen Bela Kiss walking with a young woman. Upon the finger of the corpse was a wedding-ring engraved on the inside by which she was identified with the young wife of a furrier in a large way of business in Vienna, who had before the war run away with a middle-aged man, taking with her a quantity of jewellery and the equivalent of two thousand pounds in money. She had left her husband and entirely disappeared, after sending a letter to a friend from Budapest.

Inquiries were at once instituted, of course, and it was found that her husband had been killed within the first week of the war. Therefore, as far as the police—unfortunately a very inefficient service in those days—were concerned, they could do no more. But within three months yet another body was turned up by the plough in the vicinity. The records of missing persons were inspected, and they found that the unfortunate woman was named Isabelle Koblitz, a niece of the Minister of Commerce, who was known to have studied spiritualism, and who had disappeared from Vienna in July 1913.

The chief of the detective police of Budapest then began further inquiries. From Berne a report came that a wealthy Swiss lady named Riniker, living at Lausanne, had been staying at a well-known hotel in Budapest, from which she had written to her sister in Geneva, but had, in October 1913, mysteriously disappeared. A description was given of her, together with the fact that she had a red scar upon her cheek and that she had a slight deformation of the left leg. Within three days the Hungarian police established the fact that the body of the lady was that which had, six months before, been found in a disused well at Solymar, a little place about twenty miles away, at which the festival of the Queen of the Roses is celebrated each year.

The police now became much puzzled. Yet they did not connect the stories of the women who had gazed into the crystal with the discovery of the bodies of others.

Suddenly an order to commandeer all petrol went forth, and all garages and private persons were compelled to deliver it over for military purposes and receive receipts for it, which the Government eventually paid. At first the commandeering took place only in the big towns, but after three months a further thorough 'comb-out' of petrol was ordered, and commissioners visited every village, including Czinkota. There they searched for petrol, whereupon the old woman Kalman recalled the fact that poor Kiss who had died possessed quite a stock of petrol.

This quickly reached the ears of the commissioner, who went at once to the dead man's house, broke down the iron bars, and found the big drums of spirit. From their appearance both the commissioner and a constable suspected them to be full of smuggled brandy. Indeed, the constable obtained a tin mug from the kitchen in order to sample the spirit when they bored a hole. They did so—and found it to be crude alcohol.

Further investigation, however, led to a most ghastly discovery. On cutting open the top of the big drum a quantity of female clothing was seen. This was removed, and beneath was the nude body of a woman bound with cord and so well preserved in the spirit that her features were easily recognisable. Indeed, around her neck was a thin red line, showing plainly the manner in which she had been murdered—namely, by strangulation with a cord and slip-knot!

And each of the other drums contained the body of a woman, each showing traces of strangulation. Upon these gruesome facts—perhaps the most horrible discovery ever made in the annals of the police of Europe—we need not dwell.

Search of Bela Kiss's belongings brought to light a number of receipts for advertisements inserted in several of the most important newspapers in Vienna and Budapest, and upon examination of the files of those papers the advertisements in question were easily identified.

One, which was repeated in ten different issues of the paper, read:

> Bachelor: aged 40: lonely; good income from commercial enterprises averaging £3000 per annum, is desirous of corresponding with educated lady with a view to matrimony. Address: De Koller, Poste Restante, Granatos, Budapest.

A number of other similar advertisements were traced by the receipts, all of which were either alluding to matrimony or trying to induce girls to learn their futue. Indeed, when the police came to inquire at the Post Office in Budapest they found no fewer than fifty-three letters awaiting the mysterious De Koller undelivered!

In a Vienna daily newspaper the following advertisement was found: 'Know Yourself!—Those who wish to know their future and thus frame their lives should consult Professor

Hofmann of Budapest. Write: Poste Restante, Vienna.' To this one advertisement there were twenty-three replies awaiting him, all from women eager to have their fortunes told. It then became plain that the fellow's habit was to lure women possessing even paltry sums of money or modest jewellery, either to his flat in Budapest, or to take them out by night to his house at Czinkota, and there strangle them. The tin drums of spirit he evidently used in order to preserve the bodies of his victims until he could bury them in secret or otherwise dispose of them.

A number of prisoners of war were at once set to work digging in Kiss's garden and in the acacia woods, the result being that no fewer than twenty-six other bodies of women and girls were found at various spots. Over one hundred and sixty pawn-tickets relating to women's clothing were found concealed under the carpet of the dining-room, and by the recovery of the clothing and some jewellery, fourteen of his victims were eventually identified. They were mostly of women of the better class, and in every case had worn jewellery and had money in their possession when they had gone to consult him.

The method he adopted never varied. His first crime was committed by means of a cord slipped over the head and drawn tight ere his victims could utter a cry—thus adopting the method of the notorious Frenchwoman Gabrielle Bompard— and so successful was he that he always pursued the same course. Among the bodies recovered in the garden was one which was identified as the young wife who was supposed to have fled with the artist, Paul Bihari. The latter was found in Agram, and when questioned by the police stated that one day, while at the house in Czinkota, Kiss came home unexpectedly, and after a fracas he left and had not seen the lady or heard of her since.

The monster Bela Kiss had, however, died of wounds received while fighting in Serbia, therefore the police hushed up the terrible affair, and soon the gruesome discovery was forgotten by all except the villagers of Czinkota.

About a year later, however, Inspector Resch, of the detective force of Budapest, learned that a man closely resembling Franz Hofmann had been seen a week before by the girl Luisa Ruszt—who had had such a narrow escape while gazing into the crystal globe. At first he was not inclined to believe her, but so positive was she that she had actually seen him in the flesh, that the police officer decided to go to the hospital at Belgrade and learn details at first hand of the assassin's death.

On arrival he found that Bela Kiss had died from wounds, and he was given the dead man's papers, which proved his identity beyond question. By mere chance the nurse who had tended him in his dying moments was still there, and naturally the inspector questioned her as to the end of such a callous and elusive criminal.

'But surely,' she remarked, 'such a very frank and pious-minded boy could not have committed such awful crimes!'

'Boy!' echoed the inspector. 'What do you mean? Bela Kiss was over forty years old.'

'Well, the Bela Kiss who died here was about twenty!' was her reply.

Again the surprised detective examined the identification papers, and saw that without doubt they were the genuine ones belonging to Bela Kiss of Czinkota. Hence the assassin had, no doubt, exchanged papers with the poor young fellow who had died and been buried under his name.

With this astounding knowledge Inspector Resch sped back to Budapest, and a thorough search was at once made for the assassin. The police of Europe were warned, and as it was believed that the assassin had fled to London, Scotland Yard became active, as well as the Paris Sûreté. But the fellow managed to slip through their fingers, and today they are still searching for him all over Europe and America.

AFTERWORD

Five years later, a man who has just emerged from the French Foreign Legion informed the Sûreté that a fellow-soldier called Hofmann was in the habit of amusing his friends with lurid stories of garrottings; moreover, he answered the description of the wanted man. But by the time the authorities acted, Hofmann too had deserted.

There were rumours that he had fled to the United States, and in 1932 a detective in New York's Homicide Squad claimed to have spotted Kiss in Times Square, but again he proved too elusive to be apprehended.

He was never caught.

EDMUND PEARSON

The Borden Case

EDMUND PEARSON

The Borden Case

The Borden case is without parallel in the criminal history of
America. It is the most interesting, and perhaps the most
puzzling murder which has occurred in this country. There are
in it all the elements which make such an event worth reading
about, since, in the first place, it was a mysterious crime in a
class of society where such deeds of violence are not only
foreign, but usually wildly impossible. It was purely a problem
in murder, not complicated by scandals of the kind which lead
to the *crime passionel*, nor by any of the circumstances of the
political assassination. The evidence was wholly circumstantial. The perpetrator of the double murder was protected by a
series of chances which might not happen again in a thousand
years. And, finally, the case attracted national attention, and
divided public opinion, as no criminal prosecution has done
since—nor, to the best of my belief, as any murder trial in the
United States had ever done before. People have become
disputatious, even quarrelsome, over the probability of a verdict, one way or the other, over the justice of a verdict rendered,
or over the wisdom of a commutation of sentence, in cases in
which there was no doubt at all as to the identity of the slayer.
In many celebrated cases the actual murder has been done
openly and in public.

But during the investigation of the Borden mystery, and
during the thirteen days of the trial, families throughout the
United States were divided upon the question, and argued its
points with a vehement interest for which no comparison
suggests itself to me except the excitement in France over the
Dreyfus case. And since there were no political and no racial
matters at issue, there becomes apparent the extraordinary

fascination of this case as a problem in human character and in human relations.

A murder may attract national attention for any one of a number of reasons. The actors may be persons of good position and respectability, as in the slaying of Dr Parkman by Professor Webster, which amazed everybody in the days of our grandparents, and is still discussed by many writers on criminology. In later days, those who follow the art of yellow journalism became agitated about that miserable affair in the Madison Square Garden in 1906. In this was no mystery whatever, and there would have been little interest except for the publicity of the crime, the scandals which attended it, and the fact that the victim was famous, and the other persons notorious. Otherwise, it was cheap and shabby; a carnival for the Sunday supplements. The warfare of gamblers, half a dozen years later, which came to a climax in front of the Hotel Metropole in New York, was really an incident in the history of municipal corruption; the killing of Rosenthal belongs in the class of crimes committed during feuds, rather than that of private murders. The lonely death of Mr Elwell in his own home, was the subject of great interest; the opening chapter from a novel by Anna Katharine Green had been translated into reality. But it happened upon a verge of a world where such events are neither rare nor astonishing. More unusual was that scene in De Russey's Lane, New Brunswick, upon whose horrors the discoverer casually wandered, as if stepping upon a stage laden with the dreadful quarry of an Elizabethan tragedy.

No one of these, I venture to assert, equals in peculiar interest the Borden murders in Fall River. Here were concerned neither gamblers, wasters, nor criminals, but quiet folk of a kind known to all of us. They were not members of a class among which killing is a matter of momentary impulse. They were so obscure that except for the event which put their names upon everybody's lips, we should never had heard of them. They became important in the light of what happened; the case was not like a play by a lazy dramatist who shirks his work of creation, and fills his scene with personages already famous. The crime itself—unexpected, hideous, unexplained—was the central point of interest. When the trial came to an end, ten months later, and the jury considered their verdict, there was before them, of course, only the task of answering, by yes or no, the question: was the accused person guilty? Apparently, they had little trouble in finding an answer to this, but the verdict did not clear up the astonishing puzzle. If, instead of a jury bound by our laws, they had been a committee of inquiry, charged with discovering an explanation of the crime, their task would have been as perplexing as anything which twelve men ever attempted. Each of the principal theories advanced at the time had its dark and doubtful points, and was moreover, as many reasonable men believed, in itself grossly improbable, and nearly contrary to human experience. Hardly ever was a murder committed where the limits of time and space so closed in upon the act, leaving such a narrow gap for the assassin to slip through to security.

The name Borden is found in all parts of the United States. It has been honorably associated with more than one important business, and in Canada two of the names have been eminent in politics. Many of the American Bordens are descendants of Richard and Joan Borden who came from England in 1638 to live in Rhode Island. In that State, and even more in the adjoining county of Bristol, Massachusetts (which includes the cities of Fall River, New Bedford, and Taunton), the Bordens have always been numerous. The name has often been associated with that of Durfee. In 1778, when Fall River was attacked by a detachment of British troops, a Major Durfee led the citizens in a successful defence. Two of the houses burned during the fight were owned by men named Borden; one of these men was captured. In 1844, a Borden and a Durfee represented the district in the Legislature; and, in 1892, the year of the tragedy, these family names were borne by one or the other of the victims. Orin Fowler's 'History of Fall River', in 1841, mentions the name Borden as second in frequency in the town. When the name came into painful notoriety in 1892, there were a hundred and twenty-five Bordens—representing, of course, many more than that—listed in the Fall River directory. It is illustrative of the frequency of the name that the indictment for murder, found in that year against a Borden, should have been attested by two others óf the name, father and son, clerk and assistant clerk of the Superior Court, but not related to the accused person.

Fall River, like Dover or Calais, is one of those cities to which few go for its own sake, compared with the thousands who pass through on their way elsewhere. To the traveler into New England from New York or the South, it is associated with the name of a steamship line, and with an early morning change from boat to train. Reuben Paine, the hero of Mr Kipling's 'Rhyme of the Three Sealers', as he lay dying in the fogs of Bering Sea, let his mind travel far over the world to regret:

> No more I'll see the trawlers drift below the
>   Bass Rock ground,
> Or watch the tall Fall steamer lights tear blazing
>   up the Sound.

And if nobody except Reuben Paine, that I have heard of, ever referred to them as 'Fall steamers', it is best to remember not only the exigencies of verse, but that the sight of the Fall River boats, from either shore of Long Island Sound at night, or from the water, is one that might well return to a man after many years. Current and local speech has not always been so respectful toward this steamship line, but Mr Conrad Aiken has not hesitated to make one of the Sound steamers the scene of a poetical romance of much beauty.

The overwhelming importance of one industry, the manufacture of cotton goods, is perhaps what has prevented Fall River from becoming either interesting or attractive. It has its full complement of ugly streets, but of pleasant ones, fewer than such cities as Providence and Salem. Any American can see the town in his mind's eye, for there is a tedious similarity in places of this size; and the fact has been noted in the saying that West Newton, Massachusetts, extends all the way to the Pacific Coast. All have their Main Streets, under that name or another. Fall River has both the name and the thing itself. In 1892 there were a few more trees and a few less brick buildings upon it; the street-cars were not so noisy nor so many; the motion picture theatre, the motor-car and the traffic policeman were still to arrive. Otherwise it looked nearly as it does today. The city had not then grown to have a hundred and twenty thousand inhabitants, but there were about seventy-five thousand, already including many of foreign birth, who were helping the native-born in their work, and sometimes perplexing them, and rendering them doubtful of the blessing of their presence. Citizens whose families had long been established in this country were inclined, as always, to suspect that any unusual offence was necessarily the deed of 'some of those foreigners', forgetting the strange twists and distortions of which the oldest American stock has sometimes shown itself capable.

The newspapers of August, 1892, curiously prim and almost quaint to us today, contained small matter for excitement in that hot, dull season. There were speculations upon Mr Cleveland's popularity; he was about to turn the tables on President Harrison, and defeat him in the November election. Mr Gladstone's health was not too good. That aspiring sportsman, the Emperor Wilhelm, was racing his yacht at Cowes. John L. Sullivan was training for his last fight—with Corbett. From the port of Palos had set forth a replica of the caravel *Santa Maria*, to take part in the celebration of the 400th anniversary of Columbus's discovery. Chicago was raising money for its World's Fair, and hoping that the cholera, reported in distant parts of Europe, was not coming as a guest. There were echoes of the Homestead strike and riot; Mr Frick was recovering from the assault which had nearly ended his life. The *Teutonic* had broken the ocean record by crossing from Queenstown to New York in five days and eighteen hours. And the London police had caught a strange and terrible creature, named Neill Cream, and in great perplexity were uncovering a series of crimes, fiendish and inexplicable.

On the intensely hot morning of Thursday, August 4, 1892, something more than an hour before noon, an elderly gentleman named Andrew Jackson Borden was walking through South Main Street, Fall River. He was returning to his home which was only a few steps from the principal business street, and little more than around the corner from the City Hall, and the center of the town. It is probable that his mind was chiefly concerned with business, or with his family affairs, which were disconcerting. For the personages mentioned in the morning newspapers, and for the events described in them, it is fair to suppose he had no thought. So securely is the future hidden from us, that there is no way to imagine the astonishment which would have been his, could he have had any intimation not alone of the sufficiently startling fact that the remainder of his life time was then numbered by minutes, but that his name was to engage his countrymen's attention, for weeks and months to come, as if he were somebody of national importance.

However little he may have been known elsewhere, in his own town he was certainly not obscure. He was president of the Union Savings Bank, director in one or two other banks, and a director in various companies, including the Merchants Manufacturing Company, the Globe Yarn Mills, the B.M.C. Durfee Safe Deposit and Trust Company, and the Troy Cotton and Woolen Manufacturing Company. His business affairs had taken him on that morning to one or more of these banks. In his early life he had been an undertaker, and either that, or the gloomy custom of mankind, led him to dress in black, and in black clothes he trudged along on this tropically hot morning. His hair was white, for he was about seventy years of age, and he wore a fringe of white whiskers under his chin and along the angle of the jaw. His expression could be kindly, but it was stern; the thin lips—he wore no moustache—met in a way that denoted a stubborn character. The New England phrase is suggested: 'He was as set as the everlasting hills of Zion'. I have heard him described by one who remembers him coming from his farm—a tall and erect old man, in his black clothes, carrying a little basket of eggs. That last bit is significant; Mr Borden owned farms across the Taunton River, in addition to more than one house in the city. He had built one of the best office buildings in Fall River and the value of his estate was between $250,000 and $300,000. Yet he was not averse to bringing a few eggs to town, and selling them to some dealer. His manner of living had not changed as he rose from lesser things to greater, from one small business to financial power which, in that time and place, was not so different from that of a millionaire in a large city today. His was the melancholy lot of a man grown old in the treadmill of business, with no idea that life could be enjoyed, and no diversion except the further

The Borden house.

accumulation of money. Yet a just and honorable man, respected by everybody, and loved, perhaps, by one woman. He
lived simply—many would say narrowly—in a small wooden
house, Number 92 (now 230) Second Street.

Mr Borden had married twice. His first wife was a Miss
Sarah A. Morse, by whom he had three children. After the
death of the first Mrs Borden, he married in 1865, Miss Abby
Durfee Gray, who was six years younger than himself, and
therefore in 1892 about sixty-four years old. With Mr and Mrs
Borden there lived the two surviving daughters by the first
marriage, Miss Emma L. Borden, about forty-one years old,
and Miss Lizzie Andrew Borden, about thirty-two. These four
persons, with a servant named Bridget Sullivan, made up the
family at the Borden home.

On August 4th, however, Miss Emma Borden was visiting
some friends in Fairhaven, but the number of the house in
Second Street remained the same, since John Vinnicum Morse,
a brother of the first Mrs Borden, had arrived the day before for
a short visit. This was a man of sixty years, who lived in
Dartmouth, Massachusetts. Visits to Fall River and to the
Borden house were frequent with him after his return to New
England from twenty years spent as a farmer in Iowa. Serious
and disturbing as the consequences of this visit were to Mr
Morse, it is almost impossible to regard his casual appearance
in the household, on this occasion, without amusement. Arriving, quite without baggage, on August 3rd, and solemnly
pursuing for about twenty-four hours the objects of his visit—
which seem to have been calls upon other relatives and the
inspection of Mr Borden's farms—he found himself entangled
in events of the most dreadful and sensational nature. The
innocent bystander proverbially deserves our sympathy, but
seldom gets it. Excepting young Mr Monks, embarking upon
the *Herbert Fuller*, for health, rest, and recreation (as recorded
elsewhere) it is hard to recall any figure similar to that of John
Vinnicum Morse.

Mr Borden continued through South Main Street, up Borden Street, and thence—it could have been only a few minutes'
walk, even for an elderly man—into Second Street. He arrived
at his home at ten or fifteen minutes before eleven. He had some

little difficulty getting admitted, going first to the side door and then to the front, (for it was a peculiar household as regards locks, bars, and bolts) but at last he entered. Within about thirty minutes a report came to the police that Mr Borden had died—by violence—and the investigation began.

Out of the mass of rumors and assertions, of charges and denials, it is necessary now to select certain facts which are generally admitted, and to trace the happenings of the week in Mr Borden's home. It is useless to pretend that the family was either happy or contented. The presence in one home, of a step-mother and two daughters of mature years may be a fortunate combination with people of especially sunny disposition, but the Bordens seem to have been rather dour folk, to say the least. There was an aggrieved feeling about money on the part of the daughters, and this was of long standing. There was a perfectly comprehensible dissatisfaction with the manner of living, with the lack of such modern arrangements as a bathroom—which some parents then considered new-fangled, expensive and unnecessary. When all these difficulties were discussed in court, the best that could be done was to admit some of them, but vigorously to deny that they had any bearing on the murder, or that anything of importance could be deduced from them. But we have it, on the statement of a witness who was undisputed, that there was in the mind of that member of the family most concerned not to exaggerate the lack of harmony, a sense of impending disaster, and this only the night before the murder.

It had been a disturbing week. On Tuesday, August 2nd, Mr and Mrs Borden had been violently ill during the night. They were seized with vomiting. Miss Lizzie Borden said that she herself was affected, but not so as to cause vomiting. She went, she said, to the bedroom door of the older people, and asked if she could be of any help to them, but the offer was declined. Mr Morse who came to the house after the family had eaten their dinner, at noon, on Wednesday, was served with that meal, which he ate alone. He ate again at breakfast on Thursday with Mr and Mrs Borden, but seems to have suffered no harm, nor was there any other return of this mysterious sickness, except that the servant Bridget Sullivan, was, alone of the household, sick on Thursday morning, the day of the murder, when she went into the backyard where she vomited her breakfast.

On Wednesday afternoon, after his dinner, Mr Morse went to Swansea, to Mr Borden's farm. He returned to the house on Second Street after eight o'clock, and sat talking with Mr and Mrs Borden. Miss Lizzie Borden was paying a call in a neighboring street, upon Miss Alice Russell, a friend of the family. During this call there was a remarkable conversation. Miss Borden said that she had decided to follow Miss Russell's advice, and go to Marion for a vacation. But she was apprehensive and depressed. She said:

'I feel as if somethig was hanging over me that I cannot throw off.'

She described Mr and Mrs Borden's sickness, the night before, and expressed a suspicion that the milk might have been intentionally poisoned! Miss Russell was incredulous, and in this there is little cause for wonder. The suggestion that some person, with the tendencies of the Borgias, was, in the early hours of the morning, slipping deadly drugs into the milk can of a respectable family in a New England town is not one that ordinarily commends itself to the usual lady of good sense. The caller, however, went on to say that she feared her father had an enemy. He had trouble with somebody who came to see him. One man got into a quarrel with Mr Borden and was ordered out of the house. Then there were robberies: the barn had been broken into twice. Miss Russell, who had formerly lived in a house next to the Bordens, and was still a not-distant neighbor, offered a more prosaic explanation of the barn robberies; they were merely boys coming after the pigeons. There had also been a daylight burglary, in the house, said Miss Borden. At one time or another in the conversation, this prophetess of disaster said that she slept in 'fear that they will burn the house down over us'. She was not precise as to who 'they' were, but as everybody knows there are no more dangerous nor malicious beings in the world than 'they'. After a little more lugubrious chat of this kind, Miss Borden left her friend to her meditations. Like Cassandra's, her foreboding fell upon doubting ears, but like Cassandra's, her prophecies were by no means empty.

Miss Borden returned home, and although her uncle John

Vinnicum Morse was seated in the room below, talking with her father and step-mother, and although she had not yet seen him, she did not pause nor speak to him. She went upstairs to her own room. She was the last one to enter by the front door, which she locked. Bridget was the last to enter by the side door, which she in turn locked. Mr and Mrs Borden that night as usual occupied their room in the rear of the second floor of the house; Miss Borden's room was next theirs. Mr Morse slept in the guest-room at the front. Bridget's room was on the third floor. It is hard to conceive how any person other than these five could have been in the house, and I believe that no serious contention has ever been made that any stranger was concealed.

The next morning, Thursday, Bridget Sullivan came downstairs at a little after six o'clock, built a fire in the kitchen stove, and began to prepare breakfast. Mrs Borden appeared about seven, and her husband and Mr Morse soon following, the three breakfasted together. This breakfast was subsequently discussed at more than one legal investigation, so it may be said that according to Mr Morse it consisted of mutton, bread, coffee, 'sugar cakes' and bananas. The servant, who prepared the food, said that there was *mutton-broth*, as well as mutton itself, johnny cakes, coffee and cookies. Bridget insisted, in answer to the specific question, that to the best of her belief, they had no bananas that day. At all events, for a hot morning and mid-summer it was a breakfast well adapted to set the stage for a tragedy. One trembles at the thought of beginning a day in August with mutton-soup.

A lady said to me recently that, after more than thirty years, the details of the Borden case had vanished from her mind—all except this awful breakfast.

Mr Morse departed from the house at a quarter before eight. Mr Borden let him out at the side door, and locked the screen door after him. A little later, Miss Borden came downstairs, and at first said to Bridget that she doubted if she cared for any breakfast. Finally, however, she decided to have coffee and cookies. Mr and Mrs Borden moved about the house; emptying slops and attending to other work of the kind, for Bridget was not expected to do this, nor was she even allowed in the rooms

The bodies of Mr and Mrs Borden.

on the second floor. Soon afterwards, the servant was attacked by the sickness already referred to, and went into the yard, for perhaps ten or fifteen minutes, where she was relieved by vomiting. She described her illness as a 'sick headache'. When she returned to the house, Mr Borden had gone downtown. This was between nine and half after the hour, and the three women were now, so far as anybody knows, alone in the house. Miss Borden was in the kitchen, still engaged, perhaps with her cookies and coffee, while Mrs Borden was wielding a feather-duster in the dining-room. The latter gave Bridget some orders for the morning; the windows on the lower floor were to be washed inside and out. A few minutes later, at about half-past nine, it would appear that Mrs Borden, having made up the bed in the guest-room, came downstairs again, and remarked that she was going back to put pillow-cases upon the two pillows of the bed in that room. She disappeared upstairs and nobody has ever admitted to seeing her alive again.

Bridget Sullivan went to the barn and to the cellar for brushes, pails, and other things for the window-washing. She came into the kitchen, the dining-room and the sitting-room to close the windows before beginning her work, and found those rooms empty. Neither Mrs Borden nor Miss Borden was there. She began her duties outdoors and in, washing windows on both sides of the house. It occupied some time; she had a talk over the fence with 'Mrs Kelly's girl,' and she made a number of trips to the barn for fresh pails of water. The Kellys were the next-door neighbors to the south. Neighbors' houses were close to the Borden house on both sides, and in the rear. Finally Bridget finished outside, and was occupied indoors, when she heard Mr Borden fumbling at the front door. He had already been at the side of the house where he found the wooden door open, but the screen door locked. Now he was trying his key at the front.

Bridget came from the sitting-room to let him in, but found the door not only locked, but triple-locked, with bolt, key, and spring lock. This is said to have been contrary to custom, and the slight annoyance caused her to make some exclamation, to say 'Oh, pshaw!'

At that moment she heard Miss Lizzie Borden at the head of the front stairs. She heard her *laugh*.

This little hall opens into Miss Lizzie Borden's room, and into the guest-room. Mr Borden entered his house and went to the dining-room. His daughter came to him, asked about the mail, and said:

'Mrs Borden has gone out; she had a note from somebody who was sick.'

Mr Borden took the key of his bedroom — it was a curiously well-guarded house — from a shelf, and went up the backstairs, to his own chamber. He came down again very shortly, and sat by a window in the sitting-room. Bridget finished her window-cleaning, going from one room to another. Miss Borden now appeared in the kitchen, to get an ironing board; this she took to the dining-room, and placing it on the table there, began to iron some handkerchiefs. All of this, from the entrance of Mr Borden, occupied but a few moments.

Miss Borden then made an inquiry of Bridget, addressing her, according to her custom, as 'Maggie,'' a name which had been inherited from a former servant.

'Maggie, are you going out this afternoon?'

'I don't know,' replied Bridget, 'I might and I might not; I don't feel very well.'

Apparently nobody did feel very well in that house. Miss Borden had herself made a meagre breakfast, as we have seen. But the mutton-soup may account for that.

'If you go out,' pursued the lady, 'be sure and lock the door, for Mrs Borden has gone out on a sick call, and I might go out, too.'

'Miss Lizzie,' Bridget asked, 'who is sick?'

'I don't know,' was the reply, 'she had a note this morning; it must be in town.'

And she went on ironing. Bridget rinsed the cloths she had been using, and hung them behind the kitchen stove. Miss Borden came into the kitchen, with another friendly bit of information.

'There is a cheap sale of dress goods at Sargent's at eight cents a yard.'

Bridget replied:

'I am going to have one,' and went upstairs, up the back-stairs, of course, to her own room where she lay down on the bed for a rest.

Surprise has often been expressed at this action on the part of
a servant, at eleven o'clock in the morning. But Bridget had
been up since six, she had been working steadily and there was
nothing more to be done until half-past eleven or twelve, when
she was to get the midday dinner. It was her custom, if time
allowed, to take such a rest; the Bordens were not unduly hard
or exacting towards their servant. It has been seen that she had
few of the duties of a housemaid, and none as chambermaid. No
astonishment could have been felt by any member of the family
when she went upstairs. The dinner, moreover, was to be
merely a repetition of the gruesome breakfast: 'soup to warm
over and cold mutton.'

Shortly after she reached her room she heard the City Hall
clock strike eleven. The house was quite; she heard no doors
opened nor shut, nor any other sound. She denied that she slept
or even became drowsy; on second questioning she weakened
the force of her denial a little — she did not *think* that she slept at
all. One rarely does know about this, and with many persons it
seems to be considered a confession of breach of trust ever to
admit closing the eyes, days or night. Second Street is a narrow
street; wagons and carts probably rattled and rumbled past
from time to time, but Bridget may well have failed to hear or to
notice them. Nothing unusual was abroad in the house; nothing, at least, that came to the servant's ears, until some ten or
fifteen minutes had passed. Then she heard Miss Borden's
voice, and the tone of alarm was apparent at the first words.

'Maggie, come down!'

'What is the matter?' asked Bridget.

'Come down quick; Father's dead; somebody came in and
killed him!'

Bridget descended instantly, and found Miss Borden standing near the side door. The servant started to enter the sitting-
room, but was checked.

'Oh, Maggie, don't go in. I have got to have a doctor quick.
Go over. I have got to have the doctor.'

There was no doubt who was meant by this. Dr Bowen, the
family's friend and physician, who had already been consulted
that week in regard to the strange illness, lived diagonally
across the street, within a stone's throw. Bridget hurried to his

house and reported the death to Mrs Bowen, but learned that the doctor was, at the moment, not at home. She came back and told Miss Borden, and at the same time asked the question which was destined to be asked by everybody:

'Miss Lizzie, where were you when this thing happened?'

The reply was:

'I was out in the yard, and heard a groan, and came in and the screen door was wide open.'

Bridget was then ordered to go to Miss Russell's house and bring her. She departed again. In the meantime the going and coming of Bridget, pale and agitated, had attracted the attention of the nearest neighbor, Mrs Churchill, who lived in the house to the north, hardly more than thirty feet away. Mrs Churchill went to the window, looked across at her neighbor's house, and saw the younger daughter of the family standing inside the screen door, and apparently excited or agitated. The distance was so slight as to make it possible to note that. She called to Miss Borden and asked her if there was any trouble.

'Oh, Mrs Churchill,' was the reply, 'do come over. Someone has killed Father.

Mrs Churchill hastened to her neighbor's house, went up the side-steps, and put her hand upon Miss Borden's arm.

'Oh, Lizzie!   Where is your father?'

'In the sitting-room.'

'Where were you when it happened?'

'I went to the barn to get a piece of iron.'

'Where is your mother?'

'I don't know; she had a note to go see someone who is sick, but I don't know but that she is killed too, for I thought I heard her come in . . . Father must have an enemy, for we have all been sick, and we think the milk has been poisoned.'

Mrs Churchill then learned that Dr Bowen could not be found, and she volunteered to go out in search of another doctor. She crossed the street to a stable, and asked for help. Among the men who heard her was one named Cunningham, who telephoned to the police station. City Marshal Hilliard thus received the news at 11:15 and sent an officer to the house.

Mrs Churchill returned to the Borden home, where in a few moments and before the arrival of the policeman, Bridget rejoined them, followed by Dr Bowen. Then, for the first time since the alarm was given, somebody entered the sitting-room. This was a small room, nearly square, with but two windows, both on the south side. The floor was covered with the usual garish, flowered carpet, customary in such houses at that time, and the wall paper was of a similarly disturbing pattern. The furniture was mahogany or black walnut, upholstered with the invariable black horsehair. On the north side of the room, opposite the windows, was a large sofa, and on this lay the dead body of Mr Borden with his head and face so hacked as to be unrecognizable even to his friend and physician, Dr Bowen.

The doctor noticed that Mr Borden had removed his coat, which was folded on the arm of the sofa, above the pillow on which his head rested. He had put on a cardigan jacket, in place of the coat. The body was stretched on the couch, but the legs from the knees down sloped toward the floor, and the feet rested on the carpet. It was his custom to take a nap in that position. Apparently, he had not altered his position after the attack. He wore congress shoes. There was no sign of a struggle; the fists were not clenched, and no furniture in the room was overturned. Dr Bowen believed that he had been killed by the first blow, while asleep, but as to the other wounds which had been inflicted, in order to make death certain, he added:

'Physician that I am, and accustomed to all kinds of horrible sights, it sickened me to look upon the dead man's face.'

Mr Borden had been dead, so he thought, not more than twenty minutes.

Dr Bowen asked for a sheet with which to cover the body, and then, at Miss Borden's request, went to send a telegram to her elder sister at Fairhaven. He was asked to break the sad news as gently as possible. Miss Russell had arrived by this time, and with Mrs Churchill was engaged in the humane task of comforting Mr Borden's afflicted daughter: fanning her, bathing her brow with cologne, and otherwise offering such help as would naturally be suggested. It was not observed that she asked for any of these feminine consolations, nor that she shed any tears, showed hysteria, nor betrayed great agitation. Indeed, it would not be too much to say that she was, on the whole, as calm in her demeanor, perhaps calmer, than any of

Lizzie Borden.

the women who fluttered about, and made unsuccessful attempts to 'loosen her dress' and apply other forms of first aid. Grief shows itself in different ways in different temperaments; and it has often been noticed, even after natural deaths which have not come suddenly, that the person most bereaved does not, at once, exhibit the most sorrow.

Finally, Miss Borden said that she wished that somebody would try to find Mrs Borden, as she thought she had heard her come in. Dr Bowen had been sent for, and Miss Russell, and it now seemed appropriate to notify the person most concerned: the wife of the dead man. Bridget declined to go upstairs alone, but went with Mrs Churchill from the kitchen to the front of the house, and up the frontstairs. The neighbor said:

'As I went upstairs I turned my head to the left, and as I got up so that my eyes were on the level with the front hall, I could see across the front hall and across the floor of the spare room. At the far side on the north side of the room I saw something that looked like the form of a person.'

Bridget went into the room for an instant; Mrs Churchill did not. They went downstairs again, hastily. When they had joined the others in the kitchen, Mrs Churchill sank into a chair, with an exclamation or a groan. Miss Russell asked:

'Is there another?'

And Mrs Churchill said: 'Yes; she is up there.'

The situation was quite beyond the experience of any woman; it is not surprising that Mrs Churchill had no exclamation or remark in her vocabulary. Others went upstairs within a few minutes; Dr Bowen was soon back at the house; and if the scene in the lower room was shocking, that in the upper was both ghastly and pitiful. The furnishing of the 'spare room' would be homely and familiar to most of us. It had all the heaviness of the Victorian style of decoration: the carpet with gigantic clusters of impossible roses; the ponderous bed with carved head and frontboards in some dark wood; and beyond, against the north wall, another ornate piece of furniture, a dressing table, or 'bureau', with brass knobs and handles on the drawers, slabs of white marble on the top, ornaments and framed photographs, a lace-covered pin-cushion, and two white bottles or cruets, theoretically for scent or toilet water, precisely placed but purely ornamental, since nobody ever knew such receptacles to contain anything at all. The fringed bedcover was smooth and clean, and the two pillows were covered by the white cases with ruffled borders which had been the last care of the poor woman who had gone to make up the bed which her guest had occupied.

On the floor between the dressing table and the bed, face-downward in a pool of blood, was the body of Mrs Borden. Her head had been ferociously hacked and battered, like her husband's. But her wounds, unlike his, were not so fresh nor recent; the blood had ceased to flow from them, and that on the floor had coagulated; the temperature of her body was sensibly lower; she had been dead much longer than he. She wore a light dress of some cotton cloth. She was a short, heavy woman, weighing nearly two hundred pounds; how had she fallen at full length from an upright position without shaking the house, and alarming the others who were in it? Had she been caught by the assailant kneeling at the side of the bed to tuck in the bed clothes, and had there been, in consequence, no heavy fall? The position of the body, stretched out fully, with the arms under her; did not indicate this. If it were true, what evil fate was it that caused the two victims, the old man and his wife, she kneeling and he lying down, and both helpless, to be delivered thus into such savage and merciless hands?

The first policeman to arrive at the house was one named Allen. He was the committing officer at the police station, and happened to be there and available when the City Marshal (or chief of police) received the warning by telephone. He was dispatched to look into some 'row' on Second Street, and may have thought that it was merely another 'cutting affray' between some of 'those foreigners.' Certainly he did not know that he was to make the first report upon one of the most notorious and perplexing crimes which have ever engaged American police officers. It is one of the ironical circumstances of this case that upon the day when the Fall River police were for the first and only time to be brought into national celebrity, and to start an investigation which was to call down upon themselves unlimited criticism and abuse—quite undeserved, as best I can judge—that upon this day of days in their history, more than half of them were away on their annual picnic at Rocky Point! Their chief was at his post, however, while a few members of the day force were on double duty.

Officer Allen stayed but a few moments at the Borden house. He looked upon the body of Mr Borden, but at that time no discovery had been made of the other death, and he did not search the house. Instead of finding some fruit-vender, or vagrant, bleeding from one or two unimportant wounds acquired in a casual fight with a friend, he gazed upon the horrifying spectacle of a venerable and respected citizen barbarously murdered in his own home. A friendly writer says of Allen that he was, 'to put it mildly, taken considerably aback by the sight in the house, and, to put it not too strongly, was frightened out of his wits. He left no guard upon the house when he ran back to the station' to inform the Marshal. It is, however, said that he stationed a private citizen at the side door, with orders to admit nobody except the police and physicians. There have always been many to assert that a prompt and intelligent search of the house, with all that this implies, would have solved the mystery at once. This assertion seems to be based upon the knowledge gained after the fact and upon suppositions which may or may not be sound. It is not at all impossible that the police did, within twenty-four hours, discover nearly all the evidence which it was humanly possible to find. I think it can be put even more strongly: it is probable that they did so. This statement holds true, it seems to me, whatever view one takes of the commission of the crime. If one follows the opinion of those who hold that the murders were the work of a stranger, an outsider, then this assassin certainly carried with him, when he fled from the house, all the most important evidence. And while it is not possible to discuss other theories, except as one may speculate upon a mystery, it is not unreasonable to believe that the most telling clews as to guilt were suppressed, destroyed or removed before the alarm was given. Officer Allen did not act with composure nor acumen — but it may be that his omissions were less damaging than they have been considered.

What the police did not comprehend was that they were working in the dark against a person of considerable cunning and extraordinary audacity, who was, moreover, protected by an incredible series of lucky chances.

Before a great number of people had arrived in or near the house, Mr John Vinnicum Morse strolled down Second Street. He had been calling, at some distance, upon a nephew and niece, and now, as the dinner hour approached, returned to the Borden home, part of the way by street-car, but the rest of the way on foot. Although inside the house lay the murdered forms of his host and hostess, and although a small group of agitated persons had gathered in the kitchen, Mr Morse was not aware of anything unusual. He went through the side yard, to the rear of the house, picked up two or three pears, and began to eat them. Pears enter this case more than once, and to all who are familiar with the region and the time of year, they suggest the atmosphere of an old New England garden in August. Perhaps Mr Morse, as he thought of dinner, foresaw a recurrence of the mutton-soup and was fortifying himself against the blow, but in any event we should not begrudge him his pears, nor the two or three peaceful minutes he spent with them, before he went into the house. It was to be a long time before he was to know peace again, or to go mooning about Fall River and its vicinity upon his innocent errands. From a small expedition which he attempted, a day or two later, merely as far as the post-office, he returned with an escort of about one thousand people, and under police protection. Most unjustifiable suspicions were entertained against him for a number of days, but the police discovered promptly that his alibi was perfect, and that his account of his doings that morning was truthful and fully corroborated.

From shortly after midday it is impossible to think of Second Street as quiet, or of Number 92 as a house in which silence dwelt, as it had when Bridget heard the town clock strike the hour before noon. Crowds gathered in such numbers as to drive the newspaper reporters, in describing them, to the use of the phrase, 'a surging mass of humanity.' Friends, policemen, clergymen and doctors gathered in the yard, or swarmed through the house. The utmost pity was expressed for Miss Borden, since she had suffered a double sorrow through events far more distressing than natural deaths.

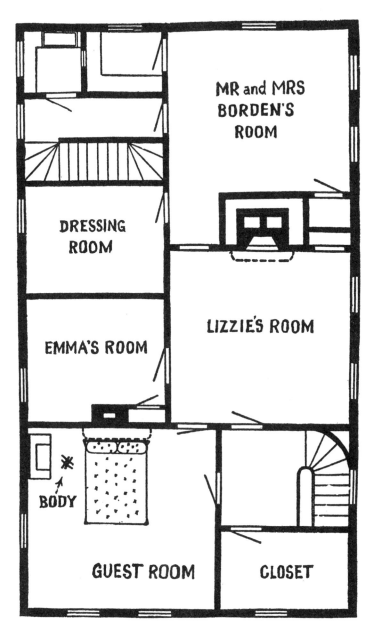

Upstairs at the Borden house.

Dr Dolan, one of the Medical Examiners for the county, had chanced to be passing the Borden house at 11:45, before the crowds had come. (Medical Examiner is the name in Massachusetts for the officer who elsewhere is called coroner. He is necessarily a physician.) Dr Dolan entered the house, and with Dr Bowen and others, viewed the dead persons. It was discovered that there had been no robbery from Mr Borden's body: he wore a ring, and had in his pockets a watch and a pocketbook; in money there was $81.65. Dr Dolan heard of the sickness in the family, two days earlier, and in consequence, took samples of the milk for analysis. He went with the police to the cellar, during their search of the house, and took note of some axes and hatchets which were found there. It was evident to all who saw the wounds in the skulls of the dead man and woman that these had been made by some heavy instrument, with a cutting edge—without any doubt, a hatchet or something similar. During a visit, later in the afternoon, Dr Dolan had the bodies photographed, and then removed the stomachs and sent them, with the samples of milk, to Edward S Wood, professor of chemistry in the Harvard Medical School, and celebrated consultant in cases of legal medicine.

The search of the house proceeded; Miss Borden was questioned and questioned again by almost every officer who arrived. It was a distressing ordeal. One of those who had an interview with her was a patrolman, named Philip Harrington, who was afterwards described by the Chief Justice of the Superior Court as 'intelligent.' To him Miss Borden said that during the time of her absence from the house, when the attack upon her father took place, she was in the barn, that she was in there for twenty minutes. He expressed surprise that she did not hear anything from the house or the yard, sounds of the attack, of the opening or closing of doors, or of footsteps in the yard. She said that she was in the *loft* of the barn. This caused him still further surprise, since, as he and others afterwards discovered, the dusty loft of that barn, on a sultry August day, was about as uninviting a place as the steam-room of a Turkish bath. He and others made investigations as to the barn and the results of them will be considered later. Harrington asked her about any men who might have borne malice against her father, and she narrated one or two semi-angry conversations between her father and some strange man, which she had overheard. The policeman warned her about talking to anybody else, and suggested that it would be well for her to make no further statements for that day. Owing to the atrocity of the crime, he suggested, she might well be confused. She answered, however, with what he called 'a stiff courtesy,' and said:

'No, I can tell you all I know now, just as well as at any other time.'

Mr Edwin H. Porter, historian of the Borden case, says that it was his conversation with Philip Harrington, as it was later reported to the City Marshal, which aroused suspicions 'in the minds of the police that the daughter knew more of the circumstances of the tragedy than she cared to tell.' The police were to pay dearly for such suspicions, but it seems hard to understand, in view of what has been related, to say nothing of what was yet to be discovered, how they could have avoided them. And yet it was a monstrous thing to suspect. As time went on, it took the form not of a mere accusation of complicity, or guilty knowledge of the crime, but of the part of principal and sole actor in it. And to suggest that a woman of good family, of blameless life and hitherto unimpeachable character, could possibly commit two such murders, is to suggest something so rare as to be almost unknown to criminology. It is beside the question to cite the many homicides of which women have been proven guilty. Nearly always, when the victim was an adult person, they have been murders by poison or by shooting. When, in modern times, the attack has taken a more brutal form, the murderess has usually been a woman of base antecedents, one from the criminal class, and acting in concert with a man. There is that about the act of battering in the skulls of an elderly man and woman which suggests the male butcher, not the more subtle though equally malicious methods of the murderess. The police of Fall River and the law officers of the county were not so inexperienced as to ignore this, and they could not have taken the step they did under the pressure of strong evidence. There was no lack of other and powerful influences working against it.

Mr Edwin Porter's book, 'The Fall River Tragedy' is a

comprehensive history of the case based upon intimate personal knowledge. It has the advantages and disadvantages of having been compiled, apparently, from current newspaper accounts, the result of the author's work as police reporter of the *Fall River Globe*. In the opening chapter, he sums up the perplexity which beset all early investigators. They were absolutely at a loss to explain how, in broad daylight, it had been possible for anybody to commit two murders and escape unseen, both by those in and outside the house. This difficulty was increased as the medical testimony made it apparent that from one to two hours had elapsed between the death of Mrs Borden and that of her husband. Mr Porter refers to the escape of the murderer in one apt sentence:

'The author of that hideous slaughter had come and gone as gently as the south wind, but had fulfilled his mission as terrifically as a cyclone.'

In the same chapter he describes the extraordinary series of chances that favored the murderer. I quote the passage:

'To those who stop to contemplate the circumstances surrounding the double murder, it was marvelous to reflect how fortune had favored the assassin. Not once in a million times would fate have paved such a way for him. He had to deal with a family of six persons in an unpretentious two-and-a-half story house, the rooms of which were all connected and in which it would have been a difficult matter to stifle sound. He must catch Mr Borden alone and either asleep, or off his guard, and kill him with one fell blow. The faintest outcry would have sounded an alarm. He must also encounter Mrs Borden alone and fell her, a heavy woman, noiselessly. To do this he must either make his way from the sitting room on the ground floor to the spare bed room above the parlor and avoid five persons in the passage, or he must conceal himself in one of the rooms upstairs and make the descent under the same conditions. The murdered woman must not lisp a syllable at the first attack, and her fall must not attract attention. He must then conceal the dripping implement of death and depart in broad daylight by a much frequented street. In order to accomplish this he must take a time, when Miss Emma L. Borden, the older daughter of the murdered man, was on a visit to relatives out of the city; Miss Lizzie A. Borden, the other daughter, must be in the barn and remain there twenty minutes. A less time than that would not suffice. Bridget Sullivan, the servant, must be in the attic asleep on her own bed. Her presence in the pantry or kitchen or any room on the first or second floors would have frustrated the fiend's designs, unless he also killed her so that she would die without a murmur. In making his escape there must be no blood stains upon his clothing; for such tell-tale marks might have betrayed him. And so, if the assailant of the aged couple was not familiar with the premises, his luck favored him exactly as described. He made no false move. He could not have proceeded more swiftly nor surely had he lived in the modest edifice for years. At the most he had just twenty minutes in which to complete his work. He must go into the house after Miss Lizzie entered the barn and he must disappear before she returned. More than that, the sixth member of the family, John V. Morse, must vanish from the house while the work was being done. He could not have been counted on by any criminal, however shrewd, who had planned the tragedy ahead. Mr Morse came and went at the Borden homestead. He was not engaged in business in Fall River and there were no stated times when the wretch who did the slaughtering could depend upon his absence. Mr Morse must not loiter about the house or yard after breakfast as was his custom; he must take a car to some other part of the city and he must not return until his host and hostess have been stretched lifeless. The slightest hitch in these conditions and the murderer would have been balked or detected red handed upon the spot. Had Miss Emma remained at home she would have been a stumbling block; had Miss Lizzie left the stable [barn] a few moments earlier she would have seen the murderer as he ran out the side door; had Bridget Sullivan shortened her nap and descended the stairs she would have heard her mistress drop, as the axe fell on her head; had Mr Morse cut short his visit to friends by as much as ten minutes the butcher would have dashed into his arms as he ran out at the front gate; had Mr Borden returned earlier from his morning visit to the post office he would have caught the assassin murdering his aged wife, or had he uttered a scream at the time he himself was cut down, at least two persons would have rushed to his assistance.

It was a wonderful chain of circumstances which conspired to clear the way for the murderer; so wonderful that its links baffled men's understanding.'

There was still another and greater difficulty for this singularly astute and favored murderer to overcome. It is not clearly mentioned by Mr Porter, for the reason, it may be, that his first chapter was written early in the history of the case and never revised in the light of subsequent knowledge. It was established that Mrs Borden had been killed not less than an hour and possibly two hours before her husband. The autopsies proved this. Therefore it was necessary, assuming the murderer to have come from outside the house, for him to have killed Mrs Borden at about half-past nine, without attracting the attention of Miss Lizzie Borden or of Bridget Sullivan; to have remained concealed in the house until eleven, still eluding them, and then to have accompliuhed his purpose with Mr Borden, and to have left the house unseen. Even for those who advanced a different theory as to the identity of the murderer, that is, for persons who agreed with the contention of the Commonwealth, there were still unexplained difficulties—especially as to the time of Mr Morse's return and of Bridget's retirement upstairs. Who could have predicted when these would take place?

For those who like to exhaust every possibility, there is, of course, the wild hypothesis of a first and second murderer: one who killed Mrs Borden and then fled, and one who tracked down and slew Mr Borden in the same fashion, and with the same or similar weapon. Difficult, even absurd, as this theory is, it is no more impossible of belief than some of the notions which were entertained. Folk were almost ready to suggest a visitation of Providence, or other supernatural act of vengeance, although why the Heavenly powers should set upon this harmless pair was unexplained. Nor was the method exactly celestial.

The investigation went on during that hot afternoon, and before midnight the police had some astounding information. Dr Bowen had related the story of the illness, and the suspected poisoning — as Miss Borden had also done to Miss Russell and to Mrs Churchill. Two officers went to various pharmacies to learn if anybody had been purchasing poison, and at D.R. Smith's on South Main Street, the clerk, Eli Bence, said that an attempt had been made to buy prussic acid. This had happened on Wednesday, the day before the murders. A lady had come in the morning and asked for this deadly drug for the purpose of killing moths in a seal-skin coat. Mr Bence had refused to sell it, except on a doctor's prescription, and she went away disappointed. He identified this lady as Miss Lizzie Borden, and, being taken to her house to see her (although it is said that he knew her perfectly well by sight), persisted in the identification. In this he was supported by another clerk in the pharmacy, Frederick E. Hart, and by a third man who was also present, one Frank H. Kilroy. On the next day, August 5, the *Fall River Globe* printed a full account of it, under the headings: 'What did Lizzie Want of Poison? She is Identified by a Drug Clerk as Having Visited his Store Recently.' Newspapers elsewhere failed to accept the information, or else gave it slight attention. I have been told by one who knew him that Bence was a careful man, who was quite aware of the serious import of his statement. The final disposition of the matter, as legal evidence, will appear in an account of the trial.

The note, which, according to Miss Borden, had been received by her stepmother, remained elusive. Who had sent it? Who brought it? Under what circumstances was it received, and what action was taken? Did she really go out? If she did go out, it is inconceivable that she went in the cotton dress in which was doing housework, and so it must have required agility to get back into that dress, for she wore it when death overtook her. A New York paper, *Once a Week*, offered $500 for the discovery of the writer of the note, and the *Fall River News* begged its readers in the name of justice, to find this writer. But the reward was unclaimed, and the appeal unanswered. Finally, Miss Borden told Dr Dolan that she believed the note must have been burned up in the kitchen stove. Nobody suggested that the person who sent it and the messenger who brought it had been carried away by giant eagles. But the land knew them no more.

Within a single day the attention of the newspaper readers of the country was directed toward the Misses Borden. Miss Emma, the elder, had returned from Fairhaven in the evening of the day of the murder. Information about her was of a rather negative quality; she was reputed to be less active in church work than her sister, and to have traveled less. As to the younger, it never appeared that her parents had called her by the glorious name of Elizabeth; her legal style was that less pleasing diminutive, for which the best that can be said is that it did not offend the delicate ear of Miss Jane Austen, since she allowed the heroine of '*Pride and Prejudice*' so to be addressed by her family. In our time, the Ford automobile has been called, in derision, a Lizzie, and it is said that Miss Mary Pickford uses this name as a sort of generic term to describe her spectators. It can hardly be given in compliment. But in the years '92 and '93 there was only one 'Lizzie' for the people of the United States, and it was that Fall River lady who was presently to be confronted with the gravest of accusations. It is almost invariably noticed that a charge of murder, or of any serious crime, acts automatically to rob a person of all right to polite address; the public promptly makes free with the first name, especially if it is a woman. There is some strange rule about this, exactly as with the custom by which a sedate middle-aged man, when he puts on military uniform, in time of war, instantly becomes a 'boy'.

Miss Lizzie Borden was a native of Fall River, and had been graduated from the high school. Some of her classmates described her as 'rather eccentric,' which, of itself, means exactly nothing. There is no human being who would not be described as 'eccentric,' by one or another of his or her acquaintances. She had traveled in Europe, with other ladies, in 1890. Perhaps the outstanding fact about her was her membership in the Central Congregational Church, in various charitable societies such as the Fruit and Flower Mission, and in the Woman's Christian Temperance Union. At her Church Mission she taught a class of young people. Her association with these religious bodies was no meaningless fact when clouds began to gather over her life, for her cause was warmly supported by them. The Rev. Mr Buck and the Rev. Mr Jubb, her pastors, became her pillars of support, and although after a time, through constant repetition of their names, some of the less devout were tempted to look upon them as the Box and Cox of the Borden cause, it could have been no small consolation and of no little value to her, when she appeared at public hearings, to enter the room on some occasions 'leaning on the arm' of the Rev. Mr Buck, and at other times escorted in similar fashion by the Rev. Mr Jubb.

The frank comments upon the case which appeared within the first few days may be typified by an interview given out on August 5th by Mr Hiram Harrington. He was the husband of Mr Borden's only sister, and is not to be confused with the officer, Philip Harrington. A few passages may be quoted:

> 'Mr Borden was an exceedingly hard man concerning money matters, determined and stubborn. . . . As the motive for the crime it was money, unquestionably money. If Mr Borden died he would have left something over $500,000, and in my opinion that estate furnishes the only motive, and a sufficient one for the double murder. Last evening I had a long interview with Miss Lizzie, who has refused to see anyone else. . . . She was very composed, showed no signs of any emotion, nor were there any traces of grief upon her countenance. That did not surprise me, as she is not naturally emotional.'

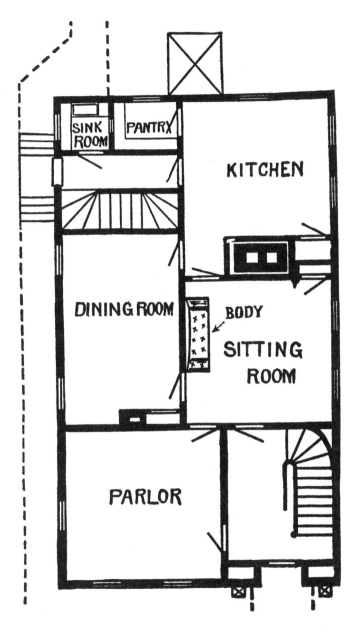

Downstairs at the Borden house.

Then followed a description, quoted by Mr Harrington, of Miss Borden's reception of her father when he returned on Thursday morning, her solicitous inquiries for his health, the assistance which she gave him in removing his coat, helping him to the sofa, and her offers to cover him with an afghan, and to lower the shades at the windows, so that he could have a 'nice nap.'

> 'On leaving the house, she says she went directly to the barn to obtain some lead. She informed me that it was her intention to go to Marion on a vacation, and she wanted the lead in the barn loft to make some sinkers. She was a very enthusiastic angler. I went over the ground several times and she repeated the same story.'

Miss Borden, when questioned as to a possible explanation of the crime, told Mr Harrington the story of the burglary in the house a year earlier, and of 'strange men' recently seen by her around the house. She had been frightened enough to tell her parents about them, and to write to her sister at Fairhaven.

On the subject of the domestic and business affairs of the Borden family, Mr Harrington said:

> 'Yes, there were family dissensions although it has been always kept very quiet. For nearly ten years there have been constant disputes between the daughters and their father and stepmother. It arose, of course, with regard to the stepmother. Mr Borden gave her some bank stock, and the girls thought they ought to be treated as evenly as the mother. I guess Mr Borden did try to do it, for he deeded to the daughters, Emma L. and Lizzie A., the homestead on Ferry Street, an estate of 120 rods of land, with a house and barn, all valued at $3,000. This was in 1887. The trouble about money matters did not diminish, nor the acerbity of the family ruptures lessen, and Mr Borden gave each girl ten shares in the Crystal Spring Bleachery Company, which he paid $100 a share for. They sold them soon after for less than $40 a share. He also gave them some bank stock at various times, allowing them of course, the entire income from them. In addition to this he gave them a weekly stipend, amounting to $200 a year. In spite of all this the dispute about their not being allowed enough went on with equal bitterness. Lizzie did most of the demonstrative contention, as Emma is very quiet and unassuming, and would feel deeply any disparaging or angry word from her father. Lizzie on the contrary, was haughty and domineering with the stubborn will of her father and bound to contest for her rights. There were many animated interviews between father and daughter on this point. Lizzie is of a repellent disposition, and after an unsuccessful passage with her father, would become sulky and refuse to speak to him for days at a time. . . . She thought she ought to entertain as others did, and felt that with her father's wealth she was expected to hold her end up with others of her set. Her

father's constant refusal to allow her to entertain lavishly angered her. I have heard many bitter things she has said of her father, and know that she was deeply resentful of her father's maintained stand in this matter. This house on Ferry Street was an old one, and was in constant need of repairs. There were two tenants paying $16.50 and $14 a month, but with taxes and repairs there was very little income from the property. It was a great deal of trouble for the girls to keep the house in repair, and a month or two ago they got disgusted and deeded the house back to their father. I am positive that Emma knows nothing of the murder.'

The faction which held strong views about the stupidity of the Fall River police, and their brutal persecution of an innocent and bereaved woman, often said that the officers neglected all opportunities to catch the real murderer. The police formed a 'theory,' said their critics, and having done so, tried by all means—some of them unusually foul—to entangle their victim in it. In the opinion of the man in the street, who is supposed to be a devotee of 'good, plain common-sense,' it is, of course, a destructive thing to say of another man that he has a 'theory.' Nobody should ever have any theories at all: but just plunge ahead. As a matter of truth, the police of Fall River spent weary hours and days in running down every report, rumor, and suspicion.

The usual crop of 'strange,' 'wild' and 'crazy' men, of tramps and vagrants, of 'foreigners,' and other guilty-looking persons was more prolific than ever. There was a suspected Portuguese, who was called a Portuguese because he was a Swede; and there were miscreants who turned up in lonely places, days and weeks after the murders, still brandishing axes or hatchets dripping with gore,—just as the Russian soldiers in England in August, 1914, still had—on their boots—the snow of their native land. Pale young men had been seen on Second Street. There was a camp of wandering horse-traders in Westport, and with them, it was alleged, Mr John Vinnicum Morse had been darkly dealing. There was a disgruntled owner of property, across the river, whose business relations with Mr Borden might have roused him to dreadful vengeance against all who bore the hated name. One Dr Handy, who was on Second Street about an hour before the murders, had seen a very peculiar looking man, who attracted the doctor's most particular attention. This man was discussed, in column after column

of newspaper space, as 'Dr Handy's Wild Eyed Man.' Some
participants in the discussion held that the Wild Eyed Man was
better, but still cryptically, known as 'Mike the Soldier.' Mike
was run down and found free from all criminous taint, excepting that he was near Second Street ten o'clock that morning,
that he was pale, as a result of a spree, and that he wore an odd
and noticeable pair of trousers. It appeared that he followed the
weaver's trade, when he was not going from one bar-room to
the next, and by talking with his fellow-weavers, and various
saloon-keepers, it was easy to learn all that he had been doing,
and to find that it was unimportant. But the Wild Eyed Man
lingered, off-stage.

A boy thought he had seen a man jump over the back fence of
the Borden house. A Frenchman had helped the same man
escape toward New Bedford, but how he knew it was the same
man, in what way he helped him, and what he was escaping
from, do not appear. Two officers found somebody like him in
the person of the chief of the gypsy horse-dealers' camp. He had
the satisfactory name of Bearsley S. Cooper, but he also had an
alibi, which prevented anybody from visiting upon him the
punishment which mankind always longs to inflict upon a
horsedealer. The terror of the murders had spread throughout
New England, and men seen getting on railroad trains, or
getting off them, with dust on their shoes, or spots on their
clothes, were asked who they were, and what they had been
doing. A Bostonian was frightened half to death by detention
and questioning. On Monday another bloody hatchet was
discovered on a farm in South Somerset; it was the property of
somebody called Sylvia, and the police rushed out there, with
the first words of the famous song trembling upon their lips. But
the blood was the blood of a chicken, and old Mr Sylvia was left
undisturbed.

Petty offences hover close to great crimes, as the sucker
follows the shark. When at some fête, during the French
Revolution, two men were discovered lurking under a platform
built for the spectators, they were charged with designs against
the Republic, and promptly lynched by the mob. They went to
their deaths, however, with the somewhat humiliating but
probably truthful confession that gunpowder plots were far

from their minds; they had gone there merely to gaze upwards at the sturdy legs of citizennesses. One man seen by a neighbor on the back fence of the Borden yard, was caught, and forced blushingly to admit that he had been attracted, as Mr Morse had been, by the pears. But his interest was, of course, illicit, and hence his confusion. The police investigated every plausible rumor, and in order to deal according to precept with unturned stones, spent much good effort in many searches which were hopeless from the start. Their work at first was undoubtedly open to criticism, although metropolitan police often do no better with perplexing crimes. They finally arrived at a conclusion, and its results will appear in the account of the four legal investigations which followed.

Something should be said now about Bridget Sullivan, since she was in the house, or within a few feet of it, when each murder was committed. It has often been asked why she was not suspected. The answer is simple: she bore a good character, she had no notive to such crimes, and she was exonerated by the person who was still nearer to the scenes of the murders, Miss Lizzie Borden herself. Vague suggestions of complicity, or guilty knowledge, arose against her, but evidently were not shared by the officers of the law. Bridget was an agitated and badly scared woman for a few days, and at last had to undergo a long cross-examination by one of the most skilful advocates in the State. It is said that she returned to her native land some years—not very long—after the trial, and there, an elderly woman, she may still abide, in the intermittent calm of the Irish Free State.

Of all the rumors as to murderers from the outside, only one had the charm of romance. Somebody attempted to inject a maritime flavor into the mystery, by recalling the trial, in 1876, of the mutineers of the schooner *Jefferson Borden*. This was not Mr Borden's name, but it was suggested that he had an interest in this vessel, and that the guilty mutineers, imbued with the combined spirits of Clark Russell and Conan Doyle, had nursed their vengeful feelings for sixteen years, only to strike at last in this telling fashion. Unluckily for the story, it was discovered that two of the accused had been acquitted on their trial, one had served his term and now lived, crippled, in St

Paul; while the two ring-leaders were safe in the State Prison at Thomaston, Maine. Mr Borden, moreover, had no connection with the schooner.

On the day after the murders, this notice was sent to and duly appeared in the newspapers:

'Five thousand dollars reward. The above reward will be paid to anyone who may secure the arrest and conviction of the person or persons, who occasioned the death of Andrew J. Borden and his wife. Signed,

Emma L. Borden and Lizzie A. Borden.'

The funeral services were held on Saturday, August 6. From three to four thousand people surrounded the house, and a passage was kept clear by twenty police officers. Other crowds of people lined the street as the hearses and the carriages with mourners proceeded to the cemetery. The coffins were not buried, but placed in a receiving tomb.

In the evening of that day, the Mayor of Fall River, Dr John W. Coughlin, with City Marshal Hilliard, went to the Borden house. The number of people standing on the sidewalks or in the street itself was still so great that the Mayor's carriage was driven with difficulty. Policemen were called and ordered to send the people away. The Mayor and the Marshal then went into the house to confer with the Misses Borden and Mr Morse. Dr Coughlin said:

'I have a request to make of the family, and that is that you remain in the house for a few days. I believe it would be better if you do so.'

Miss Lizzie raised the question:

'Why, is there anybody in this house suspected?'

The Mayor answered: 'Well, perhaps Mr Morse can answer that question better than I, as his experience last night, perhaps, would justify him in the inference that somebody in the house is suspected.'

Miss Lizzie persisted: 'I want to know the truth.'

And she repeated this remark. Then the Mayor said:

'Well, Miss Borden, I regret to answer, but I must answer yes; you are suspected.'

She replied: 'I am ready to go now.'

Her sister said: 'We have tried to keep it from her as long as we could.'

Dr Coughlin told the family that if they were disturbed in any way, or annoyed by the crowds in the street, they should either notify the officer in the yard, or sent word to him—the Mayor—who would see that the police department gave them protection. Miss Emma Borden then remarked: 'We want to do everything we can in this matter.' And the two officials departed.

On the following Tuesday an investigation began, when Bridget Sullivan was examined by the District Attorney, Mr Hosea M. Knowlton, assisted by the City Marshal, the Mayor, and the Medical Examiner. This investigation, on the same day, took the form of an inquest, before Judge Josiah C. Blaisdell of the Second District Court. A summons to attend was served upon Miss Lizzie Borden. Her family attorney, Mr Andrew J. Jennings, appeared and made an appeal to the Court for permission to be present, 'in the interest of the witnesses.' The Justice heard his argument, but denied admission. The inquest continued its sessions in secret, until Thursday, while Fall River waited in suppressed excitement and impatience, reading newspaper bulletins, and learning nothing. The case was of such importance as to attract to the city the Attorney General of Massachusetts, Mr Albert E. Pillsbury, who was in consultation with Mr Knowlton and other officers. In addition to Miss Lizzie Borden, Dr Bowen, Mrs Churchill, Mr Hiram Harrington, Mr John Vinnicum Morse, and Miss Emma Borden were examined. Another witness, who was followed about in Fall River, and unsuccessfully questioned by the newspaper reporters, was Professor Wood of the Harvard Medical School. On the third and last day of the inquest there appeared Eli Bence and the two other witnesses who were supposed to offer testimony as to the attempt to buy poison. On that same day autopsies were held, at the cemetery, upon the two bodies. Chiefly, they disclosed ten incised wounds on the head and face of Mr Borden; and on the body of his wife, one wound in the back, just below the neck, and no less than eighteen incised and crushing wounds on the head.

The inquest ended late Thursday afternoon, one week after

the murders. A short consultation was held and at the end of it, Mr Jennings was called, and Miss Lizzie Borden arrested for the murder of her father. No mention of Mrs Borden was made in the warrant. The prisoner was detained at the police station under charge of the matron, but she was not confined in the cell-room. Mr Porter writes:

'No other prisoner arrested in Bristol County had been accorded the delicate and patient consideration which Marshal Hilliard bestowed upon Miss Lizzie Borden.'

She was arraigned in the District Court, before Judge Blaisdell next morning. She entered the room 'on the arm of the Rev Mr Buck,' and is described as wearing a dark blue suit, and a black hat with red flowers. She was 'not crying, but her features were far from firm. She has a face and chin betokening strength of character, and on this occasion the sensitiveness of the lips especially betrayed itself. She was constantly moving her lips as she sat in the court-room in a way to show that she was not altogether unemotional.'

To the warrant, she pleaded not guilty. Mr Jennings protested against the proceedings as 'extraordinary,' in that the Judge had presided at the inquest and was now sitting to hear the case against her. This he called sitting in a double capacity and not ensuring his client an unprejudiced hearing. The District Attorney replied that the statutes required Judge Blaisdell to hold the inquest, which was in itself an action against no one, but an attempt to ascertain facts. The same procedure had been followed more than twenty times to his knowledge in cases which had not excited so much attention. The inquest was still proceeding, and the evidence before it had no bearing upon this hearing. The Judge was equally required by statute to hear this case. The Court overruled Mr Jennings's motion, and the point does not seem to have been raised again. The lawyers agreed upon August 22 for the preliminary hearing, and Miss Borden was taken by train to the jail at Taunton. At railway stations, and other places, crowds gathered to look at her.

On the date appointed Miss Borden was brought back to Fall River, but a postponement was made, until August 25. She remained in charge of the police matron, and was not taken back to Taunton. Finally, the hearings began. Crowds were present, inside and out of the court-room, and it is said that forty newspapers were represented by reporters. The prisoner entered the Court, leaning upon the practised arm of the Rev Mr Buck. There began a preliminary trial which lasted for six days. Few such extensive investigations, prior to the presentation of a criminal case to the Grand Jury, could ever have been held in the State. Mr Melvin O. Adams of Boston was now associated with Mr Jennings in the defence. The witnesses included the Medical Examiner, Dr Dolan; Thomas Kieran, an engineer, who gave technical details about measurements of the Borden house; officers of the banks which Mr Borden had visited the day he was killed; John Vinnicum Morse; Bridget Sullivan; Mrs Churchill; Miss Alice Russell, who testified only as to events on the day of the murder; Eli Bence and the other men from the pharmacy—whose appearance, says Mr Porter, 'in the judgment of many of the spectators . . . produced evidence of uneasiness on the part of Lizzie Borden,' and some officers of the police.

On the fifth day of the hearing, Professor Wood's evidence was given. It was to the effect that his tests and analyses of the two stomachs showed that digestion was much further advanced with Mr Borden than with his wife. No trace of prussic acid was found in either stomach; tests were not made for any other poison, but there was no evidence of irritation. He had made examinations for blood stains on a hatchet and two axes, found in the Borden house, and on a dress waist, two skirts, and shoes and stockings belonging to the prisoner. Except for a minute spot on one of the skirts, he found no blood upon any of these. This testimony was received with great relief and joy by the friends of Miss Borden; quite naturally and correctly they looked upon it as a strong point in her favor.

After some more police evidence, the District Attorney read the short-hand report of the testimony of Miss Lizzie Borden given at the inquest. This is an exceedingly interesting and important series of questions and answers. Miss Borden, as we have seen, talked to friends and neighbors and to the police, on the day of the murders. Afterwards, except for the inquest statement, she never opened her mouth. She acted upon what proved to be the best of legal advice, and at her final trial, availed herself of her right not to go upon the witness stand. Miss Borden's testimony at the inquest introduced at the preliminary trial, as part of the case of the Commonwealth, is significant not only for itself but for the point raised when it was offered as evidence at the trial before the Superior Court. It is to be found today in the press reports of that date, and in Mr Porter's book—to which I am so much indebted for information about this period in the history of the case. I quote his version of it.

My father and stepmother were married twenty-seven years ago. I have no idea how much my father was worth and have never heard him form an opinion. I know something about what real estate my father owned . . . 'two farms in Swansea, the homestead, some property on North Main street, Borden Block, some land further south and some he had recently purchased.' 'Did you ever deed him any property?' 'He gave us some land, but my father bought it back. Had no other transaction with him. He paid in five thousand dollars cash for this property. Never knew my father made a will, but heard so from Uncle Morse.' 'Did you know of anybody that your father had trouble with?' 'There was a man who came there some weeks before, but I do not know who he was. He came to the house one day, and I heard them talk about a store. My father told him he could not have a store. The man said: "I thought with your liking for money you would let anybody in." I heard my father order him out of the house. Think he lived out of town, because he said he could go back and talk with father.' 'Did you father and anybody else have bad feelings between them?' 'Yes, Hiram C. Harrington. He married my father's only sister.' 'Nobody else?' 'I have no reason to suppose that that man had seen my father before that day.' 'Did you ever have any trouble with your stepmother?' 'No.' 'Within a year?' 'No.' 'Within three years?' 'No. About five years ago.' 'What was it about?' 'About my stepmother's stepsister, Mrs George Whitehead.' 'Was it a violent expression of feeling?' 'It was simply a difference of opinion.' 'Were you always cordial with your stepmother?' 'That depends upon one's idea of cordiality. 'Was it cordial according to your ideas of cordiality?' 'Yes.' Continuing: 'I did not regard her as my mother, though she came there when I was young. I decline to say whether my relations between her and myself were those of mother and daughter or not. I called her Mrs Borden and sometimes mother. I stopped calling her mother after the affair regarding her sister-in-law.' 'Why did you leave off calling her mother?' 'Because I wanted to.' 'Have you any other answer to give me?' 'No, sir. I always went to my sister. She was older than I was. I don't know but that my father and stepmother were happily united. I never knew of any difficulty between them, and they seemed to be affectionate. The day they were killed I had on a blue dress. I changed it in the afternoon and put on a print dress. Mr Morse came into our house whenever he wanted to. He has been here once since the river was frozen over. I don't know how often he came to spend the nights, because I had been away so much. I have not been away much during the year. He has been there very little during the past year. I have been away a great deal in the daytime during the last year. I don't think I have been away much at night, except once when I was in New Bedford. I was abroad in 1890. I first saw Mr Morse Thursday noon. Wednesday evening I was with Miss Russell at 9 o'clock, and I don't know whether the family were in or not. I went direct to my room. I locked the front door when I came in. Was in my room Wednesday, not feeling well all day. Did not go down to supper. Went out that evening and came in and locked the front door. Came down about 9 next morning. Did not inquire about Mr Morse that morning. Did not go to Marion at that time, because they could go sooner than I. I had taken the Secretaryship of the Christian Endeavor Society and had to remain over till the 10th. There had been nobody else around there that week but the man I have spoken of. I did not say that he came a week before, but that week. Mr Morse slept in the spare room Wednesday night. It was my habit to close my room door when I was in it. That Wednesday afternoon they made such a noise that I closed the door. First saw my father Thursday morning down stairs reading the *Providence Journal*. Saw my mother with a dust cloth in her hand. Maggie was putting a cloth into a mop. Don't know whether I ate cookies and tea that morning. Know the coffee pot was on the stove. My father went down town after 9 o'clock. I did not finish the handkerchiefs because the irons were not right. I was in the kitchen reading when he returned. I am not sure that I was in the kitchen when my father returned. I stayed in my room long enough to sew a piece of lace on a garment. That was before he came back. I don't know where Maggie was. I think she let my father in, and that he rang the bell. I understood Maggie to say he said he had forgotten his key. I think I was up stairs when my father came in, and I think I was on the stairs when he entered. I don't know whether Maggie was washing windows or not when my father came in.' At this point the District Attorney had called Miss Borden's attention to her conflicting statements regarding her position when her father came in, and her answer was: 'You have asked me so many questions, I don't know what I have said.' Later, she said she was reading in the kitchen and had gone into the other room for a copy of the *Providence Journal*. 'I last saw my mother when I was downstairs. She was dusting the dining room. She said she had been upstairs and made the bed and was going up stairs to put on the pillow slips. She had some cotton cloth pillows up there, and she said she was going to work on them. If she had remained down stairs I should have seen her. She would have gone up the back way to go to her room. If she had gone to the kitchen I would have seen her. There is no reason to suppose I would not have seen her when she was down stairs or in her room, except when I went down stairs once for two or three minutes.' 'I ask you again what you suppose she was doing from the time you saw her till 11 o'clock?' 'I don't know, unless she she was making her bed.' 'She would have had to pass your room, and you would have seen her wouldn't you?' 'Yes, unless I was in my room or down cellar, I supposed she had gone away, because she told me she was going, and we talked about the dinner. Didn't hear her go out or come back. When I first came down stairs saw Maggie coming in, and my mother asked me how I was feeling. My father was still there, still reading. My mother used to go and do the marketing.' 'Now I call your attention to the fact you said twice yesterday that you first saw your father after he came in when you were standing on the stairs.' 'I did not. I was in the kitchen when he came in, or in one of the three rooms, the dining room, kitchen and sitting room. It would have been difficult for anybody to pass through these rooms unless they passed through while I was in the dining room.' 'A portion of the time the girl was out of doors, wasn't she?' 'Yes.' 'So far as I know, I was alone in the house the larger part of the time while my father was away. I was eating a pear when my father came in. I had put a stick of wood into the fire to see if I could start it. I did no more ironing after my father came in. I then went in to tell him. I did not put away the ironing board. I don't know what time my father came in. When I went out to the barn I left him on the sofa. The last thing I said was to ask him if he wanted the window left that way. Then I went to the barn to get some lead for a sinker. I went up stairs in the barn. There was a bench there which contained some lead. I unhooked the screen door when I went out. I don't know when Bridget got through washing the windows inside. I knew she washed the windows outside. I knew she didn't wash the kitchen windows, but I don't know whether she washed the sitting room windows or not. I thought the flats would be hot by the time I got back. I had not fishing apparatus, but there was some at the farm. It is five years since I used the fish line. I don't think there was any sinker on my line. I don't think there were any fish lines suitable for use at the farm.' 'What! did you think you would find sinkers in the barn?' 'My father once told me that there was some lead and nails in the barn.' 'How long do you think you occupied in looking for the sinkers?' 'About fifteen or twenty minutes.' 'Did you do nothing besides look for sinkers in the twenty minutes?' 'Yes, sir. I ate some pears.' 'Would it take you all that time to eat a few pears?' 'I do not do things in a hurry.' 'Was Bridget not washing the dining room windows and the sitting room windows?' 'I do not know. I did not see her.' 'Did you tell Bridget to wash the windows?' 'No, sir.' 'Who did?' 'My mother.' 'Did you see Bridget after your mother told her to wash the windows?' 'Yes, sir.' 'What was she doing?' 'She had got a long pole and was sticking it in a brush, and she had a pail of water.' 'About what time did you go out into the barn?' 'About as near as I can recollect, 10 o'clock.' 'What did you go into the barn for?' 'To find some sinkers.' 'How many pears did you eat in that twenty minutes?' 'Three.' 'Is that all you did?' 'No. I went over to the window and opened it.' 'Why did you do that?' 'Because it was too hot.' 'I suppose that it is the hottest place on the premises?' 'Yes, sir.' 'Could you, while standing looking out of that window, see anybody enter the kitchen?' 'No, sir.' 'I thought you said you could see people from the barn?' 'Not after you pass a jog in the barn. It obstructs the view of the back door.' 'What kind of lead were you looking for, for sinkers? Hard lead?' 'No, sir; soft lead.' 'Did you expect to find the sinkers already made?' 'Well, no. I thought I might find one with a hole through it.' 'Was the lead referred to tea lead or lead that comes in tea chests?' 'I don't know.' 'When were you going fishing?' 'Monday.' 'The next Monday after the fatal day?' 'Yes, sir.' 'Had you lines all ready?' 'No, sir.' 'Did you have a line?' 'Yes, sir.' 'Where was your line?' 'Down to the farm.' 'Do you know whether there were any sinkers on the line you left at the farm?' 'I think there was none on the line.' 'Did you have any hooks?' 'No, sir.' 'Then you were making all this preparation without either hook or line. Why did you go into the barn after sinkers?' 'Because I was going down town to buy some hooks and line, and thought it would save me from buying them.' 'Now, to the barn again. Do you not think I could go into the barn and do the same as you in a few minutes?' 'I do not do things in a hurry.' 'Did you then think there were no sinkers at the barn?' 'I thought there were no sinkers anywhere there. I had no idea of using my lines. I thought you understood that I wasn't going to use these lines at the farm, because they hadn't sinkers. I went up stairs to the kind of bench there. I had heard my father say there was lead there. Looked for lead in a box up there. There were nails and perhaps an old door knob. Did not find any lead as thin as tea lead in the box. Did not look anywhere except on the bench. I ate some pears up there. I have now told you everything that took place up in the barn. It was the hottest place in the premises. I suppose I ate my pears when I first went up there. I stood looking out of the window. I was feeling well enough to eat pears, but don't know how to answer the question if I was feeling better than I was in the morning, because I was feeling better that morning. I picked the pears up from the ground. I was not in the rear of the barn. I was in the front of it. Don't see how anybody could leave the house then without my seeing them. I pulled over boards to look for the lead. That took me some time. I returned from the barn and put my hat in the dining room. I found my father and called to Maggie. I found the fire gone out. I went to the barn because the irons were not hot enough and the fire had gone out. I made no efforts to find my mother at all. Sent Maggie for Dr Bowen. Didn't see or find anything after the murders to tell me my mother had been sewing in the spare room that morning.' 'What did your mother say when you saw her?' 'She told me she had had a note and was going out. She said she would get the dinner.' The District Attorney continued to read: 'My mother did not tell when she was coming back. I did not know Mr Morse was coming to dinner. I don't know whether I was at tea Wednesday night or not. I had no apron on Thursday; that is, I don't think I had. I don't remember surely. I had no occasion to use the axe or hatchet. I knew there was an old axe down stairs and last time I saw it it was on the old chopping block. I don't know whether my father owned a hatchet or not. Assuming a hatchet was found in the cellar I don't know how it got there, and if there was blood on it I have no idea as to how it got there. My father killed some pigeons last May. When I found my father I did not think of Mrs Borden, for I believed she was out. I remember asking Mrs Churchill to look for my mother. I left the screen door closed when I left, and it was open when I came from the barn. I can give no idea of the time my father came home. I went right to the barn. I don't know whether he came to the sitting room at once or not. I don't remember his being in the sitting room or sitting down. I think I was in there when I asked him if there was any mail. I do not think he went upstairs. He had a letter in his hand. I did not help him to lie down and did not touch the sofa. He was taking medicine for some time. Mrs Borden's father's house was for sale on Fourth street. My father bought Mrs Borden's half sister's share and gave it to her. We thought what he did for her people he ought to do for his own and he then gave us grandfather's house. I always thought my stepmother induced him to purchase the interest. I don't know when the windows were last washed before that day. All day Tuesday I was at the table. I gave the officer the same skirt I wore that day, and if there was any blood on it I can give an explanation as to how it got there. If the blood came from the outside, I cannot say how it got there, I wore tie shoes that day and black stockings. I was under the pear trees four or five minutes. I came down the front stairs when I came down in the morning. The dress I wore that forenoon was a white and blue stripe of some sort. It is at home in the attic. I did not go to Smith's drug store to buy prussic acid. Did not go to the rooms where mother or father lay after the murder. Went through when I went up stairs that day.' . . . 'I now ask if you can furnish any other suspicion concerning any person who might have committed the crime?' 'Yes; one night as I was coming home not long ago I saw the shadow of a man on the house at the east end. I thought it was a man because I could not see any skirts. I hurried in the front door. It was about 8.45 o'clock; not later than 9. I saw somebody run around the house last winter. The last time I saw anybody lately was since my sister went to Marion. I told Mr Jennings, may have told Mr Hanscom.' 'Who suggested the reward offered, you or your sister?' 'I don't know. I may have.'

Mr Knowlton stopped reading, and said: 'This is the case of the Commonwealth.'

The defence called Dr Bowen and Marshal Hilliard. On the sixth day of the trial, arguments of counsel were presented at a length hardly less than at a trial before a jury. At the conclusion of the speech of the prosecuting attorney, Judge Blaisdell said:

'The long examination is now concluded, and there remains for the magistrate to perform what he believes to be his duty. It would be a pleasure for him, and he would doubtless receive much sympathy if he could say, "Lizzie, I judge you probably not guilty. You may go home." But upon the character of the evidence presented through the witnesses who have been so closely and thoroughly examined, there is but one thing to be done. Suppose for a single moment a *man* was standing there. He was found close by that guest chamber, which, to Mrs Borden, was a chamber of death. Suppose a *man* had been found in the vicinity of Mr Borden; was the first to find the body, and the only account he could give of himself was the unreasonable one that he was out in the barn looking for sinkers; then he was out in the yard; then he was out for something else; would there be any question in the minds of men what should be done with such a man?'

There was a pause, and the old Judge's eyes filled with tears.

'So there is only one thing to do, painful as it may be—the judgment of the Court is that you are probably guilty, and you are ordered committed to await the action of the Superior Court.'

If the tide seemed to set against Miss Borden, and if the preliminary skirmishes had given distress to those who had already acquitted her in their minds, it must not be supposed that her friends, including a number of highly respected and influential persons, were not gathering valiantly. The painful situation in which she found herself, her sex, and her religious associations, were summoning to her aid many people from all parts of the State—persons who had hitherto been strangers to her. The points which had told against her were the seemingly impossible nature of the story about the visit to the barn or yard; the alleged attempt to buy poison; the lapse of time between the two murders, which appeared to shake the theory of an outside murderer; the failure to find the sender of the note to Mrs Borden; and the fact that from the stairs which she descended when her father entered the house, the body of her stepmother could have been visible. But, on the other hand, the glaring improbability of such murders being committed by a woman; combined with the failure to find any definitely determined weapon; and above everything, the absence of blood from the clothing or person of the accused—all these not only strengthened the faith of those who were sure of her innocence, but convinced the authorities that they were far from having a strong case.

Her defence, so far as concerns those in whose hands it was officially placed, was conducted with wisdom and ability.

Elsewhere, however, there was more than the usual amount of irresponsible agitation, gushing sentimentality, and abuse of officers of the governments who were merely bent on the disagreeable task of carrying out their plain and imperative duties. The abuse was the more disgusting since much of it originated with persons of education and self-professed moral superiority. The lynching mob exists in America in two forms, equally discouraging to those who cling to their faith in demo-.cracy: the mob which hunts down and kills some wretch of a malefactor, or alleged malefactor; and the mob which rails against legal officers who are engaged in protecting the community against crime Some newspaper writers and public personages, men and women, took up Miss Borden's cause with no other equipment than ignorance. Blatantly they abused the Judge, the District Attorney and the police. One editorial writer was outraged in his feelings because of the 'harshness' of the words used in the warrant for arrest, as if a charge of murder should be conveyed in terms of delicate insinuation. To tell him that the form of complaint was a hundred and fifty years old would have availed nothing; so excited was he in behalf of the 'unfortunate girl' that he would have suggested an agreeable form for this case. The Rev Mr Jubb said that the action of Judge Blaisdell in sitting on the bench, after presiding at the inquest, was 'indecent, outrageous and not to be tolerated in any civilized community.' To him it was mildly remarked that the statute under which the Judge acted had been in use in America nearly two hundred years, and somewhat antedated his own personal knowledge of this country, since he had come hither from England within about one year.

Associations like the Woman's Auxiliary of the Y.M.C.A. took up Miss Borden's cause, sometimes with enthusiasm and knowledge; sometimes merely with enthusiasm. Prayers were invited from religious societies all over the country, the verdict was found in advance, and Heaven was to be implored or advised to assist the 'unfortunate girl.' There was an unpleasant flavor of sectarianism about much of this agitation; innocence must be assumed because of church membership. In contradistinction to this, however, I have seen proof that some of the more thoughtful of the lady's spiritual brethren, including clergymen in different parts of the State, had no sympathy with the attempts to interfere with law by the methods of the revival and the camp-meeting. As to the term which was applied to her, it is, of course, conventional to refer to anybody accused of a capital crime as 'this girl' or 'this boy' provided that she or he is still under sixty years of age. And for the other word, Mr Porter said that throughout the whole proceeding, Miss Borden was called 'unfortunate,' but that nobody, good, bad, or indifferent, was ever heard to say that the murdered man and woman were 'unfortunate.'

Ten thousand tears are shed in America for persons accused of murder, and even for persons convicted of murder, to every word of regret spoken for the victims of the murders. And that, according to thoughtful investigators, is one of the reasons why America leads the world in its shameful record for the unlawful taking of human life—although a few semi-civilized Oriental countries, and certain turbulent provinces of Italy, may be exceptions to this statement.

Advocates of suffrage for women came energetically to the defence of Miss Borden, almost as if her sex alone proved her innocence. One especially good result of the present status of women as voters, is a nearly complete abandonment on the part of their political leaders of the belief which was prevalent thirty of forty years ago: that all women accused of grave crimes should either be cleared in advance of trial, or if convicted, should not be liable for punishment. Their present attitude is a far more reasonable acceptance of women's duties and responsibilities to the State, as no more and no less than those of men. But in 1892, Mrs Mary A. Livermore, an estimable lady of very vigorous character, Mrs Susan Fessenden, president of the Woman's Christian Temperance Union, and Miss Lucy Stone, all distinguished in the struggle for what were then termed 'Woman's Rights,' came to the aid and comfort of Miss Borden. They did it so ecstatically as to leave doubt whether they were acting from logic or from emotion.

Miss Borden's name means little today to those who do not remember the year of her trial. Perhaps the younger folk in Scotland have never heard of Madeleine Smith, although their fathers and grandfathers followed her adventures with palpitating interest. Soon, perhaps, the name of Mrs Maybrick will have completely faded from memory in England and America. One may search old books on criminology and summon one's own recollections, in vain, to recall the name of any American woman, resting under the capital charge, which was so widely known as that of Miss Borden. Perhaps the equally unfortunate Miss Nan Patterson is the only one for comparison, although far in the past there was Mrs Cunningham, while more recently arose the grim figure of Mrs Rogers of Vermont, and the adventurous Clara Phillips of California. No *Ballade des Dames du Temps Jadis* celebrates these names; they, too, are gone with the snows of yester-year. But once, upon railroad trains, in clubs, at tea-parties, and around every breakfast table could be heard conversations about 'Lizzie.' A voice would arise from a group of talkers, anywhere between the two oceans: 'I tell you, she never did it in the world! It's impossible. I *know* she never did it!' And nobody had to ask what was being discussed.

An account of the case would be incomplete if it did not record the fact that, however unjustly, the event was celebrated in rhyme, in one of those jingles which are never forgotten. Who invented it, nobody knows, but everyone heard it:

> Lizzie Borden took an axe
> And gave her Mother forty whacks;
> When she saw what she had done,—
> She gave her Father forty-one!

This has been communicated to me, in one way or another, at least half a dozen times, while I have been writing this article, by persons to whom it was the most vivid recollection of the Fall River murders—surpassing even the mutton-soup.

Similar folk-rhymes have been associated with two notorious crimes in Great Britain: one which delighted Sir Walter Scott:

> They cut his throat from ear to ear
> His brains they battered in;
> His name was Mr William Weare,
> He dwelt in Lyon's Inn,

and that even grimmer quatrain which sums up the popular notion—as these things do—of the West Port murders in Edinburgh:

Up the close and doun the stair,
But and ben wi' Burke and Hare,
Burke's the butcher, Hare's the thief,
Knox the boy that buys the beef.

In America there is hardly a notorious murder which does not evoke one or two jokes or epigrams, sometimes witty, sometimes ribald, but only one other beside the Fall River murder, has, to my knowledge, brought forth any rhyme. In the early '90's, one Isaac Sawtell, living in New Hampshire, planned to do away with his brother, Hiram. He noted with approval that the neighboring State of Maine, more considerate toward gentlemen of his disposition than his own New Hampshire, had abolished the death penalty. So he took his brother out for a drive one evening, crossed, as he thought, into Maine, and killed him. But his topographical sense was at fault; the deed had really been done in New Hampshire after all, and in that State he was tried. The incident was described in a couplet by some rhymster:

Two brothers in our town did dwell,
Hiram sought Heaven, but Isaac Sawtell.

Miss Borden went back to the jail in Taunton, to await the action of the Grand Jury. It was with her as with the Napoleonic prisoners in *Peter Ibbetson:* she could not have found her durance very vile. I have been credibly informed that she was seen on the streets of Taunton, from time to time, having been taken out for walks. Whether this privilege was accorded because of the advance decision of her innocence, or because she was joint-heiress to a considerable estate, there is no information.

In October occurred a thoroughly discredible incident. At first it seemed to be a heavy blow at Miss Borden's interests, but its effect was almost instantly reversed, and in the end probably worked in her favor. A newspaper reporter with the felicitious name of Henry G. Trickey, and a detective named Edwin D. McHenry were concerned in the production of a long newspaper article with which they hoodwinked the *Boston*

Globe. Trickey and his friends blamed McHenry for it, while McHenry and his friends blamed Trickey. Definitely it can be said that Trickey was indicted by the Grand Jury for an attempt to tamper with a Government witness, that he left the country and did not live to return, nor to meet the accusation.

A newspaper seldom publishes such an article. It began on the front page of the *Globe*, on October 10, and filled nearly two and a half of its pages. In all these columns, which purported to set forth testimony in possession of the Government, truth rarely entered. Had one-quarter of it been fact, it would have convicted the prisoner. The *prima facie* case for the prosecution must have seemed, to outsiders, to be strong indeed, or this could not have appeared. The names of the newly discovered witnesses were plausible, although they were nearly all imaginary. A man called John H. Murphy, while passing the house, had seen Miss Borden in Mrs Borden's room. Another mythical person, 'Mrs Gustave F. Ronald,' had passed the house at 9:40, had heard a terrible cry, and had seen a woman whose head was covered with a rubber cap, or hood. (It was a favorite theory, at this time, that the mysterious assassin had worn some outside covering for the hair to avoid being spattered with blood. Some newspapers and their readers found a still greater thrill in the notion that the assailant of the Bordens had dispensed with clothing altogether during the commission of the deed.) A certain 'Peter Mahany' had witnessed all that 'Mrs Ronald' had seen, and, in addition, had recognized the hooded woman as the prisoner. The street opposite must have thronged with witnesses! 'Mr and Mrs Frederick Chace,' calling at the house on Wednesday evening, had overheard a quarrel between Mr Borden and his younger daughter—about a man, a lover. This seemed at last to bring into the case the 'love interest,' for which many newspaper reporters had almost pined away and died. Bridget Sullivan (an actual person at last) was to tell of a quarrel which happened the same evening. The police matron was to amplify an adverse bit of testimony— already in evidence—and to say that she had heard Miss Borden tell John Vinnicum Morse to 'get those things out of the way in my room, and then they can do their worst.'

On the following day the *Globe* made a partial retraction. 'It [the story] has been proven wrong in some particulars.' Mr McHenry, the *Globe* said, had furnished the story, and admits that the names and addresses of witnesses were purposely false. The other Boston papers were quoted as denying the truth of the yarn. One part which was entirely withdrawn—to the sorrow of all good reporters—was the 'love interest.' Finally, on October 12, the *Globe*, in a boxed article on the front page, made a full retraction. It had been 'grievously misled,' suffered an 'imposition,' 'unparalleled. . . cunningly contrived' but 'based on facts.' It expressed its 'heartfelt apology' for the 'inhuman reflection' on Miss Borden's honor, and included in the apology, Mr John Vinnicum Morse.

Mr Trickey soon left Boston, and in November he was killed by a railroad train in Canada. It may be imagined that more than one of Miss Borden's rural neighbors and sympathizers solemnly remarked: 'It was a *jedgment* on him!' The final result of this wretched affair may well have been to add to the number of those who distrust the newspapers, and to persuade them that if this damaging story were false, everything which seemed to tell against the prisoner might equally be false.

The Grand Jury of Bristol met in November and listened to the evidence for a week. An unusual course was followed in that the District Attorney, Mr Knowlton, invited Miss Borden's counsel, Mr Jennings, to be present and offer evidence for the defence. It is not customary for the Grand Jury to hear others beside the witnesses for the prosecution. The sitting was adjourned until December 1, when a curious thing happened. Miss Alice Russell re-appeared and gave testimony which had not been offered before. On December 2, the Grand Jury found three indictments against Miss Borden: one for the murder of her father, one for the murder of her step-mother, and one in which she was charged with both murders. Mr Porter says that there were twenty-one jurymen present when the vote was taken; twenty voted 'guilty,' and one voted against that finding.

In the months which followed the preliminary trial, and especially in the autumn of 1892, the District Attorney made a careful study of the case, and pursued investigations in various directions. The members of the Grand Jury, after they completed their work, had desired to draw up a paper certifying to the impartial manner in which he had presented the case for the Government, but he advised them not to do so. The question of the prisoner's sanity had been raised, soon after the arrest, and inquiries were made into the family history, but with negative results. Miss Borden had more than once spoken of the burglary of the house, which had taken place a year before the murders, and as the police had been consulted at the time, they were asked for a report of the circumstances.

In the latter part of June, 1891, so it appeared, Mr Borden had called upon City Marshal Hilliard, and asked that officer's help. A police captain was detailed to go with Mr Borden to the house on Second Street, where they found Mrs Borden, the Misses Borden, and Bridget Sullivan. In a small room on the second floor, Mr Borden's desk had been broken open. Eighty dollars in bank-notes, twenty-five or thirty in gold, a large number of street-car tickets, Mrs Borden's watch with a chain, and some other small trinkets had been stolen. The family were at a loss to see how any one could get in and out unseen. Miss Lizzie Borden said:

'The cellar door was open, and someone might have come in that way.'

The officer visited the houses in the neighborhood and exhausted all the resources of the average detective who is not the creation of a novelist: that is, he asked if anybody had seen a mysterious stranger entering the Borden house. One 'clew' he did get: Miss Lizzie Borden presented him with 'a 6 or 8 penny nail' which she had found in the keyhole of a bedroom door. Apparently nobody seemed to think that the robber, in leaving this behind him, had made an adequate return for his thefts. Three times within two weeks, said the officer, Mr Borden remarked to him:

'I am afraid the police will not be able to find the real thief.'

He was right, and the robbery, like the greater crime in that household, remains a mystery.

We usually read, during the investigation of a notorious crime, that the police, or the prosecuting officers, or the attorneys for the defence, or the Governor, are receiving hundreds or thousands of letters from cranks and others; suggestions, insinuations, accusations, and threats. As few of us are policemen, criminal lawyers, or Governors, we take this for granted and seldom expect to see such letters; perhaps we would rather not see them. It has been my privilege to read five or six large packets of communications received by the District Attorney during his investigation of these murders, and a more curious and varied collection could not be imagined. From all parts of the United States they came; written on all possible colors and shapes of paper, in every type of handwriting, and every degree of sanity. Excitable, calm, puerile, nonsensical, pompous, intelligent (a few), preposterous, or insulting, they poured in by the dozen. A railroad conductor in the West asked Mr Knowlton to lay aside his official duties, and embark upon genealogical research, which had no reference to the crime. An embattled Protestant from Vermont called upon him to clap Bridget Sullivan and her 'confessor' into prison, and extort admissions from them—apparently by torture. He ended: 'beware of jesuits.' A man in Albany gleefully admitted that he alone was guilty in this case (he had many a rival in his claim!), but that he was 'moving about so fast' that the police could not hope to catch him. Spiritualists, clairvoyants, crystal-gazers, and other seers had discovered strange things under the flooring of the Borden house, or concealed in the stuffing of the 'sopha.' The Ouija board had been invoked, and had answered a long series of questions in its maddening fashion—half devil and half child. Its control was much interested in 'Lizzie's cat,' that doubtful animal, which, according to a cruel and unfounded bit of gossip, had been carried down cellar, by Miss Borden, and beheaded, with an axe.

One bold blade, who signed 'Voter,' wrote an abusive post-card, to inform Mr Knowlton that he deserved to be 'kicked out' and that he would never again be District Attorney—a sound prophecy, since he was soon promoted by the voters of the State to the office of Attorney General.

Many of the letters began with apologies, and assurances that the writers were acting solely in the interests of justice, but a lady from Brooklyn with a romantic name, an adherent to the most popular theory of all, closed by saying: 'If the suggestions prove of any value, I shall expect to be suitably rewarded.' The attorney was advised to hunt for the missing weapon in the piano, in the back of the kitchen stove, in the barn, the outhouses, and the well. The thought that the police might have looked in some of these places did not occur to the letter-writers. One man, who sent in some curious and rather acute messages, wrote that if the search continued unsuccessful, the house should be burned down in order to find the weapon, as nobody, in his opinion, would ever wish to live in it again. He cited the Burdell and Nathan houses in New York, in support of this theory, but he was mistaken, since the house is cheerfully occupied at the present time.

A band of letter-writers were convinced that the weapon had been, not a hatchet, but a flat-iron, and upon this contention they wrote pages. (The nature of the wounds made this theory untenable.) A serious correspondent from Danvers, Massachusetts, proposed that both men and women should be set to work battering the skulls of subjects in the dissecting-room, in order to prove experimentally the difference between blows inflicted by persons of opposite sexes. Two or three correspondents suggested that the Fall River murderer was probably Such-a-One who murdered Somebody in 1884, or Another Man who killed Some-One-Else-Again in 1879—the fancy being that there only one or two murderers in the land, and that they go about from place to place, like traveling salesmen, or the public hangman in England. But by far the most popular theory was that held by the 'water-proof' or 'gossamer' school. The idea that the clothes of the assailant of the Bordens might have been protected from blood stains by a water-proof, to be washed or destroyed, was widely entertained and vigorously argued.

Perhaps the most intelligent letter of all came from a lady, who also wrote to the Attorney General. Her suggestion was that there was something curious in the action of the discoverer of the body of the dead man, in remaining in that fatal house, where for all anybody could know, the murderer was still lurking. Another suggestion was that the absence of blood stains from clothing, might well prove too much, when that clothing was worn by the child of a murdered man, who was the first to discover the death.

Six months elapsed between the indictment and the trial

before the Superior Court, one of the almost invariable delays of our law, but one which provoked no complaint from the defence. The situation was unusual, and it is best indicated by a letter from the District Attorney to the Attorney General, written in the spring. A capital case in Massachusetts is frequently prosecuted for the State by the Attorney General, but Mr Pillsbury was not in good health. Mr Knowlton, in this letter of April 24, 1893, said, among other things:

'Personally I would like very much to get rid of the trial of the case, and fear that my own feelings in that direction may have influenced my better judgment. I feel this all the more upon your not unexpected announcement that the burden of the trial will come upon me.

'I confess, however, I cannot see my way clear to any disposition of the case other than a trial. Should it result in disagreement of the jury there would be no difficulty then in disposing of the case by admitting the defendant to bail: but a verdict either way would render such a course unnecessary.

'The case has proceeded so far and an indictment has been found by the Grand Inquest of the county that it does not seem to me that we ought to take the responsibility of discharging her without trial, even though there is every reasonable expectation of a verdict of not guilty. I am unable to concur fully in your views as to the probable result. I think it may well be that the jury might disagree upon the case. But even in my most sanguine moments I have scarcely expected a verdict of guilty.

'The situation is this: nothing has developed which satisfies either of us that she is innocent, neither of us can escape the conclusion that she must have had some knowledge of the occurrence. She has been presented for trial by a jury which, to say the least, was not influenced by anything said by the Government in the favor of the indictment . . . I cannot see how any other course than setting the case down for trial, and trying it will satisfy that portion of the public sentiment, whether favorable to her or not, which is worthy of being respected.'

This remarkable letter, so accurate in its prediction, shows how clearly the man best informed understood both the strength and the weakness of the Government's case. The fact that every investigation, so far, had resulted in a decision adverse to the interests of the accused, makes many of the final comments in the newspapers seem absurd. Yet the facts that the evidence was still purely circumstantial; that the unquestioned weapon had not been found; that the absence of blood stains upon the prisoner's clothing was a telling point in her favor; as well as the difficulty in prevailing upon a jury to convict a woman except upon the most overwhelming proof,— all these points made the District Attorney understand the hopelessness of convicting a defendant whose guilt, he sincerely believed, was nevertheless certain.

Miss Borden was arraigned before Justice Hammond of the Superior Court, in New Bedford, on May 8, when she pleaded to the indictments. Early in the next month she was taken again to the Court House, in the same city, to be put upon her trial. Newspaper readers had almost forgotten her. In the first week in June they were amusing themselves with reports of one of the damage suits of Laidlaw against Russell Sage, for injuries received in the attempt to blow up Mr Sage. An archaic problem was under debate, whether the World's Fair in Chicago should be opened on Sundays. Lord Dunraven's *Valkyrie* was winning in English waters, and seemed the probable challenger for the *America's* cup. At the end of the week, Edwin Booth died at his home, *The Players*. These far off events were news, during the week that Miss Borden came, as the reporters said, 'to face her accusers.'

Three judges were on the bench on June 5, 1893, as the trial began. They were Chief Justice Albert Mason and Associate Justice Caleb Blodgett and Justin Dewey. Mr Knowlton was assisted in the prosecution by the District Attorney for the Eastern District, Mr William H. Moody. The defence was now entrusted to Mr George D. Robinson, together with Messrs Jennings and Adams. Mr Robinson had been Governor of Massachusetts thrice; he was held in peculiar and unusual esteem by the people of the State for the integrity of his character. The story, then current, that before accepting a retainer in this case he had spent two hours in consultation with Miss Borden in the jail, and that he had come forth declaring his firm belief in her innocence, had done much to hearten her friends and convince the doubtful.

On the first day one hundred and eight talesmen were examined before twelve were selected for the jury. Almost every town and city of the county was represented on this large panel, but not Fall River, and there were no Fall River men on the jury. The fine old question and reply, between the Clerk and the prisoner, have vanished from our courts: 'How will you be tried?' 'By God and my country.' 'God send you good deliverance!' But Massachusetts keeps some of the ancient phraseology, so after the reading of the indictment, the Clerk said to the jury:

> 'To each count of which indictment Lizzie Andrew Borden, the prisoner at the bar, has heretofore pleaded and said that thereof she is not guilty, and for trial puts herself upon her country, which country you are. You are now sworn to try the issue. If she is guilty on either or both of said counts, you are to say so, and if she is not guilty on either or both of said counts, you are to say so, and no more. Good men and true, stand fast together and hearken to your evidence.'

It is one of the great sensational moments in our civilization: the trial of a woman for her life. The newspapers, for the ultimate thrill, prefer to have a trial for the murder of a lover or a husband, but this was for a crime more rare and terrible—for parricide. If anybody in the crowded Court, on that warm June day, found the scene dramatic, it was merely because he comprehended its meaning. The proceedings were quiet and dignified, but without ceremony or circumstance; the surroundings were commonplace. There entered no judge in scarlet, acclaimed by trumpeters, as in the trial of Mrs Maybrick at Liverpool; these justices did not even wear the black silk gowns of our Supreme Court. The sitting was held in a bare, white-walled room, filled with desks, chairs and long settees. Three elderly and bearded gentlemen, with palm-leaf fans, sat a little above the rest, upon the bench. Another beard, a long one, on the chin of the Clerk. Beards, side-whiskers, or heavy moustaches in the jury-box; men still liked to surround their faces with hair. The prisoner came in 'walking steadily.' She wore a 'new dress of black mohair, cut in the latest style, with leg-of-mutton sleeves, which fitted her by no means inferior form to perfection. Upon her head was a jaunty black lace hat

trimmed with rosettes of blue velvet and a blue feather. . . . She
was altogether unembarrassed.'

Perhaps the most unusual figures in the New Bedford Court
House were the thirty or forty newspaper men from Boston and
New York, and from the press associations. They alternately
amused and were amused by New Bedford. They sat upon
uncomfortable stools and rested their papers upon narrow
strips of board, called by courtesy, tables. Writers from the
metropolitan journals gave their readers what they were supposed to desire, by describing almost every man in the trial as
'stern and Puritanical' and nearly every woman as 'an angular
old maid.' The New Yorker visualizes the inhabitant of New
England as looking more or less, in features and costume, like
St Gaudens' statue of Deacon Chapin, 'The Puritan,' and if, in
his expeditions to Newport, Boston or Bar Harbor, he has seen
few of this appearance, he clings, nevertheless, to his secret
belief.

There may have been women among the reporters; the
sob-sister had made her appearance in journalism, and one
who signed herself 'Amy Robsart' had already written sympathetic articles about Miss Borden languishing in the Taunton jail. Mr Algernon Blackwood, the novelist, was on the staff
of the New York *Sun* at this time, and he refers in his autobiogra-
phy, *Episodes before Thirty*, to the Borden case. None of the
bizarre and terrible situations in Mr Blackwood's stories, with
all their appropriate setting, is stranger than the contrast
between the homely scene of the Borden house on that August
morning and the Æschylean slaughter there enacted.

Probably the most distinguished correspondent present was
Julian Ralph of the New York *Sun*, although nobody was so
conspicuous as Joseph Howard, Jr., of *The New York Recorder*
and *The Boston Globe*. At that time many citizens of New
England considered it a solemn duty, between breakfast and
church on Sunday mornings to read 'Howard's Letter' from
New York in the *Globe*. Pontifical in style, and invariably
ending with a description, in two words, of the weather in New
York, these letters had become a sort of weekly necessity, for
reasons difficult to explain today. Mr Howard had descended
upon New Bedford with something of the grandeur of an

Oriental embassy, and with every provision for his comfort and convenience. Somehow he secured a chair next the Sheriff, and there, conspicuous in his summer clothes, among all the poor wretches in doleful black, he fairly dominated the scene. Mr Howard was said to have attended every notable trial in thirty years, including that of Mrs Surratt of the Lincoln conspiracy.

Before giving any narrative of the progress of the trial, it may be useful to show what the State tried to prove. I will condense into this paragraph and the next an analysis of the case made by Professor John H. Wigmore, author of *The Principles of Judicial Proof*. The State sought to establish that the prisoner had a motive for the crime, and the design to commit it; that she had the opportunity, and the means and the capacity; and finally, that she betrayed consciousness of guilt. The motive was supposed to arise in the family history; in the fact that she was not on good terms with her stepmother; that customarily she and her sister did not eat with the others in the house; and that she had made certain remarks about her stepmother which betrayed her animosity. There was no evidence of design to use an axe, but a general intention to kill was to be shown by the attempt to buy poison. The conversation with Miss Russell on Wednesday night, and the suggestion to Bridget that she go out to buy dress goods, were to support the theory of premeditation.

For opportunity, means and capacity, the State attempted to prove that she had exclusive opportunity; that physically she was not incapable of the deeds; and that one of the hatchets produced in Court—the 'handleless' hatchet—was not incapable of being the weapon. Consciousness of guilt, with exclusive opportunity, were the strong points of the prosecution. To establish the former the State relied, first, on the alleged falsehoods to prevent detection of the first death in the story about the note sent to Mrs Borden. Second, the falsehoods as to the visit to the barn, and the contradictory versions of this story. Third, her knowledge as to the first death. Fourth, her concealment of the knowledge. Fifth, that she concealed or destroyed evidence, as will appear in the testimony. So far, Professor Wigmore.

Mr Moody opened for the Commonwealth. He had begun a

career which was to reward him, before middle-age had passed, with two of the great prizes of his profession in America. Of medium-size and sturdy figure, he had a pleasant, youthful countenance, and a manner in public speech of sincere, often intense, conviction, not unlike that of President Theodore Roosevelt, whose Cabinet Minister he became. Mr Moody gave an outline of the history of the case which need not be repeated here, since I qave already drawn upon it, as well as other sources. He described the interior of the Borden house— fortunately this description was supplemented by an inspection, for which the jury were taken to Fall River. One or two points in the address may be mentioned. When he came to the remark which Miss Borden made to her father: 'Mrs Borden has gone out; she had a note from somebody who was sick,' he said:

'That, gentlemen, we put to you as a lie, intended for no purpose except to stifle inquiry as to the whereabouts of Mrs Borden.'

In regard to the stories about the visit to the yard or to the barn, he invited the jury's attention to certain minor differences and to one important discrepancy. To Bridget, to Mrs Churchill, and to Officer Mullaly, she said that she was in the barn, and came into the house because of a noise she heard. The noise was variously described, to the different persons, as 'a groan,' 'a distress noise' and a 'scraping sound.'

'All those, gentlemen, you see in substance are stories which include the fact that while she was outside she heard some alarming noise which caused her to rush in and discover the homicide. Well, gentlemen, as inquiry begins to multiply upon her as to her whereabouts, another story comes into view, and she repeats it again and again, and finally repeats it under oath, that at the time, after Bridget went upstairs she went out into the barn to get lead to make sinkers. Now, gentlemen, having in view the character of her statements, that she heard the noise, you will find that when she gave a later and detailed account, she said that she went into the loft of the barn, opened the window, ate some pears up there, and looked over some lead for sinkers, came down, looked into the stove to see if the fire was hot enough that she might go on with her ironing, found it was not, put her hat down, started to go upstairs to await the fire which Bridget was to build for the noonday, and discovered her father. It is not, gentlemen, and I pray your attention to it, a difference of words here. In the one case the statement is that she was alarmed by the noise of the homicide. In the other case, the statement is that she came coolly, deliberately, about her business, looking after her ironing, putting down her hat, and accidentally discovered the homicide as she went upstairs.'

Mr Moody also described other portions of the case for the prosecution, and these may be mentioned as they are reached in the testimony. At the close of his speech, the prisoner fainted. The witness first called included Mr Kieran, the engineer who measured the house; Mr John Vinnicum Morse; and a number of bank employees and shop-keepers who saw Mr Borden on the day of his death.

The first important witness was Bridget Sullivan, and her cross-examination by Mr Robinson seemed to elicit the first bits of information which had not been heard at the preliminary trial. Mr Robinson dwelt upon the matter of discord in the family. The witness testified that she had never observed any quarrels. Asked the direct question if the daughters came to the table for meals with the rest of the family, the answer was:

'No, sir, they did not.'

The lawyer persisted, and she replied:

'Most of the time they did not eat with their father and mother.'

He suggested that this was because they did not arise as early in the morning, and asked about the custom at dinner. She answered:

'Sometimes at dinner; a good many more times they were not.'

She testified that Miss Lizzie and Mrs Borden did speak to each other civilly. He asked about the stepdaughter's conduct toward Mrs Borden when the latter was ill, and brought out the disconcerting reply:

'I know that she was sick one time, and none of them went into the room while she was sick.'

He quoted her testimony at the inquest, which was in some degree opposed to this, but did not get her to alter the statement. He returned to the question of their eating together, until she finally said that

'They always ate at the same dining-room.'

He then asked:

'Always ate together in the dining-room?'

The answer was 'Yes.'

His treatment of the witness on this point seems somewhat disingenuous. Bridget testified that she had no duties in the bedrooms of the family. The most important facts which he brought out in favor of the prisoner were that while Bridget was on the other side of the house, talking with the Kellys' servant, she could not have seen anyone who might have entered the house by the sideyard; and that when she came downstairs, after the murders, she saw no blood on Miss Borden's face or hands. Mr Robinson touched upon the story of the note to Mrs Borden, learned that the witness heard the prisoner tell her father that such a note had been received, but then dropped the subject, and did not ask whether the witness had heard of the note from Mrs Borden, or from anybody except the prisoner. That omission was significant.

Dr Bowen and Mrs Churchill followed Bridget Sullivan. All of these witnesses were questioned about the dress which Miss Borden was wearing when they first saw her after the murders. Dr Bowen's testimony on this point was confused; Mrs Churchill described it as 'a light blue and white ground work . . . with a dark navy blue diamond on it.' Shown a dark blue *silk* dress, given to the police by the prisoner as the one worn by her that morning, and asked if this was the one she saw, Mrs Churchill replied:

'I did not see her with it on that morning.'

On cross-examination Mrs Churchill said that she could not tell much about Bridget's dress on that day; and that she saw no blood on Miss Borden, although she stood over her and had fanned her. Mrs Churchill also said that Bridget told her the story about the note. The defence promptly tried to clinch this apparently valuable testimony and made the witness repeat it again and again. But on the redirect examination, Mr Moody asked:

'Lest there be any mistake, Mrs Churchill, you don't speak of this talk with Bridget with reference to the note as in substitution, but in addition to what Miss Lizzie Borden told you?'

'It was after Lizzie had told me.'

'Then Bridget told you what you have told us?'

'Yes, after that.'

When Miss Alice Russell was called, 'Miss Borden straightened up in her chair and began to watch the door.' Miss Russell entered, and looked, says a reporter, in every direction but toward the prisoner. She related, at length, the conversation with Miss Borden on the night before the murders. When the witness came to relate experiences at the Borden house after the murders, she said that in answer to her question:

'What did you go to the barn for, Lizzie?' the answer was:

'I went to get a piece of tin or iron to fix my screen.'

A new and important part of Miss Russell's testimony was that on the Sunday morning after the murders (following Mayor Coughlin's call on Saturday evening) she—the witness—came into the kitchen of the Borden house and saw Miss Lizzie Borden at the stove, with a dress in her hand. Her sister, Miss Emma, asked what she was going to do, and the answer was:

'I am going to burn this old thing up; it is covered with paint.'

Miss Russell left the room without speaking, but on returning saw the prisoner ripping or tearing the garment. She said:

'I wouldn't let anybody see me do that, Lizzie.'

There was no reply. On the next day, Miss Russell said to the prisoner:

'I am afraid, Lizzie, the worst thing you could have done was to burn that dress. I have been asked about your dresses.'

The prisoner answered: 'Oh, what made you let me do it? Why didn't you tell me?'

This testimony about the dress, said Miss Russell, was not given at the inquest nor at the preliminary trial, nor at her first appearance before the Grand Jury. She further said that the burned dress was a 'cheap cotton Bedford cord' with 'light blue ground with a dark figure, small figure.'

Miss Russell, on cross-examination, said that in the dining-room, on the day of the murder, she found the handkerchiefs that the prisoner had been ironing. Some of them had been

ironed; two or three had not. She saw no blood anywhere upon
the prisoner. When the dress was burned, on Sunday morning,
there was a policeman in the yard at the time. She saw no blood
on the dress, and she did not actually see the prisoner put it into
the stove.

It was the Government's contention that the few handkerchiefs left unironed were significant: that there was no good
reason for leaving this work unfinished.

One of the first of the police witnesses was the assistant city
marshal, John Fleet. He had been early to arrive, and to talk
with the prisoner. In this conversation she made what was
considered a significant remark. In reply to Mr Fleet's question
if she had any idea who could have killed her father and mother,
she said:

'She is not my mother, sir; she is my stepmother; my mother
died when I was a child.'

One gathers from various sources the impression that there
was something in Miss Borden's manner, in all these early
interviews, which tended to arouse suspicion. This, of course,
did not reach the jury, but it is often alluded to in contemporary
accounts. The cross-examination of Mr Fleet was long and
severe; it was the policy of the defence to impeach all the police
testimony as incorrect, sometimes deliberately malicious. In
the opinion of some of the reporters, the police witnesses were
badly confused by Mr Robinson; this is not apparent in reading
the stenographic report. Officer Medley, who arrived at the
Borden house at twenty minutes before twelve and heard from
Miss Borden about her visit to the barn, promptly went to the
place himself. He testified that he especially examined the floor
of the loft for footprints, and found that he could see none. He
experimented to see if his own footsteps would be left in the
accumulation of dust on the floor, and found that they were.

On the seventh day of the trial, the prosecution offered Miss
Borden's own testimony at the inquest, and on Mr Robinson's
objection, argued for its admission, after the jury had withdrawn. Mr Moody said, without dispute, that the conduct of
the inquest had been in accordance with law; that her testimony was not a confession, but rather in the nature of denials,
which were evidences of guilt. He made the usual citations of

other cases in which similar evidence had been admitted.

In reply, Mr Robinson urged that an accusation had been made against his client, by the Mayor, on August 6, that the inquest was from August 9 to 11, and that from August 6 she was under observation of the police. The house was surrounded. A warrant had been issued—but not served—on August 8; she was arrested, later, under another warrant. She was surrounded by police, a defenceless woman, denied counsel, not told by the Court or the District Attorney that she ought not testify to anything which might incriminate herself.

'If that is freedom, God save the Commonwealth of Massachusetts!'

Mr Moody replied that all this was magnificent, but it was not law. He pointed out that it was agreed that Mr Jennings was told by the District Attorney that he might confer with his client on her rights as a witness, and that it was absurd to suppose that he had not warned her of her rights not to give evidence.

The Court withdrew for consultation, and on returning said that Miss Borden was practically under arrest at the time she gave this testimony, and it was therefore excluded.

Doctors Dolan, Wood, and Draper were among the medical witnesses for the State. They were examined and cross-examined at enormous length. They agreed that between one and two hours, probably about one hour and a half, had elapsed between the two deaths—a fact deduced from the progress of digestion, the warmth of the two bodies, and the condition of the blood from each. A valuable point for the accused woman was made when Professor Wood said that he believed the assailant of the Bordens could not have avoided at least a few spatters of blood. No doctor testified that many blood stains would necessarily be received.

During the medical testimony the skull of Mr Borden was produced in Court, for purposes of illustration of the nature of the wounds. The mawkish and sentimental newspapers—and this included three-quarters of them at this stage—made great play with this fact, and dwelt upon how it affected the poor prisoner. The newspapers were few which did not speak as if the deaths of Mr and Mrs Borden ought to have been forgotten long ago; that the officers of the law were little better than brutes to have prosecuted anybody; and that the sole concern of mankind was to rescue, from her grievous position, the 'unfortunate girl,' and send her home amid a shower of roses.

Mrs Hannah Gifford, a dressmaker, testified, under objection by the defence, as to a conversation which she had with the prisoner in the month of March, preceding the murders. Mrs Gifford, in referring to Mrs Borden had used the word 'mother,' whereupon Miss Lizzie had said:

'Don't say that to me, for she is a mean, good-for-nothing thing.'

To which the dressmaker replied: 'Oh, Lizzie, you don't mean that?'

'Yes, I don't have much to do with her; I stay in my room most of the time.'

'You come down to your meals, don't you?'

'Yes; but we don't eat with them if we can help it.'

Miss Anna H. Borden (not a relative) was produced to testify to a similar but milder remark on the ship during the voyage home from Europe, in 1890, but this was excluded as remote.

A mass of conflicting evidence surrounded the testimony of Mrs Hannah Reagan, matron of the Fall River Police Station. She said she overheard a quarrel between the Borden sisters, in which the prisoner said:

'Emma, you have given me away, haven't you?'

The reply of the elder sister was: 'No, Lizzie, I have not.'

The prisoner answered: 'You have; and I will let you see I won't give in one inch.'

A controversy had arisen over Mrs Reagan's testimony, and in it were included Mr Jennings, the police, the Rev Mr Buck, and others. At the time the conversation was first reported, in August, a determined attempt was made by Miss Borden's friends to induce Mrs Reagan to sign a retraction, and thenceforth the incident was like a football, kicked about by the Borden partisans and the reporters. The original conversation was evidently believed by the prosecution, and was repeated in detail by Mrs Reagan at the trial. But it was more flatly contradicted than almost any other point in the case for the Government.

The testimony of Eli Bence, as to the poison, was excluded on the ground that it was not shown that prussic acid might not have an innocent use! At this point the Government then rested its case.

The defence, to give Professor Wigmore's analysis in one paragraph, did not shake the evidence as to motive. It had excluded the prussic acid evidence. It did not destroy the proof of exclusive opportunity, but it did show that the screen door at the side was not locked at all times. It showed no traces of another person in the house, and only vague reports of others in the vicinity. It failed to prove that the handleless hatchet might not have been used, but tried to suggest that the evidence of the police was wilfully false. It could not shake the story of the note, but suggested that the note might have been part of the murderer's plot. The inconsistent stories about the trip to the barn were attributed to excitement, and the most damaging of them—the inquest testimony—was excluded. It was shown that lead was found in the barn loft, but no fish-line was produced, and no screen in need of repair was identified. 'The inconsistent stories as to her return and discovery of the murder were in part slid over, in part ignored, and in part discredited.' The stronghold of the defence was the utter absence of blood stains on the person of the accused. Five or six persons saw her within ten minutes, and saw no stains on her. 'It is safe to say that this was the decisive fact of the case.'

Mr Jennings opened for the defence. He dwelt upon the fact that not one particle of direct evidence had been produced against her. He quoted cases to show the unreliability of circumstantial evidence—often an effective argument, for although attorneys may argue and judges expound until the end of time, persons will still be found to say: 'I don't believe in circumstantial evidence.' He pointed out that the Government, for all the array of axes and hatchets they brought into Court, were not positive about any one of them. He denied the proof of exclusive opportunity. He asserted that others had been in the barn before Medley paid his visit.

The defence had little need of any witnesses. The previous good character of the prisoner had been conceded by the Government, so no testimony was offered on that point. A number of witnesses did appear; they were solemnly heard, and

duly cross-examined; but at this distance they appear in no
other light than as comic relief. Two ladies, neighbors of the
Bordens, named Chagnon, testified that they had heard a
thumping sound in the direction of the Borden barn, the night
before the murders. (It had been investigated, and shown to be
dogs upsetting barrels of waste to get at some bones. Even had
it been other than this, did the defence suggest that the
murderer, arriving twelve hours in advance of the crime, had
taken up quarters in the barn—perhaps to get an early chance
at the sinkers—and had announced his coming by thumping on
the floor?) One Mrs Durfee had heard a man, a year before,
make threats against Mr Borden; her testimony was excluded
as remote. One or two witnesses appeared to tell of a drunken
man seen sitting on the Borden steps, the night before. Dr
Handy described his Wild Eyed Man—not satisfied that he
was 'Mike the Soldier.' The appearance of Hyman Lubinsky,
an ice-cream peddler, gave an exotic flavor to the day's proceedings. He had driven through Second Street at some time
that morning, when he 'saw a lady come out the way from the
barn to the stairs from the back of the house.' This was offered
in corroboration of the story of the visit to the barn, but it was
discarded testimony, as he had already been carefully examined by the Government, and his idea of time shown to be
faulty. The Clan Lubinsky were more of a novelty in 1893 than
today, and Hyman's tart answers to the District Attorney
('What has a person got eyes for, but to look with?') must have
amused the auditors.

Better still were a pair of youthful witnesses, Everett Brown
and Thomas Barlow, a couple of boys who had apparently
determined to get into Court one way or another. The spirit of
romance burned in them, a far hotter flame than their passion
for fact. They had not had, like Huck Finn and Tom Sawyer,
the luck to witness a murder, and to be able to take a solemn
oath by midnight. But they did almost as well. They ate their
dinners at the surprising hour of 10:30 a.m., on August 4, and
arrived at the scene almost before the crime was committed.

'We went in the side gate.'

'You say "we." Who?'

'Me and Brownie.'

They went up in the barn loft far ahead of anybody else, although they paused a while at the stairs, and dared each other to go first, each thinking that 'somebody might drop an axe on him.' They enjoyed the loft because it was 'cooler' up there than it was outdoors. The District Attorney was inhospitable toward these fairy-tales.

'The barn loft was a nice, comfortable, cool place?'

'Yes, sir.'

They had approached the Borden house 'fooling along,' and they were asked what that meant.

'He was pushing me off the sidewalk and I was pushing him off.'

Ah, 'me and Brownie,' the rest of the folk who were in the New Bedford Court House, that day, are either dead, or else they are old, old people. But you are not too old to recall with delight the day you had a trip over from Fall River, and a free ride on the train, chummed with the police, and for a while stood with the fierce light of fame beating upon you, the reporters taking down your words, to be printed that evening in all the papers. What mattered it to you if Truth blushed and turned aside while you spoke?

Joseph Lemay from Steep Brook, led forward the murderer of melodrama. On August 16 (twelve days after the crime), on a farm four miles from the city, he was in a deep wood, a savage place, holy and enchanted. Suddenly he heard a voice thrice repeating the words:

'Poor Mrs Borden!'

He looked over a wall and saw a man sitting on the ground. The man picked up a hatchet and shook it at him. Then he—the man with the hatchet—leaped over the wall and disappeared; he had spots of blood on his shirt. The Court, however, did not let Mr Lemay entertain the jury with this fable. It was unnecessary; the Court were to do far better for the prisoner than all these romancers combined.

Miss Emma Borden was one of the last witnesses for the defence, and she bore with some composure a long and skilful cross-examination. She was not allowed by the Court to tell about the custom in the family of burning old dresses. She admitted that there had been trouble between her father and

step-mother on one side, and her sister and herself on the other.
She said that it was Miss Lizzie, not herself, who had become
reconciled with the stepmother, and this statement was considered more gallant than veracious.

The prisoner did not testify in her own defence. The jury
were, of course, duly informed that she was within her rights in
refraining from the witness stand, and the justice who delivered
the charge gave a long explanation of why she might refrain.
They were warned not to consider it as telling against her. But
we, who are not jurymen, may wonder at it. She was not a
foreigner, unable to speak or understand the language, nor a
timid or feeble person, who could not make a calm appearance.
She had not an evil record in her past life, which might be
disclosed in cross-examination, unfairly to prejudice the jury.
The spotlessness of her life was acclaimed by her defenders. She
was known to have made the most unaccountable and contradictory statements about her actions at the time of her father's
murder. Here was her chance to explain them all away. She did
not accept it. Not any of the warm admirers who were soon to
throng around her, or to fill the mails and the wires with
enthusiastic messages of congratulation, ever seemed to notice
the fact. The law, in their opinion, owed her an abject apology
for having suspected her. At the close of the arguments, and
before the charge, the Chief Justice informed her that it was her
privilege to speak in person to the jury. Secure from question,
she arose and repeated the thirteen words in which her counsel
had coached her:

'I am innocent. I leave it to my counsel to speak for me.'

On the twelfth day of the trial Mr Robinson made the final
argument for his client. One gathers from reading it, that, like
his conduct of the case, it was marked by courtesy, and even
more by kindliness, and a manner of transparent honesty. The
advocate was held in respect everywhere in the State. He was
addressing a jury chiefly from the country, or from small towns
and villages, and he never failed to put himself in sympathy
with them. Although he had dwelt in the tents of wickedness
long enough to study at Harvard, to serve in the State Legislature in Boston, and for three years as Governor of the Commonwealth, and although he had even been in Washington for

number of years, as a Member of Congress, he never failed to drop a hint as to what he thought of city folks, or about the general superiority of men who lived on farms.

He described the murders as terrible and revolting beyond all imagination—so terrible that they could only be the work of a maniac, a fiend, a devil. Such acts were morally and physically impossible for the prisoner at the bar. In the days following the murders the police had been criticized for not catching somebody; they had perforce to go out and make an arrest. Once having done this, they easily persuaded themselves of the prisoner's guit. The prosecution had said that she was in the house on that morning. Well, that was a proper place for her to be. Did they wish her to be out on the street? It was where he would wish his daughter to be; at home. He made a strong argument against the contention that she necessarily would have seen the body of her stepmother from the hall at the head of the stairs, or from the stairs while descending. He said that *Bridget*, as well as Miss Borden, had been told by Mrs Borden about the note. Mr Robinson's words were:

'Both Bridget and Lizzie had learned from Mrs Borden that she had had a note. Mrs Borden had told Lizzie. Mrs Borden had told Bridget. She had given Bridget the work to do, washing the windows. She said to her: "I have got a note to go out and see someone that was sick." '

On this point, Professor Wigmore writes:

'The only blot upon an almost perfectly conducted trial was the attempt of the counsel for the defence in argument to show that the information as to the note emanated originally from Bridget, and that the accused merely repeated it. This was decidedly a breach of propriety, because it was not merely an argument suggesting the fair possibility of that explanation, but a distinct assertion that the testimony was of that purport, and therefore, in effect, a false quotation of the testimony. In truth, the accused's statement about the note was her own alone and was one of the points to be explained.'

Mr Robinson suggested that the note might have been a part of the scheme of the murderer to get Mrs Borden out of the house, or otherwise to entrap her. He made light of the supposed discomforts of the Borden home, and of the plain fare

served at their table. He held the array of hatchets up to
ridicule. In ending he asked for a prompt verdict of ' "not
guilty" that she may go back and be Lizzie Andrew Borden of
Fall River in that blood-stained and wrecked home, where she
has passed her life so many years.'

Mr Knowlton, in closing for the Government, had a much harder problem. He was asking for the conviction of a woman, and a
church member, who was supported and buttressed by friends,
and by a press which had almost ceased to do anything except
palpitate to the sentimentalism of the nosier section of the public.
He was a thickset man, with a tenacious manner, easily exager-
ated by his detractors into the air of the inquisitor or the tyrant.

No prosecuting officer in Massachusetts ever had a less
enviable task than his; none ever carried his work through with
more ability or more courageous fulfillment of a public duty.
His address was acknowledged, even in the hostile press, as far
abler than that of his opponent. Mr Robinson talked down to
the whims and prejudices of a country jury; Mr Knowlton
talked straight to citizens whom he assumed had an eye to their
duty. He argued that neither church membership nor the fact of
being a woman were proof against guilt.

'With all sympathy for the woman, in which, believe me, I
share with you; with all distrust of any evidence until it is
brought home to your convictions, in which you will let me
share with you, and all good and true men; with due regard, if
you please, to the consequences of your action, yet let me
remind you that you stand not only to deliver that woman but
to deliver the community. It was a crime which may well
challenge your most sober and sacred attention. That aged
man, that aged woman, had gone by the noonday of their lives.
They had borne the burden and heat of the day. They had
accumulated a competency which they felt would carry them
through the waning years of their lives, and hand in hand they
expected to go down to the sunset of their days in quiet and
happiness. But for that crime they would be enjoying the air of
this day. But for that assassin, many years of their life, like
yours, I hope, sir, would have been before them, when the cares
of life are past, when the anxieties of their daily advocations had
ceased to trouble them, and together they would have gone

down the hill of life, serene in an old age which was happy because the happiness had been earned by a life of fidelity and toil.

'Over those bodies we stand, Mr Foreman. We sometimes forget the past. Over those bodies we stand, and we say to ourselves, is it possible that this crime cannot be discovered? You are standing as has been suggested, in the presence of death itself. It is not only what comes hereafter, but it is the double death that comes before. There is a place, it is the chamber of death, where all these personal animosities, passions, and prejudices, have no room, where all matters of sentiment are aside, where nothing but the truth, the naked truth, finds room and lodgment. In that spirit I adjure you to enter upon the trial of this case. It is the most solemn duty of your lives.'

Illustrations of circumstantial evidence have often been given in Court, from Thoreau's playful remark about a trout in the milk, to the more familiar one of footprints. Perhaps it has seldom been more effectively presented than in Mr Knowlton's speech:

'What is called sometimes circumstantial evidence is nothing in the world but that presentation of circumstances—it may be one or fifty—there isn't any chain about it—the word chain is a misnomer as applied to it; it is the presentation of circumstances from which one is irresistibly driven to the conclusion that crime has been committed. Talk about a chain of circumstances! When that solitary man had lived on his island for twenty years and believed that he was the only human being there, and that the cannibals and savages that lived around him had not found him, nor had not come to his island, he walked out one day on the beach, and there he saw the fresh print in the sand of a naked foot. He had no laywer to tell him that that was nothing but a circumstance. He had no distinguished counsel to urge upon his fears that there was no chain about that thing which led him to a conclusion. His heart beat fast; his knees shook beneath him, he fell to the ground in fright, because Robinson Crusoe knew when he saw that circumstance that a man had been there that was not himself. It was *circumstantial evidence;* it was nothing but *circumstantial evidence*, but it satisfied *him.'*

The District Attorney emphasized the pre-decease of Mrs Borden as the key to the case, since the murderer of Mr Borden was also the murderer of Mrs Borden. No outsider could have planned it, nor lurked about the house to execute it. Mrs

Borden, he said, had no outside enemies. These men with a grudge against her husband had no grudge against her. He touched upon Mrs Gifford's testimony, and upon the prisoner's promptness in saying to the officer: 'She is not my mother.' He refused to withdraw, but re-affirmed Mr Moody's statement that the story about the note was a lie.

'No note came; no note was written; nobody brought a note; nobody was sick. . . . I will stake the case on your belief or disbelief in the truth or falsity of that proposition.'

He disputed Mr Robinson's claim that Bridget said she had heard about the note from Mrs Borden. Mr Knowlton met the argument that the prisoner had no quarrel with her father by asserting that when Mrs Borden had been killed, it became apparent to her that she must kill Mr Borden too, in order to save herself from his accusation. Her father was the one person who would be in no doubt who was guilty, as he knew who hated the stepmother. The prosecutor dwelt upon the absurdity of the stay in the barn loft on so hot a day. The defence, he said, could introduce evidence about dogs upsetting ash-barrels, why did they not explain what screen needed repair, and why did they not produce the fish-line for which sinkers were required? The prisoner's coolness was touched upon; she did not rush out of the house, nor send for police; she sent only for her friends; and public knowledge of the murders came by accident. On the difficulty of the blood stains upon her clothing, he reasoned that she had ample opportunity to remove the stains of the first murder. As for the second, he ackowledged the difficulty of the question.

'I cannot answer it. You cannot answer it.'

He did draw attention, however, to the roll of paper seen in the stove, which might have been used for protection; and to the murdered man's coat, not hanging on a hook, but folded at the head of the couch where he lay. That also might have been used as a shield. The question about the dresses was debated at great length by both counsel. The prosecution contended that, at all events, the one produced by the prisoner was not the one worn on that morning. It was silk; an unlikely material for morning housework.

The charge to the jury was given by Mr Justice Dewey. It

Lizzie Borden (left) and sister Emma at the trial.

became the subject of a great amount of discussion, and the mildest comment is that it was extremely favorable to the prisoner. Mr Howard, the newspaper correspondent, and by this time one of the warmest of Miss Borden's sympathizers, called it 'a plea for the innocent,' a description which could hardly have been enjoyed by the learned and supposedly impartial judge who delivered it.

At twenty-four minutes past three, on the afternoon of June 20, the thirteenth day of the trial, the jury went out. They stayed a little over an hour, or until about half-past four. At that time, they came in with the verdict.

'Not guilty.'

The *Boston Journal*, which was favorable to Miss Borden, said that two ballots were taken and that on the first ballot one juror voted for conviction. It is usually said, however, that they were agreed from the start, and that they stayed out an hour only to avoid suspicion of not having considered the Government's case.

The familiar scene was enacted—cheers, tears, congratulations; hand-shakings and thanks for each of the jurymen—all a matter of course as long ago as when Mark Twain and C.D. Warner wrote the court scene in *The Gilded Age*. Mr Howard had a few words of felicitation for the heroine, and received her thanks, as he modestly records in both his papers. It was a privilege to shake her hand. Mrs Livermore and Mrs Fessenden were in raptures; they wired congratulations, and spoke of the District Attorney and other officers of the Government in terms of severe condemnation. The impression given by the newspapers is that it was a popular outcome. The *Boston Journal* said that the verdict 'saves from deadly peril and vindicates from cruel suspicion a true, modest, and upright woman.' The same paper had published a poll of citizens of New England as to whether the case were 'proven' or 'not proven.' Persons were consulted in many of the larger towns, and there was a strong majority of 'not proven.'

The *Boston Globe* agreed with the verdict; The *Boston Herald* was neutral, and said that the evidence was insufficient. The *Boston Post* criticized the Government. The *Springfield Republican*, which in the early days of the case had taken a severe line with the police, was less outspoken, and intimated that many persons would still believe her guilty. Another paper of more than ordinary merit, the *Providence Journal*, said that many would find the verdict unsatisfactory. The *Fall River Globe*, which firmly supported the police and the case of the Government (and never ceased to do so) suggested that there were many in Fall River who would not agree with the jury—a sound prediction, and one which has not been falsified.

But if the press of New England were not absolutely unanimous in throwing their hats into the air, and cheering for the defendant, the newspapers of New York had no such hesitation. The *New York Herald* said: 'It will be the verdict of the great public.' The *Herald* held a poll of lawyers all over the country, and these almost unanimously voted the case of the State as 'not proven,' although here and there a lawyer said that he believed in the defendant's guilt, but did not expect a conviction. The *World* said: 'No other verdict could have been expected'; it had protested against the indictment; the trial was merely an instance of 'police blundering,' and in the meanwhile the real culprit had escaped. The *Tribune* remarked that: 'The New Bedford jury have done what they could to restore Lizzie Borden to her rightful place in a world of hope and happiness.' The advantage was all with the State in the final arguments; Knowlton's speech was much superior to Robinson's. 'We have no hesitation in pronouncing this a righteous verdict.' The cynical will say that it is a Scotch verdict of 'not proven,' but the *Tribune* cried out against such injustice.

It remained for the usually sober *New York Times* to reach the heights of ecstasy. The verdict, according to that paper, was 'a certain relief to every rightminded man and woman.' The *Times* spoke of 'this unfortunate and cruelly persecuted woman. . . .' 'There was never any serious reason to suppose that she was guilty.' The result was 'a condemnation of the police authorities of Fall River and of the legal officers who secured the indictment and have conducted the trial.' It had been 'a shame to Massachusetts.' The article, filling half a column on the editorial page, varies from severity towards the law officers, to touching sympathy for Miss Borden; it condemns the conduct of the former as 'outrageous'; they were 'guilty of a barbarous wrong to an innocent woman and a gross injury to the community.' It is a misfortune that she has not legal recourse against them and a means of bringing them to account. 'Her acquittal is only a partial atonement for the wrong that she has suffered.' The police force of Fall River is denounced as the 'usual inept and stupid and muddle-headed sort.' If the writer for the *Times* had never read a word of evidence in the case, and had turned for his information to an especially lachrymose sob-sister, who, like Miss Borden's friends in Court, held their hands over their ears when anything was uttered against her, this article might be explained.

It is not true that, on the case as it was presented to the jury, a verdict of 'guilty' was to be expected. Few lawyers have been willing to assert that the result was against the weight of evidence. The *New York Recorder*, for which Mr Howard wrote his letters, tried the case in its columns more frankly than any of the other papers, and actually organized a 'special jury' of more or less distinguished citizens, whose pictures were printed every day. They were furnished verbatim reports of each day's proceedings, and on the last day of all were asked to vote 'proven' or 'not proven.' This 'jury' included the Rev Dr Edward Everett Hale, William Sulzer, Samuel Gompers, George Fred Williams, DeLancey Nicoll, Lucy Stone, and Albert A. Pope, and these with the other five, all voted 'not proven.'

After the newspaper comments, it is instructive to read a few passages from two articles on the case both written by lawyers, who were, moreover, conversant with all the evidence. They are the only serious discussions which I have seen. Professor Wigmore, writing in the *American Law Review* for November, 1893, said:

> 'It is difficult to see how the assailant could have avoided receiving blood-marks during the assaults; it is also difficult to understand what arrangements of implements and clothing, and what combinations of opportunity, suffered to allow the accused, if she was the assailant, to remove the traces upon weapon and clothes after each assault. But, first, these are difficulties of ignorance; in other words, there is no proved fact which is inconsistent with the thing being so; we merely cannot find traces of the exact *modus operandi*; second, this difficulty is equally as great for any other person than the accused, and we may say greater; it is a difficulty that cannot change the balance of conviction. On the other hand, the

conduct of the accused after the killing was such that no conceivable hypothesis except that of guilt, will explain the inconsistencies and improbabilities that were asserted by her. The statements about the purpose of the barn visit, and about the discovery of the father's death, are frightfully inconsistent; while the story of the note requires for its truth a combination of circumstances almost inconceivable. We may add to this the inevitable query, Why did the accused not take the stand to explain these things? Of course, it was her legal right to remain silent; but the rule against self-crimination is not one of logic or of relevancy; it is a rule of policy and fairness, based on broad considerations of average results desirable in the long run. It cannot prevent us as logical beings, from drawing our inferences; and if we weigh in this case the confounding inconsistencies and improbabilities of these statements and then place with these the opportunity and the refusal to explain them, we cannot help feeling that she failed to explain them because she could not; and one side of the balance sinks heavily.

This is not saying that the evidence justified a conviction. . . .'

On the rulings of the Court, Mr Wigmore almost invariably disagrees.

'It may be suggested . . . with all deference, that . . . most of what was excluded seems admissible.'

On the prussic acid evidence the Court decided that the evidence did not come up to the offer.

'As for the authorities . . . the clear result is for the admission of the evidence.'

On the question of admitting the inquest statement, Mr Wigmore adopts Mr Moody's argument; that there was no doubt that Mr Jennings informed his client of her rights, 'and that he allowed her to go on the stand because he deliberately concluded that it was the best policy for her, by so doing, to avoid all appearance of concealment or guilt. And yet the ruling of the Court allowed them to blow hot and cold—to go on the stand when there was something to gain and to remain silent when the testimony proved dangerous to use.'

The Court ruled against the defence when it proposed to prove the family custom of burning old dresses, and this, Mr Wigmore believes, would have over-turned the verdict if it had resulted in a conviction. He further said that the charge that the police showed a spirit of persecution was 'an unfounded accusation.'

Judge Charles G. Davis of Plymouth, wrote to the *Boston Advertiser*, letters afterwards published as 'The Conduct of the

Law in the Borden Case.' They contain the severest criticisms of the rulings by the Court, and leave no manner of doubt that the author thought that these decisions led to a grave error. The ruling about the poison 'was received with almost universal surprise by the bar.' On that which excluded the inquest testimony he remarks:

'It is difficult to see how Miss Borden was under arrest when she was not under arrest.'

Judge Davis's analysis of the evidence is an extremely interesting consideration of the laws of chance and of averages to show the improbability or impossibility of the murders having been committed by a person from outside the house.

'It is a rule of law that the possession of property recently stolen and unaccounted for is sufficient for conviction . . . But the same law . . . applies to capital crimes. Here was a person who had in possession the bodies of two victims robbed of the precious jewels of their lives. Does anybody think that if this evidence had been applied to a case of robbery, or of mere property, the law administered or the verdict would have been the same?'

In the charge of the Court, writes Judge Davis, the justice went beyond his legitimate function with respect to matters of fact. On the charge and on the rulings, Judge Davis says in his second letter:

'It was not the prisoner, but the Commonwealth which did not have a fair trial.' Was Mr Justice Dewey's 'the tone of a judge or of an advocate?' Here the author referred to such words in the charge as this: 'Is it reasonable and credible that she could have killed Mrs Borden at or about the time claimed by the Government . . .?'

It is impracticable to quote more, but I am led to believe, from conversations with lawyers, that the Superior Court of Massachusetts has never been subjected to such criticism as that resulting from the conduct of its justices in the Borden case. And in this criticis, there was no hint or intimation of corruption, but of a mental infirmity or bias resulting from an unwillingness to believe that a woman could murder her father.

The sense of outrage felt by a considerable portion of the community becomes apparent in the extraordinary series of articles published annually, for many years, in the *Fall River Globe*. These were written by the city editor, the late James D. O'Neil. They always appeared about August 4, the anniversary of the murders, and were very pointed, to say the least. Thus, on August 4, 1904, an article one and a half columns long is headed: 'A Dozen Years Since the Bordens Were Brutally Butchered. Perhaps Murderers or Murderess May Be in the City. Who Can Tell?' It says that the police were abused, although they made up their minds correctly within forty-eight hours 'as to the dastard.' It jeers at the story of the 'Wild Eyed Man,' and the Portuguese farm laborer, and the man with the grudge against Andrew Borden, 'and Lubin-sky,' 'and me and Brownie,' 'and the sinkers in the barn loft and all the rest of the rot and nonsense that ran riot through the disordered imagination of a prejudiced and gullible public . . . Who knows, even now, that the vile minded murderer, may not be at large in the community, walking, stalking or driving obout in carriage or car . . .? Perhaps the good people of Fall River may be daily meeting him—or her—in hall, store, or railroad train . . .' The 'man—or woman' 'he—or she' 'him—or her' *motif* recurs throughout.

On August 4, 1905, a less indignant article had the caption: 'Great Wrong is Righted after 13 Years of Misrepresentation. No Murders were Committed On August 4, 1892. Despite the Belief that Andrew and Abby Borden Died in that Manner.' There follow nearly two columns of sarcasm, ending:

> There were No Borden Murders!
> Both the Victims of 13 Years Ago
> Died as the Result of Excessive Heat!

This persecution of the 'unfortunate girl' was probably resented by the Borden partisans in Fall River, but for some years nothing was done about it. It is one of the oddities of the case that once the acquittal was secured the Borden party began to melt and disintegrate. Finally, however, influential persons were induced to bring to bear a pressure which stopped the articles.

There is a persistent belief that the case has figured in fiction, and that more than one novelist has drawn upon it for a plot.

There is a noticeable fact about real crimes when they are put into novels or stories; they appear in the fictitious form so altered as to be almost unrecognizable. The writer has merely borrowed a hint, if anything, from the supposed source. The tale most frequently mentioned as based upon the Fall River murders is Miss Mary Wilkins's story, 'The Long Arm,' but it really contains hardly as much of the case as an analytical chemist would call a 'trace.' A woman is accused of killing somebody, but she is, of course, triumphantly innocent. Much nearer to the real thing are a few sentences in *The Summit House Mystery, or The Earthly Purgatory*, by Lily Dougall (1905). The author, a native of Canada, but living in England, had apparently slight acquaintance with the United States. She had heard something about the Borden case. The scene of her story is Georgia, and there is simply a brief reference to 'Mr Claxton and his second wife' who were 'suddenly killed.' It appeared that 'a large body of circumstantial evidence proved that Hermione,' his daughter, 'was alone in the house with them.' Hermione, needless to say, is quite innocent.

Miss Borden's name appeared again in the newspapers in February 1897, about three and a half years after the acquittal. On the 16th and 17th of that month, articles were printed in the *Providence Journal*, the first being headed:

'Lizzie Borden Again. A Warrant for her Arrest issued from a local Court. Two Paintings Missed from Tilden Thurber Co.'s Store. Said to Have Been Traced to Miss Borden's Home in Fall River.'

In the warrant, according to the second article, she was charged with larceny of a painting on porcelain, called 'Love's Dream.' 'It is known,' said the *Journal*, 'that the warrant was issued. It was never served and it is said that the two paintings are still in the possession of Miss Lizzie Borden.' The incident attracted much attention in Fall River. The Tilden-Thurber Corporation, a firm of silversmiths and jewelers in Providence, write (1924):

'We have no records regarding the Lizzie Borden case but our recollection of the situation is that the warrant for arrest was based on shoplifting episodes which were finally adjusted.'

At a later date, Miss Nance O'Neil, the distinguished actress, was involved in financial difficulties and litigation with her managers and creditors. These took the form of hearings in the equity session at the Court in Boston. Miss Borden emerged from her retirement and became an almost daily spectator at the trial. Since she can hardly have been amused by the legal proceedings, it is supposed that the attraction lay in the interest she felt for Miss O'Neil as an artist, for the latter was a tragedienne of great ability.

The closing appeal in Mr Robinson's final address to the jury has not been fulfilled with precision. He asked that she might go back 'and be Lizzie Andrew Borden of Fall River' in her old home. In later years Miss Borden lived about a mile and a half from her old home, and her name appeared in the telephone director as Lizbeth A. Borden. She was not often seen in public. Her house was spacious enough for a family of ten; a gray building in modified Queen Anne type of architecture, by no means in bad taste. A touch of romance appeared in the name *Maplecroft*, in raised letters on one of the stone steps. The street was pleasant, and the houses were fairly large, with lawns and gardens. The window shades of *Maplecroft* were methodically drawn down to the middle-sash, while white curtains screened the panes. There was a large glass sun-porch, also well-curtained. The big garage, at the rear of the lawn, had an extravagant amount of plate glass set in its doors and windows. The garden accessories included a sundial on the lawn, while thoughtfulness for small creatures was manifested in a green bird-house in one of the trees. It was a generous bird-house; no mere box for a pair of wrens, but one capable of sheltering families of bluebirds, if they cared for it.

Miss Emma Borden did not remain long with her sister. They separated when the elder lady went first to Fairhaven—where she had been on that famous 4th of August—and then elsewhere, to live. On May 11, 1923, the newspapers recorded that Miss Lizzie Borden was engaged in litigation with her sister. There was a disagreement between them about the sale of the A.J. Borden building on South Main Street, owned jointly by the two. The younger desired to sell her share, but the elder objected. Hence a petition in probate, filed by Miss Lizzie, or Lizbeth, seeking an equal distribution of the property.

Miss Lizzie Borden died in Fall River on June 1, 1927; Miss Emma, in New Market, N.H., June 10, 1927. Few others of the participants in the trial survive. When Mr Jennings died, in 1923, there were no others of the justices or the counsel living. Perhaps, on a farm in Seekonk, or another of those little villages, lingers some member of the jury which for thirteen days endured all that examination of expert, and other, witnesses; and then when they had received the thanks of the lady they had freed, stayed not a moment, but (to the great delight of Julian Ralph) strode right across the market-place to the nearest hotel-bar, and (still acting in unison) drowned the dreadful thirst which had so long accumulated. I have read of one jury—I am not sure if it was this one—who were deprived, by some severe sheriff, of the consolation of tobacco, during their long confinement. Perhaps the idea was that by making men unhappy you enable them to arrive at the truth.

Those who remember the murders in 1892, and the trial in 1893, sometimes enjoy raking up the old embers, and recalling the days when families bickered about the case over the dinner table; when husbands and wives parted in wrath after breakfast, and met again at evening to take up the controversy once more. The fact that the plot of 'Edwin Drood' is never to be solved, makes the book exasperating to some readers, but highly fascinating to others.

There are, in the Borden mystery, a dozen unanswered questions to ponder. What was the meaning of the laugh from the head of the stairs, heard by Bridget Sullivan? What is the explanation of the burglary, in 1891? What caused the mysterious illness in the family? Assuming the theory of an assassin from outside, where did he go? What did he do with the weapon? What was his motive? Why did he kill Mrs Borden? Adopting the opinion of the prosecution, how could the departure of Bridget, to her own room, be counted upon? Or the time of Mr Morse's return? What was the truth about the poison story? Could anybody have made this attempt so openly? (The answer is that such things have often been done.) Were there any grounds for the suspicions entertained against two men, and at least one other woman, all of whom testified at the trial? (Suspicions, that is, of complicity.) Will the whole truth ever come out?

AFTERWORD

Will it, indeed? Edmund Pearson's piece on the Borden case was written in 1924, and for nearly 40 years it was regarded as more or less the last word on the subject. Pearson's status as a crime-writer was (and is) very high, and if he suggested that Lizzie Borden was guilty, most people went along with that. Lizzie was even portrayed in a stage musical, brandishing a hatchet and doing a spirited can-can around the courtroom while the jury sang 'Oh you can't chop your poppa up in Massachusetts'; the song became quite a hit in the 1950s. How guilty can you get?

Then in 1971 a journalist called Edward Radin launched a scathing attack not only on Pearson's views but on his very integrity as a writer; he 'presented such a biased version of the case that it might be considered a literary hoax', said Radin, and in his own book Lizzie Borden, the Untold Story *he set out to restore the balance, naming as the murderer the parlourmaid Bridget Sullivan. Radin did a splendid job in his re-presentation of the material, analyzing events, drawing up detailed timetables and bringing out inconsistencies that Pearson certainly did gloss over. He makes out quite a convincing case for Bridget as the murderer too, failing only to suggest a plausible motive for such drastic crimes from a mere maid. Nonetheless, many readers were at least half-persuaded by his arguments, and the criminological world was split into Pearson v. Radin factions. By this time Pearson himself was dead, but his widow sprang to his defense, and for some time the controversy raged on in the press. No doubt it sold a lot of books as well.*

Whether or not you believed Bridget to be guilty, the effect of all this was certainly to make you think again about Lizzie's role in the murders, and the case seemed incapable of resolution until the publication of yet another book, Victoria Lincoln's A Private Disgrace *(1967), which at last shed some new light on the matter. The author, a native of Fall River, brought both local knowledge and a sharp female insight to the case, and she offered a totally new and very plausible explanation: Lizzie suffered from periodic bouts of psychomotor epilepsy, a rare condition, knowledge of which was suppressed even within her family, but which could have produced short spells of temporary, violent insanity, with little recall afterwards. The book cannot be recommended too highly to anyone interested in the Borden case.*

And there the matter rests at present, with the ball firmly back in Lizzie's court. Has the whole truth now come out? It seems unlikely, at least as far as crime-writers are concerned.

JULIAN SYMONS

The Death of
Sir Harry Oakes

JULIAN SYMONS

The Death of Sir Harry Oakes

There was nothing unusual about the last day in the life of the Canadian millionaire, Sir Harry Oakes. He planted trees at Westbourne, his home near the Bahamas Country Club in Nassau. In the afternoon he played tennis at the Club with his friend Harold Christie, a local estate agent and a member of the Governor's Executive Council.

That evening there was a small dinner party at Westbourne, with Christie and two other friends of Oakes' as guests. The party broke up early but Christie stayed the night, as he often did. He told Sir Harry good night, went to his own room, which was separated from Sir Harry's by a bedroom and a bathroom, undressed, crawled under the mosquito net and went to sleep.

Christie woke after daybreak. He went to the screen door of Sir Harry's room on the northern porch and called 'Hi, Harry', but got no reply. He then went into the bedroom, and there saw the millionaire's body. Oakes was lying on the bed, his body burned in several places. Fire was still smouldering in the mattress. The mosquito net was burned. There were burns on the carpet and on the wardrobe, and a fine soot was lying about the room. Christie did not notice all these things at once, but he saw enough to call a doctor and the police. Sir Harry Oakes was dead. At some time during the night he had been attacked, and his skull fractured by a hard, blunt instrument. Death was caused by this fracture, by a brain haemorrhage, and by shock.

Sir Harry's sudden and violent death shocked the whole island. The Duke of Windsor, who was Governor-General, cancelled all his appointments so that he could take a hand in the enquiry. He telephone to Miami, and the Florida police arranged to fly out two experts at once. Sir Harry Oakes died on the night of 7th July, 1943, and on the following day Captain E.W. Melchen, homicide investigator, and Captain James O Barker, fingerprint and identification expert, arrived. Sir Harry's body had been taken by plane to the United States for burial. Now the plane was recalled for an autopsy. Melchen and Barker moved swiftly. Three days after the death Sir Harry's son-in-law, Marie Alfred Fouqueraux de Marigny, was charged with murder.

So opened one of the most curious crime puzzles of this century, a puzzle still unsolved. It is remarkable partly for the characters of the participants, and partly because 'expert evidence' of identification through fingerprints has seldom, if ever, been so utterly destroyed in cross-examination.

Let us look at the people and their backgrounds. Sir Harry Oakes was a remarkable man by the standards of any period. He had tramped Canada in youth as a poor prospector. Kicked out by a railway guard when he hitched a lift in a car travelling north to Northern Ontario, he found the second richest goldfield in the world on Lake Shore, one reputed to bring him an income of a million pounds a year.

Oakes looked for the railway guard and had him pensioned. His generosity was multifold, his influence international. He gave £90,000 towards the rebuilding of St George's Hospital. He had homes in Florida and Maine, a house in Kensington Palace Gardens with separate flats for each of his five children by the Australian girl he had married, an estate of 850 acres in Sussex. When he decided to settle in the Bahamas, he financed Bahamas Airways for inter-island communication, built Oakes Airfield, and stocked a 1,000 acre sheep farm with sheep specially imported from Cuba. In the early days of the war he had made a gift of £5,000 to the Ministry of Aircraft Production for a fighter plane, and more recently had given £10,000 to provide two Spitfires, named Sir Harry and Lady Oakes.

The multi-millionaire, now in his late sixties, was a man of simple and unpretentious tastes. In the Bahamas he wore often the slouch hat, khaki shirt, corduroy breeches and top boots of a prospector. Generous in the ordinary affairs of life, and indulgent to his children, he was not a man who took kindly to having his wishes thwarted. He made no secret of his dis-

Top left: Sir Harry Oakes. Centre: Alfred de Marigny. Top right: Nancy Oakes de Marigny. Below: Sir Harry's body on the bed.

approval when, in 1942, his daughter Nancy secretly married Alfred de Marigny, two days after her eighteenth birthday. The marriage took place in New York, just after Nancy had left school. Sir Harry and his wife learned of it on the evening after the wedding. It is hardly surprising that they were displeased, and what they knew of the man generally called Count Alfred de Marigny cannot have reassured them.

He was not, as his name implied, a French nobleman, nor was his name Marigny. He had been born in Mauritius, and although his mother's name was de Marigny, his father's was merely Alfred Fouqueraux. The Count had blended the names and added the title, although his friends called him Freddie. He had come to the Bahamas in 1937 with his first wife, was active in yachting circles, bought and sold estates. He was a fast, fluent talker, a playboy devoted to all kinds of sport, lavishly hospitable. Where his money came from—whether, indeed, he had any money—was not known. In fact, he was in receipt of £100 a month from his first wife.

From the beginning Sir Harry disliked his son-in-law, and an incident a few months after the marriage widened the estrangement. Nancy became very ill with typhoid while travelling with her husband in Mexico, and her state of health on recovering from this was so bad that an operation was necessary to terminate her pregnancy. Marigny came into hospital at the same time for a tonsil operation, and occupied the room next to his wife's. Sir Harry told him to get out of this room, or he would kick him out. Marigny left the hospital. His feelings were not openly expressed at the time, but may be imagined.

On 10th February, Marigny went to see a lawyer named Foskett, who acted for the Oakes family, and asked Foskett to do his best to establish good relations with Sir Harry. He was a gentleman, Marigny said, and he was not treated as one. Foskett said that he disapproved of the way in which Marigny had pursued Nancy in New York, and had married her without the knowledge of her parents. He refused to give any help. Five days later Foskett prepared a new will for Sir Harry by which, although the body of the estate was to be divided among the five children, none of them obtained a share until they reached the age of thirty.

In the following month there was a furious scene. Sir Harry went to Marigny's house in Nassau where his eldest son, sixteen-year-old Sydney Oakes, was staying the night. He made Sydney get up, dress and leave. He was like a madman, said the foreman of Sir Harry's Nassau estate, as he called Marigny a sex maniac, said that he had better not write any more letters to Lady Oakes, and threatened to horsewhip him if he did not leave the Oakes family alone. After this Nancy wrote a letter in which she said that the Marignys were cutting themselves off from the Oakes family until they had confidence in Alfred.

So much for the background. How had Marigny spent the evening of 7th July? With his wife Nancy away in the United States, Marigny, in the company of his friend and fellow Mauritian the Marquis Georges de Visdelou Guimbeau, had entertained the wives of two R.A.F. officers to dinner. Mrs Dorothy Clark and Mrs Jean Ainslie testified that Marigny drove them home at 1:30 in the morning. This, however, did not provide him with an alibi, since the time of death was placed between half past two and five o'clock. Marigny said that he had gone straight home, and his friend the Marquis de Visdelou was prepared to support that statement.

A neighbour had seen a light on in Marigny's room between 12.30 and 4 a.m. and on the vital night. On the following morning, very early, he had come in to the local police station, with bulging mouth and wild eyes, to make some routine enquiry about a car.

Slowly the prosecution accumulated evidence. Fingerprint expert Barker found the print of Marigny's little finger on a screen drawn across Oakes's bed. He also carried out a heat test and found that Marigny's beard, and the hair on his hand, forearm and head all showed signs of scorching under a microscope.

Homicide investigator Melchen found smudge marks in the hall. He reconstructed the case to show that Sir Harry had staggered into the hall, pyjamas aflame, had gripped the stair railing and tottered against the wall. Then he had been dragged back to his room, and the bed set on fire.

Melchen said Marigny had told him: 'Oakes hated me for

marrying his daughter, Nancy. I hated him because he was a stupid old fool who could not be reasoned with.'

The prosecution suggested that Marigny, tired of attempting to reason with Sir Harry, had planned and executed his murder, and then attempted to burn the body. The strong points of their case were the expert evidence relating to finger-prints and scorched hair. It was essential to the prosecution to prove these beyond question in court.

Into the small court room at Nassau people crowded every day to watch the case, bringing sandwiches and ice cream sodas, often sitting two to a seat. The preliminary investigation in the Magistrates' Court had opened a week after Marigny's arrest. It was adjourned more than once, dragged on through August. The trial itself finally opened on 18th October in the Supreme Court, before Sir Oscar Daly, Chief Justice of the Bahamas. The Attorney-General, the Honourable Eric Halli-nan, led for the Crown, with one of the colony's leading lawyers, the Honourable A.F. Adderley, to assist him. The Honourable Godfrey Higgs led for the defence.

The trial lasted more than three weeks, with preliminary challenging for many jurors by both sides, and several others providing medical certificates to say that they were unfit to serve. During those three weeks the prosecution saw the case steadily slipping away from them, because of the inefficiency of many of the police officials who worked on it.

Consider that vivid reconstruction of the case made by Captain Melchen, when he said that Sir Harry had staggered into the hall, tottered against the wall and been dragged back to his room. In face of positive medical evidence that Sir Harry never got out of the bed in which he was found, Melchen retracted this evidence. He admitted that no analysis had been made of the material used to light the fire in the bedroom. Certain hand marks on the wall of Sir Harry's room had not been measured.

There followed the curious story of the bloodstained towels. Major Herbert Pemberton, head of the C.I.D. in the colony, had removed a bloodstained towel from Sir Harry's bed. He had also found a towel with what appeared to be bloodstains on it in Christie's bedroom.

While giving evidence in the Magistrates' Court Pemberton had forgotten all about these towels, and indeed denied seeing them. He was tired, he explained, and didn't recollect the matter. As a matter of fact the towel in Sir Harry's room had been in his possession for some weeks, and he had forgotten all about it. As for the towel in Christie's bedroom, why, it had just been left there. He had not made a note of finding the towels, Pemberton told an astonished court room, and did not think they were important.

How had bloodstains got on to Christie's towel? The estate agent explained that when he found Sir Harry's body he poured water in his mouth, wet a towel and wiped his face with it. He believed that the towel came from his own bedroom. There were certain bloodstains on the glass door and screen door of Christie's bedroom, and he said that these were probably from his own hands, after he had found Sir Harry.

A strange story was told by Captain Sears, the Assistant Superintendent of Police. Driving in Nassau on the fatal night Captain Sears had seen a station wagon with Christie sitting in the front seat, and somebody else driving. Sears, however, must have been mistaken, for Christie said positively that he did not leave Westbourne on that night.

The severest blow struck at the prosecution came with the evidence of Captain James Barker. It was evidence which at times turned the tragedy into something like a farce. It was also evidence of historical importance about the methods of obtaining fingerprints.

The first step in taking fingerprint evidence is usually to photograph the prints. This fingerprint expert, however, had left his fingerprint camera behind. Perhaps Pemberton might have one? Well, yes, he had, but it was out of commission.

Without bothering to make any further enquiries about cameras or to send for his own camera. Barker proceeded to take prints by 'lifting' them on to Scotch tape. This is a recognized method. When he ran out of tape he 'lifted' them on to rubber, a procedure which has the effect of destroying the original print. Having done this, he forgot all about the print on the screen for ten days when, he said, he examined it and found that it was Marigny's.

Judge Daly called Barker's conduct 'quite incomprehensible', and his forgetfulness was really extraordinary. In court he identified the place on the screen where the print had been found—and it turned out to be the wrong place. He said that certain lines on the screen were not made by him—and they turned out to be marked with his initials. Looking at the lifted print, this expert was unable even to say which way the finger was pointing.

There was worse to come. It was obvious that, for the fingerprint evidence to be effective, Marigny must have had no possible access to the screen before it was fingerprinted. Now, Marigny had been taken upstairs at Westbourne to be interviewed on the day Barker took the prints. Had he gone before or after the work was done? In the Magistrates' Court all the police officers agreed that it was after.

Pemberton said the screen was under constant police guard. Two other police witnesses said that Marigny, on strict instructions, had not gone upstairs in the morning, while the screen was being finger-rinted. Melchen confirmed that he had taken Marigny upstairs between 3 and 4 in the afternoon.

At the trial, however, Mrs Clark and Mrs Ainslie said that they had been summoned to Westbourne that morning, and that Marigny had been taken upstairs between eleven o'clock and noon. Now, quite suddenly, the prosecution evidence on this point collapsed. The police guards admitted that they had been mistaken about the time, and so did Melchen. It was just a mistake, he said.

'What a mistake,' defence counsel commented ironically. 'What a coincidence that you and the constables should make the same mistake.'

In his final speech for the defence Higgs plainly accused these witnesses of perjury. While Melchen was examining Marigny upstairs Barker had come to the door and asked if everything was O.K. The defence suggested that Marigny had been taken upstairs deliberately, to get his print on to the screen.

By the time that Marigny went into the witness box, the incompetence or corruption of the police had made his acquittal almost inevitable. He explained that the burnt hair on his beard and forearms had been caused when he lit a cigar over a candle in a hurricane shade. He was a confident witness, laughing, joking occasionally, winking at his wife. The jury voted 9 to 3 for acquittal. They unanimously recommended Marigny's deportation.

Talking to reporters afterwards Marigny told them to keep out of prison. 'It's a hard life,' he said. 'I could see that I had a good foreman to guide the jury. By the way, did you notice that he was the only one who was awake all the time?' Asked if he would try to solve the mystery he said, 'I'll leave that to Erle Stanley Gardner.'

Echoes of the case can be heard occasionally through the years. In 1950 a Finnish seaman said he had been told the name of the Oakes murderer by an American landscape artist, and a search was made for a blonde model named Betty Roberts, who gave evidence in the case. When found, Miss Roberts, now happily married, proved to have nothing to say. In this same year Betty Ellen Renner, who came to the Bahamas to investigate the case, was murdered and put into a well. At this time, also, Marigny was heard of, working as a part-time French translator in New York. His marriage to Nancy Oakes had been annulled. In 1953 Barker was shot dead by his son, after a quarrel. But these are mere sidelights on some of the characters. Neither Erle Stanley Gardner (who was there as a reporter) nor anyone else has ever solved the problem: who killed Sir Harry Oakes?

Any investigation of the Oakes case is bound to leave one with the feeling that much less than the whole truth has been told. But in the welter of contradictory evidence, and the evasions of police officials (the jury expressed their regret that no evidence had been obtained from Lieutenant-Colonel Erskine-Lindop, Commissioner of Bahamas Police, who left to take up another appointment between the Magistrates' hearing and the trial), some questions stand out. They are questions that seem, strangely enough, never to have been asked:

(1) Oakes was killed in his bedroom, as the result of a blow with a heavy instrument. The night of the murder was stormy, but still, there must have been considerable noise. Why was it not heard?

(2) Where did the inflammable material come from that was used to set the fire?

(3) And why, having decided to burn the body, did the murderer make such a bad job of it, when he had apparently all night at his disposal? Was he disturbed? Or was the body-burning an elaborate pretence to lead suspicion away from the real murderer?

There are other questions too, which it is not possible to ask publicly, even fifteen years after Marigny's trial. But the Oakes case is one on which the file is not completely closed. It is possible, at least, that one day an answer will be provided to one of the most remarkable murder mysteries of the twentieth century.

AFTERWORD

Plenty of people have tried to provide the answer, notably James Leasor in his book Who Killed Sir Harry Oakes? *(1983). The argument proposed is a complex one, which is not helped by its quasi-fictional form of presentation, but it goes roughly like this. The Mafia were determined to build and run hotels and casinos on Nassau, and if they were allowed to do so they would return the favour by facilitating the Allied landing in Sicily. The only real opposition to this scheme came from Sir Harry Oakes.*

He therefore had to be 'persuaded', and to this end he was lured onto a yacht where a struggle developed and he was (accidentally?) hit on the head by an engineer, unnamed in the book. In panic, Sir Harry was moved back to his house, soaked with flykiller and set alight. Captain Barker was sent over from Miami to organize a cover-up (hence the messy investigation), the Allies landed safely in Sicily, and Nassau became the gambling-place that everybody except Sir Harry wanted.

Pleasing though this may be, one must add that there is not a shred of evidence for any of it.

Postscript

We should never dismiss a murder as 'unsolved' for, as we have seen, there is always a possibility that new evidence will be found, new explanations suggested, and a solution eventually reached. Admittedly, not much progress has been made in the Starr Faithfull, Elwell and Kiss murders, but that is not to say that it never will. Other cases are far from closed and, as we have seen, there is a real possibility that the Wallace case might yet be solved, while there is still much fruitful speculation about Jack the Ripper, Lizzie Borden and Florence Bravo which, even if it does not bring solutions as such, might at least lead to some sort of consensus about what really happened.

We now know much more—though still not enough—about people who commit crimes like those of Jack the Ripper. In the 1880's the solutions proposed were highly *logical* ones based on clear-cut motives such as revenge: the sort of neat answer that Sherlock Holmes (a contemporary of the Ripper) might have found at the end of one of his cases. But crimes like those have happened more and more frequently in our own century, and they have taught us that the 'motive' is much more likely to be one of psychopathic sexual gratification than anything so obvious as vengeance or monetary gain: the sort of explanation that simply could not have been discussed at the time, and which probably would not have been understood even if it had been. Then, madmen were wild-eyed maniacs. Now we know that a psychopath can live a very normal, anonymous life and still commit atrocities.

In the Bravo and Borden cases too, the most plausible explanations come not from detective-story solutions but from our greater understanding of the sort of sexual and emotional problems that might have prompted these women to do such seemingly uncharacteristic things. In each case the 'motive' for the crimes can only be understood in terms of domestic pressures concerned with money and petty jealousies, but to understand why they should have boiled over into murder is less a matter for strict logic than of understanding the extremes of human personality and behaviour. To view these cases as mere puzzles is condescending and probably misleading. Perhaps if we knew more about the muddled motivation of someone like poor Starr Faithfull we would be able to make much shrewder guesses about the precise manner of her death.

The tragic thing is that none of this helps where help really is needed: to clear the innocent or to help the victims. In both Britain and the USA very little effort is made to increase our understanding of convicted murderers, and what we *have* learned generally proves to be of pathetically little help when the police are actually faced with the task of catching a killer or preventing further murders. Neither is there any very obvious solution. We can only hope that eventually a more enlightened attitude will prevail, and that in time we shall be able to learn something useful from those who violate the rules of behaviour.

Perhaps cases like the ones in this book, particularly when they are analyzed by such excellent writers, can help to increase our understanding a little.

While every effort has been made to trace authors and copyright holders, in a few cases this has proved impossible; the publishers would be glad to hear from any such parties so that these omissions can be rectified in future editions of the book.

Thanks are due to the following for permission to reproduce the photographs and illustrations on the following pages:

Mail Newspapers plc 19 t + b; UPI/Bettmann Newsphotos 36, 110, 162, 277 tl, tc, tr, + b; Popperfoto 52, 78; BBC Hulton Picture Library 99; The Mansell Collection 123, 140; John Topham Picture Library 168, 198 t + b.